AF527884

Migration in India

Links to Urbanization, Regional Disparities and Development Policies

SHEKHAR MUKHERJI

RAWAT PUBLICATIONS

Jaipur • New Delhi • Bangalore • Hyderabad • Guwahati

ISBN 978-81-316-0557-8

Published by
Prem Rawat for **Rawat Publications**
Satyam Apts, Sector 3, Jawahar Nagar, Jaipur 302 004 (India)
Phone: 0141 265 1748/7006 Fax: 0141 265 1748
E-mail: info@rawatbooks.com
Website: www.rawatbooks.com

New Delhi Office
4858/24, Ansari Road, Daryaganj, New Delhi 110 002
Phone: 011 2326 3290

Also at *Bangalore*, *Hyderabad* and *Guwahati*

Typeset by Rawat Computers, Jaipur
Printed at Chauhan Enterprises, New Delhi

Dedicated to the
most respected

Professor Murray Chapman

Emeritus Professor in Geography,
University of Hawaii at Manoa, Honolulu, Hawaii, USA,
under whom I did my PhD in Population Geography and Demography.

And, to whom I am most gratefully indebted for his novel, innovative and humane concepts in Migration and Mobility Studies, which provided the basis of my life-long migration research.

Contents

Part II: Census 2001

Part III: Issues, Challenges and Development Policies

List of Tables

Appendix Tables

List of Figures

Preface

This volume is a part of a series of studies that I have made during last 40 years (1970–2010) on Causal Linkages between Migration, Urbanization and Regional Disparities in India, previously using field data and census data of 1961, 1971, 1981, and 1991 and related socio-economic data. This volume is one of the products of that series, and pertains to both 1991 and 2001 Census migration-urbanization data and their analyses.

Migration is the most intriguing and most complex demographic phenomenon and, in India, according to 1991 Census, it involved the lives of over one-third (230 million) of country's total population. As per Census 2001, volume of migrants swelled much further (327 million), and the patterns, more complex. It deserves very comprehensive study and research. But, most unfortunately, this is totally lacking in India. For example, none of the National Population Policy Documents of Government of India (Ministry of Health and Family Welfare (MOHFW, N.P.P. 1994; and MOHFW, N.P.P. 2000) even mentioned the crucial human and economic problems of migration and urbanization in the country. Very soon, these problems are going to be the most burning issues of the 21st century, all over the world, specially in the most populous and high-growth developing countries, like India. Particularly this is because of huge population explosion and very rapid migration-urbanization. Unfortunately, in India, in population and demographic studies and research, adequate attention is not given as it deserves.

Migration is not a simple phenomenon, nor can it be investigated just as sheer number or insipid statistics. It involves the lives of the individuals and their families, and their complex socio-economic background and deprivation. Migration also has a deeply imbedded spatial dimension. Migration indeed is a spatial symptom of the nexus of poverty-underdevelopment and regional disparities over the national space economy, and, as such, it affects the lives of millions, over space and time. So, a complete understanding of such complexities is very urgently necessary, specially for a developing country like India, in order to alleviate the crucial human, social, economic and spatial problems. Such problems are associated with poverty-induced migration and low quality urbanization – that are happening in India, since many decades. Often migration arises out of poverty and underdevelopment, and compounds further exploitation and impoverishment. Moreover, spatial imbalance causes out-migration from deprived regions, which, in turn, accelerates further spatial inequities. Thus, migration research must explore all such dimensions, not in isolation, rather in entirety. It must also investigate the causal linkages between poverty-underdevelopment-spatial disorganization and study them over space and time. The approach should be process-oriented. The perspective must be historic, and politico-economic, untangling underlying forces and processes. The avowed goal must be to generate planning policies in order to ameliorate such human and socio-economic problems.

Very sadly, such comprehensive studies, or clear understanding, are very much lacking in India. Only with proper understanding and proper perspectives, could we come up with proper planning prescriptions – for eliminating those crucial human, socio-economic and spatial disparities. Then only, social and spatial inequities can be reduced. Otherwise, such problems will soon aggravate and compound further, reaching beyond our control.

Set within this great need for research in migration fields and the crucial task for alleviating human problems, however, there exist two great handicaps. First, there is a tremendous lacuna of comprehensive theoretical and conceptual framework for doing meaningful migration-urbanization research in India. Second, it was non-availability of correct and full migration data of 1991 and 2001 censuses. For a long time, neither preliminary, nor comprehensive analysis of causes and consequences of migration could be attempted in India, due to lack of basic Census 1991 migration data.

Likewise, Census 2001 migration and related economic data of cities, towns and regions were available only in 2005–6–7–8–9. Such inordinate delay has really hampered timely and meaningful study of migration-urbanization and regional disparities in India. In this book, Census 2001 migration and urbanization data are also analysed, and the main trends are highlighted. I hope that Census 2011 data will be available in time.

This book on *Migration in India* has explored many new grounds, and thus made many new contributions to social science research. Attempts are made here to fill up afore-mentioned lacunae in conventional migration studies. Second, historical processes underlying the nexus between poverty-induced migration, underdevelopment and spatial disorganization in India are also unfolded. Third, causal linkages between migration on one hand, and urbanization and regional disparities, on the other, are identified through many high-powered multivariate analyses (like regression techniques, factor analyses, and canonical models). Migration Field Theories and canonical analyses are very rare in migration-urbanization research in India and in the world. Since the present author has done such research continuously during the last 40 years (1970–2010), so he is considered as one of rare world authorities on Migration Field Theories and related canonical models. However, their objectives were never mere technical exercises, rather to generate useful and appropriate policies for correct solutions of those human problems. Thus, finally, specific policies and planning strategies are generated and recommended in order to alleviate human, spatial and socio-economic problems.

This study has made several canonical analyses of migration phenomena at many levels: district, state, class I city, million city and mega city levels;

everytime also incorporating the economic structure of regions under study (district, state, city, or million city), as well as encompassing the variables related to growth efforts and investments therein. And, such series of canonical linkages have generated, not only statistically very highly significant results, but also practically very meaningful findings. Those findings have great policy import. Briefly, such results are presented in the summary of findings (Chapters 9 and 18). Canonical analysis is a very powerful, but yet unexplored, mathematical technique for investigating many important geographic or demographic phenomena. This volume, by making many successful demonstration of using canonical models in Migration and Migration Field Theory, has made unique contribution to migration study and research. These are equally applicable to other geographic, demographic, and social science research.

This book is most respectfully and lovingly dedicated to Professor Murray Chapman, Emeritus Professor in Geography, University of Hawaii at Manoa, Honolulu, Hawaii, USA, to whom I am most indebted for learning my first lessons in migration studies and research, specially the most essential concepts of Migration-Circulation-Mobility Research, during my second PhD study (1970–75). I am also very much indebted to him for his classic and life-long urge to imbed migration-mobility investigations in the context of the Third World socio-economic-cultural background itself, bereft from the Western bias and Western concepts, models and theorization. My humble attempts to construct and test Migration Field Theory, Spatial Field Theory and the Theory of Migration and Underdevelopment, as narrated in this book, are also the first faltering steps towards that noble goal. Indeed, I feel deep gratitude to him for his innovative ideas and initiating me into my life-long sojourn to migration-mobility research. This book is my *Pranam* to him (Prostating before the Feet of God Inside Him).

Second, some major section (of 1991 part) of this research was carried out during my tenure as a Visiting Research Fellow in Bellagio Study and Research Center, Bellagio, Italy, under Rockefeller Visiting Research Fellowship Programme, USA. I hereby express my sincere gratitude and indebtedness to both the Rockefeller Institute and Bellagio Study Center for kindly providing me the prestigious fellowship, research facilities and wonderful hospitality at Bellagio. I treasure hallowed memories of green Bellagio hills, overlooking the beautiful blue Lake Lado, in northern Italy (north of Milan).

Third, this study also owes sincere gratitude and indebtedness to many. I am also grateful to International Institute for Population Sciences (IIPS), Mumbai, for providing institutional support for conducting rest 1991 Census part of this research, during January 2000–May 2001, before my retirement from the Institute.

Besides, I am also grateful to Mr S.S. Srinivasan, Assistant Research Officer of this project, for computer assistance, and executing my numerous Migration Field Theory formulations and canonical models, under my guidance (for first part of the book). Indeed, his computing help was very essential.

Moreover, I am also very sincerely grateful to Ms Sai Thakur, Assistant Research Officer of the project, who meticulously converted all computer outputs into finalized Canonical matrices, Factor matrices, and many tables, under my supervision. Without her help, it was difficult to give shape to first part (1991) of this book.

Many others have also helped in various ways. Four migration maps (of 1991) were prepared by Srinivasan and Anjula Saraff, under my direction. I am also thankful to Shri R.T. Randheria, former Librarian of IIPS, for providing useful materials. I am also very thankful to Shri M. Mistry, present Librarian and Information Officer for making available useful books. My thanks also go to Shri Motilal Mohare, Institute's Artist, who inked my ten draft maps. My thanks are also due to Mr Lakhan Gharve for reprographic help.

The book was though completed by May 2001, but its publication was much delayed due to various reasons. However, changes in India are rather slow, and the basic causal relationships between widespread poverty and mobility, arising out of impoverishment and regional disparities, remain very much similar, even today (2008–09). Maximum possible attempts are made, however, in Part II of this book, to update recent migration and urbanization situation, according to Census 2001 data, and provide recent references to make it a current study.

Regarding the preparation of the second part, encompassing 2001 Census, four persons were of immense help. First, Dr Thakur (now in Tata Institute of Social Sciences, Mumbai) and Ms Yogita Rathod, Research Assistant who helped me in the preparation of summary tables from Census 2001 migration and economic series, for all-India picture, and district and state-level situation. I am very especially grateful to both of them.

Top of all, I very immensely and heartily owe to my youngest brother Shri Vikram Mukherji, a veteran computer specialist, who very meticulously drawn all diagrams of 2001 part of this book, especially innumerable regression graphs and all Excel graphs. He also very meticulously prepared many migration and economic tables for Class I cities, million cities and mega cities for 2001 Census. He also converted all Excel tables to Word format; and, that was of immense help. He is headquartered at the holy city of Varanasi, and I am living at a far away metropolis, Mumbai. But his constant inputs in the form of innumerable final graphs and data tables, through computer, were of great help. Without his help, this book would not have come to this shape at all. No words of thanks can express my hearty gratitude to Vikram Bhaia (brother!).

I am also sincerely grateful to my wife, Dr Uma Mukherji, a Nuclear Physicist and Professor of Physics and Electro-Magnetic Theory, who has very nicely drawn four Migration maps of India of Census 2001 (as I was immersed in fire-fighting!). For the first time, a Nuclear Physicist (concerned with the movements of electrons and particles) has made maps of the movements of the people! Contributions by both of them have immensely enriched this volume. I am very especially grateful to both of them, Uma and Vikram.

Lastly, I am aware that there are many others, not mentioned here, but to whom I owe all my sincere gratitude and heartfelt thanks. I must profusely thank my son, Vijay Mukherji (chemical engineer), now based at London, who made frequent phone calls during last three years urging me to finish soon my Voluminous *Mahabharata*, rather take care of my failing health.

Last, but most prominently, my very special thanks and gratitude goes to Shri Pranit Rawat and all in Rawat Publications, for their professional excellence and utmost care for very nice and expert publication of this book. I very sincerely express my hearty gratitude to all of them.

I will consider that my labour is amply rewarded, if this research draws the attention of the students, scholars, planners, policy-makers, administrators, and the governments – and urge all of them to be really concerned with enormous human, socio-economic and political problems of poverty-induced migration and low quality urbanization in India. The future is very uphill, and needs very urgent solutions, before they reach a catastrophic level.

These crucial human problems really need our urgent actions to bridge the development divide between handful of privileged billionaires and over 600 millions poor in India!

Shekhar Mukherji

Part I

Census 1991

Messages of Swami Vivekananda
(1863–1902)

"Advance, forward, O ye brave souls, to set free those that are in fetters, to lessen the burden of woe of the miserable, and to illumine the abysmal darkness of the ignorant hearts!"

Swami Vivekananda (1895)
(Complete Work, Centenary Volume VII, 1963: 504)

"Stretch forth a helping hand, and open the gates of knowledge to one and all, and give the downtrodden masses once more their just and legitimate rights and privileges."

Swami Vivekananda (1894)
(Complete Work, Centenary Volume III, 1963: 461)

"I hold all the educated people of India as traitors, who being educated at the expense of the illiterate masses, do nothing for them."

Swami Vivekananda (1894)
(Complete Work, Centenary Volume III, 1963: 105)

"Don't look back – forward, infinite energy, infinite enthusiasm, infinite daring, and infinite patience – then alone can great deeds be accomplished."

Swami Vivekananda (1896)
(Complete Work, Centenary Volume VIII, 1963: 353)

1 Patterns of Migration in India

"Lay down your comforts, your pleasures, your names, fame or position, nay even your lives, and make a bridge of human chains over which millions will cross this ocean of life."

Swami Vivekananda (1894)
(Complete Work, Centenary Volume IV, 1963: 352)

Nature of Migration and Urbanization in India

Studies on migration and urbanization in India and abroad are mostly descriptive; neither analytic, nor synthetic – nor unravelling the underlying socio-economic-political processes behind the phenomena of distressed migration and acute urban decay in a developing country, like India. This study takes a different view about the whole issue of migration and urbanization in India, and emphasizes that labour migration of distressed people are occurring as "spatial" manifestations of poverty, underdevelopment, and spatial disorganization. These were caused by the past historical adversaries, and which continue due to inadequate planning that does not cater for the poor and the distressed labourers. Consequently, acute urban decay is also occurring in all mega cities of India. Planning is thus necessary to relieve such oppressive situation.

This volume has two main parts. Part I deals with situations according to 1991 Census, and Part II, discusses according to Census 2001. In Part I, thrust of the study is fourfold: (a) to unfold the true nature of migration and urbanization in India, and to discuss acute urban decay in Indian metropolises; (b) to present true explanation of the underlying processes of labour migration and urbanization, interlinking them with underdevelopment and spatial disorganization; (c) canonically to ascertain linkages between volume and patterns of migration and socio-economic attributes of regions and investments therein (performed at district, state, class I city, and million city levels); and (d) finally, to summarize the main findings of distress migration and urban deterioration. These four are intimately connected.

In Part II, the situation of migration and urbanization according to Census 2001 are analysed. Details of that part are presented there. Some relevant issues and challenges are also highlighted. Finally, planning policies and strategies are discussed at the end of the book.

Objectives

All these conditions described above urgently require remedial measures and solution. The study has four main objectives:

- First, this study attempts to unfold the on-going *complex phenomena of poverty-induced migration and consequent urban decay in India.* These phenomena are not yet adequately studied in India.
- Second, the study also briefly untangles the complex *spatial-socio-economic-political processes* that underlie and cause such complex nexus of migration-urbanization-poverty-underdevelopment systems in India. These processes have general applicability to other developing countries.
- Third, and more importantly, volume and patterns of migration of 2001 Census are meticulously analysed at six different scales of analysis: (1) All-India, (2) District, (3) State, (4) Class I City, (5) Million City, and (6) Mega City. A series of factor analysis and canonical analysis were performed between: (a) the volume and patterns of migration in the regions (as dependent matrix), and (b) the economic structure of regions (districts, or states, cities, or million cities)-cum-investment and growth efforts therein (as predictor matrix), at each scale of research. A series of final canonical linkage equations were generated, linking each time, a specific pattern(s) of migration, with a specific pattern(s) of economic structure-cum-investment pattern(s). *Such canonical linkages have yielded, as we shall see, many useful and meaningful results. Canonical analysis is a very powerful and useful analytic method, but very rarely utilized in geographic, demographic or social sciences. Thus, this volume also makes an unique and innovative theoretical and methodological contributions.*
- Finally, the study also recommends certain relevant policies and planning strategies to redress the acute human problems associated with such phenomena and processes. These strategies will also benefit other similarly placed countries in Asia-Pacific region. Because such processes are operating in many Third World nations, that need our urgent attention for remedies. In the coming decades, evidently, the problems of such distressed migration, over-urbanization, and urban decay will very fast become the greatest problems in the developing world.

One important point must be explained right at the beginning. This volume primarily focuses on various aspects of migration, and migration alone. It does not dwell with urbanization or regional disparities in India *per se* (issues that demand separate analyses), rather it discusses some aspects of urbanization or regional disparities in special ways. Discussions on such topics were highlighted wherever the "links" between migration to towns or class I cities or million cities or mega cities have emerged. Thus, the causal links between migration and urbanization are specifically focused, rather than conventional discussion on urbanization. Likewise, issues of regional disparities were emphasized, whenever migration at district or state levels are made and discussion focused on migration from backward to forward districts, or from stagnated to favoured states. In this regard, the "causal links" between migration and regional disparities are emphasized, rather than conventional discussion on regional disparity. Investigations are also made (with 1991 Census data) to mathematically compute socio-economic "distances" between states and, relate that to inter-state migration. Furthermore, attempts are also made to relate district's levels of development (new index constructed) to volume and rates of in-migration and out-migration from districts. Thus, mainly the "causal links" between regional disparities with migration are emphasized. Furthermore, full discussions on migration planning, development policies and strategies, that are necessary for redressing the problems of migration-urbanization in India are presented in the final chapter.

All-India Migration Patterns

Broad Patterns

Table 1.1 presents the patterns of male and female internal migration, according to place of last residence (1991), showing separately volume for all durations (columns 1–2), and for ten years duration, 1981–91 (columns 3–6). Figure 1.1 shows main cities of India, and Figure 1.2 portrays the levels of urbanization, during 1981–91(Census of India, 1991, Paper 2 of 1991).

According to 1991 Census (b), 64.3 million males and 167.8 million females were migrants; indicating the predominance of female mobility over male mobility in India. The sex ratio of mobility thus comes to 2609.

During 1981–91, however, 27.25 million male and 54.85 million females were recorded as migrants (columns 3–5) (Census of India, 1991(b)). The mobility sex ratio has come down to 2012, during 1981–91. Considerable variations between male and female migration patterns are also noteworthy (Table 1.1):

(i) Females mostly move from rural to rural (64.4%), while for males this share is much less (40%).

(ii) Rural-urban migration is dominated by males (29.6%), the share of females is relatively small (15.8%).

(iii) The females primarily migrate short distances, within the district (62%), between rural areas (48%). About 13.1 per cent make inter-district migration, and only 3.4 per cent cross state boundaries. Corresponding percentage for males are 49.1, 27.1, 9.1 and 3.9. Thus, inter-state migration is male selective.

(iv) Regarding rural-urban migration, volume-wise male and female migrants are not much different at intra-district, inter-district and inter-state levels, but proportion-wise the females constitute decreasingly a smaller part of total female migration, viz., 7.4., 5.5 and 2.9 per cent, respectively for intra-district, inter-district and inter-state rural-urban migration. Corresponding share of males are 12.0, 10.3, and 7.3 per cent, respectively. Thus, rural-urban migration is also male selective. Identical patterns are also seen for urban-urban migration.

(v) However, when sex ratios (females to males) are computed, then some intriguing features emerge: in general, the females predominate in rural to rural, both at intra-district (sex ratio 3572) and inter-district level (sex ratio 2895), and also in urban-urban migration in short distances, but males predominate in rural-urban migration, especially at longer or inter-state migration.

Figure 1.1 *India: Administrative Divisions and Million Cities, 1991*

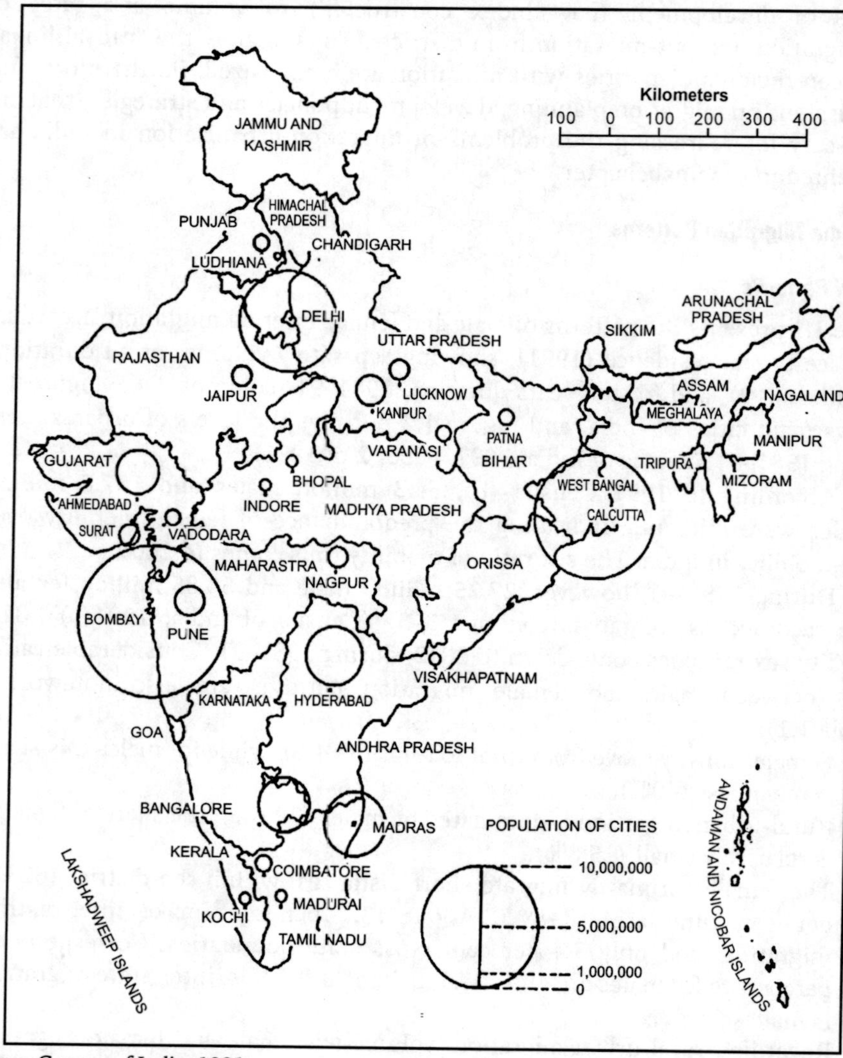

Source: Census of India, 1991.

Table 1.1 *Internal Migration by the Place of Residence, All-India, 1991*

	Total Migration All Durations		*Migration Less Than 10 Years Duration (1981–91) and Percentage of Total Migration*			
	M	*F*	*M*	*M%*	*F*	*F%*
Total Migration	64308038	167804935	27255302	100	54851873	100
Total Internal Migration	60766095	164088267	26587951	97.6	54087418	98.6
R – R	26451780	118593451	10897175	40.0	35350179	64.4
U – R	4547492	8931937	2423620	8.9	3660349	6.7

Cont'd...

...Cont'd

R – U	18237250	21672614	8072481	29.6	8692798	15.8
U – U	11529573	14890265	5194675	19.1	6384092	11.6
Intra-District Migration						
R – R	18890374	90094075	7372624	27.1	26340085	48.0
U – R	2204723	4752807	1147990	4.2	1897888	3.5
R – U	6934730	10446358	3260015	12.0	4063425	7.4
U – U	2639265	3855040	1161722	4.3	1577857	2.9
Inter-District Migration						
R – R	5439084	23100822	2474807	9.1	7165258	13.1
U – R	1557577	3064785	829409	3.0	1268345	2.3
R – U	6423111	7410161	2820815	10.3	3032377	5.5
U – U	4896727	6660202	2317692	8.5	2926713	5.3
Inter-State Migration						
R – R	2122322	5398554	1049744	3.9	1844836	3.4
U·– R	785192	1114345	446221	1.6	494116	0.9
R – U	4879409	3816095	1991651	7.3	1596996	2.9
U – U	3993581	4375023	1715261	6.3	1879522	3.4
From Other Countries						
Moved to Rural	1551401	1523319	298118	1.1	324326	0.6
Moved to Urban	1516745	1336417	248531	0.9	208970	0.4
Unclassified – R	59754	143055	11529	0.0	36126	0.1
Unclassified – U	45835	48601	15402	0.1	15770	0.0

Source: Census of India, 1991 (b) and (c), Migration Table, D-Series (CDs, data available only in 1998).

Note: Number of total migrants and their break-up do not tally: a discrepancy of 3.6 million male and 6.6 million females.

Reasons for Migration at All-India Level

Table 1.2 indicates volume of migration of males and females during 1981–91 (Census of India, 1991 (b)). It also indicates seven main reasons for migration: for the males, who moved to rural areas (first row), the most important reason was employment (22.6%), followed by miscellaneous (26.6%) and family moved (31.4%), education (8.4%), and business (5.7%). For the females, those who moved to rural areas (first row), marriage (74.3%) was the most important reason, followed by family moved (11.9%) and miscellaneous (9.4%). Among them, education, or business were still not prominent (3.5% and 1.1%, respectively). Thus, for the males the economic motives are still the most important reason for migration; whereas for the females, marriage or familial migration is still predominant. Indeed, the patterns have not changed, in spite of recent economic progress in India (Table 1.2).

As we move down the table (second row), noteworthy point is that for those who moved to urban areas, employment becomes most predominant reason for the males (38.7%), although for the females it is still low (only 5.3%). However, a large number of females are reported as moved for familial reasons (35.1%), but there are strong reasons to believe (from literatures, chapter 11), that a large part of them takes up employment later at destinations. Census data fail to capture these huge masses of women employment migration, because they

Figure 1.2 *Levels of Urbanization in India, 1991*

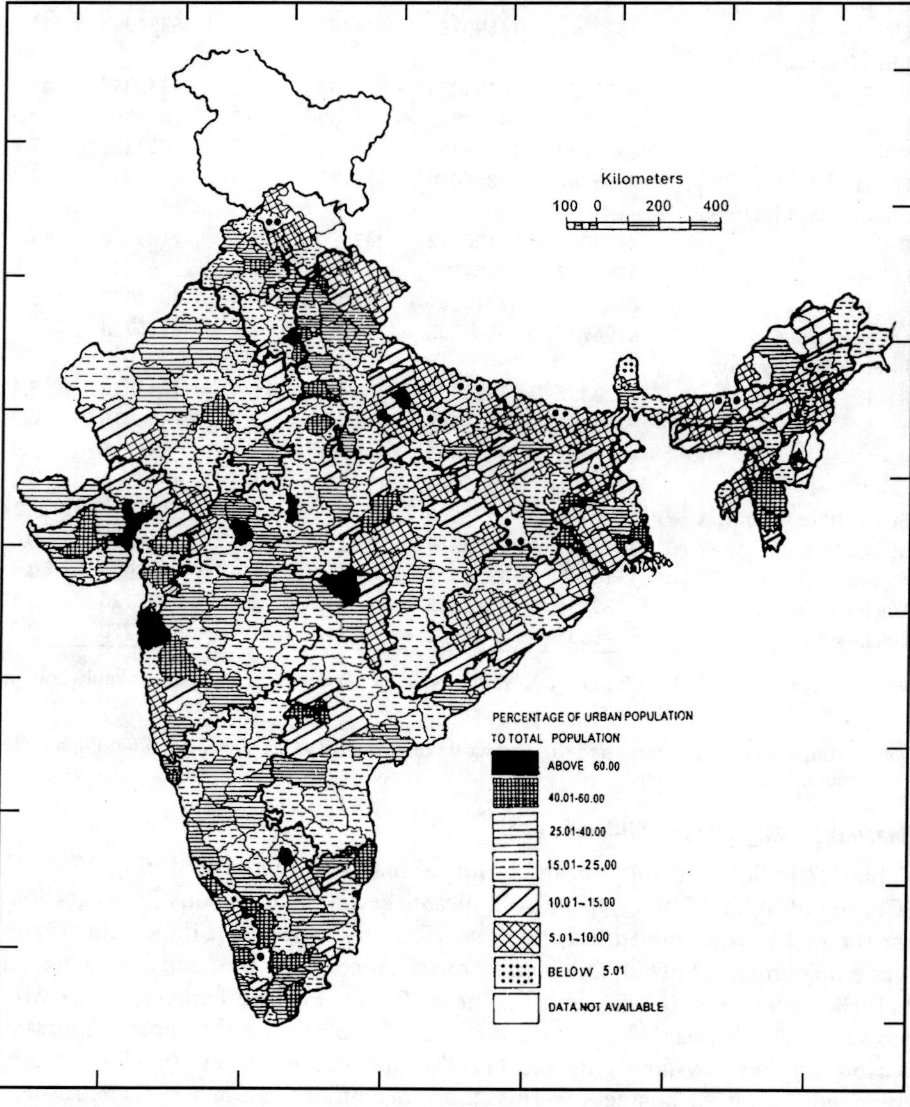

Source: Computed from Census of India, 1991(a).

focus only on the primary reasons for move, not asking second reason(s). This needs urgent correction (see Chapman, 1985a).

Further down the table, move for employment becomes increasingly more important for the males at inter-district (42%) and inter-state levels (51%), especially for rural-to-urban component. For the females, employment migration still hovers around 5 per cent, while marriage migration shows decreasingly less importance at longer distances (40–50%). A large segment of the male migrants moved for both familial and miscellaneous reasons at various types of migration, and a larger proportion of the females indicate similar trends.

Figure 1.3 *India: Male Inter-state Migration, 1981–91*

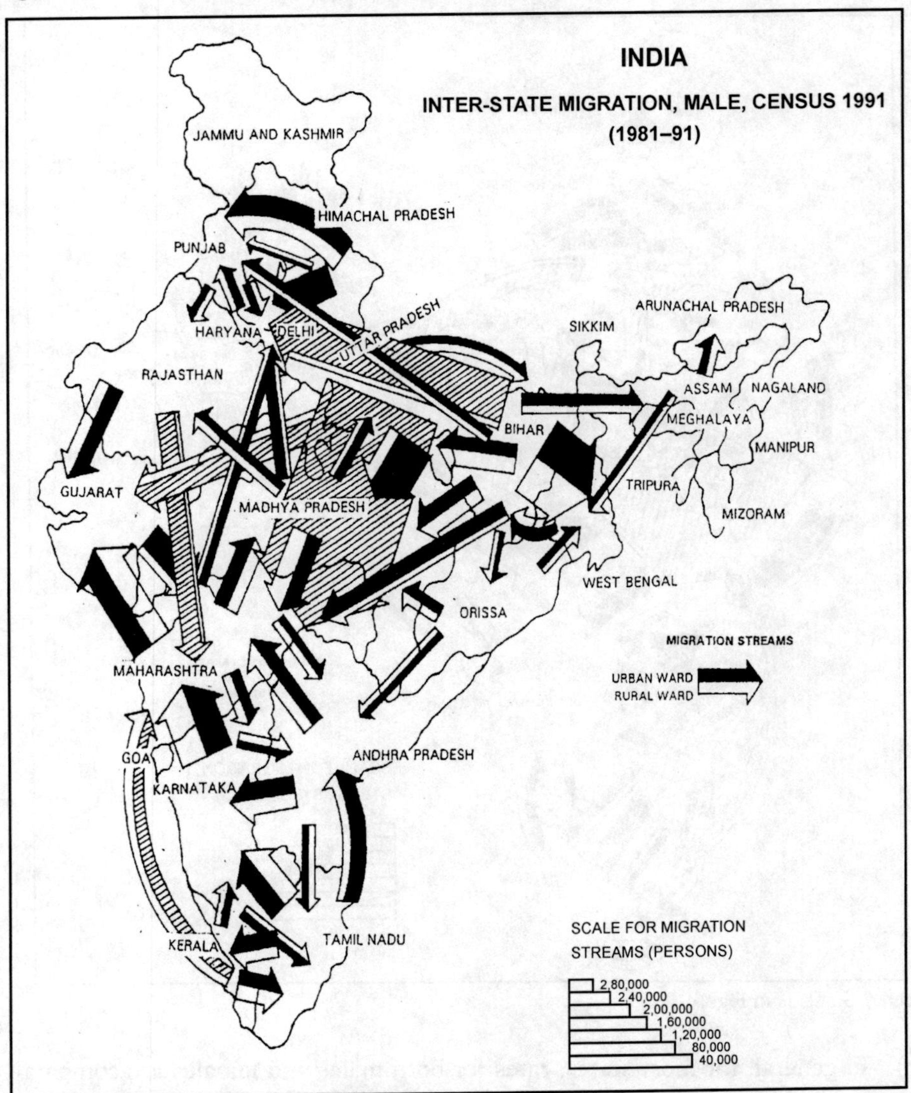

Source: Computed from Census of India, 1991 (b).

State-level Variations in Migration Patterns

Table 1.3 indicates state-level variations in reasons for migration, both for males and females (all durations of residence). However, our specific concern here is migration for employment, about which a few notable aspects may be discerned:

(a) Compared to the males, the females make much less moves for employment in all states.

(b) On average, while males record 20–40 per cent rates for employment migration, rates for females vary between 2 to 6 per cent in most states, except in Tamil Nadu and Kerala (due to higher female literacy rates), and partly in Orissa (due to specific situations).

Figure 1.4 *India: Female Inter-state Migration, 1981–91*

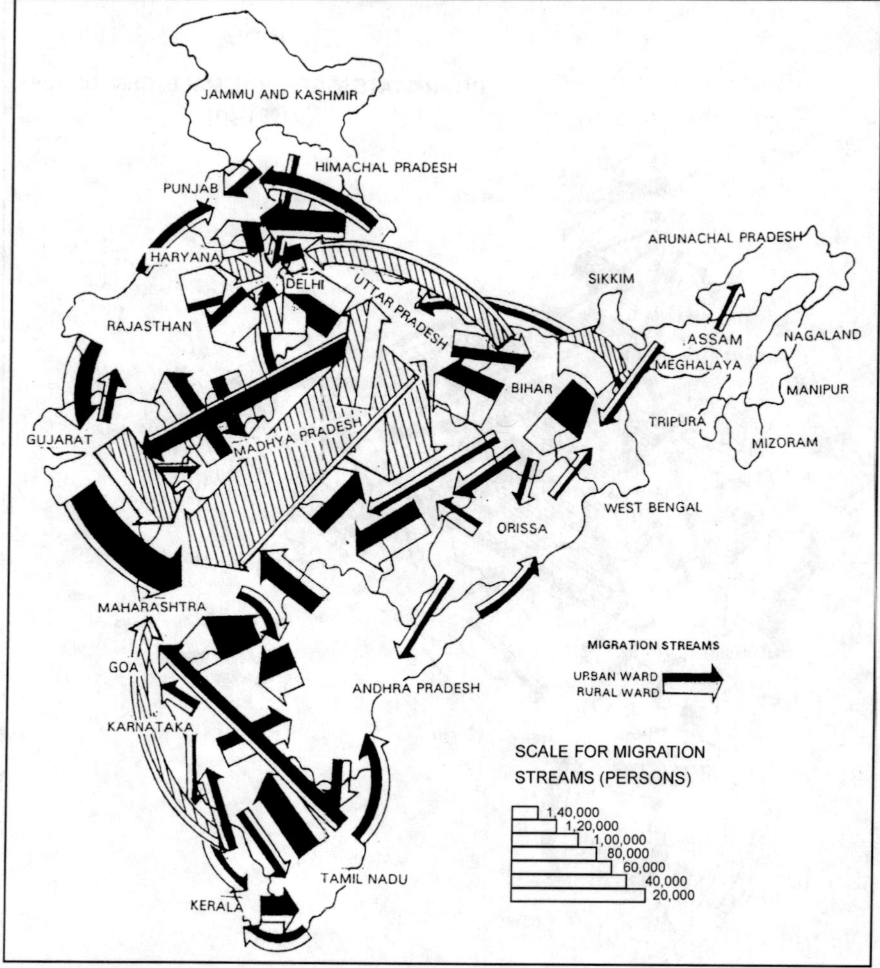

Source: Same as in Figure 1.3.

(c) In general, for most states, rates for both males and females are comparatively higher for rural-urban and urban-urban than for rural-rural and urban-rural patterns, because the migrants have the hunch that the chances of getting employment are more in cities. There are a few exceptions, especially where rural development has taken some strides (Kerala and Tamil Nadu).

Inter-State Migration Streams, 1981–1991

Figures 1.1 and 1.2 present the details of inter-state migration streams of the males and females who moved during 1981–91. Only the major streams are illustrated (Census of India, 1991(b)). Noteworthy features include:

(a) Uttar Pradesh, Bihar, Madhya Pradesh, Rajasthan, Tamil Nadu and Kerala are the main migration-source regions for the males and females. Karnataka and

Andhra Pradesh are secondary sending regions. Evidently, these are less developed states from which the males and females are forced to move out.

(b) Maharashtra, Gujarat, Karnataka, Delhi, Punjab, West Bengal, and partly Madhya Pradesh, are the main migration-destination regions for the males and females. Obviously, these are economically more developed states, towards which the males and females move for employment or subsistence. Haryana, Kerala and Tamil Nadu also receive some males and females from adjoining states.

(c) Like men, the female migrants in general are also more attracted towards the urban centres in most of the states, being the centres of production (Figures 1.3–1.4). Exceptions are seen in rural Gujarat, Haryana, Kerala and Karnataka, where agricultural development has occurred recently.

Table 1.2 *Reasons for Migration, All-India, 1991 Census, During 1981–91 (%)*

Place of Last Residence	*Total Migrants*		*Migration Less Than 10 Years of Duration, 1981–91*											
			Employ-ment		*Busi-ness*		*Educa-tion*		*Family Moved*		*Marriage*		*Others*	
	M	*F*	*M*	*F*	*M*	*F*	*M*	*F*	*M*	*F*	*M*	*F*	*M*	*F*
Total Internal Migration														
Moved to Rural	13361442	39127433	23	2	6	1	8	1	31	12	4	74	27	9
Moved to Urban	13320281	15139248	39	5	8	1	10	4	30	35	2	46	13	9
Intra-District Migration														
R – R	7372624	26340085	17	2	5	1	11	1	32	9	5	78	29	9
R – U	3260015	4063425	32	5	7	1	16	5	30	30	2	50	13	9
U – R	1147990	1897888	20	4	4	1	5	2	36	24	2	51	34	19
U – U	1161722	1577857	29	5	5	1	6	3	38	34	2	44	20	13
Inter-District Migration														
R – R	2474807	7165258	28	3	7	1	7	1	31	13	3	74	22	8
R – U	2820815	3032377	42	6	8	1	11	4	26	34	2	46	12	9
U – R	829409	1268345	31	5	5	1	7	2	32	26	2	53	23	13
U – U	2317692	2926713	37	6	6	1	8	3	34	36	1	45	13	9
Inter-State Migration														
R – R	1049744	1844836	40	5	10	2	4	1	27	19	2	65	16	8
R – U	1991651	1596996	51	5	11	1	5	2	23	43	1	39	9	9
U – R	446221	494116	35	6	8	2	5	2	28	33	1	46	22	12
U – U	1715261	1879522	41	5	9	1	7	3	31	41	1	41	11	9
From Other Countries														
Moved to Rural	298118	324326	14	3	3	1	2	1	26	27	1	30	55	38
Moved to Urban	248531	208970	28	5	5	1	4	2	28	41	1	21	34	29

Source: Census of India, 1991(b).

Note: There is a discrepancy in total figures in Table 1 and Table 2 (males – 5,73,579, females – 5,85,192). Migration data for calamities as a reason are negligible, so not shown. Unclassifiable are also not shown.

Table 1.3 *Patterns of Migration in States, Reasons for Migration, India, 1991(%)*

Last Residence	*Total Migrants*		*Employment*		*Business*		*Education*		*Family Moved*		*Marriage*		*Others*	
	M	*F*	*M*	*F*	*M*	*F*	*M*	*F*	*M*	*F*	*M*	*F*	*M*	*F*
ALL INDIA														
R – R	10897175	35350179	22	2	6	1	9	1	31	11	4	77	26	9
R – U	8072481	8692798	40	5	8	1	11	4	27	34	2	47	12	9
U – U	5194675	6384092	37	5	7	1	7	3	34	37	1	44	14	10
U – R	2423620	3660349	26	4	5	1	5	2	33	26	2	51	28	16
Andhra Pradesh														
R – R	1294013	2937277	27	5	2	0	17	2	29	14	4	68	21	10
R – U	899179	956098	43	11	4	1	15	6	27	35	1	39	10	9
U – U	506492	572574	41	10	3	1	8	4	34	41	1	34	13	10
U – R	229125	348826	35	9	2	1	10	2	32	26	2	50	19	12
Bihar														
R – R	380605	4221522	21	0	4	0	11	0	26	2	15	94	21	2
R – U	411240	547263	34	3	6	1	17	4	27	21	5	67	11	5
U – U	141764	187742	34	3	6	1	12	4	34	27	4	59	12	5
U – R	38510	115264	32	1	4	0	10	1	28	10	4	84	21	4
Gujarat														
R – R	676941	1904739	21	3	15	2	10	2	26	12	3	73	25	9
R – U	684733	729119	35	5	18	3	7	4	27	37	1	42	12	10
U – U	376535	486908	27	4	17	4	5	2	33	36	1	42	16	12
U – R	138110	209625	21	4	15	3	5	2	30	26	1	49	27	16
Haryana														
R – R	181994	830652	31	2	10	1	6	1	33	8	1	83	18	6
R – U	197754	209783	42	4	10	1	5	2	34	41	1	48	8	5
U – U	144053	209260	33	3	9	1	4	2	44	37	1	51	10	5
U – R	35480	80935	31	3	7	1	4	2	43	20	1	69	14	6
Karnataka														
R – R	839223	1838843	20	3	2	0	9	2	28	15	3	63	37	17
R – U	540657	548423	38	6	4	1	19	6	25	35	1	42	12	11
U – U	482621	526874	38	7	4	1	12	4	32	41	1	37	13	11
U – R	222579	306776	25	5	2	1	6	2	32	29	2	43	32	21
Kerala														
R – R	620088	1234754	16	3	1	0	4	2	40	21	9	59	30	15
R – U	208703	343496	26	6	2	0	8	5	37	28	6	48	22	13
U – U	147873	177528	29	8	2	0	4	4	35	38	5	31	25	19
U – R	284885	356247	15	4	1	0	3	2	30	26	5	34	45	34
Madhya Pradesh														
R – R	1240022	3603702	24	2	7	1	8	1	35	13	4	74	21	9
R – U	732029	804742	39	4	7	1	13	3	30	37	1	48	10	7
U – U	447182	588851	38	4	6	1	6	2	38	38	1	48	12	8
U – R	201802	299388	31	4	7	1	4	2	38	31	1	52	19	11
Maharashtra														
R – R	1520229	3045817	15	2	12	3	10	2	26	16	1	59	36	18
R – U	1332371	1240032	39	4	13	2	11	4	22	35	1	41	14	14
U – U	738880	859527	32	4	10	1	7	3	31	39	1	39	19	15
U – R	387565	491889	19	4	8	2	6	2	32	32	1	37	35	23

Cont'd...

...Cont'd

Orissa														
R – R	433553	1576837	19	1	4	0	14	1	30	9	7	81	23	6
R – U	256567	237701	37	5	9	1	15	5	22	40	2	40	13	9
U – U	116628	107855	40	6	8	1	9	4	30	49	1	31	11	8
U – R	57179	74690	33	6	6	1	7	2	28	27	2	53	23	11
Punjab														
R – R	276553	996610	29	2	1	0	3	1	37	10	3	80	26	6
R – U	220239	248494	48	5	3	0	3	2	33	32	1	54	11	7
U – U	183970	280287	40	4	3	1	3	2	38	29	2	57	14	7
U – R	61560	123781	35	4	1	0	3	1	38	21	2	65	21	9
Rajasthan														
R – R	564692	2219316	26	1	7	0	7	1	32	9	2	79	26	10
R – U	357224	387308	41	4	7	1	15	2	27	31	1	56	8	6
U – U	221839	320113	36	3	7	1	9	2	34	30	1	56	12	7
U – R	102627	188418	32	3	7	1	5	2	28	18	1	66	27	10
Tamil Nadu														
R – R	555455	1463571	27	4	3	1	9	2	30	14	5	69	23	10
R – U	469269	555987	45	9	5	1	9	5	27	32	2	43	12	10
U – U	516541	608427	42	9	4	1	7	4	32	37	2	37	14	12
U – R	229594	359112	29	7	3	1	7	3	35	28	2	46	23	15
Uttar Pradesh														
R – R	641131	5137209	23	1	6	0	6	0	31	4	8	90	24	4
R – U	545499	763919	36	3	8	1	11	3	31	27	3	62	10	5
U – U	393184	630596	34	3	6	1	10	2	35	28	3	60	12	6
U – R	109600	313795	31	2	6	1	5	1	33	13	3	79	21	5
West Bengal														
R – R	669843	2669866	16	1	3	0	9	1	33	8	5	82	31	7
R – U	423439	504217	39	5	5	1	9	2	28	27	2	54	17	11
U – U	215458	274326	34	5	4	1	7	2	35	32	1	49	19	12
U – R	107690	193984	19	3	3	0	6	1	39	23	2	58	31	14

Source: Census of India, 1991 (b), Migration Table.

Note: Migration data for calamities are negligible, hence not shown. Unclassifiable also not shown. Himachal and Assam not shown.

(d) Thus, noteworthy feature is that migration occurs as a response to regional disparities in the levels of socio-economic development over the national space: in general, movements arise from the less economically developed to more developed regions.

(e) The map of inter-state migration streams for the females is almost identical to that of the males. The main difference is that volumes are much greater among the males. Migration-sending regions and migration-receiving regions are also the same; so also underlying macro socio-economic-political forces that cause such regional discontinuities in economic development, and which, in turn, induce migration to occur.

(f) Usually, the conventional explanations that are offered emphasize religious or cultural constraints controlling female mobility rate (Singh and Desuza, 1980) (without explaining why is it so), In sharp contrast to that, it is argued that both the males and the females respond to the same macro socio-economic-political processes in India, that have created, and still maintain, regional imbalances and underdevelopment. These processes induce labour migration to arise and proliferate (Mukherji, 1992b).

Salient Features of Migration According to 1991 Census

Briefly speaking, the following salient aspects of migration become apparent (Tables 1.4 to 1.12):

(a) Migration according to place of birth data: About 136.2 million people were enumerated in other places but within the district of enumeration (Table 1.4) Additionally 59 million were enumerated in other districts within the same state. Thus, *intra*-state migration is very large, 195 million.

(b) Inter-state migration (according to birthplace statistics): Besides about 27 million people migrated from other states (44% males, 56% females). Of these, the largest number of migrants moved from Uttar Pradesh, followed by Gujarat, Karnataka and Tamil Nadu. Besides, substantial number also moved from Kerala, Rajasthan and Andhra Pradesh. These flows are depicted in annexed maps (Figures 1.3–1.4). Such massive migration testifies that the people move over all parts of the country (Table 1.4).

Table 1.4 *Population Classified by Place of Birth, All-India, 1991*

Birthplace	*Rural-urban status*	*PLACE OF ENUMERATION*								
		Total			*Total %*		*Rural %*		*Urban %*	
		P	*M*	*F*	*M %*	*F %*	*M %*	*F %*	*M %*	*F %*
		1	*2*	*3*	*4*	*5*	*6*	*7*	*8*	*9*
TOTAL POPULATION		838567936	435208158	403359778	52	48	52	48	53	47
A. Born in India										
	Total	831345844	431530275	399815569	52	48	52	48	53	47
	Rural	646105009	333818973	312286036	52	48	52	48	46	54
	Urban	184304070	97383538	86920532	53	47	33	68	54	46
I. Within the state of enumeration										
	Total	804045899	419371916	384673983	52	48	52	48	53	47
	Rural	629001640	326308539	302693101	52	48	52	48	43	57
	Urban	174300583	92832394	81468189	53	47	32	69	55	45
(a) Born at the place of enumeration										
	Total	608726596	371530943	237195653	61	39	63	38	56	44
	Rural	462396039	289051082	173344957	63	38	63	38	0	0
	Urban	146330557	82479861	63850696	56	44	0	0	56	44
(b) Born elsewhere in the district of enumeration										
	Total	136214054	29336682	106877372	22	79	18	82	40	60
	Rural	123350596	24900556	98450040	20	80	17	83	40	60
	Urban	12363858	4298345	8065513	35	65	31	69	39	61
(c) Born in other districts of the state										
	Total	59105249	18504291	40600958	31	69	21	79	45	56
	Rural	43255005	12356901	30898104	29	71	19	81	47	53
	Urban	15606168	6054188	9551980	39	61	33	68	41	59

Cont'd...

...Cont'd

II. States in India beyond the state of enumeration											
All States	Rural	17103369	7510434	9592935	44	56	29	71	56	44
All States	Urban	10003487	4551144	5452343	46	55	39	61	47	53
Andhra Pradesh	Rural	782093	313796	468297	40	60	*30*	*70*	50	50
	Urban	499524	223772	275752	45	55	*38*	*62*	46	54
Bihar	Rural	2418303	1282175	1136128	53	47	38	62	65	35
	Urban	689741	373085	316656	54	46	45	55	56	44
Gujarat	Rural	531419	232981	298438	44	56	23	77	50	50
	Urban	391010	175284	215726	45	55	41	59	45	55
Haryana	Rural	977054	283997	693057	29	71	*16*	*84*	47	53
	Urban	431991	162971	269020	38	62	*26*	*74*	40	60
J&K	Rural	51179	22043	29136	43	57	33	67	55	45
	Urban	79066	36080	42986	46	54	41	59	47	53
Karnataka	Rural	897260	343708	553552	38	62	*28*	*72*	50	51
	Urban	595666	255190	340476	43	57	*36*	*64*	45	55
Kerala	Rural	554564	289969	264595	52	48	45	55	55	45
	Urban	553382	291663	261719	53	47	50	50	53	47
Madhya Pradesh	Rural	1022923	281418	741505	28	73	21	*79*	43	57
	Urban	457434	156700	300734	34	66	27	*73*	37	64
Maharashtra	Rural	920126	341682	578444	37	63	28	72	47	53
	Urban	809676	327248	482428	40	60	37	63	41	59
Orissa	Rural	493217	219143	274074	44	56	*31*	*70*	62	39
	Urban	136830	67656	69174	49	51	*39*	*61*	52	48
Punjab	Rural	749211	315924	433287	42	58	36	64	51	50
	Urban	615446	276686	338760	45	55	40	60	46	54
Rajasthan	Rural	1391781	528554	863227	38	62	21	79	54	46
	Urban	596710	265093	331617	44	56	34	66	46	54
Tamil Nadu	Rural	693194	335958	357236	49	52	43	57	53	47
	Urban	823370	408238	415132	50	50	49	52	50	50
Uttar Pradesh	Rural	4116597	2180504	1936093	53	47	32	68	61	39
	Urban	1833963	924695	909268	50	50	44	56	51	49
West Bengal	Rural	579043	186517	392526	32	68	*22*	*78*	50	50
	Urban	555026	236128	318898	43	58	*31*	*69*	46	54
B. Born Abroad		6941056	3578932	3362124	52	48	51	49	53	47

Source: Same as in Table 1.3.

Note: Some states with highly skewed sex ratios are shown in italics, signifying disproportionate migration among sexes.

(c) Migration according to place of last residence: According to place of last residence total migrants were 232 million, of which majority were females. Duration of residence of the migration depicts that, compared to 1971–81 period, volume of migration has slightly changed during 1981–91 (Table 1.5).

(d) Rural-urban share and short distance versus long distance migration: Within short distance (intra-state) migration, the bulk of the male migrants came from rural (70%), and 30 per cent moved from urban areas. Corresponding components of females were 77 per cent and 23 per cent, respectively. However, these proportions changed considerably with long distance (inter-state) migration, e.g., rural male migrants comprised 59 per cent and urban male migrants, only 31 per cent; while the corresponding shares of rural female migrants were 66 per cent and urban female migrants, 34 per cent (Table 1.5). So, female migrants crossing longer distances are as numerous as the males.

(e) Migrants classified by place of last residence and duration, 1991: Table 1.5 provides the details of migrants classified by last residence. Out of total 232 million migrants, among males, 5 per cent performed for less than 1 year, 22 per cent for 1–4 years, 16 per cent for 5–9 years, 20 per cent for 10–20 years, and 23 per cent above 20 years. That is, only 43 per cent migrated within 10 years, compared to more than 57 per cent above 10 years. Rates appear to have slightly reduced. For females, corresponding rates are 32 per cent within 10 years and 61 per cent above 10 years, showing much decline. Data of state variations is given in Table 1.5(a), in the Appendix.

Table 1.5 *Migrants Classified by Place of Last Residence and Duration, India, 1991*

Place of last residence	*Total/ Rural/ Urban*	*Total migrants*			*Duration of Residence in Place of Enumeration*									
					Less than 1 year		*1–4 years*		*5–9 years*		*10–19 years*		*20+ years*	
		P	*M*	*F*	*M %*	*F %*	*M %*	*F %*	*M %*	*F %*	*M %*	*F %*	*M %*	*F %*
Total Migrants		232112973	64308038	167804935	5	2	22	15	16	15	20	25	23	36
A. Last residence elsewhere in India														
	Total	225887846	61134303	164753543	5	2	23	16	16	15	21	25	21	36
	Rural	184955095	44689030	140266065	5	2	22	15	16	15	21	25	22	38
	Urban	39899267	16077065	23822202	5	3	25	21	17	18	21	24	20	25
I. Within the state of enumeration but outside the place of enumeration														
	Total	199198251	49250417	149947834	5	2	23	15	16	15	20	25	21	37
	Rural	168738715	37687299	131051416	5	2	22	14	15	15	20	25	22	38
	Urban	29631126	11298292	18332834	5	3	26	21	17	18	20	24	18	25
(a) Elsewhere in the district of enumeration														
	Total	140357053	30819650	109537403	5	2	22	14	15	15	19	25	20	38
	Rural	126365537	25825104	100540433	5	2	21	14	15	14	19	25	21	39
	Urban	13451835	4843988	8607847	6	3	25	20	17	17	19	24	16	26
(b) In other districts of the state of enumeration														
	Total	58841198	18430767	40410431	6	3	24	17	17	16	22	25	21	33
	Rural	42373178	11862195	30510983	6	3	23	16	16	15	22	25	22	36
	Urban	16179291	6454304	9724987	5	3	26	22	18	18	21	25	19	25
II. States in India beyond the state of enumeration														
	Total	26689595	11883886	14805709	6	4	22	19	17	17	23	25	25	29
	Rural	16216380	7001731	9214649	6	4	21	17	17	16	24	26	25	32
	Urban	10268141	4778773	5489368	5	4	24	22	16	18	22	25	25	25
B. Last residence outside India														
		5927882	3068146	2859736	3	2	8	9	7	8	15	17	59	57

Source: Census 1991(b). Unclassifiable not shown. Period not stated also not shown.

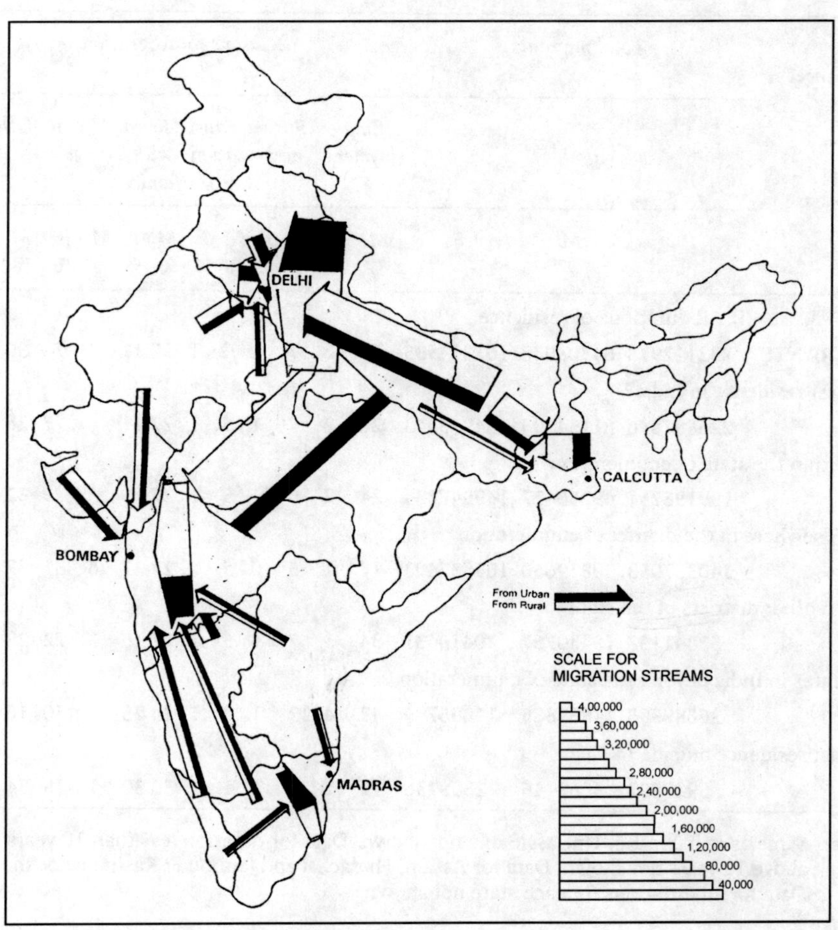
DELHI
CALCUTTA
BOMBAY
MADRAS
From Urban
From Rural
SCALE FOR
MIGRATION STREAMS
4,00,000
3,60,000
3,20,000
2,80,000
2,40,000
2,00,000
1,60,000
1,20,000
80,000
40,000

Table 1.6 *Migrants by Place of Last Residence, Duration and Reasons, India, 1991*

Last residence	*Total migrants*			*Reasons for Migration*											
				Employment		*Business*		*Education*		*Moved with family*		*Marriage*		*Others*	
	P	*M*	*F*	*M %*	*F %*	*M %*	*F %*	*M %*	*F %*	*M %*	*F %*	*M %*	*F %*	*M %*	*F %*
TOTAL (i) All durations of residence															
MIGRANTS	232112973	64308038	167804935	27	2	7	1	5	1	27	11	4	76	30	10
A. Last residence in India	225887846	61134303	164753543	28	2	7	1	5	1	27	11	4	77	28	9
I. Within the state of enumeration	199198251	49250417	149947834	24	2	6	1	5	1	27	9	5	79	32	9
(a) Elsewhere in the district of enumeration	140357053	30819650	109537403	18	1	5	0	5	1	27	7	6	81	37	9
(b) In other districts of the state	58841198	18430767	40410431	34	3	7	1	5	1	27	15	3	72	22	9
II. States in India beyond the state of enumeration	26689595	11883886	14805709	43	4	12	1	4	1	24	25	2	60	16	9
B. Last residence outside India	5927882	3068146	2859736	11	2	3	1	1	1	30	30	1	28	54	37

Source: Same as in Table 1.5. Unclassifiable not shown. Data for duration less than 10 years and above 10 years not shown. Data for Assam, Himachal and Jammu & Kashmir not shown. Data for all durations for each state not shown.

Literacy and Illiteracy among Migrants for Employment

In India, total migration for employment for all durations (which comprised 27% of all migration for various reasons) was 20.36 million. Of this 17.34 million (85%) were performed by males, and only 15 per cent by females. The majority (65%) came from rural areas, whereas the remaining came from urban areas (35%). Surprisingly, 24 per cent of male migrants were illiterate; and among the females, their proportion rose even to 49 per cent. That is, about half of the female migrants, who moved for employment, were illiterate; their proportion even rising to 57 per cent among the rural female migrants. Corresponding proportion among urban females was 30 per cent. Proportion of non-workers was 8.53 per cent among the males, rising to 53 per cent among the females. In short, considerable proportion of male migrants, who moved for employment, includes actually illiterates and non-workers. And, more than 90 per cent of female migrants, who moved for employment, were either illiterate or non-workers. These characteristics of migrants, indeed, reflect a very dismal picture.

The picture further worsens for recent migrants with durations of residence less than one year (1990–91). Forty per cent of male migrants for employment

Figure 1.6 *India: Female Migration to Mega Cities, 1981–91*

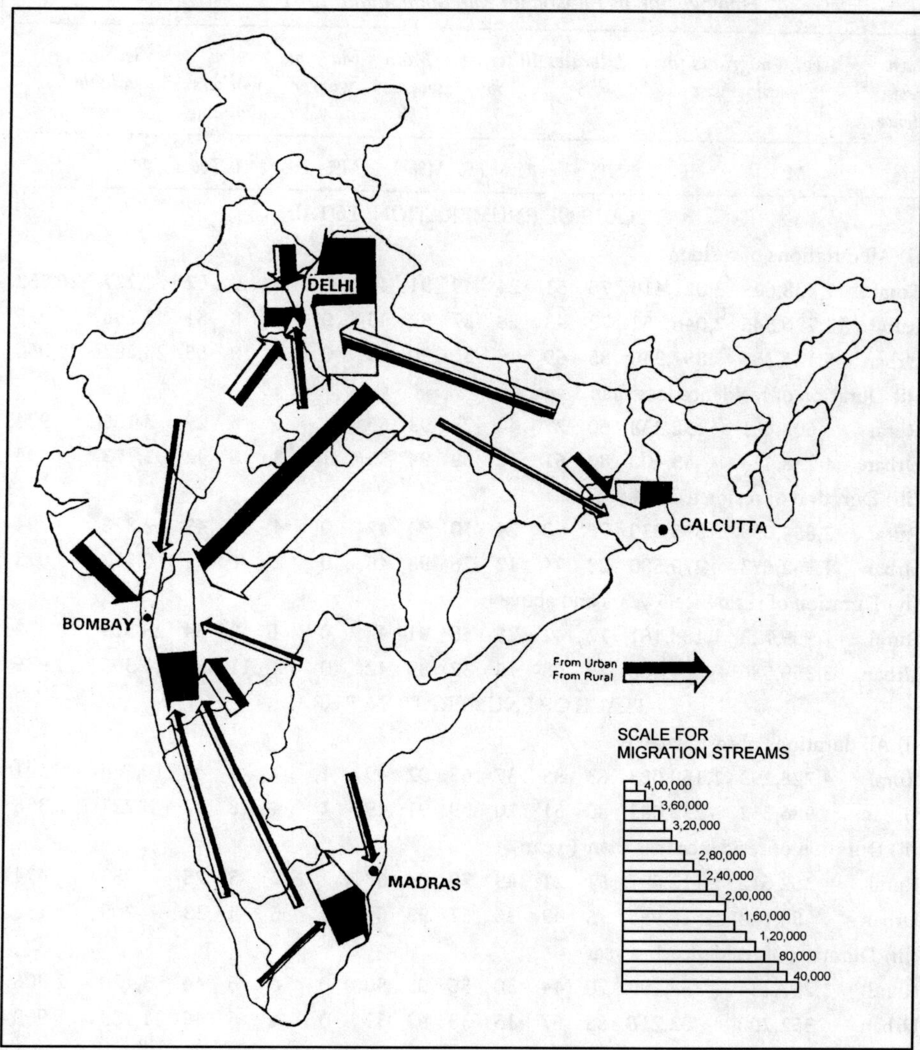

Source: Same as in Figure 1.5.

were illiterate (compared to 24 per cent during life-time migrants, for all durations); while their proportion among the females rose to even higher level, 73 per cent (compared to 49% among the life-time female migrants).

Almost similar picture arises when we examine the situation of migrants with duration of residence for 1 to 4 years or 5 years and above (Table 1.7). Compared to earlier situation, the condition of recent migrants (with duration of residence less than 1 year) has not improved much. This is again intriguing, given the context of the country's successive Five-Year Plans. Table 1.10 shows similar picture of literacy/illiteracy among all types of migrants, rather shows more precarious situation.

Table 1.7 *Main Workers, Marginal Workers and Literacy among Migrants Reporting 'Employment' as Reason for Migration, India, 1991*

Last residence	*Total migrants for employment*		*Literates %*		*Illiterates %*		*Main workers %*		*Marginal workers %*		*Non workers available*		*Seeking or available for work*	
	M	*F*	*M%*	*F%*	*M%*	*F%*	*M%*	*F%*	*M%*	*F%*	*M%*	*F%*	*M*	*F*
PLACE OF ENUMERATION: TOTAL														
(i) All durations of residence														
Total	17,338,629	3,021,416	76	51	24	49	91	44	0	4	9	52	78,227	26,552
Rural	11,796,545	2,046,753	72	43	28	57	92	45	0	4	8	51	43,288	14,915
Urban	5,121,353	887,940	85	69	15	31	90	43	0	2	10	55	23,292	9,056
(ii) Duration of residence less than 1 year														
Rural	602,481	152,238	60	27	40	73	93	65	1	6	6	29	3,156	924
Urban	238,433	43,400	82	61	18	39	94	55	1	3	6	42	1,173	494
(iii) Duration of residence 1–4 year														
Rural	2,854,098	595,030	76	50	24	50	94	47	0	4	6	49	12,828	4,794
Urban	1,362,673	279,580	88	74	12	26	93	46	0	2	6	52	6,552	3,078
(iv) Duration of residence 5 years and above														
Rural	7,959,723	1,188,161	72	42	28	58	91	42	0	4	8	54	25,519	8,379
Urban	3,359,586	524,408	85	68	15	32	89	42	0	2	11	57	14,396	4,955
PLACE OF ENUMERATION: RURAL														
(i) All durations of residence														
Rural	4,228,293	1,169,083	63	35	37	65	92	49	1	7	8	44	10,766	7,321
Urban	986,813	252,083	80	61	20	39	91	49	1	4	8	47	3,721	2,386
(ii) Duration of residence less than 1 year														
Rural	362,612	112,697	51	21	49	79	94	68	1	7	5	25	783	574
Urban	88,118	18,955	75	49	25	51	95	61	1	6	4	33	209	158
(iii) Duration of residence 1–4 year														
Rural	1,257,134	352,193	70	44	30	56	93	50	0	6	6	44	3,120	2,306
Urban	352,700	92,216	85	67	15	33	93	51	0	4	6	46	1,183	908
PLACE OF ENUMERATION: URBAN														
(i) All durations of residence														
Rural	7,568,252	877,670	77	53	23	47	92	39	0	1	8	60	32,522	7,594
Urban	4,134,540	635,857	86	73	14	28	90	41	0	1	10	58	19,571	6,670
(ii) Duration of residence less than 1 year														
Rural	239,869	39,541	74	45	26	55	91	57	2	2	7	41	2,373	350
Urban	150,315	24,445	86	70	14	30	93	51	1	1	6	48	964	336
(iii) Duration of residence 1–4 year														
Rural	1,596,964	242,837	81	60	19	40	94	42	0	1	6	57	9,708	2,488
Urban	1,009,973	187,364	89	77	11	23	93	44	0	1	6	56	5,369	2,170

Source: Same as in Table 1.6. Duration of residence 5 years and above not shown in rural and urban areas.

Illiterates and Semi-Educated Form the Majority of Migrants

Table 1.8 shows educational status of four categories of urban-ward migrants, who migrated for employment, and enumerated in urban areas:

(a) the migrants from rural areas within the state,
(b) the migrants from urban areas within the state,
(c) the migrants from rural areas, outside the state, and
(d) the migrants from urban areas, outside the state.

Table 1.8 *Migrants from Rural and Urban Areas Within and Outside State of Enumeration Reporting Employment as Reason for Migration by Education and Duration of Residence, Urban India, 1991*

Duration of Residence	*Total Migrants*		*Total %*		*Educational Level (%)*											
					Illiterate		*Literate but < matric @*		*Matric but < graduate ***		*Tech. Dip. or cert. not Equal to Deg.*		*Graduate + non-tech. Degree*		*Tech. Degree/ Diploma equal to degree or PG*	
	M	*F*	*M*	*F*	*M*	*F*	*M*	*F*	*M*	*F*	*M*	*F*	*M*	*F*	*M*	*F*
From rural areas within the state																
(i) All durations	5,040,307	707,867	88	12	19	46	35	29	28	15	2	2	13	5	3	2
(ii) < 1 year	162,048	29,705	85	15	21	52	30	26	28	13	3	2	14	5	4	2
(iii) 1–4 years	1,116,520	199,922	85	15	15	39	31	32	30	18	3	2	17	7	4	3
(iv) 5–9 years	939,521	141,683	87	13	16	41	33	32	30	17	3	2	15	6	3	3
(v) 10 years +	2,685,887	306,871	90	10	21	52	37	27	27	14	2	1	11	4	2	2
From urban areas within the state																
(i) All durations	2,478,556	446,818	85	15	11	26	27	30	30	23	4	2	22	14	6	5
(ii) < 1 year	95,114	16,564	85	15	11	28	23	27	29	22	5	2	26	15	7	5
(iii) 1–4 years	646,636	134,174	83	17	8	22	24	29	30	25	5	2	27	17	7	6
(iv) 5–9 years	460,056	90,688	84	16	10	24	26	32	30	24	4	2	24	14	6	5
(v) 10 years +	1,196,846	185,660	87	13	13	31	31	29	31	23	3	2	18	11	4	5
From rural areas of outside state																
(i) All durations	2,527,945	169,803	94	6	30	54	37	24	24	14	1	1	7	5	1	2.
(ii) < 1 year	77,821	9,836	89	11	37	65	32	19	22	10	1	1	6	3	1	2
(iii) 1–4 years	480,444	42,915	92	8	28	47	35	25	26	17	1	2	8	7	2	2
(iv) 5–9 years	451,357	30,209	94	6	29	50	37	27	25	15	1	1	7	6	1	1
(v) 10 years +	1,472,273	80,015	95	5	31	59	37	22	23	12	1	1	7	4	1	1
From urban areas of outside state																
(i) All durations	1,655,984	189,039	90	10	18	30	28	25	27	22	3	2	19	17	5	5
(ii) < 1 year	55,201	7,881	88	12	19	34	25	21	24	20	3	2	21	19	8	4
(iii) 1–4 years	363,337	53,190	87	13	16	25	25	23	25	23	3	2	23	21	7	6
(iv) 5–9 years	281,842	33,844	89	11	18	28	28	26	25	23	3	1	20	18	6	4
(v) 10 years +	918,975	86,396	91	9	18	34	30	25	28	22	3	1	17	14	4	4

Source: Same in Table 1.7. @ Often means only primary duration. ** Includes non-technical diplomas and certificates not equal to degree.

Note: 'All durations' includes unspecified durations.

Volume-wise, out of total 13.25 million migrants who moved for employment, 8.6 million came from within state (66% from rural areas and 33% from urban areas). Another 4.5 million came from outside the state (59% from rural areas and 41% from urban areas). Hence, the rural to urban migration comprised as large as 62 per cent, while urban to urban migration consisted of only 38 per cent (see also Table 1.7). We may examine the stock of illiterate plus semi-educated migrants (considering literate migrant – who are having less than matric education as the semi-educated, as most having really primary education). The following features may appear from Table 1.8:

(a) Among "intra-state" migrants from "rural areas", the proportion of illiterate plus semi-educated (less than matric) migrants (with all durations) comprised 53 per cent among males, rising to 75 per cent among females.
(b) Corresponding picture of illiterate and semi-educated migrants from "urban areas" with all durations of residence are only slightly better: 39 per cent among males and 55 per cent among females.
(c) But, corresponding proportion continued to remain worse among recent migrants from "urban areas", with duration of residence less than one year: 34 per cent for males and 55 per cent for females, respectively.
(d) Conversely, among "inter-state" migrants from "rural areas", share of illiterate and semi-literate migrants (with all durations) are again as high as 66 per cent among males, rising to 77 per cent among females.
(e) Corresponding picture among recent migrants (with less than one year duration) further worsens: 69 per cent among males and 82 per cent among females (Table 1.8).
(f) Corresponding situation of illiterate and semi-literate persons among Inter-state migrants from "urban areas" (with all durations) are 46 per cent among males and 55 per cent among females.
(g) Similar situation is also noticeable among recent migrants from urban areas with duration of residence less than one year: 44 per cent and 54 per cent, respectively.
(h) In sum, over half of male migrants from rural areas, both from intra-state and inter-state migration, comprised of illiterate and semi-educated migrants (with less than matric education). Their proportion only slightly improves, 45 per cent among migrants from urban areas. These situations further worsen among the recent migrants (with less than one year duration). Corresponding picture is further frustrating among the female migrants (55–65% among rural female migrants and 50–55% among urban female migrants). Table 1.10 provides similar picture of all kinds of migrants, who moved for various reasons, but seeking employment or available for work. Overall picture is same, rather more precarious.
(i) In short, such low quality migration of distressed people, both from rural and urban areas, and both from intra-state and inter-state migration, only dismally confirm one of the basic tenets of this study, i.e., poverty-induced migration and urban involution are occurring in India, not migration for prospect and high quality urbanization. Indeed, these are signs of underdevelopment, not development!
(j) Crucial question arises: What could be expected from masses of such illiterate and semi-educated migrants? What kind of quality of life is waiting for them in a town or city? Indeed, it is a movement from rural poverty to urban poverty. Much waste of human and national potentials and productivity.

(k) Of course, it must be reiterated that such migration occurs as their safety valve, a route to escape from acute rural poverty. Without such migration, they would be subjected to further abject poverty. So, even such migration is desirable. Migration restriction is completely out of question, as that would be most cruel and most undemocratic policy. Rather protection of migrants and elimination of barriers from their migration fields is most recommended (also see chapters 11 and 22).

Occupational Absorption of the Migrants

Whereas Table 1.9 provides the picture of occupational absorption of migrants who moved for employment, cross-classified according to rural-urban break-ups, Table 1.11 presents the same, but cross-classified according to educational status. A detailed discussion is given here about employment migration (Table 1.11). In both the tables, the occupational divisions are: Div. 0–1 refers to professional workers, Div. 2 refers to Administrative workers; likewise, Div. 3 (clerical workers), Div. 4 (sales workers), Div. 5 (services workers), Div. 6 (farm and related workers) and Div. 7–8–9 refer to production process workers. And, Div. 10 refers to unclassifiable groups (not shown).

Table 1.9 *Migrant Workers (other than Cultivators/Agricultural Labourers) from Place of Last Residence by Occupational Division, India, 1991*

Last Residence	*Rural/ Urban*	*Migrant Workers*		*Div. 0–1*		*Div.2*		*Div.3*		*Div. 4*		*Div.5*		*Div.6*		*Div. 7–8–9*	
		M	F	M %	F %	M %	F %	M %	F %	M %	F %	M %	F %	M %	F %	M %	F %
PLACE OF ENUMERATION: TOTAL																	
TOTAL		28,599,494	6,861,012	11	21	4	1	12	6	15	8	9	12	3	8	43	41
A. Last residence in India																	
	Total	27,156,662	6,689,090	11	21	4	1	12	6	15	8	9	12	3	8	44	41
	Rural	18,418,229	4,830,921	10	16	3	1	11	4	14	8	9	13	4	10	46	46
	Urban	8,653,530	1,843,061	12	34	7	2	15	12	16	7	9	12	2	3	38	28
I (a) Elsewhere in the district of enumeration																	
	Rural	7,589,021	3,040,277	13	15	3	1	12	3	14	9	9	12	5	11	41	48
	Urban	2,115,614	574,951	12	28	4	1	16	8	16	8	9	12	2	3	40	38
(b) In other districts of the state																	
	Rural	5,967,665	1,253,595	11	21	4	1	13	6	13	8	10	14	4	9	45	40
	Urban	3,500,308	786,716	15	37	7	2	17	14	14	7	9	12	2	3	35	24
II. States in India beyond the state of enumeration																	
	Rural	4,861,543	537,049	5	13	3	1	7	6	16	8	9	13	2	8	55	48
	Urban	3,037,608	481,394	10	35	9	3	11	15	18	7	8	12	1	3	40	23
B. Last residence outside India																	
	Total	1,442,832	171,922	9	24	5	2	11	8	26	6	9	14	3	12	35	32
PLACE OF ENUMERATION: RURAL																	
TOTAL		8,671,030	3,752,698	13	16	2	0	9	2	13	8	9	10	8	14	43	47
A. Last residence in India																	
	Total	8,244,600	3,691,834	13	16	2	0	10	2	13	8	9	10	8	14	43	47
	Rural	6,509,443	3,160,046	13	14	2	0	9	2	13	8	9	10	9	14	44	49
	Urban	1,714,009	525,703	13	28	4	1	12	5	13	8	10	10	6	8	41	38
I (a) Elsewhere in the district of enumeration																	
	Rural	3,906,393	2,292,351	15	13	2	0	10	2	13	8	9	11	9	14	41	49

Cont'd...

...Cont'd

Urban	702,823	265,645	13	26	3	1	13	5	14	8	10	10	4	6	41	42
(b) In other districts of the state																
Rural	1,672,468	643,169	15	19	2	1	9	2	11	8	9	9	10	15	42	44
Urban	635,729	187,671	15	32	4	1	13	6	12	8	10	10	7	9	38	33
II. States in India beyond the state of enumeration																
Rural	930,582	224,526	5	7	2	0	5	1	13	6	8	7	7	17	58	58
Urban	375,457	72,387	9	22	4	1	8	5	14	8	10	9	6	15	47	39
PLACE OF ENUMERATION: URBAN																
TOTAL	19,928,464	3,108,314	10	28	5	2	14	11	16	8	9	15	1	2	43	33
A. Last residence in India																
Total	18,912,062	2,997,256	10	28	5	2	14	11	16	8	9	15	1	2	44	33
Rural	11,908,786	1,670,875	9	21	4	1	12	8	15	9	10	17	1	2	48	40
Urban	6,939,521	1,317,358	12	37	8	2	16	15	16	7	8	13	1	1	37	24
I (a) Elsewhere in the district of enumeration																
Rural	3,682,628	747,926	11	20	4	1	15	6	16	9	9	15	2	2	42	44
Urban	1,412,791	309,306	11	31	5	1	17	11	17	8	9	13	1	1	39	34
(b) In other districts of the state																
Rural	4,295,197	610,426	10	23	4	1	14	9	13	9	10	19	1	2	46	35
Urban	2,864,579	599,045	15	39	8	2	18	16	14	7	8	12	1	1	35	22
II. States in India beyond the state of enumeration																
Rural	3,930,961	312,523	5	18	4	2	8	9	17	9	9	18	1	1	54	41
Urban	2,662,151	409,007	11	38	9	4	12	17	19	7	8	13	1	1	39	20

Source: Same as in Table 1.8. Last residence outside India not shown for rural and urban areas.

Migrants According to Place of Last Residence by Education and Duration, 1991

Table 1.10 indicates that, out of total 64 million life-time male migrants, who are seeking or now available for work, as many as 33 per cent were illiterate, and another 39 per cent had less than matric (or high school) education.

Table 1.10 *Migrants from Place of Last Residence by Sex, Education and Duration, 1991*

Duration of Residence	*Total migrants for 'employment', now seeking or available for work*			*Educational Level*											
				Illiterate		*Literate but < matric @*		*Matric But < Grad***		*Tech. Dip. not equal to deg.*		*Grad+ and Non-tech. Degree*		*Tech dip. equal to degree or PG*	
	P	*M*	*F*	*M*	*F*	*M*	*F*	*M*	*F*	*M*	*F*	*M*	*F*	*M*	*F*
(i) All durations	232,112,973	64,308,038	167,804,935	33	71	39	22	18	6	1	0	7	2	2	0
(ii) Less than 1 year	7,073,095	3,273,560	3,799,535	52	66	27	22	13	8	1	0	5	3	1	1
(iii) 1–4 years	39,824,804	13,998,584	25,826,220	35	59	36	28	18	10	1	0	8	3	2	1
(iv) 5–9 years	35,209,276	9,983,158	25,226,118	27	61	45	29	17	8	1	0	8	2	2	0

Source: Same as in Table 1.9. @ Includes literates without educational level and educational levels not classifiable. ** Includes non technical diplomas not equal to degree. 'All durations of residence' includes unspecified durations.

Hence, illiterate and semi-educated (less than matric) together comprised as high as 72 per cent of male migrants. Among 168 million female life-time migrants, the situations are terrible, huge 93 per cent. Even among recent migrants, their conditions do not improve: their proportions are 79 per cent for males and 88 per cent for females (with < 1 year duration), 71 per cent and 87 per cent among 1 to 4 year durations, and 72 per cent and 90 per cent among 5 to 9 year duration. What occupational absorption could we expect from such an ocean of illiterate or semi-skilled migrants?

Occupational Classifications of the Migrants

With reference to Table 1.11, one noteworthy point is: unlike in the Western countries, where sales and services and other occupational groups indicate higher occupational categories; but, in India, except for the first two categories, most of the occupational groups actually refer to low grade work. Thus, in India, 'sales' does not refer to computer sales work, rather refers to vegetable selling. Likewise, by service, it does not mean high level professional services like Radio or TV operation or repair services, rather it means low grade domestic servants, ayahs, or shoe-shine. These basic differences between the West and India must always be understood. Otherwise, it will give wrong notions and conclusions.

Another point that needs to be mentioned is that this particular Table 1.11 is computed very specially. Here, all the rows do not add up to 100 per cent, nor all the columns. Only the first row (where total is indicated) adds up to 100 per cent, separately for the males and the females. All small percentages in various little cells are tiny parts of that grand total percentage (100%), separately for males and females. In this way, the actual contribution of respective occupational categories to total picture becomes clear (separately for each sex).

Regarding occupational absorption of the migrants, the following features clearly emerge:

(a) As regards male migrants with all durations of residence, 19 per cent (last but one column) are found to be illiterate, and they are primarily engaged in low-grade production-processing work (Div. 7–8–9) (13%). Together, they comprise a large bulk of male migrants (44%). They are not engaged in sales, services, nor professional or administrative work, nor in clerical job. Similar feature are observed among the females migrants.

(b) Likewise, the similar picture arises among the literate male migrants (but less than matric education), i.e., they are conspicuously absent in most of the occupational categories, and crowding in low-grade production-process work. However, some males are also engaged in sales/services. The scene for the females follows the suit. Females are comparatively more engaged in services; but these are actually very low-grade services in informal sectors, like maid servants, domestic help, ayahs, or hawkers, vendors, vegetable sellers. The truth of this statement is that they are having less than secondary or matric education – often less than primary education. As such, they cannot be absorbed in highly skilled jobs.

(c) In the third educational level, those migrants who have completed matric education, but stay below graduation, most of the males are still engaged in

Table 1.11 *Migrant Workers (other than Cultivators and Agricultural Labourers) Reporting 'Employment' as Reason for Migration, by Duration of Residence, Educational Level, Occupational Division and Sex, All-India, 1991*

Educational Level	*Total 'Employment' Migrants*			*Occupational Divisions*															
				Div.0-1		*Div.2*		*Div.3*		*Div. 4*		*Div.5*		*Div.6*		*Div.7–8–9*		*Total*	
				Professional Workers		*Adminis. Workers*		*Clerical Workers*		*Sales Workers*		*Service Workers*		*Farm Workers*		*Production Process workers*			
	P	*M*	*F*	*M%*	*F%*	*M%*	*F%*	*M%*	*F%*	*M%*	*F%*	*M%*	*F%*	*M%*	*F%*	*M%*	*F%*	*M%*	*F%*
PLACE OF ENUMERATION: TOTAL																			
(i) All durations of residence																			
Total	15906339	14847987	1058352	12.9	37.5	4.1	1.2	15.3	10.5	8.3	3.1	10.7	15.3	2.5	4.7	44.5	25.9	100	100
Illiterate	3153770	2784491	369279	0.1	0.4	0.1	0.1	0.0	0.0	1.7	2.0	2.3	8.2	0.9	3.6	12.9	19.3	18.8	34.9
Literate but < matric*	5060884	4881090	179794	1.2	3.6	0.5	0.1	2.9	1.6	3.5	0.7	4.7	5.4	0.9	1.0	18.8	4.5	32.9	17.0
Matric but not graduate	4372190	4120090	252100	3.3	15.4	1.0	0.3	7.0	4.6	2.2	0.3	3.1	1.3	0.5	0.1	10.3	1.7	27.7	23.8
Tech diploma not degree	469589	419299	50290	1.4	4.4	0.2	0.0	0.2	0.1	0.1	0.0	0.0	0.0	0.0	0.0	1.0	0.1	2.8	4.8
Graduate/PG, not tech degree	2185505	2055699	129806	3.9	7.0	2.0	0.6	4.9	3.9	0.7	0.1	0.6	0.2	0.2	0.0	1.4	0.3	13.8	12.3
Tech degree	664401	587318	77083	3.0	6.7	0.4	0.1	0.3	0.3	0.1	0.0	0.0	0.1	0.0	0.0	0.2	0.1	4.0	7.3
PLACE OF ENUMERATION: RURAL																			
(i) Duration of residence less than 1 year																			
Total	454427	391655	62772	12.5	20.5	2.2	0.5	8.8	2.4	3.5	1.5	12.9	7.4	6.4	5.9	51.8	60.2	100	100
Illiterate	175555	133323	42232	0.3	0.5	0.2	0.2	0.0	0.0	1.0	1.2	1.7	3.1	2.6	5.0	27.4	56.1	34	67.3

Cont'd...

...Cont'd

Literate but < matric*	122241	115739	6502	1.5	2.1	0.3	0.0	2.0	0.5	1.5	0.2	5.2	3.4	2.0	0.7	16.7	3.3	29.6	10.4
Matric but not graduate	93993	86417	7576	3.6	9.1	0.5	0.1	4.1	1.0	0.8	0.1	5.0	0.8	1.4	0.1	6.3	0.7	22.1	12.1
Tech diploma not degree	11090	9251	1839	1.4	2.8	0.1	0.0	0.2	0.1	0.0	0.0	0.1	0.0	0.0	0.0	0.7	0.1	2.4	2.9
Graduate/PG, not tech degree	35922	33526	2396	2.9	2.8	1.0	0.1	2.4	0.7	0.2	0.0	1.0	0.1	0.4	0.0	0.7	0.1	8.6	3.8
Tech degree	15626	13399	2227	2.8	3.3	0.2	0.0	0.2	0.1	0.0	0.0	0.1	0.0	0.0	0.0	0.2	0.0	3.4	3.5
PLACE OF ENUMERATION: URBAN																			
(i) Duration of residence less than 1 year																			
Total	448706	410080	38626	12.0	27.0	6.1	1.5	14.1	10.3	6.9	2.2	17.9	22.5	1.7	1.0	39.4	34.2	100	100
Illiterate	93845	77444	16401	0.2	0.5	0.1	0.1	0.0	0.0	1.4	1.5	2.4	11.0	0.5	0.6	13.7	28.0	18.9	42.5
Literate but < matric*	120574	113963	6611	0.9	2.0	0.4	0.1	1.8	1.0	2.7	0.4	6.4	9.3	0.5	0.3	14.6	4.0	27.8	17.1
Matric but not graduate	117681	110920	6761	2.1	9.5	1.0	0.2	5.7	3.9	1.8	0.2	7.3	1.8	0.4	0.1	8.2	1.7	27	17.5
Tech diploma not degree	15241	13919	1322	1.6	3.0	0.2	0.0	0.3	0.2	0.1	0.0	0.1	0.1	0.0	0.0	1.1	0.1	3.4	3.4
Graduate/PG, not tech degree	78370	73282	5088	3.8	6.4	3.7	0.9	5.9	4.8	0.8	0.1	1.6	0.4	0.3	0.0	1.4	0.3	17.9	13.2
Tech degree	22995	20552	2443	3.5	5.6	0.7	0.2	0.4	0.5	0.1	0.0	0.1	0.1	0.0	0.0	0.3	0.1	5	6.3

Source: Same as in Table 1.10. A small proportion of unclassifiable are not shown.

Note: This table is specially computed, as grand row total (under each category) is 100 per cent separately for males and females, i.e., each small cell is a tiny part of that grand row total, indicating how many illiterate (or semi-educated) male or female migrants working as sales/services, etc. Then all row total in last column are summed up to get grand row total (100%). Zero in small cells means less than 1 per cent. Data for longer durations are not shown.
* Often means less than primary education.

low-grade production-process work, and only some do clerical work. Among the females, however, more are found engaged in sales/services.

(d) Among higher educational level (above graduation), a small share of both sexes got absorption in professional or administrative or clerical work. But, they are only a tiny part of total migrants for work.

(e) The position of males is very precarious. And, the conditions of the female migrants are further dismal.

(f) If all low-grade occupational categories of such illiterate and semi-literate (below secondary) migrants are added up, then, it will comprise 60 per cent low-grade workers among the males and 55 per cent of low-grade workers among females (for all durations). In short, majority of them were compelled being absorbed in a bazaar-type or low-grade urban informal sectors where cut-throat competition, low wages, low productivity, insecurity and exploitation predominate. These are indeed symptoms of underdevelopment, not development. In fact, these are signs of mobility from rural poverty to urban poverty. *However, as this allows escape from abject poverty, even such low-grade migration and low-grade work absorption are also much more desirable than absolute stagnation or quick death in tottering villages.*

(g) Almost similar features also emerge among the migrants with duration of residence 0–4 years, and also separately for males and females. Thus, the situation has not improved at all in recent years, in spite of tall claims of higher economic growth during the period. The poor remained in the same darkness as before. Development has not touched them. This is the most pitiable condition of the migrants.

(h) Table 1.12 provides some detailed information regarding literates, illiterates, main workers, marginal workers and non-workers among the migrants, which reiterate almost similar picture, as described above.

(i) In sum, it is a movement of distressed people from one region of poverty to another, from rural unemployment to urban underemployment, from one area of stress to another. Indeed, these are symptoms of poverty and underdevelopment. These migration tables must act as revelations for planners, administrators and social scientists. We need to act urgently for the upliftment of these masses of poor migrants in India. Many migration-urban researchers still try to camouflage real situations and try to present a good picture of their condition. Such attempts do more harm than good to these impoverished humanity!.

(j) *By this dismal description, it is not meant to argue for migration-restriction or any denigration of such low-quality migration, rather the avowed purpose is to highlight their true conditions.* And, to urge before all concerned scholars, planners, administrators, policy-makers and the governments (local, state and national) *to wake up to the grave situation and to eliminate widespread rural poverty and to help the hapless hundreds of millions of migrants to surmount their poignantly adverse situation.*

Migrants by Literacy, Main Workers, Marginal Workers and Non-workers, 1991

Table 1.12 presents a broad picture of literates, illiterates, main and marginal workers and non-workers among the migrants in India, in 1991. Thirty-three per cent of male migrants were illiterate, their share among the females were more dismal (70%). Main workers and marginal workers among male migrants were 62 per cent and 1 per cent, the situation was more precarious among the female migrants, i.e., 22 per cent and 10 per cent, respectively. Non-workers are substantial among males (37%) and among females, staggeringly high (68%). Their condition further deteriorates among the recent migrants (less than one year duration) in many respects.

Table 1.12 *Migrants by Literacy, Main Workers, Marginal Workers and Non-workers, All-India, 1991*

Rural/urban status of last residence	*Total migrants*		*Literates*		*Illiterates*		*Main workers*		*Marginal workers*		*Non-workers*	
	M	*F*	*M%*	*F%*	*M%*	*F%*	*M%*	*F%*	*M%*	*F%*	*M%*	*F%*
PLACE OF ENUMERATION: TOTAL												
(i) All durations of residence												
Total	64,308,038	167,804,935	67	30	33	70	62	22	1	10	37	68
Rural	44,689,040	140,266,065	63	24	37	76	63	24	1	11	36	65
Urban	16,077,065	23,822,202	77	58	23	42	58	13	1	4	42	83
PLACE OF ENUMERATION: RURAL												
(i) All durations of residence												
Total	32,807,219	129,660,405	56	22	44	78	61	25	1	13	39	62
Rural	26,451,790	118,593,451	54	20	46	80	61	26	1	13	38	61
Urban	4,547,492	8,931,937	68	44	32	56	51	19	1	9	48	72
(ii) Duration of residence less than 1 year												
Rural	1,652,989	2,341,629	36	24	64	76	49	23	1	9	50	68
Urban	371,062	333,453	52	40	48	60	49	14	1	5	50	81
PLACE OF ENUMERATION: URBAN												
(i) All durations of residence												
Total	31,500,819	38,144,530	78	56	22	44	64	10	0	2	35	88
Rural	18,237,250	21,672,614	76	49	24	52	67	11	0	2	33	88
Urban	11,529,573	14,890,265	81	67	19	33	60	10	0	1	39	90
(ii) Duration of residence less than 1 year												
Rural	685,239	598,538	62	48	38	52	51	10	1	1	48	89
Urban	470,864	459,040	67	61	33	39	49	8	1	1	51	92

Source: Census 1991(b), Migration Tables, D-series, R.G. Office, New Delhi, CDs 1998.

Note: 'All durations of residence' includes unspecified durations of residence. Data for other duration of residence not shown.

Literacy and Illiteracy Situation of the Migrants in Selected 52 Class I Cities

Table 1.13 shows the percentage and volume of migration according to literacy level of the selected 52 cities. Accordingly,

1. For migrants of all durations, as many as 13 cities show more than 25 per cent male migrants to be illiterate (Hyderabad, Vijaywada, Delhi, Surat, Vishakhapatnam, Solapur, Ludhiana, Amritsar, Jalandhar, Jodhpur, Meerut,

Ghaziabad and Asansol). Among them, Ludhiana (33.64%) leads, followed by Ghaziabad (32.6%).

2. The situation in case of female migrants is worse: 23 cities show more than 40 per cent of the female lifetime migrants to be illiterate (Hyderabad, Vishakhapatnam, Vijaywada, Jamshedpur, Delhi, Surat, Faridabad, Indore, Gwalior, Durg-Bhilai Nagar, Ludhiana, Amritsar, Jaipur, Jodhpur, Kota, Kanpur, Varanasi, Agra, Meerut, Allahabad, Bareilly, Ghaziabad, Gorakhpur, Asansol). And, in some, nearly half of the female migrants are illiterate: Ghaziabad (51.4%), Meerut (49.9%), Bareilly (49.7%), Jodhpur (49.6%).
3. Compare this picture with that of recent years (migrants of last 0–5 years) which shows that the situation has worsened: nine cities (Delhi, Surat, Durg-Bhilai Nagar, Greater Mumbai, Ludhiana, Amritsar, Ghaziabad and Asansol) have more than 30 per cent male migrants reported as illiterates. The number of the cities swells to 28 when we identify the cities having more than 25 per cent of its male migrants illiterate. Ludhiana (42.6%) has the highest percentage of male illiterate migrants, followed by Ghaziabad (36.8%).
4. The percentage of female illiteracy is above 40 per cent in 17 cities. While all other cities show a consistent pattern in terms of comparison between the two categories of duration of residence, one notable exception being Mumbai. Here, the comparison of literacy rates of both categories (all duration migrants and migrants for last five years) is intriguing. Only 19 per cent of the migrants of all durations were illiterate. But among the migrants of last five years more than 30 per cent are illiterate. That is, more unskilled and illiterate migrants have moved into Mumbai recently.

Occupational Absorption of Migrants in Selected 51 Class I Cities

Table 1.14 gives the volume of migration and percentage distribution of migrant workers by sex in seven occupational categories in 51 selected cities of India.

1. The percentage of migrant workers employed in low-grade production work is significant as compared to other categories. As many as 13 cities (Jamshedpur, Ahmedabad, Surat, Rajkot, Faridabad complex, Durg-Bhilai Nagar, Greater Mumbai, Pune, Nashik, Ludhiana, Coimbatore, Kolkata, Asansol) out of the total 51 cities show more than 50 per cent male migrant workers employed in such production-process work. These 13 cities include metropolises like Greater Mumbai (50.5%) and Kolkata (49.1%). Surat shows the highest proportion of male migrant workers employed in production-process work (70.7%) followed by Ludhiana (63.1%).
2. Apart from these 13 cities, another 17 cities show 40 to 50 per cent migrant workers joining in production-process work. In other words, more than 40 per cent of the total migrant workers are engaged in low-grade production process and related activities in 30 most important cities of India.
3. In case of female migrant workers the scenario is a bit different and interesting. It is true that a large chunk of female migrants is employed in production-process work, but at the same time we can also observe a considerable segment going into the professional occupations. In production work the proportion of females is low as compared to the

proportion of males. But, in the professional occupations in all cities proportion of females is higher as compared to the males. But, their volume are very small. Also noteworthy feature is that since their educational level is not very high, as we shall see in Chapter 2 (Table 2.3), most such women professional workers are actually primary teachers or nurses, not high grade technicians, or doctors.

4. Only five cities (Durg-Bhilai Nagar, Nagpur, Solapur, Aurangabad, and Salem) show more than 40 per cent females employed in the production-process work, while 10 cities (Patna, Kozhikode, Ludhiana, Amritsar, Jalandhar, Jodhpur, Lucknow, Meerut, Allahabad, Bareilly) show more than 40 per cent females employed in the professional jobs. And, in all 51 cities, more than 20 per cent of the female migrant workers are employed in the professional jobs. Nevertheless, their absolute number is still very small!

Table 1.13 *Volume and Duration of Residence of Migrants, 1991 (52 Class I Cities)*

City/UA	Population			All Durations of Residence									Duration of Residence 0–5 Years					
				No. of Lifetime Migrants				Lit. %		Illit. %			No. of Migrants		Lit. %		Illit. %	
	Total	M	F	Total	% of Pop	M	F	M%	F%	M%	F%		M	F	M%	F%	M%	F%
Hyderabad	4280261	2224718	2055543	1123185	26	571895	551290	75	57	25	43		165940	156025	71	57	29	43
Vishakhap.	1051918	542742	509176	453218	43	228652	224566	76	58	24	42		68340	65980	73	59	27	41
Vijayawada	845305	430076	415229	325810	39	154581	171229	73	57	27	43		37620	38650	70	59	30	41
Guwahati	577591	323986	253605	276835	48	157918	118917	82	68	18	32		41634	30910	78	62	22	38
Patna	1098572	600643	497929	337036	31	139649	197387	85	63	15	37		44993	38770	81	69	19	31
Jamshedpur	834535	449218	385317	311574	37	133805	177769	82	57	18	43		29696	29838	74	62	26	38
Chandigarh	574646	316946	257700	365227	64	199595	165632	78	67	22	33		53631	47114	73	68	27	32
New Delhi	8375188	4574263	3800925	3290708	39	1801830	1488878	74	55	26	45		426431	343938	69	57	31	43
Ahmedabad	3297655	1745017	1552638	1115129	34	557427	557702	81	63	19	37		89563	103860	71	64	29	36
Surat	1517076	825115	691961	739983	49	412260	327723	73	55	27	45		119914	94309	66	52	34	48
Vadodra	1115265	387643	527622	482791	43	236533	246258	83	71	17	29		50670	53570	73	67	27	33
Rajkot	651007	338158	312849	266634	41	125457	141177	81	65	19	35		25686	30920	75	68	25	32
Faridabad	613828	340341	273487	339463	55	183481	155982	77	53	23	47		50420	40237	73	56	27	44
Bangalore	4086548	2147978	1938570	1185168	29	615975	569193	82	66	18	34		169470	152360	77	64	23	36
Mysore	652246	335612	316634	220066	34	107162	112904	83	68	17	32		35220	31390	81	72	19	28
Hubli.	647640	336272	311368	224099	35	106607	117492	82	63	18	37		30494	27792	79	66	21	34
Kochi	1139543	570794	568749	284574	25	112333	172241	88	86	12	14		37610	49780	80	83	20	17
Thiruvana-thapuram	825682	409515	416167	151800	18	71340	80460	93	89	7	11		20890	21880	89	87	11	13
Kozhikode	800913	396242	404671	170250	21	65990	104260	83	82	17	18		22740	30090	71	76	29	24
Indore	1104065	582700	521365	355119	32	163512	191607	77	59	23	41		36760	39040	72	63	28	37
Bhopal	1063662	561582	502080	425736	40	215896	209840	79	58	21	42		47799	48170	74	63	26	37
Jabalpur	887188	471326	415862	263911	30	122537	141374	83	65	17	35		26940	30930	77	68	23	32
Gwalior	720068	390293	329775	183431	25	76070	107361	81	54	19	46		19720	24370	73	60	27	40

Cont'd...

...Cont'd

Durg-Bhilai	688670	364398	324272	385922	56	197782	188140	77	54	23	46	44179	47189	70	56	30	44
G. Mumbai	12571720	6875271	5696449	4436167	35	2494516	1941651	81	62	19	38	449227	396311	70	56	30	44
Pune	2485014	1304739	1180275	684765	28	339222	345543	78	62	22	38	95980	95905	70	61	30	39
Nagpur	1661409	867082	794327	303602	18	143507	160095	82	64	18	36	35310	35428	79	70	21	30
Nashik	722139	381993	340146	249648	35	120806	128842	81	65	19	35	34730	35215	76	65	24	35
Solapur	620499	318885	301614	149160	24	65548	83612	75	53	25	47	13160	15770	73	62	27	38
Aurangabad	592052	315966	276086	147954	25	72142	75812	81	55	19	45	23970	21960	79	59	21	41
Ludhiana	1012062	562880	449182	474240	47	226680	247560	66	59	34	41	56783	48849	57	60	43	40
Amritsar	709456	376721	332735	190099	27	80882	109217	71	57	29	43	19460	23420	65	61	35	39
Jalandhar	519530	277633	241897	193680	37	89730	103950	73	61	27	39	19010	19714	67	65	33	35
Jaipur	1514425	810664	703761	442598	29	220864	221734	81	56	19	44	60790	52123	77	60	23	40
Jodhpur	648621	347347	301274	115620	18	55678	59942	74	50	26	50	18020	17149	74	57	26	43
Kota	536444	287727	248717	196228	37	94410	101818	80	53	20	47	22582	22970	73	56	27	44
Chennai	5361468	2782106	1579362	1498195	28	769969	728226	86	70	14	30	165041	161740	79	69	21	31
Coimbatore	1135549	627977	507572	305010	27	150159	154851	85	67	15	33	42270	40140	82	71	18	29
Madurai	1093702	555678	538024	274198	25	130063	144135	85	68	15	32	26410	29980	79	70	21	30
Tiruchchi-rappalli	711120	362943	348177	232678	33	107440	125238	86	71	14	29	26390	29660	82	74	18	26
Salem	573685	293457	280228	100866	18	44276	56590	80	63	20	37	10680	12890	78	70	22	30
Kanpur	2111284	1149513	961771	399569	19	185915	213654	78	56	22	44	37580	38310	76	61	24	39
Lucknow	1642134	879704	762430	464991	28	226828	238163	82	63	18	37	65340	57233	77	67	23	33
Varanasi	1026467	551854	474613	74210	7	30460	43750	88	59	12	41	9160	8790	86	65	14	35
Agra	955694	518604	437090	118675	12	30929	87746	81	56	19	44	7310	16870	79	56	21	44
Meerut	846954	452549	394405	120540	14	35800	84740	74	50	26	50	9870	17930	74	58	26	42
Allahabad	858213	472709	385504	129822	15	52030	77792	83	59	17	41	8360	8320	89	68	11	32
Bareilly	607652	322827	284825	109457	18	42590	66867	78	50	22	50	11070	14100	76	58	24	42
Ghaziabad	519508	284751	234757	105382	20	39680	65702	67	49	33	51	8710	16630	63	57	37	43
Gorakhpur	489850	264214	225636	90278	18	36480	53798	87	55	13	45	10000	10390	82	65	18	35
Kolkata	10916272	5973888	4942384	2617626	24	1381157	1236469	76	63	24	37	184794	193521	72	65	28	35
Asansol	763845	417450	346395	249574	33	116556	133018	72	52	28	48	17450	21300	64	57	36	43

Source: Census of India, 1991(b) and (c), Migration Tables, D-series, R.G. Office, New Delhi.

Table 1.14 *Volume of Migration, Migrant Workers and Percentage of Migrant Workers by Occupational Division, 51 Class I Cities, All-India, 1991*

City/UA	All Migrant Workers (All Durations)			Prof. workers %		Admin. %		Clerical %		Sales %		Services %		Farmers %		Production Workers %	
	Total	Male	Female	M	F	M	F	M	F	M	F	M	F	M	F	M	F
Hyderabad	408284	345901	62383	12.2	26.1	8.5	2.4	14.7	15.0	13.2	7.3	7.3	12.2	0.6	1.0	41.3	33.9
Vishakhapatnam	153733	137304	16429	10.8	26.1	5.2	1.2	13.4	11.2	12.1	12.5	7.7	15.6	1.1	0.7	47.5	31.5
Vijayawada	115895	101475	14420	7.1	22.5	4.7	0.9	12.7	9.3	19.6	14.5	8.4	20.3	0.5	0.6	46.3	31.1
Guwahati City	127596	112347	15249	9.5	27.4	6.0	2.0	20.5	20.6	21.3	5.7	11.4	29.8	1.0	0.5	27.0	10.8
Patna	38772	33334	5438	19.6	56.6	9.1	2.2	27.7	9.7	13.5	5.4	12.8	13.6	0.8	0.7	14.0	8.9
Jamshedpur	95051	85595	9456	10.5	35.5	4.4	2.8	10.3	5.9	11.9	6.8	8.6	13.6	0.6	0.2	52.3	32.7
New Delhi	1509812	1360744	149068	7.7	30.0	6.4	3.8	12.8	15.6	17.9	7.0	9.5	19.5	0.7	0.4	43.6	21.5
Ahmedabad	400714	365784	34930	6.8	32.4	6.9	1.9	11.9	15.4	15.4	6.5	7.1	12.5	0.7	0.9	50.4	29.4
Surat	311143	295911	15232	2.8	27.4	3.2	0.9	3.6	8.5	13.9	11.3	4.1	18.2	0.4	0.7	70.7	31.2
Vadodra	166530	147523	19007	11.4	35.6	7.4	2.3	15.6	19.1	11.6	5.0	9.5	16.4	0.6	0.9	43.2	19.5
Rajkot	85844	77715	8129	6.1	30.1	5.9	1.1	12.5	12.7	17.5	7.0	5.1	10.3	0.8	1.3	51.6	36.3
Faridabad Complex	138751	129024	9727	7.2	39.4	6.0	2.4	9.7	13.1	11.3	4.7	5.6	10.3	0.5	0.2	58.7	28.5
Bangaluru	605644	510259	95385	10.6	22.5	7.1	2.8	11.9	16.4	16.4	7.0	8.6	13.1	0.7	0.7	42.7	35.7
Mysore	71048	58592	12456	13.9	30.0	6.3	1.8	15.4	15.9	17.0	7.2	9.9	12.9	1.5	1.1	34.7	29.4
Hubli-Dharwad	63898	55227	8671	11.9	29.4	5.3	1.3	19.1	16.4	16.3	10.6	11.3	14.6	1.0	0.8	33.9	25.7
Kochi	85513	61852	23661	14.2	32.7	10.7	3.2	13.3	21.7	13.9	4.7	7.8	18.9	2.3	1.6	36.0	15.9
Thiruvanathapuram	55922	39535	16387	22.5	36.7	11.6	4.2	19.8	29.8	12.1	3.2	7.8	18.1	2.4	0.3	22.7	7.2
Kozhikode	37844	28745	9099	12.1	43.8	9.4	1.9	11.4	16.0	18.0	2.3	7.5	17.6	4.3	0.8	36.9	17.3
Indore	113441	96078	17363	7.5	27.3	8.9	2.2	10.0	9.3	16.6	6.6	9.7	12.0	0.4	0.2	42.8	37.5
Bhopal	172753	145218	27535	10.5	27.3	9.0	2.8	19.5	19.3	8.8	3.2	9.4	11.4	1.0	1.0	38.3	30.9
Jabalpur	85267	74400	10867	9.6	33.1	6.0	2.1	17.4	14.0	10.4	5.6	9.3	10.4	1.2	1.1	43.2	31.5
Gwalior	50971	43512	7459	15.7	36.5	8.5	2.0	14.4	8.7	8.8	4.0	9.3	7.3	0.9	0.4	37.6	36.5
Durg-Bhilai Nagar	148943	130526	18417	6.6	18.7	6.1	1.7	7.1	5.0	11.8	11.0	6.2	14.6	0.9	1.2	59.9	45.5
Greater Mumbai	2577910	2308603	269307	5.7	22.1	4.8	2.3	10.9	17.6	17.2	10.5	9.5	20.7	0.5	0.5	50.6	25.1

Cont'd...

...Cont'd

Pune	371389	306653	64736	8.3	21.5	7.3	2.1	10.7	12.7	11.3	9.5	9.1	15.3	0.7	0.9	51.8	35.6
Nagpur	185909	157207	28702	9.8	21.9	6.3	1.7	12.2	9.1	13.6	9.6	9.6	14.3	0.6	0.7	47.3	41.4
Nashik	98700	83732	14968	9.7	24.8	5.5	1.8	12.5	9.7	10.1	10.5	9.0	14.9	1.2	1.8	50.6	34.7
Solapur	43251	33361	9890	11.0	18.9	3.8	0.9	14.3	5.4	15.1	9.1	9.8	10.5	0.6	0.3	44.8	53.9
Aurangabad	94765	80644	14121	12.4	26.0	5.0	1.2	16.3	9.9	10.6	6.8	7.8	10.9	0.5	0.9	46.3	42.2
Ludhiana	156151	146898	9253	4.7	49.4	2.6	1.0	6.3	11.6	16.2	4.3	5.4	10.3	0.8	0.5	63.1	21.3
Amritsar	59028	53469	5559	7.4	53.7	2.2	0.7	11.1	12.0	22.3	4.9	7.4	12.3	0.7	0.2	47.2	14.4
Jalandhar	63741	57233	6508	7.3	48.8	4.1	1.2	11.3	12.8	19.5	6.1	10.2	11.7	0.6	0.3	44.8	17.0
Jaipur	154703	138253	16450	12.6	39.0	6.8	2.8	16.1	10.1	16.8	6.1	9.6	12.1	0.6	1.0	36.0	26.0
Jodhpur	35856	32515	3341	9.7	43.6	3.6	1.1	11.8	8.1	13.8	5.0	13.4	7.8	0.8	0.7	38.5	29.0
Kota	69153	61836	7317	11.0	34.8	3.8	0.6	13.3	6.1	14.7	5.5	8.6	10.6	0.7	0.7	46.9	38.6
Chennai	600901	526316	74585	10.3	30.3	10.9	3.3	13.1	21.4	16.5	6.9	8.4	13.6	0.6	0.2	39.5	23.6
Coimbatore	122458	106434	16024	7.6	26.7	9.5	2.0	9.2	14.8	15.0	7.2	7.5	12.6	0.4	0.7	50.3	35.2
Madurai	58858	50089	8769	8.9	30.3	8.9	1.3	13.6	13.2	22.4	12.9	9.3	14.8	0.4	0.3	35.9	26.4
Tiruchchirappalli	73197	63789	9408	8.4	31.1	6.0	1.4	13.7	15.8	20.9	11.2	8.8	14.1	0.3	0.2	41.5	25.4
Salem	38864	31603	7261	9.0	22.8	9.6	1.4	12.1	8.6	18.0	11.4	8.5	8.6	0.4	0.3	41.9	46.2
Kanpur	128361	121274	7087	7.7	36.0	4.2	1.8	13.9	9.2	16.8	9.7	7.2	16.5	0.5	0.4	45.7	22.3
Lucknow	99544	89538	10006	15.0	40.0	8.1	3.0	24.5	17.0	13.0	6.8	10.3	10.0	0.9	0.6	21.9	15.7
Varanasi	12315	10046	2269	15.6	38.2	4.1	1.1	16.8	4.2	15.6	9.8	13.3	12.8	0.9	0.8	30.0	27.4
Agra	19339	16861	2478	9.2	34.6	2.7	0.8	14.3	6.9	17.3	6.2	8.1	13.6	0.4	0.8	37.4	31.1
Meerut	52349	47804	4545	10.4	46.6	3.7	1.6	13.8	8.6	17.1	5.2	7.6	16.3	0.9	1.1	41.6	17.2
Allahabad	13546	11349	2197	18.9	42.8	3.9	0.9	26.7	10.2	10.8	9.6	13.2	10.7	0.6	0.3	20.2	20.2
Bareilly	5899	5210	689	12.0	44.7	5.3	1.3	18.0	9.3	12.8	6.2	19.3	16.8	0.9	0.7	26.7	15.5
Ghaziabad	50660	46263	4397	7.4	33.8	3.2	0.9	13.0	10.8	14.7	4.8	4.0	11.1	0.4	0.7	47.9	27.6
Gorakhpur	20788	18599	2189	18.8	37.9	6.4	1.6	20.8	7.0	14.7	14.4	14.5	12.1	0.6	0.6	20.1	21.3
Kolkata	1067208	977535	89673	5.8	26.1	3.9	1.3	13.4	12.5	16.8	5.1	9.0	33.3	0.7	0.3	49.1	19.7
Asansol	85902	80091	5811	6.3	29.3	4.3	1.0	11.4	9.7	12.8	4.6	8.4	25.0	1.0	0.4	54.4	27.5

Source: Migration Tables, D-Series, Census 1991(b) and (c), R.G. Office, New Delhi (available only in 1998). Small 'other' categories not shown.

2 Nature of Migration and Urbanization in India

"If you want any good to come, just throw your ceremonials overboard and worship the Living God, the Man-God – every being that wears a human form. God in His universal as well as individual aspect."

Swami Vivekananda (1895)
(Complete Work, Centenary Volume VI, 1963: 264)

In this chapter, first, the nature of rural to urban migration in India, specially towards four largest metropolises (Kolkata, Mumbai, New Delhi and Chennai)is discussed. It is mainly a tale of massive poverty-induced migration of illiterate and unskilled peasants and labourers into the mega cities of India, who are virtually compelled to leave their native places and are forced to be absorbed in poor quality urban informal sectors and somehow eke out their living in urban slums in the metropolises. Thus, it is still primarily a low quality labour migration. These also lead to low quality urbanization and acute urban degradation. As a true explanation of such migration-urbanization phenomena in India, the underlying socio-economic-political processes of colonization and underdevelopment are also briefly presented (in next chapter), along with discussion on continuation of the present-day processes of poverty and underdevelopment even under-planning era. Finally, in the last chapter, some planning strategies are also suggested in order to ameliorate such poverty-induced migration and urban involution.

The large metropolitan cities are growing very rapidly in India, unfortunately with slum growing many times faster. Poverty, agony, misery, exploitation, humiliation, insecurity, inequalities and human unhappiness are also multiplying tremendously in the recent decades. These are indeed manifestations of our iniquitous society and faulty planning. These crucial problems will aggravate many times in the early part of the 21st century, specially when aided by population explosion and increasing migration. These crucial human problems need our urgent attention and immediate redress, which is the main concern of this book.

Crucial Urban Crisis

Crucial problems of massive distressed migration of people from villages to metropolises and problems of unbalanced urbanization and extreme urban decay in India call forth urgent attention of scholars, administrators and planners for immediate remedies, before such maladies reach a catastrophe. Based on earlier studies on problems of migration, urbanization, poverty, underdevelopment, etc., (Mukherji, 1975, 10–345; 1977a; 1979a: 45–61; 1979b: 1–81; 1981:1–190; 1985a; 1985b; 1991; 1992b; 1993a; and 1997d: 1–65), the complex scenario that comes to the fore is described as follows:

First, masses of the poor, landless, illiterate and unskilled agricultural labourers and petty farmers from backward states of such countries make quantum jumps towards big metropolises like Kolkata, Mumbai, Delhi, Chennai, and so forth, bypassing local small towns and small cities that fail to give them even minimum employment. Such massive rural to metropolitan migration of distressed people is a typical characteristic of migration in India, which is leading to acute urban involution, congestion and decay. Proliferation of filthy urban slums and pavement dwelling, extreme squalor and very poor level of living characterize such metros. Such metropolises have failed to provide to migrants and residents with minimum shelter and minimum subsistence employment. Overflow of urban poverty, unemployment, extreme housing shortages, and frequent breakdowns of essential urban services (like water, electricity, sewerage, transport) are visible everywhere in such metropolises (Mukherji, 1977a: 1–56). Other studies also indicated similar problems (Bose, 1978; Ministry of Urban Development, 1988).

Second, such phenomena are occurring because the metropolises have very limited employment-generating capacity under capital-intensive industrialization, and consequently, the incoming illiterate and unskilled migrants are absorbed only in very poorly paid urban informal sectors that are characterized by low productivity, cut-throat competition, insecurity and exploitation. Although such migration helps to avoid starvation (hence desirable), it does not improve their economic condition adequately, nor permits their social mobility. Rather, it leads to a colossal waste of human resources and of national potential. So, the migrants are in fact moving from rural poverty to urban poverty (Mukherji, 1981, 10–190; NIUA, 1988: 66–70).

Third, as a result, such metropolises also became very much involuted, not evolved, i.e., they grew merely in population, not in prosperity. Mega cities (with 10 million population by 2000) of India are becoming merely over-blown villages, without urban culture and urban functional characteristics.

Fourth, such mega cities are very fast degenerating into extreme filth and indescribable squalor, where very rude denial of even minimum shelter to the illiterate and unskilled migrants from pauperized villages to their metropolitan El-Dorado, and consequently, their below-human-dignity-level existence in filthy slums has been further aggravated by very cruel denial of even minimum water, sanitation and electricity (Mukherji, 1993e: 1–31). These are indeed very cruel mega cities, specially for poor children, women, the weak, the poor, the old, and the destitute.

Fifth, such metropolises are very fast becoming the scenes of extreme social and economic inequalities wherein abundant affluence among a handful few stand hanging and over-looking abject poverty among the masses down below (Mukherji, 1994a: 9–21). These kinds of situations may create a dangerously eruptive situation – which is conducive to unleash in the near future extreme social disorder, severe class conflict, crimes, widespread violence and urban civil war. These situations urgently warrant immediate plans of action (Mukherji, 1994b).

Acute Urban Environmental Degradation

First, due to uncontrolled urbanization in India, environmental degradation has been occurring very rapidly (Bose, 1978) and causes acute shortages of housing, worsening water quality, excessive air pollution, noise, dust, and heat, and the problems of disposal of solid wastes and hazardous wastes.

Second, as regards housing situation, due to heavy migration to cities and high urban fertility, housing shortages have been very acutely increasing and leading to proliferation of squatter settlements, shantytowns, stinking slums and pavement dwellers. Presently, slum dwellers comprise about 30–60 per cent of total urban population with very poor housing conditions. For instance, Mumbai had more than 56 per cent of population as slum dwellers, and Kolkata (43%) and Delhi (30%) followed the suit. Chennai also had 2 million slum dwellers, followed by Ahmedabad (1.13 million), Hyderabad (1.1 million), Bangalore (1.03 million), Kanpur (0.8 million) and Pune (0.5 million). Providing housing to such teeming million is a formidable task, especially in the facets of stringent financial shortages. In fact, preciously very insignificant attempts were made to provide any kind of housing to these urban poor and slum dwellers.

Third, as survey-based study of migrants to Greater Mumbai in 1991 has revealed (Mukherji, 1993e: 1–32), a majority of all migrants have moved to the metropolis just for survival (62%) – just somehow to eke out living in their urban El-dorado – by performing very low-grade and low-waged services in the poor urban informal sectors (as domestic servants, hawkers, vendors, maid-servants, shoe-shine, road construction labourers, etc.), followed by marriage migration (28%). The remaining very few (less than 10%) actually moved for prospect, business, transfer, or for seeking any skilled job. The wretched socio-economic conditions of these migrants may be apparent from the following facts:

(a) 48.3 per cent live in only one room;
(b) 57.5 per cent have no toilet facility;
(c) 36.1 per cent are denied water facility;
(d) 44 per cent live in kutchha or semi-pucca houses (mud-walled or rag-roofed shanty/junk houses);
(e) 32 per cent used gunny bag, straw, tin sheets, or mud as wall materials for their houses; and
(f) 45.2 per cent used similar things for roof materials in their houses.

Their such pitiable condition may also be judged with reference to their long duration of stay in the metropolis (37% lived below 10 years, 29 per cent lived 10–19 years, and 34 per cent lived more than 20 years in the city).

In sum, even after a long duration of stay in their El dorado, their wretched socio-economic condition did not improve substantially. And, swarming and overflow of such refugee migrants to a metropolis, coupled with very cruel denial of basic civic amenities to them (like water, sanitation and electricity) lead to very stinking and degenerating urban environment.

Fourth, there are various other components and reasons for acute urban environmental degradation in Indian cities and metropolises, other than slum proliferation and squatter settlements. Slum is just one such component. Other more dangerous agents are: air and water pollution created by poisonous gas-emitting chemical and fertilizer factories, petroleum refineries, and other polluting industrial factories and units located in highly crowded and populous metropolises. Innumerable carbon emitting vehicles, chemical pollutants released due to cooking gas, CFC (Chlorofluorocarbon) elements emitted by coolers and refrigerators, etc. also exist – for which the urban educated and the affluent class are responsible, not the poor slum dwellers. Unfortunately, so far these polluters themselves are not made responsible for creating such dangerous pollution, nor are they made to pay for the cost of controlling them. In any future action plan, these polluters must be made responsible. Only then an effective action for improving urban environment can be implemented.

Fifth, an earlier survey-based study on estimation of population to be affected if Bhopal-type gas-leak ever occurs in Greater Mumbai was made (Mukherji, ibid.). It showed that 2.23 million people (out of 11.3 million of the city in 1991) would be affected, within a 5 km zone around the factory in Greater Mumbai in any likely event of gas leakage from Rashtriya Chemical Fertilizers Ltd. (RCF), or from any similar chemical or petroleum factories located within the city. It must be made mandatory that such gas emitting factories should not be located in highly vulnerable metropolises.

Sixth, apart from any such gas leakage, the health hazards created by such air and water pollution are very dangerous to the urban residents, making them acutely susceptible to asthma, chronic bronchitis, pneumonia, acute respiratory diseases and other ailments, specially among the children, the women and the old. The survey-based findings show that 15 per cent of the sampled population in Greater Mumbai were suffering from pollution-related diseases, for instance, eye irritation, skin itching, sore throat and chronic headache. Children suffer mainly from skin itching and sore throat, while the adults and older people from eye irritation and chronic headache. A large proportion of older people also suffer from asthma and eczema. It is also suspected that considerably larger number of children, women and older people suffer from acute respiratory difficulties due to intense air pollution in Greater Mumbai (Mukherji, ibid.).

The above survey also showed that about 30 per cent of sampled people (numbering about 9,300), among both illiterate and the educated, demanded relocation of such poisonous and hazardous chemical and petroleum factories from the metropolitan territory. It is extremely dangerous that no serious thoughts were previously given before such huge concentration of petroleum refineries, atomic reactors, chemical and fertilizer companies, etc. were permitted to be located in Mumbai (or other centres) in India. A total change in perspective is necessary.

Seventh, henceforth, a great care has to be taken before any such polluting factories or production units are ever allowed to be located, or extended, in such cities and metropolises. Necessary rules should be framed and implemented with strict vigilance.

Eighth, Indian cities are very acutely suffering from the problems of shortage of drinkable and safe water, disposal of solid and hazardous wastes, excessive vehicular traffic and consequent emission of poisonous gases, noise, heat, warming off of urban climate, noise pollution, and concomitant health hazards. As a consequence, the people therefore are compelled to use unsafe water and get themselves disease-prone and exposed to health hazards. Cities are also unable to cope up with formidable task of collection, transport and disposal of solid wastes, leading to unhygienic sanitary conditions, which result in widespread malaria, filarial and other fatal diseases. As most industries are located within or near urban centres, the adverse effects of emissions and effluent from chemical factories lead to dangerous poisonous gases and hazardous wastes. In turn, these lead to a series of air-borne and water-born diseases, specially among the weak, the child, the women and the destitute. All these oppressive conditions urgently require remedial measures, action plans and implementation.

In short, these are the crucial problems of massive poverty-syndrome labour migration and problems of acute urban congestion, urban failure and urban inequalities in India. If effective actions are not urgently taken to redress such human problems, the process will fast reach to maximum entropy level, when the entire system will break down, resulting in dangerous volcanic eruption and calamity (Mukherji, 1993a: 3–56). In this study, the magnitude of above problems of migration-urbanization in India is briefly discussed.

Reasons for Migration

Unlike in developed economies, where migration occurs mainly for prosperity or betterment, or for vertical social mobility or higher education, unfortunately, migration in India occurs mainly for survival, for subsistence, for familial reasons, or among the females for marriage. Table 2.1 reveals that in India, as in 1991 census, people mostly migrate for economic reasons, especially for seeking employment. It ranges about 30–40 per cent of migrants, even in the largest four metropolises. The noteworthy feature is that these employment-seeking migrants in India do not move for high level managerial or professional jobs, as in the West, rather they are mostly forced to migrate from rural areas and crowd into the largest metropolises, just to eke out somehow their miserable living in their urban El-dorado. This will be revealed from the educational status of the migrants, discussed later in this chapter. If this is the condition of migrants in India's largest four metropolises (Kolkata, Delhi, Mumbai and Chennai), the so-called four nerve centres of the country, the situation of migrants in smaller metros, small cities, or rural areas can be easily understood. Table 2.2 presents some details about occupational status of migrants. Considerable amount of them are illiterate and unskilled migrants, and, as such, are absorbed in low-grade production-process work or poor tertiary sectors.

Employment-seeking migration is quite prominent in India, comprising 28–38 per cent. However, education as a reason comprises only 2 to 5 per cent in Indian metros. Family-related movements comprise around 20 per cent for both sexes in Indian metros. 'Marriage' is more important reason for migration among the females (over 40%), because in India economic activity rates among the females are much less and marriage migration among the females comprise almost half of their total migration. Unlike in developed countries, where prosperity-related migration is very much evident, in India rather survival-related migration mostly prevails.

Table 2.3 unravels further on this aspect, especially with reference to four metros. As stated above, among the males, employment is the most important reason, followed by familial reason, which appears to be related to economic reasons. Business or education comprises a very small part of migration, even in metros. Employment-seeking migration becomes more important in longer-distance inter-district, or still distant, inter-state migration. Among the females, marriage migration is most predominant, followed by family moves. Unlike in the West, where the females also migrate substantially for education and employment, among the females in India, employment migration or migration for education or business still comprises a very small part. In short, economic reasons, specifically effort for survival, is the most predominant reason in Indian migration, whereas purpose of betterment and social reasons comprise migration in the West.

Table 2.1 *Reasons for Migration Into Four Metropolises, Census 1991 (%)*

Metros	*Migration (0–10 Years)*		*Employ-ment*		*Business*		*Education*		*Family Moved*		*Marriage*		*Others*	
	M	*F*	*M*	*F*	*M*	*F*	*M*	*F*	*M*	*F*	*M*	*F*	*M*	*F*
Mumbai	827507	718267	45.8	4.2	11.6	1.1	5.5	2.7	21.9	36.0	0.6	39.1	14.4	16.7
Kolkata	347584	367426	36.2	5.7	4.4	0.5	6.3	1.7	30.9	32.4	1.4	44.5	20.5	15.0
Delhi	771281	635735	54.2	3.5	6.8	0.6	3.2	1.4	29.6	55.4	0.4	34.1	5.7	4.9
Chennai	291111	291375	45.5	8.2	4.4	1.0	5.5	2.7	31.7	40.2	1.1	37.0	11.3	10.7

Source: Migration Tables, Census 1991 (b), R.G. Office, New Delhi, 1998. A small percentage under reason "calamity" not shown.

Occupational Status of Migrants

Majority of migrants are absorbed in low-grade work in metros. This is evident from accompanying tables, which are self-explanatory, hence not elaborated. Notable feature is that in all metros illiterate and semi-educated migrants being engaged in low-grade production-process work constitute a large majority.

Educational Status of Migrants in Metros

Tables 2.3 (a) and 2.3 (b) vividly present the nature of low quality migration that is occurring in India, specially towards largest metros, even recently. The majority of the migrants are illiterate or semi-educated peasants and labourers who are virtually compelled to move from stagnant villages and shanty towns into mega cities. They move somehow to eke out their miserable living in their urban El-dorado's. They are forced to leave villages because of lack of any employment. But, the mega city also failed to provide them with adequate employment, because of limited job opportunities created due to capital-intensive industrialization. So, these masses of migrants are forced to

Table 2.2 *Occupational Status of Migrants in Four Largest Metros, 1991*

Educational Level	*Vol. of Migration, 0–4 Years*				*Div.1*		*Div.2*		*Div.3*		*Div.4*		*Div.5*		*Div.6*		*Div.7–8–9*		*Div.10*	
					Professional workers etc.		*Adminis-trative workers, etc.*		*Clerical workers*		*Sales workers*		*Service workers*		*Farmers and related workers*		*Production process workers*		*Unclassified workers*	
	M	*F*	*M%*	*F%*	*M*	*F*	*M*	*F*	*M*	*F*	*M*	*F*	*M*	*F*	*M*	*F*	*M*	*F*	*M*	*F*
MUMBAI																				
Total	237093	14088	100.0	100.0	5.7	21.0	3.3	1.5	10.6	17.0	10.8	2.3	13.5	32.7	0.4	0.2	55.1	24.1	0.7	1.1
Illiterate	38818	4078	16.4	28.9	0.1	0.3	0.1	0.0	0.0	0.0	1.7	0.7	3.2	13.8	0.2	0.1	10.9	13.6	0.3	0.4
Literate but below matric*	96392	3601	40.7	25.6	0.6	1.0	0.4	0.1	1.9	0.9	5.0	0.6	6.9	16.8	0.2	0.0	25.6	6.0	0.2	0.1
Matric but not graduate*	68877	3066	29.1	21.8	1.0	7.6	0.8	0.3	4.6	7.7	3.2	0.6	3.0	1.6	0.0	0.0	16.3	3.9	0.2	0.1
Tech dip, not degree	4655	753	2.0	5.3	0.8	4.8	0.1	0.0	0.2	0.2	0.1	0.0	0.0	0.1	0.0	0.0	0.7	0.1	0.0	0.0
Grad/PG, not tech degree	22655	2008	9.6	14.3	1.7	3.7	1.6	0.9	3.7	7.9	0.8	0.3	0.4	0.5	0.0	0.0	1.4	0.4	0.1	0.5
Tech degree, equal to grad/PG	5696	582	2.4	4.1	1.5	3.6	0.4	0.1	0.2	0.3	0.1	0.0	0.0	0.0	0.0	0.0	0.2	0.1	0.0	0.0
KOLKATA																				
Total	58411	7643	100.0	100.0	6.0	10.3	3.4	0.5	13.5	4.8	8.1	0.8	17.8	58.3	0.6	0.1	48.3	24.1	2.3	1.1
Illiterate	15545	4846	26.6	63.4	0.1	0.1	0.1	0.1	0.0	0.0	1.9	0.3	4.1	40.6	0.2	0.1	19.6	21.4	0.6	0.9
Literate but below matric*	20824	1572	35.7	20.6	0.5	0.7	0.3	0.0	2.3	0.9	3.6	0.3	7.9	16.5	0.2	0.0	20.5	2.1	0.4	0.1
Matric, not graduate**	10714	524	18.3	6.9	0.8	3.9	0.4	0.0	4.2	1.5	1.7	0.1	4.4	0.9	0.1	0.0	5.8	0.4	0.9	0.0
Tech dip, not degree	498	65	0.9	0.9	0.4	0.8	0.0	0.0	0.1	0.0	0.0	0.0	0.0	0.0	0.0	0.0	0.3	0.0	0.0	0.0
Grad/PG, not tech degree	9224	498	15.8	6.5	2.5	3.1	2.1	0.4	6.6	2.3	0.9	0.1	1.3	0.4	0.0	0.0	2.0	0.2	0.3	0.0
Tech deg, equal to Grad/PG	1606	138	2.7	1.8	1.8	1.6	0.4	0.0	0.3	0.1	0.1	0.0	0.0	0.0	0.0	0.0	0.2	0.0	0.0	0.0

Cont'd...

...Cont'd

DELHI																				
Total	213695	8907	100.0	100.0	6.5	23.9	4.7	3.3	10.5	16.8	11.9	2.9	14.2	32.8	0.6	0.1	49.9	18.8	1.81	1.36
Illiterate	59403	3020	27.8	33.9	0.1	0.1	0.1	0.1	0.0	0.0	3.3	1.1	4.4	19.6	0.2	0.1	19.0	12.0	0.67	0.91
Literate but below matric*	65931	1391	30.9	15.6	0.5	1.1	0.3	0.1	1.7	0.7	4.1	0.5	5.5	10.5	0.2	0.0	18.3	2.6	0.36	0.13
Matric, not graduate**	52667	1833	24.6	20.6	1.0	7.0	0.6	0.3	4.5	6.5	3.4	0.7	3.6	2.3	0.1	0.0	11.0	3.5	0.48	0.12
Tech dip, not degree	2494	492	1.2	5.5	0.6	5.1	0.1	0.0	0.1	0.2	0.1	0.0	0.0	0.0	0.0	0.0	0.3	0.1	0.01	0.01
Grad/PG, not tech degree	27086	1643	12.7	18.4	2.6	5.6	2.9	2.5	4.0	8.8	1.1	0.5	0.6	0.4	0.0	0.0	1.3	0.5	0.23	0.13
Tech degree, equal to grad/PG	6114	528	2.9	5.9	1.7	5.0	0.7	0.3	0.2	0.5	0.1	0.0	0.0	0.0	0.0	0.0	0.1	0.1	0.06	0.04
CHENNAI																				
Total	73263	6094	100.0	100.0	11.7	28.7	10.3	3.3	12.6	19.3	13.8	3.5	9.7	16.9	0.5	0.1	40.7	27.8	0.52	0.44
Illiterate	6396	1463	8.7	24.0	0.1	0.2	0.1	0.0	0.0	0.0	1.0	0.9	1.2	8.2	0.1	0.0	6.0	14.4	0.20	0.23
Literate but below matric*	23838	1065	32.5	17.5	0.8	1.4	1.4	0.1	1.2	0.6	6.9	1.1	4.7	6.8	0.2	0.1	17.2	7.4	0.12	0.02
Matric, but not grad**	22178	1618	30.3	26.6	2.1	11.0	2.2	0.6	5.5	7.6	4.2	1.1	3.2	1.4	0.1	0.0	12.9	4.8	0.11	0.08
Tech dip, not degree	3805	175	5.2	2.9	1.8	1.7	0.4	0.1	0.4	0.4	0.2	0.0	0.0	0.0	0.0	0.0	2.3	0.5	0.02	0.05
Grad/PG, not tech degree	13170	1227	18.0	20.1	3.6	6.5	5.1	2.2	5.2	10.0	1.4	0.4	0.6	0.4	0.0	0.0	1.9	0.6	0.05	0.03
Tech degree, equal to Grad/PG	3876	546	5.3	9.0	3.3	7.8	1.2	0.3	0.3	0.7	0.2	0.0	0.0	0.0	0.0	0.0	0.3	0.1	0.01	0.03

* Literate but below matric (actually below primary). ** Matic not graduate (actually just matric).

Source: Computed from data of Census of India, 1991 (b), Census Commissioner's Office, New Delhi, CDs available in 1998.

Table 2.3(a) *Educational Status of Migrants in Indian Metropolises, 1991 Census (continued)*

Metros	Last Residence	All Durations of Residence (%)						Duration of Residence < 1 year (%)					
		No. of Migrants		Literate		Illiterate		No of Migrants		Literate		Illiterate	
		M	F	M	F	M	F	M	F	M	F	M	F
Mumbai	Total	2116093	1563081	81.9	61.6	18.9	38.3	34690	33920	59.2	49.5	40.8	50.5
	Rural	1494013	1021390	80.0	55.5	19.9	44.5	23400	22710	57.2	42.5	42.8	59.4
	Urban	575380	541691	83.6	72.4	16.4	27.6	9780	10250	61.9	63.7	38.0	36.3
Kolkata	Total	5476221	12394560	66.3	38.5	33.7	61.5	148775	174288	45.7	39.2	54.3	60.8
	Rural	3146415	9866287	61.6	34.9	38.3	65.1	105230	131718	42.1	36.9	57.9	63.1
	Urban	836497	1197378	77.8	66.0	22.2	34.2	26265	27570	55.6	55.0	44.4	45.0
Delhi	Total	2002615	1415675	73.5	63.4	26.5	36.4	81202	60170	57.2	46.4	42.8	53.6
	Rural	1064666	824574	67.9	37.4	32.1	62.5	48283	32180	49.1	31.2	50.9	68.8
	Urban	768297	754845	78.4	65.7	21.6	34.3	29024	25577	68.7	63.9	31.3	36.1

Table 2.3(b) *Educational Status of Migrants in Indian Metropolises, 1991 Census (concluded)*

Metros	Last Residence	Duration of Residence 1–4 years						Duration of Residence over 5 years					
		No. of Migrants		Literate (%)		Illiterate (%)		No of Migrants		Literate (%)		Illiterate (%)	
		M	F	M	F	M	F	M	F	M	F	M	F
Mumbai	Total	291664	249171	70.2	55.5	29.9	44.5	1638109	1187930	83.9	63.4	16.0	36.5
	Rural	212614	168110	69.9	50.3	30.1	49.7	1160929	752500	82.8	42.8	17.2	57.2
	Urban	74100	77841	71.2	66.7	28.8	33.3	441890	404670	86.7	74.3	13.2	25.7
Kolkata	Total	810217	1783453	61.3	47.8	38.7	52.2	3969756	9862824	68.8	36.6	31.2	63.4
	Rural	533048	1438591	58.3	45.4	41.7	54.6	2132350	7860075	64.2	32.8	35.8	37.2
	Urban	162090	225300	71.3	67.1	28.7	32.9	569995	873333	82.3	66.4	17.7	33.6
New Delhi	Total	439965	363626	69.2	55.6	30.8	44.4	1447943	1271715	75.8	51.7	24.2	48.3
	Rural	245419	181047	65.2	47.5	34.8	56.5	756023	600634	70.1	36.1	29.9	63.9
	Urban	179272	172767	74.6	68.1	25.4	31.8	546918	545951	80.4	65.2	19.6	34.8

Source: Computed from Data of 1991 (b) and (c), Census of India, D- Series, Migration Tables, CDs. Registrar General and Census Commissioner's Office, New Delhi, 1998.

take up whatever employment is available to them in bazaar economy or urban informal sector, where not only wages and productivity are very low, but also high cut-throat competition.

Poverty-Induced Migration in India

Table 2.4 vividly describes poverty-induced migration phenomena that have been occurring in India, and also indicate consequent urban decay and urban involution. Rather, it leads to a colossal waste of human resources and national potential. So the migrants are in fact moving from rural poverty to urban poverty (Mukherji, 1981, 10–150). McGee (1973) also studied proliferation of such urban informal activities among migrants in Malaysia Based on such evidences, a generalized picture emerges, discussed in next section.

Table 2.4 *Absorption of Illiterate and Semi-educated Migrants in Low Grade Urban Informal Sectors of Large Metros of India, 1981 Census (life-time migrants who moved for employment)*

Metropolis	*Male Migrants (%)*					*Female Migrants (%)*				
	No. of male migrants	*Illiterate*	*Semi-educated*	*Total (3+4)*	*Absorbed in low-grade work*	*No. of female migrants*	*Illiterate*	*Semi-educated*	*Total (8+9)*	*Absorbed in low-grade work*
Kolkata	670,059	38.4	41.3	79.7	84.7	24,638	72.5	16.0	88.5	89.0
Mumbai	1,414,655	24.2	44.4	68.6	79.6	43,283	42.5	21.5	64.0	66.5
Delhi	676,016	30.9	32.5	63.4	72.3	22,493	54.2	11.1	65.3	65.8
Chennai	340,249	11.4	37.5	48.9	62.6	13,256	28.1	15.6	43.7	48.2

Source: Computed from Census of India, 1981 (1988), Migration Tables, D Series.

Note: Low-grade workers are considered as to include those working in petty sales, petty services, farm, low grade production process – transport-labour work, and all other categories of work done by illiterates and semi-educated, and also those low-grade farm, production-process-transport-labour workers among migrants who have even high school or above education. These exclude high-grade professional, administrative, technical, or clerical workers among educated migrants.

The Three Phenomena

The Phenomenon of Distressed Migration

With reference to rural-urban migration, especially to large cities, a very complex scenario emerges. In the rural sector, such factors as demographic explosion, increasing land inequality, continuous fragmentation of land holdings, and almost a total lack of rural industries and rural non-agricultural employment have virtually compelled the small farmers and landless agricultural labourers or other operatives to leave the tottering villages and to crowd in the cities (Mukherji, 1993a: 1–56). They increasingly gravitate towards larger metropolises, bypassing smaller towns and cities, as they somehow know that employment opportunities are more available in the cities of larger size

(Mukherji, 1985a: 253–287). However, their dreams often remain unfulfilled and their lives end up in filthy slums and dirty pavements. Bastees, squatter settlements, shanty towns and pavement dwellers in most mega cities of India demonstrate this truth. In short, this process can be termed as the *phenomenon of distressed migration* (Mukherji, 1985b: 279–299).

The Phenomenon of Involutionary Urbanization

In the urban sector, conversely, a very weak urban economic base, very rapid urban growth, heavy emphasis only upon export (mainly raw materials), neglect of internal domestic markets, the growth of only light branches of industries, and a very low level of technology – all these have resulted in the growth of parasitic urban centres with a feet of clay! In short, urban growth has occurred, but without development and without internal socio-economic strength. Metropolises serve more as focal points of collection of raw materials for export, rather than as poles of development to diffuse growth impulses to their respective hinterlands! Since these cities have very limited employment-generating capacity, under capital-intensive industrialization, and very limited absorptive capacity in the organized sector, the incoming illiterate and unskilled labour migrants, thus, find salvage only in informal sector, such as porters, domestic servants, hawkers, vendors, construction workers, etc. So, involutionary urbanization, rather than evolution, is taking place. That is, metropolises are now becoming merely overblown villages, without internal consolidation and prosperity. Quality of life is fast deteriorating, instead of evolving. This can be termed as the *phenomenon of involutionary urbanization* (Mukherji, 1991: 203–249). Taken together, the entire phenomenon can be termed as *distressed migration and involutionary urbanization* (Mukherji, 1993a, 1–30).

The Phenomenon of Polarized Capital Accumulation

To make the matter worse, there has been a markedly uneven distribution of new production enterprises and excessive concentration of capital investments only to a few large metropolises (viz., Kolkata, Mumbai, Delhi, Chennai), at the expense of the vast majority of smaller cities, smaller towns, and countryside (Mukherji, 1985c, 54–61). But this capital was not utilized to create more employment; not for incoming migrants. This process is termed as the *phenomenon of polarized capital accumulation* in a few mega cities. Their poverty-induced migration has ended up in absorption in poverty-stricken urban informal sectors. It is indeed a movement from rural poverty to urban poverty (Mukherji, 1985a: 252–289).

Hence, the three basic elements of the system in India, i.e., distressed rural-urban labour migration, weak economic structure of metropolitan cities, and a polarized distribution of growth efforts/production enterprises, can be seen as causally linked (Mukherji, 1985c: 54–60; 1993a: 64–80).

During successive Five-Year Plans (1951–2010), there has been a markedly uneven distribution of new production enterprises and excessive concentration of capital investments only to a few metropolises (like Kolkata, Mumbai, New Delhi, Chennai, Hyderabad, Ahmedabad, Bangalore, etc.) at the expense of the vast majority of smaller cities, smaller towns and the countryside. Even where capital is available, most of this merchant capital is not invested for industrialization in the cities, but is rather utilized in collecting agricultural goods and commodities from the surrounding countryside for petty trade and low-grade commerce.

As regards the economic structure, the majority have a weak economic base haying petty trade-commerce and services and a very minor proportion in manufacturing. Manufacturing comprises 20 to 43 per cent of workers, while poor tertiary sectors comprise as much as 54 to 73 per cent. Over 20 per cent of adult population even in million cities are estimated to be non-workers. As regards migration, data reveal following features: First, in most metropolises, bulk of migrants came from rural areas. Secondly, for larger metropolises, volume of inter-state migration exceeds that of intra-state migration, i.e., rural migrants mostly came from far-flung rural areas. Thirdly, intra-state migration still forms the rule for smaller metropolises. Fourthly, employment was the most important reason for migration; and a large segment of migration that occurred for "familial reason", is suspected to be employment-linked migration. Fifthly, 40 to 80 per cent of migrants are illiterates or semi-literate, both males and females. Sixthly, they have little skill or training and majority are absorbed in low-grade processing activities, indigenous transport, petty trade, or low-grade services. Very few are in administrative, professional or technical services. Conditions of women migrants are more precarious, greater proportion of them are illiterate or semi-literate and are compelled to take up still lower kinds of job, as domestic/maid servants, hawkers or vendors (Mukherji, 1990: 1–38; Mukherji, 1995a: 1–65).

Such type of distressed migration, parasitic cities, cancerous metropolises, involutionary urbanization, and polarized capital investment and growth efforts are indeed symptoms of underdevelopment, not development (Mukherji, 1985a). Such distress migration merely helps as a survival strategy, but very little scope exists for their vertical mobility, even after long stay in city (Mukherji, 1985b). No statistics can adequately describe sadness, agony, and pain associated with processes of massive city-ward migration of illiterate/semiliterate peasants and labourers, and concomitant urban involution. It is a tale of cancerous growth of shantytowns, slums, bastees and squatter settlements. It is a sad story of overflow of urban unemployment, digression of per capita consumption levels of daily necessities (food, clothing, shelter), and a very sharp decline of basic human values in extremely congested Indian metropolises that are occurring over 1981–91 period and which will accelerate in future (Mukherji, 1995a).

Table 2.5 *Persistence of Weak Tertiary Activities in Indian Metropolises, Males, 1901–91*

Metro City	*Econ. Sectors*	*1901*	*1911*	*1921*	*1931*	*1951*	*1961*	*1971*	*1981*	*1991*
Kolkata	Secondary	21.8	18.7	17.5	16.3	29.1	34.1	35.1	43.6	40.8
	Tertiary	75.8	79.3	80.6	82.9	70.3	65.7	63.8	51.7	56.9
Mumbai	Secondary	32.8	30.9	29.8	28.9	39.9	44.7	46.9	44.4	44.3
	Tertiary	64.5	66.3	68.9	69.1	58.8	53.6	51.6	51.8	54.3
Delhi	Secondary	41.0	34.1	30.0	28.6	29.4	27.4	30.5	35.2	34.3
	Tertiary	54.4	52.5	65.6	65.5	69.9	71.2	67.9	61.6	64.4
Chennai	Secondary	31.3	29.6	26.7	22.5	28.8	32.7	33.7	37.6	35.2
	Tertiary	62.5	64.0	68.0	72.2	68.5	65.8	64.7	57.1	61.0

Sources: (i) Up to 1951, Census of India, 1961 (a) and (b), Paper 1 and II of 1967, Tables B Series, Registrar General's Office, New Delhi, (ii) Census of India, 1961–1981, General Economic Tables, R.G. Office, New Delhi, B-series, 1961–81, (iii) Census of India, 1991 (d), Workers Data in Urban Areas, CDs, 1993, New Delhi.

Table 2.6(a) *Poverty-Induced Migration and Urban Involution in India (continued)*

Metros	*Pop (Mill) (2000)*	*I. Poverty-Induced Migration Characteristics*			
		Main Causes of Migration	*Main Purpose of Move*	*Education Level of Migrants*	*Absorption of Migrants in Informal Sector*
Mumbai	18.0	Poverty Subsistence	Search jobs	68% Illiterates	80% in informal sector
Kolkata	12.7	Unemployment Poverty	Search jobs (unskilled)	70%+ Illiterates	85% informal sector
Delhi	11.7	Poverty	Search jobs	66% Illiterates	72% informal sector
Chennai	8.0	Unemployment	Search jobs	50% Illiterates	Informal sectors

Source: UN Reports on Population Growth in Mega Cities (Calcutta – 1986a, Bombay – 1986b, Delhi – 1986c, and Madras – 1987 a) and UN (1993b-World Urbanization Prospects), UN (1995a, 1995b, 1995c, 1995d, and 1995e).

Table 2.6(b) *Poverty-Induced Migration and Urban Involution in India (concluded)*

Metros	*II. Urban Involution Characteristics*				*III. Urban-Industrial Polarization*
	Growth of Poor Tertiary Sector	*Slums*	*Urban Decay*	*Housing Shortages*	
Mumbai	54% in tertiary sec.	56% slums	Acute	Extreme	Excessive polarization (50% of state industries)
Kolkata	57% in tertiary sec.	45% slums	Extreme	Extreme	42% of state industries concentrated
Delhi	65% in tertiary sec	35% slums	Considerable	Acute	Considerable polarization
Chennai	50% in tertiary	30% slums	Considerable	Acute	Much polarization

Sources: Same as before: UN Reports on Population Growth in Mega Cities (Calcutta, Bombay, Delhi, Madras, 1986–87) and UN 199b and UN 1995 (a to e).

The path to the future is thus uphill. To alleviate such conditions will require Herculean strength. Not only in South Asia, but also in South-East and East Asia, similar problems of very rapid urbanization, massive influx or migrants from rural areas, and querulous growth of industrialization-urbanization are taking place (e.g., around Bangkok, Jakarta, Manila, etc.). These problems are very rapidly accelerating in pace. Hence, planning-oriented research is immediately required to unravel and to mould the processes.

3 Migration Theory I

Socio-economic and Spatial Processes of Underdevelopment and Spatial Disorganization

"You should go to the sinking millions of India, and take them by the hand."

Swami Vivekananda (1894)
(Complete Work, Centenary Volume III, 1963: 433)

Last chapter brings us to the issue of spatial-social-economic-political processes that underlie such low quality migration and low quality urbanization. The relevant crucial questions are: Why are such phenomena repeatedly found over all developing countries across all the three southern continents? Around Metro Manila, Jakarta, Bangkok, Kolkata, Mumbai, Colombo, Cairo, Lagos, Nairobi, Sao Paulo, Mexico city, and elsewhere? Why are such phenomena absent in the Western countries? Why do such types of low quality urbanization, urban involution, and proliferation of stinking slums occur *only* in the Third World countries, where dependent nature of economy prevails? What are the spatial-social-economic-political-cultural processes? What are the underlying mechanisms? How could we rectify them? Unfolding these complex webs of spatial-economic-social processes are very necessary, before we could understand or mould them through effective planning strategies for the welfare of the poor (Mukherji, 1992b, 20–75; 1993a, 1–45; 2006, 191–208).

Over time, migration-mobility researchers have attempted to provide some explanatory models as the causal reasons for mobility in the Third world nations. In a classic study, Chapman and Prothero (1985: 1–26 and last chapter) have succinctly summarized them mainly in four categories:

(a) Circulation and modernization (i.e., circulation and migration are integral parts of the modernization process, and are in various stages of mobility transition (ibid.: 15–17).
(b) Circulation, social field and social network (i.e., workers are tossed between the centrifugal attraction of wage employment and the centripetal power of village obligations, social relationships, and kinship ties (ibid.: 17–19).
(c) Circulation, family welfare and risk aversion (i.e., labourer household attempts to maximize family welfare and risk aversion) (ibid.: 19–21).
(d) Circulation and capitalist penetration (i.e., penetration of tribal and peasant societies by capitalism increases local demands for cash, due to new

currencies and new taxes imposed, thus forcing labourers to migrate to meet needs (ibid.: 21–23).

These perspectives also equally apply to migration phenomena. Chapman and Prothero (ibid.: 24–26) have also very critically evaluated all these perspectives, discussed their respective merits and limitations, and finally, emphasized upon the great need for an integrated explanation. Unfoldment of afore-mentioned crucial processes underlying migration and urbanization in India and similar countries will need similar in-depth research.

The present attempt (discussed below) to unfold the underlying processes, however, is *not* claimed as an integrated perspectives in that sense, rather it takes a *historical perspective on the macro socio-economic-spatial processes that caused, and still cause, "poverty, underdevelopment and spatial disorganization" in a developing country,* like India and similarly placed nations (Mukherji, 1985b: 279–298). The present attempt is, thus, immensely indebted to Professor Chapman's afore-mentioned clarion call for an integrated explanation.

Although Professor Chapman may not subscribe to this historical-politico-economic view, which I claim, is not at all follow or related to God-forsaken Marxist view. Many do not know that Marx very much lauded bombarding of thousands of Indian Freedom Fighters by the British colonists by attaching these people to canons and blowing them over into pieces, during India's First War for Freedom (1857–59). He commended upon such unjust acts through his writings – ennobling such criminal acts – during exactly the same time and writing from London for *New York Times* (1857–59). So, the Marxist view is completely anti-human. So, I do not subscribe to such inhuman viewpoint!

Rather, I claim that my perspective is a purely humanist view of wretchedly poor conditions of the peasants and labourers who were exploited in India through many millenniums (who continued being exploited and migrating, even now), much before Marx were born!! My views mainly owe to Great Savior Swami Vivekananda (1863–1902), who upheld the Divine cause of salvation of these masses of the Poor in India, as evidenced in his Divine messages (1886–1899), given at the beginning of this book, much before anybody in India ever heard of Marx!!

Besides, the Idea of socialism is very inherent and indigenous in Bharat or India, since many millenniums, since the days of the Sacred Books of Upanishads (over 10,000 years old) – which declared to the Universe –"Shrinwentwu Vishwey Amritatsya Putraa" (Hearken the Universe! Ye all are the children of God, nay, You are all God Himself). India also gave birth to God Buddha, who assured 2600 years ago, that He will take endless reincarnations until the last blade of grass of this entire creation attains the enlightenment! Such immense humanistic equity and spiritual equity were always present in India, many millenniums before the earth heard of Marx or any socialist (who believe that "people's power comes out of barrels of gun"). These equities continued for many millenniums.

Only much later, the caste-based discrimination between the peoples was imposed in India, due to mischievous priest-craft. Even then, the lower castes were merely discriminated; they were not killed, as happened in many continents throughout the history. Of course, that was very much condemnable, but that was much safer than total annihilation of the entire civilizations and wiping out of entire indigenous peoples, as happened in Australia, North America, South America, Africa, Middle East, and every where else.

Besides, Dadabhai Naoroji (1869) also wrote about the torture and exploitation of the Indians by the colonialists in his classic book in 1869 (much before Marx was known). Also wrote Ramesh Chunder Dutt (1892), the most renowned historian of the 19th century – who fully unraveled in his books written during 1875–1892 the exploitation, poverty and underdevelopment in India by prolonged colonial domination. These realities were very much well known, much before Marx ever said that colonialism is the forerunner of capitalism.

I have read all these historical explanations of poverty and underdevelopment in India in my childhood days, decades before I plunged into study of Geography and Demography in college or university. So, the divine writings of Swami Vivekananda influenced my thoughts and writings. Not Marx. This must be clearly stated at the outset.

Another writer, Professor A.L. Basham (1968, 1970) of Australian National University wrote classic history books, *"The Wonder that was India, till 1020 AD"*, before the Muslim invosions and so forth. These described how rich and prosperous India was for many millenniums, before waves of severe murderous Muslim invasions from India's NW border countries made it extremely impoverished and exploited. No wonder, that India was dominated, colonized, and exploited, since last 1,000 years. *Now, all the maladies of an impoverished humanity permeated India's entire life, even now*. Generations after generations, people have slave mentality. Its citizens became narrow and selfish. No commitment exist to the Nation!

Processes of Underdevelopment and Spatial Disorganization Underlying Migration

Main ideas are briefly discussed below in *three parts* (A, B and C) and are illustrated in Figures 3.1 and 3.2, the details are given in Mukherji (1977a: 1–56; 1979a: 45–61; 1981: 1–190; 1985a, 252–289; 1985b, 289–299; 1993a; 2001b: 20–65, 2006: 191–208). Evidently, these ideas were developed during 1975–76 and published in 1977 onwards, much before Armstrong and McGee (1985) and Shrestha (1989) developed their theories of Underdevelopment and Third World urbanization. These are discussed in following three sections:

A. Poverty, Underdevelopment, Spatial Disorganization, and Migration

Figure 3.1 provides the basis of entire discussion of this section. It is a schematic diagram showing the macro processes of under-development, spatial disorganization, and labour migration in developing economies, like India and other similarly placed nations. The discussion is deliberately brief:

1. *Anti-development*: Crucial to this understanding is that underdevelopment is not a lower stage of development, nor a lagging behind, but rather a product of a "specific development", induced by the imposition of a colonial economy. It is an anti-development!
2. *Poverty was Induced:* In India, this imposition came in the disguise of a mercantile economy, and through successive invasions and annexations, exploitation and consolidation, rose to widespread colonialism. India was not really a poor country in 16th and 17th centuries, when these European powers jumped upon India to rob it, because no robber loots a poor person

or a poor country, rather loots only a rich country. So, poverty was induced in India by colonialism, plunder or loot.

3. *Colonization first occurred into coastal ports and foreign enclaves:* And soon the country's all economic activities were given a total orientation to export promotion, but mainly for the benefit of the colonial masters. Soon ports and new settlements were set up at Calcutta, Bombay and Madras (they were totally absent then), forts created therein, army brought in and installed, and all these were utilized for such colonial drain from India.
4. *Induced Spatial Disharmony*: Capitals, ports, and intermediary urban centres were used as collecting points to pump out resources and raw materials from agricultural regions, plantations, and mines. Arteries of railways and roadways were constructed, but only to aid this draining out from outlying rural areas in the hinterland. Penetration thus reached all parts of the country, where its devastating effects were noticeable primarily in following three ways.
5. *First, introduction of commercialized farming* and concomitant exploitation and coercion of the labour (Figure 3.1).
6. *Second, Creation of Unjust Land Settlement, Colonial Land Use and Land Inequality*: introduction of permanent land settlement and private ownership of land in a society where the systems were blissfully absent earlier, and consequently, created induced land inequality. Local stooges of colonization were made big property owners (*Jamindars and Rajas),* as rewards for their betrayal to the Motherland. Others were more exploited. These mechanisms initiated process of marginalization of vast majority of cultivators, who eventually were relegated to sharecroppers, tenant farmers, or landless agricultural labourers.
7. *Third, neglect of the indigenous village industries* to facilitate advances for an evolving mercantile capitalism.
8. *Colonial Loot of India and Start of Industrial Revolution in UK and Europe*: Famous economists John Stuart Mill and Adams Smith had admitted long ago that those loots of enormous gold, jewellery, and mining, agricultural and plantation resources from India were at the root of industrial revolution in Manchester, Birmingham, and elsewhere in UK. The same were also true with French, Portuguese, and Dutch powers who colonized some parts of India. Without them, industrial revolution surely would not have started in UK and Europe. History is witness of this truth.
9. *Exploitation and Rural Exodus of Labourers:* The end result of such process of continuous exploitation of the peasants, workers, labourers, and village artisans was the initiation of the process of massive exodus of these pauperized groups from the marginalized countryside to the filth and dirt of slums in the coastal ports. Like Calcutta, Bombay, Madras, etc. and national regional capitals like Delhi, Lucknow, Patna, Ahmedabad, Hyderabad. The same macro socio-economic-political processes and the same patterns of labour migration can be seen still today in India (Mukherji, 1981: 1–65; 1995a: 1–56).
10. *Poverty and Regional Imbalances:* Exploitation of labour continued unabated in both rural and urban areas by appropriating huge profits from commodities,

Figure 3.1 *Processes of Poverty-induced Migration and Urban Decay in India*

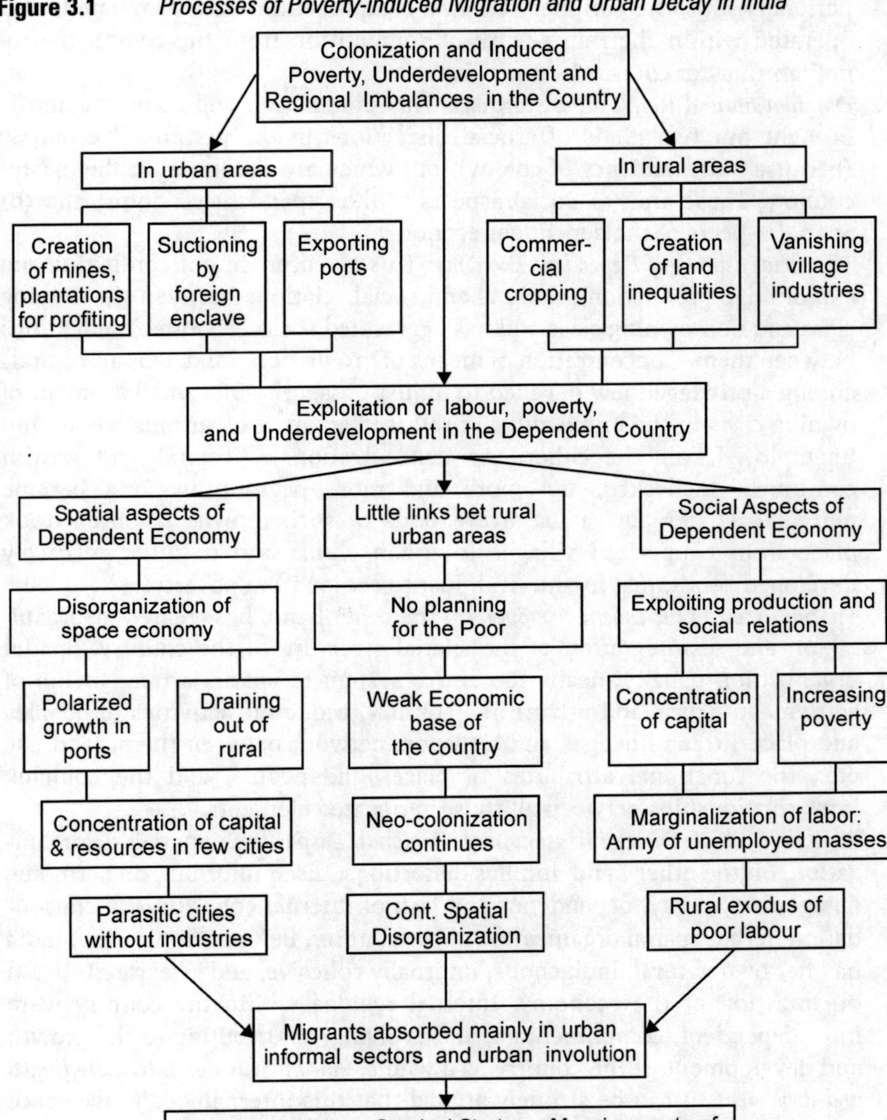

Source: Author

initially through unequal exchange. Later, huge profits were appropriated through monopoly and industrial capitalism. But, per capita income of the masses perpetually remained at the lowest level. Poverty was thus induced, created, and maintained in India. Consequently, regional imbalances and disparities also widened.

11. *Peripheral and Dependent Capitalism:* Over time, private accumulation of capital led to the formation of peripheral capitalism in a vigorous form within the colony. This is an extension of metropolitan capitalism to the

periphery. But, the periphery became complimentary and dominated, as it operated within the frame-work of competition from the central metropolitan (master country's) capitalism.

12. *Domination and Resultant Distortions:* This domination and complimentarily brought out two kinds of crucial distortions in the peripheral economy (because of dependency of colony), but which are not found in the master country. These are: (a) Social aspects of the dependent economy, and (b) Spatial aspects of the dependent economy.
13. *The social aspects of Dependent Economy:* This has brought out conflicting and exploitative production relations and social relations between the owning class and non-owning class and has aggravated socio-economic inequalities between them. Concentration of means of production (land, labour, capital) among a privileged few have led to unjust prosperity of a small segment of owning class in the one hand, and released an army of surplus labour and unemployed, on the other. As concentration of capital and wealth continued unchecked, the more and more peasants/workers became marginalized. Finally, a massive exodus of such refugee labourers took place from pauperized villages to urban slums and to other relatively developed zones, just for survival. Just to escape from poverty.
14. *Spatial aspect of dependent economy,* on the other hand, has created disorganization and disintegration of the spatial structure of the country. Spatial organization usually means the entire system of spatial arrangements of settlements (rural and urban) in a country, economic activities of peoples and places, trade linkages and transport network between them, land use etc., the functional attributes of places and people, and the complex inter-relationships between all those variegated elements.
15. *Induced Spatial Disorganization and Regional Disparities:* Spatial disorganization, on the other hand, implies distortions, disequilibrium, disharmony, antagonism, decay, dependency and lack of internal cohesion and consolidation in that spatial organization of the country. Before colonization, India had her own natural, indigenous, internally cohesive, and integrated spatial organization of the economy. Internal regions within the country were inter-dependent, complimentary, and evolving, contributing to the growth and development of the country as a whole. *And, it was not externally linked and dependent.* It can be strongly argued that this internally cohesive space economy, in spite of a number of negative economic and regional constraints, might have developed into a more spatially integrated structure, had India not undergone colonial domination. (Mukherji, 1981: 1–65).
16. *Destruction of Old Indian Education Systems and Imposition of Colonial Education System to dominate:* On February 2, 1835, Lord Macaulay gave the following evidences and reasoning before the British Parliament for introduction of his new Education Bill into India (later known as Macaulay's Bill, 1835). He said: "I have travelled across the length and breadth of India and I have not seen one person who is a beggar, who is a thief, such wealth I have seen in this country, such high moral values, people of such caliber, that I do not think we would ever conquer this country. Unless we break the backbone of this

nation which is spiritual and cultural heritage and therefore I propose that we replace her old and ancient education system, her culture for it (so that) the Indians think that all that is foreign and English is good and greater than their own, they will lose their self esteem, their native culture and they will become what we want them, a truly dominated nation" (Macaulay, Lecture before British Parliament, February 2, 1835) (www.fordhams.edu).

Thus, from 1835 onwards, the Indian age-old education system was destroyed and replaced by colonial education, and generations after generations of Indian contingent of clerks and low-grade operatives were produced by colonial systems to *enslave* and dominate the country. They were taught and they actually started firmly believing that anything Indian were low and brutish, and anything English and foreign were great. Generations after generations, they were made to believe that: "Your forefathers were inferior, and our forefathers belonged to a civilised society" (as if civilised society invades a country!). "Your ancient wisdom was nothing, but our knowledge was scientific.". "We are superior than you, so we dominate your country." "We came to civilize you." ... Indeed, as village elders used to say: "When they arrived, they had Bibles in their hands, and we had all the lands. Soon, we had Bibles in our hands, and they had all the lands!

17. *Bonded Man, Bonded Country and Dependent Space Economy:* As in a human being, who is externally dependent, cannot become free, internally developed and emancipated; similarly a nation which was externally linked and dependent, could not develop its own, spontaneous, self-sustaining, internally consolidated spatial organization, economy and the society. *Internal development pre-supposes freedom from external dependency. May it be a human, or a nation!*

18. *Distorted Space economy, Widening Regional Disparities, Consequent Migration:* The former national spatial structure of India was thus pulled out of shape. It was substituted by a colonial space economy (Mukherji, 1981: 1–65). Mainly due to suctioning mechanism by which raw materials were collected and exported to the world market at throw-away prices. Consequently, certain new ports/cities emerged and grew up at the expenses of the former towns/cities: and certain specific regions became favoured and prosperous, to the neglect of the interior regions of the country. Consequently, marked regional disparities and imbalances have sprung up and the gulf between growing regions and lagging regions widened. Under such a situation, evidently, labour migration of males and females occurred, and is still occurring, from neglected regions to relatively favoured regions. These are the end results of induced spatial disorganization – created by colonialism, capitalism, export-orientation, external dependency and induced poverty and underdevelopment.

19. *Three crucial distortions also occurred in the spatial organization:*
    (a) a crucial distortions towards continued export activities which usurped the major part of capital and investments (not available to other sectors);
    (b) a distortion towards mushroom growth of low-grade tertiary activities (arose from special contradictions newly introduced in dependent economy); and

(c) a distortion towards growth of only light branches of industries, and low level technology (Mukherji, 1993a: 1–48).

20. *Rural-Urban Gaps Widened:* The linkages between rural and urban areas are severely disarticulated, so also between industry and agriculture. Consequently, internal contradictions flourished. Growth of the national economy is retarded. Urban growth has occurred without development. Parasitic urban centres have grown and multiplied, without industrial strength and without a strong economic base.
21. *Resultant Migration of Landless Peasants and Labourers:* In the final analysis, there has been migration of rural refugee labourers, in the one hand, to a few coastal ports and parasitic urban centres, on the other. Labourers are leaving rural areas and moving into such urban centres. Since there has been only limited employment opportunities in towns under capital-intensive industrialization, the labour migrants could find salvage only in urban informal sectors, like vendors, hawkers, domestic servants, construction workers, rag-pickers, and so forth. Under competition from male migrants, females are relegated to bottom of informal sectors (Mukherji, 1997a: 283–304). *Urban unemployment* has also been overflowing, creating concurrently a dangerous involutionary situation.
22. *Poverty and Mobility:* Thus, migration of labourers, both males and females, in an underdeveloped economy is taking place from rural poverty to urban poverty, from one stress region to another, compounding further poverty and underdevelopment. It tells a poignantly sad story. And the waste of human and national potential is massive (Figure 3.1).

B. Underdevelopment Continued in the Post-Independent and Planning Era

23. *Past Unjust Forces Continue Determining Migration-Urbanization during Post Independent Period:* The forces set in motion by historical adversaries still largely determine labour migration and urbanization in India at present. This is because the development measures – taken during successive Five-Year Plans – were not adequate to ameliorate acute poverty, spatial disorganization, widespread unemployment, increasing land inequality, and neglect of the poor farmers and labourers in stagnating states (UP, Bihar, Rajasthan, etc.). So, there still has been tremendous rural exodus of uprooted labourers from such backward states to relatively favoured or prosperous states. And also movement to a few urban centres, ports, and administrative capitals (like Kolkata, Mumbai, Delhi, Chennai, Hyderabad, Bangalore, Lucknow, Kanpur, Ahmedabad). Even after 63 years of planning, the economy of India continues to be oriented towards export of mainly raw materials. Railways and roadways mainly feed export centres, or primate cities, instead of the interior areas within the country. Similar features can also be seen in other Asia-Pacific regions (Mukherji, 1995a: 1–56; 1995b: 1–8).
24. *Parasitic Cities:* But, these so-called metropolises and mega cities fail to provide the migrants with proper and gainful employment even today; they are engaged in very low-grade and poorly paid urban activities. This is because these metro cities have very limited employment-generating capacity, under capital-intensive industrialization. These realities amply testify the validity of the conceptual framework presented.

25. *Continued Spatial Disorganization Even under Planning Era:* Thus, spatial disorganization persists even now, in spite of a few attempts to correct it. Consequently, internal trade circuits remain stultified. Breaks in settlement hierarchy continue, impeding free flow of goods, commodities, and services across all parts of a country. It is very symbolic that no big city has ever emerged in between Kolkata, Mumbai, Delhi, or Chennai during last 300 years. Investments, capital, and industries continue to be polarized, as in the past, only in a few selected urban nodes and ports. Rarely there has been any real attempt for rural development; or development of hitherto neglected regions (Mukherji, 1994a: 9–21; 1997b: 1–81; 1997d: 1–65).
26. *Urban Development Bias:* Persistent development bias only towards metropolises and large cities continued unabated since a long time. In India, almost all urban services, capital, and development efforts have always been concentrated only at a few favoured centres and foreign enclaves (Mumbai, Kolkata, Delhi and Chennai), neglecting and impeding growth of other settlements (Mukherji, 1992b: 1–96). Investments and industries continue to be polarized, as in colonial era, only in a few selected and favoured nodes/ports. Never vigorous attempts were made for rural development, nor attempts for development of hitherto-neglected states (Mukherji, 1996b; 1999b).
27. *Urban Thrombosis Likely:* Evidently, if all the blood in a human body rushes only towards its head, then that is not a sign of health; rather a sure recipe for death due to thrombosis. Exactly similar things are happening in the mega cities and in the space economy of India and South and SE Asia. This implies acute spatial disorganization.
28. *Stagnant Villages:* Numerous villages are thus reeling under poverty, unemployment, under-employment and stagnation.
29. *Migration only as Survival Strategy:* No wonder that masses of illiterate, unskilled, and poor labourers keep crowding to the largest metros to find any job, no matter how unskilled or low the pay, nor how unbearable the filthy slums.
30. *Cities were not development Poles:* Small towns and cities of India still act (as they did earlier) primarily as agricultural collecting centres, as points of suctioning mechanism, for further onward movement of raw materials to coastal exporting centres, rather than as poles of development to diffuse development impulses to the surrounding hinterlands. Evidently, these nodes lack those spatial linkages that are necessary for rural development.
31. *Centrifugal Forces and Labour Migration:* Naturally, rural migrants (males and females) have to make quantum jump to coastal metropolises, by-passing such small towns. Because, like flow of capital and commodities to such ports, the human labour is also compelled to move under the same suctioning mechanism and centrifugal forces.
32. *Dependence and Internal Structure*: Further, as Dos Santos puts it: "the concept of dependence itself cannot be understood without reference to the articulation of dominant interests in the hegemonic centres and in the dependent societies. Domination is practicable only when it finds support among those local groups who profit by it. Dependence defines internal situation and is

structurally linked to it. The only solution therefore would be to change its internal structure" (Dos Santos, 1973: 76–77).

33. *Persistence of Non-egalitarian Society:* Clearly, it is dependent economy within an underdeveloped country which maintains enslavement and hinders all efforts for developmental change in the internal structure: the structure of the non-egalitarian society, the structure of concentrated ownership of means of production; and the structure of spatial disarticulations and imbalances.
34. *Planning not for the Poor*: In India, the planning is never meant for the poor! All tall talks of poverty alleviation are games for vote bank politics. As Desai stated: "the state instead of becoming a funnel to pump out resources from the rich for distributing them to the poor, in fact works in the opposite direction through an elaborate system of deficit financing, loans (foreign of internal) and indirect taxation – a system which hurts the poor most" (Desai, 1974: 89–99).
35. *Ad-hocism and Regional Inequalities*: Consequently, whatever developmental planning has been attempted has actually increased the gulf between the rich and the poor; and whatever regional developmental programmes have been taken, are characterized by ad-hocism and maintenance of the status-quo. In fact, these have increased regional inequalities, instead of narrowing down (Rao, Misra, and Sundaram, 1974: 79–120; Singh 1987).
36. *Prolonged Rural Neglect:* Prolonged rural neglect, on the other hand, have stagnated the countryside; where unfortunately utter lack of even a primary school, or drinking water, or minimum means of livelihood persist over many decades. So, the processes of prolonged rural neglect in the one hand and pronounced metropolitan bias in the development policies, on the other, have been at the root of such phenomena of distressed migration.
37. *Proliferation of Poor Tertiary Sectors in the Post-Independence Period:* Excessive export-oriented economy (mainly of raw materials at throw-away prices) and distortion in urban economy, on the other hand, resulted in the growth of only parasitic cities and proliferation of low-grade trade and services, without strong manufacturing base. As Figure 3.1 shows, therefore, we have parasitic urban centres without proper industrialization, on the one hand, and marginalization of peasants, on the other; with weak economic base of the country in between.
38. *Waste of Human Potentials and National Productivity:* Although they somehow survive in the mega city at the most minimum level of living, but there is very little scope for upward social mobility. They continue to live at the same low level of existence in the cruel city, even after 30–40 years. This results in massive waste of human resources and national potentials. Briefly this is the central idea of underlying processes. Various planning strategies are illustrated and discussed in the last chapter.
39. *Resultant Rural Exodus and Labour Migration of Unemployed:* Consequently, massive and continuous rural exodus of refugee labourers occurs from rural to urban centres. This is the economic-historical context of such low quality labour migration and urbanization in a developing economy.
40. *In short, unemployment, poverty, inequality, and spatial disparities persist:* Such imbalance persist even now and still impel the poverty-induced male and

female labourers to migrate in between one area of stress to another (Mukherji, 1997b: 1–61).

41. *Poorer Female Migrants:* Within this overall context, the situation of the female labourers are more precarious as they are the victims of double colonialism; external and internal; and are relegated to the poorer class.
42. *True Explanation of the Processes:* This is the true conceptual explanation of such distress migration and lopsided urbanization in India. Proper understanding of such complex processes is absolutely necessary; based only upon that may we be able to find ways and means of correcting such mechanism of underdevelopment and spatial disorganization (Mukherji, 1997a: 283–304; 2000e: 1–145).
43. *The Theory Holds true for most Developing Countries:* What have been described with reference to India, also hold very much true for other similarly placed developing countries of Asian, African and Latin American countries. Excessive primacy of Bangkok, Metro Manila, Jakarta, Lagos, Sao Paulo, Mexico City, etc., and utter neglect of other settlements in those countries – provide ample testimonies of such ongoing iniquitous socio-economic- political-spatial processes; and consequent lopsided patterns of migration and urbanization (Mukherji, 1997b; 1998b: 10–20; and 2011, chapter 11).

C. Globalization and Its Adverse Effects on Migration

44. *Current Processes:* What is the present and the future scenario? Figure 3.2 highlights these processes. Under the current trends of liberalization, privatization, and globalization, evidently the more and more resources, capital, investments, production units, and growth efforts are polarized only around mega cities/ports (and mainly in elitist-consumption oriented industries), thus neglecting all-round development of the interior countryside, villages, innumerable small towns, and hinterland of India. As a result, much more skewed forms of afore-mentioned types of distressed migration and urban decay will increasingly manifest in the present century. The true nature of such processes are never truly unfolded. We really need more socially committed social scientists – who will undertake such research and will help the poor and the common people (Mukherji, 2002: 525–559).
45. *Global Processes and Further Pauperization of Labour:* Process of liberalization in fact has placed common people at the mercy of international market forces and privileged industrialists, buried issues of equity and social justice, and widened the gaps between the rich and the poor. Process of privatization, on the other hand, that involves dis-investment of Public Sector Units (PSUs) at throw away prices, has actually usurped huge amount of public money, benefiting only a handful of the rich, at the cost of an ocean of the poor. Third, the ongoing processes of globalization is hurting the poor most, as prices of daily necessities are sky-rocketing, beyond the reach of common people. New capital or investments, if any, are mainly concentrated in mega cities. benefit only a few privileged families or corporate houses (Figure 3.2). These capital and investments are not available for

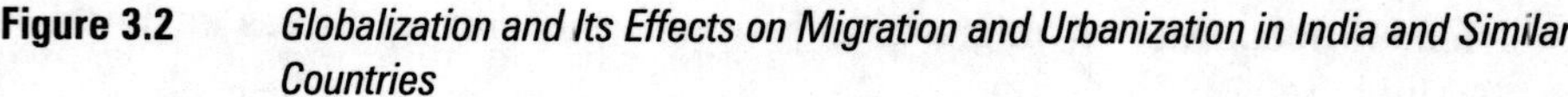

Figure 3.2 *Globalization and Its Effects on Migration and Urbanization in India and Similar Countries*

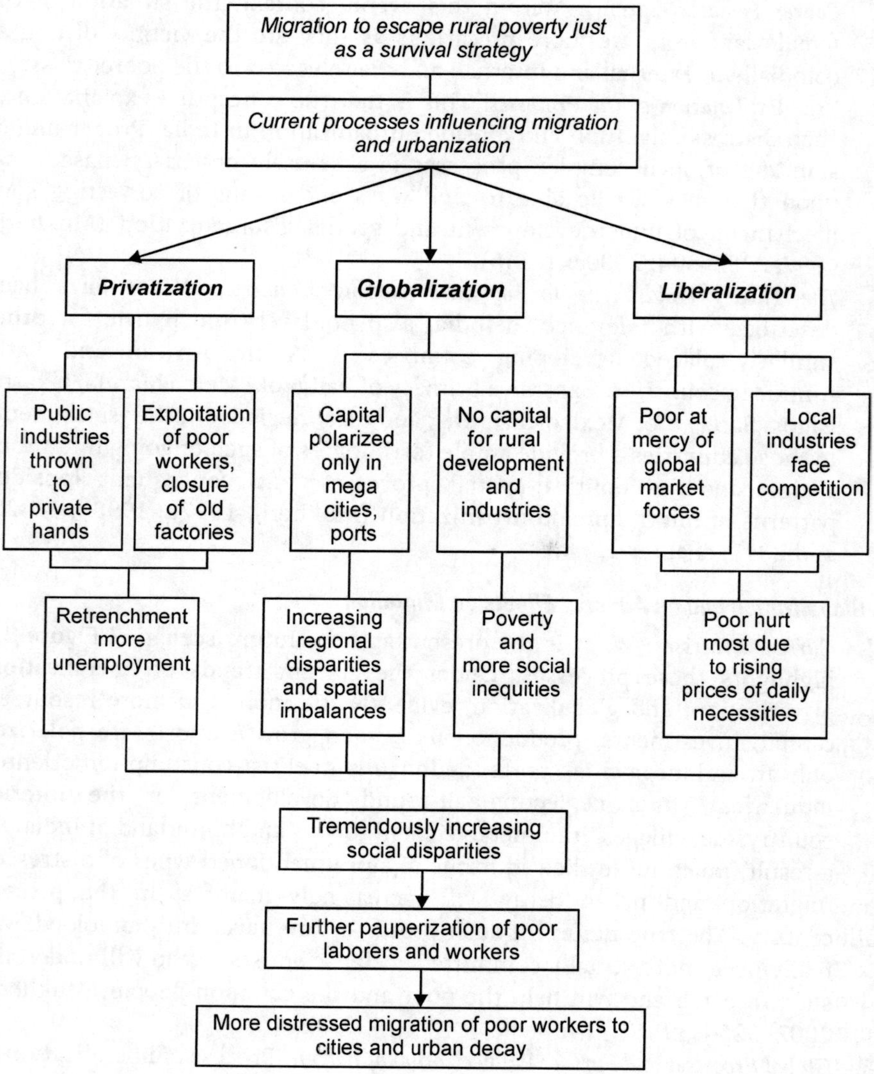

agricultural regeneration or rural development. Rural areas, thus devoid of any development efforts and capital, are reeling under abject poverty, acute unemployment and widespread illiteracy.

46. *The masses of dispossessed farmers and labourers:* They are further compelled to swell in urban slums and construction sites around large cities for minimum sustenance. Recently, a study of such migrant labourers is made in Gujarat, which amply testified such agonizing process of migration under globalization and privatization. Authors noted: "The down and out (migrants) produce wealth from which they however remain excluded as beneficiaries. Most of them are the working poor who continue to live in a

state of misery and oppression because of the low wages paid for long hours of work" (Bremen and. Das, 2000: 12–46.). So, policies are needed to organize working poor, so also greater state intervention. Otherwise, they will be victims of predatory capitalism (ibid.: 40–45).

47. *Adverse effects of Globalization on Local Labour Market:* Another example is: due to intrusion of globalization and import of cheap and subsidized foreign clothes into Indian markets, the local handloom workers of Bhiwandi (near Mumbai) became jobless and pauperized. These examples amply testify ongoing agonizing processes of globalization and consequent marginalization of workers and resultant migration from rural to urban poverty. Briefly, this is the main ideas of entire underlying processes (Mukherji, 1997b:1–80; 1998b, 10–20; 2006: 191–206).
48. *Globalization and Migration:* In a recent study on impact of globalization on migrants in a small village in southeast Nigeria, Onyeiwu, et al. (2007) studied mechanism by which globalization affects poverty and inequality. It investigates whether individuals who migrate from village to take advantage of urban-biased globalization process do better than non-migrant villagers, and concludes that while migrant villagers earn slightly higher incomes than non-migrants, poverty of both categories are essentially same. Contrary to conventional wisdom, globalization has not succeeded in alleviating poverty amongst poor villagers who took advantage of process, because by changing relative prices in towns, structural adjustment have eliminated any advantage that globalization may have given to migrants.

In a significant study titled "India Untouched" George (2004) tells a powerful story as he seeks solutions that would reduce the hardships faced by hundreds of millions of Indians still living in poverty and social deprivation, which are made much more difficult due to impact of globalization on the indigenous markets.

In my view, nowadays in India, under the present-day most unjust economic systems, the number of dollar billionaires is daily swelling (127,000 on June 10, 2010, and still counting) (*Times of India*, June 24, 2010), while over 500 millions poor people survive just less than Rs 24 per day per person (US $1 = Rs 20 at purchasing-power-parity)! What more evidences do we need of very adverse effects of liberalization-privatization-globalization process upon the poor masses and migrants? Those who can afford to move, are forced to leave the tottering villages and migrate to cities for survival. And, those who are more frustrated, angry, politically vulnerable and misguided, often take up guns and turn Maoists and Naxalites (Maoist terrorists) killing thousands of innocents.

India is not at all well. India needs mass awakening, soulful consciousness, and real patriotism among her all people. As discussed earlier (item 16 above), Macaulay's education systems has completely destroyed age old Indian spiritual and ethical values, and made India a Nation of slave mentality and corruption.

As Swami Vivekananda thundered over a century ago (1894): "We want that education by which character is formed, strength of mind is increased, the intellect is expanded and by which one can stand on one's own feet." He further cautioned: "A Nation is formed, not by amassing wealth, rather by forming character of its citizen" (ibid.).

The only hope lies in re-introducing the character building and Nation building education systems.

4 Migration Theory II

Canonical Model: Linking Spatial Structure and Spatial Flows – Inter-state Migration and Regional Disparities

"Let us pray, "Lead, Kindly Light" – a beam will come through the dark, and a hand will be stretched forth to lead us"

Swami Vivekananda (1894)
(Complete Work, Centenary Volume V, 1963: 57–58)

Different Mobility Behaviour in the Third World

There has been *a basic difference* in the processes of migration in developing countries from that of the developed countries; and most often such a difference is neither adequately spelt out, nor properly understood. Unlike in developed economies where inter-regional migration of people occurs in association with a qualitative shift in the labour force from the agricultural sector to urbanized-industrial sector, conversely, migration of people in search of employment in the developing countries, as in India, on the other hand, occurs as spatial manifestation of underdevelopment, rural poverty and regional disparities in the economy. In India, such migration of workers are occurring, not so much in response to any structural changes in the labour force or in the economy, nor moves occur mainly for prospect or prosperity, as happened in the West. Rather, these occur as displacements of poor peasants and labourers from backward regions, which are characterized by lack of irrigation, capital and investments, and of development efforts, and by persistent regional inequalities.

In short, migration in the developed countries is intimately connected with the process of development and prosperity of the migrants; whereas migration in the developing countries, as in India, is tightly linked with the processes of underdevelopment, poverty, and social and regional inequalities. Such types of migration take place, not due to the so-called attractive pull forces of the destination regions, but basically occur due to acute stress situations and underdevelopment in the migrant-origin regions; and little opportunities exists for the migrants for upward or vertical social mobility, as usually happened in the Western countries. These basic differences between the two worlds and between essentially two different types of migration are not highlighted in the existing literatures. Nor are they investigated in conventional research. Obviously, when the perspective of migration process are incorrect, the planning prescriptions are also bound to be wrong. Formulation of policies and planning strategies must be based upon correct perspective of the complex processes of migration – that occurring in the developing countries, like India. Hence, to analyse the processes in India, and to suggest suitable policies to affect them, is the primary concern of this study. Objective is also to unfold causal links between migration of workers and regional disparities in the country.

In order to perform this, a conceptual model is tentatively developed, and a canonical model to test it is also explained. Before these are discussed, there is an important *prologue* to evolutionary steps in my theory construction. This chapter, thus, has the following three parts:

(a) Discussion on very useful mobility concepts of Professor Murray Chapman, my PhD research guide (1970–75), and overwhelming influence of his concepts on my mobility theories and research;
(b) Brief discussion on a conceptual model, linking spatial flows and spatial structure; and
(c) Canonical model to test the linkages between spatial flows and spatial structure. These parts are tightly connected, each ensuing from previous one.

Useful Mobility Concepts of Professor Murray Chapman

Professor Murray Chapman, an internationally renowned Population Geographer and Mobility Specialist, and a foremost pioneer in the Circulation and Mobility studies, has evolved many ennobling and new concepts of mobility studies and research, which have great relevance to the entire world, specially the Third World.

Professor Chapman greatly promoted the study of population geography and study of mobility (not just migration), specially circulation and circular migration, when these were neglected and given less importance and recognition. In fact, he is considered as the Grand Father of "Circulation and Mobility studies" in the world. His innumerable research papers, spanned over last five decades (1960–2010), provide ample testimonies (Chapman, 1970; 1975, 129–145; 1976: 127–142; 1978: 558–569; 1979, 111–114; 1981, 71–87; 1985a: 1–6; 1985b; 1991b: 263–292; 1995: 247–259, and many others).

His treatises on circulation research are now considered authoritative and classics (Chapman and Prothero, 1977; Chapman 1985c: 1–371; Prothero and Chapman, 1985a; Chapman and Prothero, 1983: 597–632; Chapman and Prothero, 1985a: 1–26 and 436–440; Chapman and Prothero, 1985b; Chapman and Prothero, 1985c: 1–12, Chapman, 1991a: 75–98; 1992; and many others).

Consider his emphatic focus in the following writings, which are equally applicable to migration and mobility studies:

1. "Reciprocal flows of people, goods, and ideas have persisted over time; links are maintained between places of origin and of destination and traditional mode of circulation are manifest in contemporary mobility behaviour" (Chapman, 1970; Chapman and Prothero, 1985a: 436).
2. "To comprehend its complex nature more adequately, circulation needs to be investigated and analysed at a variety of different scales. These range from the micro (individual, family), through meso (community, settlement systems, region), to macro (country, continent, world). Integration of these different scales of enquiry will be achieved through the better understanding of each and of the ways in which they relate to one another"

(Chapman, 1975; Chapman and Prothero, 1985a: 438). And, in this respect, the role of "an astute mix of intuition and a detailed awareness of the inner workings of a piece of social reality is very useful" (Chapman, 1981: 86–87).

3. "Study of circulation is very necessary, as earlier it were mostly between rural areas, and extended to towns and other centers of wage employment, and now based on towns from which there is circulation to the rural areas ..." "The implications of such changes for the planning of administrative services and for social provision in spheres such as housing, education and health are considerable" (Chapman and Prothero, 1985a: 437). This makes a very strong argument for inclusion of circulation studies in urban and regional planning, as well.
4. "The importance of investigating indigenous concepts, beliefs, and terms related to the movements of people needs to be much more emphasized .... Only through this may unique meanings of mobility be captured. They are not accommodated by the western concepts and terms which are most frequently used in the Third world studies in mobility .... Only in this way can we establish more accurately what people are actually doing and from this develop policy-making which is realistic" (Chapman and Prothero, 1985a: 439).
5. "Field investigation is essential since its very nature circulation is excluded from most census and other conventional forms of data collection on the movements of population. The forms of data collection presently employed in the Third World are based very largely on the experience employed in the developed world; within the times, terms, and techniques which are used circulatory forms of movement cannot be accommodated" (Chapman, 1978: 559–569; Chapman and Prothero, 1985a: 439).
6. "Techniques for studying circulation must be both cross-sectional and longitudinal. The former have been mostly employed, the latter have been sorely neglected. ... Static concepts and techniques are inadequate for the study of phenomena which are so dynamic." "There is a need to experiment more widely with retrospective data collection like movement histories and longitudinal studies" (Chapman, 1981: 71–87).
7. "There is a broader contribution to be made by the Third World studies of circulation through the transfer of concepts and methods to societies and populations very different from those for which they are developed initially and in which they were first tested (cf, Marshall, and Mukherji, in Prothero and Chapman, 1985a). Such transfers would be the reverse of that normally found in scholarship; the flow of concepts and techniques would be from Third to First World realities" (Chapman and Prothero, 1985a: 440). What a benediction showered upon his Third world students and followers.
8. "With reference to studies of circulation in particular and of population mobility in general, we hope that the growing involvement of scholars from the Third World will continue on similar lines, with heightened vigour and resulting in ever increasing understanding and explanation" (Chapman and Prothero, 1985a: 440).
9. Chapman strongly observed that micro studies of mobility have their practical ramifications: "First, results from micro studies reveal far more common ground, and consequently a much greater ability to generalize,

than is usually assumed. Second, careful comparison of field investigations and their particular context can identify different mobility reactions to changing sets of socio-economic conditions – and in a way not possible from more aggregative research" (Chapman, 1985c).

10. "Yet administrative mechanisms to restrict, control, or even forbid movement within a country have failed virtually everywhere they have been attempted, because they focus attention on the act of movement rather than on the cultural, social, economic, and political conditions of which movement itself is a visible and perhaps final expression. *To constrain the individual freedom of movement is contrary to the UN Declaration of Human Rights"* (Chapman, 1991: 95) (italics mine).
11. "Even attempts from the late 1960s to employ "circulation" as metaphor to draw attention to the repetitive dynamism and reciprocal character of much island mobility (Chapman and Prothero, 1985a) have ended in a scholarly cul-de-sac. The perverse result of a vigorous debate among Pacific specialists has been to ossify "circulation" as in diametrical opposition to "migration" and to ignore the obvious fact that each is an integral part of a broader, regional system of mobility connecting the individuals, the families, and the wider communities ..." (Chapman, 1992: 289).

For my research, Professor Murray Chapman's two most ennobling ideas and concepts, out of many, have deep-seated and all pervading impacts, namely the following:

First, that migration, or circulation, of the individuals or people between the places or regions must be considered as *only one, out of many*, forms of *Mobility Behaviour*. More importantly, that migration or mobility must be studied, not merely as statistical numbers, but as psycho-social-cultural responses, or *"ebbs and flows of the human beings to the socio-economic needs, limitations and realities"* (Chapman, 1970: 1–60). Thus, he religiously urged for the great need to focus upon investigating migration (mobility) at the *micro scale, at the level of the individuals*. According to him, minute details of movement behaviour can be ascertained mainly at the micro level, specially performed through field-based study (Chapman, 1970: 1–125; 1976: 127–142).

Second, he also greatly emphasized upon the basic need to study mobility of the people, or the individuals, *as couched in their specific socio-economic and cultural context of the society – in which they are situated, as specific Third World realities. These should not be viewed from the perspective of the Western norms and concepts* (Chapman, 1970: 1–175; 1975: 129–145; Chapman and Prothero, 1985a: 1–29).

During my formative years, for my second PhD degree (1970–75), under the expert guidance of Professor Murray Chapman, in the University of Hawaii and East West Population Institute, East West Center, Honolulu, his such two ennobling ideas, out of many, have percolated into my mind to such a great extent that I frantically searched for 5 years to find suitable ways to translate these two ideas into mathematically testable theories and models. The latter were, of course, my personal objectives (as a graduate student of Physics and Mathematics previously, as well)! But, the existing knowledge or wisdom in social sciences at that time, were not at all developed enough to construct such a suitable and mathematically verifiable theory and model, either in geography or demography (nor even now). Top of all, I had, in my mind, the task of explaining why people move in a highly populous country, India, where hundreds of millions of migrants move from one place to another in search of barest sustenance, and the great tasks of formulating the steps for migration planning (hitherto unheard concept, then, and even now!). Hence, my all efforts for developing a mathematically verifiable theory of migration seemed in the beginning, all in vain. But, those two novel concepts of Professor Chapman were not thrown into barren mind. They were deeply rooted in my veins and worked very subtly over those 5 years, and all through my life. *The pervasive influences of Professor Chapman's ideas and concepts were very subtle, sublime, and all-absorbing in my all efforts of theory construction, during those five formative years and also life long!* These efforts continued the entire decade of 1970s and later.

Thus, I struggled very hard and finally was able to evolve *three* new theories of migration-mobility myself, namely:

1. The Mobility Field Theory (during 1970–75) (Mukherji, 1971a, 1974, 1975),
2. Theory of Underdevelopment and Migration (during 1975–76) (Mukherji, 1979a, 1981),
3. The Spatial Field Theory of Migration (during 1972–92) (Mukherji, 1971a, 1971b, 1992b, 1993c).

The first theory greatly emphasized upon the mobility behaviour of the "individuals" and need to study at the "micro scale" *(a la Professor Chapman)*, and upon the need-stress of the individuals. Thus, I learnt and heavily borrowed from Professor Chapman – the concepts of making the basic four-fold foci in my research, namely:

(a) Focus upon the study of total mobility behaviour (migration, circulation, oscillation; not just migration).
(b) Focus upon study at micro scale, at the level of the individuals,
(c) Focus upon detailed field investigations, not on secondary data, and
(d) Take a humane perspective about movers, not just as a statistical number. This last one has led me to think and consider seriously about focusing upon the "need-stress-poverty-attributes" of the individual movers in my theory construction. I gave it a supreme and the pivotal importance in my "mobility field" concept and the M F Theory.

Eventually, the *Mobility Field Theory* was evolved, by the present author, *as a theory causally linking the need-stress-attribute sets of the individuals, and, in relation to that, the place-utility distances between the places of origins and the destinations, and their resulting mobility behaviour that arises out of those needs and stresses.* Thus, in my Mobility Field Theories and the present Spatial Field Theory, the great emphasis are given upon the individuals or people (or regions), and also upon their needs-stresses-attributes, and also to investigate migration as a behaviour, as responses, arising out of those needs, stresses, poverty and locational stresses, and, thus, somewhat attempted to fulfill Professor Chapman's ennobling *first* idea.

Thus, considerable emphasis are given on both the noble concepts of Chapman, viz.:

(a) to investigate migration phenomena as a behaviour of the human beings (as responses to their socio-economic stresses, and not just mere as statistical numbers), and
(b) to imbed that behaviour of the people (or the individuals), in the specific *context* or *field* of socio-economic-cultural context of the society in which they are situated.

He always encouraged students to question the relevance of Western concepts and models to the Third World realities, and to couch mobility in the Third World country's specific context. So, that has encouraged me to build a completely new theory of mobility (M F Theory), which is capable of explaining why people move in Third world countries.

Mobility Field Theory (1970–75) was presented elsewhere in great details and with all applications to the Indian situation (Mukherji, 1975: 1–370; 1979b: 1–81; 1979c: 40–51; 1980a: 45–60; 1980b, 254–284; 1980c: 39–66; 1982a, 1–278). So it is not repeated here. However, this was my starting point of evolving various theories and its pervasive influence can also be seen in my later *two* theories, briefly presented in this volume. Notable point here is, that the Mobility Field Theory is a very organized, structured and mathematically and empirically verifiable theory, unlike most theories in social sciences.

In my second theory, titled, *Underdevelopment and Poverty-Induced Migration (1975–76)*, again, the great emphasis were given upon the causal links between the nexus of poverty, underdevelopment and spatial disorganization in a developing country, in the one hand, and, distressed migration and urban decay, on the other. Thus, Chapman's second idea of linking and couching migration within the context of the Third World Realities (away from the Western models), was also attempted. His ideas were very super-fine, and they very subtly affected my thoughts, and thus have also influenced my construction of the theory – the *Theory of Underdevelopment and Migration in Developing Countries.*

This theory was presented with all details in a book titled, *Mechanisms of Underdevelopment, Labour Migration, and Planning Strategies in India* (1981), and was dedicated to Professor Murray Chapman in 1981. In Chapter 3 (this volume), a brief and much revised version of that theory is presented.

One thing must be said at the outset. *Prof. Chapman does not subscribe to my Theory of Underdevelopment and Migration, which many wrongly and conventionally consider being influenced by the Marxist perspective.* NO! My theory of Underdevelopment and Labour Migration in India and developing countries is "not" anyway related, nor it has anything to do, with the Marxist view. It arises out of my own thoughts as a soulful witness of endless human miseries in my country, India. The exploitation of the poor farmers, social and economic inequality, and injustice are universal phenomena – and which causes migration to arise – and these phenomena have persisted over many millenniums in this planet, specially in the Third World. Any humane person can feel these, without ever subscribing to God-forsaken Marxist thought.

Professor Chapman, as a very humane person and a very humane social scientist, has seen and deeply felt such phenomena in the Weather Coast, South Guadal-Canal, Solomon Islands, in his field studies throughout 1960s and in 1970s, and all through his life-long research in the Melanesia and the South Pacific. He makes almost annual visits to those fields. Even in 2008–9.

His such humane research perspective have greatly influenced my research too, during my formative years under him (1970–75), and continued throughout my life. Indeed, I am greatly indebted to him. I have also viewed oppressive phenomena of poverty-induced migration, and appalling human condition of the migrants (also non-migrants) all over India, and have attempted to unfold the crucial nexus between poverty and underdevelopment, in the one hand, and the migration of the dispossessed, on the other. We are thus not Marxist, rather humanist!!

Top of all, Swami Vivekananda's soulful ideas have imbibed me from childhood, and were my guiding spirit in life long research, and specially in constructing Theory of Underdevelopment and Migration (discussed in Chapter 3).

In a felicitation volume in the honour of Professor Chapman, his world-wide students and followers celebrated through a novel publication in the journal of *Pacific Viewpoint* (1999), and lovingly commended upon immense influence of his research and very humane personality upon their life-long mobility research. Another felicitation volume in his honour appeared in a special volume of *Asia-Pacific Population Journal* (2003), in which his many notable colleagues and mobility researchers lauded upon his great contributions to population mobility research and to the promotion of population geography in the World, especially in the Asia-Pacific.

In a recent paper in *Geo-journal,* Yvonne Underhill-Sem (2004) has also celebrated Professor Murray Chapman's strong influence among Asia-Pacific scholars studying population and population mobility. Also see Bedford (1999) which made detailed review of Prof. Chapman's contributions to geography. In her paper, she (Underhill-Sem, 2004) "traces some trajectories from the teachings of population geography at the University of Hawaii that successfully engendered this geographical scholarship at the same time as other American geographers have rendered it insignificant" *(*ibid.*)*.

She studied under Professor Chapman perhaps during 1990s. She observed that: "Circulation in population movement, especially in the Western Pacific was the intellectual passion of Professor Murray Chapman at University of Hawaii at Manoa and East-West Centre (Chapman and Prothero, 1985a). And, building on his experiences as an antipodean scholar in North America, Chapman's efforts to instill in his graduate students a concept of population mobility went further than he might have expected" *(*ibid.*)*.

She further observed that: "Far from being cloned followers of Professor Chapman, many of his graduate students, the majority of whom were from Asia-Pacific, became mobility scholars (not just circulation researchers). Rather than faithfully working to a source of authority, Chapman's students took the possibilities provided by a fluid concept to develop an enquiry that was able to be inventive and applicable to non-English-speaking countries" *(*ibid.*)*. Indeed, I know that they were from Bangladesh, India, Indonesia, Thailand, Nepal, Fiji, Hawaii, the USA, Melanesia, Solomon Islands, Papua New Guinea. And also from other countries: Australia, New Zealand, New Caledonia, and so forth.

She further noted: "More recently, in the context of geo-political reconfigurations wrought by globalization, the concept of population mobility retains a critical framing many of the problems associated with people moving between territorial boundaries at a variety of scales. Successful engagement with theorizing mobility has occurred where population geography has engaged with social theory" ... *(*ibid.*)*. She concluded: "that the fertility of working with the concept of mobility rather than migration, has contributed to more inclusionary geographical imaginations ... (I)n the current geo-political situation, personal politics centered on the concerns of post-colonialism and feminism provides a more nuanced analysis that advances both critical thinking and eventually more progressive social policy" (Underhill-Sem, 2004).

Very recently, an UNDP study on "Migration and Development in India" has appeared in the internet (Deshingkar and Akter (2009), UNDP: 1–90). The subject matter of the paper again reminded me of old memories of classes of Prof. Murray Chapman in the University of Hawaii, during 1970–75. He is the Pioneer of Circulation Studies in the World. His most enlightening, innovative and pioneering thoughts were centred around circulation, circular migration, its causes and consequences, the need for continuous population register for good mobility data, and limitations of census and conventional migration data, etc., in Asia and in Western Pacific.

I was very pleasantly surprised by reading in above paper the very same thoughts and observations about data limitations, concepts of circular-migration, lives of the dispossessed, and so forth, about which I had the great opportunity to learn for five years under Professor Murray Chapman, forty years ago (1970–75). Most were *actually* his pioneering ideas and now classic concepts, expressed 40–50 years ago, and now percolated through UNDP publications. Although, he investigated in South Pacific Islands, but the concepts are equally applicable World wide, specially in India and the Third World. That is, his ideas have pervaded through the minds of all mobility researchers, world-wide; sometimes the researchers, at far away places, not knowing where the original concepts came from! Of course, I attempted to make them aware of the research of the original thinker, Professor Chapman!

Recently, there have been increasing interests from UN agencies and International forums about the study of circulation, circular migration, temporary and permanent migration in developing countries, because of their great importance as means of poverty reduction and development (UNDP, 2009: Overcoming Barriers: Human Mobility and Development). In these contexts, Professor Murray Chapman's classic contributions to mobility research are receiving renewed attention and recognition. Publishers of his classic 1985(a) book (with Prothero)*"Circulation in the Third World Countries"* are now making a new edition. These testify renewed research and practical interests of UN and International agencies. I very firmly believe that these will have transcending effects over time and space!

Present Three Theories of Migration

As we shall unfold in this study, other two noble ideas of Prof. Chapman have led to the formation of my three migration theories, mentioned in this volume:

1. The Mobility Field Theory of Human Spatial Behaviour (Migration and Circulation) (Mukherji, 1975),
2. Spatial Field Theories of Migration (Mukherji, 1971a, 1971b, 1974, 1992b, 1993c), and
3. Theory of Underdevelopment and Poverty-Induced Migration in Developing Countries (Mukherji, 1977a, 1981).

. The Mobility Field Theory, presented in details in other books (Mukherji, 1975, 1979b, 1982a), is excluded from this volume.

However, it must be stated that his all ennobling concepts were not fully presented in these studies, because only those aspects could be included which can be translated into mathematically and analytically verifiable Field Theories (as in first two cases). Or, as migration phenomenon couched in the context of poverty and underdevelopment in a developing economy (as in the third case). As can be easily understood, mathematically linking poverty, underdevelopment and mobility – in linear or non-linear models – are most difficult tasks, not yet accomplished in social or population sciences, neither in 1970s, nor 40 years later. During the next three decades (1976–2007), I have modified and upgraded these theories and mathematically verified with current data, countless times. They are still evolving!

Thus, his new and novel concepts rather acted like the great seeds of thoughts, *acted as sweet theme music, percolating my all theoretical and empirical thoughts, behind the past and present models and theories of migration.* I am, indeed, very sincerely grateful to him all through my life, for his most ennobling and guiding principles in mobility research. This book is, thus, most reverently dedicated to my most respectable Professor Murray Chapman, Emeritus Professor, Department of Geography, University of Hawaii at Manoa Campus, and East West Center, Honolulu, Hawaii. Since 2007, however, he lives in Hilo city, Big Island, Hawaii, but continues as Emeritus Professor in the University of Hawaii at Manoa, supervising over two dozens PhD students.

Conceptual Model Linking Spatial Structure and Spatial Flows

Migration behaviour can also be termed as *Spatial Behaviour,* because such behaviour occur over the space and have spatial connotations and ramifications (Berry, 1969: 1–29). On the other hand, the main basis dimensions of the socio-economic attributes or characteristics of different regions within a country can be regarded as the *Spatial Structure* of the economy (Berry, 1966: 5–151). It can also be termed and understood as the structure of the space economy of a country, or the overall spatial organization of economic activities over the national space. In short, the spatial dimensions of the socio-economic system over various regions of the country is emphasized here.

According to the present theoretical and conceptual model, the basic proposition is: that *the Spatial Behaviour and Spatial Structure of regions of a country are interdependent, isomorphic, and causally linked.* Before we elaborate on the model further, a brief discussion on previous studies made along these lines will be pertinent here.

Previous Studies

In geography, although there have been a lot of studies on spatial organization (Abler, Adams and Gould, 1971: 1–25) and spatial behaviour (Wolpert, 1965: 152–180; Brown and Moore, 1971: 118–132), but so far very little research done to *link and integrate the spatial behaviour to spatial structure.* Essentially, such linkages and integration between the structure of attributes (of places, or people, or individuals) and the patterns of spatial behaviour between them (migration, circulation, etc.) required a field-theoretic approach. An approach which would causally link the spatial behaviour of the movers towards the places (of origins and destinations) and also link the attributes of the movers with the socio-economic differences between the dyads of places – all seen in an integrative manner. Evidently, for a long time, there has been a gap between the research need felt and the theoretical-cum-methodological ways of achieving such an integrative design. It was indeed a very difficult task.

It was the classic work of German psychologist Kurt Lewin (1951: 1–250) which showed the pathway towards such an integrative approach, but only for "delinquent behaviour of adolescents". For the first time in social sciences, Lewin presented a Psychological Field theory in which he attempted to explain the behaviour of the juvenile delinquents in German prisons by integrating their "behaviour" with their "social attributes" and couching both behaviours and attributes in the context of the "specific environment" in which the delinquents were placed.

However, Lewin's field theory was merely descriptive, loosely fashioned, and not structurally organized; nor it was presented in a form that could be mathematically verifiable or testable. According to his own statements, his field theory was not a theory, rather a method, and *a philosophy to view behaviour and attributes in their causal relations*.

The credit for formulating and successfully testing a theoretically organized and mathematically testable field theory in social sciences goes to Rudolf J. Rummel (1965: 183–197) who contributed a new *Field Theory of Social Action* in order to explain the "conflict behaviour" within nations and between nations. Rummel, in his life-long contributions to field theories, also provided new formulations, titled as "Dynamic Psychological Field" (1975a: 1–170) in which he dealt with the dynamics of conflict and war between the individuals and the peoples, as well as between the nations. I sincerely owe to Professor Rummel (Department of Political Science, University of Hawaii) for his pioneering thoughts on social field theory and application of canonical model for testing it. It was Professor Rummel, who for the first time, used Canonical analysis for testing field theory. That was a great innovative work. His classic work also include books on Factor Analysis (Rummel, 1970), Analysing Population Policy and Demographic Change (Rummel, 1975b), and Field Theory Evolving (Rummel, 1980) (Also see, Rummel and Mukherji, 1981: 1–90).

It must be mentioned that, in Geography, especially in the Studies of Spatial Behaviour, the credit goes to Brian J.L Berry (1966, 1969) who for the first time gave a spatial translation of the above-mentioned attempts of field theory formulation in psychology (of Lewin) and in political sciences (of Rummel). Berry, in his pioneering study of *Commodity flows and the Spatial structure of the Indian Economy* (1966: 1–151) had made a very laudable contribution by providing a spatial transformation of field theories of other sciences by referring it specifically to the spatial interactions between the places. In this study, he investigated the relationship between spatial economic structure and the commodity flows amongst the states of India, and postulated and tested that spatial pattern of attributes of places and of interactions between them are interdependent and isomorphic. *That study, however, dealt with the commodity flows between various regions (states of India), not human behaviour, nor migration*. That was a limitation.

However later, in another pioneering study, Berry (1969: 21–31) extended his earlier work, postulated about the *interdependency of spatial structure and spatial behaviour*, and formulated a general field theory of spatial behaviour in which he referred to "migration". In the former study, he successfully tested his model by applying canonical analysis to data on commodity flows; whereas his second study was a general formulation of the theory which referred to all spatial interactions, including migration between places, but, which *he did not test in that study with real migration data*. The present author is not aware of Berry's later papers in which he have tested his above-mentioned field theory model employing migration data. Nevertheless, it must be said that some major building blocks of the field theory model, linking spatial behaviour between regions (viz., migration) to spatial structure was there.

The third major attempt of field theory construction in geography and social sciences was that of the *Mobility Field Theory* of Mukherji (1975: 10–383), in which the present author provided a full spatial rendering of Lewin's psychological field theory to spatial behaviour or mobility and migration behaviour of the individuals, along with *philosophical perspective, theoretical text, and mathematical models*. It was also mathematically tested and empirically verified, with fine-grained field survey data.

In this connection, it must be clearly indicated that although Berry's attempt was pioneering and very commendable, but it essentially referred to "passive interactions between the regions". It did "not" refer to migration "behaviour of the individual movers themselves", who actually suffer locational stresses, who struggle to fulfill their basic needs, who evaluate various place utilities, who are the "decision-makers themselves", and who perform the act of migration. *All such complex aspects were not considered in Berry's both the models. These were great lacunae in Berry's both the models. Top of all, Professor Berry did not at all focus upon the "need-stress-attributes-aspirations of the movers themselves" – main pivot of individual movers decision to move, around which all other elements are fastened. All these lacunae were filled up and resolved in the Mobility Filed Theory of Mukherji (1975)*.

In the Mobility Field Theory, thus, attempts were made to provide answers to all these crucial issues; by indicating causal relationships between: (a) the individuals' basic needs and attributes, (b) as filtered through their place utility considerations of places of origins and destinations, and (c) the resultant migration-mobility behaviour of the individuals that arises from attempting to satisfy those needs (Mukherji, 1975: 25–121; 1979b: 1–80). All these three sub-systems were linked and integrated, both theoretically and mathematically. It was a novel, useful and a verifiable theory. The theory was tested with fine-grained data and was found very successful and useful to explain migration behaviour of the individuals and people, capable of generating concrete policy prescriptions to alleviate the problems associated with migration under duress (Mukherji, 1979c: 45–51; 1982a: 1–275; 1985c: 27–34).

One important thing must be stated very clearly. Though, Lewin's Psychological field, Rummel's Field theory of International conflict and violence, and Berry's field theory relating commodity flows and spatial structure were of much help, but my Mobility Field Theory (MFT) does not originate from there, or from any other sources. It is completely my own theory, a new, novel and unique theory, termed as the Mobility Field Theory – which none of the above or any other, remotely ever thought or conceptualized. Just the name "field' is common, but that kind of misinterpretation or misgivings must be clearly stated right at the outset. Because, Lewin was concerned with juvenile delinquent behaviour; Rummel was concerned with violence and war between nations; and Berry with commodity flows between regions, or at best, with gross migration flows between regions, and not with need-stress-attributes-poverty of the individual migrants and their decision-making processes (as Mobility Field Theory does). So, these are completely different formulations!

However, my that model referred to the individual mobility behaviour. On the other hand, if we want to explain migration behaviour of population or flows between places or regions, we will need to redesign the entire structure of above Mobility Filed Theory (MFT). This is the concern of the present model, discussed below. In doing so, Berry's second model (1969) about spatial behaviour and spatial structure provided considerable guidelines. But he used only two matrices, but in my formulations, there are scope for handling with *n-number of predictor matrices*. Indeed, this is a novel contribution.

The Conceptual Model: The Spatial Field Theory

Taking cue from the sections above, it may be stated that the central tenet of this model is the theoretical proposition: that the *spatial behaviour* of regions towards each other and *spatial structure* of economic activities of those regions in any country will be interdependent, isomorphic, and causally linked. That is, the matrix of migration behaviour between regions and the matrix of socio-economic differences between those regions are interdependent, causally linked, and isomorphic. By inter-dependence and isomorphism it is meant that there will be an *one-to-one correspondence* between the two matrices; between the matrix of migration between spatial regions *(spatial behaviour)* and the matrix of socio-economic attributes of those spatial regions *(spatial structure)* (see all details in Mukherji, 1993c: 250–280). The Spatial Field Theory was first formulated in 1971 (Mukherji, 1971a, and 1971b) and repeatedly tested and upgraded in the next two decades (Mukherji, 1974; 1979d; and 1993c).

The theoretical model states and proves that in any country, volume and nature of migration between various regions will be determined by *differences* in socio-economic attributes in those regions. In short, *as is the spatial economic differences between various regions in a country, correspondingly will be migration flows between them; and vice-versa. Each of the matrices can be generated with the help of other.*

Briefly, this is the essence of present conceptual model, termed as *Spatial Field Theory*, in which it is postulated that both the matrices of spatial behaviour and of spatial structure, together, will make a Field or a System, called *Spatial Field*, and changes in one sub-system, within the system, will bring corresponding changes in the other. Both matrices and sub-systems will be *interdependent, causally linked, integrated, and isomorphic (one to one relationship)* (Mukherji, 1993c: 250–280).

Secondly, besides this overall correspondence between two matrices, it is also postulated that specific pattern(s) of migration behaviour will be causally linked with specific kind(s) of socio-economic attributes or characteristics, which co-exist and belong to a particular "field" within the overall general Spatial Field, excluding other attributes, which do not belong to that particular "field". Thus, the *underlying causal socio-economic reasons beneath a specific migration behaviour will be unfolded, and will be linked together, producing a particular field, or a sub-system – which indeed causally co-exist in reality. This is the essence of these field theories.*

Causal linkage equations to be generated between the two sets (spatial behaviour and spatial structure) will not only test and prove the Spatial Field

Theory, but will also validate its central proposition of inter-dependence and one-to-one correspondence between the two sets. Besides, it will also equip us to change the future patterns of migration streams and the spatial economic structure of the regions in a country.

Evidently, such policy and planning oriented research design and generating such linkage equations will be of great practical importance to urbanization-migration-development research, especially for developing countries.

The idea of this Spatial Field theory is yet evolving. However, these are capable of modifications. The crux of the theory is that it permits a mathematical mapping of migration behaviour matrix and socio-economic attribute matrix of spatial regions, and shows causal reasons between various elements of the two matrices, or the two sub-systems. So, in a modified model, instead of socio-economic "differences", rather socio-economic "attributes" themselves are used as predictor matrix. In these ways, migration (spatial behaviour) and socio-economic factors of different regions (spatial structure) are causally linked. *My main contributions to such new formulations are: the pivotal importance given to matrices and variables that depict poverty, underdevelopment, locational stress, spatial disorganization, and social and economic inequalities – in short, the Third World Realities – which are lacking in the western conceptualizations! Besides, it deals with n-number of matrices simultaneously, as independent matrices (e.g., investment matrix, growth effort matrix, poverty indices matrix, and so forth which were never attempted before (Figure 4.1).*

Canonical Model: Linking Spatial Flows (Migration) and Spatial Structure of Economy (Socio-economic System of Regions)

Being wedged between discussions on Spatial Field Theory and Canonical model, two crucial things must be stated right at the outset. First, canonical model is the most appropriate technique for testing and verifying the Field Theory, as both focus upon testing isomorphism and degree of interdependences between behaviour and attribute matrices, with reference to the same subjects. Theoretically and analytically, the Field theory is so formulated that canonical model becomes an integral part of the theoretical structure and of operational theoretical model. In this way, the relationship between the theory and the analytic method is thus made structured, organized, and very tightly connected; and, consequently, it fulfils all the essential requirements of theory construction.

The second noteworthy thing is that canonical analysis can also be performed independently, as a general analytic technique, without referring to the field theory. In short, canonical analysis can be undertaken without field theory (as a loner), but the field theory cannot be done without canonical model (as lovers united).

Developed by Hotelling (1936: 321–377), canonical analysis basically elicits the maximum correlation between linear functions of two sets of variables describing the same subject(s). It can be employed to find statistical relationships between any two data matrices of behaviour and attributes describing, for example, nations, or states, or regions, cities or individuals. It is successfully utilized to assess the interlinks between violence, conflict and war between the nations of the world in the one hand and socio-economic-political distances between them, on the other, as done in Social Field Theory (Rummel, 1965: 185–197). Or, between patterns of commodity flows between regions and spatial structure of economy of regions, as done by Berry (1966). Or, between mobility-migration behaviour of the individuals, in the one hand, and place-utility distances between origins and destinations-cum-the needs-stresses-socio-economic attributes of movers, on the other, as done in Mobility Field Theory (Mukherji, 1975: 1–363). Or, it can also be utilized to ascertain causal linkages between demographic behaviour in the one hand and the combination of socio-economic characteristics of population of regions-cum-population policies adopted in those regions, on the other, as done in Demographic Field Theory (Mukherji, 1983a: 1–144). The Demographic Field Theory is also successfully tested by employing a field-theoretic approach and performing canonical models to all major nations of the world (Mukherji, 1992a: 1–96). Other field theory studies were also made which yielded very meaningful canonical results (Mukherji, 1982b: Ch 3; 1982c: 1–30). The model can also be fruitfully employed to investigate many other demographic, geographic, socio-economic, or political inter-relations. It has indeed immense potentials, specially investigating migration and regional disparities (Mukherji, 1992b: 1–96).

Detailed analytic technique of canonical model and its utility, elegance, appropriateness, its high statistical power, and interpretation of ensuing results are very much elaborated in successive studies made since 1970 by the present author (Mukherji, 1971a, 1971b, 1974, 1975, 1977b, 1979d). In such studies, canonical models are also successfully utilized by taking three data matrices simultaneously, which was not done originally by Hotelling, nor by Rummel or Berry. That is done here, by taking one as the dependent matrix, and the combination of the other two (or more) matrices as the independent matrix (Mukherji, 1980a, 1982a, 1983a, 1985c, 1989a) Every-time, the canonical model yielded very significant and meaningful results (also see Mukherji, 1989a, 1992a, 1992b, 1993a, 2001a and 2001b).

Although canonical model is very powerful and useful, but so far it has been very rarely applied and known in demographic, geographic, or social sciences; because often detail literature are not available and people are not familiar with it, and, as such, have many misconceptions. To fill these lacunae, it is surmised worthwhile to briefly discuss sere. A very brief description of the canonical model and the way it is applied in the present research design is now in order. Factor analysis is a quite well known technique, and, as such, it is not elaborated here (see Rummel, 1970).

Canonical Model

Given the two sets of data on migration behaviour between regions and socio-economic structure of those regions, canonical analysis may yield answers to two related basic research questions (Phillip, 1973):

1. What is the overall *general* relationship between migration behaviour in the one hand and the socio-economic structure of spatial regions, on the other? and
2. Given this overall general relationship, what are the underlying *causal* relationships between specific combination of migration behaviour variables and specific combinations of socio-economic structure variables of regions?

What canonical analysis does is to delineate independent patterns in two sets of data in such a way as to ascertain maximum inter-relationships between the new sets of patterns or dimensions. Just as factor analysis separates out distinct clusters of variables that vary together over a set of observations, canonical analysis uncovers clusters of patterns in two sets of observations or matrices by *maximizing the correlation between linear combinations of variables* (Anderson, 1958; Cooley and Lohnes, 1962: 35–45). Details are presented elsewhere (Mukherji, 1979b, 20–65; 1982a, 32–140). Such combinations of factors or patterns delineated in each set are independent of other patterns in the same matrix, but each is maximally correlated with a specific patterns found in the other matrix (Mukherji, 1983a: 1–144). Simultaneously, each pattern in the original matrix is independent of all but one pattern in the second matrix (Berry, 1969: 21–31). In short, each linear combination of variables becomes independent of all the previously-derived linear combinations, just as factors are independent of each other in factor analysis.

The nature of canonical correlation analysis probably can be best explained through the algebraic model of a set of simultaneous equations (Cooley and Lohnes, 1962; Mukherji et al.: 1981: 1–35; 1983a):

$$U_1 = b_1 y_1 + b_2 y_2 + b_3 y_3 = a_1 x_1 + a_2 x_2 + a_3 x_3 + a_4 x_4 = V_1 \qquad \ldots(1)$$

$$U_2 = b_1 * y_1 + b_2 * y_2 + b_3 * y_3 = a_1 * x_1 + a_2 * x_2 + a_3 * x_3 + a_4 * x_4 = V_1 \qquad \ldots(2)$$

$$U_3 = b_1 ** y_1 + b_2 ** y_2 + b_3 ** y_3 = a_1 ** x_1 + a_2 ** x_2 + a_{13} ** x_3 + a_4 ** x_4 = V_3 \qquad \ldots(3)$$

Where b (betas) and a (alphas) are coefficients like regression coefficients, weighting Y and X sets of variables, respectively, in two data matrices, Here, the Y's represent three behaviour variables (i.e., migration behaviour) and the X's represent four attribute variables (i.e., socio-economic structure of regions). The asterisks indicate that the coefficient assume different values in three equations. Canonical correlation analysis, then, simply attempts to maximize the correlations between the pairs of weighted combinations of X's and Y's. Within each equation (1 to 3), if the weighted combination of Y's (migration behaviour) on the left hand side of the equation is termed as the new vector U, then the weighted combination of X's (socio-economic structure) on the right hand side can be termed as the new vector, V.

These new pairs are called as Canonical variates. Within each equation, these new pairs of vectors U and V are matched in such a way that the correlation between them is maximized. Successively, three matched pairs of U and V can be extracted, as in regression analysis, subject to the criterion that these should be independent of previously derived linear combinations (for technical details, see Cooley and Lohnes, 1962: 35–45, Anderson, 1958; Wood, 1973).

Conceptual and Analytical Design of the Spatial Field Theory

Canonical Model

For example, equation (1), referred to as the first matched pair of canonical variates, delineated the combination of those behaviour and attribute variables which have the strongest interrelationships in the two sets of data; the second matched pair of variates, as in equation (2), delineates the next strongest pattern of relationships that is orthogonal or uncorrelated to the first; and so on.

Figure 4.1 *Conceptual and Analytical Design of the Spatial Field Theory: Canonical Model*

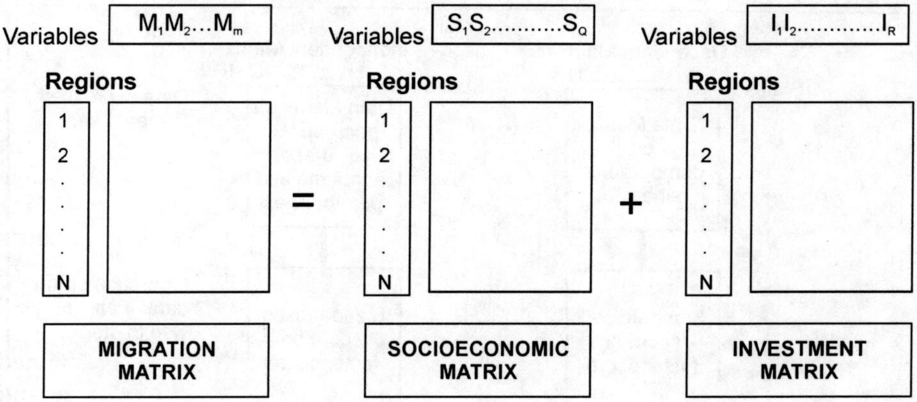

Variables $M_1M_2...M_m$ | Variables $S_1S_2..........S_Q$ | Variables $I_1I_2............I_R$

Regions 1, 2, ..., N — MIGRATION MATRIX = Regions 1, 2, ..., N — SOCIOECONOMIC MATRIX + Regions 1, 2, ..., N — INVESTMENT MATRIX

$$\sum \beta_m M_m = \sum \alpha_Q S_Q + \sum \alpha_R^* I_R$$

Source: Mukherji, 2001b, 2007

By its very nature, canonical analysis delineates a set of solutions or variates, which will be as large as there are independent patterns in both the data matrices, usually as many as there, are variables (or factors) in the smaller of the two matrices. Thus, the main difference between regression analysis and canonical analysis is that in the latter both multiple dependent variables and multiple predictor variables are involved. In regression, a multiple coefficient of correlation (R) measures the strength of the relationship between one dependent and a number of independent variables. By comparison, in canonical analysis *a series of canonical correlations (rho's)* specify the degree of inter-dependencies or causal inter-relationships between different matched pairs of dependent and independent sets of variables, and, instead of one, a set of canonical correlations is derived. Canonical analysis yields a much higher level analysis than that of regression or simultaneous equations, as they can handle only one dependent variable, not a whole matrix of dependent variables; and can generate only one single solution at a time, not a series of *independent* solutions, as canonical model does.

Thus, successive iterations linearly recombines both sets of variables (or factors) in order to uncover newer combinations, which maximizes the remaining variables. Such iteration continues until all patterns are discovered and the matrix with the least number of variables is exhausted. Each combination is orthogonal and independent of all previously derived linear combinations, and, as such, we can visualize which behaviour and attribute are indeed causally linked and matched, independent of all other causal linkages. Evidently, such advantages are not available in other simple techniques.

Application of Canonical Model

In general, canonical analysis is performed on two data matrices: Behaviour (B) and Attribute (A). Here, the first matrix is of (n x k) dimensions (n = number of

Figure 4.2(a) *Steps in Canonical Analysis (continued)*

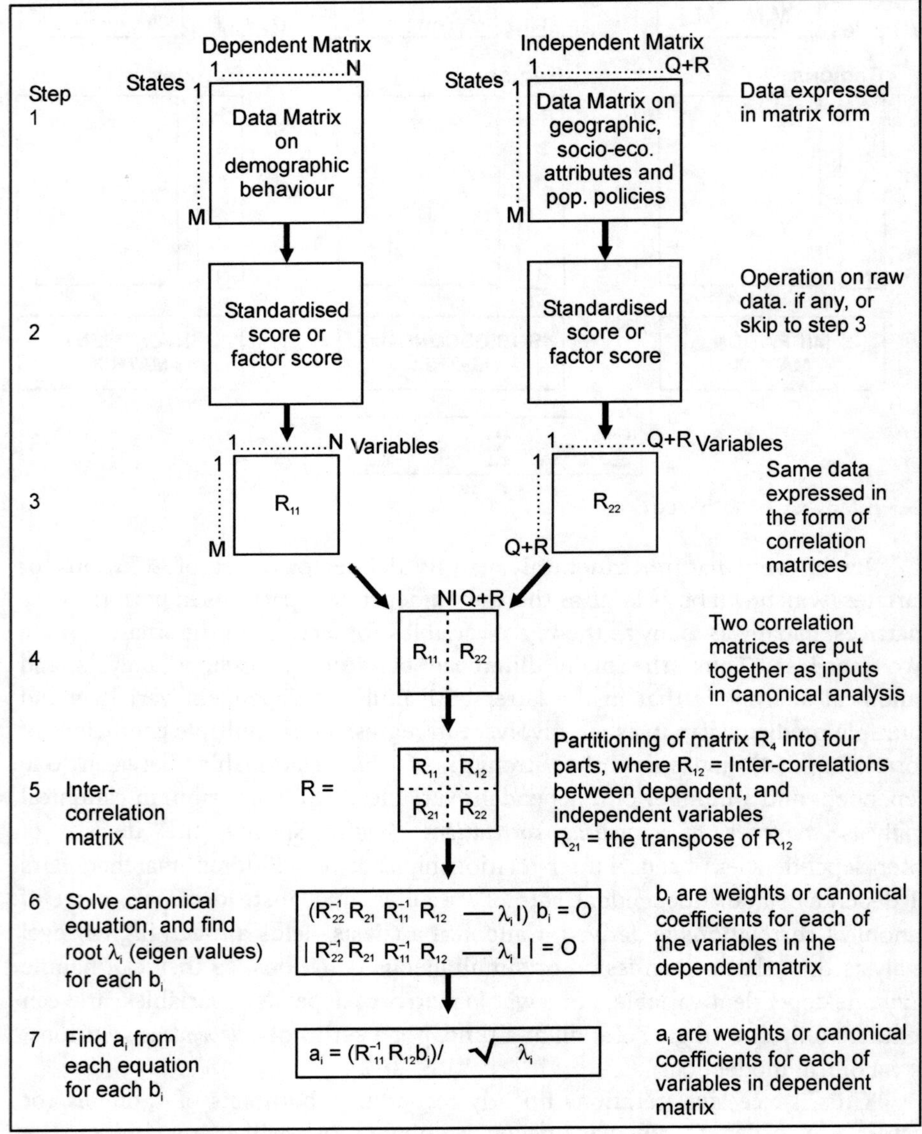

regions or states, 16; k = number of migration variables, 4). Here, general behaviour matrix B becomes Migration behaviour matrix, M. Second matrix A is of (n x r) dimensions (n = number of regions 16; r = number of variables related to socio-economic structure of regions, 13). Here, general matrix A becomes the predictor matrix S (socio-economic matrix, or termed as matrix of spatial structure of economy of regions) (S can be combinations of two/more matrices).

In canonical analysis, these two matrices are put together, considering behaviour matrix (M) as the dependent set and the attribute matrix (A, or S) as

Figure 4.2(b) *Steps in Canonical Analysis (concluding part)*

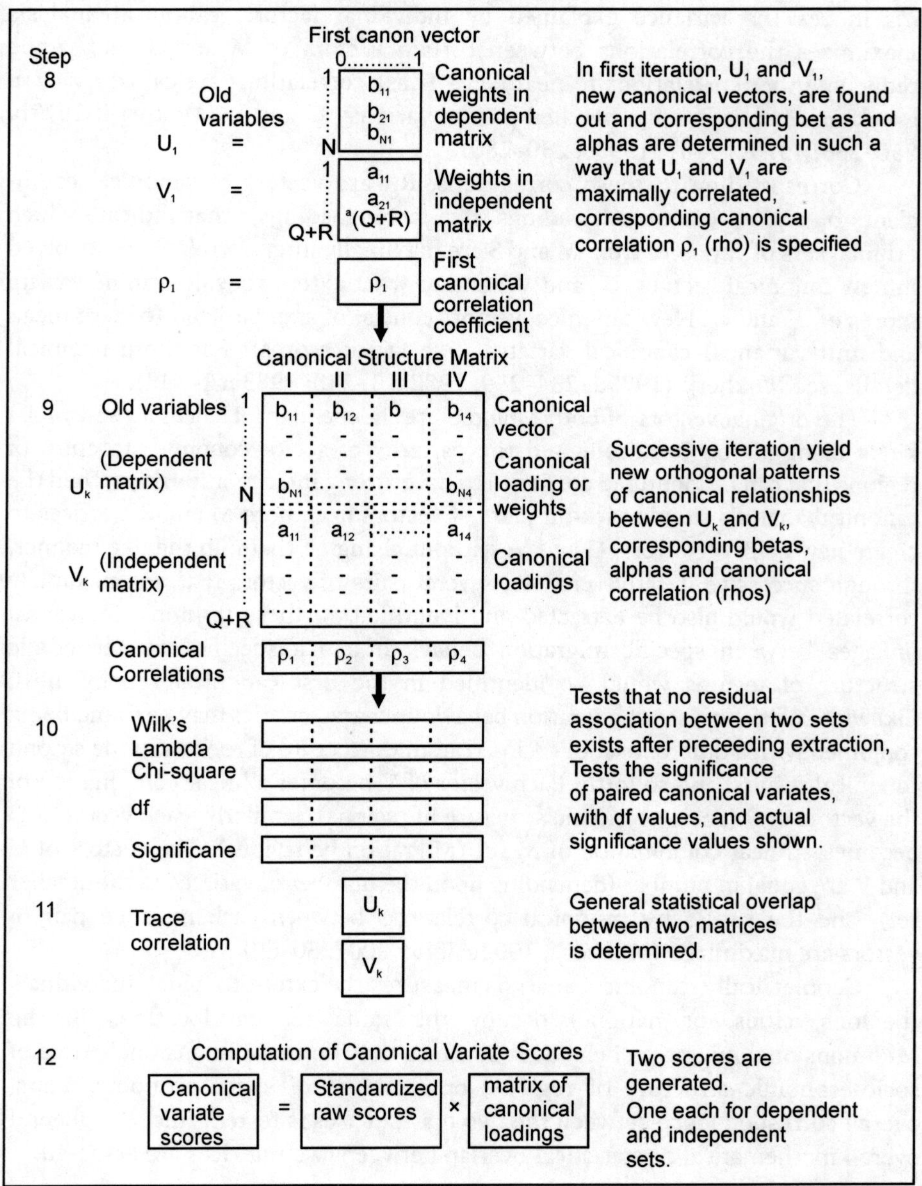

the independent set (see diagram). Canonically, the field theory can be expressed as (i.e., proportionally related to each other, not exactly equal),

$$M \approx S$$

Each vector of M provides a measure of an independent kind of migration behaviour of regions, and each vector of S provides the same for socio-economic structure of regions. Through computer, canonical analysis of these two matrices transforms the vectors from M and S to an independent pair of vectors, U and V, in both the matrices without changing them. Unlike factor analysis, which maximizes the variance explained by individual factors, canonical analysis maximizes the correlations between certain vectors of M and S sets, while reducing other correlations to near zero. These correlations are called *canonical correlations* between each matched pair of variates, U and V (Mukherji, 1977b: 250–266; 1979b: 1–81, 1993c: 250–280).

Corresponding to these correlations, R_c, are vectors of canonical coefficients b_K and a_K (canonical loadings, like factor loadings), that indicate which original sets of variables from M and S are maximally inter-correlated or involved in new canonical vectors, U_k and V_k; and to what extent they determine variate scores of u_k and v_k. New canonical vectors consist of standardized (of zero mean and unit variance) canonical variates (like factor scores). For more technical details, see Mukherji (1979d: 234–249; 1982a: 1–248; 1983a: 1–145).

The original vectors of both M and S are independent. Hence, if the various kinds of migration behaviour and the patterns of socio-economic structure of regions that can be identified are found to have strong inter-relationships, then the canonical analysis should pick-off pairs of vectors from both M and S matrices to create new pairs of vectors, U and V, without changing them. In the like manner, through successive iterative process, several pairs of vectors that are maximally correlated would also be extracted and identified. In these fashions, the causal linkages between specific migration behaviour and a specific socio-economic structure of regions would be identified in the first canonical relationships. Likewise, a different set of migration behaviour characteristics may be found being conjoined with a different set of socio-economic structure of regions in the second canonical results; and so forth. Each vector of V becomes a linear combination of the vectors of S (Socio-economic structure of regions); similarly, each vector of U becomes a linear combination of M set (Migration behaviour). The vectors of U and V are equal in number (depending upon the number of variates in the smaller set), and the successive canonical correlations between each matched pair of vectors are maximized (Mukherji, 1993c: ibid.; 2007: 50–69)

Geometrically, canonical analysis measures the extent to which individuals (persons, cities, or nations) occupy the same relative locations in the M-dimensional migration behaviour space as they do in S-dimensional space of socio-economic structure of regions, or structure of space economy. Thus, overall correspondence between the two matrix bases is tested. And, the general overall mathematical or statistical overlap between two matrices are assessed.

Number of Statistics Provided

Canonical analysis provides a number of statistics for assessment of the statistical significance of the inter-relationships. First is called the *Trace correlation* which indicates overall general goodness of fit between the two sets of input variables or two matrices; that is, it measures the amount of variance in the one set being explained by the variance in the other set. The higher the value of Trace correlation, the greater the statistical overlap between the two spaces; between behaviour and attributes sets. Usually, the trace correlation squared multiplied by 100 indicates the total amount of variance in the dependent set which is being explained by the independent set. However, since the size of the overall trace correlation depends upon total data sets, its magnitude can be reduced by the presence of less significant variables. This may happen, as close to the end of the analysis, successive iterative cycles may keep producing less and less meaningful results, and thus account for lesser amount of variance explained (Wood, 1973: 477–482).

Generally, thus, it is more meaningful to observe the second set of statistic, that is, the successive sets of *canonical correlations* (Rc or rho) which measure the degree of interdependences or associations between each matched pair of variates. Here too, the square of canonical correlation times 100 indicates the amount of variance explained in the variate of the dependent set by the variate in the independent set.

Third feature of canonical analysis is the *Chi-square statistic,* which indicates the statistical significance of these canonical correlations between each matched pair of variates or linear combinations of input variables (or factors).

Fourth feature is the *canonical coefficients* (similar to factor loadings) which relate each input variables to a canonical variate. Examinations of such coefficients permit precise interpretation of a canonical variate in terms of those input variables which constitute that specific variate and indicate high loadings.

The fifth statistic is *canonical variate scores*. These are standardized scores of zero mean and unit variance, and are obtained by the sum of the weights (canonical loadings) times the data products for each observations for all input variables in a specified matrix (behaviour or attribute). This gives one score each for pair of variates, Behaviour and Attributes. Plotting of these scores may reveal the geometrical mapping of relative location of each individual (nations, states, cities, persons or the like) on the canonical space, defined by the given set of variates. The residuals thus obtained from plotting may be the measures of unknown factors, not accounted for, or not considered in the data set.

Thus, in short, this mathematical tool can be a very powerful technique of assessing causal inter-connections between the socio-economic structure of regions in the one hand, and different patterns of migration behaviour of people in those regions in a country, on the other. The model is a general one, and can be equally applied to the study of fertility, as done in 'The Demographic Field Theory' (Mukherji, 1977b, 1983a, 2007), or other types of migration-circulation behaviour, as done in 'Mobility Field Theory' (Mukherji, 1975, 1979b, 1982b), or any other demographic/geographic problems (Mukherji, 1993c, 2001c: 1–25; 2001d: 1–21).

Variables Selected and Analysed

What follows now is the data corresponding to 443 districts of India (out of many, for which complete data available). It includes following variables. In all analysis, all 443 districts (belonging to 18 major states) are analysed, but due to lack of space, in tables, only data of very few districts are shown (as most tables run several pages). This is true for all tables and all analyses of this chapter, and subsequent chapters. The variables selected are:

CULT	Per cent cultivators	POPGRO	Population growth rate
AGL	Per cent agricultural labourers	POPDENS	Population density
LIVES	Per cent livestock workers	URBANISA	Per cent urbanised
MINS	Per cent workers in mining	GLITERA	General literacy
HH	Per cent workers in household industry	PERWOR	Per cent workers
MNF	Per cent workers in manufacturing	PERFAREA	Per cent forest area
CONS	Per cent workers in construction	PERNSA	Per cent net sown area
TC	Per cent workers in trade and commerce	VINMIGM	Volume of in-migration, males
TRANS	Per cent workers in transport	VOMIGM	Volume of out-migration, males
PCBDEP	Per capita bank deposit	INMIGRTM	In-migration rate, males
PCBCRED	Per capita bank credit	OMIGRTM	Out-migration rate, males
PCBCAGI	Per capita bank credit to agriculture	INTRADMA	*Intra*-district migration, males
PCBCSSI	Per capita bank credit to small industry	TOTMIGM	Total migration, males
PCBCIND	Per capita bank credit to industry	INTRADMR	*Intra*-district migration rate, males

These data are used as the input for Regression analysis (Chapter 5), Canonical and Factor analysis (Chapter 6)

Tables 4.1(a) and (b) show migration and socio-economic variables of 80 high in-migration districts, while Tables 4.1(c) and (d) present the same for 56 high out-migration districts (in Appendix). However, analyses are performed on all 443 districts. Male migration are mainly considered as they move for economic purposes. Female migration are very difficult to analyse as they mostly move for marriage.

In Retrospect

A conceptual model is presented linking spatial structure of economic activities of various regions and spatial flows of migration between them. Canonical model is used to assess *degree of inter-dependences* between two matrices and to ascertain *causal relations* between various elements within them. Canonical analysis was performed between inter-state migration matrix and states' socio-economic factors matrix. Migration matrix included volume and rates of in-migration and out-migration (dependent set) and matrix of four socio-economic factors, which themselves were results of factor analysis of former 13 indicators (predictor set). Factor scores were used as inputs for canonical analysis. Trace correlation between two sets emerged as 0.67, showing high degree of interdependence between two. Besides, successively four canonical correlations also emerged, which had not only high statistical significance, but also practical meaning. Findings show that large out-migration occur from states having high rural poverty and less plan outlay; and large in-migration occur into states having high per-capita income, less rural poverty, and fertilizer and irrigation. Findings show: *regional disparities* must be corrected before balanced spatial flow can be expected.

In retrospect, it must be mentioned that recently another attempt is made to extend Mobility Field Theory to International Mobility Field Theory (IMFT): Linking Internal and International Migration (Mukherji, 2001(d): IUSSP, Brazil: 1–20). This provides pathways to explain and predict international migration (details elsewhere).

Table 4.1(a) *Socio-economic and Migration Variables of Selected 80 Districts (showing high in-migration), 1991*

SL NO	DISTRICT	CULT	AGL	LIVES	MINS	HH	MNF	CONS	TC	TRANS	SERV	PCBDEP	PCBCRED	PCBCAGI	PCBCSSI	PCBCIND	PERWOR	PERFAREA	PERNSA
1	Vishakhapatnam	36.3	23.6	2.3	0.5	2.7	6.5	2.5	7.4	5.0	13.3	3147	2484	162	107	906	43.1	41.5	22.9
2	East Godavari	14.9	50.4	2.6	0.2	3.3	5.3	1.1	8.2	3.0	11.0	1763	1129	303	126	379	38.5	29.9	35.6
3	West Godavari	15.1	55.2	1.7	0.2	2.2	5.1	1.0	7.3	2.7	9.5	1767	1333	505	108	340	43.4	10.4	53.3
4	Krishna	15.7	48.6	2.0	0.5	2.4	6.2	1.6	8.6	5.3	9.2	2348	1598	446	125	361	43.3	7.5	56.2
5	Guntur	20.5	51.5	1.4	0.5	1.2	5.4	1.3	7.2	3.0	8.1	2094	1577	390	176	426	47.9	13.8	52.9
6	Nellore	21.3	47.7	2.9	0.4	3.0	4.1	1.9	6.8	2.7	9.3	1522	1297	446	98	195	45.6	7.5	24.5
7	Chittoor	37.7	35.0	2.1	0.4	2.3	4.1	1.4	6.1	2.5	8.4	1712	1057	388	72	182	45.9	30.3	31.5
8	Anantapur	35.5	38.6	1.7	0.2	3.3	3.6	1.7	5.7	2.5	7.2	1375	870	326	57	186	46.2	15.0	60.6
9	Kurnool	24.7	49.5	0.9	1.8	2.4	3.8	1.7	5.7	2.0	7.4	1295	1019	303	66	261	46.5	18.1	49.1
10	Rangareddy	25.3	28.5	1.9	1.6	1.0	13.8	4.5	7.9	4.3	11.1	1599	1849	302	381	1037	40.8	9.7	40.4
11	Hyderabad	0.2	0.3	0.3	0.1	0.5	18.6	7.6	28.7	12.3	31.5	12826	13349	609	831	4934	27.4	0.0	2.1
12	Adilabad	33.9	35.0	1.2	6.2	4.9	5.4	0.9	4.4	1.4	6.8	1330	478	113	25	123	44.4	42.4	37.4
13	Karimnagar	31.0	35.7	1.3	2.9	7.9	7.0	1.3	4.0	1.4	7.4	1640	689	271	42	153	50.3	21.2	33.7
14	Warangal	32.4	42.1	1.1	0.5	3.5	5.1	1.6	4.6	2.3	7.0	1295	846	344	70	181	47.8	28.9	31.8
15	Khammam	27.2	48.4	1.3	3.2	1.9	3.4	1.3	4.7	1.7	6.9	1135	639	216	32	122	45.9	48.0	27.2
16	Nalgonda	32.3	43.0	1.3	0.3	5.3	4.1	1.5	4.6	1.7	5.8	798	552	210	45	187	48.3	6.0	42.1
17	Kamrup	35.1	8.2	2.2	0.2	2.4	6.4	3.2	13.3	7.0	22.2	4586	2401	269	268	748	32.6	31.5	37.4
18	Dhanbad	19.6	9.4	0.9	24.9	1.6	12.3	2.5	10.1	5.4	13.2	2769	716	46	220	493	27.6	7.9	21.7
19	Rajkot	34.1	14.7	2.4	0.2	1.1	18.6	2.3	11.6	4.6	10.4	3845	1704	180	320	576	36.9	3.2	63.7
20	Junagadh	40.8	23.3	3.3	1.3	1.2	7.5	1.7	8.7	4.0	8.2	3006	1183	220	127	610	38.5	18.8	57.0
21	Mahesana	33.0	25.1	7.2	0.5	1.2	10.5	2.0	8.4	3.5	8.6	1492	755	193	151	406	42.6	1.8	74.9
22	Vadodara	26.2	28.1	1.7	0.6	0.9	14.3	2.7	9.2	3.9	12.5	6758	5407	329	567	3061	40.5	10.6	69.4

Cont'd...

...Cont'd

23	Surat	19.7	23.8	1.3	0.3	1.8	29.8	2.0	9.8	2.9	8.7	4958	2067	234	522	1254	43.2	18.3	51.8
24	Valsad	34.5	25.0	2.6	0.1	0.9	17.6	1.7	6.2	3.1	8.2	5509	1883	334	665	1376	45.6	24.3	57.4
25	Bangalore	5.9	4.6	1.0	0.8	1.3	30.1	8.1	19.6	7.6	21.0	12402	10867	413	1165	4435	34.3	0.0	0.0
26	Belgaum	40.7	29.5	1.6	0.1	3.1	6.6	2.2	6.4	2.1	7.7	1880	1085	419	81	291	42.4	14.2	66.2
27	Bijapur	31.5	43.2	1.7	0.3	3.2	4.6	1.6	5.8	1.7	6.5	1140	741	322	39	118	41.6	4.9	73.7
28	Chitradurga	37.1	32.2	2.4	0.4	2.2	6.0	2.2	8.1	1.9	7.5	1200	1031	314	81	292	43.0	8.0	53.1
29	Dakshin Kannad	19.7	16.1	6.7	0.4	1.1	28.1	3.2	10.4	3.9	10.4	6021	2826	416	389	771	43.2	27.1	26.0
30	Dharwad	30.0	39.1	1.4	0.2	2.3	6.6	2.0	8.3	2.9	7.3	1893	1143	359	119	259	42.1	8.2	68.8
31	Mysore	37.8	28.2	3.2	0.5	1.6	7.5	2.6	8.0	2.5	8.3	2302	1626	300	209	679	40.2	27.2	41.3
32	Shimoga	37.5	35.3	1.9	0.4	1.6	5.2	1.8	7.1	1.9	7.3	1720	1596	468	113	473	40.9	31.1	29.9
33	Kozhikode	6.2	13.6	12.5	2.4	1.6	12.4	6.1	18.4	9.8	17.1	2492	1470	277	117	328	26.6	17.7	69.9
34	Thrissur	9.2	22.8	6.4	0.7	4.5	14.8	4.4	14.5	6.8	15.9	5390	1665	209	213	443	32.0	34.6	52.1
35	Thiruvanathapur	11.5	29.7	5.8	0.5	2.3	9.7	4.0	11.1	5.8	19.7	5651	2317	289	122	411	32.0	22.8	65.4
36	Indore	18.5	14.8	0.9	0.1	1.3	17.5	4.0	16.6	6.3	19.9	6442	5313	210	732	2886	34.3	13.6	67.6
37	Bhopal	13.6	9.2	1.7	0.4	1.1	14.5	8.8	15.9	6.9	27.8	8740	5589	n.a	n.a	n.a.	44.7	39.4	42.2
38	Jabalpur	29.0	24.8	1.6	0.8	3.7	12.5	2.4	8.6	4.0	12.6	2772	2284	455	161	640	37.0	15.7	46.2
39	Bilaspur	55.0	24.6	1.5	1.3	1.3	3.0	1.4	3.8	1.7	6.4	1059	397	58	58	208	41.0	10.0	40.5
40	Raigarh	60.4	24.2	0.9	0.1	2.7	2.0	0.6	2.8	0.8	5.5	607	325	96	31	80	49.2	31.0	41.2
41	Rajunandgaon	63.7	20.3	2.0	0.2	1.5	2.9	0.7	3.1	1.0	4.6	611	396	99	54	104	52.4	35.1	45.7
42	Durg	43.3	25.0	1.7	1.4	1.2	9.9	2.1	5.2	2.3	8.1	1997	1075	105	151	442	43.9	11.4	63.9
43	Rajpur	49.3	28.8	1.8	0.3	1.6	4.5	1.2	5.0	1.8	5.8	1193	769	94	164	353	47.1	36.5	44.2
44	Bastar	73.2	14.7	1.1	0.6	1.3	1.1	0.8	1.9	0.7	4.8	545	244	74	22	54	46.7	40.5	40.4
45	Greater Bombay	0.1	0.1	0.5	0.2	1.5	35.3	4.2	24.9	11.3	21.9	52985	32791	89	1515	10578	35.3	4.0	0.0
46	Raigarh	44.8	17.7	3.0	0.4	1.5	11.4	2.8	6.3	3.4	8.8	2189	808	131	183	1036	43.9	23.5	26.7
47	Nashik	43.3	24.2	1.2	0.1	1.4	10.6	2.0	5.9	2.8	8.6	1581	978	279	120	283	43.6	22.3	57.6

Cont'd...

...*Cont'd*

48	Jalgaon	30.0	44.3	1.4	0.1	1.3	5.0	1.4	6.0	2.8	7.7	1122	784	163	58	124	42.9	14.8	69.9
49	Ahmadnagar	47.4	26.6	1.5	0.1	1.4	7.6	1.6	5.1	1.8	7.1	11330	879	325	70	250	46.0	10.9	68.2
50	Pune	31.4	14.0	1.6	0.2	1.5	16.3	5.5	9.8	4.8	15.0	5386	3416	300	437	2106	40.3	11.8	63.6
51	Satara	49.3	21.6	1.8	0.2	2.2	6.2	1.8	5.5	2.7	8.8	1497	877	293	96	234	44.5	13.8	53.8
52	Sangli	43.4	24.2	2.0	0.1	1.3	7.8	2.0	6.9	2.8	9.4	1722	1124	331	135	377	44.1	5.5	69.6
53	Solapur	33.7	31.6	2.1	0.2	2.4	10.4	2.0	6.8	2.7	8.3	1256	890	333	84	239	43.1	2.3	75.6
54	Kolhapur	45.9	17.0	1.6	0.2	2.2	12.3	2.3	7.5	2.5	8.5	1503	1146	262	179	394	46.1	18.5	53.2
55	Buldana	39.0	43.4	1.0	0.1	0.9	2.7	1.2	4.4	1.4	5.9	608	463	173	18	41	47.6	12.2	70.9
56	Akola	26.1	50.8	0.9	0.1	1.0	3.7	1.6	5.9	2.4	7.5	847	674	154	48	79	43.8	6.7	75.7
57	Amravathi	21.5	52.4	1.5	0.0	1.3	3.4	2.0	6.0	2.5	9.3	1278	634	285	51	85	44.4	27.2	59.2
58	Yavatmal	27.0	53.5	1.4	0.6	1.2	2.8	1.6	4.4	1.3	6.2	829	548	205	27	74	47.7	18.3	63.8
59	Nagpur	18.4	24.0	2.0	2.2	2.2	12.5	5.4	11.6	6.0	15.7	4082	2254	168	259	643	37.5	17.7	56.0
60	Koraput	50.8	32.8	1.3	0.1	1.4	2.0	0.7	3.6	0.9	6.3	527	355	134	13	146	49.0	45.5	28.5
61	Puri	38.2	22.6	3.8	0.3	2.9	4.1	1.7	8.8	3.0	14.7	2634	2025	307	117	563	30.2	30.9	25.1
62	Ludhiana	20.0	16.7	1.4	0.0	0.5	25.3	3.8	13.6	5.3	13.4	8726	6989	531	1504	2705	31.3	2.0	86.7
63	Ganganagar	52.4	18.3	1.7	0.0	1.2	5.0	1.5	7.7	2.2	10.1	1597	1215	595	52	104	37.2	1.9	76.1
64	Jaipur	45.6	5.9	1.6	0.5	3.3	9.8	4.1	10.4	4.1	14.9	3934	2271	192	234	655	34.2	4.6	56.6
65	Madras	0.1	0.0	0.9	0.1	0.7	23.6	6.4	25.7	10.7	31.9	22630	22117	341	1714	9417	0.9	0.0	0.0
66	Chengalpattu	16.2	33.7	1.4	0.3	3.8	14.4	3.3	8.9	4.5	13.7	1587	1224	270	197	742	38.1	5.4	39.6
67	South Arcot	34.5	44.8	0.9	1.3	1.5	3.1	1.0	4.4	1.6	7.0	956	802	372	31	241	43.7	4.7	54.7
68	Salem	25.8	34.3	0.9	0.5	5.9	13.2	1.9	6.8	3.3	7.4	2095	1502	473	192	502	49.3	19.3	44.0
69	Periyar	23.8	39.1	0.6	0.1	4.1	12.1	2.3	7.8	3.0	7.1	2652	1675	623	193	366	52.3	28.3	38.0
70	Thanjavur	22.1	48.9	1.3	0.0	1.9	4.3	1.5	8.6	2.1	9.2	1921	906	363	53	106	40.6	1.4	62.6
71	Nainital	41.2	18.5	2.9	0.3	0.9	7.6	2.9	8.3	3.3	14.1	3033	1658	367	279	706	38.6	57.7	29.4
72	Lucknow	29.7	8.7	1.5	0.1	2.1	8.5	3.4	14.2	4.8	26.9	8345	3799	225	267	1159	29.6	4.5	59.7

Cont'd...

...Cont'd

73	Jalpaiguri	29.4	16.9	22.4	0.1	1.1	6.0	1.8	8.9	4.3	9.2	879	409	84	125	421	33.8	28.0	53.1
74	Murshidabad	31.5	29.3	1.9	0.0	13.6	4.3	3.5	7.7	1.9	6.1	620	262	54	19	36	31.5	0.2	74.0
75	North 24 Prgn	17.1	17.2	1.5	0.1	2.2	22.8	2.8	15.9	6.4	14.1	2288	552	57	81	229	28.8	–	67.8
76	South 24 Prgn	27.8	29.8	2.0	0.1	4.2	11.4	1.5	9.6	4.4	9.2	987	288	62	136	595	28.3	41.4	36.3
77	Calcutta	0.2	0.2	0.5	0.2	0.5	26.0	3.4	29.7	11.4	28.0	38456	21835	323	1621	9117	33.0	–	–
78	Haora	10.7	14.8	1.1	0.1	3.6	33.1	2.5	15.3	6.3	12.6	2523	693	40	325	881	29.1	–	62.3
79	Hugli	21.1	26.6	1.0	0.1	2.9	19.6	2.0	11.6	4.2	10.8	1915	563	91	102	546	31.1	0.1	71.0
80	Medinipur	42.1	25.4	1.8	0.1	4.9	5.2	1.6	6.9	3.2	8.9	925	371	89	46	100	35.2	12.7	64.3

CULT Per cent cultivators
AGL Per cent agricultural labourers
LIVES Per cent livestock workers
MINS Per cent mining workers
HH Per cent workers in household industry
MNF Per cent workers in manufacturing
CONS Per cent workers in construction
PCBDEP Per capita bank deposit
PCBCRED Per capita bank credit
PCBCAGI Per capita bank credit to agriculture
PCBCSSI Per capita bank credit to small industries
TC Per cent workers in trade/commerce
TRANS Per cent workers in transport
PCBCIND Per capita bank credit to industry
PERWOR Percentage of workers
PERFAREA Per cent forest area
PERNSA Per cent net sown area

Source: Computed from data of Census of India, 1991©, Economic Tables, B-Series and Migration Table(b), D-Series, Census Commissioner and Registrar General's Office, New Delhi, CDs available in 1996–7–8.Plus, Data of Centre for Monitoring Indian Economy(CMIE, 1991), Mumbai, were also used. Note: In all analysis, all 443 districts (belonging to 18 major states) are analysed, but due to lack of space, in tables, only data of very few districts are shown (as most tables run several pages). This is true for all tables and all analyses of this chapter, and all subsequent chapters.

Table 4.1(b) *Socio-economic and Migration Variables of Selected 80 Districts (showing high volume of in-migrants), India, 1991*

SL NO	District Name	POPGRO	POPDENS	URBANISA	GLITERA	VINMIGM	VOMIGM	INMIGRTM	OMIGRTM	INTRADMA	INTERDM	TOTMIGM	INTRADMR
1	Vishakhapatnam	2.4	294	39.8	45.5	159737	76272	9.6	4.6	253425	160607	454812	55.7
2	East Godavari	2.1	420	23.8	48.8	89563	120266	3.9	5.3	401665	89803	504048	79.7
3	West Godavari	2.1	454	20.7	53.4	89563	169211	5.1	9.6	304862	119213	430185	70.9
4	Krishna	1.9	424	35.8	53.2	151581	140887	8.1	7.5	316367	152711	482338	65.6
5	Guntur	1.8	361	28.9	46.4	103152	149663	5.0	7.2	300734	103662	412536	72.9
6	Nellore	1.7	183	23.8	47.8	52116	55090	4.3	4.6	166780	52436	233539	71.4
7	Chittoor	1.8	215	19.8	49.8	39103	34253	2.4	2.1	152706	39433	232314	65.7
8	Anantapur	2.2	166	23.5	42.2	38180	33340	2.3	2.0	179815	38280	242019	74.3
9	Kurnool	2.1	168	25.8	40.0	47552	55333	3.1	3.6	181170	47702	237582	76.3
10	Rangareddy	4.8	341	47.2	49.1	254768	26667	19.4	2.0	89431	256678	396518	22.6
11	Hyderabad	3.2	14497	100.0	72.5	184543	76644	11.3	4.7	0	186053	254375	0.0
12	Adilabad	2.4	129	23.1	33.0	67265	23364	6.4	2.2	136900	67915	222535	61.5
13	Karimnagar	2.2	257	20.6	37.2	51402	83121	3.4	5.4	157922	51912	220744	71.5
14	Warangal	2.0	219	19.4	39.3	50712	91492	4.5	8.1	152418	95122	254175	60.0
15	Khammam	2.4	138	20.2	40.5	94762	43386	6.6	3.0	173520	51222	229322	75.7
16	Nalgonda	2.3	200	11.9	38.0	46180	86987	3.2	6.0	205250	46580	255300	80.4
17	Kamrup	2.5	460	32.8	65.0	103441	51129	9.7	4.8	74414	104131	235601	31.6
18	Dhanbad	2.5	893	51.3	55.5	262976	15085	18.0	1.0	53213	265616	406237	13.1
19	Rajkot	1.8	224	47.1	67.0	107405	92880	8.3	7.2	146576	107635	269881	54.3
20	Junagadh	1.3	225	32.5	60.3	48050	86168	3.9	7.1	147746	48220	206321	71.6
21	Mahesana	1.4	325	22.0	65.1	62331	186971	4.1	12.4	134721	62491	218772	61.6
22	Vadodara	1.9	396	43.0	63.6	152454	80092	9.4	5.0	164473	153314	389452	42.2

Cont'd...

...Cont'd

23	Surat	3.1	443	50.6	64.4	248706	51660	13.9	2.9	116954	249676	624951	18.7
24	Valsad	2.1	415	24.5	64.4	56508	38816	5.1	3.5	90252	57148	205070	44.0
25	Bangalore	3.2	2210	86.2	76.3	336618	76482	13.2	3.0	73416	344958	708075	10.4
26	Belgaum	1.7	267	23.5	53.0	71450	72870	3.9	4.0	280521	72770	406192	69.1
27	Bijapur	2.0	172	23.5	55.1	60120	96403	4.0	6.5	233876	60830	314830	74.3
28	Chitradurga	2.1	201	27.0	55.5	76265	68230	6.8	6.1	128016	77665	222591	57.5
29	Dakshin Kannad	1.3	319	28.3	75.9	34072	99565	2.6	7.6	228621	34782	309940	73.8
30	Dharwad	1.7	255	34.9	58.7	121307	127615	6.7	7.1	338777	122527	480234	70.5
31	Mysore	2.0	265	29.7	47.3	70957	89455	4.4	5.5	151575	71367	257122	59.0
32	Shimoga	1.4	181	26.5	61.5	92961	73710	9.5	7.6	124143	93391	238074	52.1
33	Kannur	1.5	759	50.9	91.5	91926	43085	8.4	3.9	198748	92186	303636	65.5
34	Kozhikode	1.5	1117	38.3	91.1	75187	50294	5.8	3.9	221820	75887	313737	70.7
35	Thrissur	1.2	903	26.3	90.2	72524	66885	5.5	5.1	254362	72954	339902	74.8
36	Thiruvanathapur	1.3	1344	33.9	89.2	49060	61730	3.4	4.3	132890	49410	205150	64.8
37	Indore	2.7	471	69.4	66.3	112242	59403	11.7	6.2	45687	113542	230719	19.8
38	Bhopal	2.5	191	17.0	25.3	126404	26588	17.7	3.7	12109	126854	223352	5.4
39	Jabalpur	1.9	261	45.5	59.1	83857	54099	6.1	3.9	106916	84607	249948	42.8
40	Bilaspur	2.7	133	19.3	35.2	70354	74829	3.7	3.9	253328	71134	376144	67.4
41	Durg	2.4	281	35.3	58.7	98722	67924	8.1	5.6	161080	99762	365673	44.1
42	Rajpur	2.4	184	19.7	48.1	77230	82604	3.9	4.2	272849	78850	424910	64.2
43	Bastar	2.5	118	18.6	45.9	34293	12350	3.0	1.1	131093	35013	200600	65.4
44	Greater Bombay	1.9	16460	100.0	82.5	820043	172082	15.0	3.2	0	834693	2E+06	0.0
45	Raigarh	2.0	255	18.0	64.0	73388	104760	8.1	11.5	104905	73828	221701	47.3
46	Nashik	2.5	247	35.6	62.3	126753	112500	6.4	5.7	329082	127943	489015	67.3
47	Jalgaon	2.0	270	27.4	64.3	98173	149953	6.0	9.1	329501	98403	462242	71.3

Cont'd...

...*Cont'd*

48	Ahmadnagar	2.2	197	15.8	61.0	112898	149540	6.5	8.6	257385	121388	388903	66.2
49	Pune	2.8	353	50.7	71.1	236192	202260	8.3	7.1	226085	238632	573927	39.4
50	Satara	1.8	233	12.9	66.7	118423	201010	9.8	16.6	255998	118793	396281	64.6
51	Sangli	1.8	257	22.7	62.6	79904	150724	7.1	13.4	141175	80114	257628	54.8
52	Solapur	2.2	216	28.8	56.4	97635	174035	5.8	10.4	240557	97935	380030	63.3
53	Kolhapur	1.9	389	26.3	66.9	96305	99600	6.3	6.5	233875	96665	414008	56.5
54	Buldana	2.2	195	20.6	61.7	63774	77491	6.6	8.0	155538	63824	227992	68.2
55	Akola	1.9	209	28.7	65.8	86410	93280	7.6	8.2	162888	86560	260558	62.5
56	Amravathi	1.7	180	32.6	70.1	53517	87602	4.7	7.7	127798	54067	201315	63.5
57	Yavatmal	1.8	153	17.2	58.0	63491	75561	6.0	7.1	177887	63731	252638	70.4
58	Nagpur	2.4	332	61.8	73.6	80137	63488	4.7	3.7	71299	81517	235203	30.3
59	Cuttack	1.8	495	12.3	63.3	63391	117612	2.3	4.2	159531	63931	251072	63.5
60	Koraput	1.9	111	11.2	22.7	51083	8900	3.4	0.6	126409	51953	205932	61.4
61	Puri	2.0	352	19.7	63.8	90628	49615	4.9	2.7	98918	90758	204126	48.5
62	Ludhiana	2.9	640	50.3	67.4	93109	47123	7.0	3.5	106450	94569	320029	33.3
63	Ganganagar	2.6	127	21.1	41.8	53884	23676	3.9	1.7	201115	54394	357000	56.3
64	Jaipur	3.2	336	39.5	47.9	120422	43389	4.8	1.7	122865	121652	307003	40.0
65	Madras	1.5	22076	100.0	81.6	324262	92333	16.3	4.7	0	341442	461308	0.0
66	Chengalpattu	2.5	592	44.9	66.4	268583	62217	11.3	2.6	205092	280623	561785	36.5
67	South Arcot	1.5	447	15.8	52.9	70440	98230	2.8	4.0	157168	79425	253724	61.9
68	Salem	1.3	450	29.2	53.3	58258	113457	2.9	5.6	184117	65768	257465	71.5
69	Periyar	1.2	282	24.7	53.8	98600	68660	8.3	5.8	164897	105550	279347	59.0
70	Thanjavur	1.1	547	22.9	66.0	89035	137770	3.9	6.1	311257	91235	412472	75.5
71	Nainital	3.4	226	32.7	56.5	168845	16950	20.5	2.1	50224	170015	255522	19.7
72	Lucknow	3.1	1092	62.7	57.5	183010	27335	12.4	1.9	26976	183850	242886	11.1

Cont'd...

...*Cont'd*

73	Jalpaiguri	2.3	449	16.4	45.1	37617	23490	2.6	1.6	121512	38397	213869	56.8
74	Murshidabad	2.5	890	10.4	38.3	27190	69473	1.1	2.9	169978	31610	210498	80.8
75	North 24 Pargan	2.8	1779	51.2	66.8	123700	65328	3.2	1.7	145160	126040	464050	31.3
76	South 24 Pargan	2.7	574	13.3	55.1	71708	49050	2.4	1.7	122839	72658	220450	55.7
77	Calcutta	0.6	23782	100.0	77.6	98300	102284	4.0	4.2	0	100010	325073	0.0
78	Haora	2.3	2542	49.6	67.6	50248	49840	2.5	2.5	66847	51318	222125	30.1
79	Hugli	2.0	1383	31.2	66.8	75430	52806	3.3	2.3	129656	75920	293674	44.2
80	Medinipur	2.2	591	9.9	69.3	45762	103500	1.1	2.4	363489	47046	447715	81.2

POPGRO	Population growth rate	VINMIGM	Volume of in-migration, males
PPDENS	Population density	VOMIGM	Volume of out-migration, males
URBANISA	Urbanisation	INMIGRTM	In-migration rate, males
GLITERA	General literacy	OMIGRTM	Out-migration rate, males
INTERDM	Inter-district migration, males	TOTMIGM	Total migration, males

Source: Computed from data of Census of India, 1991©, Economic Tables, B-Series and Migration Table (b), D-Series, Census Commissioner and Registrar General's Office, New Delhi, CDs Note: In all analysis, all 443 districts (belonging to 18 major states) are analyzed. But due to lack of space, in tables, only data of very few districts are shown (as most tables run several pages). This is true for all tables and all analyses of this chapter, and all subsequent chapters.

5 Findings of District-level Regression Analysis of Migration, Urbanization and Socio-economic Variables, 1991

"Do not be frightened. Awake, be up and doing. Do not stop till you have reached the goal."

Swami Vivekananda (1893)
(Complete Work, Centenary Volume II, 1963: 410)

In this chapter, results of many regression analyses are briefly presented. Analyses were performed at the district-level. Results of Factor and Canonical analyses are presented in the next chapter.

District-level Analysis

District level analysis of inter-relationships between migration and socio-economic variables were done at following three stages:

1. By performing step-wise regression analysis between *intra*-district and inter-district migration and the district-level socio-economic variables, for All-India (443 districts) specially for the males (Tables 5.1 to 5.8). Results for the females are not shown due to lack of space and they mostly move for non-economic reasons, which are difficult to explain.
2. Step-wise regression analyses are performed between inter-district in-migration and out-migration and selected socio-economic variables, done separately for all major states of India (Tables 5.9 to 5.12) (see Appendix).
3. Step-wise regression analysis between inter-district in-migration and out-migration and the composite development indices evolved and computed for the districts (Tables 5.13 and 5.14).

These three sets of results are greatly elaborated through several Tables (Tables 5.1 to 5.14), and are briefly discussed below. Before discussion starts, a brief note on the limitations of census migration data is pertinent here.

Limitations of Census Migration Data and Other Data

Indian census migration data have several shortcomings, which have handicapped the present analysis:

(a) District-level data were not available for separate reasons for migration, and, as such, no study could be attempted separately for employment migration, educational migration, or the like. Evidently, it is primarily the employment migration, which has direct relation with the socio-economic attributes of the districts, not all heterogeneous categories of migration. Thus, while predictor variables were quite distinct, but the right kind of dependent variable (employment migration) was missing! Therefore, this was a serious shortcoming.

(b) District-level migration data were not available according to duration of residence, and, as such, study of decadal migration or recent migration could not be made. Data referred to life-time migration which included all the impurities and data noise.

(c) District-level migration data showed only in-migration (according to birth-place statistics), not out-migration. So, out-migration could not be explained satisfactorily. Another deficiency is lack of data of out-migration from districts with reference to *inter-state migration*, for instance, it can not be deciphered from which districts of Uttar Pradesh state massive out-migration occurs to the state of Maharashtra or Delhi or West Bengal.

(d) Rudimentary data on in-migration and out-migration, however, could be extracted at inter-district level, but it included only life-time migrants, not sub-classified according to different duration of residence, nor according to different purposes of moves. So, such limitations have considerably handicapped our present analysis.

(e) In census data enumerating process, the reason for migration is asked and reported only for the *main* reasons, not for second reason of move; as a result, a huge proportion of migrants (specially females) are reported being moved for familial migration (i.e., moved with family), or for other miscellaneous purposes, which actually may be employment-related migration.

(f) Another very serious lacuna is that no economic indicators of the migrants' condition are available, like income, poverty situation, housing, existence of water and toilet facilities, and so forth. In their absence, extreme difficulty arise to relate poverty and mobility among hundreds of millions of migrants in India. Evidently, not only migration research has greatly suffered, but also concrete planning for mitigating their poverty never took place.

(g) Another serious handicap was that corrected and fully computerized version of Indian census 1991 migration data were available but only in 1999, after so many years! So it greatly delayed analysis of census 1991 data. Similarly, 2001 migration data were also available only after 5–6–7 years (in 2005 or 2007, some in 2008).

(h) According to Prof. Chapman (1970: 1–30; Chapman and Prothero, 1985a: 436–437) migration data *per se* is most inadequate, as it is capable of revealing only one shot picture of movement, not a continuum of mobility, Thus, it fails to unfold the true nature of people's mobility (like circulation, oscillation, commuting, temporary migration and so forth). These movements have great ramifications for planning for administrative services and social provisions in spheres of housing, education, and health (Chapman, ibid.).

(i) In India, another source of migration data is National Sample Survey Organization's (NSSO) occasional survey encompassing migrants (NSSO, 2001). Recently, some migration studies based on NSSO data wrongly show that it is the literate and more educated people who are migrating, than poor segments of rural society (Kundu, 2007; Raju, 2009). But, NSSO migration data are highly biased against the illiterate and the poor sections of the villages. This is recently found by some studies (Deshingkar and Aktar, 2009: 1–90). And, such wrong analyses, thus, gives wrong results and make incorrect prescriptions!! If these were true, then, why do 500 million poor exist in India in 2005 (and still increasing)? Why are filthy and stinking urban slums mushrooming everywhere in all mega cities of India? Why are sad incidences of 100,000 farmers' suicides coming from many southern states of India? Why are hordes of migrants leaving tottering villages and crowding in dirty urban slums? Recently, other studies also expressed doubts about the reliability of NSSO data on poverty and other surveys: "There are still so many poor people, so many hovels, so many mounds of filth and so many beggars. This is why we need the smell check" (Gupta, 2010: 22).

So, much more penetrating and revealing research are really necessary, before we may opine otherwise. We indeed need facts, based on nation-wide migration surveys and censuses, and their deep and high-level mathematical and statistical analyses (like canonical models, field theories, matrix analyses), before we can arrive at contrary observations. Otherwise, wrong analyses of the few sampled and biased data (biased against the poor), may mislead migration research in India and end up with wrong prescriptions for the hundreds of millions of the poor migrants. *Elitist perspectives are dangerous!*. And, the conventional or arm-chair researchers in the area of migration (or fertility) do much harm to the country.

Socio-economic Variables

At the district level, data of about 30 socio-economic variables from various sources were collected and utilized for socio-economic matrix, and for explaining district level migration of 443 districts (out of total 525), belonging to 17 major states of India (out of total 25), for which some kind of data were available (plus Delhi Union Territory). Most such data refer to proportion of 10 major categories of workers to total workers in each district (i.e., workers in cultivation, agricultural labour, livestock, mining, household industry, manufacturing, construction, trade-commerce, transport and services). Besides, other variables are also selected: population size, density, population growth rate, per cent urban, proportion of total workers to population, size of operational holdings, value of agricultural productivity, per cent irrigated area, and per cent of net sown area of total geographical area. Other socio-economic variables are also chosen, like per cent general literacy, female literacy, per capita fertility consumption, consumption of fertilizers per hectare of gross cropped area, per capita bank credit given to all industries, to small-scale industries, or to service sectors, etc. In step-wise regression analysis, not all such variables emerged in the final results, but only those few specific variables emerged which survived rigorous statistical test, and showed significant results. Tables 5.1 to 5.14 present details of such results.

Brief Note on Regression Analytic Technique

Bi-variate regression analysis or multivariate regression analysis are well known, and any standard textbook on statistics may help easy understanding. For instance, Introduction to Modern Statistics by Dixon and Massy (1970) or Advanced statistics by S.C. Gupta (1969), may be of considerable help. Here, basic rudimentary ideas are presented for the newly initiated. Table 5.1 to 5.8 are of considerable help to easily understand the essential of regression analysis. Many regression plots are given throughout chap. 12 to 16, along with associated statistics of regression lines.

There is an essential difference between correlation and regression. Correlation between two variables shows only the "degree of relationships" between the two variables (which vary together), but it does not tell about the "direction of causality" or "cause-and-effect relationship", which regression does. Thus, regression is much superior statistical technique, as it tells both the "degree of relationship" between two variables, which vary together, but also indicates the "direction" of relationship, i.e., it also points out which is the causal variable and which is the effect variable. However, spurious cause and effect relationships must always be avoided, and the researcher must have a prior idea or knowledge (as far as possible, from research literature) about the cause and effect relationship between the two variables. The meaning of the following useful statistical terms are explained below:

1. Dependent variable (Y) = Variable which is to be explained or the "effect" variable (e.g., volume or rate of migration).
2. Independent variable (X) = Predictor variable or "causal" variable (e.g, manufacturing sector in the city).
3. Correlation coefficient = shows degree of relationships between the dependent and independent variables.
4. Regression = shows how much variation in dependent variable is brought about by unit change in independent variable.
5. Regression line of fit = the best line of fit between the dependent and independent variables on a scatter diagram.
6. R-Square = Square of the correlation coefficient between the two variables, or Coefficient of Determination.
7. Adjusted R-Square = Standardized R-Square value of the Coefficient of Determination.
8. Explanation = Adjusted R-Square times 100, "explains" the variations in the dependent variable by the variations in the independent variable. *This is the simplest meaning of relationship between the two variables.*
9. Beta Coefficient = Regression weights on the independent variable, showing how much change in the dependent variable would occur due to "unit" change in the independent variable.
10. Angle Theta (θ) = Angle of the regression line of fit with the X-axis, showing the slope of the line with X-axis.
11. Beta = Tan Theta = indicates the above beta coefficient i.e., how much change in dependent variable is caused by unit change in independent variable

12. Direction = Positive or negative Beta would show the direction (positive or negative) of relationships.
13. Intercept = Length of intercept of Regression line with the Y-axis.
14. Regression Equation = Consists of (Y) dependent variable is being explained by the intercept and Beta coefficient-weighted independent variable.

    For example: Y (Dependent variable) = Intercept + Beta weights (X) (Independent Variable), as in Y = 123 + 0.35 (X).
15. Meaning of Relationships = The simplest meaning is given in the last column of each regression table. For example: "volume of out migration in the districts increases as the proportion of marginal workers increases" or "In-migration rates in the Class I cities increases as the proportion of manufacturing sectors in the cities increases", and so forth.
16. *The most readers are best advised just to focus on the last column of each regression table, that describes the "Meaning of Relationships" in simple words, without bothering much about the statistical parameters.* Anybody can very easily understand the simple regression line of fit and this meaning of that line describing the "cause and effect relationship" between the two variables, amidst masses of data, tables, observations, and complex entities. Thus, used in this way, the regression analysis is the best effective way to untangle the hidden complexities.
17. In step-wise regression, the same methods are followed, except that here we deal with one dependent variable and multiple independent or predictor variables, and in the first step, the most important predictor variable will emerge as the most significant and most meaningful explanatory variable, based on the strength of correlations between the dependent variable and all predictor variables. In the next step, the next important variable will emerge as the second most explanatory variable, based on the same strength of correlations. Such steps will go on, until all meaningful steps in the regression are completed. Interpretations are also similar.
18. Canonical analysis is much higher form of these regression analysis, but instead of just two variables, it uses many variables (*both* in dependent and independent sides), and does that between many "data matrices", treating them simultaneously (not simply between two variables, or one dependent and many independent variables). The beauty, elegance and the utility of canonical analysis are elaborated in Chapter 4.

All-India Results: Step-wise Regression Analysis of *Intra*-District and Inter-District Migration (Males) and Socio-economic Variables (1991)

Table 5.1 to 5.8 present the salient findings of eight sets of analysis performed between district-level migration rates and selected socio-economic variables for the males: summary of the main findings are also given in the annexed summary table. Most tables are self-explanatory, and all major relationships are elaborated in the 'Remarks/Explanation' column of each table.

1. Volume of in-migration into a district is explained by per cent of manufacturing workers (to total workers) (explains 36%), followed by per capita bank credit explaining another 8%. It appears that in-migration is positively

related to development level of a district. It is a good sign (see attached summary table).

2. Volume of out-migration from a district, on the other hand, is negatively related to proportion of cultivators (to total workers) in the district, i.e., less cultivators causing more out-migration. This explain 15%. Likewise, presence of less service workers in a district causes more out-migration (explains another 8%). Together, they explain 23% of variations in volume of out-migration from a district.
3. In-migration rates are explained by higher per capita bank credit (19%) and less population density (8%) (see annexed summary table).
4. Conversely, out-migration rates are explained by higher general literacy rates (12%), and presence of less service workers in a district (8%) (see Table). This also makes sense.
5. Volume of *intra*-district migration is explained by higher proportion of agricultural labourers (19%), and higher proportion of transport workers (10%). Evidently, these sectors attract more job- seekers, at *intra*-district level.
6. Volume of inter-district migration on the other hand, is explained by presence of stronger manufacturing sector (explains 36%), and higher per capita bank credits to general industries (another 9%). Total 44%, which is simply remarkable.
7. Similarly, other migration patterns can be easily interpreted and understood summary table and Tables 5.1 to 5.8.

Tables 5.1(a) *Summary of Regression Findings of District-level Migration, All-India, 1991*

Equation	*Main two explanatory variables*	*Explains (%)*	*Relation (+/–)*
Volume of In-migration	1. Per cent of manufacturing workers 2. Per capita bank credit	36 8	+ +
Volume of out-migration from district (Males)	1. Per cent cultivators 2. Per cent service workers	15 8	– –
In-migration rates of districts (Males)	1. Per capita bank credit 2. Population density	19 8	+ –
Out-migration rate from districts (Males)	1. General literacy 2. Per cent service workers	12 8	+ –
Volume of *intra*-district migration (Males)	1. Per cent agricultural labourers 2. Per cent transport workers	19 10	+ +
Volume of *inter*-district migration (Males)	1. Per cent of manufacturing workers 2. Per capita bank credit	36 9	+ +
Volume of total migration (Males)	1. Per cent of manufacturing workers 2. Per cent agricultural labourers	30 9	+ +
Intra-district migration rate	1. Per cent service workers 2. Per capita bank credit to small scale industry	31 7	– –

Table 5.1(b) *All-India Results: Findings of Step-wise Regression Analysis between Migration Variables and Socio-economic Variables, Districts, Males, 1991. Equation 1: VINMIGM (Volume of In-migration)*

Eq. No.	*Dependent Variable*	*Step No.*	*Independent Variables*	*Adjusted R-square*	*Indivi. Expl. (%)*	*Cumul. Expl. (%)*	*Beta*	*T*	*Sig. T*	*Constant (Intercept)*	*Remarks/Explanation*
1	*2*	*3*	*4*	*5*	*6*	*7*	*8*	*9*	*10*	*11*	*12*
1	Volume of in-migration to district, males (VINMIGM)	1	Per cent of Manufacturing Workers (MNF)	.36	36	36	.60	15.1	.0000	8645.6	More manufacturing workers, more volume of in-migration
		2	Per Capita Bank Credit (PCBCRED)	.44	8	44	.36	7.9	.0000	8299.7	More bank credit, more volume of in-migration
		3	Per cent of Mining Workers (MINS)	.49	5	49	.22	6.1	.0000	5219.5	More workers in mining, more in-migration
		4	Agricultural Labour (AGL)	.53	4	53	.19	5.6	.0000	–10785.4	More agricultural labourers, more in-migration
		5	Per Capita Bank Credit to SSI (PCBSSI)	.54	1	54	–.19	–3.3	.0011	–10781.4	Less credit to SSI, more in-migration
		6	Per Capita Bank Credit to Industry (PCBCIND)	.55	1	55	.29	3.0	.0032	–10068.8	More credit to industry, more in-migration
		7	Population Density (POPDENS)	.56	1	56	–.19	–3.5	.0005	–10580.4	Less density of population, more in-migration
		8	Urbanisation (URBANISA)	.57	1	57	.14	2.9	.0045	–14568.1	More urbanization, more in-migration

Note: When Sigma T is 0.0000, it means that the result is statistically significant at 0.0000 level, i.e., the chances of this relationship being valid is 9999 out of 10,000 observations or tests, i.e., error term is only 1 out of 10,000 tests (observations). Likewise all other meaning of sigma. T, in all tables.

Table 5.2 *All-India Results: Findings of Step-wise Regression Analysis between Migration Variables and Socio-economic Variables, Districts, Males, 1991. Equation 2: VOMIGM (Volume of Out-migration, males)*

Eq. No.	*Dependent Variable*	*Step No.*	*Independent Variables*	*Adjusted R-square*	*Indiv. Expl. (%)*	*Cumul. Expl. (%)*	*Beta*	*T*	*Sig. T*	*Constant*	*Remarks/Explanation*
1	2	3	4	5	6	7	8	9	*10*	*11*	*12*
2	Volume of out-migration from District, males (VOMIGM)	1	Per cent Cultivators (CULT)	.15	15	15	–.39	–8.6	.0000	80650.6	Less cultivators, more out-migration
		2	Service Workers (SERV)	.23	8	23	–.29	–6.3	.0000	110990.7	Less workers in services, more out-migration
		3	Per cent General literacy (GLITERA)	.31	8	31	.39	7.0	.0000	57997.8	More literacy, more out-migration
		4	Per cent Livestock Workers (LIVES)	.36	5	36	–.24	–5.7	.0000	60359.9	Less livestock workers, more out-migration
		5	Per cent Net Sown Area (PERNSA)	.38	2	38	.16	3.6	.0003	37359.4	More net sown area, more out-migration
		6	Per cent Total Workers (PERWOR)	.40	2	40	.16	3.5	.0005	5054.5	More total workers, more out-migration

Table 5.3 *All-India Results: Findings of Step-wise Regression Analysis between Migration Variables and Socio-economic Variables, Districts, Males, 1991. Equation 3: INMIGRTM (In-migration rates)*

Eq. No.	*Dependent Variable*	*Step No.*	*Independent Variables*	*Adjusted R-square*	*Indi. Expl.(%)*	*Cumul. Expl (%)*	*Beta*	*T*	*Sig. T*	*Constant*	*Remarks/Explanation*
1	*2*	*3*	*4*	*5*	*6*	*7*	*8*	*9*	*10*	*11*	*12*
3	In-migration rates of Districts, males (INMIGRTM)	1	Per Capita bank Credit(PCBCRED)	.19	19	19	44	9.8	.0000	3.0	More credit, higher in-migration rate
		2	Population Density (POPDENS)	.27	8	27	–.45	–6.6	.0000	2.8	Less density, higher in-migration rates
		3	Per cent General literacy (GLITERA)	.31	4	31	23	4.9	.0000	0.2	More literacy, higher in-migration rate
		4	Per cent of mining workers (MINS)	.35	4	35	.20	5.1	.0000	–0.1	More mining, higher in-migration rate
		5	Per Capita bank Credit to Agriculture (PCBCAGI)	.38	3	38	.21	4.7	.0000	–0.5	More credit to agri., higher in-migration rate
		6	Per Capita Bank Credit to SSI (PCBSSI)	.40	2	40	–.1	–3.6	.0004	-0.6	Less credit to SSI, higher in-migration rate
		7	Per Capita Bank Credit to Industry (PCBCIND)	.41	1	41	.36	3.1	.0019	–0.6	More credit to industry, higher in-migration rate
		8	Per cent Forests (PERFAREA)	.42	1	42	.11	2.9	.0046	–0.9	More forest, higher in-migration rate
		9	Per cent of Manufacturing Workers (MNF)	.43	1	43	.12	2.1	.0403	–0.8	More manufacturing (MNF), higher in-migration rate

Table 5.4 *All-India Results: Findings of Step-wise Regression Analysis between Migration Variables and Socio-economic Variables, Districts, Males, 1991. Equation 4: OMIGRTM (Out-migration rates)*

Eq. No.	*Dependent Variable*	*Step No.*	*Independent Variables*	*Adjusted R-square*	*Indiv. Expl. (%)*	*Cumul. Expl.(%)*	*Beta*	T	*Sig. T*	*Constant*	*Remarks/Explanation*
1	2	3	4	5	6	7	8	9	*10*	*11*	*12*
4	Out-migration rates, males (OMIGRTM)	1	Per cent Literates (GLITERA)	.12	12	12	.35	7.6	.0000	0.1	More general literacy more out-migration rate
		2	Per cent Service Workers (SERV)	.20	8	20	–.34	–6.2	.0000	0.2	Less service workers, higher out-migration rate
		3	Per cent Total Workers (PERWOR)	.23	3	23	.17	3.8	.0002	–3.0	More workers, higher out-migration rate
		4	Per cent Urbanisation (URBANISA)	.24	1	24	–.15	–2.8	.0048	–2.9	Less urbanization, higher out-migration rate
		5	Per cent Net Sown Area (PERNSA)	.26	2	26	.17	3.4	.0007	–5.5	More net sown area, higher out-migration rate

Note: Higher work participation rate (as in third row), causes higher out-migration rate. This also makes sense: more pressure of labourers, more push for out-migration.

Table 5.5 *All-India Results: Findings of Step-wise Regression Analysis between Migration Variables and Socio-economic Variables, Districts, Males, 1991. Equation 5: INTRADMA (Volume of Intra-district migration)*

Eq. No.	*Dependent Variable*	*Step No.*	*Independent Variables*	*Adjusted R-square*	*Indiv. Expl. (%)*	*Cumul. Expl. (%)*	*Beta*	*T*	*Sig. T*	*Constant*	*Remarks/Explanation*
1	*2*	*3*	*4*	*5*	*6*	*7*	*8*	*9*	*10*	*11*	*12*
5	Volume of *Intra*-district migration, males (INTRADMA)	1	Per cent Agricultural labour (AGL)	.19	19	19	.44	9.9	.0000	17451.7	More agricultural labourers, more intra-dist. migration
		2	Per cent Transport Workers (TRANS)	.29	10	29	.31	7.3	.0000	–15082.4	More transport workers, more intra-district migration
		3	Per cent Total Workers (PERWOR)	.35	6	35	.28	6.6	.0000	–115893.9	More total workers, more intra-dist. migration
		4	Per cent Net Sown Area (PERNSA)	.38	3	38	.18	3.9	.0001	–147802.1	More net sown area, more intra-dist. migration
		5	Per cent Service Workers (SERV)	.39	1	39	–.16	–2.9	.0035	–114470.1	Less service workers, more intra-dist. migration
		6	General Literacy Rate (GLITERA)	.41	2	41	.19	3.8	.0002	–126942.2	More literacy, more-intra-dist. Migration.

Table 5.6 *Findings of Step-wise Regression Analysis between Migration Variables and Socio-economic Variables, Districts, Males, 1991. Equation 6: INTERDM (Volume of Inter-district migration)*

Eq. No.	*Dependent Variable*	*Step No.*	*Independent Variables*	*Adjusted R-square*	*Indiv. Expl.(%)*	*Cumul. Expl. (%)*	*Beta*	*T*	*Sig. T*	*Constant*	*Remarks/Explanation*
1	*2*	*3*	*4*	*5*	*6*	*7*	*8*	*9*	*10*	*11*	*12*
6	Volume of Inter-district migration (males) (INTERDM)	1	Per cent of Manufacturing Workers (MNF)	.36	36	36	.60	15.1	.0000	8743.2	More manufacturing, more inter-district migration
		2	Per Capita Bank Credit (PCBCRED)	.45	9	45	.37	8.1	.0000	8382.8	More bank credit, more inter-district migration
		3	Per cent of Mining Workers (MINS)	.49	4	49	.21	6.0	.0000	5331.1	More mining workers, more inter-district migration
		4	Agricultural Labour (AGL)	.53	4	53	.19	5.7	.0000	–11312.9	More agricultural labourers, more inter-district migration
		5	Per Capita Bank Credit to SSI (PCBSSI)	.54	1	54	–.19	–3.3	.0012	–11308.9	Less credit to small scale industry(SSI), more inter-district migration
		6	Per Capita Bank Credit to Industry (PCBCIND)	.55	1	55	.29	3.0	.0030	–10580.6	More credit to general industries, more inter-district migration

Table 5.7 *All-India Results: Findings of Step-wise Regression Analysis between Migration Variables and Socio-economic Variables, Districts, Males, 1991. Equation 7:TOTMIGM (Volume of Total Migration)*

Eq. No.	*Dependent Variable*	*Step No.*	*Independent Variables*	*Adjust. R-square*	*Indiv. Expl.(%)*	*Cumul. Expl.(%)*	*Beta*	*T*	*Sig. T*	*Constant*	*Remarks/Explanation*
1	*2*	*3*	*4*	*5*	*6*	*7*	*8*	*9*	*10*	*11*	*12*
7	Total Migration, males (TOTMIGM)	1	Per cent of Manufacturing Workers (MNF)	.30	30	30	.55	13.3	.0000	55699.6	More manufacturing workers, more total migration
		2	Agricultural Labour (AGL)	.39	9	39	.30	7.8	.0000	–7082.4	More agricultural labourers, more total migration
		3	Transport Workers (TRANS)	.42	3	42	.24	4.4	.0000	–28882.4	More transport, more total migration
		4	Per cent Total Workers (PERWOR)	.46	3	45	.20	5.1	.0000	–153452.3	More total workers, more total migration
		5	Per cent of Mining Workers (MINS)	.47	1	47	.12	3.4	.0008	156055.1	More mining, more total migration
		6	Per Capita Bank Credit (PCBCRED)	.48	1	48	.16	3.3	.0011	–160214.3	More bank credit, more total migration
		7	Per cent Cultivators (CULT)	.49	1	49	.29	3.3	.0010	–314422.8	More cultivators, more total migration

Table 5.8 *All-India Results: Findings of Step-wise Regression Analysis between Migration Variables and Socio-economic Variables, Districts, Males, 1991. Equation 8: INTRADMR (Intra-district migration rates)*

Eq. No.	*Dependent Variable*	*Step No.*	*Independent Variables*	*Adjusted R-square*	*Indiv. Expl. (%)*	*Cumul. Expl. (%)*	*Beta*	*T*	*Sig. T*	*Constant*	*Remarks/Explanation*
1	*2*	*3*	*4*	*5*	*6*	*7*	*8*	*9*	*10*	*11*	*12*
8	*Intra*-district Migration Rate (INTRADMR)	1	Per cent Service Workers (SERV)	.31	31	31	–.56	–13.4	.0000	71.6	Less service workers, higher *intra*-district migration rate
		2	Per Capita Bank Credit to Small Scale Industry (PCBCSSI)	.38	7	38	–.30	–7.1	.0000	70.8	Less SSI, higher *intra*-district migration rate
		3	Per cent of Mining Workers (MINS)	.40	2	40	–.15	–3.9	.0001	71.8	Less mining workers, higher *intra*-district. Migration rate
		4	General Literacy Rate (GLITERA)	.42	2	42	.18	3.9	.0001	65.2	More literacy, higher *intra*-district migration rate

State-level Result: Step-wise Regression Analysis of *Intra*-District and Inter-District Migration of Males and Socio-economic variables, 1991

Tables 5.9(b) to 5.12 provide these results (Appendix), which are quite self-explanatory. Further, annexed summary table [Table 5.9(a)] presents the relationships between migration variables and socio-economic variables, and hence not repeated.

Table 5.9(a) *Summary Table of Causes of In-migration and Out-migration in India, District-level Analysis, done for States*

Dependent Variable	*Predictor Variables*	*Relation*	*States (in same order as in col. 3)*
1 In-migration			
(a) Volume of in-migration	Per capita bank credit	+, +, +, +, +, +	Assam, Maharashtra, Meghalaya, Manipur, Nagaland, Punjab
	Population growth rate	+, +, +, +	Andhra Pradesh, Gujarat, Tamil Nadu, Uttar Pradesh
	Per cent workers in mining	+, –, +, +	Bihar, Karnataka, Madhya Pradesh, West Bengal
	Per capita bank credit to agriculture	+, –, +, +	Himachal Pradesh, Nagaland, Rajasthan, Uttar Pradesh
	Per cent workers in manufacturing	–, +, +, –	Karnataka, Madhya Pradesh, Sikkim, Uttar Pradesh
(b) Rate of in-migration	Per cent agricultural labourers	–, +, +,–,+	Assam, Haryana, Madhya Pradesh, Punjab, West Bengal
	Per capita bank credit to agriculture	+, +, +, –, +	Karnataka, Kerala, Manipur, Nagaland, Uttar Pradesh
2 Out-migration			
(a) Volume of out-migration	Population density	+, +, +, +	Himachal Pradesh, Madhya Pradesh, Manipur, Orissa, Uttar Pradesh
	Per cent workers in trade/commerce	+, –, +, +, +	Assam, Madhya Pradesh, Orissa, Punjab,
	General literacy rate	+, +, +, +	Bihar, Himachal Pradesh, Kerala, West Bengal
	Population growth rate	–, –, +, –	Haryana, Orissa, Sikkim, Uttar Pradesh
(b) Rate of out-migration	Population growth rate	–, –, –, –, –, –	Andhra Pradesh, Haryana, Himachal Pradesh, Maharashtra, Nagaland, Tamil Nadu
	Per cent net sown area	–, –	Assam, Uttar Pradesh
	General literacy rate	+, –	Bihar, Kerala
	Per cent urbanized	+, +	Bihar, Rajasthan
	Per capita bank deposit	–, –	Gujarat, Mizoram
	Population density	+, +	Haryana, Madhya Pradesh
3 *Intra*-district migration			
(a) Volume of *intra*-district migration	Per cent urbanized	+, +, +, +	Arunachal Pradesh, Gujarat, Haryana, Tamil Nadu
	Per cent livestock workers	–, +, +, +	Arunachal Pradesh, Bihar, Haryana, Mizoram
(b) Proportion of *intra*-district migration to total migration	Per capita bank credit	–, –, –, –, –	Assam, Himachal Pradesh, Karnataka, Rajasthan, Tamil Nadu
	Per cent transport workers	+, –, +, –	Karnataka, Manipur, Punjab, Rajasthan

Further state-level results of such regression analyses are given in Appendix in Tables 5.9(b) to 5.12.

Development Measures Evolved: Analysis of Inter-district In-migration and Out-migration

The following development measures are devised at the district level and are computed for all 443 districts of India. Here, the factor scores (or FS_i), generated from factor analysing 29 socio-economic variables of the districts are weighted by the corresponding variance explained by respective factors or dimensions:

$$DI_1 = (\Sigma\ W_i\ FS_i) + 100 \qquad \ldots(1)$$

$$DI_2 = (\Sigma W_i/100 * FS_i) \qquad \ldots(2)$$

Where, weights are given to factor scores according to per cent of variance explained by respective factors or dimensions, converted into a total of 100 per cent.

Thus, $W_1 = 30.79$; $W_2 = 28.11$; $W_3 = 14.75$; $W_4 = 11.20$; $W_5 = 8.03$; and $W_6 = 7.10$.

Hundred is added to avoid negative scoring in the development index.

Where, FS_i are factor scores with reference to the following factors:

F_1 = URBNZCAP = More urbanized, economically developed and more capital invested to industry/service sector dimension.

F_2 = LITCOM = General literacy and trade-commerce dimension.

F_3 = SERVCON = Service and construction workers dimension.

F_4 = POPWORK = High population growth and more workers dimension.

F_5 = LIVESTOCK = Livestock workers dimension.

F_6 = MINING = More mining workers dimension.

The ensuing result is a composite development index indicating the levels of development of the district, measuring with reference to those six main factors or basis dimensions of the socio-economic factor structure of districts of India (Table 5.13). Most of these dimensions are positively related to development. DI_1 is always positive, and it ranges between 0 to 200 or above; higher scores showing greater socio-economic development. On the other hand, DI_2, may be either positive or negative, and it ranges between –1.0 to + 4.0. Negative scores show backwardness; positive scores indicate relatively more development. The end result of this exercise is the identification of over 200 backward districts of India, which having 100 or less scores on DI_1 development index, and a few relatively more developed districts which having more than 100 scores. Thus, 443 districts of India (for which data were available, out of total 525) were scaled according to these indices of economic development. Considered in this way, we get a very good measure of levels of regional development and *regional disparities*. Data are analysed, but this voluminous table is not shown, due to lack of space.

Results of Regression Analysis between Development Indices of Districts and Flows of Inter-district In-migration and Out-migration

Table 5.14 presents such results of step-wise regression between volume and rate of district-level in-migration and out-migration (as dependent variable(s) and development index score (DI_1) as predictor variable. Following findings emerged:

Table 5.13 ***Factor Results Used for Preparing the Development Index***

Variables	*FACTORS*					
	1	*2*	*3*	*4*	*5*	*6*
	Meaning of the Factors					
	Economic developmen, urbanization, high investment in industry and SSI dimension	*General literacy, transport, trade/ commerce, manufac-turing, credit to agriculture dimension*	*Service and const-ruction dimen-sion*	*High work partici-pation, more forests and high population growth dimension*	*Live-stock*	*Minin g*
Per capita bank credit to industry (PCBCIND)	**0.9**	0.2	0.1	0.0	0.1	0.0
Per capita bank credit (PCBCRED)	**0.9**	0.3	0.1	0.0	0.1	0.0
Population density (POPDENS)	**0.8**	0.0	0.1	–0.2	0.0	0.0
per capita bank credit to SSI (PCBCSSI)	**0.8**	0.3	0.1	0.0	0.0	0.0
Per capita bank deposit (PCBDEP)	**0.7**	0.5	0.3	–0.1	0.1	0.0
Percentage of cultivators (CULT)	–0.3	**–0.8**	0.3	0.1	0.0	–0.1
General literacy (GLITERA)	0.2	**0.8**	0.2	0.1	0.1	–0.1
Percentage of workers in transport (TRANS)	**0.5**	**0.7**	0.1	–0.2	0.0	0.1
Percentage of workers in trade/commerce (TC)	**0.5**	**0.7**	0.1	–0.2	0.0	0.0
Percentage of workers in manufacturing (MNF)	**0.5**	**0.6**	–0.1	–0.1	–0.2	0.0
Urbanization (URBANIZA)	**0.6**	**0.6**	0.0	0.0	–0.2	0.0
Per capita bank credit to agriculture (PCBCAGI)	0.2	**0.4**	–0.4	0.1	0.4	–0.3
Percentage of agricultural labourers (AGL)	–0.1	0.1	**–0.8**	0.0	–0.1	0.0
Percentage of workers in service (SERV)	0.3	0.5	**0.7**	–0.1	0.1	–0.1
Percentage of workers in construction (CONS)	0.2	0.5	**0.6**	0.1	0.0	0.0
Per cent net sown area (PERNSA)	0.0	0.2	**–0.5**	**–0.5**	–0.2	–0.3
Per cent total workers (PERWOR)	–0.2	–0.1	–0.1	**0.8**	0.0	–0.1
Per cent forest area (PERFAREA)	–0.1	0.0	0.2	**0.6**	0.1	0.3
Population growth (POPGRO)	0.0	0.1	0.0	**0.6**	–0.3	–0.2
Percentage of workers in household industry (HH)	–0.1	0.2	–0.2	0.0	**–0.6**	0.1
Percentage of livestock workers (LIVES)	–0.1	0.4	0.1	0.0	**0.6**	0.1
Percentage of workers in mining (MINS)	0.0	0.1	0.0	0.0	0.0	**0.9**
Eigen value	4.9	4.4	2.3	1.8	1.3	1.1
Percentage of Variance	22.1	20.2	10.6	8.0	5.8	5.1
Cumulative % of variance	22.1	42.3	52.9	60.9	66.7	71.8

Note: The input data for Factor Analysis are taken from Table 4.1

1. Volume of in-migration into a district is positively related to and caused by development index DI_1 (adjusted $R^2 = 0.29$, explaining 29 per cent of variance, and significant at 0.000 level).
2. Rate of in-migration into a district is also positively related and caused by the same development index, DI_1 (adjusted $R^2 = 0.27$, explaining 27 per cent of variance, significant at 0.000).
3. Volume of in-migration (males) is found to be positively related to first factor (economic development-cum-urbanization dimension, 28%), followed by second factor (literacy-cum-agricultural investment, 13%). Together these explain 41 per cent of volume of in-migration. These imply that more in-migration is caused due to economic development, and people migrate from backward to more developed districts. These findings have considerable policy implications.
4. Volume of out-migration from a district is very slightly related to development index, showing that development of a district only slightly encourage out-migration from it As is well known, Indian census migration data provide some details of only in-migration to a district, *not that of out-migration.* Inter-district out-migration data are available (used here), but that do not refer to a particular duration of stay or particular time point. It includes life-time out-migration. So, the lack of fine-grained migration data in the Indian censuses, specially of out-migration from the district, have handicapped in-depth analysis of causes of district-level out-migration. However, *out migration is found to be more where service and construction dimension is less in a district. It is negatively related. Policy-wise, more employment in the service and construction sectors within a district will discourage out-migration.*

Links between Development Index (1) of Districts and Volume of Male In-migration into them

Regression analysis shows that higher the development index (I) of the districts, the more male in-migration into the districts (Figure 5.1, Table 5.15). Multiple R (coefficient of determination) value is 0.39, and value of adjusted R-square is 0.12, indicating that about 12 per cent of variations in the volume of male in-migration into the districts are being explained by the variations in the predictor variable, development index(i) of the districts. In simple words, higher the level of development of a district, the more male in-migration. This causal relationship is statistically significant at 0.01 level of significance. That is, the error term is only 1 out of 100 such observations or tests that this relationship could be wrong, and the chances are 99 out of 100 tests that the result will be correct and statistically significant. Policy-wise, this result implies more economic development of districts may arrest male out-migration from them, and may provide more opportunities to the male in-migrants. So, economic development is the key to the solution of migration problems.

Table 5.14 *Summary of Results of Regression Analysis between District's In-migration/Out-migration and District's Development Index*

Sr. No.	Dependent Variable	Independent Variable	Multiple R	Adjusted R^2	Individual Explanation	Cumulative Explanation	Beta	T	Sig T	Constant
1	Volume of in-migration (Males) (VINMIGM)	1. Development Index (D_1)	0.54	0.29	28.9	28.9	0.54	12.8	0.000	–16934.8
2	In-migration rate (Males) (INMIGRTM)	1. Development Index (D_1)	0.52	0.27	26.9	26.9	0.52	12.2	0.000	–0.46
3	Volume of in-migration (Males) (VINMIGM)	1. Factor Score on Factor 1 (Economic dev-Urbanization)	0.53	0.28	28.0	28.0	0.53	12.5	0.000	25936.4
		2. Factor Score on F2 (Literacy-Trade-Transport-Agricultural investment)	0.64	0.41	13.0	41.2	0.37	9.6	0.000	17845.6
		3. Factor Score on F6 (Mining)	0.68	0.46	4.2	45.5	0.21	5.7	0.000	10239.6
		4. Factor Score on F3 (Service-Construction)	0.70	0.49	3.3	48.8	–0.18	–5.5	0.000	–8980.3
4	Volume of out-migration (Males) (VOMIGM)	1. Factor Score on F3 (Service-Construction)	0.40	0.51	15.40	15.4	–0.40	–8.6	0.000	–15719.1
		2. Factor Score on F2 (Literacy-Trade-Transport-Agricultural investment)	0.51	0.25	10.00	25.4	0.32	7.4	0.000	12717
		3. Factor Score on F1 (Economic development-urbanization)	0.53	0.27	1.70	27.1	0.13	3.1	0.002	5329.4
		4. Factor Score on F5 (Livestock)	0.53	0.28	0.60	27.7	–0.09	–2.1	0.040	–3479.9
		5. Factor Score on F6 (Mining)	0.54	0.28	0.50	28.2	–0.09	–2.0	0.041	–3440.6

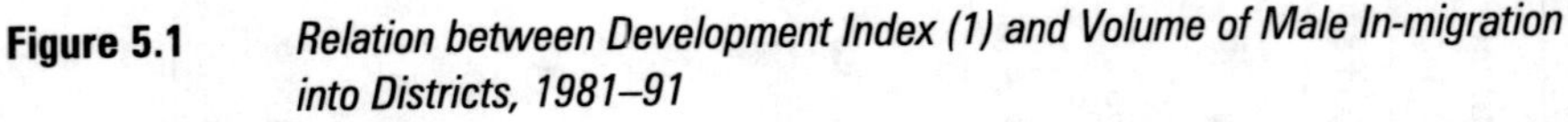

Figure 5.1 *Relation between Development Index (1) and Volume of Male In-migration into Districts, 1981–91*

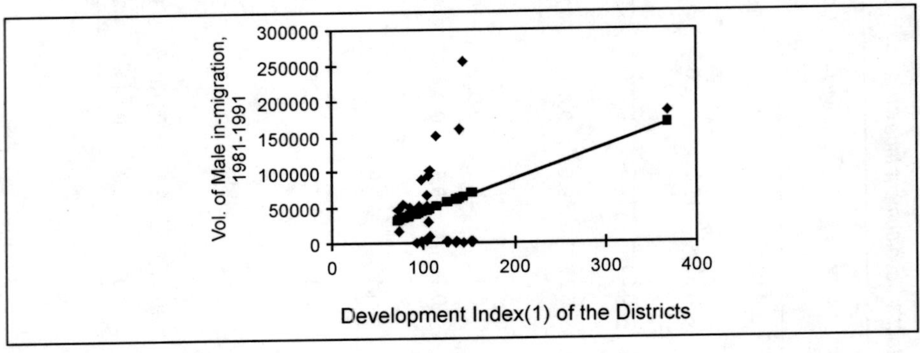

Table 5.15 *Regression Statistics for Links between Development Index (1) of Districts and Volume of Male In-migration into Districts, India, 1991 (N = 34 selected districts)*

Dependent Variable	*Indep. Variable*	*Mult. R.*	*Adj R Sq*	*Expln.*	*Beta*	*T.*	*Sig. T*	*Intercept*	*Meaning of Relation*
Vol. of male in-migration	Development Index-1 of districts	.39	.12	12%	.45	2.2	.01	–606.2	Higher the development index of districts, the more male in-migration into them

Links between Development Index (2) of Districts and Volume of Male In-migration into them

Here also, the causal relationship shows that higher the development index (2) of districts, the more male in migration into districts. All other related findings are also the same (Table 5.16, Figure 5. 2). So, it reiterates that socio-economic development is the key to the solution of most problems of distressed migration in India.

Table 5.16 *Links between Development Index (2) of Districts and Volume of Male In-migration into Districts, India, 1991 (N = 34 selected districts)*

Dependent Variable	*Indep. Variable*	*Mult. R.*	*Adj R Sq*	*Expln.*	*Beta*	*T.*	*Sig. T*	*Intercept*	*Meaning of Relation*
Vol. of male in-migration	Development Index (2) of districts	.38	.12	12%	–.29	2.3	.01	453857	Higher the development index (2) of districts, the more male in-migration into them

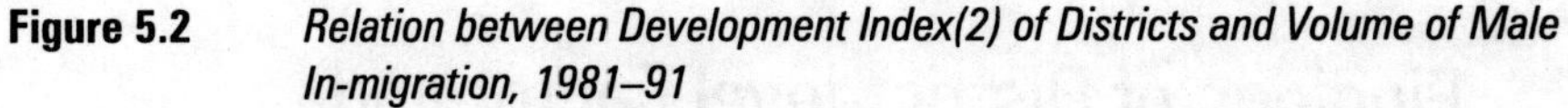

Figure 5.2 *Relation between Development Index(2) of Districts and Volume of Male In-migration, 1981–91*

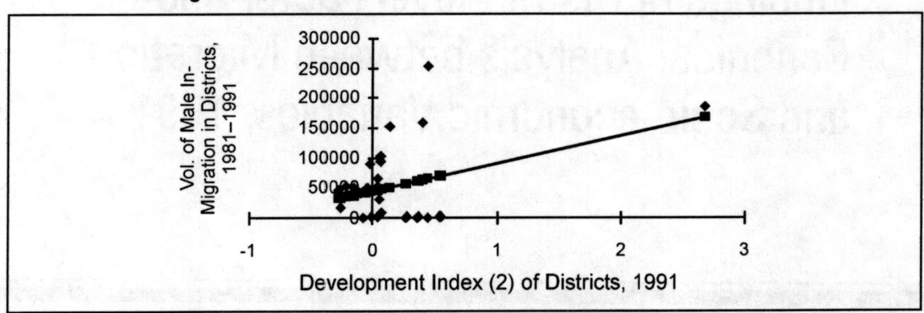

Links between Service-construction Sectors of Districts and Volume of Male Out-migration

Regression finding points out that the less service and construction sectors in districts, the more male out-migration from districts (Table 5.17, Figure 5.3). Relationship is negative, i.e., more male out-migration occurs from those districts where service and construction sectors are less prevalent. Value of adjusted R-Square is high, 0.51, explaining 51% of variations. Causal relationship is statistically significant at 0.001 level of significance, i.e., error term is only 1 out of 1,000 observations. This is simply remarkable!

Figure 5.3 *Relation between Service and Construction Sectors of Districts and Volume of Male Out-migration, 1981–91*

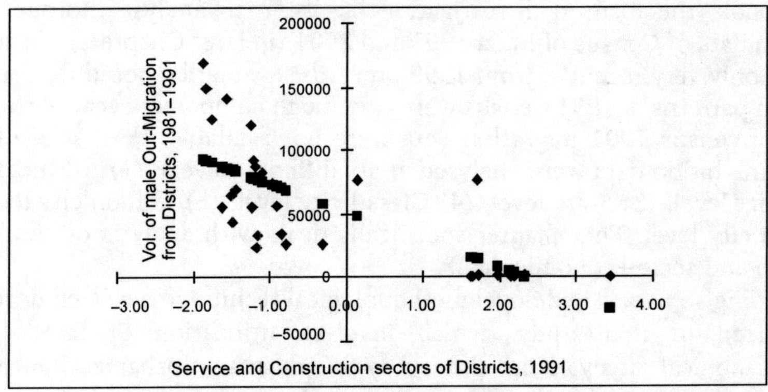

Table 5.17 *Links between Service-construction Sectors of Districts and Volume of Male Out-migration from Districts, India, 1991 (N = 34 selected districts)*

Dependent Variable	*Indep. Variable*	*Mult. R.*	*Adj R Sq*	*Expln.*	*Beta*	*T.*	*Sig. T*	*Intercept*	*Meaning of Relation*
Vol. of male out-migration	Service-construction in Dist.	.73	.51	51%	–.12	–5.7	.001	51543.9	Less service and construction sectors in districts, more male out- migration from them

Policy-wise, this causal relationship implies that construction and service sectors are the main job-providers and capable of arresting mass male out migration from districts. Strategy should be to invest therein for generating more jobs.

6 Findings of District-level Factor and Canonical Analysis between Migration and Socio-economic Variables, 1991

"Arise, awake, for your country needs this tremendous sacrifice."

Swami Vivekananda (1894)
(Complete Work, Centenary Volume III, 1963: 318)

Methodology

In this book, the focus of investigation has been to analyse thoroughly the migration data of Census of India 1991 and 2001 (in later Chapters) – which are available only very recently, from 1999 onwards. It must be noted that study of migration patterns of 1991 Census were very much hampered, because corrected version of census 1991 migration data were not available, until 1998. In this volume, migration data were analysed at six different levels: (1) All-India level, (2) District level, (3) State level, (4) Class I city level, (5) Million city level and (6) Mega city level. This chapter specifically deals with analysis of *district level* migration and socio-economic data.

In doing so, a new and novel methodological technique has been developed and utilized in this study, which involves utilization of factor analysis-cum-canonical analysis in the study of migration-urbanization-regional disparities. A series of canonical analyses were made, at each of the above domains. The causal relationships between volume and patterns of migration, urbanization, and of regional development were analysed, at each of these domains of research: districts, states, class I city and metropolitan levels.

A series of high powered factor analyses and Canonical linkage analysis were made between:

(a) *Volume and patterns of migration (as the Dependent matrix), and*
(b) *Economic Structure of districts (or states or cities or metropolises), cum*
(c) *Growth efforts or investments made therein (last two matrices (b + c) as combination of Independent matrices);*

And, as a result, each time, a series of final canonical linkage equations were generated, linking each time, a specific pattern(s) of migration, with a specific pattern(s) of economic structure-cum-investment pattern(s).

These canonical linkages are not only statistically very powerful, but are also practically very meaningful. They have generated many useful planning directives for reducing poverty induced migration, querulous urbanization and acute regional disparities that adversely affect the economy of India. Hence, this research monograph offers both new methodological pathways in population studies, as well as substantive findings for migration-urbanization research and for alleviating human problems associated with low quality migration and urban decay in India. The study incorporates findings of hundreds of regression analyses (at district and state levels), results of a dozen factor analyses, and 20 canonical analysis, done at various levels of investigation; even a brief account of all these findings cannot be presented here. *Only a few major* findings are very briefly highlighted.

Major All-India Findings: District Level Analysis

These analyses were done at three levels:

- Factor analysing all 30 socio-economic, investment variables and migration variables all taken together,
- In another set, first, factor analysing only socio-economic and investment variables within themselves, and then, canonically linking them with *four* migration variables in a Final Canonical correlation (linkage) analysis; and
- Canonical analysis of four migration variables and 18 socio-economic plus investment variables together, without factoring them.

Results are shown in three parts, (A), (B) and (C), as follows.

(A) *Inter-Relationships between Patterns of Migration and Socio-Economic situations at District Level (Results of Factor Analysis of taking All such 30 variables together) (Table 6.1):* The following *seven* main factors (with eigen-values greater than 1.0) were generated, linking migration and socio-economic variables, and explaining 73 per cent of total variance:

1. Where economic development more, urbanization high, investments are also more, there the volume of in-migration is also high, and also inter-district migration more (explains 28 per cent of variance). Thus, during the decade of 1981–91, more in-migration has occurred to urban centres, manufacturing centres, and where more capital investments are made.
2. Where general literacy is high, and percentage of service and construction workers are also high, intra-district migration rate is low and in-migration rate is moderate (explains 11.3%).
3. High volume and high rate of out-migration occur, where less manufacturing prevails and less service workers exist (explains 9.9%).
4. Moderately high *intra*-district migration rate occurs where agricultural labourers are more, cultivators less, net sown area high and agricultural investment is moderate (explains 7.85%).
5. High volume of in-migration and of total migration occur where mining centres exist (explains 6.8%).
6. Very low in-migration occurs where population growth is high and forest is more (5.2%).
7. Little in-migration occurs to places of high household industry (4.4%).

Table 6.1 *Factor Analysis Results: Rotated Factor Structure of Migration Variables (Males) and Socio-economic Variables of 443 Districts, All-India, 1991*

VARIABLES	*FACTORS*						
	1	*2*	*3*	*4*	*5*	*6*	*7*
Meaning of Factors	*Economic development high, volume of in-migration high, inter-district migration high*	*Literacy, percentage of service and construction workers high, intra-district migration rate low, moderate in-migration rate*	*High volume and rate of out-migration, where less manufacturing and service workers*	*Moderately high intra-district migration rate, where agricultural labour more, cultivators less, net sown area high and agricultural investment moderate*	*High in-migratio n and high total migration to mining centres*	*Very low in-migration where population growth is high and forest more*	*Little in-migration to household industry centres*
Per capita bank credit (PCBCRED)	**0.9**	0.1	0.0	–0.1	0.0	0.0	–0.1
Per capita bank credit to industry (PCBCIND)	**0.9**	0.1	0.0	0.0	0.0	0.0	–0.1
Per capita bank deposit (PCBDEP)	**0.9**	0.2	0.0	–0.1	0.0	–0.1	–0.1
Population density (POPDENS)	**0.8**	–0.1	0.0	–0.1	-0.1	–0.1	–0.1
Per capita bank credit to SSI (PCBCSSI)	**0.8**	0.2	–0.1	0.1	-0.1	0.0	–0.1
Per cent workers in trade/commerce (TC)	**0.7**	0.4	0.0	0.3	0.0	–0.1	0.2
Urbanization (URBANIZA)	**0.7**	0.3	0.0	0.2	0.1	0.1	0.2
Inter-district migration (INTERDM)	**0.7**	0.0	0.3	0.0	**0.5**	0.0	–0.1
Volume of in-migration (VINMIGM)	**0.7**	0.0	0.3	0.0	**0.6**	0.0	–0.1
Percentage of workers in manufacturing (MNF)	**0.7**	**0.3**	0.1	0.3	0.2	0.0	0.2
Percentage of workers in transport (TRANS)	**0.7**	0.5	0.1	0.2	0.1	–0.1	0.2
Total migration (TOTMIGM)	**0.6**	–0.1	**0.5**	0.1	**0.5**	0.1	0.0
General literacy (GLITERA)	0.3	**0.7**	0.3	0.1	0.0	0.0	0.1

Cont'd...

...Cont'd

Percentage of workers in services (SERV)	0.4	**0.7**	**–0.2**	–0.1	–0.1	0.0	0.1
Percentage of workers in construction (CONS)	0.3	**0.7**	–0.1	–0.2	0.0	0.1	0.2
Percentage of livestock workers (LIVES)	–0.1	**0.6**	0.0	0.1	0.1	–0.1	–0.2
Volume of migration, males (VOMIGM)	0.3	0.0	**0.9**	0.2	0.0	0.0	0.1
Out-migration rate, males (OMIGRTM)	–0.1	0.3	**0.8**	0.0	–0.2	0.0	–0.2
Intra-district migration, males (INTRADMA)	0.0	–0.1	**0.7**	0.3	0.3	0.1	0.2
Intra-district migration rate, males (INTRADMR)	–0.5	**–0.5**	**0.5**	0.0	–0.2	0.1	0.2
Per cent net sown area (PERNSA)	0.0	–0.2	0.1	**0.7**	–0.1	–0.3	0.1
Per capita bank credit to agriculture (PCBCAGI)	0.1	0.3	0.1	**0.7**	0.0	0.1	–0.4
Per cent agricultural labourers (AGL)	–0.2	–0.4	0.3	**0.6**	0.1	0.0	0.1
Per cent cultivators (CULT)	–0.4	–0.4	–0.1	**–0.6**	–0.2	0.1	–0.2
Per cent workers in mining (MINS)	0.0	0.0	–0.1	–0.1	**0.7**	0.0	0.1
In-migration rate, males (INMIGRTM)	0.3	0.4	0.2	0.1	**0.6**	0.1	**–0.4**
Population growth (POPGRO)	0.1	0.0	–0.1	0.1	–0.2	**0.8**	0.1
Per cent total workers (PERWOR)	–0.2	–0.1	0.3	–0.2	0.0	**0.7**	–0.2
Per cent forest area (PERFAREA)	–0.2	0.1	0.0	–0.3	0.2	**0.5**	–0.1
Percentage of workers in household industry (HH)	–0.1	0.0	0.1	0.0	0.1	0.0	**0.7**
Eigen value	8.4	3.4	3.0	2.4	2.0	1.5	1.3
% of variance	28.0	11.3	9.9	7.8	6.8	5.2	4.4
Cumulative % of variance	28.0	39.3	49.2	57.0	63.8	68.9	73.3

Note: The input data for the factor analysis are taken from Table 4.1. Eigen-values greater than 0.4 are highlighted and which help to identify those specific variables which contributed and made the particular factor. Factors with eigen-values greater than 1.0 are considered, ignoring less important ones. Over 73 per cent variance is explained, showing very high explanation of original data set.

Table 6.2 *Factor Analysis Results: Rotated Factor Structure of Socio-economic Variables and Bank Investment Variables of 443 Districts, India, 1991*

VARIABLES	*FACTORS*					
	1	*2*	*3*	*4*	*5*	*6*
Meaning of Factors	*Economic development, urbanization, manufacturing, more bank deposit and credit dimension*	*General literacy, bank credit to agriculture and livestock dimension*	*Service and construction workers, less agricultural labourers and less net sown area dimension*	*Per cent total workers and forest area dimension*	*Household industry and population growth dimension*	*Mining dimension*
Per capita bank credit (PCBCRED)	**0.9**	0.0	0.1	0.0	–0.1	0.0
Per capita bank credit to industry (PCBCIND)	**0.9**	0.0	0.1	0.0	–0.1	0.0
Per capita bank deposit (PCBDEP)	**0.9**	0.1	0.2	0.0	–0.1	0.0
Population density (POPDENS)	**0.8**	–0.2	0.1	–0.1	–0.1	0.0
Per capita bank credit to SSI (PCBCSSI)	**0.8**	0.2	0.1	–0.1	0.0	–0.1
Percentage of workers in trade/commerce (TC)	**0.7**	0.4	0.1	–0.3	0.2	0.1
Urbanization (URBANIZA)	**0.7**	0.3	0.1	–0.1	0.2	0.1
Percentage of workers in manufacturing (MNF)	**0.7**	0.3	0.0	–0.2	0.2	0.1
Percentage of workers in transport (TRANS)	**0.7**	0.5	0.2	–0.2	0.2	0.2
Per cent cultivators (CULT)	**–0.5**	**–0.7**	0.2	0.2	–0.3	–0.2
General literacy (GLITERA)	0.3	**0.7**	0.3	0.0	0.1	0.0
Per capita bank credit to agriculture (PCBCAGI)	0.2	**0.6**	–0.2	–0.1	–0.2	–0.3
Percentage of livestock workers (LIVES)	–0.1	**0.6**	0.2	0.1	–0.2	0.1
Per cent agricultural labourers (AGL)	–0.1	0.2	**–0.8**	–0.1	0.2	0.0

Cont'd…

...Cont'd

Per cent workers in services (SERV)	0.4	0.3	**0.7**	–0.1	0.1	–0.1
Per cent workers in construction (CONS)	0.2	0.4	**0.7**	0.1	0.2	0.0
Per cent total workers (PERWOR)	–0.2	0.0	–0.1	**0.8**	0.0	–0.1
Per cent forest area (PERFAREA)	–0.1	0.0	0.1	**0.7**	0.0	0.2
Per cent net sown area (PERNSA)	0.1	0.1	–0.5	**–0.6**	0.1	–0.2
Per cent workers in household industry (HH)	–0.1	0.0	0.0	–0.1	**0.7**	0.1
Population growth (POPGRO)	0.1	–0.1	0.0	0.4	**0.5**	–0.2
Per cent mining workers (MINS)	0.0	0.0	–0.1	0.1	0.0	**0.9**
Eigen value	6.7	2.7	2.3	1.9	1.2	1.1
Percentage of variance	30.3	12.1	10.4	8.5	5.7	5.2
Cumulative % of variance	30.3	42.4	52.8	61.3	67.0	72.2

Note: The input data are taken from Table 4.1. The same notes as in below Table 6.1 also apply here. In this factor analysis results, over 72 per cent (last column, last row) of variance of original data matrix is explained showing very highly successful findings. (Also note SSI mean small-scale industries).

(B) *Causal Linkages Between Migration and Socio-economic variables-cum-Investment Variables:* Factor Analysis-cum Canonical Analysis at District Level.

(i) *Factor Results (District Level):* As stated above, at the initial step, factor analysis of socio-economic variables-cum-investment variables of 443 districts of India (for which complete data available) is done, which has yielded following *six* main factors, *depicting the main economic structure* of all districts of India (Table 6.2):

1. More economic development, higher urbanization, more manufacturing, more bank deposit, and more bank credit dimension (explains 30%).
2. General literacy, more bank credit to agriculture, and livestock dimension (explains 12.1%).
3. More service and construction workers, less agricultural labourers, and less net sown area dimension (10.4%).
4. Higher work participation and forested areas (8.5%).
5. Household industry and high population growth areas (5.7%).
6. Mining dimension (5.2%).

(ii) *Canonical Results:* Factor scores were also generated on each of these six dimensions for each district; and those become inputs for the next linking step, the canonical analysis. Here, volume and rate of in-migration and out-migration at the district level were treated as the Dependent matrix, and those 6 factor scores on those six economic structure-cum-investment variables, as the Independent Matrix. A final canonical analysis is then performed on these two matrices – which has generated four Canonical Linkages, linking each time, a specific migration variable(s) (from Dependent matrix) with a specific set of socio-economic variable(s), or factors (from Independent matrix), with which it is causally linked. Following four final Canonical linkage equations were generated:

Table 6.3 *Canonical Structure Matrix: District-level Canonical Results between Four Migration Variables and Six Factor Scores of Socio-economic Variables*

	Canonical Variate Pairs			
	1	2	3	4
A. Dependent matrix (Migration Variables)		*Canonical Loadings*		
1. Volume of In-migration	**0.96**	–0.48	–0.44	0.38
2. Volume of Out-migration	0.18	**0.77**	0.08	–0.29
3. In-migration rate	–0.12	0.15	**0.87**	–0.47
4. Out-migration rate	–0.19	–0.40	0.20	**0.75**
B. Independent Matrix (Socio-economic variables)				
1. Economic Development, Urbanization, Capital Investment	**0.93**	–0.23	–0.03	0.20
2. General Literacy, Agricultural Investment	0.09	**0.31**	**0.90**	–0.17
3. Service, Construction	–0.25	**–0.79**	0.15	–0.15
4. Per cent Workers, Forest Area	–0.02	–0.26	0.36	**0.52**
5. Household Ind., Population Growth	0.08	0.33	–0.19	–0.09
6. Mining	0.23	–0.18	0.03	**–0.79**

Cont'd...

...Cont'd

C. Canonical Correlation	**0.74**	**0.53**	**0.52**	**0.14**
D. Meaning of Canonical Relationships	*In-migration high where economic dev. high*	*Out-migration high where service & constn. less although ag. inv. more*	*In-migration rate high, where literacy high, pop. growth less*	*Out-migration rate high, mining less, forest more*
E. Trace Correlation	= **0.53**			
Wilk's Lambda	= 0.24			
Chi Square	= 633.4			
Significance	= 0.0001			

Note: Data for input taken from previous Tables 6.1 and 6.2 and from factor scores of factor analyses of socio-economic matrix.

These are statistically significant, and are also practically very meaningful:

(a) High volume of In-migration occurs in those districts where more economic development-cum-high urbanization-cum-high investment prevail (Canonical Equation No 1: Canonical Correlation 0.74).

(b) High volume of Out-migration occurs from those districts where service and construction were less, and where general literacy and agricultural investment were also less (Canonical Linkage equation 2; Canonical Correlation is 0.53).

(c) In-migration rate is high in those districts where general literacy is high and investment to agriculture is more (Canonical Linkage equation No 3; Canonical Correlation is 0.52).

(d) Higher Out-migration rate occurs in those districts where mining is less, and forest area is more (Canonical Equation No 4; Canonical Correlation 0.14).

Caution: A caution is necessary here. These kinds of canonical linkages may appear (to the uninitiated) to be telling merely the axiomatic truth; but two noteworthy aspects must be indicated:

1. First, these final canonical causal linkages do actually emerge, not as simple general statements, or as loose observations, rather emerge as final, determining, causal linkages. They emerge after processing of massive amount of data, their statistical analyses, and final determination of eigen-value-eigen-vector solution of the dependent and independent matrices (involving massive numbers of variables and data). They emerge after mathematically assessing respective canonical correlations and overall Trace correlation between the Dependent matrix and the Predictor Matrix. And, they do emerge as the final cause-and-effect relationships between migration variables and socio-economic conditions, arising out of masses of input variables, data, and a multitude of initial relationships, hidden in data matrices. So, these canonical linkages are not emerging as simple statements, rather as precisely measured General Rules or Laws of Migration Behaviour of people (in India). As in Physics, one law emerges that 'light always travels in a straight line', or 'water always flows downhill'. Similarly, in this Migration-Urbanization research, these laws,

or Canons that have emerged – mathematically states that: "In-migration occurs into economically more developed districts or regions", or "Out-migration occurs from economically backward districts or regions". So these must be considered in their true perspective.

2. Second, these canonical linkages do, in fact, mathematically confirm the truth, no matter though they may appear sometimes as axiomatic truth. Besides, such rules do have great practical significance for planning – they do indicate the great need for reducing regional disparities between districts (or states/cities), if we are really desirous of redirecting migration flows to more desirable places, or arresting crowding in overburdened cities.

Table 6.4 *Canonical Structure Matrix: Canonical Results between Migration Variables and Economic Variables-cum-Investment Variables, 432 Districts, India 1991 (without factor analysis)*

Variables	*Canonical Variate Pairs*			
	1	*2*	*3*	*4*
A. Dependent Matrix (Migration Variables)	*Canonical Loadings*			
1. Volume of In-migration	**–0.95**	–0.54	–0.51	–0.01
2. Volume of Out-migration	–0.19	**0.64**	0.23	0.61
3. In-migration rate	0.08	0.18	**0.82**	–0.49
4. Out-migration rate	0.25	–0.52	0.14	**0.63**
B. Independent Matrix (Socio-economic Variables)				
1. Cultivators	**–0.42**	**0.68**	–0.35	–0.62
2. Agricultural labourers	**–0.39**	**0.52**	–0.18	–0.17
3. Livestock workers	–0.08	0.16	0.08	–0.29
4. Mining workers	–0.10	–0.01	0.10	–0.21
5. Household industry	–0.06	0.11	–0.11	–0.02
6. Manufacturing	–0.23	0.16	0.10	–0.10
7. Construction	–0.03	0.14	0.17	**–0.37**
8. Trade/commerce	–0.13	0.22	**–0.47**	–0.28
9. Transport	–0.14	0.26	0.03	0.13
10. Service	–0.05	–0.01	–0.09	–0.04
11. Bank deposit	0.07	0.01	–0.38	–0.06
12. Bank credit	**–0.61**	–0.19	0.09	0.01
13. Credit to agriculture	0.08	0.05	**0.48**	–0.09
14. Credit to SSI	0.14	–0.07	–0.10	0.04
15. Credit to industry	–0.11	0.08	0.12	–0.16
16. Population growth	–0.18	–0.02	0.04	–0.11
17. Urbanization	–0.08	–0.01	–0.01	–0.09
18. General literacy	–0.03	0.05	**0.34**	**0.32**

Cont'd...

...Cont'd

C. Canonical Correlations	**0.84**	0.71	0.56	0.48
D. Meaning of Canonical Linkages	*High vol. of in-migration where more cultivators, agricultural labourers and more bank credit, moderate manufacturing*	*More vol. of out-migration where more cultivators and agricultural labourers and little bank credit*	*High in-migration rate where more credit to agriculture, high literacy less trade/ commerce*	*High out-migration where literacy moderate, little construction and little mining*
E. Trace Correlation	= **0.66**			
Wilks Lambda	= 0.08			
Chi Square	= 1025.6			
Significance	= 0.0001			

Note: Input data is taken from Table 4.1. Loading above 0.03 also taken for important variables.

(C) *Canonical Linkages between Migration Variables and Socio-economic Structure-cum-Investment Variables, District Level Analysis (without Factor Analysis):* Another Canonical analysis is performed at the district level, without first doing factor analysis of socio-economic variables. This test has generated the following four canonical linkages:

1. Volume of in-migration into the district is high where more bank investment have gone in, and where moderately high manufacturing sector are present (Canonical correlation 0.84).
2. Higher volume of out-migration occurs from the districts where share of cultivators and agricultural labourers are more and manufacturing less (Canonical correlation 0.71).
3. High in-migration rate occurs where credit to agriculture is high, general literacy also high, and trade-commerce relatively less (Canonical correlation 0.56).
4. High out-migration rate prevails where literacy is moderate and construction sector is less (Canonical correlation 0.48).

As stated above, likewise, these canonical linkages have considerable statistical significance, practical meaning, and policy import. These indicate that considerable out-migration occurs from those districts where already heavy burden of agricultural labourers persist; conversely, it also indicates that considerable in-migration also happens into those districts where investment are made and where scope of some manufacturing employment are available. These findings have much policy significance for achieving a more balanced spatial flows.

Theoretical Significance

Here, as various canonical linkages demonstrated, a specific kind of migration is found to be linked to a specific component of economic structure of the districts, and with a specific kind of capital investments. Thus, these three components of this migration-urbanization system of India are causally linked, producing respective "Migration Fields", as conceptually thought and canonically formulated. So time and again, these "Migration Fields" are generated by a series of canonical linkages and a series of canonical tests. These prove the central notion of Migration Field Theory, thus propounded and briefly presented in this volume.

Policy Import

Apart from theoretical contribution, various substantive findings also have considerable policy implications. They indicate that if we are seriously desirous of redirecting migration flows to more desirable destinations, instead of over-crowding into stinking slums of a few major mega cities (Mumbai, Kolkata, Delhi, Chennai), then, we really need to develop strong economic sectors of rural and urban economy. And, we also need to provide all growth efforts and investment in those hitherto neglected districts, instead of excessive polarization of these factors into over-congested and favoured regions. Evidently, these prescriptions are substantiated by above findings, and as such they have tremendous importance.

7 Findings of State-level Factor and Canonical Analysis between Migration and Socio-economic Variables, 1991

"Proclaim at the top of thy voice: "The Indian is my brother, the Indian is my life, India's gods and goddesses are my God. India's society is the cradle of my infancy, the pleasure-garden of my youth, the sacred heaven, the Varanasi of my old age."

Swami Vivekananda (1894)
(Complete Work, Centenary Volume IV, 1963: 480)

Introduction

At state level, a series of high powered factor analyses and canonical linkage analysis were made between:

(a) Volume and patterns of migration in the states (as the Dependent matrix), and
(b) Economic Structure of states, cum
(c) Growth efforts or investments made therein (as combination of Independent matrices).

Each time, a series of final canonical linkage equations were generated, linking each time, a specific pattern(s) of migration, with a specific pattern(s) of socio-economic structure-cum-investment variable(s).

State-level Analysis: Canonical Results

Causal Canonical Linkages between volume and rate of in-migration variables, in the one hand and socio-economic variables and investment variables, on the other, are done according to *two* analytical strategies (Models I and II):

1. *In Model I,* taking raw variables in both Dependent (migration) and Independent matrices (Socio-economic Matrices), and
2. *In Model II,* first factor analysing the socio-economic matrix, and then generating the factor scores for each state on each of those identified factors, and taking these factor scores as inputs for final linking Canonical analysis (Independent Matrix), and linking them with Migration variables (as Dependent matrix). Both these models of analyses have yielded useful and meaningful results.

Table 7.1 *State-level Analysis – Socio-economic Variables and Investment Variables of Selected States, India (%), 1991*

	State	PCI	POP GRO	URBA NIZA	GLIT ERA	CULT	AGL	MNF	TC	TRA NS	SERV	PERF AREA	PER NSA	FERT CON	VMCR OPPH	PROF OOD	PCBC AGI	PCBC SSI	PCBCI ND
1	Andhra Pradesh	4738	2.2	27	44	28	41	5	7	3	9	21	38	131	4392	150	338	131	525
2	Arunachal Pradesh	5397	3.1	13	42	60	5	3	3	1	19	94	3	3	4167	210	82	71	607
3	Assam	4281	2.1	11	53	51	12	3	7	3	11	25	34	11	3875	119	112	90	332
4	Bihar	2665	2.1	13	38	44	37	2	4	1	8	17	44	58	3017	118	110	57	143
5	Goa	8797	1.5	41	76	15	9	13	15	8	22	28	24	350	3702	90	352	384	2102
6	Gujarat	5917	1.9	34	61	33	23	14	9	4	10	10	51	67	2446	77	227	309	1121
7	Haryana	7508	2.4	25	56	39	19	9	9	3	16	3	82	114	4564	474	505	307	888
8	Himachal Pradesh	4910	1.8	9	64	63	3	4	4	2	14	27	18	35	2343	203	194	167	403
10	Karnataka	4605	1.9	31	56	34	29	9	8	3	9	16	53	82	3495	146	386	219	732
11	Kerala	4200	1.3	26	90	12	26	12	13	6	15	28	56	79	8034	37	276	188	563
12	Madhya Pradesh	4053	2.4	23	44	52	24	4	5	2	8	32	4	38	2170	208	181	97	317
13	Maharashtra	7367	2.3	39	65	33	27	12	9	4	10	17	59	61	2202	115	204	319	1784
15	Meghalaya	4530	2.8	19	49	55	12	2	5	1	15	38	9	15	2957	75	162	44	166
17	Nagaland	5498	4.6	17	62	73	1	1	3	1	17	26	16	4	2084	93	204	169	302
18	Orrisa	3077	1.8	13	49	44	29	4	5	2	10	38	41	22	2425	162	140	63	210
19	Punjab	8341	1.9	30	59	31	24	11	11	4	15	4	83	177	6856	827	599	466	1062
20	Rajasthan	4191	2.5	23	39	59	10	5	6	2	10	6	45	25	1559	163	198	98	288

Cont'd…

...Cont'd

21 Sikkim	5302	2.5	9	57	58	8	3	5	2	13	4	13	12	2108	217	79	132	225
22 Tamil Nadu	5071	1.4	34	63	25	35	11	9	3	10	16	44	124	6622	124	365	312	1190
23 Tripura	3370	3.0	15	60	38	23	3	8	3	19	58	24	25	3431	156	120	57	163
24 Uttar Pradesh	3590	2.3	20	42	53	19	5	6	2	10	17	58	90	4502	220	159	101	271
25 West Bengal	4710	2.2	27	58	28	25	12	11	4	11	12	60	95	5139	152	90	184	851

PCI	Per capita income
POPGRO	Population growth rate
URBANIZA	Urbanization
GLITERA	General literacy
CULT	Per cent of total workers as cultivators
AGL	Per cent agricultural labourers
MNF	Per cent workers in manufacturing
TC	Per cent workers in trade/commerce
TRANS	Per cent workers in transport
SERVE	Per cent service workers
PERFAREA	Per cent forest area
FERTCON	Consumption of fertilizers
VMCROPPH	Value of crop per hectare
PROFOOD	Food production
PCBCAGI	Per capita bank credit to agriculture
PCBCSSI	Per capita bank credit to SSI (Small Scale Industries)
PCBCIND	Per capita bank credit to general industry

(A) *First Model of State-level analysis connecting Migration and Socio-economic variables yielded the following four Canonical Linkages (Tables 7.1 and 7.2):*

1. High volume of out-migration occurs from the states where proportion of cultivators are less, agricultural labourers less, and trade-and commerce are also less prevalent (Canonical Equation No. 1; Canonical correlation 0.99).
2. High volume of in-migration occurs into those states where share of manufacturing is high, per capita income is also high, and moderate level of credit to agriculture are also present (Canonical Equation No 2; Canonical correlation 0.98).
3. High rate of out-migration prevails from those states where per capita income is less, credit to small scale industries are less, and investment to general industries are moderate (Canonical correlation 0.97).
4. High rate of in-migration occurs into those states where proportion of cultivators are more and transport workers also more (Canonical correlation 0.84).

The *Trace correlation* or general statistical overlap between the Dependent and Independent matrices is very high, 0.97, explaining more than 87 (i.e., square of trace correlation, times 100) per cent of total variance in the dependent (Migration) matrix. This is simply remarkable. Besides, the various canonical linkages are not only statistically very powerful, but are also practically meaningful. They indicate useful planning directives for reducing regional disparities. in the level of development between states, and to reduce concomitant massive migration from backward and neglected states (Orissa, UP, Bihar) to relatively favoured or developed states (Punjab, Haryana, and Maharashtra).

Table 7.2 *Canonical Structure Matrix: State-level Canonical Results between Four Migration Variables and 16 Socio-economic Variables*

	Canonical Variate Pairs			
Variables	*1*	2	3	4
		Canonical Loadings		
A. Dependent Matrix (Migration Variables)				
1. Volume of In-migration	0.29	**0.79**	0.15	–0.03
2. Rate of In-migration	–0.74	0.01	–0.59	**0.70**
3. Volume of Out-migration	**0.60**	–0.58	–0.08	**–0.63**
4. Rate of Out-migration	0.05	–0.15	**0.79**	–0.33
B. Independent Matrix (Socio-economic variables)				
1. PCI (Per capita income)	0.00	**0.39**	**–0.32**	–0.12
2. Pop growth	0.03	0.11	0.09	0.09
3. Urbanization	0.10	0.00	–0.00	0.24
4. Literacy	-0.04	0.12	0.21	0.02
5. Cultivators	**–0.75**	0.23	–0.27	**0.65**
6. Agriculture labourers	**–0.46**	–0.00	–0.19	**0.34**
7. Manufacturing	–0.00	**0.47**	0.03	0.03
8. Trade-commerce	**–0.36**	–0.08	–0.23	–0.01
9. Transport	–0.20	0.22	0.21	0.40
10. Services	0.02	–0.36	0.07	0.22
11. Forested area	–0.03	0.21	–0.22	–0.14
12. Value of agriculture products	–0.06	0.01	–0.04	0.06
13. Food production	0.14	0.07	0.28	0.11
14. Credit to Agriculture	–0.04	**0.20**	0.22	–0.02
15. Credit to small-scale industry	0.13	–0.50	**–0.48**	–0.28
16. Creit to general industry	0.01	–0.13	**0.47**	0.22

Cont'd...

...Cont'd

C. Canonical Correlation	**0.99**	**0.98**	**0.97**	**0.88**
D. Meaning of Canonical Relationships	*High out-migration where cultivators less, agricultural labourers less, trade-commerce less*	*High vol. of in-migration where MNF high, PCI high, and moderate credit to, agriculture*	*High out-migration rate where PCI less, SSI less, industrial investment moderate*	*High in-migration rate and less volume of out-migration, where cultivators agricultural labourers high*
E. Trace Correlation	= **0.97**			
Chi Square	= 230.1			
Significance	= 0.0001			

Note: The input for canonical analysis is taken from Table 7.1.

(B) *Second Model of State-level analysis connecting Migration variables and Factors of Socio-economic Matrix yielded following three Canonical Linkages equations (Tables 7.1, 7.3 and 7.4):*

1. Where service sectors of the economy of the state are high, in-migration rate is also high (Canonical correlation is 0.86).
2. Volume of out-migration is high from the states where agricultural development is low, and proportion of agricultural labourers are more (Canonical correlation 0.72).
3. Volume of in-migration into the states is high and out-migration low, where the level of economic development are high and urbanization is also high (Canonical correlation 0.38). (The fourth relationship was not significant).

The *Trace correlation* is also high, 0.59. Respective canonical correlations are also high, generating meaningful linkage equations that are having useful policy import. It indicates the great need for reducing wide regional disparities in the levels of agricultural and economic development between the states, and the need to a have a balanced migration flows between them.

Table 7.3 *Factor Analysis Results: Rotated Factor Structure Matrix of Socio-economic Variables and Investment Variables, States, India 1991*

Variables	*FACTORS*			
	1	2	3	4
Meaning of Factors	*Urbanization and economic development dimension*	*Value of agriculture, agricultural labourers and trade/commerce dimension*	*Agricultural development dimension*	*Service sector as significant aspect of economic structure of states*
Per capita bank credit to industry (PCBCIND)	**0.9**	0.0	0.1	0.0
Percentage of workers in transport (TRANS)	**0.9**	0.4	0.0	0.1
Urbanization (URBANISA)	**0.9**	0.1	0.1	–0.3

Cont'd...

...Cont'd

Per cent of workers in manufacturing (MNF)	**0.8**	0.3	0.2	–0.2
Per cent of workers in trade/commerce (TC)	**0.8**	**0.5**	0.1	0.0
Per capita bank credit to SSI (PCBCSSI)	**0.8**	0.0	0.6	–0.1
Consumption of fertilisers (FERTCON)	**0.8**	0.3	0.3	0.0
Per capita income (PCI)	**0.7**	–0.2	0.5	0.2
General literacy (GLITERA)	**0.7**	0.3	–0.1	0.3
Value of crop per hectare (VMCROPPH)	0.2	**0.8**	0.4	0.2
Per cent of cultivators (CULT)	–0.7	–0.7	0.0	0.2
Population growth (POPGRO)	–0.4	–0.6	0.0	0.3
Per capita food production (PROFOOD)	–0.1	0.1	**0.9**	0.0
Per capita bank credit to agriculture (PCBCAGI)	0.4	0.2	**0.7**	-0.1
Per cent net sown area (PERNSA)	0.3	0.4	**0.6**	–0.5
Per cent of workers in services (SERV)	0.3	–0.1	0.1	**0.9**
Per cent forest area (PERFAREA)	–0.3	0.1	–0.4	0.7
Agricultural labourers (AGL)	0.0	**0.6**	0.0	–0.6
Eigen Value	7.0	2.8	2.8	2.5
Percentage of Variance	38.9	15.7	15.4	13.7
Cumulative % of Variance	38.9	54.6	70.0	83.7

Note: Input data for factor analysis taken from Table 7.1. Negative high loadings often ignored.

Table 7.3 (contd.)

S. No.	*STATE*	*VINMIG M*	*INMIG RTM*	*VOMIGM*	*OMIG RTM*	*FS1*	*FS2*	*FS3*	*FS4*
1	Andhra Pr.	189714	0.6	173126	0.5	–0.3	0.8	0.0	–0.9
2	Arunachal Pr.	46526	10.0	8691	1.9	–1.0	–0.2	–0.1	2.3
3	Assam	82078	0.7	88092	0.8	–0.6	0.1	–0.4	0.2
4	Bihar	162590	0.4	454092	1.0	–1.2	0.5	–0.5	–1.2
5	Goa	37003	6.2	10576	1.8	3.1	–0.2	–0.6	1.5
6	Gujarat	203158	1.0	79481	0.4	1.3	–0.7	–0.6	–1.1
7	Haryana	309360	3.5	241631	2.7	0.2	–0.1	2.2	0.0
8	Himachal Pr.	78458	3.0	46583	1.8	–0.4	–0.7	0.0	0.7
10	Karnataka	256825	1.1	251047	1.1	0.2	0.2	0.0	–1.1
11	Kerala	135000	0.9	91558	0.6	0.6	2.7	–0.8	0.9
12	Madhya Pr.	378895	1.1	313605	0.9	–0.5	–0.6	–0.5	–0.6
13	Maharashtra	331876	0.8	303445	0.7	1.6	–1.1	–0.4	–1.0
15	Meghalaya	13882	1.5	9544	1.1	–0.7	–0.5	–0.5	0.7
17	Nagaland	10566	1.6	6649	1.0	–0.4	–2.1	0.2	1.1
18	Orrisa	98700	0.6	118494	0.7	–1.0	0.5	–0.6	–0.5
19	Punjab	226410	2.1	178719	1.7	0.3	0.7	3.6	0.1

Cont'd...

...Cont'd

20	Rajasthan	305754	1.3	304177	1.3	–0.3	–1.2	–0.1	–0.9
21	Sikkim	8505	3.9	5289	2.4	–0.4	–1.1	–0.1	0.2
22	Tamil Nadu	91417	0.3	240469	0.8	0.6	1.1	0.0	–0.6
23	Tripura	12046	0.8	12509	0.9	–0.7	0.8	v0.7	1.4
24	Uttar Pradesh	378770	0.5	573453	0.8	–0.8	0.2	0.3	–0.6
25	West Bengal	200635	0.6	172599	0.5	0.5	0.7	–0.5	–0.5

VINMIGM Volume of in-migration (males)
INMIGRTM In-migration rate (males)
VOMIGM Volume of out-migration (males)
OMIGRTM Out-migration rate (males)
FS 1 Economic development-cum-urbanization dimension
FS 2 Agricultural labourers, trade/commerce, moderately high agricultural productivity dimension
FS 3 Agricultural development, high NSA, high food production dimension
FS 4 Service sector of economy

(C) *Theoretical and Policy Implications*

As various canonical equations demonstrated, a specific kind of migration type is linked to a specific component of the economic structure of the states, and with a specific kind of investments. Hence, these three components of this migration-development system are found to be causally linked, yielding respective "Migration Fields", as conceptually thought and canonically tested. So, time and again, these kinds of "Migration Fields" are generated by a series of canonical equations and a series of canonical tests. They testify the central tenet of Migration Field Theory and Spatial Field theory, propounded here. Apart from this theoretical contribution, manifold substantive findings also have considerable policy significance.

As they indicate, we really need to develop strong economy of states. We also need to provide all growth efforts and investment in hitherto neglected states, instead of excessive polarization of these resources and investments only into progressive states. Obviously, these policies are substantiated by the above findings, and as such have much policy import.

Table 7.4 *Canonical Structure Matrix: Canonical Linkages between Migration and Socio-economic Factors of States, India, Males, 1991*

Variables	*Canonical Variate Pairs*			
	1	*2*	*3*	*4*
A. Dependent Matrix (Migration Variables of States)	*Canonical Loadings*			
1. Volume of In-migration	–0.34	–0.53	**0.70**	0.05
2. In-migration rate	**0.81**	0.24	0.17	–0.73
3. Volume of Out-migration	–0.46	**0.31**	**–0.63**	–0.60
4. Out-migration rate	–0.11	–0.75	–0.30	0.32

Cont'd...

...Cont'd

B. Independent Matrix (Socio-economic Factors of States)				
1. Economic development-cum-urbanization dimension	0.13	–0.14	**0.95**	0.24
2. Agricultural labourers, trade/Commerce, moderately high agricultural productivity dimension	–0.19	**0.42**	-0.13	0.88
3. Agricultural development high NSA, high food production dimension	–0.10	**–0.90**	–0.21	0.38
4. Service sector of economy	**0.97**	0.01	–0.18	0.18
C. Canonical Correlations	**0.86**	**0.72**	**0.38**	0.01
D. Meaning of Canonical Linkages	*Where service is high, in-migration rate also high*	*Vol. of out-migration high where agricultural development is low and agri-labourers more*	*Vol. of in-migration high and out-migration low, where economic development-urbanization high*	*Not significant*
E. Trace Correlation	= **0.59**			
Chi Square	= 39.5			
Significance	= 0.0001			

Note: Input for canonical analysis taken from Table 7.1. High negative loadings often ignored.

State-level Canonical Analysis between Inter-State In-and Out-migration and Socio-economic Distances (Differences) between Them

The Model Linking Inter-State Migration and Inter-State Socio-economic Distances

A new and novel methodology is evolved and applied here. Socio-economic distances or differences are calculated between each pair of states, according to the formula given below.

In the beginning, two separate matrices are prepared:

(a) Inter-state in-migration flow matrix (or out-migration matrix), M.

(b) Inter-state socio-economic distance matrix, S.

It is now appropriate to dwell on the concept of functional distance or socio-economic distance. Socio-economic distance (d_{ij}) can be computed between any two specific states *i* and *j* and this would determine the functional distance or difference between the two areas, says, states *i* and *j*. This distance can be computed by subtracting one states' (say, the *i*th state) score from the score of another state (say *j*th state) on each of the factors or variables considered. Or a composite distance can also be calculated with reference to all the variables or dimensions. This composite distance between any pair of states *i* and *j* is given by:

$$d_{ij} = [\Sigma_{k=1}^{m}(S_{ij} - S_{jk})^2]^{1/2}$$

where

d_{ij} = composite distance between *i* and *j* states with reference to m number of variables or dimensions,

k = number of variables or dimensions involved (*k* = 1, 2...*m*),

S_i = score of the ith state,
S_j = score of the jth state.

The smaller the distance, the closer the states are in the socio-economic attribute space and they are more or less similar. Conversely, larger the distance separating them, the more dissimilar they are. In this way, we can link and differentiate between any pairs of states or regions (or any objects like nations or districts), with reference to a selected number dimensions or variables. These distance measures provide indicators for functionally differentiating or clustering of states (details of method given in the next section).

This yields a 16–state by 16–state socio-economic distance matrix, as shown in Table 7.8(a) This table is derived from the socio-economic indicators matrix of the states, as given in Tables 7.5 and 7.6. The distance shown in each cell of this Table indicate the socio-economic differences between them (i and j). Larger the distance separating them, the greater is the difference between them. Conversely, smaller the distance between the states, the more is similarity between them.

It is hypothesized that larger the socio-economic differences between the states, greater will be the volume of migration taking place between them. Conversely, smaller the socio-economic distances or differences between the states, lesser will be the volume of migration occurring between them.

Inter-state in-migration Matrix (M) (Table 7.10) is also factor analysed to find out the main basis dimension of this matrix (Table 7.11 Appendix). Following four dimensions are found, which explains 83 per cent of variance:

1. Migration from UP to Maharashtra and MP (explaining 35.4% of variance; eigen-value is 5.67);
2. Migration flows from Bihar to West Bengal (explains 23.9% variance; eigen-value is 3.83);
3. Migration from Tamil Nadu to Kerala (explains 16% variance; eigen-value is 2.61)
4. Migration from Kerala/Karnataka to Tamil Nadu (explains 7.6%, eigen-value 1.2).

Factor scores are generated for all these 16 states (Table 12, appendix). Out of a total of 16 states, 11 were finally taken for factor analysis, excluding Andhra Pradesh, Assam, Haryana, Himachal Pradesh and Orissa, as factor analysis required that the number of variables should be less than the number of cases considered, and these states had comparatively less in-migration. Similar adjustments were also made in the socio-economic distance matrix, S_D. As a result the inputs for Table 7.13 become the following two modified matrices:

(a) Inter-state in-migration flow matrix, M' (4 factor scores for 11 states); and
(b) Inter-state socio-economic distance matrix, S_D (16 pairs of distances between 16 states, finally taken 11 states).

These two matrixes are analysed further through canonical model. It is pertinent here that method is explained now, before we unfold emerging canonical inter-relationships between inter-state migration and state's socio-economic distances.

Table 7.5 *Basic Data for Socio-economic Variables of States, 1991*

STATE	*PBPR*	*PBPU*	*PCI*	*URBAN*	*GLITERA*	*CULT*	*AGL*	*MNF*	*CONS*	*TC*	*SERV*	*NSA*	*IRRI*	*FERCON*	*VCROP*	*PCBCA*	*PCBCS*	*PCBCI*
Andhra Pradesh	34	26	4738	27	44	28	41	6	2	7	9	38	36	131	4392	338	131	525
Bihar	43	30	2665	13	39	44	37	2	1	4	8	44	36	58	3017	110	57	143
Gujarat	21	13	5917	35	61	33	23	15	2	9	10	51	25	67	2446	227	309	1121
Haryana	12	12	7508	25	56	39	19	9	3	9	16	82	66	114	4564	505	307	888
Himachal Pradesh	10	2	4910	9	64	63	3	4	5	4	14	18	17	35	2343	194	167	403
Karnataka	36	24	4605	31	56	34	29	9	3	8	9	53	18	82	3495	386	219	732
Kerala	16	19	4200	26	90	12	26	12	4	13	15	56	14	79	8034	276	188	563
Madhya Pradesh	42	21	4053	23	44	52	24	4	2	5	8	4	13	38	2170	181	97	317
Maharashtra	37	17	7367	39	65	33	27	12	3	9	10	59	12	61	2202	204	319	1784
Orissa	48	24	3077	13	49	44	29	4	1	5	10	41	23	22	2425	140	63	210
Punjab	7	7	8341	30	59	31	24	11	3	11	15	83	91	177	6856	599	466	1062
Rajasthan	26	19	4191	23	39	59	10	6	2	6	10	45	21	25	1559	198	98	288
Tamil Nadu	40	21	5071	34	63	25	35	11	2	9	10	44	48	124	6622	365	312	1190
Uttar Pradesh	37	27	3590	20	42	53	19	5	1	6	10	58	51	90	4502	159	101	271
West Bengal	30	21	4710	28	58	28	25	12	2	11	11	60	24	95	5139	90	184	851

Sources: Centre for Monitoring Indian Economy (CMIE) Reports, 1991–2, Various States, Mumbai.

PBPR	Population below poverty line in rural areas (1987)	NSA	Per cent net sown area
PBPU	Population below poverty line in urban areas (1987)	IRRI	Per cent irrigated area
PCI	Per capita income	FERCON	Per hectare consumption of fertilizers
Urban	Per cent urban	VCROP	Value of output of major crops
Glitera	General literacy rate	PCBCA	Per capita bank credit to agriculture
Cult	Per cent cultivators	PCBCS	Per capita bank credit to SSI (small-scale industry)
Agl	Per cent agricultural labourers	PCBCI	Per capita bank credit to industry
Mnf	Per cent workers in manufacturing	TC	Per cent workers in construction
Cons	Per cent workers in construction	SERV	Per cent workers in services

State-level Canonical Interrelationships

Further on Methodology

Table 7.5 presents raw data of socio-economic variables of major states, which are factor analysed. The analysis yielded four main basis dimensions or factors, (shown in Table 7.6). Corresponding factor score of those major states are also generated, as provided in Table 7.7. Socio-economic distances between pairs of states are computed, as presented in Table 7.8(a). Square of these distances are computed and shown in Table 7.8(b) Then, volume of interstate (male) migrations during 1981–91 decade are computed (Table 7.9), and their proportion of total state migration is calculated (Table 7.10).

Using data of inter-state migration matrix of Table 7.9, with respect to each state, then, the proportions of all other states' contribution to total in-migration of that state are calculated, as shown in last row of Table 7.10. This matrix (7.10) become inputs for the next step of factor analysis (see Table 7.11 and 7.12 in Appendix), and final canonical analysis (as in Tables 7.13 and 7.14). Factor analysis of this inter-state migration matrix is performed, as shown in Table 7.11 (Appendix) and their corresponding factor scores also generated, as in Table 7.12 (Appendix).

Accordingly, as discussed above, a canonical analysis is performed between these two matrices, M and S_D taking the migration flow matrix as the dependent set and the square of socio-economic distances between the states as the independent set (see Table 7.13).

Table 7.6 *Factor Analysis of Socio-economic Matrix of States, 1991*

Variables	*Factors*			
	1	2	3	4
	Economic development, urbanization, bank investment dimension	*Less agri. labourers, less rural poverty and more service dimension*	*More investment in agriculture dimension*	*Higher value of agricultural productivity dimension*
Per capita bank credit for industry (PCBCIND)	**0.95**	0.04	0.13	0.12
Per cent urban (URBANISA)	**0.91**	–0.21	0.05	0.22
Per cent workers in manufacturing (MNF)	**0.83**	0.17	0.02	0.42
Per capita bank credit to SSI (PCBCSS)	**0.78**	0.33	0.47	0.16
Per capita income (PCI)	**0.74**	0.42	0.47	–0.06
Below poverty line, urban (PBPU)	–0.18	**–0.88**	–0.27	–0.13
Percentage of workers in service (SERV)	0.08	**0.84**	0.33	0.35
Per cent agricultural labourers (AGL)	0.10	**–0.82**	0.22	0.42
Per cent irrigated area (IRRI)	0.03	0.14	**0.94**	0.03
Per capita bank credit to agriculture (PCBCA)	0.35	0.28	**0.73**	0.18

Cont'd...

...Cont'd

Rate of unemployment (UNEMPRT)	0.10	–0.05	**0.60**	0.11
Value of crop per hectare (VCROP)	0.06	0.13	0.42	**0.84**
Per cent cultivators (CULT)	–0.46	0.22	–0.13	**–0.83**
General literacy (GLITERA)	0.40	0.48	–0.23	**0.71**
Eigen Value	4.13	2.91	2.71	2.55
Percentage of Variance	29.47	20.80	19.37	18.18
Cumulative percentage of variance	29.47	50.27	69.64	87.83

Note: Input for factor analysis taken from Table 7.5. Other variables did not emerge. Loadings of higher value (above 0.4) taken for identifying a factor.

Table 7.7 *Factor Score of Socio-economic Matrix*

	States	*Economic development, urbanization, bank investment dimension*	*Less agri. labourers, less rural poverty and more service workers*	*More investment in agriculture dimension*	*Higher value of agricultural productivity*
		FS1	*FS2*	*FS3*	*FS4*
1	Andhra Pradesh	–0.32	–1.27	0.72	0.35
2	Bihar	–1.39	–1.24	0.14	–0.12
3	Gujarat	1.49	0.15	–0.80	–0.35
4	Haryana	0.17	1.13	1.73	–0.25
5	Himachal Pradesh	–0.96	2.22	–0.71	–0.76
6	Karnataka	0.50	–0.56	–0.35	0.02
7	Kerala	–0.38	1.10	–1.25	2.88
8	Madhya Pradesh	–0.32	–0.53	–0.80	–0.86
9	Maharashtra	2.20	–0.31	–0.98	–0.62
10	Orissa	–1.18	–0.78	–0.08	–0.11
11	Punjab	0.68	0.96	2.25	0.15
12	Rajasthan	–0.38	0.46	–0.51	–1.47
13	Tamil Nadu	0.65	–0.95	0.81	0.92
14	Uttar Pradesh	–0.95	–0.08	0.04	–0.44
15	West Bengal	0.22	–0.29	–0.22	0.66

Source: Computed from above factor analysis. Factor score as a state's specific weighted score on that factor.

Factor Analysis of Inter-State Migration Matrix of India, 1981–91

Inputs of Table 7.10 are factor analysed to identify the main dimensions of the State's migration matrix of India. Factor analysis results are given in Table 7.11 (in Appendix). Their corresponding factor scores are also generated, and given in Table 7.12 (in Appendix, due to shortage of space). Then, finally in Table 7.13, all these inputs are provided for major states, which involve two sets of data: (1) Factor score data for migration variables (proportion of migration of states in Inter-state migration matrix, as dependent matrix), and (2) Square of the socio-economic distances between those pairs of states (socio-economic differences between states, as predictor matrix).

Table 7.8(a) *Socio-economic Distances between 15 Major States, India, 1991*

	States	*AP*	*Bi*	*Gj*	*Har*	*HP*	*Kar*	*Ker*	*MP*	*Mah*	*Ori*	*Pun*	*Raj*	*TN*	*UP*	*WB*
		V1	*V2*	*V3*	*V4*	*V5*	*V6*	*V7*	*V8*	*V9*	*V10*	*V11*	*V12*	*V13*	*V14*	*V15*
1	Andhra Pradesh	0.0	1.3	2.9	2.7	4.0	1.6	4.0	2.1	3.3	1.4	2.9	2.8	1.2	1.7	1.5
2	Bihar	1.3	0.0	3.4	3.3	3.6	2.1	4.2	1.8	3.9	0.6	3.7	2.5	2.4	1.3	2.1
3	Gujarat	2.9	3.4	0.0	3.0	3.2	1.4	3.9	2.0	0.9	2.9	3.3	2.2	2.5	2.6	1.8
4	Haryana	2.7	3.3	3.0	0.0	2.9	2.7	4.4	3.1	3.7	3.0	0.8	2.7	2.6	2.4	2.6
5	Himachal Pradesh	4.0	3.6	3.2	2.9	0.0	3.3	3.9	2.8	4.1	3.1	3.7	2.0	4.2	2.4	3.2
6	Karnataka	1.6	2.1	1.4	2.7	3.3	0.0	3.5	1.3	1.9	1.7	3.0	2.0	1.5	1.6	0.8
7	Kerala	4.0	4.2	3.9	4.4	3.9	3.5	0.0	4.1	4.6	3.8	4.6	4.5	3.7	3.8	2.9
8	Madhya Pradesh	2.1	1.8	2.0	3.1	2.8	1.3	4.1	0.0	2.6	1.4	3.7	1.2	2.6	1.2	1.7
9	Maharashtra	3.3	3.9	0.9	3.7	4.1	1.9	4.6	2.6	0.0	3.6	3.9	2.9	2.9	3.3	2.5
10	Orissa	1.4	0.6	2.9	3.0	3.1	1.7	3.8	1.4	3.6	0.0	3.5	2.0	2.3	0.8	1.7
11	Punjab	2.9	3.7	3.3	0.8	3.7	3.0	4.6	3.7	3.9	3.5	0.0	3.4	2.5	3.0	2.9
12	Rajasthan	2.8	2.5	2.2	2.7	2.0	2.0	4.5	1.2	2.9	2.0	3.4	0.0	3.2	1.4	2.4
13	Tamil Nadu	1.2	2.4	2.5	2.6	4.2	1.5	3.7	2.6	2.9	2.3	2.5	3.2	0.0	2.4	1.3
14	Uttar Pradesh	1.7	1.3	2.6	2.4	2.4	1.6	3.8	1.2	3.3	0.8	3.0	1.4	2.4	0.0	1.6
15	West Bengal	1.5	2.1	1.8	2.6	3.2	0.8	2.9	1.7	2.5	1.7	2.9	2.4	1.3	1.6	0.0

Source: Socio-economic distances between states are computed according to formula given in the middle of this chapter, and from data of Table 7.7.

Table 7.8(b) *Square of the Socio-economic Distances between the Selected Major States, 1991*

	State	*Bi*	*Gj*	*Kar*	*Ker*	*MP*	*Mah*	*Pun*	*Raj*	*TN*	*UP*	*WB*
		V1	*V2*	*V3*	*V4*	*V5*	*V6*	*V7*	*V8*	*V9*	*V10*	*V11*
1	Andhra Pradesh	1.7	8.2	2.4	15.9	4.3	11.1	8.4	7.8	1.4	2.9	2.2
2	Bihar	0.0	11.2	4.3	17.4	3.1	15.3	13.7	6.1	5.8	1.6	4.2
3	Gujarat	11.2	0.0	1.9	15.1	4.0	0.8	10.9	5.0	6.2	6.8	3.2
4	Haryana	10.6	9.2	7.4	19.0	9.8	13.7	0.7	7.2	6.8	5.6	6.6
5	Himachal Pradesh	13.3	10.5	10.6	15.2	8.0	16.5	13.9	4.0	17.8	6.0	10.0
6	Karnataka	4.3	1.9	0.0	12.5	1.7	3.8	9.1	4.1	2.3	2.7	0.6
7	Kerala	17.4	15.1	12.5	0.0	16.9	21.0	20.9	19.9	13.4	14.4	8.3
8	Madhya Pradesh	3.1	4.0	1.7	16.9	0.0	6.5	13.6	1.4	6.9	1.5	3.0
9	Maharashtra	15.3	0.8	3.8	21.0	6.5	0.0	14.9	8.2	8.4	11.1	6.1
10	Orissa	0.3	8.6	3.0	14.5	1.9	12.8	12.0	4.2	5.3	0.7	2.8
11	Punjab	13.7	10.9	9.1	20.9	13.6	14.9	0.0	11.6	6.3	9.0	8.1
12	Rajasthan	6.1	5.0	4.1	19.9	1.4	8.2	11.6	0.0	10.5	2.0	5.5
13	Tamil Nadu	5.8	6.2	2.3	13.4	6.9	8.4	6.3	10.5	0.0	5.8	1.7
14	Uttar Pradesh	1.6	6.8	2.7	14.4	1.5	11.1	9.0	2.0	5.8	0.0	2.7
15	West Bengal	4.2	3.2	0.6	8.3	3.0	6.1	8.1	5.5	1.7	2.7	0.0

Source: Square of socio-economic distances between states are computed according to formula given in the middle of this chapter, and using data of Table 7.8 (a).

Cononical Analysis and Emerging Results

Finally, four statistically very highly significant and practically meaningful canonical inter-relationships are generated (Table 7.14). *Trace correlation* is very high (0.850), explaining about 73 per cent of total variance of the dependent matrix (i.e., migration flows). Successively four canonical inter-links have also emerged; with very high canonical coefficients (e.g., 0.97, 0.94, 0.78 and 0.70). These are not only statistically very highly significant, but also having considerable policy import. (Table 7.14). Now all these data input Tables 7.9 to 7.13 are presented, before we can embark upon the final cononical results in Table 7.14 (unfolded at the end of the chapter).

Final Canonical Links: Testing of Spatial Field Theory – Inter-State Migration and Socio-economic Distances

Finally, findings of canonical inter-relationships between these two sets of data are shown in Table 7.14. These four canonical linkages are identified as follows:

1. Larger in-migration flows occur from Karnataka and Kerala to Tamil Nadu, mainly because of large socio-economic differences or distances between the states of Tamil Nadu and these states (Canonical linkage equation 1, canonical correlation is 0.97).
2. Larger in-migration flows take place from UP to Maharashtra, especially due to larger socio-economic differences or distances of UP from this state (Canonical linkage equation 2; canonical correlation is 0.94).

Table 7.9 *Volume of Inter-state Migration, 1991 Census*

	Origin States	*Destination States*															
		AP	*AS*	*Bi*	*Gj*	*Hr*	*HP*	*Kar*	*Ker*	*MP*	*Mah*	*Ori*	*Pun*	*Raj*	*Tam*	*UP*	*WB*
1	Andhra Pradesh	1	590	1160	3680	330	138	23396	1132	5890	19250	3960	370	1260	9320	910	1410
2	Assam	520	1	410	440	130	134	290	170	550	1280	320	350	570	220	850	3840
3	Bihar	4370	12100	1	10130	19120	4285	1970	320	22278	22140	8920	35238	9989	950	35792	83029
4	Gujarat	1080	330	350	1	220	116	1020	330	3680	19230	300	470	4370	560	1060	560
5	Haryana	440	300	940	1190	1	1550	290	50	1740	1740	190	11431	8110	230	3750	650
6	Himachal Pradesh	190	320	260	310	2882	1	210	20	620	790	220	11519	1070	40	1570	330
7	Karnataka	13080	90	490	1970	150	100	1	3760	1080	39230	360	220	820	5900	640	450
8	Kerala	7642	520	910	6430	1330	241	23060	1	5970	27480	900	680	2480	28327	1620	840
9	Madhya Pradesh	2380	390	2330	6600	1350	930	770	260	1	13360	2030	1787	11880	650	9860	1870
10	Maharashtra	10940	390	580	44960	650	329	9311	1950	23914	1	480	750	2670	2970	2910	930
11	Orissa	8200	1090	4750	17957	880	995	1270	160	11450	6070	1	1280	1280	450	1920	13040
12	Punjab	940	450	1130	1540	12324	5073	650	180	2960	3450	310	1	7730	470	5292	1320
13	Rajasthan	3740	1500	1100	31126	15360	882	3740	260	15955	16470	330	8010	1	2150	4690	2150
14	Tamil Nadu	22380	330	650	3170	400	60	49481	40941	2140	20900	650	600	1070	1	1240	1150
15	Uttar Pradesh	3700	2990	10596	41760	57031	7178	2630	340	53137	134562	1890	60687	24410	1360	1	16070
16	West Bengal	3180	3700	16826	3040	1870	295	1600	480	7308	9920	5510	1970	2680	1060	4870	1

Cont'd...

...Cont'd

17	Arunachal Pradesh	360	460	190	60	20	35	80	10	160	90	80	60	40	160	220	150
18	Goa	180	20	130	110	20	22	740	100	120	2090	60	20	90	110	80	70
19	Jammu & Kashmir	280	110	160	450	380	2338	250	110	650	1280	148	2090	600	240	1470	400
20	Manipur	20	230	120	80	10	62	50	40	240	210	90	40	30	20	80	190
21	Meghalaya	50	1180	60	40	40	17	30	20	90	120	120	40	90	90	100	200
22	Mizoram	60	160	50	230	0	11	50	20	120	320	20	20	50	10	30	40
23	Nagaland	30	390	60	110	0	15	60	20	50	150	80	50	40	20	150	50
24	Sikkim	270	10	20	50	0	37	130	0	130	130	10	30	40	140	190	150
25	Tripura	270	830	110	80	40	6	30	0	200	160	50	100	120	60	190	710
26	Delhi	1100	260	380	1130	4360	1053	1260	460	2480	3570	280	2410	3170	1210	6200	680
	Total	85403	28741	43763	176644	116698	25903	122369	51134	162913	343993	27309	140223	84660	56718	85685	130280

Note: Numeric 1 is purposefully inserted in the place of zero, in the diagonal; in regard to own state to own state migration, in order to avoid dividing by zero in Factor Analysis and Canonical Analysis, which results into infinity, when a numeric in numerator is divided by zero. States No. 17 to 26 are just shown to give a complete picture of inter-state migration in India, they are not included in final factor and canonical analysis.

Source: Computed from Census of India, 1991 (b), D-Series, Migration Tables, Census Commissioner's Office, New Delhi, CDs available only in 1998.

Table 7.10 *Proportion of Inter-state Migration*

	Origin States	*Destination States*															
		AP	*AS*	*Bi*	*Gj*	*Har*	*HP*	*Kar*	*Ker*	*MP*	*Mah*	*Ori*	*Pun*	*Raj*	*Tam*	*UP*	*WB*
1	Andhra Pradesh	0.0	2.1	2.7	2.1	0.3	0.5	19.1	2.2	3.6	5.6	14.5	0.3	1.5	16.4	1.1	1.1
2	Assam	0.6	0.0	0.9	0.2	0.1	0.5	0.2	0.3	0.3	0.4	1.2	0.2	0.7	0.4	1.0	2.9
3	Bihar	5.1	42.1	0.0	5.7	16.1	16.5	1.6	0.6	13.7	6.4	32.7	25.1	11.8	1.7	41.8	63.7
4	Gujarat	1.3	1.1	0.8	0.0	0.2	0.4	0.8	0.6	2.3	5.6	1.1	0.3	5.2	1.0	1.2	0.4
5	Haryana	0.5	1.0	2.1	0.7	0.0	6.0	0.2	0.1	1.1	0.5	0.7	8.2	9.6	0.4	4.4	0.5
6	Himachal Pradesh	0.2	1.1	0.6	0.2	2.4	0.0	0.2	0.0	0.4	0.2	0.8	8.2	1.3	0.1	1.8	0.3
7	Karnataka	15.3	0.3	1.1	1.1	0.1	0.4	0.0	7.4	0.7	11.4	1.3	0.2	1.0	10.4	0.7	0.3
8	Kerala	8.9	1.8	2.1	3.6	1.1	0.9	18.8	0.0	3.7	8.0	3.3	0.5	2.9	49.9	1.9	0.6
9	Madhya Pradesh	2.8	1.4	5.3	3.7	1.1	3.6	0.6	0.5	0.0	3.9	7.4	1.3	14.0	1.1	11.5	1.4
10	Maharashtra	12.8	1.4	1.3	25.5	0.5	1.3	7.6	3.8	14.7	0.0	1.8	0.5	3.2	5.2	3.4	0.7
11	Orissa	9.6	3.8	10.9	10.2	0.7	3.8	1.0	0.3	7.0	1.8	0.0	0.9	1.5	0.8	2.2	10.0
12	Punjab	1.1	1.6	2.6	0.9	10.4	19.6	0.5	0.4	1.8	1.0	1.1	0.0	9.1	0.8	6.2	1.0
13	Rajasthan	4.4	5.2	2.5	17.6	12.9	3.4	3.1	0.5	9.8	4.8	1.2	5.7	0.0	3.8	5.5	1.7
14	Tamil Nadu	26.2	1.1	1.5	1.8	0.3	0.2	40.4	80.1	1.3	6.1	2.4	0.4	1.3	0.0	1.4	0.9
15	Uttar Pradesh	4.3	10.4	24.2	23.6	48.0	27.7	2.1	0.7	32.6	39.1	6.9	43.3	28.8	2.4	0.0	12.3
16	West Bengal	3.7	12.9	38.4	1.7	1.6	1.1	1.3	0.9	4.5	2.9	20.2	1.4	3.2	1.9	5.7	0.0
	Total	96.9	87.3	97.1	98.7	95.9	86.1	97.8	98.5	97.4	97.6	96.6	96.5	95.0	96.4	89.8	98.0

Source: Using data of Inter-state migration matrix of Table 7.9, With respect to each state, the proportions of all other states' contribution to total In-migration of that state are calculated, as shown in last row. This table become inputs for the next step of factor analysis (see Tables 7.11 and 7.12 in Appendix) and final canonical analysis (in Tables 7.13 and 7.14).

Table 7.13 *Input Data for Canonical Analysis at State Level: Inter-state Migration Variables and Socio-economic Distances, 1991*

State	*Factor Scores for Migration Variables*				*Square of Socio-economic distances between states*										
	FS1	*FS2*	*FS3*	*FS4*	*BI*	*GJ*	*KAR*	*KER*	*MP*	*MH*	*PJ*	*RAJ*	*TN*	*UP*	*WB*
Andhra Pradesh	–0.3	0.2	0.2	1.7	1.7	8.2	2.4	15.9	4.3	11.1	8.4	7.8	1.4	2.9	2.2
Bihar	0.3	4.7	0.0	–0.4	0.0	11.2	4.3	17.4	3.1	15.3	13.7	6.1	5.8	1.6	4.2
Gujarat	–0.2	–0.3	–0.3	–0.2	11.2	0.0	1.9	15.1	4.0	0.8	10.9	5.0	6.2	6.8	3.2
Haryana	0.0	–0.2	–0.4	–0.6	10.6	9.2	7.4	19.0	9.8	13.7	0.7	7.2	6.8	5.6	6.6
Himachal Pradesh	–0.3	–0.2	–0.4	–0.4	13.3	10.5	10.6	15.2	8.0	16.5	13.9	4.0	17.8	6.0	10.0
Karnataka	–0.1	–0.4	0.6	0.5	4.3	1.9	0.0	12.5	1.7	3.8	9.1	4.1	2.3	2.7	0.6
Kerala	0.0	–0.1	0.5	4.1	17.4	15.1	12.5	0.0	16.9	21.0	20.9	19.9	13.4	14.4	8.3
Madhya Pradesh	0.0	0.2	–0.3	–0.2	3.1	4.0	1.7	16.9	0.0	6.5	13.6	1.4	6.9	1.5	3.0
Maharashtra	0.5	–0.4	0.8	0.4	15.3	0.8	3.8	21.0	6.5	0.0	14.9	8.2	8.4	11.1	6.1
Orissa	0.1	–0.1	0.2	–0.1	0.3	8.6	3.0	14.5	1.9	12.8	12.0	4.2	5.3	0.7	2.8
Punjab	0.3	–0.1	–0.4	–0.8	13.7	10.9	9.1	20.9	13.6	14.9	0.0	11.6	6.3	9.0	8.1
Rajasthan	0.5	–0.2	0.0	0.1	6.1	5.0	4.1	19.9	1.4	8.2	11.6	0.0	10.5	2.0	5.5
Tamil Nadu	–0.4	–0.2	4.6	–1.1	5.8	6.2	2.3	13.4	6.9	8.4	6.3	10.5	0.0	5.8	1.7
Uttar Pradesh	4.6	–0.6	–0.1	–0.3	1.6	6.8	2.7	14.4	1.5	11.1	9.0	2.0	5.8	0.0	2.7
West Bengal	0.1	0.7	–0.4	0.9	4.2	3.2	0.6	8.3	3.0	6.1	8.1	5.5	1.7	2.7	0.0

Note: Assam not taken finally. Only 16 origin states and only 11 destination states are considered, which show higher values.

3. Larger volume of in-migration flowing from Bihar to West Bengal, due to larger socio-economic distances or differences of Bihar from West Bengal (Canonical linkage 3; canonical correlation is 0.78)
4. Migration from Tamil Nadu to Kerala and Karnataka also occurs, and these are related to socio-economic distances of Tamil Nadu from these states (Canonical equation no 4, canonical correlation 0.70).

Policy Implications of Final Canonical Linkages

These are very meaningful and useful canonical inter-relationships. These are not repeating the usual geographical map of inter-state migration-flow matrix. Rather these canonical equations very significantly and indisputably tell us that such migration streams from a particular backward origin state to a particular relatively prosperous destination state have been occurring primarily due to the large socio-economic differences or disparities separating them. Those also warn us that such migration streams have persisted in the past, and unfortunately, will also persist for a long time so that such regional disparities and inequalities will continue and proliferate in future. The immediate policy implication of such crucial findings are that such regional imbalances must be given now a final burial. Of course, here it is not meant that the states like West Bengal, Maharashtra, Punjab, or Haryana are economically much better than the backward states of Bihar and Uttar Pradesh; but the urgent policy imperative of such findings is to fully comprehend that such regional disparities and regional underdevelopment are indeed artificially and historically created by colonialism.

Table 7.14 *Canonical Structure Matrix: Canonical Links between Socio-economic Distances between States and Inter-state Migration, 1991*

	Canonical Variate Pairs			
	1	*2*	*3*	*4*
A. Dependent Matrix (Migration Variables)		*Canonical Loadings*		
1. Migration from UP to Maharashtra	–0.57	**0.54**	0.53	–0.31
2. Migration from Bihar to West Bengal/UP	0.37	0.01	**0.78**	0.56
3. Migration from Tamil Nadu to Karnataka/Kerala	0.03	**0.71**	–0.30	**0.52**
4. Migration from Kerala/Karnataka to Tamil Nadu	**0.73**	0.43	0.12	–0.56
B. Independent matrix (Socio-economic Distances)				
1. To Bihar from other states	0.06	–0.06	0.15	**0.29**
2. To Gujarat from other states	–0.14	0.01	–0.03	0.32
3. To Karnataka from other states	**0.43**	–0.39	–0.29	–0.29
4. To Kerala from other states	–0.07	0.09	–0.14	0.09
5. To Madhya Pradesh from other states	0.14	–0.28	–0.17	–0.02
6. To Maharashtra from other states	–0.32	0.39	0.38	–0.29
7. To Punjab from other states	0.16	–0.22	0.07	–0.08

Cont'd...

...Cont'd

8. To Rajasthan from other states	0.20	0.03	–0.41	0.45
9. To Tamil Nadu from other states	–0.31	0.41	–0.47	**0.40**
10. To Uttar Pradesh from other states	**–0.64**	**0.54**	0.35	–0.48
11. To West Bengal from other states	0.29	–0.30	**0.43**	–0.17
C. Canonical Correlation	**0.97**	**0.94**	**0.78**	**0.70**
D. Meaning of Canonical Correlation	*Migration from Karnataka and Kerala to Tamil and socio-economic distance of Karnataka from other stats*	*Migration from UP to Maharashtra and socio-economic distance of UP from other states (Also migration from TN to Kerala and Socio-economic distance of TN from other states)*	*Migration from Bihar to West Bengal and socio-economic distance of Bihar*	*Migration from Tamil Nadu to Kerala and Karnataka and socio-economic distance from other stats*
E. Trace Correlation	= **0.85**			
Chi Square	= 46.40			
Significance	= 0.0001			

Inputs are taken from Tables 7.9 to 7.13. Also see Table 7.11 and 7.12 in Appendix as inputs.

And, these were also accentuated by the lack of soulful concern for the poor, during the Post-Independent period of Planning era, that has been marked by the same old neo-colonial legacy of favouring coastal and exporting states, at the expense of the interior states of Bihar, Uttar Pradesh, and the like – which remained neglected and underdeveloped. In sum, no noteworthy change has occurred in the space economy of India, during last 63 years. Unless and until such regional disparities are urgently corrected, the patterns of poverty-induced migration of pauperized and marginalized peasants and labourers from Uttar Pradesh and Bihar to relatively developed and favoured states of Maharashtra, West Bengal, Punjab, Haryana, and Delhi will continue unabated. Unfortunately, these migration patterns may persist for another 100 years!

8 Findings of Class I City-level, Million City-level and Metropolitan Level Canonical Analysis

"Stretch forth a helping hand, and open the gates of knowledge to one and all, and give the downtrodden masses once more their just and legitimate rights and privileges."

Swami Vivekananda (1894)
(Complete Work, Centenary volume III, 1963: 461)

Finally, the crucial analysis linking volume and patterns of migration to class I cities and metropolises, the economic structure of those cities or metropolises, and capital investment made therein are presented in this chapter. *First part deals with findings of class I cities, while later section deals with million cities and metros.*

Regarding such kinds of analysis of migration to 289 class I cities and 23 million cities, different canonical models are employed. Findings from various models are presented in Tables 8.3, 8.4, 8.6, 8.7, 8.8, 8.9, 8.11, 8.12, 8.14, and 8.15. The corresponding matrix inputs for them are given in Tables 8.1 and 8.5(a) and 8.5(b). *Results of one factor analysis are given in Appendix (Tables 8.2). Besides, results of female migrants (Tables 8.13 to 8.15) are also given in Appendix.*

The nature of variables in the dependent (migration) matrix and independent matrix (socio-economic matrix) are elaborated in corresponding tables, hence not repeated here.

Canonical Findings of Class I Cities

Complete data were available for only 289 class I cities (missing 10 cities). Bank investment data were available again for only 200 Class I cities. So, different kinds of analyses were performed for these sub-sets of class I cities, detailed as follows. *Results of factor analysis of Table 8.1 are given in Table 8.2 (Appendix)*. Factor scores from that matrix are used as inputs in final linking Canonical analysis, displayed in Table 8.3. On the other hand, in Table 8.4 canonical analysis is performed, without factor analysing the socio-economic variables

(A) *Canonical Analysis between Reasons for Migration of Males and Economic Structure of 289 Class I Cities of India:* Following *four* final canonical linkages were generated, *after factor analysing the socio-economic variables* (see Tables 8.1 and 8.3).

Table 8.1 *Per cent of Migrants by Reasons for Migration and Industrial Categories, Inputs for Factor and Canonical Analysis of 289 Cities, India 1991(only 92 cities shown)*

CITY	*RME MP*	*RMB USI*	*RME DU*	*RMFA MMOV*	*RMOT HER*	*MI NS*	*HHI ND*	*MNF*	*CO NS*	*TC*	*TRA NS*	*SE RV*
Hyderabad	43.9	5.1	5.3	26.9	17.6	0.6	0.4	30.0	9.1	21.4	10.8	27.1
Vijayawada	46.0	4.2	4.0	23.7	20.2	0.4	1.0	15.1	4.8	27.9	25.8	24.3
Warangal	42.5	3.7	12.2	15.5	24.5	0.5	2.8	11.9	7.6	24.2	18.7	32.9
Nellore	44.7	4.8	7.1	24.0	17.4	0.1	2.9	15.6	7.6	28.7	14.5	28.9
Tirupati	45.1	4.6	12.4	24.4	12.0	0.0	0.9	8.3	7.6	27.0	14.0	41.2
Guwahati City	35.1	14.9	7.7	17.2	24.0	0.5	0.4	10.1	6.6	28.4	15.4	35.9
Patna	32.6	8.5	12.9	23.7	16.2	0.1	1.9	4.6	2.1	19.6	5.2	65.7
Jamshedpur	53.3	6.3	6.1	20.8	10.5	0.1	1.7	46.9	4.0	14.7	6.2	25.7
Dhanbad	55.9	8.1	7.3	17.8	9.4	46.3	1.0	7.3	2.1	14.4	8.0	19.5
Ranchi	45.4	7.1	12.9	21.7	9.7	0.1	2.2	4.9	1.9	15.4	5.3	69.5
Bokaro	47.9	10.3	6.6	23.8	8.7	0.5	1.0	48.6	5.5	15.6	7.0	19.6
Gaya	25.8	5.4	9.2	15.1	18.4	0.0	2.5	6.6	3.7	21.1	15.5	50.2
Muzaffarpur	34.0	7.5	16.4	20.5	12.8	0.2	1.0	8.4	3.5	30.1	10.1	44.2
Delhi	52.4	7.7	1.9	28.4	8.9	0.1	1.1	22.1	9.6	24.2	9.1	33.3
Ahmedabad	34.6	17.4	3.0	19.5	23.5	0.6	0.5	38.6	4.9	23.6	9.0	22.2
Surat	44.4	16.7	1.4	20.8	15.9	0.2	0.3	62.3	3.9	17.5	4.2	11.1
Vadodra	31.9	14.5	4.1	21.5	24.3	1.7	0.4	37.1	7.0	18.2	9.0	25.8
Rajkot	19.0	23.3	3.6	22.8	29.7	0.3	1.2	31.5	7.2	25.4	10.4	22.8
Bhavnagar	19.4	21.7	4.5	24.6	28.4	0.2	0.6	39.7	4.4	21.4	11.2	20.8
Jamnagar	18.5	20.0	4.5	28.7	25.8	0.1	0.2	31.6	5.0	20.9	11.4	28.9
Faridabad	50.9	7.9	1.7	29.1	9.7	1.0	0.7	54.3	6.0	13.9	4.7	18.8
Rohtak	26.6	9.4	3.3	40.4	18.7	0.0	0.6	13.5	7.0	29.8	9.4	36.3
Panipat	37.6	11.0	1.0	32.9	16.8	0.0	5.6	39.2	3.7	22.5	5.9	22.8
Ambala	19.9	8.9	1.7	33.6	34.8	0.0	1.9	31.8	6.3	18.4	11.2	29.3
Shimla	51.0	8.8	10.0	20.5	9.2	0.0	0.4	5.0	12.4	16.6	9.4	53.3
Bangalore	49.0	5.4	6.7	22.5	14.9	0.3	0.8	32.9	9.3	26.1	8.6	21.5
Mysore	36.2	4.7	14.6	26.5	16.8	0.1	0.6	23.3	7.7	26.2	10.2	29.4
Hubli-Dharwad	38.5	3.1	12.1	20.8	24.5	0.2	1.0	20.9	6.3	29.7	13.3	26.9
Mangalore	33.2	2.3	7.5	34.6	20.3	1.1	0.4	18.6	9.4	26.3	14.8	26.5
Belgaum	28.8	9.2	9.7	23.4	27.7	0.2	3.1	24.7	5.2	27.9	9.1	28.4
Shimoga	37.0	7.3	7.9	26.2	19.4	0.1	1.6	13.9	7.2	33.9	11.0	29.4
Kochi	35.7	2.6	3.3	32.5	22.2	0.5	0.9	26.6	7.1	27.3	13.4	21.6
Thiruvanathapuram	35.6	3.1	5.7	25.6	18.2	0.2	1.2	10.9	5.3	26.3	10.6	42.6
Kozhikode	18.9	1.6	5.5	39.2	30.7	0.6	1.3	18.1	7.7	30.5	13.3	23.7
Indore	43.6	8.6	5.2	23.1	18.4	0.0	0.9	26.5	6.2	28.6	10.1	27.1
Bhopal	50.9	5.7	6.0	24.8	11.4	0.3	0.6	20.2	13.3	19.6	8.7	35.2
Jabalpur	44.4	7.0	4.9	25.9	16.2	0.3	1.2	28.0	5.8	18.2	11.6	31.9
Gwalior	36.0	7.1	9.1	26.0	19.6	0.4	1.0	23.3	7.6	17.7	7.7	40.8
Durg-Bhilai Nagar	51.6	7.2	3.6	25.5	10.7	0.3	0.6	42.9	7.8	16.2	9.7	21.1
Ujjain	37.7	7.7	5.0	26.3	22.2	0.4	1.1	23.3	6.9	20.9	10.7	35.2
Satna	41.4	10.9	7.1	26.4	13.0	0.2	1.5	29.5	5.8	25.1	10.9	24.1
Morena	25.0	11.6	7.1	33.8	20.6	0.2	1.3	9.8	8.9	19.8	13.8	44.0
Korba	49.8	9.3	3.3	25.2	10.3	3.1	0.7	28.3	6.5	17.1	8.8	33.5
Greater Mumbai	46.5	12.9	4.8	17.1	17.6	0.2	1.3	37.1	5.3	24.4	12.5	18.8

Cont'd...

...Cont'd

Pune	30.6	12.6	4.2	21.9	28.7	0.2	1.0	36.2	12.6	17.3	8.3	23.7
Nagpur	29.6	18.5	8.8	22.5	19.0	1.2	1.3	20.4	11.8	21.9	14.5	27.2
Nashik	29.6	13.1	4.6	21.5	30.5	0.1	1.2	34.4	9.3	15.5	7.6	30.0
Solapur	23.5	13.9	7.6	18.5	34.9	0.2	2.6	28.9	5.2	22.1	11.1	28.1
Aurangabad	28.3	19.3	13.2	21.4	16.4	0.1	0.8	31.0	9.4	17.8	7.4	31.1
Amravati	24.0	14.5	11.6	25.3	23.1	0.1	1.5	12.4	8.7	22.6	12.3	39.7
Kolhapur	21.9	16.3	8.2	17.9	34.1	0.3	1.2	21.7	8.9	29.6	11.1	26.1
Bhiwandi	51.6	19.6	1.4	14.5	11.9	0.0	0.3	79.7	2.1	10.0	2.9	4.9
Jalgaon	24.7	15.9	5.2	21.7	31.4	0.1	1.1	22.9	6.6	23.7	11.1	31.9
Wardha	27.8	11.9	12.5	25.7	21.1	0.1	0.3	10.0	6.4	20.9	14.0	46.3
Cuttack	42.4	12.1	9.5	16.6	17.3	0.1	1.5	17.7	3.4	23.7	11.4	39.8
Bhubaneshwar	43.2	11.2	7.2	19.5	16.8	0.5	0.7	8.9	7.6	21.3	8.4	49.3
Raurkela	48.3	11.4	6.5	17.6	14.9	0.3	0.8	43.0	4.0	16.0	12.3	21.9
Ludhiana	48.0	2.9	1.6	19.7	23.7	0.0	0.2	47.8	7.1	19.7	7.5	15.2
Amritsar	35.4	2.6	2.1	31.4	24.3	0.0	0.2	31.4	4.8	27.2	9.9	25.3
Jalandhar	34.3	2.0	1.5	34.2	26.3	0.0	3.8	25.5	4.2	26.0	10.2	29.3
Jaipur	43.5	9.0	6.8	26.2	13.6	0.9	1.4	19.2	7.7	26.6	9.3	33.7
Jodhpur	37.7	5.8	8.2	22.1	24.7	4.8	2.2	16.7	6.7	19.9	9.9	38.3
Kota	49.4	9.1	5.7	24.9	9.7	0.9	0.3	26.5	10.3	20.5	11.9	27.2
Bikaner	36.3	5.4	8.6	33.6	13.6	0.7	1.3	12.2	17.7	17.0	11.7	37.0
Ajmer	34.9	6.3	7.7	25.6	22.1	0.5	1.6	19.3	5.1	21.1	13.9	36.8
Udaipur	40.1	8.9	11.1	22.4	16.5	3.1	0.6	17.7	4.9	25.0	14.0	32.7
Bhilwara	50.6	10.7	4.2	21.6	11.6	0.7	1.1	38.2	5.8	21.6	8.2	22.8
Ganganagar	29.2	3.4	1.1	38.3	22.4	0.0	1.9	22.9	5.8	29.3	9.2	29.5
Chennai	47.2	5.6	4.1	26.8	14.8	0.2	0.3	19.8	5.9	33.8	9.9	29.7
Coimbatore	48.9	4.6	3.1	22.3	18.6	0.1	2.2	38.5	5.1	25.8	7.5	20.5
Madurai	37.6	5.3	5.1	21.5	27.6	0.0	0.7	20.5	5.3	36.4	12.4	24.2
Tiruchchirappalli	42.3	5.0	6.6	24.6	19.0	0.4	1.5	28.2	4.9	30.2	11.7	22.7
Erode	46.7	6.3	2.0	26.1	17.3	0.0	1.4	36.0	5.2	30.5	11.2	15.1
Kanpur	36.9	9.5	5.1	21.1	24.1	0.0	0.4	30.5	2.3	22.5	11.0	32.6
Lucknow	38.3	8.0	8.8	25.5	16.8	0.0	0.5	10.4	6.9	22.5	8.8	48.2
Varanasi	33.2	8.4	17.4	19.9	18.2	0.1	1.9	17.4	2.4	21.4	17.6	37.6
Agra	27.4	7.3	2.0	24.7	21.8	0.0	3.0	17.3	3.6	22.2	11.4	41.7
Meerut	34.9	6.9	2.0	27.3	20.6	0.0	3.8	21.8	4.9	22.6	8.5	36.3
Allahabad	21.6	5.0	13.5	13.2	43.3	0.1	2.1	8.6	2.9	19.6	10.9	54.7
Bareilly	33.3	4.8	3.5	28.3	22.2	0.0	2.7	8.8	3.2	17.2	14.7	50.7
Dehradun	38.3	6.3	8.1	29.7	15.0	0.2	0.5	15.3	7.0	19.9	7.5	47.2
Muzaffarnagar	30.9	9.6	4.3	31.9	20.9	0.0	2.2	14.0	5.4	30.8	10.6	35.1
Mathura	30.3	7.2	3.6	35.7	21.1	0.0	2.5	14.6	3.5	20.7	11.5	46.1
Hardwar	48.0	4.6	5.2	25.4	15.9	0.2	0.3	42.2	4.4	17.8	6.7	26.4
Kolkata	36.0	5.2	2.9	25.4	28.7	0.2	0.5	23.8	4.0	27.4	14.8	28.6
Asansol	49.6	6.3	4.0	21.3	14.9	21.6	0.5	26.9	3.3	17.4	11.7	17.1
Durgapur	51.0	5.3	3.7	19.3	16.5	0.4	1.2	51.1	3.1	12.0	5.1	26.0
Kharagpur	35.9	5.3	8.3	22.6	26.0	0.1	0.4	12.5	1.9	17.5	39.2	27.7
Barddhaman	35.0	6.2	5.7	26.0	24.2	0.3	0.7	15.8	5.6	27.9	18.2	28.5
Siliguri	36.0	13.1	3.3	29.9	15.4	0.0	0.5	10.8	5.5	38.0	19.1	24.6
Medinipur	36.8	5.6	10.2	24.4	22.1	0.1	0.4	12.5	4.2	23.4	9.4	45.6

Sources: Census of India, 1991©, All-India, B-Series, Economic Tables, and D-Series, Migration Tables (b), Registrar General and Census Commissioner's Office, New Delhi.

RMEMP	Employment as the reason for migration, males	MNF	Percentage of workers in manufacturing, total
RMBUSI	Business as the reason for migration, males	CONS	Percentage of workers in construction, total
RMEDU	Education as the reason for migration, males	TC	Percentage of workers in trade/commerce, total
RMFAMMOV	Movement of family as reason for migration, males	TRANS	Percentage of workers in transport, total
RMOTHER	Reason for migration other categories, males	SERV	Percentage of workers in services, total
MINS	Percentage of workers in mining, of total workers	HHIND	Percentage of workers in household industry, total

1. Employment migration to service centres (Canonical correlation, 0.61).
2. Migration for employment, business and education, but not to any specific centres. They are not going to service and construction centres (Canonical correlation, 0.40).
3. Business migration to trade-commerce and service centres (Canonical correlation, 0.26).
4. Employment migration and familial migration to manufacturing centres (Canonical correlation, 0.16).

These canonical linkages are self-explanatory. These state and confirm that male migration for employment and business are attracted to manufacturing centres amidst class I cities; and migration for familial reasons occurs to construction centres or household industry centres.

Table 8.3 ***Canonical Structure Matrix: Canonical Linkages between Reasons for Migration and Factor Scores on Economic Structure of 289 Class I Cities (1991) (Males) (after factor analysing socio-economic matrix)***

	Canonical Variate Pairs			
	1	*2*	*3*	*4*
A. Dependent Matrix (Reasons for migration)		*Canonical Loadings*		
1. Employment	**0.61**	**0.55**	–0.30	**0.49**
2. Business	0.41	**0.44**	**0.82**	–0.16
3. Education	–0.64	**0.66**	–0.15	0.02
4. Family Moved	–0.24	0.25	0.46	**0.86**
B. Independent Variables (Socio-economic Factors: Economic structure of cities)				
1. Service sector	**0.73**	**–0.49**	**0.45**	0.19
2. Manufacturing sector	–0.33	–0.25	–0.11	**0.90**
3. Trade/Commerce	–0.57	–0.21	**0.77**	–0.18
4. Construction sector	–0.18	**–0.81**	–0.44	–0.34
C. Canonical Correlations	**0.61**	**0.40**	**0.26**	**0.16**
D. Meaning of Canonical Linkages	*Employment migration to service centres*	*Migration for employment business, education, but not to any specific centres. They not going to service and construction centres*	*Business migration to trade/ commerce centres and service centres*	*Employment migration and migration of family to manufacturing centres*
E. Trace Correlation	= **0.39**			
Chi Square	= 208.8			
Significance	= 0.0001			

Inputs are from Table 8.1. and factor scores of Table 8.2 (see Appendix). Negative high loadings often not considered.

(B) *Canonical Analysis between Reasons for Migration of Males and Economic Variables of 289 Class I Cities of India:* Following *five* final canonical linkages were found out, *without factor analysing socio-economic variables* (Tables 8.1 and 8.4).

1. Employment migration of the males occurs to manufacturing centres of class I cities (canonical correlation 0.65).
2. Migration of the males for other miscellaneous kinds of reasons occur where service sector of the economy is less and household industry more (canonical correlation 0.47).
3. Migration of the males for familial reasons occurs to construction centres (canonical correlation 0.35).
4. Migration of the males for business purpose occurs to manufacturing centres (canonical correlation 0.24).
5. The fifth one is not significant. Results of Tables 8.3 and 8.4 have much similarities, thus confirming the realities occurring.

Table 8.4 *Canonical Structure Matrix: Linkages between Reasons for Migration (Males) and Economic Variables of 289 Class I Cities, India, 1991 (without factor analysing socio-economic variables)*

	Canonical Variate Pairs				
	1	2	3	4	5
A. Dependent Matrix (Reasons for Migration)	*Canonical Loadings*				
1. Employment	**0.71**	0.39	**0.56**	–0.76	–0.55
2. Business	**0.43**	0.05	0.40	**0.38**	–0.30
3. Education	–0.44	–0.06	0.28	–0.29	–0.43
4. Family moved	–0.15	0.37	**0.53**	–0.38	–0.06
5. Others	0.31	**0.84**	0.39	–0.30	–0.65
B. Independent Matrix (Socio-economic Variables)					
1. Mining workers	0.34	–0.25	0.32	–0.66	–0.23
2. Household Ind.	–0.29	**0.49**	0.10	–0.09	0.22
3. Manufacturing	**0.63**	–0.19	0.45	**0.65**	–0.48
4. Construction	–0.24	–0.17	**0.71**	–0.01	0.10
5. Trade/Commerce	–0.37	0.32	0.23	0.04	–0.38
6. Transport	0.14	0.01	0.20	–0.17	–0.59
7. Service workers	–0.44	**–0.73**	0.30	0.33	–0.42
C. Canonical Correlation	**0.65**	**0.47**	**0.35**	**0.24**	0.04
D. Meaning of Canonical Linkages	*Employment migration to manufacturing centres*	*Other kinds of migration where service is less and HH industry more*	*Family moved to construction centres, also some employment migration*	*Migration for business to manufacturing centres*	*Not significant*
E. Trace Correlation	= **0.41**				
Chi Square	= 281.2				
Significance	= 0.0001				

Note: Input data for canonical analysis taken from Table 8.1. High negative loadings often not considered.

Table 8.5(a) *Migration Variables (Males), Economic Structure of Class I Cities and Investment, Selected 82 Cities, India, 1991 (out of total 200 Class I cities analysed)*

CITY	LTMI GTOT	LTM IGM	VRU TOTM	VUU TOTM	PRUT OTM	PUUT OTM	MINS	MNF	CONS	TC	TRANS	SERV	PCB DEP	PCB CSSI	PCBC IND
Hyderabad	1114725	566985	302749	262956	53	47	0.6	30.0	9.1	21.4	10.8	27.1	12826	831	4934
Vijayawada	325270	154281	101561	52710	66	34	0.4	15.1	4.8	27.9	25.8	24.3	2348	125	361
Warangal	142074	64364	40624	23620	63	37	0.5	11.9	7.6	24.2	18.7	32.9	1295	70	181
Nellore	108081	51481	34917	16564	68	32	0.1	15.6	7.6	28.7	14.5	28.9	1522	98	195
Tirupati	93783	46368	25981	20387	56	44	0.0	8.3	7.6	27.0	14.0	41.2	1712	72	182
Dibrugarh	38040	19784	10833	8931	59	41	0.2	7.5	6.6	27.3	18.7	35.3	2259	524	1163
Patna	334716	138549	97012	41187	70	30	0.1	4.6	2.1	19.6	5.2	65.7	5085	206	631
Dhanbad	367875	187703	156783	30200	84	16	46.3	7.3	2.1	14.4	8.0	19.5	2769	220	493
Ranchi	225067	104607	67347	36980	65	35	0.1	4.9	1.9	15.4	5.3	69.5	3519	241	655
Gaya	54770	9640	7540	2010	78	21	0.0	6.6	3.7	21.1	15.5	50.2	1173	43	87
Muzaffarpur	81909	36091	27381	8710	76	24	0.2	8.4	3.5	30.1	10.1	44.2	1265	78	128
Delhi	2988924	1637479	936449	698518	57	43	0.1	22.1	9.6	24.2	9.1	33.3	25009	1194	4948
Ahmadabad	1089518	544417	339193	204734	62	38	0.6	38.6	4.9	23.6	9.0	22.2	8478	700	3113
Surat	735963	410150	309840	99170	76	24	0.2	62.3	3.9	17.5	4.2	11.1	4958	522	1254
Vadodara	473961	232133	148742	81771	64	36	1.7	37.1	7.0	18.2	9.0	25.8	6758	567	3061
Rajkot	260464	122357	69886	52391	57	43	0.3	31.5	7.2	25.4	10.4	22.8	3845	320	576
Bhavanagar	109609	47499	31655	15814	67	33	0.2	39.7	4.4	21.4	11.2	20.8	2275	169	573
Jamnagar	88914	36478	20708	15740	57	43	0.1	31.6	5.0	20.9	11.4	28.9	3594	202	849
Faridabad	320026	173061	101492	70379	59	41	1.0	54.3	6.0	13.9	4.7	18.8	4546	964	3432
Gurgaon	55788	23874	10210	13514	43	57	0.0	22.7	5.5	23.5	9.0	37.4	3734	381	1458
Shimla	68061	39632	23310	16229	59	41	0.0	5.0	12.4	16.6	9.4	53.3	6734	82	388
Mysore	219096	106552	45190	60892	43	57	0.1	23.3	7.7	26.2	10.2	29.4	2302	209	679

Cont'd...

...*Cont'd*

Hubli-Dharwar	222599	105657	52805	50732	51	48	0.2	20.9	6.3	29.7	13.3	26.9	1893	119	259
Mangalore	130001	59140	29300	29060	50	50	1.1	18.6	9.4	26.3	14.8	26.5	6021	389	771
Belgaum	151520	69054	39212	28842	57	43	0.2	24.7	5.2	27.9	9.1	28.4	1880	81	291
Gulbarga	90061	43820	30380	13440	69	31	0.1	10.0	7.9	25.6	14.1	38.5	1170	91	171
Shimoga	82237	40731	21163	19558	52	48	0.1	13.9	7.2	33.9	11.0	29.4	1720	113	473
Kochi	281564	110613	62983	47430	57	43	0.5	26.6	7.1	27.3	13.4	21.6	7136	472	2223
Thiruvanath.	148280	69370	39080	29800	57	43	0.2	10.9	5.3	26.3	10.6	42.6	5651	122	411
Kozhikode	168950	65210	46190	18530	71	29	0.6	18.1	7.7	30.5	13.3	23.7	2492	117	328
Kannur	97809	43859	26112	17577	60	40	0.6	23.5	7.6	29.8	10.4	21.1	2832	119	231
Indore	341759	156582	81312	75210	52	48.	0.0	26.5	6.2	28.6	10.1	27.1	6442	732	2886
Jabalpur	256621	118557	57563	60094	49	51	0.3	28.0	5.8	18.2	11.6	31.9	2772	161	640
Gwalior	176291	72400	40150	30350	56	44	0.4	23.3	7.6	17.7	7.7	40.8	3697	315	1021
Durg-Bhilai	382802	196162	133751	61781	68	32	0.3	42.9	7.8	16.2	9.7	21.1	1997	152	442
Raipur	210051	101843	60273	41560	59	41	0.3	17.6	6.5	27.7	17.8	25.6	1193	164	353
Ujjain	117013	47644	21914	25620	46	54	0.4	23.3	6.9	20.9	10.7	35.2	2239	156	777
G. Mumbai	4339787	2442426	1693112	745954	69	31	0.2	37.1	5.3	24.4	12.5	18.8	52985	1515	10578
Pune	673705	333542	188632	144570	57	43	0.2	36.2	12.6	17.3	8.3	23.7	5386	437	2106
Nagpur	296302	139627	79832	59465	57	43	1.2	20.4	11.8	21.9	14.5	27.2	4082	259	643
Nashik	247458	119636	65657	53929	55	45	0.1	34.4	9.3	15.5	7.6	30.0	1581	120	283
Solapur	148770	65328	41498	23830	63	37	0.2	28.9	5.2	22.1	11.1	28.1	1256	84	239
Aurangabad	147324	71742	46502	25140	65	35	0.1	31.0	9.4	17.8	7.4	31.1	1456	185	648
Amravati	125934	57083	37546	19507	66	34	0.1	12.4	8.7	22.6	12.3	39.7	1278	51	85
Kolhapur	148890	67783	40453	27320	60	40	0.3	21.7	8.9	29.6	11.1	26.1	1503	179	394
Bhiwandi	215173	141898	95362	46476	67	33	0.0	79.7	2.1	10.0	2.9	4.9	3687	432	1594
Jalagaon	109389	49707	29364	20343	59	41	0.1	22.9	6.6	23.7	11.1	31.9	1122	58	124
Cuttack	155084	82610	61830	20530	75	25	0.1	17.7	3.4	23.7	11.4	39.8	1388	77	256

Cont'd...

...Cont'd

Bhubanesh.	181483	105056	71408	33178	68	32	0.5	8.9	7.6	21.3	8.4	49.3	2634	117	563
Raurkela	164904	91103	63873	27160	70	30	0.3	43.0	4.0	16.0	12.3	21.9	2289	207	449
Ludhiana	431550	203530	92697	107943	46	54	0.0	47.8	7.1	19.7	7.5	15.2	8726	1504	2705
Amritsar	162919	66092	38282	27710	58	42	0.0	31.4	4.8	27.2	9.9	25.3	6436	497	971
Jalandhar	153606	68050	33610	34160	50	50	0.0	25.5	4.2	26.0	10.2	29.3	14414	757	1157
Jaipur	423338	210824	116704	93030	56	44	0.9	19.2	7.7	26.6	9.3	33.7	3934	234	655
Jodhpur	110780	53168	33305	18573	63	35	4.8	16.7	6.7	19.9	9.9	38.3	2256	249	413
Kota	190828	91480	52256	38374	57	42	0.9	26.5	10.3	20.5	11.9	27.2	1966	124	657
Bikaner	76940	34880	19080	15690	55	45	0.7	12.2	17.7	17.0	11.7	37.0	2306	102	147
Ajmer	88898	33360	14340	18850	43	57	0.5	19.3	5.1	21.1	13.9	36.8	2690	166	396
Udaipur	77396	38393	20780	17593	54.	46	3.1	17.7	4.9	25.0	14.0	32.7	1885	100	391
Bhilwara	72013	31646	20591	10955	65	35	0.7	38.2	5.8	21.6	8.2	22.8	1173	185	747
Ganganagar	58191	26663	16378	10215	62	38	0.0	22.9	5.8	29.3	9.2	29.5	1597	52	104
Coimbatore	301430	148239	68470	79359	46	54	0.1	38.5	5.1	25.8	7.5	20.5	5294	1005	2630
Madurai	270368	128113	55640	71723	44	56	0.0	20.5	5.3	36.4	12.4	24.2	2116	194	576
Tiruchchi.	222628	102540	52100	50280	51	49	0.4	28.2	4.9	30.2	11.7	22.7	2090	192	481
Salem	98616	43116	23720	18896	55	44	0.7	21.0	4.2	31.3	10.8	24.5	2095	192	502
Tirunelveli	99470	43500	26380	16920	61	39	0.5	19.3	4.5	30.7	11.1	32.1	1894	107	318
Erode	161061	77367	38344	38753	50	50	0.0	36.0	5.2	30.5	11.2	15.1	2562	193	366
Thanjavur	65709	28744	14534	14190	51	49	0.0	10.8	5.0	34.7	9.4	37.8	1921	53	106
Lucknow	451261	219778	103740	114918	47	52	0.0	10.4	6.9	22.5	8.8	48.2	8345	267	1159
Varanasi	72960	29870	17100	12410	57	42	0.1	17.4	2.4	21.4	17.6	37.6	2968	282	386
Agra	116765	30129	15180	14929	50	50	0.0	17.3	3.6	22.2	11.4	41.7	3243	380	642
Meerut	115770	33790	17970	14663	53	44	0.0	21.8	4.9	22.6	8.5	36.3	2801	201	700
Allahabad	127772	51050	18940	27010	37	53	0.1	8.6	2.9	19.6	10.9	54.7	2333	74	200
Jhansi	97542	35286	14126	21020	40	60	0.1	11.9	4.5	13.5	28.0	37.8	2237	56	193

Cont'd...

...Cont'd

Dehradun	147972	70977	34868	35999	49	51	0.2	15.3	7.0	19.9	7.5	47.2	10105	124	901
Mathura	67051	20933	10570	10353	51	49	0.0	14.6	3.5	20.7	11.5	46.1	1722	104	184
Asansol	237534	109856	76716	32290	70	30	21.6	26.9	3.3	17.4	11.7	17.1	2287	79	387
Siliguri	82401	45237	24232	20785	54	46	0.0	10.8	5.5	38.0	19.1	24.6	2748	227	432
Medinipur	37154	15810	10610	5120	67	32	0.1	12.5	4.2	23.4	9.4	45.6	925	46	100
Bankura	32546	11623	7244	4379	62	38	0.3	11.0	5.0	26.6	15.2	36.3	838	27	89
Basirhat	16357	5407	3830	1577	71	29	0.0	15.0	4.9	33.1	11.6	28.2	2288	81	229
Kolkata	1381157	324572	192296	132276	59	41	0.2	34.5	3.5	24.9	10.1	23.3	34856	1621	9117

Sources: Census of India, 1991, All-India(b), D-Series, Migration Tables, and B-Series(c), Economic Tables.

LTMIGTOT	Volume of lifetime migration, total
LTMIGM	Lifetime migration, males
VRUTOTM	Volume of rural to urban migration, males
VUUTOTM	Volume of urban to urban migration, males
PRUTOTM	Percentage of rural to urban migration, males
PUUTOTM	Percentage of urban to urban migration, males
MINS	Percentage of total workes in mining
MNF	Percentage of total workers in manufacturing
CONS	Percentage of total workers in construction
TC	Percentage of total workes in trade/commerce
TRANS	Percentage of total workers in transport
SERV	Percentage of total workers in services
PCBDEP	Per capita bank deposit
PCBCSSI	Per capita bank credit to small scale industries
PCBCIND	Per capita bank credit to general industry

(C) *Canonical analysis between Volume of Rural to Urban Migration and Urban to urban Migration of males and Economic Structure-cum-Investment variables of 200 Class I cities of India:* The following four canonical linkages emerged out (Tables 8.5(a) and (b), Table 8.6).

Basic data are presented in Tables 8.5(a) and (b), and the final canonical findings shown in Table 8.6.

Table 8.5(b) *Occupational Categories and Reasons for Migration of Male Migrants to 200 Class I Cities of India, 1991 (data of only 78 cities shown here, out of 200 analysed)*

CITY	*OPR OFM*	*OAD MINM*	*OCL ERK*	*OSA LES*	*OSE RV*	*OPR OD*	*RME MP*	*RMB USI*	*RME DU*	*RMF AMM OV*	*RMOT HER*
Hyderabad	12.2	8.5	14.7	13.2	7.3	41.3	43.9	5.1	5.3	26.9	17.6
Vijayawada	7.1	4.7	12.7	19.6	8.4	46.3	46.0	4.2	4.0	23.7	20.2
Warangal	13.8	4.2	16.5	15.8	7.9	39.8	42.5	3.7	12.2	15.5	24.5
Nellore	8.4	3.3	13.8	21.7	8.6	42.3	44.7	4.8	7.1	24.0	17.4
Tirupati	13.4	5.7	18.7	18.5	11.1	30.4	45.1	4.6	12.4	24.4	12.0
Dibrugarh	9.7	3.5	14.9	23.3	12.8	32.8	35.2	20.9	9.0	15.8	17.6
Patna	19.6	9.1	27.7	13.5	12.8	14.0	32.6	8.5	12.9	23.7	16.2
Dhanbad	7.7	2.5	9.5	12.0	6.8	58.6	55.9	8.1	7.3	17.8	9.4
Ranchi	23.0	9.3	21.2	11.3	13.1	18.3	45.4	7.1	12.9	21.7	9.7
Gaya	21.9	5.0	21.7	16.0	9.8	22.3	25.8	5.4	9.2	15.1	18.4
Muzaffarpur	18.0	7.3	21.2	19.7	11.4	18.0	34.0	7.5	16.4	20.5	12.8
Delhi	7.7	6.4	12.8	17.9	9.5	43.6	52.4	7.7	1.9	28.4	8.9
Ahmedabad	6.8	6.9	11.9	15.4	7.1	50.4	34.6	17.4	3.0	19.5	23.5
Surat	2.8	3.2	3.6	13.9	4.1	70.7	44.4	16.7	1.4	20.8	15.9
Vadodara	11.4	7.4	15.6	11.6	9.5	43.2	31.9	14.5	4.1	21.5	24.3
Rajkot	6.1	5.9	12.5	17.5	5.1	51.6	19.0	23.3	3.6	22.8	29.7
Bhavanagar	7.3	4.7	13.5	14.5	5.8	52.0	19.4	21.7	4.5	24.6	28.4
Jamnagar	8.1	4.6	13.3	14.8	8.4	46.9	18.5	20.0	4.5	28.7	25.8
Faridabad	7.2	6.0	9.7	11.3	5.6	58.7	50.9	7.9	1.7	29.1	9.7
Gurgaon	16.4	9.2	17.2	16.1	6.8	32.4	29.1	7.5	1.6	38.4	21.9
Shimla	13.6	6.0	29.9	8.7	13.1	25.8	51.0	8.8	10.0	20.5	9.2
Mysore	13.9	6.3	15.4	17.0	9.9	34.7	36.2	4.7	14.6	26.5	16.8
Dharwad	11.9	5.3	19.1	16.3	11.3	33.9	38.5	3.1	12.1	20.8	24.5
Mangalore	9.7	5.5	12.9	15.0	10.6	43.0	33.2	2.3	7.5	34.6	20.3
Belgaum	11.6	6.9	15.9	15.1	12.1	36.6	28.8	9.2	9.7	23.4	27.7
Shimoga	10.9	5.4	16.3	21.6	9.8	33.6	37.0	7.3	7.9	26.2	19.4
Kochi	14.2	10.7	13.3	13.9	7.8	36.0	35.7	2.6	3.3	32.5	22.2
Thiruv. puram	22.5	11.6	19.8	12.1	7.8	22.7	35.6	3.1	5.7	25.6	18.2
Kozhikode	12.1	9.4	11.4	18.0	7.5	36.9	18.9	1.6	5.5	39.2	30.7
Indore	7.5	8.9	10.0	16.6	9.7	42.8	43.6	8.6	5.2	23.1	18.4
Jabalpur	9.6	6.0	17.4	10.4	9.3	43.2	44.4	7.0	4.9	25.9	16.2
Gwalior	15.7	8.5	14.4	8.8	9.3	37.6	36.0	7.1	9.1	26.0	19.6
Bhilai	6.6	6.1	7.1	11.8	6.2	59.9	51.6	7.2	3.6	25.5	10.7
Ujjain	11.4	5.3	13.4	13.3	9.2	43.2	37.7	7.7	5.0	26.3	22.2
Gr. Mumbai	5.7	4.8	10.9	17.2	9.5	50.6	46.5	12.9	4.8	17.1	17.6
Pune	8.3	7.3	10.7	11.3	9.1	51.8	30.6	12.6	4.2	21.9	28.7
Nagpur	9.8	6.3	12.2	13.6	9.6	47.3	29.6	18.5	8.8	22.5	19.0
Nashik	9.7	5.5	12.5	10.1	9.0	50.6	29.6	13.1	4.6	21.5	30.5
Solapur	11.0	3.8	14.3	15.1	9.8	44.8	23.5	13.9	7.6	18.5	34.9

Cont'd...

...Cont'd

Amravati	13.2	3.9	18.1	15.9	9.6	37.6	24.0	14.5	11.6	25.3	23.1
Kolhapur	11.9	5.9	17.3	17.5	7.8	38.3	21.9	16.3	8.2	17.9	34.1
Jalgaon	11.1	4.0	17.0	15.2	9.9	41.6	24.7	15.9	5.2	21.7	31.4
Wardha	17.5	3.8	25.1	14.1	8.1	29.6	27.8	11.9	12.5	25.7	21.1
Cuttack	11.4	7.0	17.1	15.2	13.5	33.8	42.4	12.1	9.5	16.6	17.3
Bhubaneshwar	13.1	8.5	23.1	13.6	9.1	29.6	43.2	11.2	7.2	19.5	16.8
Raurkela	7.9	5.5	10.7	13.4	8.3	50.1	48.3	11.4	6.5	17.6	14.9
Ludhiana	4.7	2.6	6.3	16.2	5.4	63.1	48.0	2.9	1.6	19.7	23.7
Amritsar	7.4	2.2	11.1	22.3	7.4	47.2	35.4	2.6	2.1	31.4	24.3
Jalandhar	7.3	4.1	11.3	19.5	10.2	44.8	34.3	2.0	1.5	34.2	26.3
Pathankot	10.3	2.8	14.5	24.7	7.3	35.8	29.2	3.4	1.1	38.3	22.4
Jaipur	12.6	6.8	16.1	16.8	9.6	36.0	43.5	9.0	6.8	26.2	13.6
Jodhpur	9.7	3.6	11.8	13.8	13.4	38.5	37.7	5.8	8.2	22.1	24.7
Kota	11.0	3.8	13.3	14.7	8.6	46.9	49.4	9.1	5.7	24.9	9.7
Bikaner	21.0	5.4	17.9	11.3	11.4	28.8	36.3	5.4	8.6	33.6	13.6
Ajmer	15.0	5.3	18.8	14.3	12.6	31.6	34.9	6.3	7.7	25.6	22.1
Udaipur	14.4	6.4	17.2	16.2	12.2	31.4	40.1	8.9	11.1	22.4	16.5
Ganganagar	9.2	3.5	11.8	21.8	10.5	40.4	29.2	3.4	1.1	38.3	22.4
Coimbatore	7.6	9.5	9.2	15.0	7.5	50.3	48.9	4.6	3.1	22.3	18.6
Madurai	8.9	8.9	13.6	22.4	9.3	35.9	37.6	5.3	5.1	21.5	27.6
Tiruchch.i	8.4	6.0	13.7	20.9	8.8	41.5	42.3	5.0	6.6	24.6	19.0
Salem	9.0	9.6	12.1	18.0	8.5	41.9	36.2	5.8	3.0	21.6	30.6
Tirunelveli	10.7	5.0	18.3	20.2	9.8	35.1	36.1	3.2	10.0	24.6	23.3
Thanjavur	13.2	5.8	18.5	26.5	7.5	27.8	32.0	5.1	7.5	21.7	30.9
Lucknow	15.0	8.1	24.5	13.0	10.3	21.9	38.3	8.0	8.8	25.5	16.8
Varanasi	15.6	4.1	16.8	15.6	13.3	30.0	33.2	8.4	17.4	19.9	18.2
Agra	9.2	2.7	14.3	17.3	8.1	37.4	27.4	7.3	2.0	24.7	21.8
Meerut	10.4	3.7	13.8	17.1	7.6	41.6	34.9	6.9	2.0	27.3	20.6
Allahabad	18.9	3.9	26.7	10.8	13.2	20.2	21.6	5.0	13.5	13.2	43.3
Gorakhpur	18.8	6.4	20.8	14.7	14.5	20.1	33.8	8.5	12.7	24.0	17.1
Jhansi	8.9	2.3	18.5	10.0	11.5	38.2	39.4	6.6	3.8	27.6	19.7
Dehradun	14.7	7.5	16.2	14.3	8.9	32.5	38.3	6.3	8.1	29.7	15.0
Mathura	13.6	3.4	14.6	15.8	9.5	36.6	30.3	7.2	3.6	35.7	21.1
Asansol	6.3	4.3	11.4	12.8	8.4	54.4	49.6	6.3	4.0	21.3	14.9
Siliguri	5.6	6.2	12.4	28.6	8.7	36.4	36.0	13.1	3.3	29.9	15.4
Medinipur	13.8	3.1	24.3	17.5	13.2	25.5	36.8	5.6	10.2	24.4	22.1
Bankura	13.0	3.3	18.8	21.0	12.6	28.7	41.6	4.3	5.3	22.0	21.8
Basirhat	11.5	4.4	12.9	24.6	7.9	36.4	13.6	3.8	4.3	24.7	51.8
Kolkata	6.0	3.4	13.5	8.1	178	48.3	36.2	4.4	6.3	31.0	20.5

Source: Census of India, 1991 (b), D-Series, Migration Tables, R.G. and Census Commissioner's Office, New Delhi.

OPROFM	Occupational category, professional, males
OADMINM	Occupational category, administration, males
OCLERK	Occupational category, clerical. males
OSALES	Occupational category, sales, males
OSERV	Occupational category, service, males
OPROD	Occupational category, production, males
RMEMP	Reason for migration – employment, males
RMBUSI	Reason for migration – business, males
RMEDU	Reason for migration – education, males
RMFAMMOV	Reason for migration – family moved, males
RMOTHER	Reason for migration – other than specified, males

Final Canonical Links (of 200 Class I Cities)

In Table 8.6, the following four canonical inter-relationships emerged by performing canonical analysis of data of Table 8.5(a). Overall Trace correlation is also high and significant. Linkages are:

1. Volume of rural to urban male migration to Class I cities is more, where bank deposit more and investment to industries also high (Canonical correlation 0.94).
2. Volume of urban to urban male migration is more, where service sectors of economy more important, and credit available to small scale industries high (Canonical correlation 0.49).

Table 8.6 *Canonical Structure Matrix: Canonical Linkages between Migration Variables and Economic Structure of Cities and Investment therein, 200 Class I Cities, Males (1991)*

	Canonical Variate Pairs			
	1	*2*	*3*	*4*
A. Dependent Matrix (Migration Variables)		*Canonical Loadings*		
1. Volume of rural to urban migration (Males)	**0.94**	–0.62	**0.54**	–0.02
2. Volume of urban to urban migration (Males)	–0.16	**0.64**	–0.59	0.02
3. Percentage of rural to urban migration to total migration (Males)	0.14	0.30	0.26	**–0.71**
4. Per cent of urban to urban migration to total migration (Males)	0.25	0.35	**0.54**	–0.70
B. Independent Matrix (Socio-economic Variables: Economic Structure of Cities)				
1. Mining workers	0.07	0.06	–0.24	**0.36**
2. Manufacturing	0.14	0.21	**0.62**	**0.58**
3. Construction	–0.01	**0.31**	–0.19	–0.01
4. Trade/commerce	0.05	0.20	0.21	0.24
5. Transport	0.08	0.09	0.34	0.22
6. Service workers	0.06	**0.36**	0.07	**0.65**
7. Bank deposit	**0.73**	–0.33	**0.38**	–0.07
8. Credit to SSI	–0.36	**0.73**	–0.16	0.07
9. Credit to industry	**0.54**	–0.19	**–0.43**	0.02
C. Canonical Correlations	**0.94**	**0.49**	**0.28**	**0.14**
D. Meaning of Canonical Linkages	*Vol. of rural to urban male migration is high, where bank deposit and investment in industry is also high*	*Vol. of urban to urban male migration is more, where service is more and credit to SSI is more*	*Percentage of urban to urban male migration and vol. rural to urban male migration is high in MNF centres and where deposit is more but where industrial investment less*	*In manufacturing, service and mining centres, percentage of urban to urban and rural to urban migration is low*
E. Trace Correlation	= **0.55**			
Chi Square	= 482.1			
Significance	= 0.0001			

Note: The data for canonical input are taken from Table 8.5(a).

3. Share of urban to urban male migration (to total volume of migration) and volume of rural to urban male migration is high in manufacturing centres among Class I cities, and where bank deposit is also more (Canonical correlation is 0.28).
4. In manufacturing, service, and mining centres, the percentage share of urban to urban migration (of total volume of migration) and of rural to urban migration are low (Canonical correlation 0.14).

(D) *Other Important Canonical Findings of Class I Cities*

Tables 8.5(a) and (b) give data of occupational absorption of migrants in 200 class I cities, and related data. Tables 8.5(a) and (b) are canonically analysed. Their corresponding canonical findings are presented in Tables 8.7 to 8.9. These have different sets of dependent variables, and, as such, each time reveals new kinds of causal relationships. Ensuing tables are self-explanatory, hence not elaborated, except listing main canonical linkages.

Links Between Lifetime Migration and Economic Structure of Cities

With respect to Table 8.7, following two canonical linkages are identified. Overall *Trace correlation* is very high (0.71), explaining 50% of migration matrix:

Table 8.7 *Canonical Structure Matrix: City-level Canonical Analysis of 200 Class I Cities between Two Migration Variables and Nine Socio-economic Variables, 1991 Census*

Variables	*Canonical Variate Pairs*	
	1	2
A. Dependent Matrix (Migration Variables)	*Canonical Loadings*	
1. Lifetime migration, total	–0.04	**0.71**
2. Lifetime migration, males	**0.99**	–0.71
B. Independent Matrix (Socio-Economic Variables)		
1. Mining workers	0.10	0.16
2. Manufacturing workers	0.13	**0.23**
3. Construction workers	0.03	0.14
4. Trade/commerce workers	**0.50**	0.10
5. Transport workers	0.07	0.21
6. Service workers	0.09	**0.41**
7. Per Capita bank deposit	**0.72**	–0.53
8. Investment to small scale industry	–0.32	**0.63**
9. Industrial investment	**0.59**	0.09
C. Canonical Correlation	**0.92**	**0.40**
D. Meaning of Canonical Relationship	*Higher vol. of lifetime mig. of males occurs to trade/commerce centres, where bank deposit and industrial investment are high*	*Lifetime total mig. to service centres, partly manufacturing centres and where SSI investment available*
E. Trace Correlation	= **0.71**	
Chi Square	= 412.91	
Significance	= 0.0001	

Note: The data for canonical input are taken from Table 8.5(a)

1. Higher volume of lifetime migration of males occurs to trade-commerce centres, where bank deposit and industrial investment are high (Canonical correlation, 0.92).
2. Lifetime migration to service centres, partly to manufacturing centres and where investments to small-scale industries available (Canonical correlation, 0.40).

Links Between Occupations of Migrants and Economic Structure of Class I Cities

With respect to Table 8.8, following *six* canonical linkages are found between occupations of migrants and economic centres where they have moved [inputs taken from Tables 8.5(a) and 8.5(b)]. *Trace correlation* is high (0.59):

1. Migrants absorbed in sales and production work are moving to trade-commerce centres (canonical, 0.92).

Table 8.8 *Canonical Structure Matrix: City-level Canonical Linkages between Migration Variables (Occupations) and Socio-economic Variables, Males, 1991*

Variables	*Canonical Variate Pairs*					
	1	*2*	*3*	*4*	*5*	*6*
A. Dependent Matrix (Migration Variables: Occupations)	*Canonical Loadings*					
1. Prof. workers	0.07	–0.03	**0.66**	0.32	0.20	0.21
2. Admin. workers	0.32	0.08	0.02	0.20	–0.17	0.20
3. Clerical workers	0.04	0.01	–0.01	**0.44**	**0.50**	0.24
4. Sales workers	**0.68**	**0.54**	0.30	0.27	0.33	0.27
5. Service workers	0.11	0.08	0.18	0.12	0.20	**0.48**
6. Production workers	**0.64**	–0.83	**0.67**	**0.76**	**0.73**	**0.75**
B. Independent Matrix (Socio-economic Variables: Economic Structure of Cities)						
1. Mining	0.13	–0.18	**0.57**	0.29	**0.45**	0.33
2. Manufacturing.	0.14	–0.28	**0.39**	**0.45**	**0.53**	**0.61**
3. Construction	–0.05	–0.10	0.00	0.23	0.05	–0.01
4. Trade/commerce	**0.79**	**0.72**	**0.48**	0.29	0.22	0.29
5. Transport	0.01	0.01	–0.32	0.10	**0.40**	0.21
6. Service	–0.52	**0.57**	**0.41**	**0.46**	**0.45**	**0.60**
7. Bank deposit	0.01	–0.07	–0.11	–0.23	0.14	–0.06
8. Credit to SSI	0.24	–0.06	–0.11	–0.31	–0.19	–0.05
9. Credit to industry	–0.09	0.15	–0.01	**0.46**	–0.21	0.13
C. Canonical Correlation	**0.92**	**0.91**	**0.45**	**0.36**	**0.24**	**0.18**
D. Meaning of Canonical Linkages	*Migrants in sales and prod. work moving to trade, and commerce centres*	*Migrants in sales moving to trade, commerce, and service centres*	*Prof. and prod. workers moved to mining, service and MNF centres*	*Migrants as clerks and production moved to MNF/service centres where investment high*	*Prod. and clerks moved to mining-transport service centres*	*Prod. workers gone to MNF and service centres*
E. Trace Correlation	= 0.59					
Chi Square	= 779.3					
Significance	= 0.0001					

2. Migrants absorbed in sales are moving to trade-commerce and service centres (Canonical, 0.91).
3. Professional and production-process workers moved to mining, service and manufacturing centres (Canonical, 0.45).
4. Migrants absorbed as clerks and production-process work moved to manufacturing and service centres, where investment high (Canonical, 0.36).
5. Migrants absorbed as production-process workers and clerks moved to mining, transport and service centres (Canonical, 0.24).
6. Production-process workers gone to manufacturing and service centres (Canonical, 0.18).

All these canonical linkages have meaning, they show causal relations between migrant's occupation patterns and economic structures of the centres – where they moved in for jobs. Migration is not a random phenomenon, rather follows a specific pattern. This is a very meaningful revelation.

Table 8.9 *Canonical Structure Matrix: Linkages between Reasons for Migration and Economic Structure of Cities-cum-Investment, Cities, 1991, Males*

Variables	*Canonical Variate Pairs*				
	1	*2*	*3*	*4*	*5*
A. Dependent Matrix (Migration Variables)			Canonical Loadings		
1. Employment	**0.73**	0.09	**0.53**	**0.67**	–0.13
2. Business	0.33	–0.28	**0.41**	–0.05	–0.57
3. Education	–0.50	–0.31	0.25	**0.48**	–0.33
4. Family moved	–0.22	0.20	**0.51**	0.18	**0.34**
5. Others	0.25	**0.88**	0.47	**0.54**	–0.66
B. Independent Matrix (Economic Variables: Economic Structure of Cities and Investment)					
1. Mining workers	**0.53**	–0.37	0.03	**0.51**	–0.11
2. Manufacturing	**0.73**	**–0.49**	0.26	**0.50**	–0.59
3. Construction	–0.05	–0.26	**0.67**	0.05	0.01
4. Trade/commerce	0.06	–0.07	0.11	0.35	–0.20
5. Transport	0.25	–0.13	0.02	0.21	–0.14
6. Service	0.32	**–0.70**	–0.24	**0.51**	–0.41
7. Bank deposit	0.03	0.09	**0.32**	0.07	0.22
8. Credit to SSI	0.12	0.10	–0.55	–0.22	**0.43**
9. Investment to industry	0.03	–0.18	–0.01	0.04	**–0.43**
C. Canonical Correlations	**0.67**	**0.44**	**0.42**	**0.25**	**0.23**
D. Meaning of Canonical Linkages	*Mining and MNF causes employment migration*	*Migration for other reasons occurs where MNF and service less*	*Family moved and employment migration, where construction high and bank deposit more*	*Educational, employment and other migration more, where service high, also MNF/mining high*	*Family moved where credit to SSI more*
E. Trace Correlation	= **0.43**				
Chi Square	= 215.3				
Significance	= 0.0001				

Note: The data for canonical input are taken from Table 8.5(a) and 8.5(b).

Table 8.10 *Migration Variables (Males), Economic Structure and Investment Variables, 23 Million Cities, India, 1991*

CITY	LTMIGM	MIG (< 1 YR)	MIG (1–9 YR)	MIG (10+YR)	VOLMIG (10+YR)	RMEMP	RMBUS	RMEDU	RMFMOV	RMOTHER	TOTPOP
Greater Mumbai	2,494,516	2.5	33.4	64.1	827507	45.8	11.6	5.5	21.9	14.4	12,596,243
Kolkata	1,381,157	2.5	23.5	74.0	347584	36.2	4.4	6.3	31.0	20.5	11,021,918
Delhi	1,801,830	3.2	40.3	56.5	771281	54.3	6.8	3.2	29.6	5.7	8,419,084
Chennai	769,969	1.3	39.9	58.8	291111	45.2	4.4	5.5	31.7	11.3	5,421,985
Hyderabad	571,895	3.6	52.6	43.8	280647	45.8	3.8	7.5	31.0	10.7	4,344,437
Bangalore	615,975	4.0	45.1	50.9	273560	49.5	4.7	9.7	25.8	9.1	4,130,288
Ahmedabad	557,427	2.0	33.9	64.2	170903	33.0	17.3	5.5	27.8	14.7	3,312,216
Pune	339,222	7.5	46.6	45.9	152620	30.8	12.2	6.4	28.7	20.7	2,493,987
Kanpur	185,915	2.8	39.6	57.6	62710	33.9	9.8	8.9	31.2	14.2	2,029,889
Lucknow	226,828	3.9	49.1	47.1	106170	35.2	7.5	13.5	30.7	11.2	1,669,204
Nagpur	143,507	3.3	41.4	55.3	58165	31.2	15.7	14.4	23.9	13.6	1,664,006
Surat	412,260	3.3	55.4	41.3	215105	48.9	16.2	1.8	24.0	8.5	1,518,950
Jaipur	220,864	4.0	46.5	49.5	103533	42.2	7.7	10.6	29.6	9.3	1,518,235
Kochi	112,333	7.7	48.0	44.3	56383	38.3	2.6	5.4	35.9	15.1	1,140,605
Vadodara	236,533	3.3	39.4	57.3	86350	32.4	13.4	7.7	27.4	15.7	1,126,824
Indore	163,512	4.2	42.0	53.8	63650	45.1	7.1	8.0	26.9	12.2	1,109,056
Coimbatore	150,159	4.3	45.6	50.1	67070	51.8	4.0	4.6	26.7	11.2	1,100,746
Patna	139,649	7.5	46.6	45.9	NA	NA	NA	NA	NA	NA	1,099,647
Madurai	130,063	2.3	38.4	59.3	70643	27.3	6.3	17.8	28.7	14.0	1,085,914
Bhopal	215,896	3.8	38.9	57.3	45300	38.3	5.1	9.1	26.1	18.8	1,062,771
Vishakhapatnam	228,652	3.5	51.7	44.9	113550	44.6	3.5	6.2	29.6	14.6	1,057,118
Ludhiana	226,680	4.4	45.9	49.7	96503	59.7	2.2	2.8	22.2	10.5	1,042,740
Varanasi	30,460	4.5	47.3	48.2	13910	27.4	8.1	29.0	23.2	10.4	1,030,863

Cont'd...

...*Cont'd*

CITY	*MINS*	*HH*	*MNF*	*CONS*	*TC*	*TRANS*	*SERV*	*PCBDEP*	*PCBCSSI*	*PCBCIND*
Greater Mumbai	0.22	1.41	35.7	4.7	24.1	11.2	21.6	52985	1515	10578
Kolkata	0.15	1.36	34.5	3.5	24.9	10.1	23.3	34856	1621	9117
Delhi	0.11	1.37	23.5	7.6	25.1	8.2	33.1	25009	1194	4948
Chennai	0.12	1.11	25.9	6.6	23.0	10.2	30.2	22630	1714	9417
Hyderabad	0.44	0.50	23.1	8.4	24.3	11.3	28.6	12826	831	4934
Bangalore	0.19	1.42	31.1	8.4	24.3	8.8	24.2	12402	1165	4435
Ahmedabad	0.37	0.80	35.7	4.7	25.1	9.2	22.4	8478	700	3113
Pune	0.17	1.70	30.7	11.1	18.3	7.9	27.4	5386	437	2106
Kanpur	0.02	0.65	27.9	2.0	27.4	7.6	30.6	7974	695	1991
Lucknow	0.08	2.76	13.4	5.0	23.1	7.9	40.6	8345	267	1159
Nagpur	0.83	3.02	20.8	9.6	23.0	12.5	27.3	4082	259	643
Surat	0.17	2.20	55.7	3.4	18.7	4.5	13.3	4958	522	1254
Jaipur	0.58	3.90	22.2	6.4	24.0	8.1	31.8	3934	234	655
Kochi	0.46	1.07	20.4	9.6	21.4	13.9	23.4	7136	472	2223
Vadodra	1.14	0.58	31.9	5.7	20.1	9.0	27.7	6758	567	3061
Indore	0.05	1.29	26.5	5.6	26.2	9.3	27.9	6442	732	2886
Coimbatore	0.09	2.49	36.9	6.1	20.0	7.4	20.1	5294	1005	2630
Patna	0.06	2.46	6.6	2.4	20.3	5.3	48.5	5085	206	631
Madurai	0.09	2.61	27.0	5.5	29.3	9.3	20.5	2116	194	576
Bhopal	0.37	1.05	18.4	11.0	20.3	8.9	35.3	8740	NA	NA
Vishakhapatnam	0.61	0.82	19.3	7.9	15.0	15.2	34.6	3147	107	906
Ludhiana	0.00	0.19	44.5	6.3	20.5	6.2	14.1	8726	1504	2705
Varanasi	0.03	23.42	16.3	2.4	27.1	6.1	20.8	2968	282	386

Note: Bhopal not included in the analysis because of incomplete data.

LTMIGM	Lifetime migration, males	MINS	Per cent workers in mining	CONS	Per cent workers in construction
MIG (< 1 Y)	Migration for less than 1 year, males	HH	Per cent workers in household industry	TC	Per cent workers in trade/commerce
MIG (1–9 Y)	Migration during last 1–9 years, males	PCBDEP	per capita bank deposit	TRANS	Per cent workers in transport
MIG (10+ Y)	Migration for more than 10 years, males	PCBCSSI	Per capita bank credit to SSI	SERV	Per cent workers in service
VOLMIG (10+Y)	Vol. of migrants above 10 years, males	PCBCIND	Per capita bank credit to industry		
TOTPOP	Total population	MNF	Per cent workers in manufacturing		

Links Between Patterns of Migration and Economic Structure of Class I Cities

On the other hand, with regard to Table 8.9, the following *five* canonical links are identified between patterns of migration and the economic structure of the cities:

1. Mining and manufacturing causes employment migration (Canonical correlation, 0.67).
2. Migration for other reasons occurs where manufacturing and service less (Canonical correlation, 0.44).
3. Family migration and employment migration occur, where construction and bank deposit more (Canonical, 0.42).
4. Educational, employment, and other migration more, where services, manufacturing and mining high (Canonical, 0.25).
5. Family moved where credit to small scale industries are more (Canonical, 0.23).

All these are self explanatory, and make sense. That is, there is *almost a one-to-one relationship* between patterns of migration and the economic structure of class I cities of India. Findings may sound axiomatic, but their mathematical proof were so for lacking. Here, canonical models provide that proof of complimentarily or *isomorphism* between the two matrices. *For migration planning, these findings have great policy import: indicating the need to provide essential infrastructure and employment for migrants and economic development of cities.*

Canonical Findings of Migration to Million Cities

Migration of both males and females to 23 Million Cities were separately analysed by performing a series of canonical analyses. Here we present only findings of the analysis of the male migration. Findings of the females are presented in Tables 8.13 to 8.15 (all in Appendix):

(a) *Canonical Linkages between Types of Migration of Males for Various Durations and Economic Structure of Million Cities:* This have generated *three* meaningful linkages (see Tables 8.10 for data and 8.11 for result), as follows:

1. Lifetime migration is high where total population of Million cities is large and bank deposit is high (Canonical correlation 0.98).
2. Migration for 1 to 9 years duration and migration for 10 years or more duration are more to manufacturing and service centres (Canonical correlation is 0.87).
3. Old migration for more than 10 years is more where manufacturing and service sectors were relatively less (Canonical correlation 0.54). The fourth relationship is not statistically significant.

All these canonical linkage equations have very high canonical correlations, 0.98, 0.87, and 0.54, respectively. *Trace correlation* is also high, 0.71, reflecting general overlapping of the two matrices, dependent and independent.

(b) *Canonical Linkages between Reasons for Migration of the Males and Economic Structure of Million Cities-cum-Investment made therein:* It has generated following *seven* canonical equations [using raw socio-economic variables, without factoring upon them, see Tables 8.10 and 8.12]:

Table 8.11 *Canonical Structure Matrix: Linkages between Volume of Migration (Males) and Economic Structure of Million Cities and Investment, 1991*

Variables	*Canonical Variate Pairs*			
	1	*2*	*3*	*4*
A. Dependent Matrix (Migration Variables)		*Canonical Loadings*		
1. Lifetime migrants	**0.99**	–0.09	–0.07	–0.01
2. Migrants (< 1year)	0.06	0.02	0.29	–0.16
3. Migrants (1 to 9 years)	–0.06	**0.62**	**0.52**	–0.66
4. Migrants (10 years +)	0.10	**0.78**	**0.80**	–0.74
B. Independent Matrix (Socio-economic Variables)				
1. Total Population	**0.53**	-0.01	**0.29**	–0.68
2. Mining	0.03	0.10	0.06	–0.01
3. Household Industry	0.04	0.19	–0.29	–0.02
4. Manufacturing	0.23	**0.59**	**–0.63**	–0.09
5. Construction	0.10	–0.17	–0.13	0.14
6. Trade/commerce	0.07	0.30	–0.09	0.07
7. Transport	–0.01	0.35	–0.20	–0.12
8. Service	0.18	**0.45**	**–0.52**	–0.11
9. Bank deposit	**0.69**	–0.34	–0.28	0.40
10. Credit to SSI	0.04	0.23	–0.03	–0.20
11. Credit to industry	–0.37	0.01	0.10	0.52
C. Canonical Correlations	**0.98**	**0.87**	**0.54**	**0.03**
D. Meaning of Canonical Linkages	*Lifetime migration high where total population large and deposit high*	*1–9 yr. mig. and 10 yr. + migration more where MNF and service high*	*1–9 yr. migration and 10 yr. + migration more, where MNF and service less, but city size large*	*Not significant*
E. Trace Correlation	**= 0.71**			
Chi Square	= 73.9			
Significance	= 0.0001			

Note: The input date are taken from Table 8.10 (males).

1. Migration for employment, business, and education occur to large million cities, where manufacturing and service sectors predominate, and where bank deposit is high (Canonical correlation 0.99).
2. Migration for employment, business, and education occur to smaller million cities, where manufacturing and service sectors are more, but where little bank deposit gone (Canonical correlation 0.98).
3. Migration for education occurs to manufacturing centres, service centres and partly to household industry centres (Canonical correlation 0.97).
4. Lifetime migration occurs more where manufacturing is more, and bank deposit more (Canonical correlation 0.85).
5. Employment migration prevails to transport centres and where investment to small scale industries are more (Canonical correlation 0.75).

Table 8.12 *Canonical Matrix: Linkages between Reasons for Migration (Males) and Economic Structure of Cities, Million Cities, 1991*

Variables	*Canonical Variate Pairs*						
	1	*2*	*3*	*4*	*5*	*6*	*7*
			Canonical Loadings				
A. Dependent Matrix (Migration Variables)							
1. Volume of migration (1981–91)	0.04	0.22	0.37	–0.69	–0.12	–0.55	**0.57**
2. Volume of lifetime migrants	0.22	–0.25	–0.39	**0.64**	0.08	**0.50**	–0.56
3. Employment (as reason)	**0.61**	**0.66**	0.52	–0.12	**0.74**	**0.45**	–0.05
4. Business (as reason)	**0.31**	**0.36**	0.27	0.01	0.21	0.26	–0.16
5. Education (as reason)	**0.56**	**0.40**	**0.49**	–0.07	0.50	0.31	0.03
6. Family movement (as reason)	0.28	0.23	0.23	–0.16	0.23	0.24	–0.37
7. Other reasons	0.31	0.33	0.28	–0.26	0.30	0.16	**0.44**
B. Independent Matrix (Socio-economic Variables)							
1. Total Population of city	0.36	–0.10	–0.04	–0.37	–0.18	0.18	0.10
2. Mining workers	–0.03	–0.06	–0.05	0.11	–0.24	–0.01	–0.03
3. Household industry	0.41	0.24	**0.53**	0.28	0.25	0.07	–0.23
4. Manufacturing workers	**0.45**	**0.73**	**0.44**	**0.44**	0.14	0.23	**–0.55**
5. Construction	0.19	0.23	0.29	–0.01	0.09	–0.30	–0.06
6. Trade/commerce	0.18	0.17	0.22	0.13	0.04	0.11	–0.16
7. Transport workers	0.15	0.19	0.10	0.08	**0.39**	**0.39**	–0.20
8. Service workers	**0.47**	**0.49**	**0.55**	0.34	0.12	0.06	**–0.64**
9. Bank deposit	**0.40**	0.12	–0.13	**0.49**	0.11	0.64	0.02
10. Credit to SSI	–0.13	–0.10	–0.21	0.25	**0.62**	0.16	–0.33
11. Credit to industry	–0.14	–0.08	0.10	–0.38	–0.50	**0.46**	0.21
C. Canonical Correlations	**0.99**	**0.98**	**0.98**	**0.85**	**0.75**	**0.62**	**0.51**
D. Meaning of Canonical Linkages	*Migration for employment, business, education to cities, where MNF service, deposit high*	*Migration for employment, business, education to small cities, where MNF service more, deposit less*	*Educational migration to MNF, household industry and service centres*	*Lifetime migration more where MNF high, bank deposit more*	*Employment migration to transport centres and where SSI more*	*Lifetime and employment migration to transport centre, where industrial investment high*	*Recent and other migration, not to MNF, service centres*
E. Trace Correlation	= 0.83						
Chi-Square	= 258.2						
Significance	= 0.0001						

6. Lifetime migration and employment migration are more attracted to transport centres, where investment to industries are also more (Canonical correlation is 0.62).
7. Recent migration and other kinds of migration also occur to other centres, not specifically to manufacturing or service centres (Canonical correlation 0.51).

All these canonical linkage equations are both statistically very highly significant, and also practically very meaningful. Their canonical correlation coefficients are as high as 0.99, 0.98, 0.97, 0.85, 0.75, 0.62, and 0.51. Almost never such high multiple canonical correlation coefficients have emerged, repeatedly and successively such as these, in social sciences, nor even in physical sciences, specially in *a single* canonical test. This is simply wonderful, and very rare in entire sciences. These are not simple correlation or regression coefficients, rather multiple coefficients between *matrices,* not between variables, and have powerful statistical and practical meaning.

Those who do not know canonical model, or the power of canonical analysis, and of the Field Theory, most naively write or say that such results could have been obtained through simple regression analysis, or simultaneous equations. In fact, one canonical analysis yields the results equal to a hundred of multiple regression analyses, and generate *high powered and hidden results, which regression or any multivariate analysis is not at all capable of generating. This is the power, elegance, and utility of canonical model, and the field theory perspective.* Trace correlation is also very high, 0.85, that is, 0.85 squared times 100, equal to 72.3 per cent of variations in the dependent migration matrix is explained by the combination of economic structure of cities and investment matrices. Unexplained factors, or the play of randomness, or play of free will of the migrants, are very low. What more do we expect from demographic or geographic or social sciences? Very rarely such comparable results are ever achieved!

(c) *Canonical Findings for Migration of Females in Million Cities*: For the females, data are presented in Table 8.13 (Appendix), and canonical findings are presented in Tables 8.14 and 8.15. These are self-explanatory; hence not elaborated. *The results of female migrants to million cities are also given in the Appendix (Tables 8.13 to 8.15).*

Policy Implications and Main Trends

Even in this chapter, numerous canonical linkages have proved, that a specific kind of migration is linked to a specific component of economic structure of the cities, and with a specific kind of investments. Thus, these three components of the migration-urbanization system of India are causally linked, producing respective "Migration Fields", as conceptualized and canonically formulated. These "Migration Fields" have emerged in many canonical linkage equations, which amply testify the central notion of Migration Field Theory evolved.

Apart from various canonical results, investigations were also made about the characteristics of migrants to million cities and to 289 class I cities; which revealed the following basic trends (see attached Tables):

(a) Most such cities indicate that migrants largely come from far flung rural areas.
(b) Most of these migrants are either illiterate, or having less than primary education.

(c) Most of these migrants are absorbed in low-grade production process work, or low-grade sales and services – where wages are low, competition severe, and insecurity predominate. It is very low quality migration of poor and illiterate people; who are compelled to crowd in city slums as low-grade workers.
(d) It leads to tremendous waste of human and national potentials.
(e) Most such cities are also having poor tertiary sectors as the main component of their economic structure, not manufacturing sectors or strong secondary sectors.
(f) In sum, the patterns of poverty-induced migration of masses of illiterate and unskilled migration occurs to Indian metropolises and class I cities, even in 1981–91 decade, and these leads to acute urban involution and acute urban decay.

Summary of Findings at Metropolitan Level

(a) Most canonical tests have proved the existence of very high degree of inter-dependence between the two sets, i.e., between migration patterns for various reasons (or duration of migration) or volume of migration to metropolises in the one hand, and the economic structure of metropolises and bank investments given to them, on the other. Thus, the central notion of inter-dependence between the spatial flows (migration) and the spatial structure (economic structure and growth efforts/investments made there) is verified, times and again.
(b) Successive canonical inter-links are also generated in each model that are found to be statistically very highly significant and also practically very meaningful. They indicate that the findings are having considerable policy implications.

Concluding Remarks

In sum, in the context of ongoing globalization, liberalization, and privatization, more and more such poverty-induced migration and urban involution will occur in India in future. This is, because under globalization, the survival and existence of the poor people are hurt most. Under liberalization, cheap imports of goods are adversely affecting the poor, especially rural people's lives and their economy. In addition, under privatization, considerable stringencies and very often retrenchments of the workers are going on (see *Times of India*, "Jobless in Bhiwandi", May 16, 2006). All these negative processes are adversely affecting the lives and livelihood of the poor peasants, farmers, agricultural labourers, artisans, and village operatives; as well as urban slum dwellers.

9 Summary of Findings

1991 Census Situation

"Let your life be as deep as the ocean, but let it also be as wide as the sky"

Swami Vivekananda (1894)
(Complete Work, Centenary Volume V, 1963: 227)

Summary of Patterns of Migration and Urbanization in India (1991)

The highlights of migration-urbanization phenomena in India can be summarized as follows:

- The most predominant pattern shows that massive migration of landless agricultural labourers, peasants and village workers occur from marginalized villages directly to India's largest and over congested metropolises; the migrants often bypassing local small towns, cities, and district headquarters. These masses of unskilled, illiterate and distressed migrants are forced to make quantum jumps from stagnated villages to metropolises, leading to urban over-congestion, acute urban decay, growth of urban poor tertiary sectors, overflow of urban unemployment, and very frequent break down of essential urban amenities and services.
- Such poverty-induced migration, of both male and females, from villages occur because of very acute shortage of employment opportunities in villages, excessive population pressure on limited amount of land, lack of irrigation facilities and small scale industries, and of basic amenities of life (like school, drinking water, jobs, hospital, etc.). Pauperized and landless agricultural labourers and peasants are therefore compelled to escape from stagnation by moving out from rural areas. This is the most basic and fundamental picture of migration and urbanization pattern in India. Picture remain persistently stagnant and deadly stable over time.
- Benefits of development activities, if any, were not adequate for all classes and all regions. So, regional disparities and social inequalities have continued over space and time, and have induced further out-migration from marginalized villages to metropolises or large cities.
- But, such urban centres could not provide even barest means of subsistence and shelter to massive influx of rural peasant and unskilled and illiterate/semi-literate migrants, who are thus forced to get absorption in very poor urban informal sectors, such as, domestic servants, porters, road construction workers, maid servants, hawkers, vendors, shoeshine, ayahs,

etc. These are very low-paid services where wages are low, competition cut-throat, and exploitation very severe. Such distressed migration thus does not lead to development and higher qualitative change in urbanization. To unfold such complex processes in the Indian situation and to recommend alternative planning strategies to alleviate such problems are very urgent requirements.

- Indian cities/metropolises have very limited employment generating capacity under capital-intensive industrialization.
- Indeed, rural-to-metropolitan migration in India is mainly characterized by massive poverty-induced migration of illiterate and semi-literate people, who are compelled to move for survival, and who find absorption primarily in poor urban informal sectors, not in organized sector. Such migration helps them in their survival strategy, but it does not permit them upward social mobility or prosperity. This process is termed as *poverty-induced migration* in India.
- Consequently, huge urban population growth is occurring in the metropolises, but without prosperity and without structural changes in the urban economy. Our cities are merely growing as over-blown villages without essential urban functions, characteristics, urban infrastructure and services; and without a strong economic base. This process is called the process of *urban involution* in India. Taken together, the entire phenomenon can be termed as the *process of poverty-induced migration and urban involution* in India.
- Capital investments, growth efforts, and production units have a markedly uneven spatial concentration around a few larger and cities metropolises, neglecting smaller towns and cities.
- The three sub-systems, i.e. rural-urban distressed labour migration, weak economic structure of Indian cities, and polarized capital investments therein, are causally linked. Thus, as the spatial economic structure of city systems prevails in various regions of the country, so is the pattern of migration towards them, and vice-versa. Inter-relationships between these three systems are minutely examined in this study, and, repeatedly, the causal relationships between them are testified, at various levels – district, state, class I city, and million cities.
- This is one of the main contributions of this research.
- Massive poverty-induced migration, growth of parasitic cities and cancerous metropolises, proliferation of urban slums, consequent urban involution, and polarized capital investment and growth efforts, therefore, characterize India's migration-urbanization system. *These are indeed manifestations of spatial disorganization and underdevelopment, not development!*
- All these complex phenomena indicate the great need for research for assessing causal inter-relationships between migration, urbanization, and regional development in India; specially with reference to socio-economic inequities and regional disparities in the levels of development and polarized capital investment. Such analysis are done in this book at the micro-level (district), meso level (state) and at the macro level (metropolitan).
- Such situations call forth vast changes in our existing pro-metropolitan development bias in planning, requiring more sincere efforts towards

development of hitherto neglected small towns, intermediate cities, and especially the rural areas all over the national space.

- The problems of stagnated rural areas and massive rural-to-metropolitan migration in the Indian context, in the one hand, and of over-urbanization and urban involution in a few metropolises, on the other, were the consequences of the same kind of socio-economic processes of prolonged rural neglect and polarization of capital, investment, and growth efforts only to a few chosen metropolises. It is very much doubtful whether such crucial problems can be relieved simply by adopting a few palliative measures; or by advocating policies of efficient urban management alone, or just infrastructure development at some centres, or by continuing the policy of industrial concentration in the mega cities, and the like.
- In other words, if we are really desirous to be free from alcoholism or smoking, one has to quit alcohol or smoking entirely. In short, it requires vast systems transformations. That is, gradual but complete reversal of current pro-urban development bias in our planning; and more effective and maximum possible decentralization, in the true sense, of capital, investments, growth efforts, industrial locations, etc., in favour of small towns, small cities, intermediate cities, and innumerable villages, and more equitable distribution of production units over the entire national space. Instead of continuation of current trends in which a few Black-Holes-like cancerous metropolises gulp off all capital, investments, materials, resources, and growth efforts of the entire nation. In short, it calls for maximum possible reversal of all the flows (i.e. flows of capital, control, innovations and growth efforts, all now focused at the big metropolis) – and their re-orientation towards the smaller urban centres and the poor countryside. Such measures will be very much needed to relieve these problems. Otherwise, a few palliatives would not make a frontal attack at the crucial problems of ill-health, or distress migration or urban involution. Such problems will aggravate in future, sadly, with much more vigorous magnitudes, aided by population explosion.
- *It must be very clearly stated at the outset, that migration-restriction never can be a desirable option or strategy. Control of migration is never meant, nor advocated anywhere in this book, nor in any of my previous writing, because that will be the most undesirable and most undemocratic action. Although for most of the migrants, the choice is limited between quick death in the villages, or slow starvation in the stinking urban slums, still migration is their only escape route from rural poverty, hence, very much desirable, no matter how small is the pay, nor how unbearable is the stay in the urban slums.* If migration is not allowed, then, most would probably die in the stagnated and tottering villages. Hence, migration is most desirable for these masses of the poor as a survival strategy, as an escape route from poverty and also to enhance their incomes and skills, no matter how small is the betterment.
- Study of various regression and canonical inter-relationships between migration patterns and socio-economic variables (at district, state, city, and metropolitan level) show the great need for rural regeneration and relieving regional inequalities. Great efforts must be made for development of economy of backward districts and undeveloped states, by setting up small-scale and agro-based industries.

Findings of Regression Analyses

1. *District-level Analysis:* District level analysis of inter-relationships between migration and socio-economic variables were done at following stages:
   (a) By performing step-wise regression analysis between *intra*-district and *inter*-district migration and the district-level socio-economic variables, for All-India (443 districts), separately for males and females.
   (b) Step-wise regression analysis between *inter*-district *in-migration and out-migration* and selected socio-economic variables done, separately for each major states of India.
   (c) Step-wise regression analysis is also done between *inter-district in-migration and out-migration* and the *composite development indices evolved and computed* for the districts.

These three sets of results are greatly elaborated through several Tables in Chapter 6. At the district level, data of about 22 socio-economic variables from various sources were utilized for explaining district level migration of 443 districts, belonging to all major states of India (for which data available). Most such data refer to proportion of 10 categories of workers to total workers in each district. That is, workers in cultivation, agricultural labour, etc., per cent urban, proportion of agricultural workers to total workers, value of agricultural productivity, per cent area irrigated, per cent of net sown area, per cent general literacy, female literacy, per capita fertility consumption, per capita bank credit to all industries, to small-scale industries, or to service sectors, and so forth. In step-wise regression analysis, only those few specific variables have emerged which survived the rigorous statistical test.

2. *District-level Migration Rates and Socio-economic Variables:* In the following, the salient findings of three sets of analysis performed between district-level migration rates and selected socio-economic variables for the males are given:
   (a) Volume of in migration is found to be positively related to proportion of manufacturing workers in a district. Other details are elaborated in many tables (chapter 5).
   (b) Volume of out-migration is found to be negatively related to the proportion of cultivators in a district; that is, less work opportunity in a district, the more out-migration. Other details are given in various tables (chapter 5).
3. *Result of Step-wise Regression analysis* between District level In-migration and Out-migration and selected Socio-economic variables, Different States: Considerable variations were found when analyses were made for the districts of each separate state, and focusing upon in-migration and out-migration data. The details are presented in chapter 6.
   (a) Briefly speaking, in spite of some state-wise variations, certain common causes of in-migration and out-migration emerged. For instance: in-migration seems to have been caused to those districts where the general literacy rate is high, per cent irrigation is more, level of urbanization is higher, bank credit to agriculture is more, per cent of agricultural workers is less, proportion of agricultural labourers is less and employment in mining activities available. That is, in-migration is

occurring to those relatively developed districts where these factors are on the higher side.

(b) Conversely, out-migration seems to have been caused from those districts where per cent irrigation is less, level of urbanization is low, proportion of agricultural workers is high, proportion of landless agricultural labourers is also high. In short, regression results confirm, in general, that out-migration has been occurring from relatively backward districts to relatively prosperous districts.

4. *One development measure is devised* and computed for all 443 districts of India (for which data available). The factor scores, generated from factor analysing 22 socio-economic variables of the districts, are weighted by corresponding *eigen-values* or variance explained by respective factors; and converted into a total of 100 per cent. The ensuing result is a composite development index showing the levels of development, measured with reference to six main factors of socio-economic structure of Indian districts. Most such dimensions are positively related to development. The index, $DI_{1,}$ is always positive, ranging between 0 to 200+, higher scores indicating more socio-economic development. This exercise equips us in identification of about 250 backward districts of India, which having 100 or less scores on DI_1 development index, and about 200 comparatively more developed districts having excess of 100 scores. Considered in this way, we get a very good measure of levels of regional development, and all 443 districts of India were scaled according to this index.

5. *Then, regression analysis, performed between Development Index of districts and flows of Inter-district in-migration and out-migration* (dependent set), present following results:
   (a) Volume of in-migration into a district is caused by level of development, explaining 29 per cent of variance.
   (b) Rate of in-migration into a district is caused by the same factor, development index, explaining about 18 per cent of variance.
   (c) Volume of out-migration from a district is not clearly related to development index. Census migration data do not provide full and detailed information about out-migration. So, a lack of fine-grained data of out-migration has handicapped efforts of such analysis of out-migration.

Methodology of Factor Analyses and Canonical Analyses

In this book, methodologically and statistically migration data were analysed at *six* different levels: (1) All-India, (2) District, (3) State, (4) Class I city, (5) Million city, and (6) Metropolitan level.

In doing so, a new and novel methodological technique has been developed and utilized in this study, which involves utilization of factor analysis-cum-canonical analysis in the study of migration-urbanization-disparities. A series of canonical analyses were made, at each of the above domains.

The causal relationships between volume and patterns of migration, urbanization, and of regional development were analysed, at each of these domains of research: all-India, districts, states, class I city, Million city and Metropolitan levels. A series of high powered factor analyses and Canonical linkage analysis were made between:

(a) Volume and patterns of migration (as the Dependent matrix), and
(b) Economic Structure of districts (or states or cities/metropolises) – cum-
(c) Growth efforts or investments made therein (as combination of Independent matrices); and, each time, a series of final canonical linkage equations were generated, linking, every-time, a specific pattern (s) of migration, with a specific pattern(s) of economic structure-cum-investment. This unique type of analytical marriage is the most elegant phenomenon of this canonical analysis.

These canonical linkages are not only statistically very powerful, but are also found to be practically very meaningful. They have generated very many useful planning directives for reducing poverty-induced migration, querulous urbanization and acute regional disparities that adversely affect the economy of India.

Hence, this research offers both new methodological pathways in population studies, as well as substantive findings for migration-urbanization research and for alleviating human problems associated with low quality migration and urban decay that are occurring in India.

Major Findings of Factor and Canonical Analyses

The study incorporates findings of about hundreds of regression analyses (at district), results of a dozen factor analyses and 18 canonical analysis, done at various levels of investigation *(district, state, city, and metropolitan levels)*. However, only a few major findings are very briefly highlighted, at each level of analysis performed:

All-India Findings: District Level Analysis

(A) *Inter-relationships between Migration and Socio-economic Variables, District Level (Results of Factor Analysis):* The following seven main factors were generated, linking migration and socio-economic variables, and explaining 73 per cent of total variance:

1. Where economic development is more, urbanization high, investments also more, there the volume of in-migration is also high, and also inter-district migration more. Thus, during the decade of 1981–91, more in-migration has occurred to urban centres, manufacturing centres, and where more capital investments are made (explains 28 per cent of variance).
2. Where general literacy is high, and percentage of service and construction workers are also high, intra-district migration rate is low and in-migration rate is moderate (11.3%).
3. High volume and high rate of out migration occur, where less manufacturing prevails and less service workers exist (9.9%).
4. Moderately high intra-district migration rate occurs where agricultural labourers are more, cultivators less, net sown area high and agricultural investment is moderate (7.85%).
5. High volume of in-migration and high volume of total migration occur where mining centres exist (explains 6%).

6. Very low in-migration occurs where population growth is high and forest is more (5.2%).
7. Little in-migration occurs to places of high household industry (4.4%).

(B) *Causal Linkages between Migration and Socio-economic Variables-cum-Investment:* Factor Analysis-cum Canonical Analysis (District Level).

(i) *Factor Results (District Level):* Initially, factor analysis of socio-economic variables-cum-investment variables of all 443 districts of India has yielded the following 6 main factors, depicting the main economic structure of India:
   (a) More economic development, higher urbanization, more manufacturing, more bank deposit, and more bank credit dimension (explains 30%).
   (b) General literacy, more bank credit to agriculture, and livestock dimension (12%).
   (c) More service and construction workers, less agricultural labourers, and less net sown area dimension (10.4%).
   (d) Higher work participation and forested areas (8.5%).
   (e) Household industry and high population growth areas (5.7%).
   (f) Mining dimension (5.2%).

(ii) *Canonical Results at District Level:* Factor scores were also generated on each of these six dimensions for each district; and these become inputs for next linking step, canonical analysis. Here, volume and rate of in-migration and out-migration at district level were treated as Dependent matrix, and those 6 factor scores on six economic structure-cum-investment variables were treated as the Independent Matrix. And, a final canonical analysis is performed on these two matrices – which generated four Canonical Linkage equations, linking each time, a specific migration variable(s) (from Dependent matrix) with a specific set of Socio-economic variable(s), or factors (from Independent matrix), with which it was causally linked. So, four final Canonical equations were generated. These are statistically significant, and are also practically very meaningful:

(a) High volume of in-migration occurs in those districts where more economic development-cum-high urbanization-cum-high investment prevail (Canonical equation No. 1: Canonical correlation 0.74).

(b) High volume of out-migration occurs from those districts where services and construction were less, and where general literacy and agricultural investment were also less (Canonical correlation is 0.53).

(c) In-migration rate is high in those districts where general literacy is high and investment to agriculture is more (Canonical correlation is 0.52).

(d) Higher out-migration rate occurs in those districts where mining is less, and population growth rate is more (Canonical correlation 0.14).

It must be reiterated here, that such canonical rules or laws do have great practical significance for planning – they do indicate the great need for reducing regional disparities between districts (or states or cities), if we are really desirous of redirecting migration streams to more desirable destinations, or want to arrest crowding of migrants in already overburdened districts and cities.

(C) *Canonical Linkages between Migration and Socio-economic Variables-cum-Investment at District Level (without factor analysis):* Another Canonical analysis is performed at district level, without first doing factor analysis of socio-economic variables. This test has generated the following *four* canonical linkages:

1. Volume of in-migration into the district is high where more bank investments have gone in, and where moderately high manufacturing sector are present (Canonical correlation 0.84).
2. Higher volume of out-migration occurs from the districts where share of cultivators and agricultural labourers are more (Canonical correlation 0.71).
3. High in-migration rate occurs where credit to agriculture is high, general literacy is also high and trade-commerce is relatively less (Canonical correlation 0.56).
4. High out-migration rate prevails where literacy is moderate and construction sector is less (Canonical correlation 0.48).

As stated before, such canonical linkages have considerable statistical significance, as well as practical meaning, and considerable policy implications. These indicate that considerable out-migration occurs from those districts where already heavy burden of agricultural labourers persist; conversely, it also indicates that considerable in-migration also occurs in those districts where investments are made and where scope of manufacturing work are also available. These findings have much policy significance to achieve more balanced spatial flows.

State-level Analysis of Factor and Canonical Models

Causal canonical linkages between volume and rate of in-migration variables, in the one hand, and socio-economic variables and investment variables, on the other, are generated according to three analytical strategies (Chap. 7):

1. Taking the raw variables in both Dependent (migration) and Independent matrices (socio-economic matrices), and
2. First, factor analysing the socio-economic matrix, and, then, generating the factor scores for each state on each of those identified factors, and taking these factor scores as inputs for final Canonical linkage analysis (Independent Matrix), and connecting them with Migration variables (as Dependent matrix). Both these models have yielded very useful and very meaningful results.
3. Canonical analysis is also made between Inter-state migration matrix and socio-economic distances between the states.

(A) *First Model of State-level Analysis linking Migration and Socio-economic Variables yielded four Canonical Linkages:*

1. High volume of out-migration occurs from the states where proportion of cultivators are less, agricultural labourers less, and trade-and commerce are also less prevalent (Canonical correlation 0.99).
2. High volume of in-migration occurs into those states where share of manufacturing is high, per capita income is also high, and moderate level of credit to agriculture are also present (0.98).
3. High rate of out-migration prevails from the states where per capita income is less, credit to small scale industries are less, and investment to industries are moderate (0.97).

4. High rate of In-migration occurs into the states where proportion of cultivators is more and transport workers are more (0.84).

Trace correlation or general mathematical mapping between dependent and independent matrices is very high, 0.97, explaining more than 87 (i.e., 0.97 squared times 100) per cent of total variance in dependent (migration) matrix. This is simply remarkable. Besides, various canonical linkages are not only statistically very powerful, but are also practically very meaningful. They indicate useful planning directives for reducing regional disparities in the level of development between states, and to reduce concomitant massive migration from backward and neglected states (Orissa, UP, Bihar) to relatively favoured or developed states (Punjab, Haryana, Maharashtra).

(B) *Second Model of State-level Analysis linking Migration and Factors of Socio-economic Matrix generated three Canonical Linkages:*

1. Where service sectors of state economy are high, in-migration rate is also high (Canonical correlation is 0.86).
2. Volume of out migration is high from the states where agricultural development is low, and proportion of agricultural labourers is more (0.72).
3. Volume of in-migration into the states is high and out-migration low, where the level of economic development are high and urbanization is also high (0.38) (Fourth result was not significant).

The *Trace correlation* is also high, 0.59. Respective canonical correlations are also high, generating meaningful linkage equations that are having useful policy significance. It indicates the great need for reducing wide regional disparities in the level of agricultural and economic development between the states, and the need to a have a balanced migration flows between them.

(C) *Third Model performed between Socio-economic Distances between States and Inter-state Migration Matrix:* At the state level, another canonical analysis is performed between the two matrices, Inter-state In-migration matrix (M') and Inter-state Socio-economic Distance Matrix (S_d), by taking migration matrix as the dependent and the latter as the independent set. As a result, the following *four* statistically very highly significant and practically meaningful canonical inter-relationships are generated. Trace correlation is very high (0.85), explaining about 73 per cent of total variance of the dependent matrix (i.e., migration flows). Successively four canonical inter-links have also emerged; with very high canonical coefficients (e.g., 0.97, 0.94, 0.78 and 0.70). These are not only statistically very highly significant, but are also indicating relationships having considerable policy import. These are identified as follows:

1. Larger in-migration flows occur from Karnataka and Kerala to Tamil Nadu, mainly because of large socio-economic differences or distances of Karnataka from other southern states of this region (Canonical linkage equation 1, canonical correlation is 0.97).
2. Larger in-migration flows take place from UP to Maharashtra, due to larger socio-economic differences or distances of UP from other states of this region (Canonical linkage equation 2; canonical correlation 0.94).

3. Larger volume of in-migration flowing from Bihar to West Bengal due to larger socio-economic distances or differences of states of Bihar from other states of this region (Canonical linkage 3; canonical correlation 0.78).
4. Migration from Tamil Nadu to Kerala and Karnataka occurs, and these are related to socio-economic distances of Tamil Nadu from other states of this region (canonical correlation 0.70).

Policy Implications of above findings are very clear. These are very meaningful and useful canonical inter-relationships. They are not repeating the usual geographical map of inter-state migration-flow matrix. Rather these canonical equations very significantly and indisputably tell us that such migration streams from a particular backward origin state (UP or Bihar) to relatively prosperous destination state (Maharashtra or West Bengal) have been occurring primarily due to the large socio-economic differences or disparities separating them.

It also warns us that such migration streams have persisted in the past, and unfortunately, will also persist in the 21st century as long as such regional disparities and inequalities will continue and proliferate in future. The immediate policy implication of such crucial findings are that such regional imbalances must be given now a final burial. Of course, here it is not meant that the states like West Bengal, Maharashtra, Punjab or Haryana are economically much better than the backward states of Bihar and Uttar Pradesh; but the urgent policy imperative of such findings is to fully comprehend that such regional disparities and regional underdevelopment are indeed artificially and historically created by colonialism and its legacy. And, it continued later also due to the lack of soulful concern for the poor during the Post-Independent period of Planning era. The era that has been marked by the same old neo-colonial legacy of favouring the coastal and exporting states, at the expense of the interior states of Bihar, Uttar Pradesh, and the like – which remained persistently neglected and underdeveloped!

Unless and until such regional disparities are urgently reduced, the patterns of poverty-induced migration of pauperized and marginalized peasants and labourers from Uttar Pradesh and Bihar to relatively developed and favoured states of Maharashtra, West Bengal, Punjab, Haryana and Delhi will continue unabated for another 100 years – the very same patterns which were initiated in 1870/1880's and have persisted until now. *Such migration patterns are the signs of underdevelopment, not development!*

Such migration-urbanization process are causing tremendous urban congestion and very rapid growth of stinking urban slums. The nodes are characterized by untold stories of agony and misery of the poor migrant people in the so-called mega cities, *where the lives of the millions of urban destitutes are daily grounded by the unjust political economy of the cruel metropolis!*

Findings of Class I City Level Analysis

Complete data were available only for 289 class I cities (missing for 10 cities). Bank investment data were available again only for 200 Class I cities. So, different analytic strategies were adopted for these sub-sets of class I cities, explained below (Chapter 8):

(A) *Canonical analysis between Reasons for Migration and Economic Structure of 289 Class I Cities:* Following four canonical Linkages were generated:

1. Employment migration of males occurs to manufacturing centres of class I cities (Canonical correlation (0.65).
2. Migration of the males for other miscellaneous reasons occur where service sector of the economy is less and household industry more (0.47).
3. Migration of the males for familial reasons occurs to construction centres (0.35).
4. Migration of the males for business purpose occurs to manufacturing centres (0.24).

The fifth one is not significant.

These canonical linkages are self-explanatory. They confirm that male migration for employment and business are attracted to manufacturing centres; and migration for familial reasons occurs to construction centres, or household industrial centres.

(B) *Canonical Analysis between Rural-urban migration and Urban-urban migration and Economic Structure-cum-Investment of 200 Class I Cities: The following canonical linkages emerged:*

1. Volume of rural to urban male migration to Class I cities is more, where bank deposit is large and investment to industries is also considerable (Canonical correlation 0.94).
2. Volume of urban to urban male migration is large, where service sector is more predominant, and more credit are available to small scale industries (0.49).
3. Share of urban to urban male migration (to total volume of migration) and volume of rural to urban male migration is high in manufacturing centres, and where bank deposit is also more (0.28).
4. In manufacturing centres, or service or mining centres, the percentage share of urban to urban migration (of total migration) and of rural to urban migration are low (0.14).

Findings of Patterns of Migration to Million Cities

Migration of both males and females to 22 Million cities were separately analysed by performing a series of canonical analyses. However, only findings of the male migration are summarized here (Chap. 8) (for the females see Appendix).

(A) *Canonical Linkages between Reasons for Migration of Males and Economic Structure of Million Cities-cum-Investment generated seven canonical equations (using raw data, without factoring):*

- Migration for employment, business, and education occur to large-sized million cities, where manufacturing and service sectors predominate, and where bank deposit is also high (Canonical correlation 0.99).
- Migration for employment, business and education occur to smaller million cities, where manufacturing and service sectors are more, but where little bank deposit gone (0.98).
- Migration for education occurs to manufacturing centres, service centres and also partly to household industry centres (0.97).

- Lifetime migration occur more where manufacturing is more, and bank deposit is also more. This also happens in smaller million cities (0.85).
- Employment migration prevails to transport centres and where investment to small scale industries are more (0.75).
- Lifetime migration and also employment migration are more to transport centres, and where investment to industries are also more (0.62).
- Recent migration and other kinds of migration also occur to other centres, not specifically to manufacturing or service centres (0.51).

(B) *Canonical Linkages between Migration for Various Durations (Males) and Economic Structure of Million Cities have generated three meaningful linkages:*

1. Lifetime migration is high where total population of million cities is large and bank deposit is high (Canonical correlation 0.98).
2. Migration for 1 to 9 years duration and migration for 10 years or more duration are more to manufacturing and service centres (0.87).
3. Migration for more than 10 years is less where manufacturing and service sectors were relatively less (0.54). The fourth relationship is statistically not significant.

(C) *Summary of the Findings at Million Cities*

(a) Both the canonical tests have proved the existence of very high degree of inter-dependence between the two sets, i.e., between migration patterns for various reasons (or duration of migration) and volume of total and decadal in-migration to metropolises in the one hand, and economic structure of metros and the Five Year Plan/Bank investments to them, on the other. Thus, the central notion of inter-dependence between the spatial flows (migration) and the spatial structure (economic structure and growth efforts/investments) is fully verified.

(b) Various successive canonical inter-links are also generated in each model that are found to be statistically very highly significant and also practically very meaningful. They indicate findings having considerable policy implications. Further details are given in Chapter 8.

These analyses were much handicapped due to lack of full and fine-grained data on capital investment, both from public and private sectors, Five Year plans or non-plan investment, banks or entrepreneurs, the individuals or corporate sectors. Furthermore, we did not have any information about the investment available in the informal sectors. Were such necessary data available, we could have unravelled more incisive inter-relationships between the service sectors of urban economic structure and in-migration into the metropolises.

Theoretical Significance

As various canonical linkages demonstrated, a specific kind of migration is found to be linked to a specific component of the economic structure of the cities, and with a specific kind of capital investments. Thus, these *three* components of this migration-urbanization system are causally linked, producing respective "Spatial such Migration Fields", as conceptually thought and canonically formulated. So time and again, such "Spatial Migration Fields" are generated by a series of canonical equations and a series of canonical tests. These prove the central notion of Spatial Field Theory, propounded and briefly presented in this volume.

Policy Implications

Besides, various substantive findings also have considerable policy implications. They indicate that if we seriously want redirecting migration flows to more desirable destinations, instead of over-crowding into filthy slums of a few mega cities (Kolkata, Mumbai, Delhi, Chennai, etc.), then, we really need to develop all economic sectors of urban economy, and also provide all growth efforts, infrastructure and investment in those hitherto neglected small cities, instead of excessive polarization of these factors into over-crowded mega cities. Obviously, such policy prescriptions are substantiated by the above findings, and, as such, they have tremendous significance.

Characteristics of Migrants

Apart from various canonical and factor results, and multitudes of regression results, investigations were also made about the characteristics of migrants to Million cities and to 299 class I cities; which have revealed the following main trends:

- Most such cities indicate that migrants largely come from far flung rural areas.
- Most of these migrants are either illiterate, or having less than primary education.
- Most of these migrants are absorbed in low-grade production process work, or low grade sales and services – where wages are low, competition severe, and insecurity predominate. So it is very low quality migration of poor and illiterate people; who are compelled to crowd in city slums as low grade workers.
- It leads to tremendous waste of human and national potentials.
- Most such cities are also having poor tertiary sectors as the main component of their economic structure, not manufacturing sectors or strong secondary sectors.
- In sum, the patterns of poverty-induced migration of masses of illiterate and unskilled migration occurs to Indian metropolises and class I cities, even in 1981–91 decade, and these leads to acute urban involution and acute urban decay.
- It also implies low quality urbanization in India.

Overview of Findings of Migration and Urbanization in India

In sum, it may be reiterated that the rural migrants make quantum jump to Mumbai, Kolkata, New Delhi and the like, by-passing the smaller towns or the district headquarters. This is, simply because larger metropolises at least provide some absorptive capacity, albeit at a very low level of employment and human consumption; but even these are just not available at the district headquarters, or in smaller towns/cities. Past migration streams have also ensured a network of kinsmen, friends and relatives in those metropolises for the incoming migrants – such that the new arrivals get at least some kind of means of subsistence without waiting for a long time. Unless the labour absorptive capacity of the local district headquarters and intermediate towns and cities are greatly enhanced, both in organized and unorganized sectors, it is incorrect to assume that future migration streams can be attracted to them.

Thus, this reversal of migration streams requires tremendous structural transformations in the urban economy of both small towns/intermediate cities as well as of the metropolises. Neither were such measures clearly thought about in the existing studies or planning designs, nor are such transformations easy to take place shortly. *For such changes call forth vast changes in the existing polarized investment patterns, concentrated industrial licensing policies, in employment-generating capacities of towns, promoting pro-rural against pro-urban development policies, restructuring of spatial structure of economic activities of entire national space and changes in rural and regional development policies.*

Conclusion of Part I of the Book

Further, in the context of ongoing globalization, liberalization, and privatization, more and more such poverty-induced migration and urban involution will occur in India in future. This is simply because under globalization, survival and existence of the poor people are hurt most. Under liberalization, cheap imports of goods are adversely affecting the poor and rural people's lives and their economy. And, under privatization, considerable financial stringencies and retrenchments of the workers are going on. All these negative processes are adversely affecting the lives and livelihood of the poor peasants, farmers, agricultural labourers, artisans, and village operatives; as well as urban slum dwellers.

Unless and until their economy and subsistence are adequately protected, there will be considerably much more such kinds of poverty-induced migration and urban involution in India in future. Of course, 1991 census migration data did not adequately equip us to investigate the ongoing globalization, privatization and liberalization processes, as these were strengthened after 1991; but the main socio-economic forces of underdevelopment and poverty were prevalent since Independence and much before, and which continued uninterrupted even during planning era (1951 onwards). And, such phenomena were amply present before 1991. Evidently, these processes are now strengthened (after two decades), and will adversely affect migration-urbanization in India with much more vigorous forms in the future, specially in impending many decades. Some literatures are already showing such signs of adverse affect on lives of labourers and their migration. Hence, tremendous research in these directions is very much needed, and much more planning and policy-oriented actions will be urgently required.

Part II
Census 2001

Messages of Swami Vivekananda
(12th January, 1863–4th July, 1902)

"It may be that I shall find it good to get outside my body – to cast it off like a worn-out garment. But I shall not cease to work, I shall inspire men everywhere, until the world shall know that it is one with God."

Swami Vivekananda (1899)
(Complete work, Centenary Volume V, 1963)

"Let each one of us pray day and night for the downtrodden millions in India who are held fast by poverty, priest craft, and tyranny – pray day and night for them."

Swami Vivekananda (1896)
(Complete Work, Centenary Volume V, 1963: 58)

"Love the poor, the miserable, the downtrodden, and the Lord will bless you."

Swami Vivekananda (1896)
(Complete Work, Centenary Volume III, 1963: 368)

"Ay, let every man and woman and child, without respect of caste or birth, weakness or strength, hear and learn that behind the strong and the weak, behind the high and the low, behind every one, there is that Infinite Soul, assuring the infinite possibility and the infinite capacity of all to become great and good."

Swami Vivekananda (1895)
(Complete Work, Centenary Volume III, 1963: 193)

"We must rouse India and the whole world."

Swami Vivekananda (1896)
(Complete Work, Centenary Volume V, 1963: 61)

10 Patterns of Migration in India

Census 2001

"Remember the only sign of life is motion and growth."

Swami Vivekananda (1894)
(Complete Work, Centenary Volume V, 1963: 38)

"Each soul is potentially divine. The goal is to manifest this divinity within by controlling nature, external and internal. Do this either by work, or worship or psychic control or philosophy – by one or more or all of these and be free."

Swami Vivekananda (1894)
(Complete Work, Centenary Volume IV, 1963: 1)

Migration and Urbanization in India, Situation in 2001 Census

There is a great dearth of study and research on migration in India. Most studies are merely descriptive, not analytic, neither synthesizing, nor policy-oriented. Research is also not attempted to unfold complex phenomena encompassing migration, nor complexity of spatial-socio-economic-political processes that underlie nexus of migration-urbanization-underdevelopment and spatial disorganization in India. Moreover, there is a great lacuna of research which ever identified or enunciated planning strategies – which are urgently required to ameliorate the wretched conditions of teeming millions of migrants – who crowd into city slums, or move from one area of poverty to another, from one region of stress to the next one.

Answering to such very crucial questions and issues, the present study, in Part II, aims at filling up such great lacunae. Especially Part II thoroughly unfolds the patterns of migration, according to 2001 census, and analyses various aspects of migration at *six* levels of investigation: (1) All-India, (2) districts, (3) states, (4) class I cities, (5) million cities, and (6) metropolises.

Great emphasis is laid upon analysing the vast amount of data with simple statistical techniques, like regression analysis. The focus is given upon unfolding the general trends of migration and urbanization in India, and presents them, based on statistical results, through simple generalized statements and illustrations.

The human dimension of migration is also highlighted in the next chapter. There are hundreds of millions of very poor, landless peasants, workers and unemployed, who are forced to migrate from rural poverty to urban poverty, from one area of stress to another. No sordid statistics can tell their poignantly sad stories of endless suffering! Each migrant has his or her own pathetic story to tell, and we should remember that behind the massive number of migrants, in the tables, there exists a sea of sad faces!

The subsequent chapters also unfold the causal links of migration with urbanization and regional disparities over the national space of India. This is done in special ways, detailed below and in subsequent chapters.

Part II of the volume also provides a great wealth of recommendations and policies and strategies for alleviating the great human problems associated with such poverty-induced migration and urban involution in India. Thus, the study is both analytic and synthetic, both systematic and policy-oriented. It also attempts to draw the attention of the students, scholars, policy- planners, and the governments to these burgeoning issues of migration and urbanization problems, which will swell to great calamity in India in the coming decades, specially when population explosion, poverty, and deprivation are on its sides.

Six Objectives and Organization of Part II

All these condition described above urgently require remedial measures and solution. The study thus has six main objectives.

- First, the volume and patterns of migration of 2001 census are meticulously analysed at *six* different scales of investigation: (1) All-India, (2) districts, (3) state, (4) class I city, (5) million city, and (6) mega city levels. A series of simple *bi-variate* regression analyses were performed between: (a) the volume and rates of migration in the geographical units (as dependent variable), and (b) the socio-economic variables of the units (districts, states, class I cities, or million cities) (as independent variable), at each scale of investigations, and each time, a series of regression equations were generated, linking each time, a specific migration, with a specific socio-economic variable. *Such regression linkages have yielded, as we shall see later, very many useful and meaningful results.* These comprise the subject matter of Chapters 10 to 16. Finally, Chapter 18 summarizes all the major findings of analysing data of 2001 census.
- Second, the study also briefly untangles the complex *spatial-socio-economic-political processes* that underlie and cause such complex nexus of migration-urbanization-poverty-underdevelopment in India. Most conventional studies do not delve into the meso and macro processes, which affect the lives of hundreds of millions of migrants in India. As such, this discussion (chapter 17) has filled a great lacuna in migration-urbanization research. These processes also have general applicability to other developing countries.
- Third, India faces acute problems of massive illegal migration from Bangladesh and concomitant adverse effects on India's demographic structure, economy, society, culture, political stability, and her very existence! Such crucial issues are never discussed in existing literature. Some of these aspects are highlighted in order to draw attentions of scholars, policy makers and government. This is briefly discussed in Chapter 19.

- Fourth, India's recent growing population and growing economy has many pitfalls and many ramifications. India will surpass China in population size (after a few decades), with a great demographic dividends of massive youthful and potentially productive population. If this burgeoning labour force can be adequately educated and effectively trained into skilled manpower, then, India may emerge as an economic super-power. Conversely, if we fail to provide adequate education, health, and employment to them, then, this huge tide of population will overwhelm as a great devastating Tsunami for India's economy, society and civilization. Coupled with huge population explosion, then, much more accelerated poverty-induced migration and urban involution may create tremendous adverse impacts on India's migration-urbanization system, leading to maximum entropy level and a great catastrophe. These are briefly highlighted in Chapter 20.
- Fifthly, the major issues and challenges of India's migration-urbanization-poverty-underdevelopment nexus are briefly analysed in Chapter 21.
- Finally, in Chapter 22, the volume also recommends certain alternative policies and planning strategies to redress the acute human problems associated with such phenomena and processes. These strategies will also benefit other similarly placed countries in Asia-Pacific region. Because, such processes now operate in many developing countries and need urgent remedies. In the coming decades, evidently, the problems of such distressed migration, over-urbanization, and urban decay will very fast become the greatest problems in the Developing World.
- One important caveat must be emphasized, right at the outset. This book mainly focuses on various aspects of migration alone. It does not deal with urbanization or regional disparities *per se*, rather it investigates some aspects of urbanization or regional disparities in a *special way*. Discussions on such topics were focused – wherever the *"links"* between migration to cities or mega cities emerged. So, the causal "links" between migration and urbanization are unraveled, rather than simple study on urbanization. Similarly, issues of regional disparities were highlighted, whenever discussion focused on migration from backward to forward districts, or from stagnated to favoured states. Thus, the causal *"links"* between migration and regional disparities are explained, instead of usual discussion on regional disparities.

All-India Migration Patterns

Table 10.1 presents the patterns of male and female internal migration, according to place of last residence (2001), showing volume for all durations (cols. 1–2), and for 10 years duration, 1991–2001 (cols. 3– 6).

According to 2001 Census, 93.4 million males and 221.2 million females were migrants; indicating the predominance of female over the male mobility in India. Sex ratio of mobility thus comes to 2368 (females per 1,000 males). During 1991–2001, however, 32.9 million male and 65.4 million females were reported as migrants. Mobility sex ratio has come down to 1988 during 1991–2001. Considerable variations between male and female migration patterns are also note-worthy (Table 10.1):

Table 10.1 *Internal Migration by the Place of Residence, All-India, 2001*

Last Residence	*Total Migrants*			*Migration less than 10 years duration (1991–2001) (and per cent of Total Migration of Males and Females)*					
	Persons	*Males*	*Females*	*Persons*	*Males*	*M%*	*Females*	*F%*	*Sex Ratio*
Total Migration	**314541350**	**93361809**	**221179541**	**98301342**	**32896986**	**100**	**65404356**	**100**	1988
Total Internal Migration	309385525	90677712	218707813	97560320	32510444	**98.8**	65049876	**99.5**	2001
R-R	171735606	26080122	145655484	53354376	11745104	35.7	41609272	63.6	
R-U	51686356	24505949	27180407	20595231	10307198	31.3	10288033	15.7	
U-R	12999403	4547409	8451994	6266503	2580705	7.8	3685798	5.6	
U-U	36562314	16500680	20061634	14388774	6589445	20.0	7799329	11.9	
Intra-district Migration	193592938	47337924	146255014	54108439	14147939	**43.0**	39960500	**61.1**	2824
R-R	127972370	17364499	110607871	37944751	7299453	22.2	30645298	46.9	
R-U	19090398	7484323	11606075	7414824	3198277	9.7	4216547	6.4	
U-R	7113314	2401165	4712149	3296851	1293641	3.9	2003210	3.1	
U-U	10813540	4839563	5973977	3654899	1596613	4.9	2058286	3.1	
Inter-district Migration	74626322	24241706	50384616	26625002	9850344	**29.9**	16774658	**25.6**	1703
R-R	32742262	5614139	27128123	10935323	2686128	8.2	8249195	12.6	
R-U	17255955	8094328	9161627	6807452	3305184	10.0	3502268	5.4	
U-R	3958093	1321608	2636485	1916300	764148	2.3	1152152	1.8	
U-U	15033103	6516092	8517011	6243395	2790950	8.5	3452445	5.3	
Inter-state Migration	41166265	19098082	22068183	16826879	8512161	**25.9**	8314718	**12.7**	976
R-R	11020974	3101484	7919490	4474302	1759523	5.3	2714779	4.2	
R-U	15340003	8927298	6412705	6372955	3803737	11.6	2569218	3.9	
U-R	1927996	824636	1103360	1053352	522916	1.6	530436	0.8	
U-U	10715671	5145025	5570646	4490480	2201882	6.7	2288598	3.5	
From Other Countries	5155423	2683914	2471509	740867	386461	**1.2**	354406	**0.5**	917
Moved to rural	2603601	1317588	1286013	392807	188518	0.6	204289	0.3	
Moved to urban	2551822	1366326	1185496	348060	197943	0.6	150117	0.2	

Source: Census of India, 2001(b), Migration Tables, D-Series, Census Commissioner's Office, New Delhi, CDs, available only in 2006–7. Large number of migrants are unclassified, and not shown here.

(a) The females mostly move from rural to rural (64%), while for males this share is much less (36%).
(b) Rural-urban migration is predominated by the males (31%), share of females is relatively small (16%).
(c) The females primarily move short distances, within the district (61%), especially between rural areas (47%). About 25.6 per cent cross district boundaries, and only 12.7 per cent cross state boundaries. Corresponding share of males are 43.0, 22.2, 29.9 and 25.9, respectively. Inter-state migration is male selective.
(d) In rural-urban migration, volume-wise male and female migrants are not different at *intra*-district, inter-district and inter-state levels. But, proportion-wise the females depict decreasingly a smaller share of total female migration. Thence, rural-urban migration is also male selective.
(e) Similar patterns are seen for urban-urban migration.
(f) In general the females are in majority in urban-urban migration, while males predominate in rural-urban migration, especially at longer distances.

Broad Reasons for Migration, 1991–2001

Table 10.2 depicts migration of males and females during 1991–2001. Out of total 98.3 million during 1991–2001, 61.8 million (62.8%) moved to rural and 36.5 million (37.1%) moved to urban. Rural to rural migration was 53.4 million (56.8%), rural to urban migration 20.6 million (21.8%), urban to rural moves were only 6.3 million (6.6%) and urban to urban migration 14.4 million (15.2%). Thus, majority was rural-ward migration (63%) and urban-ward migration was still 37 per cent. Rural-urban migration was still mere 22 per cent of total decadal migration. However, it increased from 16.8 million (20.8%) during 1981–91 to 21 million during 1991–2001, an increase of 23 per cent. Even such increase cause great urban problems.

Seven basic reasons for move are also shown: for the males, who moved to rural areas (first row), the most important reason was employment (29%), followed by 'moved with the family' (25%) and 'other reasons' (20%) and moved after birth (15%), education (5.7%) and business (2%). For the females, for those who moved to rural areas (first row), marriage (74%) was the most important reason, followed by family moved (11%) and other reasons (6%). Among them, education, or business were still not important, 0.8 per cent and 0.2 per cent, respectively. Thus, for the males the economic motives are still the most important reasons for migration; while for the females, marriage or familial migration are still very important. Indeed, the patterns have not changed from 1981 or 1991 censuses, in spite of recent economic growth in India, during the first development decade, 1991–2001 (Table 10.2).

Noteworthy aspect is that for those who moved to urban areas (second row), employment becomes most significant reason for migration for males (45%), although for the females it is still low (5%). However, a large number of females moved with the family (25%), but field studies indicate (chapter 11) that many take up employment later at the destinations. Census data fail to capture such huge masses of women migrating for work, because they ask only single reason, ignoring secondary reasons. Such gaps must be corrected.

Table 10.2 *Reasons for Migration, All-India, 1991–2001*

Place of Last Residence	*Total migrants*		*Reasons for Migration for Less Than 10 Years of Duration (%)*													
			Work		*Business*		*Education*		*Marriage*		*Moved after birth*		*Moved with family*		*Others*	
Total	*M*	*F*	*M*	*F*	*M*	*F*	*M*	*F*	*M*	*F*	*M*	*F*	*M*	*F*	*M*	*F*
Moved to rural	15214947	46606289	29	3	2	0	6	1	4	74	15	5	25	11	20	6
Moved to urban	17682039	18798067	45	5	4	0	7	3	1	41	7	6	25	37	12	8
Intra-district Migration																
R – R	7299453	30645298	21	2	2	0	7	1	5	80	18	4	25	8	22	6
U – R	1293641	2003210	19	3	2	0	4	1	2	47	35	21	24	21	15	8
R – U	3198277	4216547	36	4	4	0	11	4	1	48	6	4	28	32	13	8
U – U	1596613	2058286	29	4	4	1	4	2	1	40	15	10	34	35	15	8
Inter-district migration																
R – R	2686128	8249195	37	4	2	0	5	1	3	74	11	3	27	13	15	5
U – R	764148	1152152	31	4	3	0	7	2	2	51	15	9	26	26	17	8
R – U	3305184	3502268	48	6	4	0	8	3	1	43	6	5	23	36	10	8
U – U	2790950	3452445	37	4	3	0	7	3	1	41	9	7	31	38	12	7
Inter-state migration																
R – R	1759523	2714779	57	9	3	0	2	0	2	61	3	2	24	23	10	6
U – R	522916	530436	41	5	3	1	5	2	1	40	5	5	24	39	20	9
R – U	3803737	2569218	65	6	3	0	3	1	0	35	3	5	18	46	8	7
U – U	2201882	2288598	48	5	4	1	7	3	1	37	5	4	26	43	10	7
From other countries																
Moved to rural	5449	12002	33	3	2	0	5	2	2	68	5	2	19	13	35	12
Moved to urban	18306	16539	36	5	3	1	11	7	1	21	4	4	23	44	23	19

Source: Same as before

Figure 10.1 *India: Inter-state Migration, Males, 1991–2001*

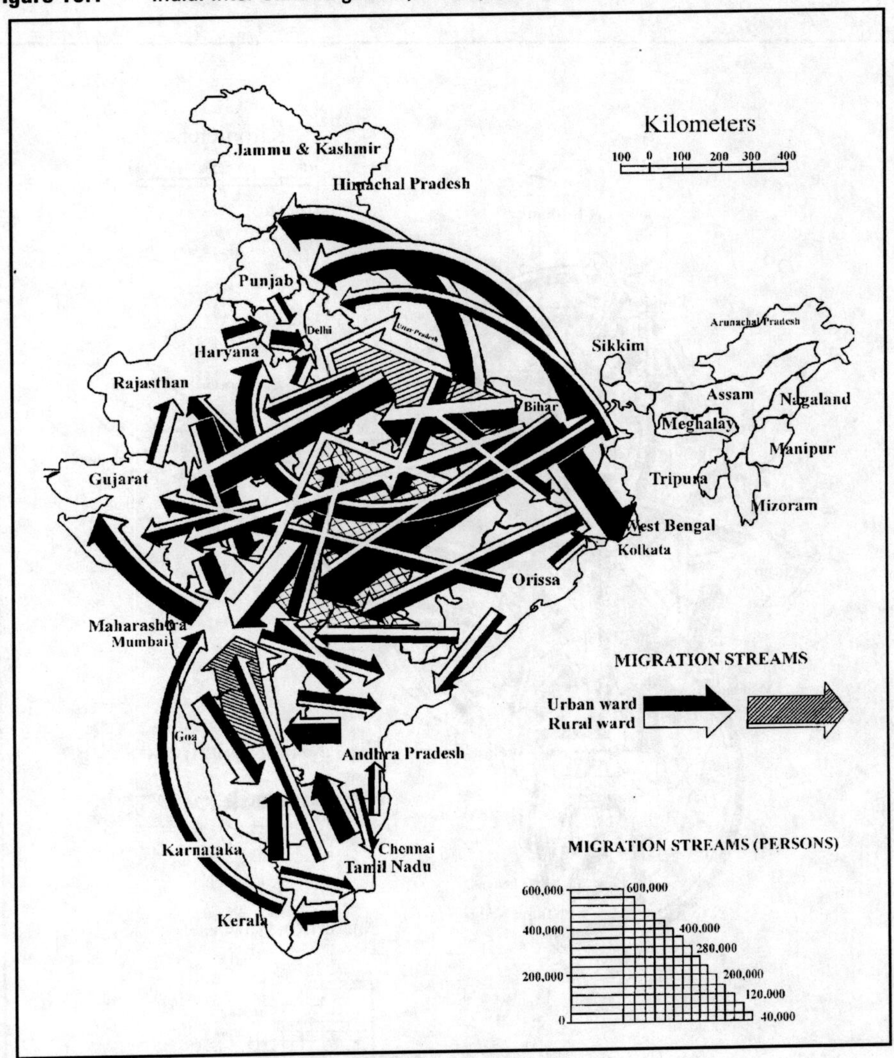

Source: Computed from Data from Census of India, 2001 (b).

Further, down the Table, move for employment becomes increasingly more important for the males at inter-district (48%) and inter-state migration (65%), for rural-to-urban part. For females, employment migration are still low (3–4%), while marriage migration shows decreasingly less importance at longer distances (35%). A large chunk of males migrated for familial (25%) and other reasons (12%) at various components of migration, and a still larger share of the females, indicate similar trends (37% and 8%).

Variations in State-level Migration Patterns

Table 10.3 presents state-level variations in reasons, for both for the sexes (all durations). Our specific concern here is migration for employment, about which some aspects may be noted:

Figure 10.2 *India: Inter-state Migration, Females, 1991–2001*

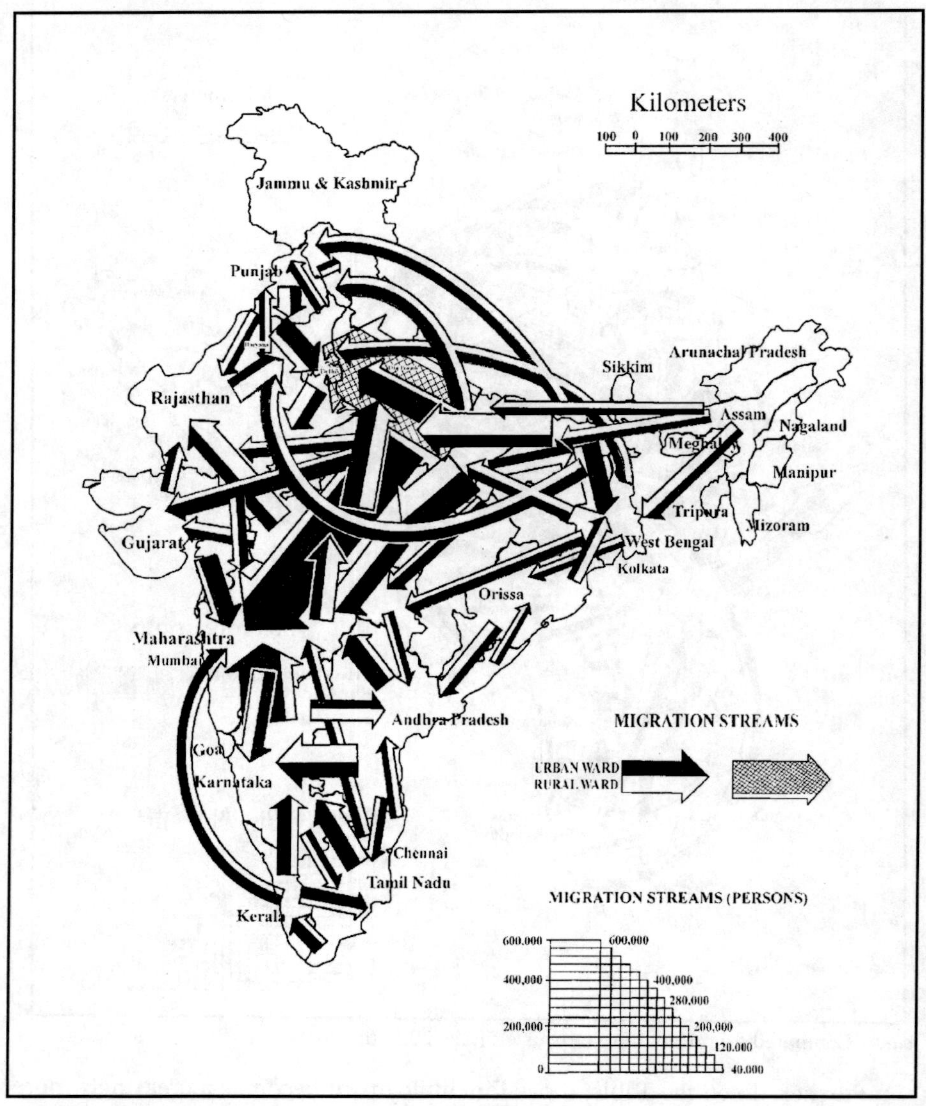

Source: Computed from Data of Census of India, 2001(b), New Delhi

(a) Compared to the males, the females make much less moves for employment in all the states.

(b) In short, while male report 30–60 per cent rates for employment migration (higher than 1981–1991 rates), rates for females vary between 4–8 per cent in most states, except in four southern states, like Andhra Pradesh, Karnataka, Tamil Nadu and Kerala (due to higher female literacy and recent economic progress), and partly in Orissa (due to mining).

Table 10.3 *Patterns of Migration in the States, Reasons for Move, 1991–2001*

Place of Last Residence	*Total migrants*		*Reasons for Migration (%)*													
			Work		*Business*		*Education*		*Marriage*		*Moved after birth*		*Moved with family*		*Others*	
	M	*F*	*M*	*F*	*M*	*F*	*M*	*F*	*M*	*F*	*M*	*F*	*M*	*F*	*M*	*F*
J-K																
R – R	11548	21377	51	4	2	1	7	1	2	72	1	0	23	18	15	5
U – R	7432	5975	33	4	2	1	10	5	0	19	2	2	31	61	23	9
R – U	13192	9492	54	4	3	0	7	3	0	27	1	2	25	58	9	7
U – U	25081	25003	36	4	4	0	12	6	0	19	2	1	35	62	12	8
Himachal Pradesh																
R – R	14932	27538	51	4	1	0	4	1	1	64	5	2	26	23	11	5
U – R	3949	3867	38	5	2	0	11	3	1	36	3	3	28	46	18	8
R – U	36469	31532	58	4	1	0	7	2	0	35	4	3	23	48	7	7
U – U	20856	22123	45	5	2	1	12	6	1	35	4	3	28	45	9	6
Punjab																
R – R	51093	108199	41	3	1	0	1	0	1	67	9	3	33	21	14	5
U – R	20110	23154	39	4	2	0	4	2	1	38	5	4	33	45	17	8
R – U	49686	59304	47	4	3	0	4	2	1	40	5	3	32	45	10	6
U – U	76707	98867	38	4	4	0	6	3	1	41	4	3	34	44	13	6
Haryana																
R – R	40162	161541	38	2	2	0	3	0	2	80	7	1	33	12	15	5
U – R	12987	19153	37	3	2	0	4	1	1	55	5	3	29	31	22	6
R – U	79055	97149	47	3	2	0	4	1	1	44	3	2	35	45	9	5
U – U	66621	95307	39	3	4	0	7	2	1	47	4	2	36	40	9	5
Delhi																
R – R	5446	21508	39	2	2	0	5	1	3	83	2	1	28	10	21	4
U – R	41859	47054	30	3	1	0	4	2	1	43	2	2	33	41	30	10
R – U	12235	15725	46	4	2	1	6	1	1	47	2	2	30	39	12	6
U – U	135297	168448	34	4	3	1	5	2	1	34	3	2	40	51	15	7
Rajasthan																
R – R	96780	207738	49	6	8	1	1	0	1	68	5	2	26	18	10	6
U – R	20889	23142	39	4	9	1	4	1	1	42	4	3	30	42	14	8
R – U	215504	160827	56	4	10	1	2	1	0	38	5	6	20	45	7	7
U – U	120299	126105	42	3	11	1	6	1	0	42	6	5	27	42	8	6
Uttar Pradesh																
R – R	341952	417312	64	7	3	0	2	0	1	59	1	1	24	29	7	4
U – R	63945	58709	51	5	4	1	5	2	1	36	2	2	26	48	12	7
R – U	1E+06	764917	68	3	2	0	2	1	0	34	3	4	17	51	7	8
U – U	405987	368515	55	3	3	0	5	2	0	40	3	3	24	45	9	7
Bihar																
R – R	303189	251619	69	9	3	0	2	0	1	55	1	1	17	30	7	5
U – R	36768	26363	55	5	5	1	8	2	1	40	2	2	19	44	11	6
R – U	829534	393932	69	5	3	0	3	1	0	31	2	3	16	52	8	8
U – U	199772	136017	54	4	4	1	10	3	0	34	2	3	20	48	9	8
Assam																
R – R	40902	76970	43	5	5	0	2	0	3	65	1	1	29	22	18	7
U – R	12156	10992	43	7	7	1	4	2	1	35	2	2	24	45	19	9
R – U	32015	27419	54	10	7	1	6	2	0	32	1	1	22	45	10	9
U – U	36834	35080	43	5	6	1	9	4	0	26	2	2	30	55	11	8

West Bengal

Cont'd...

...Cont'd

R – R	59486	103342	67	5	4	0	2	0	2	75	1	1	16	15	9	4
U – R	33478	33284	52	5	4	0	4	1	1	53	2	2	18	32	20	7
R – U	130994	69176	75	8	4	0	3	1	0	38	1	2	12	44	6	6
U – U	151885	129360	59	7	5	1	6	3	0	36	3	3	19	44	8	7
Orissa																
R – R	61113	80334	71	10	2	0	1	0	2	63	2	1	16	21	7	5
U – R	11401	10153	57	6	3	0	4	1	1	43	5	5	19	36	13	8
R – U	132690	53646	80	8	2	0	2	1	0	36	2	4	9	43	5	8
U – U	45145	36019	59	6	3	0	8	2	0	37	3	4	19	44	8	7
Madhya Pradesh																
R – R	111613	229897	52	8	2	1	1	0	2	63	3	2	30	22	10	5
U – R	21978	30780	41	4	2	0	5	1	1	50	7	4	29	34	16	7
R – U	119661	108117	60	9	3	0	3	1	0	37	4	4	23	44	7	6
U – U	85970	116353	45	4	3	0	7	2	1	47	7	4	29	37	9	6
Gujarat																
R – R	25157	57020	40	4	3	0	3	0	3	69	9	3	26	17	17	6
U – R	30654	21774	27	4	2	1	4	2	0	28	7	8	20	44	41	14
R – U	63524	66934	49	3	4	0	3	1	1	42	10	9	22	34	11	11
U – U	79115	96302	37	3	4	1	7	2	0	39	11	8	29	39	12	9
Maharashtra																
R – R	83053	152169	40	8	7	2	1	0	2	55	13	7	28	23	10	6
U – R	55308	53752	30	3	4	1	3	1	1	37	10	9	23	37	31	12
R – U	103533	111545	50	5	6	1	2	1	0	40	12	9	23	38	8	7
U – U	143216	176365	39	4	6	1	4	1	1	37	9	7	29	43	12	7
Andhra Pradesh																
R – R	58321	105389	53	10	3	0	2	0	3	60	5	3	23	20	12	6
U – R	22036	23437	47	7	3	1	9	2	1	39	5	4	22	38	14	8
R – U	100835	96094	58	10	3	1	4	1	1	38	6	6	19	37	9	8
U – U	104616	111247	47	6	3	1	11	3	1	36	7	6	24	41	8	7
Karnataka																
R – R	96311	157032	49	12	1	0	1	0	2	52	11	7	26	23	9	6
U – R	27024	34413	40	7	2	0	4	1	2	44	12	9	24	30	16	9
R – U	125280	120565	59	9	1	0	2	1	1	37	10	10	20	35	8	9
U – U	88676	102282	49	6	3	0	4	2	1	38	11	9	23	36	10	9
Kerala																
R – R	25109	25946	55	13	4	0	7	5	2	39	8	8	16	26	10	9
U – R	14961	13748	48	18	4	1	16	12	1	21	7	7	15	30	10	11
R – U	80282	75106	63	17	3	0	6	8	1	32	8	8	13	27	7	8
U – U	89695	94316	54	15	3	1	10	11	1	27	7	7	17	32	8	8
Tamil Nadu																
R – R	73339	79898	60	16	3	1	1	1	5	47	4	3	19	26	8	6
U – R	32292	31762	46	10	5	1	3	2	3	35	8	8	22	36	13	9
R – U	102585	89882	62	12	5	1	2	2	2	40	5	5	16	33	8	8
U – U	123760	123130	53	8	5	1	4	3	2	34	6	6	21	40	9	8

Source: Computed from Census of India, 2001(b), Migration Tables. R-R means rural to rural migration; R-U means rural to urban migration, etc. Only Seventeen major states and Delhi Union Territory are shown.

(c) In general, for most states, both the rates for males and females are comparatively higher for rural-urban and urban-urban, than for rural-rural and urban-rural patterns; because they have some notion that the chances of obtaining work are higher in urban nodes. However, there are some exceptions, where rural development has progressed (Kerala, Tamil Nadu, Andhra and Karnataka).

Inter-state Migration Flows, 1991–2001

Figures 10.1 and 10.2 present inter-state migration streams of the males and females, respectably, who moved during 1991–2001 Only major streams are illustrated. Noteworthy features are:

(a) Uttar Pradesh, Bihar, Tamil Nadu, Kerala, Madhya Pradesh, and Rajasthan are the main migration-source regions for the males and females. Karnataka and Andhra Pradesh are secondary sending regions. These are less economically developed states from which males and females moved out.

(b) Maharashtra, Delhi, Gujarat, Karnataka, Madhya Pradesh, Punjab, Haryana, and West Bengal are the main migration-destination states for both the sexes. These are economically more developed states towards which they move searching for employment, subsistence, or shelter. Kerala, Tamil Nadu, and Andhra also receive some migrants from neighbouring states.

(c) Like the males, the females are also drawn towards urban nodes in most states, to the centres of production and trade-commerce. Exceptions are rural parts of Haryana, Kerala, Karnataka, and Gujarat where agricultural development has progressed recently.

(d) In sum, migration occurs as a response to regional disparities in the levels of economic development over India: moves arise from the less economically developed states (Uttar Pradesh, Bihar, etc.) to comparatively more developed states (Maharashtra, Delhi, Punjab, Haryana, and West Bengal).

(e) Maps of inter-state migration for females are almost identical to that of males. Only difference is that volumes are much higher for the latter. Migration-source states and migration-receiving states are same; so also the underlying macro spatial-socio-economic-political forces that cause such regional disparities in the levels of development and which, in turn, induce migration to occur over space.

(f) Figures 10.3 and 10.4 show migration flows towards four mega cities (Mumbai, Kolkata, Delhi, and Chennai), by males and females, respectively. Migration patterns are strikingly similar between both the sexes, and also for inter-state streams, and to mega cities. Difference is only in volume, but the patterns remain the same. They indicate remarkable spatial responses to distinct regional disparities. The same patterns can also be visualized, if compared with that of prior five decades (since 1951–61) (see Mukherji, 1981: 11–65).

(g) In fact, the same patterns were prevailing since the first Indian census, from 1872 onwards. The migration patterns did not change since last 130 years, because the spatial disorganization persisted all these years. Unfortunately, it might also continue many decades more, unless and until we make very strong efforts to develop small towns and cities and re-configure India's spatial organization in favour of development of internal domestic markets. Further details are discussed in last chapter.

(h) Such evidences stand in sharp contrast to the conventional wisdom that emphasizes religious cultural constraints causing low female mobility rate (without explaining why is it so), or Todaro's model for male mobility, or the like, as explanatory factors. Rather it can be argued that, in India, both the males and the females, are under the influence of the same nexus of macro historic-economic-political forces and spatial processes that generated, and still maintain, poverty, regional imbalances and under-development over the national space and induce migration to arise and proliferate (for details, Mukherji, 1992b). These processes are still in force.

Figure 10.3 *India: Male Migration to Mega Cities, 1991–2001*

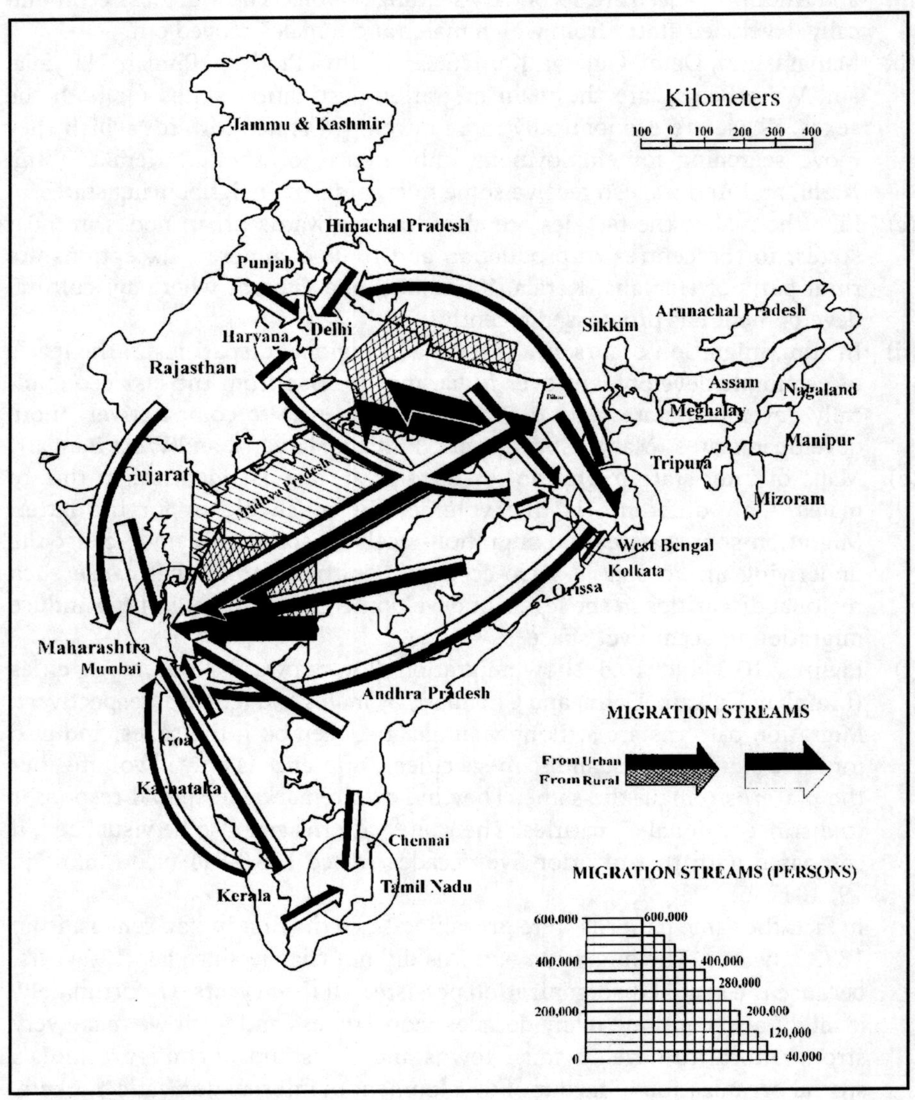

Source: Same as in Figure 10.1.

Various Aspects of Migration According to 2001 Census

Briefly, the following salient aspects of migration are apparent (Tables 10.4 to 10.16):

Figure 10.4 *India: Female Migration to Mega Cities, 1991–2001*

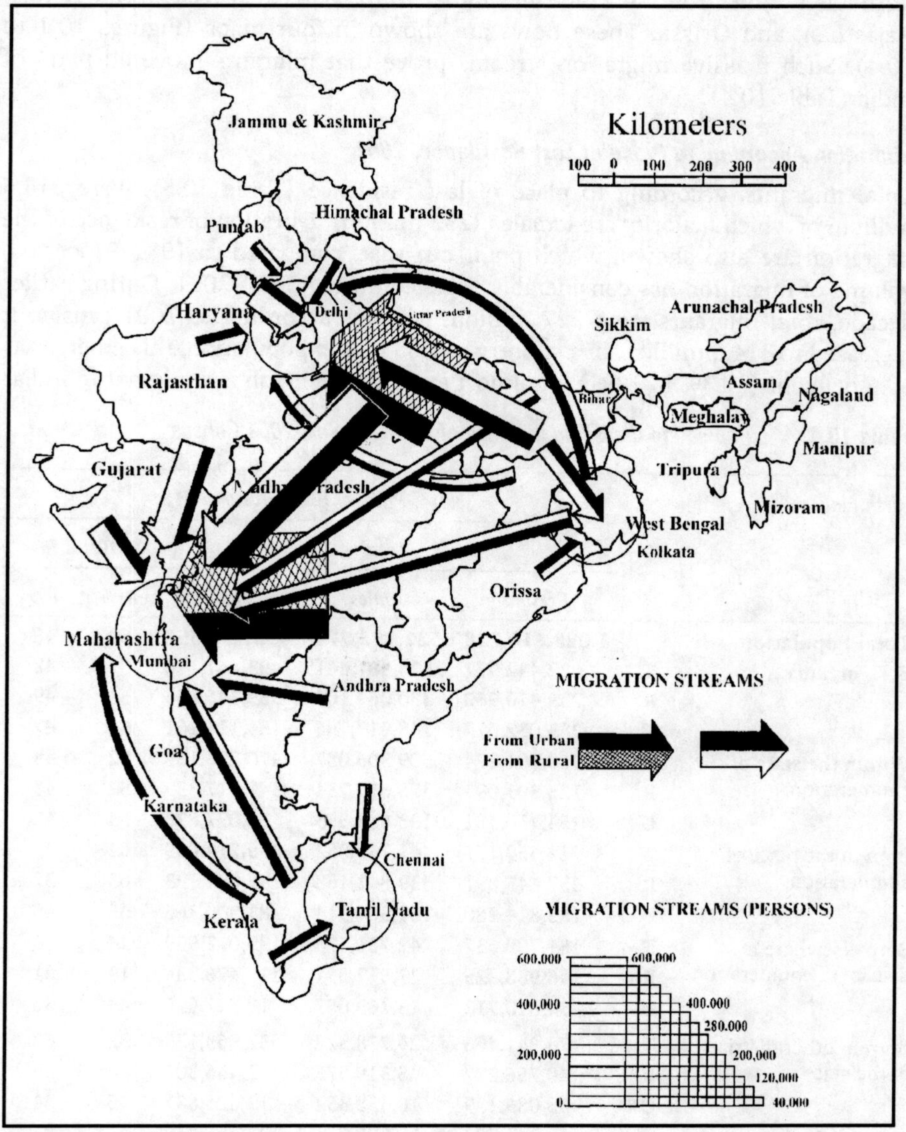

Source: Same as in Figure 10.1.

Migration According to Place of Birth Statistics

About 181.8 million people were enumerated in other places but within the district of enumeration (Table 10.4). Additionally 76.8 million were enumerated in other districts within the same state. Thus, intra-state migration is very large, 258 million.

Inter-state Migration (According to Birth-place Data)

Besides, about 42.3 million people migrated from other states (47% males, 53% females, males' share increased from last census). Of them, largest number of migrants moved from Uttar Pradesh, followed by Bihar, Madhya Pradesh, Karnataka, and Andhra Pradesh. Some were also displaced from Kerala, Rajasthan, and Orissa. These flows are shown in four maps (Figures 10.1 to 10.4). Such massive migration streams prove that migrants move all parts of India (Table 10.4).

Migration According to Place of Last Residence, 2001

Total migrants, according to place of last residence (Table 10.5), were 314.5 million; of which majority are females (232 million). Duration of residence of the migration are also shown, which point out that, compared to 1981–91 period, volume of migration has considerably changed during 1991–2001. During earlier decade, total migrants were 227 million, whereas according to 2001 census, it increased to 314.5 million. In a country of 1.03 billion population, this emerges as 30.6 per cent (27.3% in 1991), or almost every third person is a migrant in India.

Table 10.4 *Population Classified by Place of Birth and Sex, 2001 Census*

Birth place		*Place of Enumeration*				
		Total			*Total %*	
		Persons	*Males*	*Females*	*M%*	*F%*
Total Population		**1,028,610,328**	**532,156,772**	**496,453,556**	**52**	**48**
Born in India	T	1,022,442,977	528,981,861	493,461,116	52	48
	R	739,410,960	380,064,105	359,346,855	51	49
	U	283,032,017	148,917,756	134,114,261	53	47
Within the state of enumeration	T	980,101,274	509,306,087	470,795,187	52	48
	R	725,391,093	375,673,734	349,717,359	52	48
	U	254,710,181	133,632,353	121,077,828	53	47
Born in the place of enumeration	T	721,460,171	441,746,082	279,714,089	61	39
	R	537,645,891	339,841,168	197,804,723	63	37
	U	183,814,280	101,904,914	81,909,366	55	45
Born elsewhere in district of enumeration	T	181,799,637	42,781,678	139,017,959	24	76
	R	146,988,925	27,512,591	119,476,334	19	81
	U	34,810,712	15,269,087	19,541,625	44	56
Born in other districts of the state	T	76,841,466	24,778,327	52,063,139	32	68
	R	40,756,277	8,319,975	32,436,302	20	80
	U	36,085,189	16,458,352	19,626,837	46	54
States in India beyond state of enumeration	T	42,341,703	19,675,774	22,665,929	47	53
	R	14,019,867	4,390,371	9,629,496	31	68
	U	28,321,836	15,285,403	13,036,433	54	46
Jammu & Kashmir	R	95,767	26,139	69,628	27	73
	U	129,124	65,704	63,420	51	49
Himachal Pradesh	R	137,592	41,718	95,874	30	70
	U	314,050	166,589	147,461	53	47
Punjab	R	651,744	213,336	438,408	33	67
	U	998,094	467,081	531,013	47	53

Cont'd...

...Cont'd

Haryana	R	726,465	116,090	610,375	16	84
	U	1,018,569	448,586	569,983	44	56
Delhi	R	194,871	39,303	155,568	20	80
	U	553,365	203,852	349,513	37	63
Rajasthan	R	971,560	229,353	742,207	24	76
	U	1,781,258	941,451	839,807	53	47
Uttar Pradesh	R	2,203,427	765,162	1,438,265	35	65
	U	7,423,209	4,390,711	3,032,498	59	41
Bihar	R	1,518,891	665,912	852,979	44	56
	U	4,024,233	2,555,685	1,468,548	64	36
Assam	R	405,066	124,624	280,442	31	69
	U	290,241	146,490	143,751	51	49
West Bengal	R	638,887	183,314	455,573	29	71
	U	1,101,461	585,122	516,339	53	47
Orissa	R	383,078	124,586	258,492	33	67
	U	581,105	362,639	218,466	62	38
Madhya Pradesh	R	1,026,722	248,448	778,274	24.	76
	U	1,040,806	459,028	581,778	44	56
Gujarat	R	286,606	69,142	217,464	24	76
	U	1,054,221	511,752	542,469	49	52
Maharashtra	R	817,292	245,997	571,295	30	70
	U	1,335,529	597,760	737,769	45	55
Andhra Pradesh	R	552,822	169,769	383,053	31	69
	U	1,076,066	528,612	547,454	49	51
Karnataka	R	733,450	229,825	503,625	31	69
	U	1,243,765	614,422	629,343	49	51
Kerala	R	198,621	96,160	102,461	48	52
	U	1,023,240	534,752	488,488	52	48
Tamil Nadu	R	525,844	231,028	294,816	44	56
	U	1,212,670	627,038	585,632	52	48

Source: Same as in Table 10.1. Only 17 major states and Delhi Union Territory are shown.

Table 10.5 *Migrants Classified by Place of Last Residence, 2001*

Last residence	*Total migrants*			*Duration of Residence (%)*											
				Less than 1 year		*1–4 years*		*5–9 years*		*10–19 years*		*20+ years*		*Duration not stated*	
	Persons	*Males*	*Females*	*M*	*F*	*M*	*F*	*M*	*F*	*M*	*F*	*M*	*F*	*M*	*F*
INDIA	**314541350**	**93361809**	**221179541**	**5**	**2**	**18**	**14**	**13**	**14**	**18**	**24**	**21**	**37**	**26**	**10**
Last residence elsewhere in India															
Total	309385525	90677712	218707813	5	2	18	14	13	14	18	24	20	36	26	10
Rural	223421962	50586071	172835891	6	2	21	14	16	14	23	26	25	41	9	4
Urban	49561717	21048089	28513628	5	3	22	20	17	17	22	25	23	27	12	8

Cont'd...

...Cont'd

Within the state of enumeration but outside the place of enumeration															
Total	268219260	71579630	196639630	4	2	17	14	12	13	17	24	19	37	31	10
Rural	197060985	38557289	158503696	6	2	21	14	16	14	22	26	25	42	10	4
Urban	36918050	15078428	21839622	5	3	22	20	17	17	22	25	22	26	14	9
Elsewhere in the district of enumeration															
Total	193592938	47337924	146255014	4	2	15	13	11	13	15	24	16	38	39	11
Rural	147062768	24848822	122213946	5	2	21	13	16	14	22	26	24	42	12	4
Urban	17926854	7240728	10686126	5	3	20	19	16	16	20	24	20	26	20	12
In other districts of state of enumeration															
Total	74626322	24241706	50384616	5	3	20	16	15	15	21	25	23	34	15	8
Rural	49998217	13708467	36289750	7	3	21	15	16	15	23	26	27	38	6	4
Urban	18991196	7837700	11153496	5	3	23	21	18	18	23	26	24	27	8	6
States in India beyond state of enumeration															
Total	41166265	19098082	22068183	6	4	22	18	16	16	22	25	25	31	8	7
Rural	26360977	12028782	14332195	7	4	22	17	17	16	24	26	26	34	4	4
Urban	12643667	5969661	6674006	5	4	24	22	16	17	22	25	27	28	5	5
Himachal Pradesh															
Rural	285505	125717	159788	4	4	21	18	16	15	25	25	29	34	5	4
Urban	125304	61120	64184	4	3	23	21	15	16	22	24	33	31	5	5
Punjab															
Rural	884009	334735	549274	4	3	14	14	12	13	22	25	44	43	4	3
Urban	669295	303183	366112	4	3	16	17	12	14	25	27	38	35	4	4
Haryana															
Rural	1136668	313903	822765	4	2	18	15	16	14	26	27	32	39	4	3
Urban	516417	209466	306951	4	3	20	19	14	15	23	26	35	33	5	4
Delhi															
Rural	138294	32167	106127	7	2	30	18	18	15	20	24	16	37	9	4
Urban	738109	299034	439075	8	4	32	26	19	19	20	23	14	22	7	6
Rajasthan															
Rural	1749264	686148	1063116	7	4	22	16	17	15	24	26	26	36	5	3
Urban	730563	344709	385854	4	3	21	20	16	16	23	26	31	31	5	5
Uttar Pradesh															
Rural	6673933	3596345	3077588	5	4	21	18	19	17	27	28	24	30	4	4
Urban	2173727	1111559	1062168	4	3	22	21	17	17	25	26	29	29	5	5
Bihar															
Rural	4100923	2389842	1711081	5	4	23	17	19	17	24	27	25	30	4	5
Urban	875562	494688	380874	4	3	26	22	18	18	22	25	24	26	6	6
West Bengal															
Rural	851740	347833	503907	8	3	30	16	18	16	19	27	22	36	4	3
Urban	750720	361018	389702	6	3	28	22	18	17	21	25	23	28	5	4
Orissa															
Rural	693166	344216	348950	7	4	30	19	19	16	20	25	20	33	4	4
Urban	195537	101173	94364	5	4	32	27	19	18	19	24	20	22	5	5

Cont'd...

...Cont'd

Madhya Pradesh															
Rural	1331460	421579	909881	13	5	26	17	16	15	20	25	20	35	6	3
Urban	589812	226613	363199	6	3	26	21	16	16	21	25	26	30	5	4
Gujarat															
Rural	694254	285331	408923	6	3	14	14	12	14	21	25	44	42	4	3
Urban	586300	276548	309752	9	4	19	19	13	15	19	23	37	34	5	4
Maharashtra															
Rural	1089931	400249	689682	12	7	19	16	16	15	23	25	26	33	5	4
Urban	946121	413010	533111	8	4	24	22	16	17	21	25	25	27	6	5
Andhra Pradesh															
Rural	911489	363117	548372	7	4	22	18	15	15	21	24	30	35	5	4
Urban	555281	257959	297322	6	4	28	25	15	16	19	22	26	27	6	6
Karnataka															
Rural	1164109	471823	692286	11	7	21	18	15	16	21	24	27	32	5	4
Urban	594415	269837	324578	6	4	22	21	15	17	21	24	31	29	5	5
Kerala															
Rural	497148	257392	239756	4	3	22	23	15	16	22	24	33	30	4	4
Urban	477193	243260	233933	4	4	25	27	15	16	21	22	30	26	5	6
Tamil Nadu															
Rural	847665	412284	435381	5	4	22	19	16	16	23	25	30	32	4	4
Urban	712013	353531	358482	4	4	24	23	16	17	22	24	29	27	5	6
Last residence outside India															
Rural	2603601	1317588	1286013		2	6	6	6	8	17	21	62	59	7	5
Urban	2551822	1366326	1185496		2	7	6	6	6	12	13	66	67	8	8

Source: Same as in Table 10.1. Large numbers of migrants are also unclassified and not shown here. Only 15 major states and Delhi Union Territory are shown.

Rural-Urban Components and Short Distance vis-à-vis Long Distance Migration

Within short distance (*intra*-state) migration, majority of the male migrants moved from villages (54%), and 46 per cent moved from urban places (changed considerably from 1991). Corresponding share of female migrants were 80 per cent and 20 per cent, respectively (same as in 1991). However, their proportions changed much in regard to long distance (inter-state) migration: viz., rural male migrants constituted 63 per cent (59% in 1991) and urban male migrants comprised 37 per cent (31% in 1991); whereas corresponding share of the rural female migrants were 65 per cent (66% in 1991) and urban female migrants, 35 per cent (34% in 1991) (Table 10.5). Thus, the female migrants moving longer distances are as numerous as the male migrants. Table 10.6 provides a broad picture of such components of migration. *Intra*-district migration is 61.5 per cent, inter-district migration 23.7 per cent, inter-sate migration 13.1 per cent and international migration, 1.6 per cent (shown in Figure 10.5 and 10.6).

Broad Migration Patterns and Its Features

Total Migration

According to Census 2001, there were a total of 314.54 million migrants, in a country of 1016 million, i.e., almost every third Indian was a migrant! (Table 10.6, Figure 10.5)

Table 10.6 *Total Migration in India, All Durations, Males and Females, Census 2001*

Components	Total Migrants, All-India, All Durations, 2001	
	Persons	Per cent
Total migration	314,541,350	100.0
Total internal migration	309,385,525	98.4
Intra-district migration	193,592,938	61.5
Inter-district migration	74,626,322	23.7
Inter-state migration	41,166,265	13.1
From other countries	5,155,423	1.6

Source: Same as in Table 10.1.

Figure 10.5 *Total Migrants in India 314.6 million, All Durations, Census 2001*

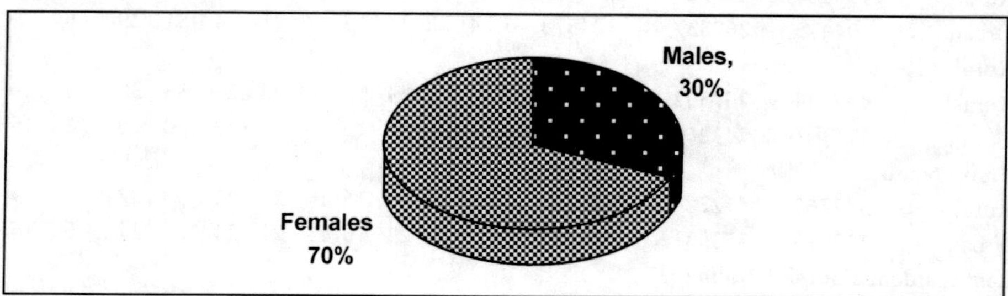

Source: Census of India, 2001

Components of Migration

During 1991–2001, about 32.9 million males and 65.4 million females were

Figure 10.6 *Total Migration in India, All Durations, Males and Females, Census 2001*

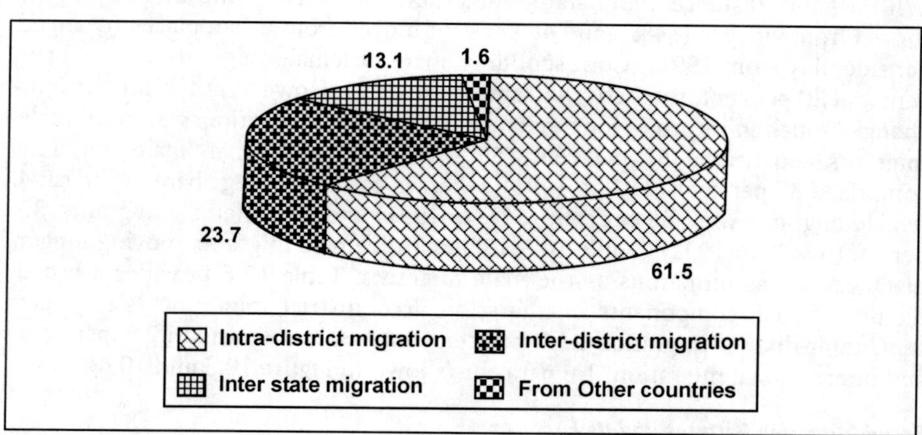

migrants. Of them, mostly were short distance intra-district migrants (males 43% and females, 61%). Inter-state migrants were only 26 per cent among males, and 12.7 per cent among females (Table 10.7, Figure 10. 6).

Table 10.7 *Total Migration by Types, All-India, Males and Females, 1991–2001*

Total Migration	*Migrants for 0–9 Years, All-India, 1991–2001*				
	Persons	*Males*	*Females*	*Males %*	*Females %*
Total migration	98,301,342	32,896,986	65,404,356	100.0	100.0
Total internal migration	97,560,320	32,510,444	65,049,876	98.8	99.5
Intra-district migration	54,108,439	14,147,939	39,960,500	43.0	61.1
Inter-district migration	26,625,002	9,850,344	16,774,658	29.9	25.6
Inter-state migration	16,826,879	8,512,161	8,314,718	25.9	12.7
From other countries	740,867	386,461	354,406	1.2	0.5

Total Population Migration, Persons, All-India, 1991–2001 and Its Parts

During 1991–2001, 98.3 million migrated, of which majority were intra-district migrants (51%), followed by inter-district (26%), inter-state (20%) and international migration (3%) (Figure 10.7, Table 10.7).

Figure 10.7 *Total Migration, 1991–2001, All-India, Persons, 2001 and Its Parts, Total Migration 98.3 Million*

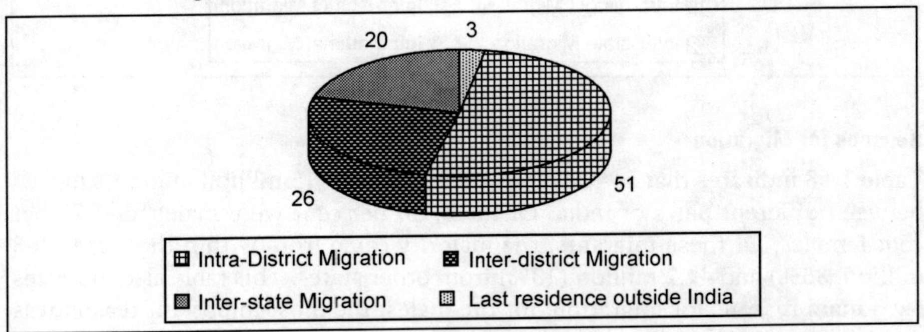

Total Male Migration, All-India, 1991–2001 and Its Parts

However, for the males, those components changed considerably: out of total 32.9 million male migrants, only 43 per cent moved *intra*-district, 29 per cent inter-district, and another 26 per cent moved for inter-state migration. These emerge in much contrast to the picture of total migration (for all persons) (Table 10.7, Figure 10.8).

Figure 10.8 *Total Migration, All-India, 1991–2001, Males and Its Components (32.9 Million)*

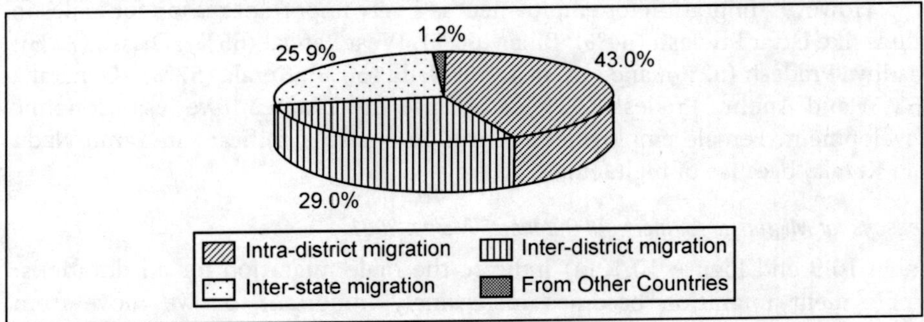

Total Female Migration, All-India, 1991–2001 and Its Parts

In comparison, for the females, such components changed substantially: out of a total 65.4 million female migrants, 60 per cent moved for short distance *intra*-district migration, whereas 26 per cent did for inter-district, and only 13 per cent moved inter-state migration. Thus, majority of the females moved short distances (Figure 10.9).

Figure 10.9 *Total Female Migration, All-India, 1991–2001, and Its Parts Total Female Migration 65.4 Million*

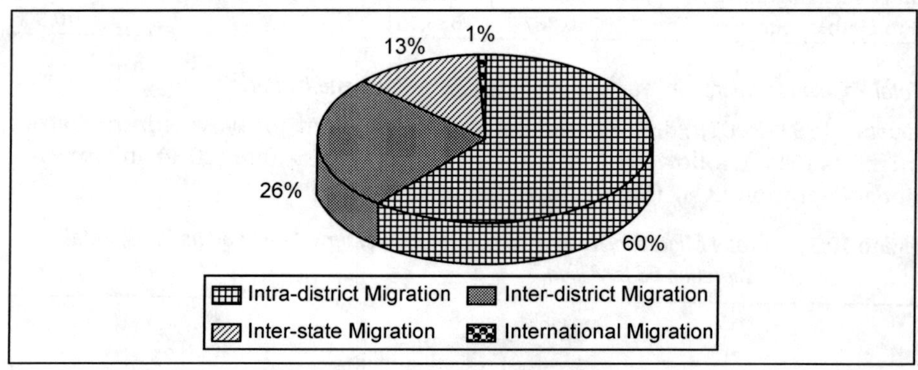

Reasons for Migration

Table 10.8 indicates that according to 2001 Census, 315 million migrants moved between different parts of India. Of them, 30 per cent were males, and 70 per cent females. Of these migrants, the majority came from within the state (268 million, 85%) and 41.2 million (13%) from other states. This table also indicates *seven* main reasons for migration: for the males, the most important reason was employment (28%), followed by miscellaneous (34%) and family moved (19%), business (3%), and education (3%). For the females, marriage (70%) was the most important reason for migration, followed by family moved (11%) and miscellaneous (14%). Among the females, education, or business was still not prominent reason, 0.2 per cent and 0.3 per cent, respectively. Thus, for the males the economic motives are still the supreme reason for migration; whereas for the females, marriage or familial migration is still important. Indeed, the patterns have not changed, in spite of recent economic development in India (Table 10.6) (Figures 10.1–10.2).

However, migration for employment is a very important reason for males in states like Uttar Pradesh (64%), Bihar (66%), West Bengal (65%), Orissa (72%), Madhya Pradesh (52%), and also in Tamil Nadu (56%), Kerala (57%), Karnataka (52%) and Andhra Pradesh (52%) – because these states have less economic development. Female employment migration is also significant in Tamil Nadu and Kerala, because of high female literacy.

Reasons for Migration, All-India, All Durations, Males, 2001

Table 10.9 and Figure 10.10(a) indicate the male migration for all durations: employment migration becomes increasingly important, as we move from

Table 10.8 *Migrants and Reasons for Migration, India and States, 2001*

Last residence	*Total migrants*			*Reasons for Migration (%)*													
				Work		*Business*		*Education*		*Marriage*		*Moved after birth*		*Moved with family*		*Others*	
	Persons	*Males*	*Females*	*M*	*F*	*M*	*F*	*M*	*F*	*M*	*F*	*M*	*F*	*M*	*F*	*M*	*F*
1	2	3	4	5	6	7	8	9	10	11	12	13	14	15	16	17	18
	All Durations of Residence																
Total	314541350	93361809	221179541	28	2	3	0	3	0	2	70	10	3	19	11	35	14
Last residence elsewhere in India	309385525	90677712	218707813	29	2	3	0	3	0	2	70	10	3	19	11	35	14
Within the state of enumeration but outside place of enumeration	268219260	71579630	196639630	22	1	2	0	3	0	3	72	12	3	19	9	40	14
Elsewhere in the district of enumeration	193592938	47337924	146255014	15	1	2	0	2	0	3	74	13	3	17	7	48	15
In other districts of the state of enumeration	74626322	24241706	50384616	36	3	3	0	3	1	2	66	10	3	23	16	24	12
States in India beyond the state of enumeration	41166265	19098082	22068183	52	4	4	0	2	1	1	55	5	3	20	27	16	11
Jammu & Kashmir	249450	106514	142936	38	3	3	0	6	2	1	52	2	1	27	31	24	11
Himachal Pradesh	435883	200747	235136	51	3	2	0	4	1	1	53	5	3	22	29	17	11
Punjab	1632410	677793	954617	41	3	3	0	2	1	1	56	6	3	30	29	18	9
Haryana	1738559	562926	1175633	43	2	4	0	2	0	1	69	5	2	29	20	17	8
Delhi	927593	353958	573635	31	3	3	0	3	1	1	51	4	2	35	31	23	12
Rajasthan	2609555	1093980	1515575	44	3	11	1	2	0	1	61	6	3	21	23	16	10
Uttar Pradesh	9255257	4930458	4324799	62	3	3	0	1	0	1	51	3	2	18	33	13	9
Bihar	5260659	3049437	2211222	60	4	5	0	2	1	1	49	2	2	16	34	15	12
Assam	708374	276597	431777	36	3	6	0	3	1	2	59	2	1	26	23	26	13
West Bengal	1687690	751523	936167	55	4	5	0	2	1	1	59	3	2	18	24	16	10
Orissa	937148	471555	465593	64	5	3	0	2	0	1	59	3	2	14	23	14	10
Madhya Pradesh	2011922	689729	1322193	47	4	3	0	2	0	1	64	6	2	24	20	17	9
Gujarat	1346817	592927	753890	39	2	6	0	3	1	1	55	12	7	20	23	19	12

Cont'd...

...Cont'd

Maharashtra	2145868	864534	1281334	37	3	6	1	1	0	1	54	13	6	23	25	19	11
Andhra Pradesh	1564768	666893	897875	48	5	3	0	3	1	2	53	7	4	19	24	18	13
Karnataka	1862289	788935	1073354	48	6	2	0	2	0	1	53	13	7	19	21	16	12
Kerala	1053407	540549	512858	54	12	4	0	4	4	1	36	8	7	14	26	16	15
Tamil Nadu	1668200	819359	848841	51	8	4	1	2	1	3	45	6	5	18	27	16	14
Last residence outside India	5155423	2683914	2471509	15	2	2	0	1	0	1	25	1	1	37	43	43	29
	Duration of Residence 0–9 Years																
Total	98301342	32896986	65404356	38	3	3	0	6	1	2	65	10	5	25	19	16	7
Last residence elsewhere in India	97560320	32510444	65049876	38	3	3	0	6	1	2	65	11	5	25	19	16	7
Within the state of enumeration but outside the place of enumeration	80733441	23998283	56735158	31	3	3	0	7	1	3	68	13	5	26	16	18	7
Elsewhere in the district of enumeration	54108439	14147939	39960500	25	2	3	0	7	1	3	72	16	5	26	13	21	7
In other districts of the state of enumeration	26625002	9850344	16774658	40	4	3	0	7	2	2	58	9	5	27	24	13	7
States in India beyond the state of enumeration	16826879	8512161	8314718	57	6	3	0	4	1	1	44	4	4	22	37	10	7
Himachal Pradesh	165776	78444	87332	51	4	1	0	8	3	1	44	4	3	25	39	10	7
Punjab	501285	204152	297133	40	4	3	0	4	2	1	50	6	3	33	35	14	6
Haryana	588001	205519	382482	41	2	3	0	5	1	1	61	4	2	34	29	12	5
Delhi	457919	199397	258522	34	3	2	1	5	2	1	41	3	2	37	45	18	7
Rajasthan	997196	465546	531650	49	4	10	1	3	1	1	51	5	4	24	33	9	7
Uttar Pradesh	3810701	2156885	1653816	64	4	2	0	3	1	0	42	3	3	20	43	8	7
Bihar	2241413	1408676	832737	66	6	3	0	4	1	0	39	2	2	17	44	9	7
West Bengal	730226	386540	343686	65	6	4	0	4	1	1	50	2	2	16	34	9	6
Orissa	440893	256231	184662	72	8	2	0	3	1	1	48	2	3	13	33	7	7
Madhya Pradesh	842937	347338	495599	52	7	3	0	4	1	1	52	5	3	27	31	10	6
Gujarat	451458	203340	248118	39	3	4	1	5	1	1	46	10	7	25	33	17	9
Maharashtra	896988	393097	503891	41	5	6	1	3	1	1	43	11	8	26	35	14	7
Andhra Pradesh	637360	292667	344693	52	9	3	1	6	2	1	44	6	5	22	33	10	8
Karnataka	769111	345298	423813	52	9	2	0	2	1	1	43	11	9	23	30	10	8
Kerala	431821	216129	215692	57	16	3	0	8	9	1	30	7	7	15	29	8	9
Tamil Nadu	674304	340617	333687	56	11	5	1	3	2	3	39	5	5	19	34	9	8
Last residence outside India	740867	386461	354406	40	5	2	1	5	2	1	36	1	1	25	40	26	16

Source: Same as in Table 10.1.

intra-district migration (15%) to inter-state migration (52%). To a lesser extent, similar trend also is also noticeable in migration for business (*intra*-district 1.8%; inter-state 3.9%). The importance for miscellaneous purpose linearly decreases, as migration distances increases (48% for intra-district, and 16% for inter-state migration), as cost for moves increases with distance. So, a distance-decay function operates.

Table 10. 9 *Migrants and Reasons for Migration, All Durations, Males, 2001*

Last Residence	*Reasons for Migration (Males, %)*							
	Males	*Work*	*Business*	*Education*	*Marriage*	*Moved after birth*	*Moved with family*	*Others*
Total Migration	93361809	28.1	2.6	2.5	2.3	9.9	19.4	35.2
Intra-District Migration	47337924	15.3	1.8	2.4	3.2	12.6	16.5	48.2
Inter-district Migration	24241706	35.5	3.1	3.3	2.0	9.7	22.6	23.7
Inter-state Migration	19098082	52.2	3.9	2.1	0.9	4.9	19.9	16.0
International Migration	2683914	14.9	1.9	1.2	0.6	0.7	37.4	43.4

Source: Same as in Table 10.1.

Reasons for migration, All-India, all Durations, Females, 2001

Likewise, Table 10.10 and Figure 10.10 (b) provide the details of purpose of migration among the females, for all durations. Even in 2001, the females moved much less for employment (only 1.7%), and marriage migration consists a huge (70%). Familial reason was also significant (11%), and other purposes (14%). However, as mentioned earlier, a large chunk of those females who moved for familial reason also take up work later in the destinations. Only minute field based investigation of their migration-mobility may reveal such truth. Here lies tremendous importance of field-based migration and circulation research.

Figure 10.10(a) *Reasons for Migration, All-India, All Durations, Males, 2001 Census (%)*

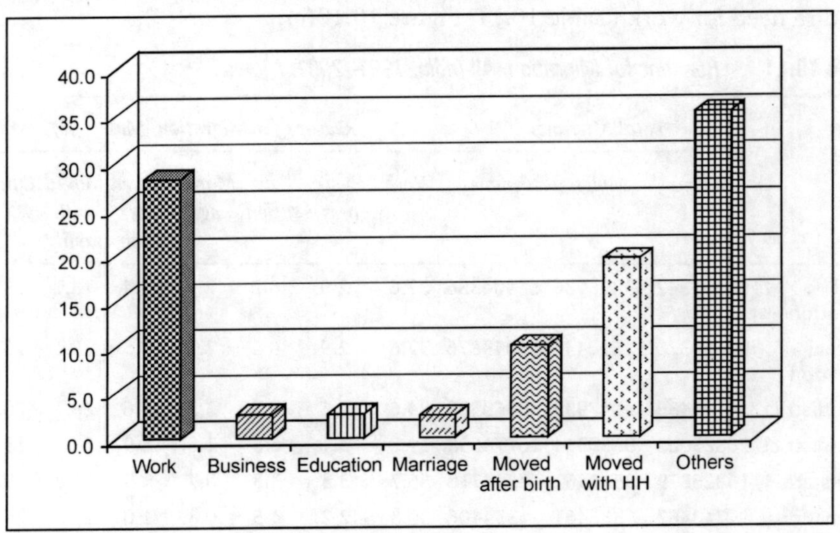

Table 10.10 *Reasons for Migration, All-India, All Durations, Females, 2001 Census*

All-India	*Migrants*	*Reasons for Migration (Females, %)*						
(All Durations)	*Females*	*Work*	*Business*	*Education*	*Marriage*	*Moved after birth*	*Moved with HH*	*Others*
All-India	221179541	1.7	0.2	0.4	69.6	2.9	11.3	13.9

Figure 10.10(b) *Reasons for Migration, All-India, All Durations, Females, 2001 Census (%)*

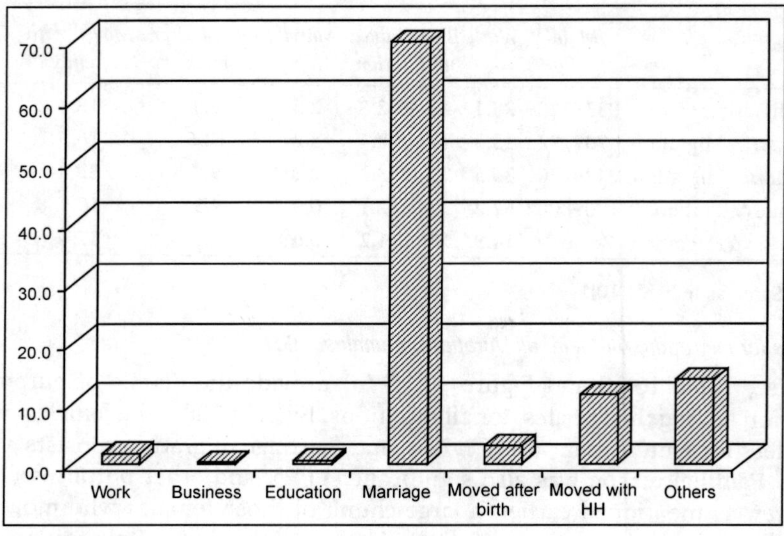

Reasons for Migration, All-India, 1991–2001, Males

During 1991–2001, male migration for employment shoots up noticeably from 25 per cent for *intra*-district moves to as high as 57 per cent for inter-state moves, viz., long distance migration were undertaken only with a major trigger effect of the dire need for work (Table 10.11, Figure 10.10(c).

Table 10.11 *Reasons for Migration, All-India, 1991–2001, Males*

Types	*Total Migrants*			*Reasons for Migration, Males (%)*						
	Persons	*Males*	*Females*	*Work*	*Business*	*Education*	*Marriage*	*Moved after birth*	*Moved with family*	*Others*
Total Migration	98301342	32896986	65404356	37.6	2.9	6.2	2.1	10.4	25.1	15.7
Internal Migration	97560320	32510444	65049876	37.6	2.9	6.2	2.1	10.5	25.1	15.6
Intra-district	54108439	14147939	39960500	24.6	2.6	7.3	3.2	15.6	26.1	20.6
Inter-district	26625002	9850344	16774658	39.8	3.1	6.8	1.6	8.9	26.5	13.3
Inter-state	16826879	8512161	8314718	56.7	3.3	3.8	0.7	3.9	21.8	9.8
International	740867	386461	354406	40.3	2.2	4.5	0.8	1.0	25.2	26.0

Figure 10.10(c) *Reasons for Male Migration, All-India, 1991–2001 (%)*

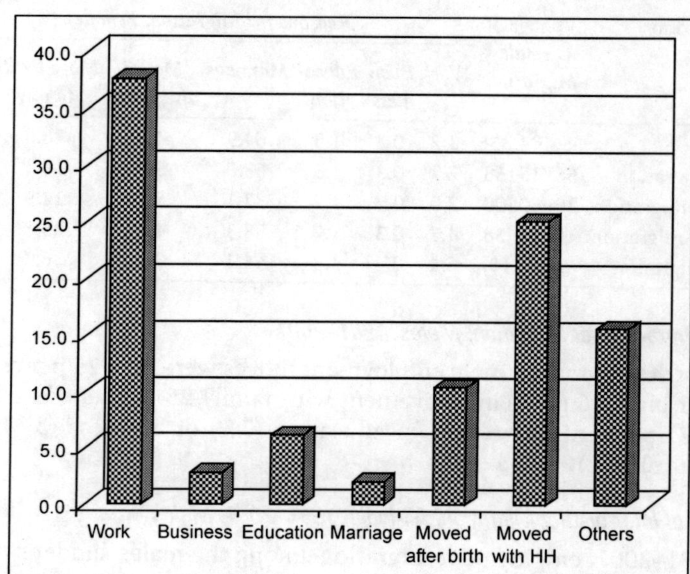

Reasons for Migration, All-India, 1991–2001, Females

Similarly, one notable aspect regarding employment migration among females is that they are more visible with respect to long distance inter-state migration, rather than short distance intra-state migration. Likewise, the same with familial moves (moved with family). Conversely, female marriage migration represents a distinct distance-decay function (decreasing from *intra*-district to inter-state migration). That is, females take up long distance inter-state migration mainly for work, or familial reason (Figure 10.11, Table 10.12).

Figure 10.11 *Reasons for Female Migration, All-India, 1991–2001, Total Female Migration 65.4 Million (%)*

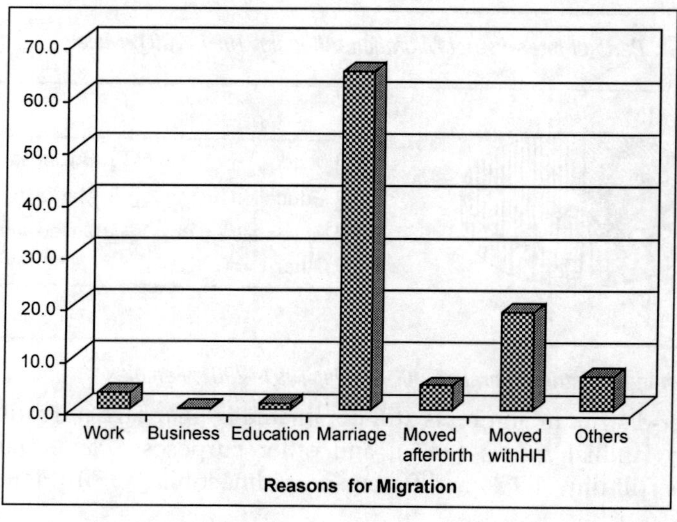

Table 10.12 *Reasons for Migration, Females, Duration of Residence, 1991–2001*

Types of Migration	*Volume of Female Migration*	*Reasons for Migration, Females (%)*						
		Work	*Business*	*Education*	*Marriage*	*Moved after birth*	*Moved with family*	*Others*
Total	65,404,356	3.2	0.3	1.3	64.9	4.8	18.9	6.7
Intra-state migration	56735158	2.7	0.3	1.3	68.0	5.0	16.1	6.5
Intra-district migration	39960500	2.0	0.2	1.2	72.1	5.1	12.9	6.5
Inter-district migration	16774658	4.3	0.3	1.7	58.3	4.8	23.8	6.7
Inter-state migration	8314718	6.4	0.4	1.4	44.4	3.7	36.7	7.0

Reasons for Intra-district Migration, Males, 1991–2001

In intra-district migration, male employment moves were only 25 per cent, while moves after birth 16 per cent, movement with family 25 per cent, and for other purposes, 21 per cent. Migration for education (7%) or business (3%) was still small (Figure 10.12).

Components of Inter-district Migration, All-India, 1991–2001, Males

During 1991–2001, employment migration among the males suddenly increases to 39 per cent with respect to inter-district moves, while all other types remain more or less same as in intra-district moves (Figure 10.13).

Figure 10.12 *Parts of Intra-district Migration, All-India, 1991–2001, Males*

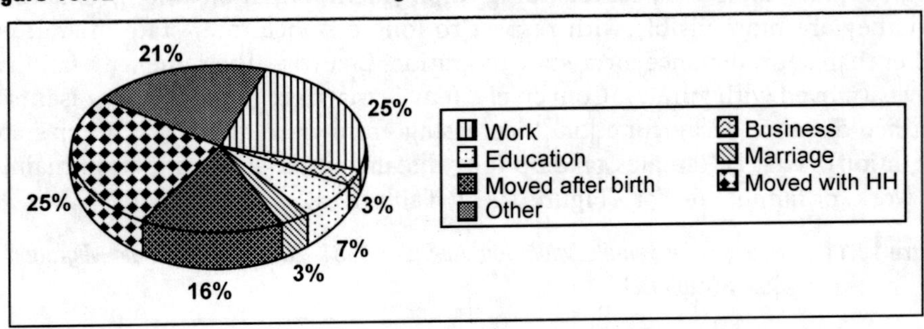

Figure 10.13 *Parts of Inter-district Migration, All-India, 1991–2001, Males*

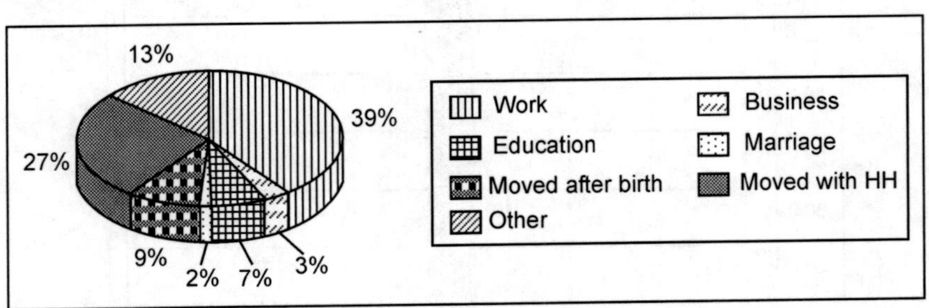

Components of Inter-District Migration, All – India, 1991–2001, Females

Female inter-district migration is still dominated by marriage migration (58%), followed by familial moves (24%), and other purposes (7%). Migration for education is still tiny (1.7%) and for business almost nil (0.3%) (Figure 10.14).

Figure 10.14 *Parts of Inter-district Migration, All-India, 1991–2001, Females*

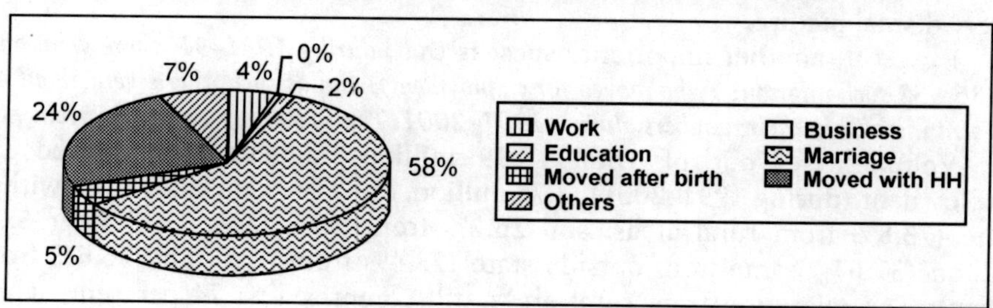

Reasons for Inter-State Migration, All-India, 1991–2001, Males

Figure 10.15 depicts different components of male inter-state migration. Most important reason is moves for work (57%), followed by familial moves (22%), and other purposes (10%). Migration for education (3.8%) and for business (3%) are still very minor.

Figure 10.15 *Reasons for Inter-state Migration, All-India, 1991–2001, Males*

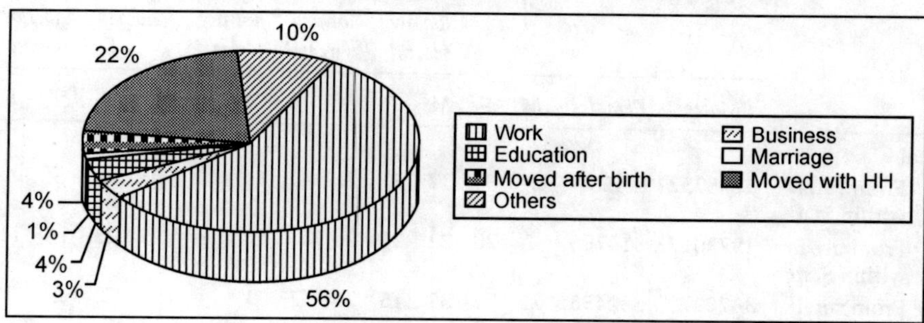

Literacy and Illiteracy among Migrants for Employment, 1991–2001

Table 10.13 is a revelation. It shows educational status of four categories of migrants, who migrated for employment:

(a) the migrants from rural areas within the state,
(b) the migrants from urban areas within the state,
(c) the migrants from rural areas, outside the state, and
(d) the migrants from urban areas, outside the state.

In India, total migration for "employment" for 1991–2001 was mere 13.99 million. Of this, 12.0 million (86%) were performed by males, and only 1.98 million (14%) by females (Table 10.13). The majority (74%) moved from rural areas; the rest migrated from urban centres (26%). Surprisingly, 29 per cent of all rural male migrants were illiterate; and among the rural females their proportion rose even to 61 per cent. That is, about two-thirds of the rural female migrants who moved for employment were illiterate. Corresponding proportion among urban males and urban females were 10 per cent and 26 per cent, respectively. In short, considerable proportion of male migrants (60% of those moving from rural areas and 38% from urban areas), who moved for employment were actually illiterate or semi-educated (below secondary school). In addition, more than 80 per cent of rural female migrants who moved for employment, were either illiterate or having less than secondary education (47% among urban female migrants) (Table 10.13). These characteristics of migrants, indeed, reflect a very dismal picture.

However, another important aspect is that, *during 1981–91, there were only 9,936,653 such migrants (who moved for employment), and as such, there were about 41 per cent increase in their numbers, during 1991–2001. This is a remarkable improvement.*

Volume-wise, out of Total 13.99 million migrants who moved for employment (during 1991–2001), 8.73 million, or 62 per cent came from within state (73.8% from rural areas, and 26.2% from urban areas). Another 5.26 million (37.6%) came from outside state (73.4% from rural, and 26.6% from urban). The migration from rural areas still comprised as 74 per cent; while migration from urban areas only 26 per cent.

Table 10.13 *Migrants from Rural/Urban Areas within and outside State Reporting Employment as Reason for Migration, Urban India, 1991–2001 (%)*

Moved from last area	*Migrants with 'Work' as reason for migration*		*Levels of Education of Migrants (%)*											
			Illiterate		*Literate but below second.*		*Secon-dary but not deg-ree*		*Tech. Diploma, not deg-ree*		*Gradu-ate and above*		*Tech. Diploma and Post Grad*	
	Males	*Females*	*M*	*F*	*M*	*F*	*M*	*F*	*M*	*F*	*M*	*F*	*M*	*F*
Total														
(i) From rural within State	5295732	1145036	21	54	32	21	26	12	3	2	13	6	5	4
(ii) From urban within State	1973017	314796	7	20	22	21	30	23	5	3	26	23	10	11
(iii) From rural outside State	3478970	382455	27	71	39	15	25	7	1	1	6	3	2	3
(iv) From urban outside State	1260541	137800	11	24	26	16	27	20	3	3	23	26	10	11
Rural														
(i) From rural within State	2545222	781662	29	61	33	19	21	9	2	2	10	4	5	6
(ii) From urban within State	480333	104876	10	26	28	21	30	22	4	4	19	17	9	9
(iii) From rural outside State	1009840	231786	38	82	35	12	20	3	1	0	4	1	2	2
(iv) From urban outside State	214444	28089	14	39	31	18	29	17	3	3	15	16	8	8
Urban														
(i) From rural within State	2750510	363374	14	39	31	25	31	18	3	3	16	10	6	5
(ii) From urban within State	1492684	209920	6	17	20	21	30	24	5	3	28	25	10	12
(iii) From rural outside State	2469130	150669	23	55	41	21	27	13	1	1	7	6	2	5
(iv) From urban outside State	1046097	109711	10	20	25	16	26	20	3	3	25	29	11	30

Source: As in Table 10.10. In last column, technical diploma equal to degree and post-graduate shown together.

We may examine the stock of illiterate plus semi-educated migrants (considering literate migrant – who are having less than secondary education as the semi-educated, as most having really primary education or can just sign their names). The following additional features may appear from Table 10.13:

(a) Among "*Intra*-state" migrants from "rural areas", the proportion of illiterate plus semi-educated migrants comprised 53 per cent among males, rising to as high as 75 per cent among the females.

(b) Corresponding picture of illiterate and semi-educated migrants from "urban areas" with all durations of residence are only slightly better: 29 per cent among males and 41 per cent among females (slightly improved from previous decade).

(c) Among the "Inter-state "migrants from "rural areas", the proportion of illiterate and semi-educated migrants are again as high as 66 per cent among males, rising to 86 per cent among the females (slightly worsened among females from previous decade).

(d) Corresponding situation of illiterate and semi-educated persons among Inter-state migrants from "urban areas" are 37 per cent among males, and 40 per cent among females (considerably improved from previous decade).

(e) Summing up, more than half of male migrants from rural areas (53 to 66%), both from *intra*-state and inter-state migration, are illiterate and semi-educated migrants (having less than secondary education). Their proportion improves to 30 to 37 per cent among urban male migrants. Corresponding picture is further frustrating among female migrants (75 to 86% among rural female migrants; and 40 per cent among urban female migrants). Thus, compared to earlier decade, the situation has further deteriorated among rural female migrants, although some improvements are noticeable among urban female migrants. Table 1.15 provides similar picture of all kinds of migrants, who moved for various reasons, but seeking employment. Overall picture is more precarious.

(f) Such low quality migration of distressed people only confirm one of the basic tenets of this research, i.e., poverty-induced migration and urban involution are occurring in India, not yet migration for prospect and high quality urbanization. Thus, these are signs of anti-development!

(g) The serious issues are: what could be expected from masses of such illiterate and semi-educated migrants? Indeed, it is a human mobility from rural poverty to urban poverty. And, involves an utter waste of human potentials and national productivity!

(h) *However, it is never meant, that "migration restriction" could be any solution. On the contrary, it is always suggested that such masses of deprived people would die in the villages, if their only escape route – "migration" – is restricted. Thus, even such a low-quality migration is far better than starvation or slow death in deadly stagnating villages. So, even these kinds of distressed migration is highly desirable. It is only meant here, that in India, the migrants are not receiving any scope of upward economic mobility in their urban or rural destinations, and, as such, their lives and rights must be protected, and all possible humane policies should be enacted and their proper implementation must be made urgently.*

Illiterates and Semi-educated are Majority among Migrants, 1991–2001

Table 10.14 presents a summary picture of all migrants, classified according to their levels of education, and according to their duration of residence in the place of destinations, Total male migration for all durations were 93.6 million, and total female migration for all durations were 221.7 million. Of them, the proportion of illiterate among male migrants was 26 per cent and among females increased to 58 per cent.

Table 10.14 *Migration Classified by Duration of Residence and Educational Levels, 2001*

Duration of Residence	*Total Migrants*		*Level of Education (%)*											
			Illiterate		*Lit. but below secondary.*		*Secondary but below grad*		*Tech. dip. not degree*		*Grad. and above*		*Tech. deg, and post grad*	
	Males	*Females*	*M*	*F*	*M*	*F*	*M*	*F*	*M*	*F*	*M*	*F*	*M*	*F*
Total														
All durations of residence	93,361,809	221,179,541	26	58	39	28	21	9	1	0	9	3	4	2
Duration of residence < 1 yr	4,173,469	4,712,255	50	58	29	25	13	11	1	0	5	4	2	2
Duration of residence 1–4 years	16,587,389	30,693,834	31	44	35	33	20	15	2	0	9	5	4	3
Duration of residence 5–9 years	12,136,128	29,998,267	21	45	44	35	20	13	1	0	9	4	3	3
Duration of residence 10 yrs+	36,607,202	133,956,410	18	65	41	24	25	7	2	0	11	2	4	2
Rural														
All durations of residence	43,846,535	166,530,857	34	66	43	26	15	6	1	0	4	1	4	2
Duration of residence < 1 yr	2,700,508	3,359,829	56	64	29	25	10	8	1	0	3	2	2	1
Duration of residence 1–4 years	7,544,871	21,409,212	40	50	37	34	14	12	1	0	5	2	3	2
Duration of residence 5–9 years	4,969,568	21,837,248	29	52	49	34	14	10	1	0	5	2	3	2
Duration of residence 10 yrs+	14,330,911	106,571,955	25	72	48	22	18	4	1	0	4	1	4	2
Urban														
All durations of residence	49,515,274	54,648,684	18	34	36	35	27	19	2	1	13	8	4	2
Duration of residence < 1 yr	1,472,961	1,352,426	37	43	29	27	20	19	2	1	9	9	3	2
Duration of residence 1–4 years	9,042,518	9,284,622	24	31	32	32	24	23	2	1	12	11	5	3
Duration of residence 5–9 years	7,166,560	8,161,019	16	27	41	39	25	21	2	0	12	10	4	2
Duration of residence 10 yrs +	22,276,291	27,384,455	13	37	36	35	30	18	2	0	15	7	4	2

Source: Same as in Table 10.1.

Note: Post graduates are shown together with Technical diplomas in last column.

Situation further worsens among recent migrants with duration of residence less than one year (2000–1). Fifty per cent of male migrants were illiterate (compared to 26% among migrants for all durations); while their proportion among the females rose even to higher level, 58 per cent (same among female migrants for all durations). When semi-educated migrants (having less than secondary education, in fact, less than primary school) are also considered, then, their proportion rises even to 65 per cent for males, and 86 per cent for females. For migrants with less than 1 year duration, their proportions are 79 per cent and 83 per cent, respectively.

Almost similar picture arises among migrants with duration of residence for 1–4 years or 5 years and above (Table 10.14). Compared to earlier situation, condition of recent migrants have further deteriorated (viz., 31% illiterates for males and 44% among females, with duration of residence 1–4 years). When semi-educated (<secondary school) are also included, their share rises to 66 per cent and 77 per cent, respectively.

This is very surprising, given India's high economic growth (over 8% during 1991–2001). High economic growth have failed to provide "inclusive growth" to the poor! Tables 10.13 and 10.14 show similar pictures of literacy/illiteracy among all types of migrants, rather show precarious situation.

Occupational Categories of Migrants (All Durations and Rural-Urban), 2001

Table 10.15 presents the picture of occupational absorption of migrants who reported moved for employment, cross-classified according to their rural-urban residence. In the Table, occupational divisions are: Division 0–1 refer to professional workers, Div 2 Administrative workers; likewise, Div 3 (clerical workers), Div 4 (sales workers), Div 5 (services workers), Div 6 (farm related workers), and Div 7–8–9 refer to production process workers. And, Div 10 refers to unclassifiable groups (not shown).

One notable aspect is that, their total numbers according to census 2001 were 66 million (44 million males, and 20.9 million females), who reported themselves as "migrant workers" in Census 2001. And, their numbers differ considerably from "employment migration" recorded for all durations as 30.6 million (26.1 million males and 4.4 million females), and also from 1991–2001 "decadal employment migration" of only 14 million (12 million males and 1.98 million females). It implies that these huge numbers of migrants joined "later" to labour force, though their "initial reasons" were perhaps recorded as other than employment (familial or other purpose). So, discrepancy between two sets arise. However, such patterns of occupation are valid for both the sets. Besides, number of such migrant workers has swelled tremendously from 36 in 1991 to 66 million in 2001 (83% increase) (compare with Tables 1.2 and 1.3).

Another point is: unlike in the West, where sales and services and other occupation indicate high occupational activities; but, in India, except for the first two categories, most of the occupational groups actually refer to low grade work. Such basic differences between the West and India's service sectors must be understood. Otherwise, it may lead to wrong conclusions.

Regarding occupational absorption of the migrants, the following features clearly emerge:

(a) With respect to total male migrants, with all durations, 50 per cent are engaged in low-grade production-processing work (Div 7–8–9) (last but one column). They comprise a large chunk of total male migrant workers, not many engaged in sales, services, nor in professional or administrative work. Similar feature are also seen among the females (44%).
(b) Some male workers are also engaged in sales (5% in rural, 8% in urban) and services (18% in rural, 21% in urban). Situation for the females follows the suit. The females are comparatively more engaged in services (8% in rural, and 11% in urban), and few in sales (1% in rural, 7% in urban); but these are in fact very low-grade services in informal economy, like maid servants, or low-grade hawkers or vendors.
(c) With respect to *intra*-district migration, most of the males are still engaged in low-grade production process work (49% in rural, 43% in urban), only few in administrative work (6% in rural, 8% in urban), or clerical work (8% in rural, 7% in urban). Substantial part are also engaged in services (19% in rural, 22% in urban). Among females, similar features can be noticed. However, more are engaged in clerical work (5% in rural, 15% in urban), or in services (8% in rural, 11% in urban).
(d) Among inter-district migrants, large part of males are still engaged in low-grade production process work (53% in rural, 36% in urban), but a small share got absorption in professional (4% in rural, 9% in urban), or administrative (7% in rural, 12% in urban), or clerical work (7% in rural, 9% in urban). Likewise, among females, a large chunk still work mainly in low-grade production-process work (44% in rural, 32% in urban). But, some also got jobs in administrative work (4% in rural, 15% in urban), or clerical work (8% in rural, 19% in urban), sales (2% in rural, and 8% in urban) or services (9% in rural, 11% in urban). However, their number are still very few.
(e) Position of males is very precarious. And, the condition of female migrants are further dismal!
(f) If all low-grade occupational groups of migrants are added up, then, it comprises as high as 60 per cent low grade workers among males, and 65 per cent among females (for all durations). The majority of them were absorbed only in a *bazaar*- type or low-grade urban informal sectors, which are characterized by cutthroat competition, low wages, low productivity, insecurity, exploitation, and humiliation. These are indeed signs of under-development, or anti-development! *In fact, these are symptoms of syndrome of poverty and mobility.*
(g) Almost similar features also emerge among the "inter-state" migrant workers, separately for males and females. As high as 66 per cent of rural male workers got absorbed only in low-grade production-process work. Likewise, 57 per cent among the rural females. Their urban proportions are 41 per cent and 30 per cent, respectively. The proportions of clerks or service workers, however, increased, among both the sexes, specially in urban nodes. In sum, the situation has not improved much in recent years, in spite of tall claims of fast economic spurts during the development decade period (8–9% annual growth). The poor remained in the same darkness as before (viz., George, *India Untouched, The Face of Rural Poverty,*

Table 10.15 *Migrant Workers by Occupational Divisions (among those who stated employment as reason for migration)(other than cultivators/Agricultural labourers), 2001*

Rural/Urban Last residence	Total Migrant Workers		Occupational Divisions (%)													
			Div. 0–1– Prof.		Div. 2–Admn		Div. 3– Clerical		Div. 4– Sales		Div. 5–Services		Div. 6– Farm		Div. 7–8–9–Prod.	
	Males	Females	M%	F%	M%	F%	M%	F%	M%	F%	M%	F%	M%	F%	M%	F%
PLACE OF ENUMERATION:TOTAL																
Total	44041435	20915300	5	1	7	5	6	8	6	2	19	9	2	17	50	44
Last residence elsewhere in India																
Total	42642110	20601408	5	1	7	5	6	8	6	2	19	9	2	17	50	44
Rural	24999151	15622796	3	1	5	3	6	6	5	1	18	8	3	20	56	46
Urban	11674467	3407412	8	3	11	14	8	18	8	7	21	11	1	4	40	34
Within state of enumeration but outside place of enumeration																
Total	29664232	18021957	5	1	7	4	7	8	7	2	20	9	3	18	47	44
Rural	16481773	13980467	4	1	6	3	8	6	6	1	19	8	3	21	51	45
Urban	7800334	2582572	7	2	10	12	9	17	9	7	21	11	1	4	39	36
Elsewhere in district of enumeration																
Total	16774685	12755776	4	1	6	3	7	6	6	1	20	9	3	19	48	45
Rural	9097005	10375237	3	1	6	2	8	5	6	1	19	8	4	22	49	46
Urban	3365390	1221886	6	2	8	9	7	15	8	5	22	11	1	5	43	40
In other districts of state of enumeration																
Total	12889547	5266181	6	2	9	7	8	11	7	4	19	9	2	15	46	40
Rural	7384768	3605230	4	1	7	4	7	8	6	2	18	9	3	20	53	44
Urban	4434944	1360686	9	3	12	15	9	19	10	8	20	11	1	3	36	32
States in India beyond state of enumeration																
Total	12977878	2579451	5	2	6	8	4	10	4	4	18	9	1	10	58	48
Rural	8517378	1642329	3	1	3	3	3	5	3	2	16	8	2	13	66	57
Urban	3874133	824840	10	5	11	18	7	19	6	8	21	10	1	3	41	30

Source: Same as in Table 10.10 Unclassifiable and unclassified not shown. Last residence outside India not shown.

2004). Development has not touched their lives. *Happiness is the most unfortunate lady, who has not seen their faces*! This is the most pitiable condition of the migrants.

(h) In sum, it is a "continuing trends" of movement of distressed people from one region of poverty to another. From rural unemployment to urban under-employment. From one area of stress and humiliation to another next one. What dismal situations were found during 1981–91, have not changed substantially even during 1991–2001. And, whatever recent rudimentary news are available in 2008–09, the things appeared to have rather worsened recently. Indeed, these are symptoms of poverty and under-development. These findings about migration in India must act as revelations to the scholars, social scientists, planners, administrators, and the government. We really need to act urgently for the upliftment of these millions of poor migrants in India.

(i) *We really need to act urgently for the upliftment of such hundreds of millions of poor migrants in India, before these problems lead to a great calamity and reach a point of no return!*

Characteristics of Migrants, Main/Marginal Workers, and Non-workers, All Durations, 2001

Table 10.16 portrays overall picture of literates and illiterates among life-time male and female migrants, as well as decadal migrants according to 2001 census. These characteristics are also illustrated in Figures 10.17 through 10.23.

Table 10.16 *Migrants by Literacy, Main Workers, Marginal Workers, Non-workers, 2001 (%)*

Place of residence	*Total Migrants*		*Illiterate*		*Literate*		*Main workers*		*Marginal workers*		*Non-workers*	
	Males	*Females*	*M*	*F*	*M*	*F*	*M*	*F*	*M*	*F*	*M*	*F*
Place of Enumeration: Total			*(1) All durations of residence*									
Total	93361809	221179541	26	58	74	42	57	22	6	17	38	62
Rural	52246555	174420993	27	63	73	37	60	24	6	19	34	57
Urban	21532764	28941304	16	28	84	72	56	13	3	5	42	82
			(2) Duration of residence less than 1 year									
Total	4173469	4712255	50	58	51	42	45	19	8	12	46	69
Rural	3038688	3624145	54	62	46	38	45	22	10	14	45	65
Urban	1006170	931944	36	41	64	59	46	10	4	4	49	86
			(3) Duration of residence 1–4 years									
Total	16587389	30693834	31	44	69	56	49	17	4	14	47	69
Rural	10946898	24018394	33	48	67	52	49	19	4	17	47	64
Urban	4758465	5781192	27	28	74	72	47	10	2	4	50	86
			(4) Duration of residence 5–9 years									
Total	12136128	29998267	21	45	79	55	54	20	4	17	43	63
Rural	8300906	24485022	23	50	77	50	55	22	4	19	40	59
Urban	3501836	4844109	16	22	84	78	51	11	2	4	47	84

Cont'd...

...Cont'd

Place of Enumeration: Rural			*(1) All durations of residence*								
Total	43846535	166530857	34	66	66	35	52	25	8	21	40	54
Rural	27018785	146629392	35	67	66	33	55	26	8	22	38	52
Urban	4617865	8509213	25	40	76	60	47	18	5	12	48	71
			(2) Duration of residence less than 1 year									
Total	2700508	3359829	56	64	44	36	45	23	9	15	46	62
Rural	2175050	2883625	60	65	40	35	45	24	10	16	45	60
Urban	447279	370510	41	52	59	48	48	12	6	7	47	81
Place of Enumeration: Urban			*(1) All durations of residence*									
Total	49515274	54648684	18	34	82	66	61	12	3	3	36	85
Rural	25227770	27791601	19	42	81	58	66	12	4	4	30	84
Urban	16914899	20432091	14	23	86	77	58	11	3	2	40	87
			(2) Duration of residence less than 1 year									
Total	1472961	1352426	37	43	63	57	46	11	7	4	48	86
Rural	863638	740520	40	50	60	50	47	12	9	5	45	83
Urban	558891	561434	32	33	68	67	45	9	3	2	52	90

Source: Census of India, 2001 (b), Migration Tables, Series D-04 and D-06. Data of durations above 1 year not shown, in rural and urban enumeration areas.

Out of total 93.3 million such male migrants (for all durations), 26 per cent were illiterates, 74 per cent literates, only 57 per cent were main workers (working more than 6 months per year) and another 6 per cent marginal workers (working less than 6 months per year). Proportionally, male non-workers are quite large (38%). Corresponding pictures of 221 million female migrants for all durations are far worse: 58 per cent are illiterates, only 42 per cent literates, merely 22 per cent main workers, additionally 17 per cent marginal workers, and a large chunk (62%) non-workers! These characteristics reveal a very pathetic condition of the movers. Rural situations are only slightly different from above overall picture, while urban situation, is slightly on the positive side.

Strangely, among the recent migrants with durations less than one year, the share of male illiterate have increased to 50 per cent, whereas of female illiterates remained 58 per cent, as before. The share of male main workers worsens to 45 per cent, while female main workers to 19 per cent. Male non-workers swells to 46 per cent and that of females to 69 per cent. However, migrant's condition appear to have degraded from longer durations (5–9 years) to recent duration (less than 1 year). In short, nothing spectacular gain accrued to the hapless millions of movers, in spite over 8 per cent economic growth in the development decade.

Indeed, the government has institutionalized a globalized and privatized economy in India, sub-servient to a handful of business families, permitting an increasing number of billionaires, in the one hand, and allowing them to exploit hundreds of millions of poor people, on the other.

Nowadays, the number of billionaires are swelling everyday in India, while the number of extremely poor people have already crossed 500 million in 2005 (who survived less than Rs 24 per day per capita, i.e., less than US$ 1.25 PPP (at purchasing power parity). We shall discuss more on these in chapter 21.

Accompanying Figures 10.17 to 10.23 vividly illustrates some of these trends and characteristics. They are self-explanatory; so not elaborated further.

Figure 10.16 *Male Migration, All Durations, Per cent Main Workers, Marginal Workers and Non-workers, 2001 Census*

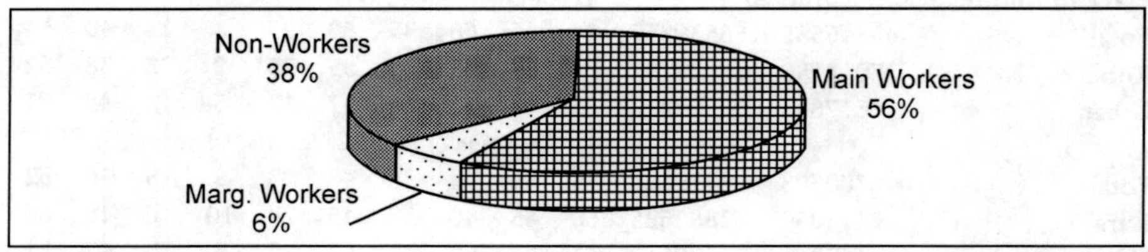

Figure 10.17 *Male Migration, 5–9 Years Durations, Per cent Main Workers, Marginal Workers and Non-workers*

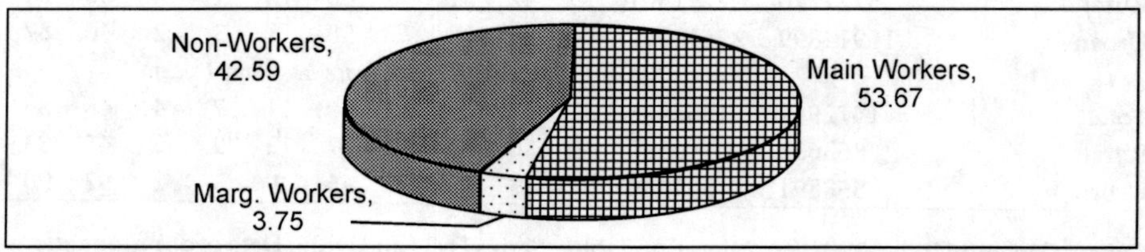

Figure 10.18 *Female Migrants, All Durations, 221 Million, Per cent Literates and Illiterates, 2001*

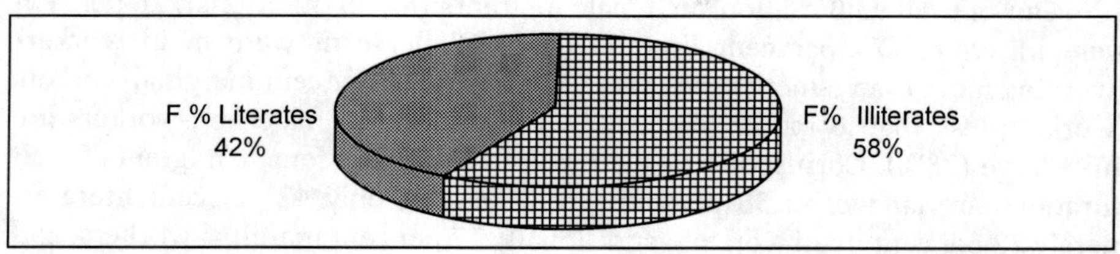

Figure 10.19 *Female Migration, All Durations, Per cent Main Workers, Marginal Workers, and Non-workers, 2001 Census*

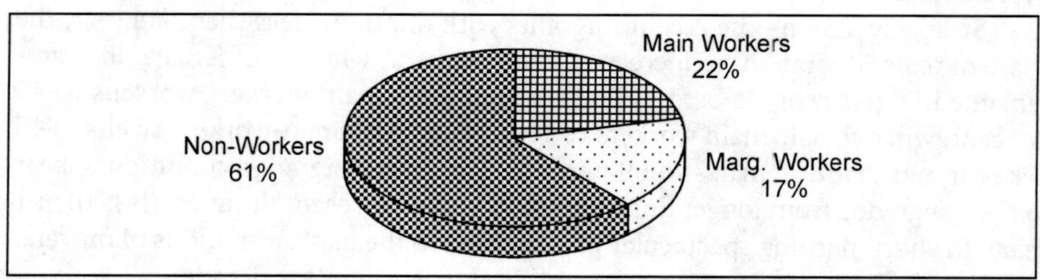

Figure 10.20 *Female Migration, 5–9 Years Durations, Per cent Main Workers, Marginal Workers and Non-workers, 2001 Census*

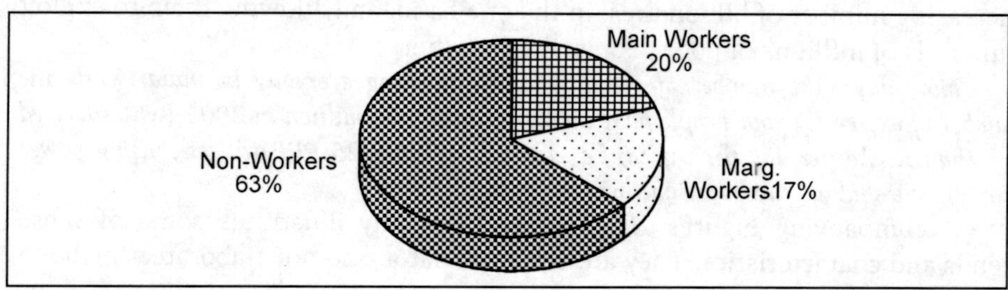

Figure 10.21 *Male Migration for 5–9 Years Durations, and Literates and Illiterates among them (12 million), 2001*

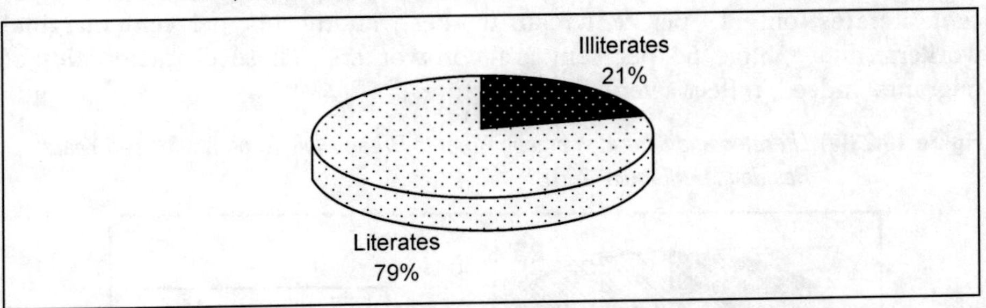

Figure 10.22 *Female Migrants, 5–9 Years Durations, 30 Million, Per cent Literates and Illiterates, 2001*

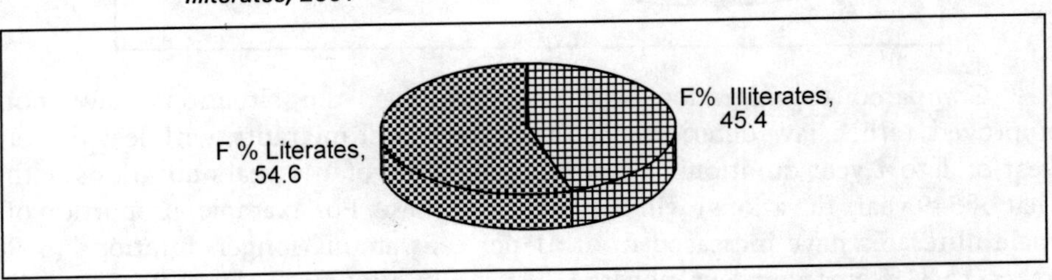

Characteristics of Migrants by Literacy, Main Workers, Marginal Workers, and Non-workers, Duration of Residence 1–4 years (1998–2001)

Table 10.17 presents broad picture of literacy and illiteracy among male and female migrants, who moved for 1 to 4 years duration, prior to 2001. Some characteristics are illustrated in Figures 10 23 (a) and (b).

10.17 *Migrants by Literacy, Main Workers, Marginal Workers and Non-workers among Them, Duration of Residence 1–4 Years (%)*

Place of last residence	*Total Migrants*		*Illiterate*		*Literate*		*Main workers*		*Marginal workers*		*Non-workers*	
	Males	*Females*	*M%*	*F%*	*M%*	*F%*	*M%*	*F%*	*M%*	*F%*	*M%*	*F%*
			Place of Enumeration: Total									
Rural	10,946,898	24,018,394	33	48	67	52	49	19	4	17	47	64
Urban	4,758,465	5,781,192	26	28	74	72	47	10	2	4	50	86
			Place of Enumeration: Rural									
Rural	5,739,771	19,000,898	40	51	60	49	42	21	5	20	53	58
Urban	1,295,871	1,824,834	37	37	63	63	40	13	3	8	56	79
			Place of Enumeration: Urban									
Rural	5,207,127	5,017,496	25	36	75	64	56	9	3	3	41	88
Urban	3,462,594	3,956,358	23	24	77	76	50	9	2	1	48	90

They refer to movers of 1998–2001 period. Out of total 10.9 such rural male migrants, 33 per cent were illiterates, another 67 per cent just literate, only 49 per cent were main workers and 4 per cent marginal workers. The proportion of non-workers is very large, 47 per cent. Corresponding pictures among 24 million recent rural female migrants are no better either: 48 per cent illiterates, 52 per cent literates, only 19 per cent main workers, another 17 per cent marginal workers, and a huge 64 per cent are non-workers! These characteristics of migrants, indeed, reflect a very dismal picture!

Figure 10.23(a) *Literates and Illiterates among Rural to Urban Male Migrants for 1–4 Years Residence, All-India, 2001*

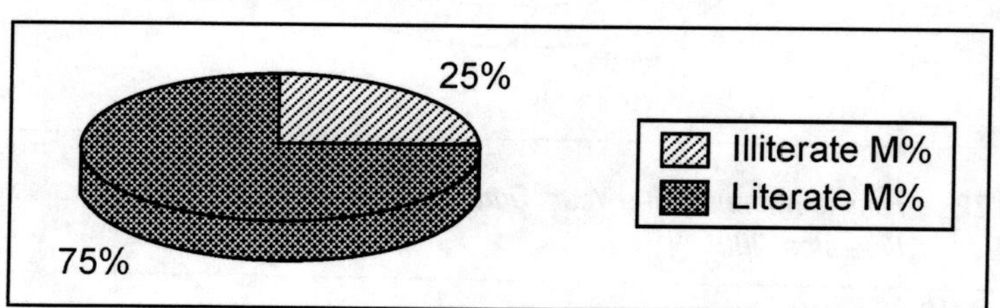

Compared to migration with all durations, the situations have not improved, rather have deteriorated among the recent migrants, with less than 1 year or 1 to 4 year durations. Comparing numbers of 1–4 years durations with that of 5–9 years durations) will easily unravel these. For example, proportion of male illiterates have increased from 21 per cent among longer durations (5–9 years) to 31% among recent movers (1–4 year durations); so also the proportion of "main" or permanent workers among them (decreased from 54% to 49%). Similar trends are also noticed among female migrants. These are depicted in annexed diagrams.

Figure 10.23(b) *Literates and Illiterates among Rural to Urban Female Migrants for 1–4 Years Residence, All-India, 2001*

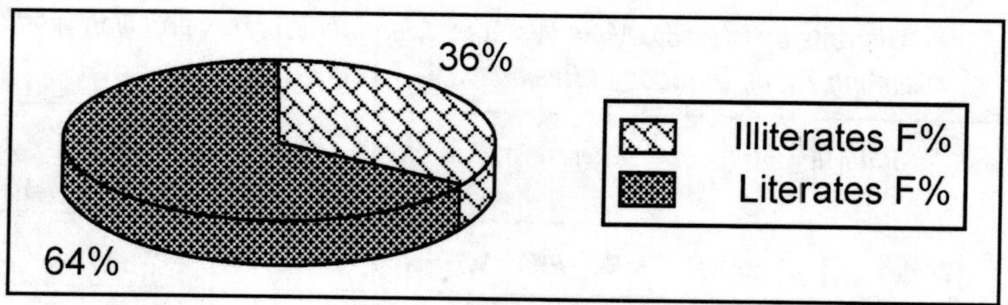

Occupational Absorption of Migrants in Class I Cities

This is discussed in much detail in chapters 15 and 16.

Circular Migration in India

A recent study on Internal migration and development emphasized upon roles of circulation and circular migration in India (Deshingkar, 2006: 1–2), with following observations:

(a) Statistics from 55th Round of National Sample Survey (1999–2000) put number of short term out-migrants staying away from their usual residence at 12.6 million. Recent micro-studies on large and increasing numbers of internal migrants (often hundreds of thousands) suggest this is an underestimate. Informal estimates show 30 million temporary migrants.

(b) Labour-sending areas are typically agriculturally backward and poor. Destinations are towns and cities, industrial zones, stone quarries and coastal areas for fish processing and salt panning. High productivity agricultural areas continue to be important destinations, but more migrants are opting for non-farm employment in both rural and urban areas because of greater returns. Permanent migration rates are higher among the more educated. Unlike East and South-east Asia, illiterate and unskilled people appear to dominate seasonal labour migration in India.

However, other studies point out that National Sample Survey Organization's (NSSO, 2001) data are much biased against illiterate and less educated migrants, and hence give a distorted picture. Permanent migration is also higher among illiterate and semi-educated people, which is very much evident from annexed Tables.

11 Human Dimensions of Migration, Urbanization and Regional Disparities in India

"To the hungry the bread itself is God."

Swami Vivekananda (1893)
(Complete Work, Centenary Volume I, 1963: 108)

"Arise and awake, O mighty one, this sleep does not become you. Awake and arise, it does not befit you. Think not that you are weak and miserable. Almighty, arise and awake, and manifest your own nature."

Swami Vivekananda (1893)
(Complete Work, Centenary Volume II, 1963: 304)

"Never lose faith in your self; you can do anything in the universe."

Swami Vivekananda (1893)
(Complete Work, Centenary Volume I, 1963)

In Retrospect

"Imagine!
There are hundreds of millions of very poor, landless peasants, workers and unemployed, denied of any education, hope and aspirations for betterment, chained to fatalism, submissiveness and traditionalism, designedly and deliberately pauperized through centuries of exploitation, murderous invasions, colonization and induced underdevelopment, and ceaselessly struggling throughout their lives for barest sustenance!

Imagine!
Their emaciated faces, moist eyes and tattered clothes!
And, you will begin to hear the roaring sound of their struggle for survival and silent suffering! Perhaps then, you may begin to understand their real situations. No insipid statistics can tell their poignantly sad stories of dismal existence!!"

Mukherji
(The Mobility Field Theory ... in the Indian Situation, 1975: 226)

The above passage was written in mid-April 1975, when I was completing my second PhD thesis on "Migration in India" in the University of Hawaii, under Professor Murray Chapman. The lines came out in the dead of the night, effortlessly, as if as a Divine message from the sky above. In fact, I did not compose it, rather – when I was writing about the wretchedly miserable conditions of hundreds and thousands of rural to urban migrants in Varanasi city, Uttar Pradesh (where I did my field studies in 1973), it poured out from my heart, unknowingly and unconsciously. And, I did not change even a word. My research guide, Professor Murray Chapman, did not change even a comma. He was such a large-hearted and magnanimous Professor and very well understood the limitless pain of his Indian student. Rather, he told: "You better write much more such evocative lines, instead of your usual writing about canonical models and statistical findings" ....

> Alas!, if I could do that ....
>
> Thirty-five years have gone since then! Many trillion of cusecs of water have flowed down the Holy river Ganga, on whose side was situated the Holy city of Varanasi. (the only living city in the world since last 3500 years).

According to 2001 census, in India, about 314.6 million migrants have changed their residents, for some duration or other. Of them, 93.1 million were male migrants, and 221.2 million female migrants. During 1991–2001 decade alone, about 98.2 million migrants (33.8 million males, and 65.4 million females) have moved from rural to rural areas, or from green fields to the stinking urban slums. For the majority of them, it is a move from rural poverty to urban poverty. Move from one area of stress to another. For the most, migration is still a severe struggle for just for survival. An escape route from abject poverty. For them, it is a choice between quick death in the deadly stagnant villages, or slow starvation in dirty urban slums.

How true the above lines, written 35 years ago!

Even after 35 years, the pathetic condition of hundreds of millions of migrants in India remains poignantly sad, wretchedly poor, hopelessly stagnant. No planning exists for the poor. No empathy is left for the poor. No work opportunities exist for them in the tottering villages. Nor any shelter awaits them in the cruel metropolises!.

According to World Bank Report (World Bank, 2008) about 500 million poor people exist in India in 2005, who lived below $1.25 dollar a day (or below Rs 24 per day, at purchasing power parity, PPP). And according to Census 2001, about 98 million migrants moved during 1991–2001 decade alone, the majority of whom moved just for barest sustenance, for the basic instinct of just for survival. Unfortunately, the Census of India does not record migrant's economic condition, but that can be indirectly inferred from their poor occupational levels of the masses of the illiterate, semi-literate, or less than secondary education levels. Set against such an unjust and iniquitous context, the Indian government, the privileged class, handful of educated and elite groups, and the favoured industrialists still feel fully complacent. They belong to Young and Radiant India – as citizens of a dynamic and vibrant economy and emerging software superpower in the world, but doing absolutely nothing for the alleviation of such a pathetic situation of 500 millions poor. For hundreds of millions of poor migrants! Still they consider themselves as civil society.

Completely corrupt administrations thrive at all levels. Evil politicization of all walks of life have completely permeated and controlled the fate of hapless citizens. Rampant corruption and all-pervading evil politics do not permit eradication of poverty in India. The empathy for the poor masses have completely evaporated and absent among the scholars. Planning always strengthen the hands of exploitation by the rich. Planning in India is never meant for the masses of the poor. Times moves on ... Decades and centuries fly away. And, quite flows the ancient great river Ganga ... under huge debris and mud ....

Some Evidences of Human Dimensions of Agonizing Process of Migration and Urbanization in India

Here are some real life experiences about the lives of migrants, as recorded by the author at different periods:

1. "We are about two thousands people ... gathered here ... you see they are standing or sitting under this very large *Banyan* tree ... we coming from all surrounding districts ... Jaunpur, Ballia, Deoria, Ghazipur, Azamgarh, and others also ... where we going? we heading towards Varanasi city ... you saying ... still twenty miles away? ... we walk all through nights, and take rest during daytime ... impossible to walk under this very scorching sun ... Sun God also very unkind to us ... blazing with so much heat ... during this month of May ... it is so unbearable ... why we traveling? to get some work in Varanasi city ... this is our only hope left ... we walking since last five days, without food ... without water.... I am 72 years old, but this little boy is only seven years ... all hoping that ... we may get some manual work in Varanasi city ... can't we get? What you say? Any chance? Why you silent? ..."

Gaya Ram, a 72 years old landless labourer, amidst a crowd of 2000 labourers under a Large Banyan tree, 20 miles away from Varanasi city (May 2, 1973).

(Mukherji, May 1973, Field Notes from Varanasi, India to East West Center, Hawaii)

2. "Did you ask how many years I am pulling this rickshaw? Twelve years! I was only thirteen then ... when village money lender took away my father's little land. How could I buy this rickshaw? It costs 1500 rupees. I earn only seven or eight rupees daily, after 14 hours of sweating. But its owner takes away four rupees, daily. I don't mind this terrible heat ... if only I could feed my parents and my wife in the village ... last time I saw her was three months back when I went to my village ... soon rainy season will come ... the time for union ... she weeps all through the rain, alone, separated, agonized and humiliated ..."

Halku, A rickshaw-wala in Varanasi City, India, (May 30, 1977)
(Mukherji, 1977c, 1–12; and 1985b: 279)

3. "You asking how many years I am coming from Bihar to work in this brick-kiln? Look at that boy working there ... in the water ... preparing bricks out of the mud ... he is my grandson ... I have been coming to this place every year even before his father was born. No change in our fate ... even after three generations! How could change come? We have no land in the village ... no work there ... only two month's work ... as a *mazdoor* on other's farm ... one month during sowing and one month during harvesting. How could we survive? What could we eat? during those ten long months? Can you tell? We are bound to beg for loans from the village money lenders ... and from the *thikadar (agents)* ... they fleece you out ... and you become a bonded labourer and lumbered here ... to prepare bricks ... 'go, prepare bricks' ... from four in the morning ... till the dead of the night ... you sweat, you weep, you cry, you starve ... but no ... you cannot escape ... you must work hard ... harder ... till you can repay through your nose, and blood .... I am not afraid of such back-breaking hard work ... in the mud, in the water, and in the filth ... even at this old age ... if

only ... if only ... even after all this toiling I could only feed my children and grand children back home .... They are hungry, starving, groaning, separated, and deeply frustrated ... no future ... no light ... to arrive in their lives ..."

Bhola, a brick-layer in Birbhum district, West Bengal (February 14, 1981)
(Mukherji, 1983b: 44–43)

4. "Did you ask why my husband is in deep sleep below the blazing sun in such a hot month of May? He is lying there unconscious since last three days ... without food ... we all are starving ... nothing to eat ... no work in this village ... he cannot even get up to search work ... because he survives only by drinking water ... no work for me also in this new village. I don't mind starvation...but look at our nine-month old daughter ... what will happen to her?"

Mangala, a Santhal Tribal Migrant Woman labourer in Birbhum District, West Bengal (May 21, 1981)
(Mukherji, 1990: 1–2)

5. "Why am I traveling in this lone compartment in the dead of the night? I was so much afraid of robbers and police ... good that you came in this railway compartment ... My daily work starts at four in the morning ... daily I catch the first train from Calcutta to Murshidabad-Bihar border... and purchase two-three kilos of rice in non-cordoned zone ... outside West Bengal .... Now I am returning to Calcutta; tonight I have to sell that rice to a Marwari businessman,... he fleeces you out, he pays only two rupees per kilo ... police and robbers also take their shares; ... very little money remains for feeding my two little children ... Where could I leave them? Their father have left us ... they also travel daily with me from four in the darkness to midnight ... tired, hungry, famished, and all the time weeping ..."

Karuna, a Migrant rice-seller in a Calcutta slum, traveling in a train in the dead of night (December 3, 1982)
(Mukherji, 1990: 1–2)

6. "I started this small roadside vegetable stall four years ago ... since I came from Ratnagiri ... I can make very little earning ... it is so difficult ... so much heat and rain ... and frequent raids by police ... My heart jumps to my throat as soon as I see police coming ... I start running with my little son in one arm and whatever bits of vegetables can carry in another arm ... Police comes and ransacks everything ... only ruins scattered on the streets ... Will they not allow us to survive?"

Amba, A street vegetable seller in Nerul, New Mumbai (September 18, 1989)
(Mukherji, 1997a: 283)

These six quotations encapsulate the essence of this entire book. The first quotation comes from an old labourer – whom I met – during my field survey in and around Varanasi City (in 1973). I met this large crowd of about 2000 landless labourers and peasants gathered under a very large Banyan tree where they took shelter for a shade from blazing sun in very hot summer of 1973. I remember their tattered clothes, moist eyes, and deep anxiety writ large on their faces. No bland statistics, no census, no economic or demographic survey, nor any description can truly narrate their agony, misery and pain. Nor arm-chair geographers, demographers, or policy-makers can fully understand their pathetic situation and exploitation, unless they personally go and meet them. Patiently listen to their woos. Without ego. With full compassion!

The investigation further revealed that migration of labourers from eastern Uttar Pradesh to Varanasi City mainly reflected that the rural dispossessed are moving in search of jobs and better living conditions. As landless agricultural labourers, most were virtually forced to leave villages and accept any manual work they could find in the towns and cities (viz., quote of *Gaya Ram*). A great majority live in urban squalor, hoping to acquire sufficient money to buy land in their home village or find a long-term livelihood in the town. Some had gone to the nearest town, but many more had moved to Varanasi, the largest city within a distance of 100–150 miles. Many of them traveled hundreds of miles to the country's largest metropolises (Kolkata, Mumbai, and Delhi), probably because they had a faint hunch that the chances of obtaining any manual job increases with the city size. Many have experienced prolonged urban unemployment, and were forced to return to their village, to look after their family or tiny parcel of land. Many oscillated between the same village and town, but their hopes were never fulfilled, and the next generation repeats the same miserable drama of life (Mukherji, 1985a: 252–289).

In the second quotation, *Halku* vividly narrates the sad story of all circular or temporary migrants like rickshaw-pullers and other low-grade operatives in India – who were uprooted from the countryside and have come to eke out a miserable living in towns. It is the story of pauperization of labourers in the village, of dirt and filth of the slums in their urban "El-dorado", and of back-breaking hard work and in-human exploitation. It is a tale of disrupted families and the dual responsibilities of circular migrants, both in the village and in the town. "Migration or circular migration' is such an insipid term for such an agonizing process" (Mukherji, 1985b,: 279–298, see also 1977c: 1–12).

In the third quotation, *Bhola*, a sixty-two years old landless agricultural labourer-cum-brick-layer, very vividly describes a very cruel story of all migrating wage labourers or low-grade operatives in India. They have been marginalized and displaced from one part of the country and have moved into another part in search of any subsistence!. It is a very sad story of acute unemployment and pauperization of labourers in villages, of mud, filth, and bondage at their new work places, of cruel hard work and exploitation, and of hunger, agony, misery, and sadness. It is a tale of disrupted families and dual responsibilities of migrants. No cold statistics is capable of narrating their very sad state of poverty, frustration, and misery. Indeed, "migration" is such a non-committed phrase for such a humiliating process! (Mukherji, 1983b: 35–69)

In the fourth quotation, *Mangala* vividly narrates the sad story of many migrating female labourers in the origin village, of acute poverty and unemployment in the destination, and of extreme helplessness and starvation.

In fifth quotation, *Karuna*, describes the poignantly sad condition of female migrants in a cruel metropolis. It is a tale of their agonizing struggle for existence in their dream city, and severe exploitation by all!

In sixth quotation, *Amba*, manifests not only absorption of such female migrants in lower rungs of urban economic activities for which usual term "informal sector" is wholly insipid, but also narrates their frustration, agony, and hopelessness.

In all six different cases, these distressed migrants ask the crucial questions: what will happen to our children? How long could children remain hungry and famished? Will they not allow us to survive? These burning questions stare at our faces. The situations have not improved even in recent time, as further evidences testify:

7. "Even dogs are better off: The ongoing battle between capital and labour in the cane-fields of Gujarat".

Breman, Jan (1990)

8. A detailed field-based study of sampled 13,855 persons in central part of Mumbai in 1990–91 (Mukherji, 1993e) revealed the presence of 9,330 migrants out of them. The survey further unraveled that:

(a) a majority of all migrants moved just for survival (62%), to eke out some kind of living in their urban El-dorado, performing very low grade services in informal sectors, followed by marriage migration (28%) and rest (< 10%) actually moved for prospect, business, transfer, or seeking any skilled job. The wretched socio-economic conditions of these migrants may be apparent from following facts:
(b) 48 per cent live in only one room,
(c) 58 per cent have no toilet facility,
(d) 36 per cent are denied water facility,
(e) 44 per cent live in Kutchha or semi-pucca houses (mud-walled or rag-roofed shanty/junk houses);
(f) 32 per cent used gunny bag, straw, tin sheets, or mud as wall materials, and
(g) 45 per cent used similar things for roof materials in their houses.
(h) Their such pitiable condition must be judged in the context of their long duration of stay in Mumbai (37% lived below 10 years), 29 per cent lived 10–19 years, and 34 per cent lived more than 20 years in the mega city).

Mukherji, Migration to Greater Bombay (1993e: 10–24; 1996, 20–40)

9. "Our cities are growing very rapidly everywhere in India, but unfortunately slums are growing four times faster; and the poverty, agony, misery, pain, exploitation, humiliation, insecurity, inequities, and unhappiness are also multiplying tremendously. These are indeed manifestations of our iniquitous society and faulty planning. The wretchedly poor urban slum dwellers in many large cities and mega cities of India, specially the old, the destitute, the weak, the helpless women, and orphaned children spread out their hands to the dark sky above, and cry out of their souls: "Hai, Vagaban! (Oh, God!) How long! How many more years I have to suffer?" Do we have an answer?

Slum Dwellers in Mumbai (May 10, 1991)
(Mukherji, 1997d: 1;1999a).

10. "The down and out (migrants) produce wealth from which they however remain excluded as beneficiaries. Most of them are the working poor who continue to live in a state of misery and oppression because of the low wages paid for long hours of work."

(Bremen and Das, 2000: 20–46)

11. "I am driving taxi in Mumbai since 30 years ... I came from a village in Jaunpur district, Uttar Pradesh ... long time ago ... I was young then ... now I am 68 or 69 ... don't know, ... no, no, I do not own this taxi ... very costly. I only drive on rent .... I earn roughly 400–500 rupees daily, but have to hand over minimum 200 rupees to owner ... Otherwise he will hire another driver ... so, I get only 200 or something daily .... How could I save? I have a grown-up son ... no, he is not at all studious ...

in class tenth ... very worried for him ... my daughter matured ... she studied up to twelve ... no money ... how could I manage all expenses? No, I do not think of going back to my village ... no work, no land there ... nothing. Now here I have to live, and here I have to die ... What to do? no, not much gain by coming to Mumbai. ... I survived here ... my family also got shelter here ... but last 30 years gone same way ... drudgery ... driving even in dead of night ... now I cannot see properly in night ... need operation ... other night ... had a near accident ... police asked for my taxi license .... I had to hand over bribes ... entire income gone. My main worries about my son ... don't want him to be a driver, like me ... suffering all through life ... in cruel city. Do you know any good teacher? for my son?" ...

Sharma, a migrant farmer from Uttar Pradesh driving Taxi since 30 years in Mumbai (July 12, 2005)
(Mukherji, "Migration Field Notes", Mumbai, 2005b)

12. "I have a little child of 2 years ... I am 16 ... my father got me married three years ago, as our custom. We came to Mumbai from a village ... near Kolkata ... very far ... Also have three little sisters and a little brother ... My father died last year ... my mother also works, mopping floors and cleansing utensils, as I do ... I work in 5 houses, she works in 9 houses, from morning to night ... to feed so many mouths. Where I leave my child? in neighbour's house. He often weeps ... I rush back late afternoon, cook little rice for him ... he becomes so hungry. No, his father deserted us ... he worked as assistant to house-painter ... as a *mistri*, but he was drinker and squandered his all money ... stolen my little earning also .... He gone one year, no news ... We could also do such work in Kolkata, but rates higher here. Now, have to rush to next house ... cleansing utensils and mopping. They give little money ... prices gone so high ... very difficult to survive" ...

Jui, a 16–year old migrant girl from a village near Kolkata, working as a maidservant in Mumbai since age 10 (August 5, 2008)
(Mukherji, "Migration Field Notes", Mumbai, 2008b)

13. In a recent paper, Kothari (2002: 1–32) also narrated the links between chronic poverty and migration in India, in the context of mover-stayer framework: "The poor are not a homogenous group, the poor are diverse reflecting differential access to resources, power and control" ... "Consequently, it cannot be assumed that all amongst the poor always have the option to migrate, or the poorest of the poor will migrate" (ibid.) ... "Thus, not everyone is similarly mobile for a range of reasons ... lack of knowledge ... social and cultural ties which bind them to their home place, physical immobility, gender and age" (ibid.).

Kothari (2002)

14. "Such poverty-induced migration from villages occur because of a great shortage of employment opportunities in rural areas, excessive population pressure on meagre amount of land, lack of irrigation and small scale industries, and of basic amenities of life (like school, drinking water, hospital, etc.). Marginalized landless agricultural labourers and peasants therefore try to escape from poverty and stagnation by moving out from tottering villages."

Mukherji (2006: 185–186)

15. The poignantly sad stories of rickshaw-walas, which I have narrated way back in 1977, is again repeated in a recent investigation on the rickshaw-pullers in India's capital city, New Delhi. The situation did not improve, not even after 30 years (2007), vide the paper "Rural-Urban Migration and Urban Poverty: Socio-Economic Profiles of Rickshaw Pullers and Owner-Contractors in North-East Delhi."

Kurosaki, et al. (2007)

Such poignantly sad stories are innumerable And, quite flows the ancient great river Ganga ... under many barriers and clogs ....

Need Migration Planning to Reduce Human Problems in Migration

Planning for the Poor

What is now required are, programmes and policies for rural reconstruction and development of hitherto neglected regions and neglected communities, and which would directly benefit the poor, the weak, the destitute, and the humiliated. Only then, the problems of those people, out of which the majority of migrants come, will be considerably relieved.

A change-embracing perspective is first necessary (Mukherji, 1982: 1–278). The objective of planning has to be positively in favour of the rural poor. Since the majority of the poor people of India live in rural areas and since the countryside suffer from stagnation, unemployment, and underemployment, thence the planning strategies should be so envisaged as to change the mechanisms that maintain poverty and under-development in the rural sector. Besides, development of economic base of urban centres, especially of small towns, and small cities should get priority (ibid.).

Migration Planning

Secondly, the crux of the problem is, first, to reckon with the need for planning for migration and circulation or circular migration, and the need for integrating this with overall economic planning for regional and national development (Mukherji, 1981:10–160). So far, very little has been thought about such integration. The problems of human mobility bear directly upon problems of regional development, as movements occur mainly due to regional imbalances in the natural, economic, human, and social resources and in their levels of utilization. Unless these inequities and disparities are corrected, there would be little chance to redress the socio-economic and human problems associated with the people's migration and mobility.

On the other hand, steps in migration planning (for movers' employment, socio-economic welfare, stability and security, and assimilation, etc.) are also intimately related to steps in planning for alleviating the problems of agricultural under-development. Also related are problems of economic development, population explosion, urban involution, squatter settlements, rural stagnation, acute unemployment, etc. Their mutual linkages are to be identified and concrete planning should be envisaged and properly implemented, for the welfare of both the uprooted movers and common people.

Eliminations of Barriers in Mobility Fields of the Migrants

Thirdly, there are many different kinds of socio-economic-cultural-political barriers in the individual mover's mobility fields, which block need gratification and restrain free field adjustments within the individual's life space (Mukherji, 1975: 316–318; 1979b: 75–77, 1982: 265–278). Caste system is one such barrier. Illiteracy is another. Language bar, lack of information about places or opportunities in destinations or restriction of jobs only for the "sons of the soil" are other examples of barriers. Rural indebtedness is another kind of barrier, which bind the villagers to perpetual serfdom (Mukherji, 1983b: 60–70).

"Sometimes the administration's coercive actions against the hawkers or vendors, or squatters, or lack of subsidy to petty entrepreneurs, act as barriers in the fields hampering free field adjustments in the individual's life space. The field solution, then, involves identifying these different kinds of barriers in the individual's or community's mobility fields and finding ways and means of eliminating them from the social nexus of the population. The objective should be to relieve these barriers so that the individuals, or families, or groups, are enabled to forge out their best abilities and right to decide their own lives" (Mukherji, 1981:172–173; 1983b: 61–62; 1983c: 1–32).

Strangely enough, above ideas were first developed by the present author in 1975, in his PhD thesis on The Mobility Field Theory (Mukherji, 1975: 1–375) in University of Hawaii and East-West Center, and subsequently were repeatedly published in 1976, 1979a and 1979b, 1981, 1982, 1983b, 1985a, 1985b, and later. But, very recently, UNDP (Human Development Report 2009, titled as Overcoming Barriers: Human Mobility and Development, New York: 1–80) is recommending the same things, i.e., overcoming barriers in human mobility and development, 35 years after I had first evolved and propagated those ideas. It seems that these ideas are borrowed, without acknowledging to the original thinker!

Then, it is greatly amusing: whom shall I refer? to my own original ideas of 1975, or UNDP (2009)? It is an example of plagiarism.

However, the crucial issue here is to help the poor masses of illiterate/semi-literate and unskilled/semi-skilled migrants, the world over. If researchers under UNDP organization have found the right ways and propagates these useful ideas and programmes, even after 35 years of its origin and evolution, then, very good for the humanity!.

Concluding Remarks

The urgent need now is to undertake mobility planning, as discussed above, for the alleviation of human problems that are associated with poverty-induced migration and urban decay and urban involution. The crucial requirement is also to reduce, as much as possible, the polarization and concentration of economic, social and political power in the hands of a few urban elites and rural novo-rich, rather provide a much better deal in favour of the impoverished humanity that inhabit India's rural countryside. In short, it urges, for a more equitable and more just distribution of the levels of income, wealth, resources and consumption among various strata of Indian society (Mukherji, 1985 b: 279–298). Similar steps for mobility planning are also recommended for similarly-placed developing countries (Mukherji, 1985a: 252– 289; 1997: 1–65).

When these requirements would be fulfilled, only then the vicious syndrome of poverty and mobility (and migration) will break and de-link (Mukherji, 1983: 33–66: 2006: 260–330). Perhaps then, the human dimensions of distressed migration and low quality urbanization will improve in India (Mukherji, 2007: 259–305).

And, then, perhaps only then, the roaring sounds of their age-old suffering will dissipate in the thin air!

12 Findings of District-level Analysis of Migration and Spatial Disparities, 2001

"Remember that the nation lives in the cottage."

Swami Vivekananda (1894)
(Complete Work, Centenary Volume V, 1963: 29)

Introduction: District-level Analysis

District level analysis of inter-relationships between male migration and socio-economic variables were done in the following ways. Analysis is restricted mainly for the males. Analysis for the females are not done for 2001 census (except some discussion of tables), because their migration, occurring mostly for non-economic reasons, are very difficult to explain. Analyses are done as follows:

1. First volume and rates of district-level male in-migration and male out-migration are computed for each of 470 selected districts. From these, net migration rates are computed for each district. Results are identification of two sets of districts: (a) with high in-migration rates, for the males and (b) with high out-migration rates, also for the males. In two separate sets of tables, these high in-migration districts and their related socio-economic variables are shown in Tables 12.1(a) and 12.1(b); and those with high out-migration districts and their related socio-economic variables are presented in Tables 12.2(a) and 12.2(b).
2. A series of regression analysis are performed between *intra*-district and *inter*-district volume and rates of in-migration and out-migration and selected socio-economic variables (Tables 12.3 to 12.4).
3. By performing a few regression analyses between district's migration and district-level socio-economic variables. for the males (Tables 12.5 to 12.17).

These three sets of results are elaborated through several subsequent Tables (Tables 12.1 to 12.17). One point must be stated right at the outset, that out of total 605 districts in India in 2001, only 470 districts belonging to 17 major states and Delhi Union Territory were considered for analysis here. All these 470 districts were analysed in this chapter, but data for only a few districts are shown in subsequent tables, to avoid long tables that run several pages. The same is true for all tables and all analyses.

Migration Variables

Five migration variables at the district-level were constructed and considered, as follows: (1) volume of in-migration, males, (2) volume of out-migration, males, (3) in-migration rate, males, (4) out-migration rate, males, and (5) intra-district migration, males. These migration variables were explained by socio-economic variables, through a series of regression analyses.

Socio-economic Variables

At district level, data of about 10 socio-economic variables from various sources were collected and utilized for preparing the socio-economic matrix, and for explaining district level migration of 470 districts belonging to all major states of India, for which some kind of data were available. Most such data refer to proportion of 9 or 10 major categories of workers to total workers in each district (i.e., workers engaged in cultivation, agricultural labour, livestock, mining, household industry, manufacturing, construction, trade-commerce, transport and services). Besides, other variables are also selected: male population size, per cent urban, proportion of main and marginal workers to total workers. Moreover, other socio-economic variables are also chosen like per cent literates, per cent illiterates, and so forth. In regression analysis, not all such variables did emerge in ensuing results; but only those few specific variables emerged which survived rigorous statistical test, and show high significance. Annexed Tables present details of such regression results.

Brief Note on Regression Analysis Technique

Bi-variate regression analysis or multivariate regression analysis are very much well known, and any standard textbook on statistics may help easy understanding. For instance, Introduction to Modern Statistics by Dixon and Massy (1970) or Advanced statistics by Gupta (1970), may be of much help. Here, basic ideas are presented for newly initiated. Many regression tables in chapters 12 to 16 are much helpful to understand the essential of regression analysis. Many regression plots are also given throughout these chapters, along with associated statistics of regression lines.

There is an essential difference between correlation and regression. Correlation between two variables shows only the "degree of relationships" between the two variables (which vary together), but it does *not* tell about the "direction of causality" or "cause-and-effect relationship", which regression *does*. Thus, regression is much superior statistical technique, as it tells both "degree of relationship" between them, which vary together, but also indicates the "direction" of relationship, i.e., also points out which is the 'causal' variable and which is the 'effect' variable. However, spurious cause and effect relationship must be avoided, and researcher must have a prior idea or knowledge (as far as possible, from research literature) about the cause and effect relationship between two variables. Meaning of following useful statistical terms are explained below:

1. Dependent variable (Y) = Variable which is to be explained or the "effect" variable (volume or rate of migration).
2. Independent variable (X) = Predictor variable or "causal" variable (e.g., manufacturing sector in the city).

3. Correlation coefficient = shows degree of relationship between the dependent and the independent variable.
4. Regression = shows how much variation in the dependent variable is brought about by unit change in independent variable.
5. Regression line of fit = the best line of fit between the dependent and independent variable on a scatter diagram.
6. R-Square = Square of the correlation coefficient between the two variables, or Coefficient of Determination.
7. Adjusted R-Square = Standardized R-Square value of the Coefficient of Determination.
8. Explanation = Adjusted R-Square times 100 "explains" the variations in the dependent variable by the variations in the independent variable. This is the simplest *meaning* of relationship between the two variables.
9. Beta Coefficient = Regression weights on the independent variable, showing how much *change* in the dependent variable would occur due to each "unit" change in the independent variable.
10. Angle Theta = Angle of the regression line of fit with the X-axis, showing the slope of the regression line with X-axis.
11. Beta = Tan Theta = indicates the above beta coefficient i.e., how much change in dependent variable is caused by unit change in independent variable
12. Direction = Positive or negative Beta would show the *direction* (positive or negative) of relationship.
13. *Intercept* = Length of intercept of Regression line with the Y-axis.
14. Regression Equation = Consists of (Y) depende variable which is being explained by the intercept and Beta coefficient weighted independent variable. For example:
    Y (Dependent variable) = Intercept + Beta weights (X) (Independent Variable), as in, Y = 123 + 0.35 (X).
15. Meaning of Relationships = The simplest meaning is given in the last column of each regression table. For example: "volume of out-migration in the districts increases as the proportion of marginal workers increases", or "In-migration rates in the Class I cities increases as the proportion of manufacturing sectors in the cities increases", and so forth.
16. The most readers are best advised just to focus on the last column of each regression table, that describes the "Meaning of Relationships" in simple words, without bothering much about the statistical parameters. Anybody can very easily understand the simple regression line of fit and meaning of that line describing the "cause and effect relationship" between the two variables, amidst masses of data, tables, observations and complex entities. Thus, used in this way in this book, the regression analysis is the best effective technique to untangle the hidden complexities.
17. In step-wise regression, the same methods are followed, except that here is one dependent variable and multiple independent or predictor variables, of which the most important predictor variable will emerge as the most significant and most meaningful explanatory variable, in the *first* step, based on the *strength of* correlations between the dependent variable and all predictor variables. In the next step, the next important variable will emerge as the

second most explanatory variable, based on the same strength of correlations. These steps will go on, until all meaningful steps in the regression are completed. Interpretations are also similar. However, in Part II, no step-wise regression is done. Nor further canonical analysis is shown in Part II of this volume.

High In-migration Districts and their Socio-economic Correlates

Table 12.1(a) presents detailed data of nine industrial categories of main workers of 47 selected high *in*-migration districts, out of 470 studied (belonging to 17 major states of India). Many other in-migration districts also exist, but this set indicates comparatively high in-migration (above 4% rates). 'Main' workers are primarily considered, but 'marginal' workers also analysed. *By Indian census definition, marginal workers are those who have no work for six months or more in a year.* During 1991–2001, their numbers swelled, implying that more workers now have temporary work. Instead of only "male" workers, *total* workers (males and females) both are considered, because that better reflect true character of a district's economic functions. In tables, due to shortage of space (widthwise), details of marginal workers not shown; only nine industrial categories of "main" workers are presented.

Table 12.1(a) *Main Workers (Persons) and Nine Industrial Categories in 47 High Male In-migration Districts, 2001(out of 470 districts analysed, data for only few shown here)*

Districts	*Total Workers*	*Main Worker %*	*Marg Worker %*	*Per cent of "Main" Workers engaged in*								
				Cult %	*Agrl %*	*Plant %*	*HHI %*	*Mnf %*	*Const %*	*Trade %*	*Trans %*	*Serv %*
Jammu	534,910	81.9	18.1	20.4	2.3	1.9	1.1	6.3	7.3	11.2	5.5	43.9
Kullu	215,358	76.6	23.4	73.3	1.8	0.8	1.1	1.8	2.8	3.3	1.4	13.6
Shimla	377,896	82.9	17.1	57.9	2.2	1.1	1.1	1.6	3.7	3.9	1.4	27.2
Panchkula	176,679	84.2	15.8	14.2	3.7	3.8	2.7	14.9	7.9	10.0	4.2	37.3
Bikaner	661,483	78.8	21.2	54.4	3.5	2.9	2.6	5.3	4.3	6.5	3.7	16.0
Jaipur	1,872,558	85.0	15.0	35.1	2.4	2.9	4.2	14.0	6.7	10.8	5.1	18.4
Jaisalmer	212,992	72.0	28.1	42.7	5.1	15.0	2.5	3.3	5.0	5.5	2.8	17.1
Kota	541,531	77.1	22.9	27.2	7.0	2.2	3.7	10.3	7.4	12.4	6.9	18.1
Ghaziabad	934,485	86.0	14.1	17.6	5.0	3.6	4.1	18.1	7.1	15.2	6.6	22.5
Gautam Nagar	361,765	84.3	15.7	27.3	5.7	3.3	3.4	11.7	4.8	10.5	4.1	29.0
Lucknow	1,085,404	82.8	17.2	21.1	6.5	1.7	4.4	10.7	5.1	13.4	7.0	30.1
Kanpur Nagar	1,249,858	83.4	16.6	18.5	7.6	1.1	3.5	16.4	4.1	17.5	6.1	25.1
Sonbhadra	539,178	67.0	33.0	41.6	23.9	1.5	3.0	6.9	2.1	4.7	2.0	12.6
Patna	1,428,250	81.2	18.8	23.4	27.1	2.7	3.6	5.1	2.9	11.1	4.9	19.4
Barpeta	513,360	79.2	20.8	43.2	12.0	2.9	4.1	4.0	3.2	10.6	4.4	15.4
Kamrup	838,136	82.9	17.1	24.3	5.0	2.4	3.5	5.9	4.5	13.7	7.6	32.6
Dhemaji	246,609	61.7	38.3	72.2	3.5	1.0	1.4	1.6	1.6	5.3	1.5	11.7
Tinsukia	468,281	74.9	25.1	26.6	2.9	30.7	1.5	6.8	2.6	10.1	3.1	13.3
Karbi Anglong	324,815	70.4	29.6	63.8	6.5	3.5	2.3	2.2	2.2	4.7	1.7	13.0
North 24 Pargana	2,991,118	87.8	12.2	10.4	11.8	2.3	3.4	18.8	5.1	17.3	7.9	22.9

Cont'd...

...Cont'd

Jharsuguda	191,287	70.0	30.0	24.3	13.9	3.2	5.8	7.1	8.1	7.9	5.4	14.7
Sundargarh	736,036	64.9	35.1	32.9	13.6	1.7	2.1	13.2	5.6	8.4	5.1	14.9
Khordha	573,866	83.4	16.6	14.3	10.7	4.3	2.6	6.2	9.3	13.5	6.9	30.2
Malkangiri	243,105	62.7	37.3	70.5	12.9	1.7	1.6	1.2	2.8	2.3	0.6	6.3
Indore	897,321	86.0	14.0	16.2	10.3	1.2	3.8	15.6	7.0	16.4	6.5	22.7
Bhopal	594,674	84.6	15.4	11.3	6.6	1.1	1.8	12.8	9.1	15.3	7.3	34.1
Gandhinagar	552,590	83.9	16.1	20.4	16.8	14.1	1.2	10.2	4.4	10.9	4.5	17.0
Ahṃedabad	2,011,022	89.5	10.5	6.3	7.7	2.2	2.1	25.5	7.2	19.5	7.9	21.5
Surat	2,170,482	90.7	9.3	11.6	18.4	2.4	2.1	35.1	3.8	11.6	3.9	11.1
Navsari	548,904	84.4	15.6	21.7	29.3	2.9	1.8	16.2	3.5	8.7	3.4	12.2
Nagpur	1,530,998	83.1	16.9	15.7	19.0	1.8	2.1	11.5	7.4	12.2	7.1	21.2
Aurangabad	1,174,991	87.0	13.0	39.1	21.2	1.5	1.4	8.3	5.2	7.0	3.7	12.4
Thane	3,196,919	87.4	12.6	10.5	6.3	1.7	1.9	28.1	5.3	12.9	9.1	23.4
Mumbai (Sub)	3,013,275	94.1	5.9	0.1	0.1	0.7	2.7	26.9	6.7	18.2	12.5	31.8
Pune	2,952,450	89.5	10.5	26.9	10.5	1.9	2.4	14.5	7.3	9.2	6.1	21.1
Hyderabad	1,123,284	92.0	8.0	1.0	0.5	0.4	2.6	12.4	8.9	23.3	11.0	39.6
Rangareddi	1,425,076	87.6	12.4	21.8	17.0	1.8	2.5	12.3	7.7	9.4	5.8	20.3
Bangalore	2,585,585	92.5	7.5	3.3	1.6	0.8	2.4	26.8	9.7	15.7	8.9	30.2
Kasaragod	326,512	NA	NA	5.3	7.8	24.4	8.9	11.2	8.2	11.4	7.1	13.9
Kannur	723,669	NA	NA	5.6	10.1	13.6	2.5	14.2	10.5	14.3	9.4	18.4
Wayanad	367,932	NA	NA	19.4	23.4	20.5	1.2	4.1	3.9	8.1	5.6	13.3
Kozhikode	719,336	NA	NA	3.3	5.6	14.4	1.9	11.0	12.8	15.8	11.8	22.1
Idukki	605,966	NA	NA	22.2	24.9	23.7	1.3	3.4	2.8	5.8	4.2	11.4
Thiruvallur	1,035,094	81.7	18.3	9.4	18.8	2.3	4.4	13.6	6.6	10.6	6.5	27.3
Chennai	1,489,481	92.8	7.2	1.1	0.4	1.1	1.9	15.1	7.8	19.2	10.1	43.1
Kancheepuram	1,130,889	79.8	20.2	12.6	18.8	1.7	6.1	12.6	5.9	9.7	5.4	26.3

Source: Computed from Data of Census of India, 2001(c), Economic Tables, B-Series, CDs available only in 2005–7. A small share of mining workers not shown. Out of total 605 districts in India (in 2001), only 470 districts of 17 major states and Delhi Union Territory considered for analysis. All these districts were analysed, but data for only a few shown here, to avoid long tables. This holds true for all tables and all analyses. Categories are cultivators, agricultural labourers, plantation workers, household industry workers, manufacturing, construction, trade, transport and service workers.

On the other hand, in Table 12.1(b), corresponding migration variables of the same 47 "high in-migration" districts are presented, as correlates. Volume of in-migration and out-migration are shown, as also their rates. These four variables pertain to inter-district migration, during 1991–2001. Besides, *volume and rates of intra*-district migration are also shown and analysed. In computing migration rates, volume of (male) migration is divided by the respective (male) population of the district, multiplied by 100, to arrive at the district's rates (instead of conventional use of mid-year population of district, as the divisor). So this can be termed as "migration as the proportion of population in the district", as some economists (viz., Todaro, 1975) and population specialists have also followed. The ensuing results show much meaningful explanation and high correlation with socio-economic variables. The results are also statistically significant, and practically very meaningful.

Table 12.1(b) *Socio-economic and Migration Variables, 47 High In-migration (Males) Districts, 2001(out of 470 districts analysed, data for few shown here)*

Name of District	Total Male Pop.	Per cent Urban	Per cent Illite-rate	Per cent Workers	Intra-district Migration	Intra-district Mig. Rates	Inter-district Migration	Inter-district Mig. Rates	Volume of In-migration	In-mig. Rates	Vollume of Out-mig.	Out-mig. Rates	Diff. bet In-mig. and Out-mig. Rates	High In-mig Rates
Jammu	850302	44	33	33	27423	3.2	16579	1.9	63754	7.5	11127	1.3	6.2	In-mig.
Kullu	198016	8	37	57	6162	3.1	7764	3.9	13317	6.7	4268	2.2	4.6	In-mig.
Shimla	380996	23	30	51	25480	6.7	17439	4.6	34109	9	11065	2.9	6	In-mig.
Panchkula	256939	45	36	38	5368	2.1	9802	3.8	22572	8.8	3246	1.3	7.5	In-mig.
Bikaner	886075	36	54	40	30200	3.4	32360	3.7	65739	7.4	25825	2.9	4.5	In-mig.
Jaipur	2768203	49	42	36	35195	1.3	81303	2.9	180132	6.5	38951	1.4	5.1	In-mig.
Jaisalmer	279101	15	60	42	6885	2.5	12666	4.5	18079	6.5	5450	2	4.5	In-mig.
Kota	827128	54	38	35	19337	2.3	27588	3.3	72875	8.8	23427	2.8	6	In-mig.
Ghaziabad	1769042	55	42	29	30561	1.7	98987	5.6	229899	13	24178	1.4	11.6	In-mig.
Gautam Nagar	652819	37	44	30	7281	1.1	31468	4.8	55641	8.5	7323	1.1	7.4	In-mig.
Lucknow	1932317	64	42	30	12986	0.7	86681	4.5	223977	11.6	28646	1.5	10.1	In-mig.
Kanpur Nagar	2247216	67	36	30	10790	0.5	71086	3.2	231710	10.3	50974	2.3	8	In-mig.
Sonbhadra	770897	19	61	37	9261	1.2	16490	2.1	52717	6.8	3476	0.5	6.4	In-mig.
Patna	2519942	42	48	30	33042	1.3	68139	2.7	163943	6.5	27936	1.1	5.4	In-mig.
Kamrup	1326981	36	36	33	37614	2.8	41658	3.1	135534	10.2	40250	3	7.2	In-mig.
Dhemaji	294643	7	47	44	6217	2.1	4674	1.6	39101	13.3	8496	2.9	10.4	In-mig.
Tinsukia	601099	20	49	41	12203	2	8718	1.5	36581	6.1	11800	2	4.1	In-mig.
Karbi Anglong	422250	11	53	41	11610	2.7	5222	1.2	27563	6.5	10704	2.5	4	In-mig.
N. Cachar Hills	99822	32	44	37	3513	3.5	3844	3.9	11333	11.4	1808	1.8	9.5	In-mig.
North 24 Prgn.	4638756	54	31	33	120788	2.6	134524	2.9	383857	8.3	74536	1.6	6.7	In-mig.
Jharsuguda	261941	37	39	37	4945	1.9	9491	3.6	22017	8.4	8157	3.1	5.3	In-mig.

Cont'd…

...Cont'd

Sundargarh	935601	34	45	40	32867	3.5	27174	2.9	80372	8.6	24501	2.6	6	In-mig.
Khordha	986886	43	30	31	25093	2.5	110090	10.4	208635	21.1	26926	2.7	18.4	In-mig.
Malkangiri	252507	7	75	49	5328	2.1	4217	1.7	14207	5.6	2001	0.8	4.8	In-mig.
Indore	1289352	70	36	36	21040	1.6	74036	5.7	152948	11.9	59019	4.6	7.3	In-mig.
Bhopal	972649	80	37	32	5861	0.6	60829	6.3	149950	15.4	26410	2.7	12.7	In-mig.
Gandhinagar	697999	35	34	42	26831	3.8	61344	8.8	137440	19.7	29393	4.2	15.5	In-mig.
Ahmedabad	3074556	80	31	35	81714	2.7	113759	3.7	402994	13.1	173973	5.7	7.4	In-mig.
Surat	2722539	60	36	44	109134	4	245029	9	490999	18	56813	2.1	15.9	In-mig.
Navsari	628988	27	33	44	33880	5.4	20056	3.2	49461	7.9	24517	3.9	4	In-mig.
Nagpur	2105314	64	27	38	91489	4.3	78168	3.7	189584	9	101101	4.8	4.2	In-mig.
Aurangabad	1505363	38	39	41	82849	5.5	95570	6.3	188869	12.5	111064	7.4	5.2	In-mig.
Thane	4377747	73	31	39	185131	4.2	555994	12.7	1E+06	23.2	69539	1.6	21.6	In-mig.
Mumbai (Sub.)	4741720	100	23	37	0	0	175444	3.7	729527	15.4	14050	0.3	15.1	In-mig.
Pune	3769128	58	30	41	233845	6.2	320376	8.5	678211	18	271871	7.2	10.8	In-mig.
Hyderabad	1981173	100	31	29	23418	1.2	84531	4.3	229563	11.6	113902	5.7	5.8	In-mig.
Rangareddi	1839227	54	43	40	43659	2.4	178405	9.7	432262	23.5	27101	1.5	22	In-mig.
Visakhapatnam	1930197	40	48	42	94806	4.9	59581	3.1	157626	8.2	60039	3.1	5.1	In-mig.
Bangalore	3426599	88	27	39	56278	1.6	222729	6.5	526956	15.4	86870	2.5	12.8	In-mig.
Kasaragod	588083	19	27	35	19501	3.3	14158	2.4	39856	6.8	11309	1.9	4.9	In-mig.
Kannur	1152817	50	18	32	141343	12.3	23931	2.1	88659	7.7	39980	3.5	4.2	In-mig.
Wayanad	391273	4	26	40	11936	3.1	13681	3.5	68521	17.5	14061	3.6	13.9	In-mig.
Idukki	566682	5	22	43	23917	4.2	18377	3.2	101232	17.9	51927	9.2	8.7	In-mig.
Thiruvallur	1397407	55	32	38	43787	3.1	88110	6.3	278346	19.9	20785	1.5	18.4	In-mig.
Chennai	2219539	100	23	34	0	0	96830	4.4	357003	16.1	218759	9.9	6.2	In-mig.
Kancheepuram	1457242	53	32	40	57976	4	68954	4.7	184396	12.7	60015	4.1	8.5	In-mig.

Source: Computed from Data of Census of India, 2001(b), Migration Tables.

Likewise, Table 12.2(a) provides data of main and marginal workers and the sub-categories of "main" workers in 67 high *out*-migration districts, though all 470 districts are statistically analysed by regression technique. The very many meaningful findings are discussed subsequently. Regression technique is a more useful method that unfolded the latent causal relationships between the worker variables and migration variables.

Another deficiency is lack of data of out-migration from districts with reference to *inter-state migration*, viz., it cannot be identified from which districts of UP massive out-migration goes to Maharashtra. In fact, heavy out-migration occurs from all districts of En. Uttar Pradesh to Maharashtra (viz., Baliia, Basti, Gorakhhpur, Azamgarh, Jaunpur, Mirzapur, Varanasi, Allahabad); but these cannot be seen from inter-district migration data. Such discrepancy in Census data need correction.

Table 12.2(a) *Main Workers and Nine Industrial Categories of 67 High Out-migration Districts, 2001*

Districts	*Total Worker (Person)*	*Main Worker (%)*	*Marg Worker (%)*	*Per cent of "Main "Workers (Persons) in*							
				Cult %	*Agrl %*	*HHI %*	*Mnf %*	*Const %*	*Trade %*	*Trams %*	*Serv %*
Leh (Ladakh)	59117	66	34	25	1	1	3	3	4	4	50
Hamirpur	211162	60	40	55	1	2	4	9	6	4	20
Hoshiarpur	510558	81	19	26	11	2	11	7	11	4	21
Nawanshahr	258492	92	9	23	10	2	9	8	8	3	13
Fatehgarh Sahib	202539	89	11	25	11	2	15	5	10	4	16
Moga	361593	84	16	32	21	5	6	3	9	3	14
Faridkot	206634	87	13	27	19	3	6	4	10	3	18
Bathinda	502581	83	18	32	18	2	5	3	9	3	19
Mansa	282517	80	20	39	20	3	5	3	9	2	11
Sangrur	801862	87	13	32	16	3	9	3	9	3	13
Kanpur Dehat	512697	74	26	59	16	3	5	2	5	2	8
Barpeta	513360	79	21	43	12	4	4	3	11	4	.15
Nalbari	373819	76	24	41	9	4	3	3	9	4	22
Kolkata	1719286	95	6	0	0	3	17	4	24	11	41
Kendrapara	391275	76	24	44	21	2	4	4	7	2	12
Nayagarh	267677	71	29	38	26	5	3	3	6	2	13
Puri	446915	83	17	39	20	2	3	3	9	3	15
Ganjam	1301874	63	37	32	21	4	5	5	9	3	16
Balangir	560048	63	37	40	22	6	4	5	6	2	13
Bhind	528424	75	25	60	12	2	2	2	5	2	9
West Nimar	698604	84	17	49	31	1	3	2	4	1	7
Mahesana	845752	80	20	26	19	1	9	4	11	4	10
Sabar Kantha	940434	70	30	44	16	2	4	3	8	3	11
Surendranagar	652227	79	21	32	25	2	10	4	8	4	10
Jamnagar	740848	85	15	34	11	2	13	5	11	6	13
Junagadh	994986	78	22	38	20	1	7	4	10	4	9

Cont'd...

...Cont'd

Amreli	600339	78	22	37	21	2	15	3	8	3	8
Bhavnagar	941436	83	17	23	16	4	26	5	10	4	10
Kheda	909190	77	23	32	24	1	5	3	8	4	10
Panch Mahals	976601	64	37	60	11	2	4	3	5	3	9
The Dangs	91655	74	26	67	17	1	2	2	2	1	7
Dhule	740210	78	22	31	35	3	5	3	7	4	11
Jalgaon	1563619	83	17	26	42	2	4	3	7	4	10
Buldana	1017363	89	11	36	44	1	2	2	5	2	7
Akola	648669	90	10	20	47	1	5	3	8	4	11
Bhandara	534736	68	32	29	34	6	5	4	5	2	11
Parbhani	643440	87	13	38	36	1	3	3	6	2	9
Jalna	713455	85	15	48	30	2	4	2	5	2	7
Mumbai	1312119	95	5	0	0	3	23	4	21	12	36
Raigarh	911216	73	27	29	12	2	14	5	8	7	17
Ahmadnagar	1858254	87	13	47	22	3	6	2	5	3	10
Bid	954148	87	13	51	26	1	3	2	4	2	8
Latur	841231	85	15	37	34	2	4	3	6	3	10
Osmanabad	654532	85	15	42	35	2	3	2	4	2	8
Solapur	1746906	85	15	35	25	5	8	3	7	3	10
Satara	1300176	80	20	50	18	2	5	3	5	4	10
Ratnagiri	760470	73	27	53	8	2	5	5	6	4	12
Sindhudurg	399602	58	42	46	10	3	4	5	6	5	15
Sangli	1219889	78	22	46	20	3	6	3	6	3	11
Srikakulam	1196257	72	28	27	37	4	5	2	6	3	11
Prakasam	1535790	85	15	28	39	4	4	4	6	2	9
Bijapur	717493	77	23	36	30	3	3	4	7	3	12
Chitradurga	722965	80	20	43	25	3	4	3	6	3	10
Udupi	490617	85	15	20	14	13	9	6	8	5	16
Tumkur	1319080	80	20	50	16	5	5	3	6	3	10
Kolar	1243380	82	18	40	21	3	6	3	7	3	9
Mandya	839728	82	19	54	17	2	4	3	6	2	10
Hassan	866046	81	19	58	9	2	3	2	6	3	9
Chamarajanagar	447884	75	25	35	34	4	4	2	6	2	10
Kottayam	624718	NA	NA	8	11	3	9	8	12	9	23
Tiruvannamalai	1057586	78	22	39	30	5	5	3	5	2	9
Thanjavur	899521	84	17	17	40	4	6	3	9	3	15
Madurai	1086398	87	13	13	25	3	13	5	13	5	21
Ramanathapuram	514677	83	17	39	18	5	4	3	8	2	13
Thoothukkudi	675548	87	14	12	21	6	19	4	10	5	17
Tirunelveli	1281543	88	12	12	25	22	10	3	8	3	15
Kanniyakumari	549711	83	17	3	12	5	13	17	10	5	22

Source: Same as in Table 12.1(a). Small percentage of mining and livestock workers not shown.

Socio-economic and Migration Variables of High Out-migration Districts (Males)

Table 12.2(b) presents migration variables and socio-economic variables of sixty-six high male out-migration districts, out of total 470 districts studied. Only those districts are shown which indicate more than 4.0 out-migration rates,

Table 12.2(b) *Socio-economic and Migration Variables of 66 High Out-migration (Males), Districts, 2001*

Name of District	*Tot. Male Pop.*	*Per cent Urban*	*Per cent Illiterate*	*Per cent Wor-kers*	*Intra-district Migration*	*Intra-district Mig. Rates*	*Inter-district Migration*	*Inter-district Mig. Rates*	*Volume of In-migration*	*In-migration Rates*	*Volume of Out-mig.*	*Out-migration Rates*	*Diff. bet In-mig. and Out-mig. Rates*	*High Out-mig. Districts (Males)*
Lahul and Spiti	18441	0.0	35.0	63.5	1465	7.9	1368	7.4	1894	10.3	3169	17.2	–6.9	High Out-mig.
Hamirpur	196593	7.3	27.7	49.8	6432	3.3	4276	2.2	4640	2.4	14586	7.4	–5.1	High Out-mig.
Hoshiarpur	765132	19.7	29.1	34.7	14622	1.9	9173	1.2	4421	0.6	48282	6.3	–5.7	High Out-mig.
Nawanshahr	306902	13.8	32.9	44.9	4533	1.5	5088	1.7	1902	0.6	17373	5.7	–5.0	High Out-mig.
Fatehgarh	290137	28.1	35.4	38.3	3560	1.2	6445	2.2	709	0.2	15011	5.2	–4.9	High Out-mig.
Moga	474139	20.0	44.7	40.1	5029	1.1	5134	1.1	1626	0.3	20995	4.4	–4.1	High Out-mig.
Faridkot	292596	35.1	46.3	38.1	2791	1.0	5281	1.8	1392	0.5	19710	6.7	–6.3	High Out-mig.
Bathinda	632809	29.7	46.5	42.3	10580	1.7	12092	1.9	1121	0.2	26315	4.2	–4.0	High Out-mig.
Mansa	366446	20.7	54.9	40.9	6089	1.7	5331	1.5	422	0.1	15762	4.3	–4.2	High Out-mig.
Sangrur	1069289	29.2	47.9	40.7	26401	2.5	14370	1.3	942	0.1	44458	4.2	–4.1	High Out-mig.
Kanpur Dehat	844339	6.9	45.5	32.8	12616	1.5	5856	0.7	14174	1.7	81997	9.7	–8.0	High Out-mig.
Barpeta	848578	7.7	54.3	31.4	19507	2.3	3212	0.4	8560	1.0	66960	7.9	–6.9	High Out-mig.
Nalbari	592375	2.4	42.7	33.4	9192	1.6	2079	0.4	18153	3.1	49429	8.3	–5.3	High Out-mig.
Kolkata	2500040	100.0	26.0	37.6	0	0.0	42740	1.7	144168	5.8	358786	14.4	–8.6	High Out-mig.
Kendrapara	646438	5.7	33.5	29.8	7178	1.1	4658	0.7	8142	1.3	50991	7.9	–6.6	High Out-mig.
Nayagarh	446177	4.3	38.7	33.3	8022	1.8	3534	0.8	6148	1.4	38951	8.7	–7.4	High Out-mig.
Puri	763389	13.6	31.8	30.0	10384	1.4	7798	1.0	16098	2.1	47169	6.2	–4.1	High Out-mig.
Ganjam	1581986	17.6	48.4	41.3	59361	3.8	12462	0.8	16916	1.1	112982	7.1	–6.1	High Out-mig.
Balangir	673985	11.5	52.3	41.9	13104	1.9	6300	0.9	12818	1.9	40200	6.0	–4.1	High Out-mig.
Bhind	780902	23.7	42.1	36.8	15392	2.0	3085	0.4	5083	0.7	39867	5.1	–4.5	High Out-mig.

Cont'd...

...Cont'd

Rewa	1016687	16.2	49.8	43.7	19722	1.9	8867	0.9	14523	1.4	59838	5.9	–4.5	High Out-mig.
W. Nimar	784604	15.4	49.0	46.1	36131	4.6	16236	2.1	31097	4.0	67838	8.6	–4.7	High Out-mig.
Mahesana	953842	22.4	35.3	45.1	46432	4.9	17194	1.8	40265	4.2	211956	22.2	–18.0	High Out-mig.
SabarKantha	1069554	10.8	43.7	45.2	27467	2.6	6873	0.6	17650	1.7	67910	6.3	–4.7	High Out-mig.
Surendranagar	787650	26.6	48.4	42.7	32542	4.1	15619	2.0	35403	4.5	92716	11.8	–7.3	High Out-mig.
Jamnagar	981320	43.9	43.1	38.6	47888	4.9	17667	1.8	43623	4.4	100365	10.2	–5.8	High Out-mig.
Junagadh	1252350	29.1	42.5	40.9	84963	6.8	16225	1.3	41031	3.3	122043	9.7	–6.5	High Out-mig.
Amreli	701593	22.5	43.3	43.1	30557	4.4	15109	2.2	33248	4.7	183080	26.1	–21.4	High Out-mig.
Bhavnagar	1274920	37.9	44.6	38.2	54606	4.3	25174	2.0	55595	4.4	178842	14.0	–9.7	High Out-mig.
Kheda	1052823	20.1	38.6	44.9	32427	3.1	15668	1.5	48405	4.6	128647	12.2	–7.6	High Out-mig.
Panch Mahals	1044937	12.5	49.3	48.2	24306	2.3	9021	0.9	19979	1.9	94534	9.0	–7.1	High Out-mig.
The Dangs	93974	0.0	52.0	49.8	5693	6.1	2070	2.2	3969	4.2	11449	12.2	–8.0	High Out-mig.
Dhule	878372	26.1	39.1	43.2	61873	7.0	31217	3.6	85980	9.8	137003	15.6	–5.8	High Out-mig.
Jalgaon	1905493	28.6	35.3	42.5	139976	7.3	29002	1.5	73430	3.9	283488	14.9	–11.0	High Out-mig.
Buldana	1147403	21.2	35.8	45.5	71030	6.2	28967	2.5	63690	5.6	114854	10.0	–4.5	High Out-mig.
Akola	841253	38.5	30.4	39.8	46550	5.5	28158	3.3	69946	8.3	113229	13.5	–5.1	High Out-mig.
Bhandara	573445	15.5	32.2	47.3	32870	5.7	15392	2.7	27979	4.9	79022	13.8	–8.9	High Out-mig.
Parbhani	780191	31.8	44.8	42.2	35583	4.6	20435	2.6	42505	5.4	92040	11.8	–6.3	High Out-mig.
Jalna	826903	19.1	46.0	44.4	37703	4.6	18336	2.2	35718	4.3	111161	13.4	–9.1	High Out-mig.
Mumbai	1878246	100.0	22.4	39.3	0	0.0	82101	4.4	278630	14.8	514288	27.4	–12.5	High Out-mig.
Raigarh	1117628	24.2	34.0	41.4	78767	7.0	64523	5.8	114118	10.2	159551	14.3	–4.1	High Out-mig.
Ahmadnagar	2083053	19.9	35.7	46.0	163892	7.9	82481	4.0	160726	7.7	273821	13.1	–5.4	High Out-mig.
Bid	1116356	17.9	42.6	44.3	50941	4.6	22483	2.0	43730	3.9	214585	19.2	–15.3	High Out-mig.
Latur	1075257	23.6	39.7	40.4	50359	4.7	23171	2.2	40767	3.8	98413	9.2	–5.4	High Out-mig.

Cont'd...

...Cont'd

Osmanabad	769368	15.7	41.3	44.0	26901	3.5	19928	2.6	40411	5.3	123615	16.1	–10.8	High Out-mig.
Solapur	1989623	31.8	39.3	45.3	126111	6.3	42474	2.1	78868	4.0	281992	14.2	–10.2	High Out-mig.
Satara	1408326	14.2	32.0	46.4	133323	9.5	53880	3.8	109145	7.7	321190	22.8	–15.1	High Out-mig.
Ratnagiri	794498	11.3	35.4	45.0	62885	7.9	35462	4.5	53284	6.7	328616	41.4	–34.7	High Out-mig.
Sindhudurg	417890	9.5	29.5	46.6	30071	7.2	14229	3.4	24626	5.9	173941	41.6	–35.7	High Out-mig.
Sangli	1320088	24.5	33.5	47.2	86928	6.6	35676	2.7	83333	6.3	190543	14.4	–8.1	High Out-mig.
Srikakulam	1260020	11.0	52.0	47.4	60508	4.8	9640	0.8	15464	1.2	105104	8.3	–7.1	High Out-mig.
Prakasam	1552332	15.3	49.9	50.3	74249	4.8	21940	1.4	39582	2.5	127358	8.2	–5.7	High Out-mig.
Bijapur	926424	21.9	52.0	39.7	36757	4.0	13267	1.4	27539	3.0	80301	8.7	–5.7	High Out-mig.
Chitradurga	776221	18.1	44.0	47.6	26607	3.4	10631	1.4	22267	2.9	60069	7.7	–4.9	High Out-mig.
Udupi	522231	18.6	27.1	43.9	43053	8.2	17460	3.3	30601	5.9	55658	10.7	–4.8	High Out-mig.
Tumkur	1313801	19.6	41.0	51.0	49538	3.8	27512	2.1	48305	3.7	122980	9.4	–5.7	High Out-mig.
Kolar	1286193	24.7	45.5	48.7	31766	2.5	9918	0.8	20621	1.6	80820	6.3	–4.7	High Out-mig.
Chamarajanagar	489940	15.3	55.2	46.4	8711	1.8	3614	0.7	7653	1.6	30255	6.2	–4.6	High Out-mig.
Kottayam	964926	15.3	14.6	32.9	42744	4.4	27121	2.8	60414	6.3	223591	23.2	–16.9	High Out-mig.
Tiruvannamalai	1095859	18.3	40.7	48.7	13071	1.2	5602	0.5	14572	1.3	66423	6.1	–4.7	High Out-mig.
Thanjavur	1096638	33.8	33.4	40.5	32840	3.0	13229	1.2	37141	3.4	107455	9.8	–6.4	High Out-mig.
Madurai	1303363	56.0	31.1	42.2	28869	2.2	12770	1.0	43706	3.4	125778	9.7	–6.3	High Out-mig.
Ramanathapuram	583376	25.5	36.2	43.8	13054	2.2	5728	1.0	11272	1.9	62684	10.7	–8.8	High Out-mig.
Tirunelveli	1333939	48.0	32.9	47.0	35377	2.7	7959	0.6	19176	1.4	130399	9.8	–8.3	High Out-mig.
Kanniyakumari	832269	65.3	21.9	32.7	15925	1.9	2341	0.3	5875	0.7	41308	5.0	–4.3	High Out-mig.

Source: Same as in Table 12.1(a).

during 2001, e.g., *intra*-district and inter-district migration rates, volume, and rates of out-migration, volume and rates of in-migration, etc. Some relevant socio-economic correlates are also considered, viz., urban per cent, per cent of illiterates, per cent literates, per cent of workers, and volume of total workers. In subsequent series of regression analyses, these two sets of variables (migration and socio-economic sets) are analysed. These exercises yielded many meaningful and statistically significant results.

District-level Regression Analysis

Regression Analysis of *Intra-district and Inter-district Migration (Males) and Socio-economic Variables (2001)*

Tables 12.3 to 12.17 present the salient findings of various regression analyses performed between district-level volume of migration and migration rates and selected socio-economic variables for the males: summary of the main findings are given in annexed tables. Most tables are self-explanatory, and all major relationships are elaborated in the last column, titled "Meaning of Relationship" in each table.

Positive Links between Total Workers of Districts and Male In-migration Rates

The more volume of total workers of the districts, the higher male in-migration rates of the districts (Figure 12.1, Table 12.3). Multiple R is 0.45, adjusted R-square is 0.25, showing that 25 per cent (i.e., multiple R squared times 100) of variations in dependent variable (male in-migration rates) is explained by variations in predictor variable (total workers, persons). Statistical significance is 0.001, i.e., error term is only 1 out of 1,000 observations or tests that this relationship could be wrong. Not only this is practically very meaningful, but also statistically very significant. Policy implication is that more male in-migration will occur into those districts where more jobs will be generated. So, the present-day jobless economic growth are incapable of attracting in-migration.

Figure 12.1 *Relations between Total Workers of Districts and Male In-migration Rates, 2001*

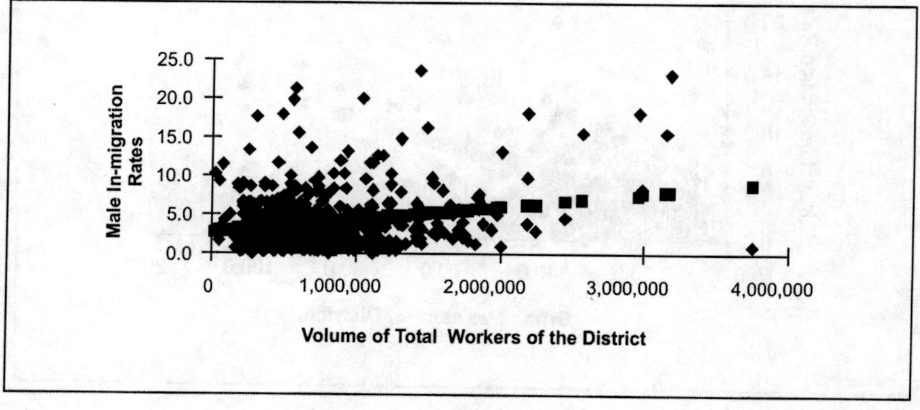

Table 12.3 *Regression Statistics for Relationships between Volume of Total Workers of Districts and Male In-migration Rates of Districts, 2001 (N = 470 Districts)*

Dependent Variable	*Indep. Variable*	*Mult. R.*	*Adj R Sq*	*Expln.*	*Beta*	*T.*	*Sig. T*	*Inter-cept*	*Meaning of Relation*
Male in-migration rates	Volume of total workers in districts	.45	.25	25%	.13	1.2	.001	1.0	More volume of total workers of districts, higher male in-migration rates of districts.

Links between Urbanization and Male In-migration Rates of Districts, 2001

Regression analysis indicates that the more urbanization of the districts, the more male in-migration occurs into the districts. Relationship is bi-polar, i.e., acts in both directions, showing that more male migration into districts also leads to more urbanization. Multiple R is 0.55, adjusted R-square is 0.31, explaining 31 per cent of variations in male in-migration rates of the districts by predictor variable. Sample size is very large, 470 districts. Result is statistically highly significant at 0.001 level, i.e., error term is only 1 out of 1,000 observations. Given these, the finding has great policy import. More urbanization and more male migration are working in unison, both reinforcing each other. In future, India's urbanization will attract more in-migration, which, in turn, will reinforce more urbanization. This will have attendant plus and minus points, that is, more swelling of urban poverty, urban slums, urban congestion, and shortages of water, electricity, etc. But, migration *per se* is not at fault, rather lack of government's clear urban and migration policies are. Increased migration and higher urbanization is almost inevitable in today's world, and many countries have experienced manifold benefits from them. India may also have positive benefits, provided we have clear vision and strategies to tackle negative offshoots!

Figure 12. 2 *Causal Links between Urbanization and Male In-migration Rates of Districts, 2001*

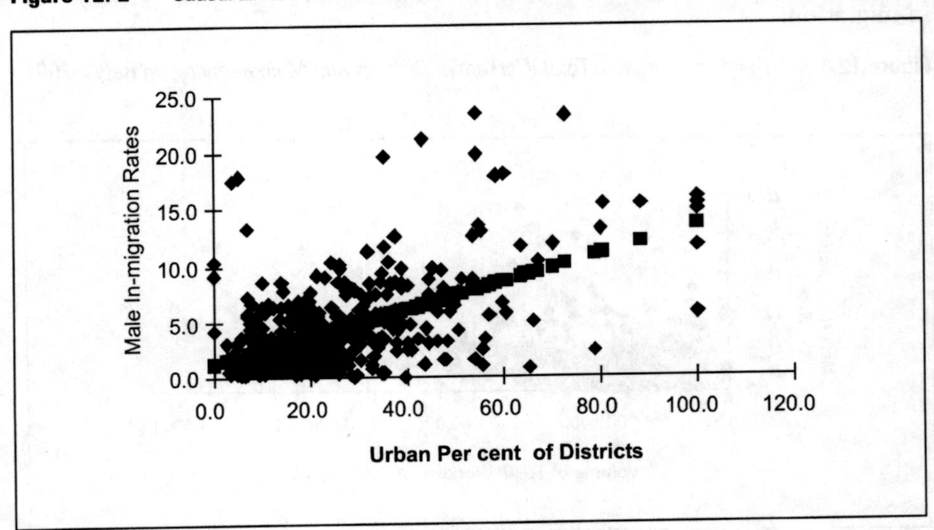

Table 12.4 *Relations between Urban Per cent of Districts and Male In-migration Rates of Districts, 2001 (N = 470 Districts)*

Dependent Variable	*Indep. Variable*	*Adj R Sq*	*Expln.*	*Beta*	*T.*	*Sig. T*	*Intercept*	*Meaning of Relation*
Male in-migration rates	Urban per cent	.31	31%	.12	14.4	.001	1.15	More urbanization of districts, more male in-migration into districts (bi-polar).

Relations between Male In-migration Rates and Service Sectors of Districts

The more workers in the service sectors in the districts, higher is the male in-migration rates of the districts. Adjusted R-square is 0.16, explaining 16 per cent of variations. Statistical significance is 0.001, considerably high. Relationship is not only statistically significant, but also practically meaningful. Policy significance is that more service sectors will attract more in-migration into districts, instead of their out-migration into far away metros. Strategy-wise, generating local self – employment in service sectors within the villages will pay great dividends in arresting overcrowding in cities. Services must be more in formal sectors, not only in informal sectors. Otherwise, the problems would continue.

Table 12.5 *Links between Male In-migration Rates and Service Sectors of Districts, 2001 (N = 470 Districts) (Beta = 0.77, Sig. T = 0.001, Intercept = 10.2)*

Dependent Variable	*Independent Variable*	*Mult. R.*	*Adj. R Sq.*	*Explanation*	*Meaning of relations*
Male in-migration rates	Service sectors	.40	.16	16%	The more service sectors, higher male in-migration rates

Figure 12.3 *Relations between Male In-migration Rates of Districts and Service Sectors of Economy, 2001*

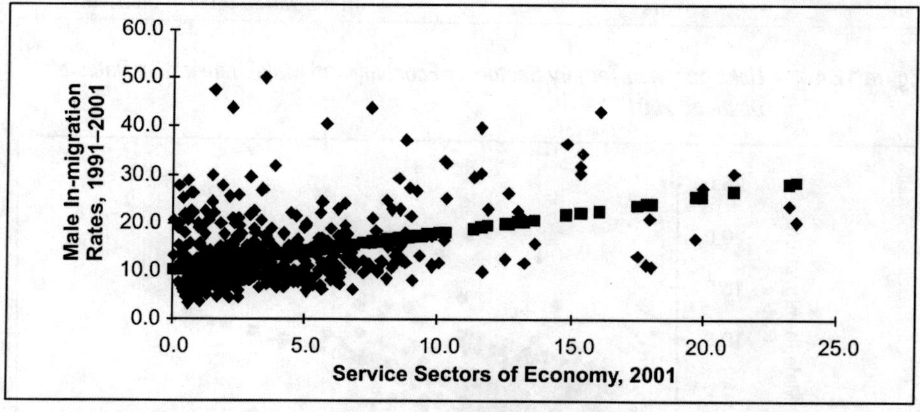

Causal Links between Tertiary Sectors and Male In-migration Rates of Districts

Regression finding shows that the more tertiary sectors in districts, the higher is the rates of male in-migration into them. (Table 12.6, Figure 12.4) It explains 21 per cent, at 0.001 level of significance. In India, tertiary sectors comprised of three parts: trade-commerce, transport and services. *This result testifies one of the main tenet of this volume that, in India, most of the migrants find salvage mainly in poor tertiary sectors, not in manufacturing or secondary sectors.* Unlike in the West, where tertiary sectors comprise of high level administrative and professional services, and high level transport, commerce or business, conversely, in India, tertiary sectors comprise of mainly low level hawkers and vendors, low-grade transport workers, and low-grade sales and services. So, swelling of tertiary sectors does not signify economic development. Even then, it provides a safety valve to in-coming migrants, who somehow eke out their livings in such low-grade unorganized sectors. This is much better alternative than quick death in tottering origin villages, where nothing is available for even minimal subsistence. *Hence, even this is highly desirable to the in-migrants.*

Such findings provide ample evidences to my main tenet, contrary to most conventional migration and urbanization researchers in India, and abroad (dealing with India) – who propagate that these are "not" poverty-induced migration, nor "distressed migrants", rather migrants who are attracted to "neon signs" of mega cities, having promising lives in destinations!. The truth is opposite! *At the same time, these are somewhat dismal findings – only urging us to think more seriously for "Planning for the Poor" and to provide more protection to the hapless hundreds of millions of the poor migrants.* Truth must be told bravely! Once we face truth bravely, then only will come the lion-hearted courage and steely Will to help the poor selflessly!

Table 12.6 *Relations between Tertiary Sectors of Districts and Male In-migration Rates of Districts, 2001 (N = 470 Districts, Beta = 0.11, Sig. T = .001, intercept = 2.3)*

Dependent Variable	*Indep. Variable*	*Adj R Sq*	*Expln.*	*Meaning of Relationships*
Male In-migration rates	Tertiary sectors	.21	21%	More tertiary sectors, higher male in-migration rates of districts

Figure 12.4 *Links between Tertiary Sectors of Economy and Male In-migration Rates of Districts, 2001*

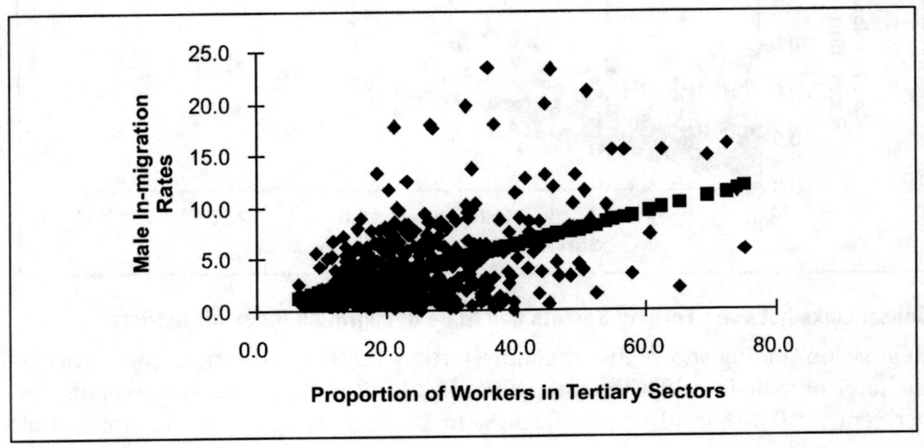

Relations between Secondary Sectors of Districts and Male In-migration Rates

Figure 12.5 shows causal links between secondary sectors of the districts and male in-migration rates of them. Line of fit is almost perfect, indicating that as the secondary sectors increases, the male in-migration also linearly rises. Causal links is not only statistically significant, but also meaningful. Adjusted R Square is 0.19, explaining 19 per cent of variations in dependent variable (male in-migration rates) (Table 12.7). This is substantive. Implication is: developing secondary sectors (manufacturing, mining, construction) will attract more male migrants, and open up new opportunities. Policy-wise also it has great importance: by generating economic development in manufacturing and construction will re-direct migrants to them, instead of crowding in slums. For migration planning, this has great significance.

Figure 12.5 *Relations between Secondary Sectors of Economy and Male In-migration Rates of Districts, 2001*

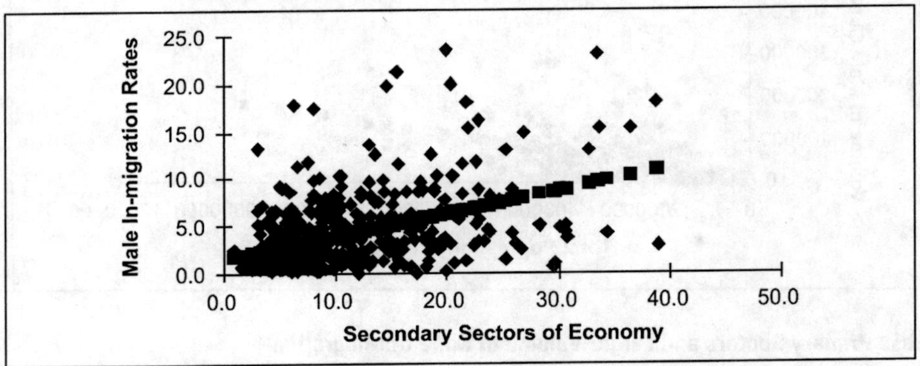

Table 12.7 *Relations between Secondary Sectors of Economy of Districts and Male In-migration Rates of them, 2001 (N = 470, Beta = 0.24, Sig. T = 0.001, Intercept = 1.4)*

Dependent Variable	*Independent Variable*	*Multi. R*	*Adj R Sq*	*Expln.*	*Meaning of Relationship*
Male in-migration rates	Secondary sectors	.43	.19	19%	More secondary sectors, the more male in-migration rates

Relations between Population of Districts and Volume of Male Out-migration

More population pressure in the districts, the more male out-migration from them (explains 18%, at 0.001 level) (Table 12.8, Figure 12.6). This is a classic example of population dynamics – as population pressure increases, out-migration from them also linearly increases. The dispossessed have no alternative, but to leave backward villages/districts in search for survival. Another study also found close relationship between surplus labour and rural to urban migration in India (Dubey et al., 2006). Policy implications are very evident: the need for control of fertility, reduction of population pressure, generation of rural employment, diversification of agriculture, and creation of more non-farm work.

Table 12.8 *Links between Total Population of Districts and Volume of Male Out-migration, 2001 (N = 470, Beta = 0.02, Sig. T = 0.001, Intercept = 11198.3)*

Dependent Variable	*Independent Variable*	*Mult. R.*	*R Sq.*	*Adj R Sq*	*Expln.*	*Meaning of Relation*
Vol. of male out-migration	Total population	.43	.18	.18	18%	More population pressure, more male out-migration

Figure 12.6 *Regression Line between Total Population and Volume of Male Out-migration, 2001*

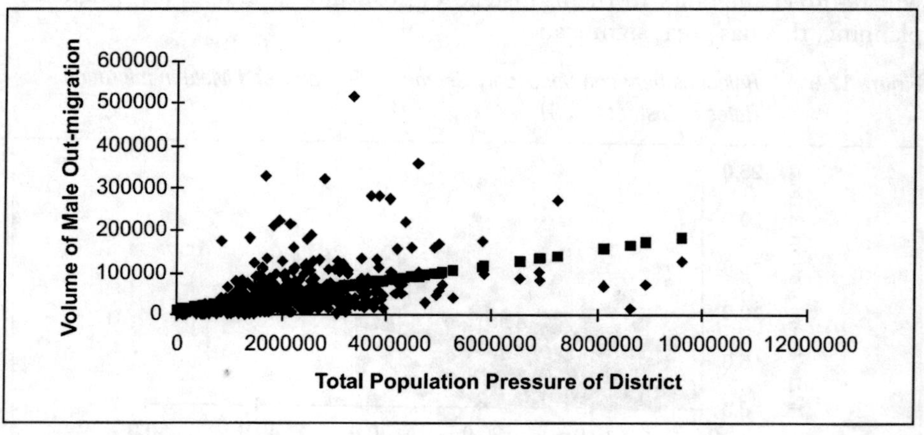

Less Primary Sectors and Larger Volume of Male Out-migration

This shows that male out-migration from districts increases as work in primary sectors (cultivation, agricultural labour and livestock) decreases. Indicates uprooting and out-migration from villages, and consequent migration of dispossessed, confirming the same sad story (explains 7%).

Figure 12.7 *Less Workers in Primary Sectors in Districts, the Larger Volume of Out-migration, 2001*

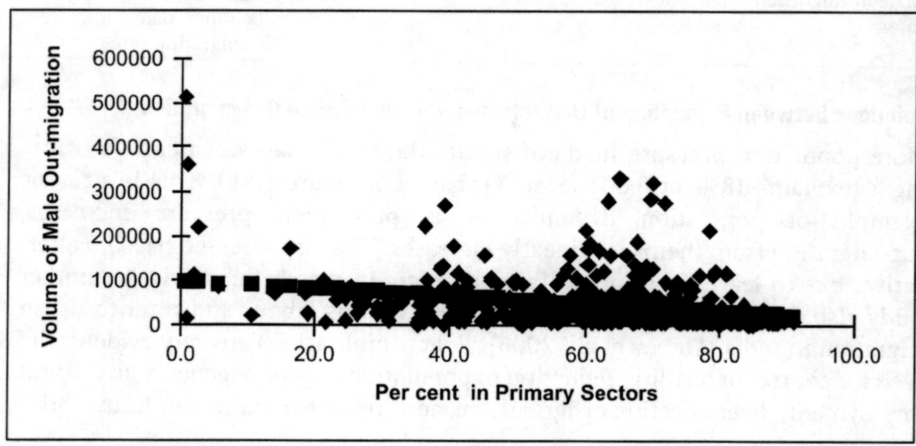

Table 12.9 *Relations between Primary Sectors of Districts and Volume of Male Out-migration, 2001 (N = 470, Beta = –0.23, Sig. T = .01, Intercept = 98807.2)*

Dependent Variable	*Indep. Variable*	*Mult. R.*	*Adj R Sq.*	*Expln.*	*Meaning of Relation*
Volume of male out-migration	Primary sectors (cultivation, agl. labour)	.27	.07	7%	Less primary sectors in district, the larger volume of male out-migration

More Urbanization, More Out-migration 2001

More urbanization of the districts, larger the volume of male out-migration from districts. This reflects the aspiration and innovativeness of the youth, explaining 14 per cent (at 0.001 level). Movement may be education-related or search for better prospects in destinations. Policy-wise, this finding has great meaning, i.e., in recent years (1991–2001) increased urbanization in some districts is synchronized with rise in both male in-migration and out-migration in those districts (see Table 12.4). Perhaps, this shows a beginning of high quality migration and urbanization in India. However, this has a caveat, since so far only small privileged segment of rural population usurps such benefits.

Table 12.10 *Relations between Urbanization in Districts and Volume of Male Out-migration, 2001 (N = 470, Beta = .12, Sig. T = .001, Intercept = 19646.8)*

Dependent Variable	*Indep. Variable*	*Mult. R.*	*Adj R Sq.*	*Expln.*	*Meaning of Relationship*
Volume of male out-migration	Urban per cent	.37	.14	14%	More urbanization, larger volume of male out-migration

Figure 12.8 *More Urbanization, More Out-migration of Males from Districts, 2001*

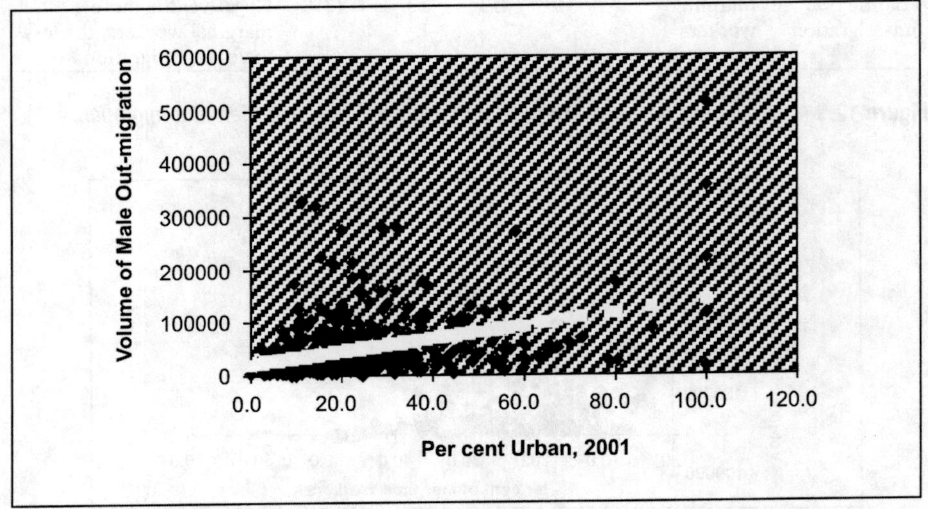

In general, in India, more urbanization has its benefits, as it breaks the shackles of caste barriers of migrants in which he (she) was previously bound in caste-ridden village society, and prompts him (her) to search for better luck in a free urban society. Thus, urbanization and migration are not evil some *per se*, rather both offer some benefits, though with attendant problems of over-congestion, breakdown of urban services, and mushrooming slums. So policy significance is: better urban governance and gainful migration must be encouraged. Urban slums are, indeed, creation of evil builders and slumlords, who keep artificially sky-rocketing urban land and housing prices, with the connivance of city authorities and politicians. Such corruption must be stopped, rather than migration-restriction.

Links between Marginal Workers in Districts and Volume of Male Out-migration

Relation is negative: the more marginal workers, the less male out-migration from districts. But, the meaning is rather positive: less male out-migration occurs where more marginal work available within the district, no matter how small is the pay, nor how short working period. This acts as *a safety valve* for migrants (explains 13%). Tables 12.10 and 12.11 must be seen together. These imply that 13 per cent of petty farmers and landless agricultural labourers prefer to stay within district (even in marginal work), instead of out-migrating (Table 12.11); while a privileged part (14%), move out from more urbanized districts for better prospects education or business. Both can exist side by side. *Because, after economic reforms and globalization in India (since 1991), now many dollar billionaires live side by side with 500 million of absolutely poor. Indeed, this has become a land of unspeakable contrast and tremendous socio-economic inequities. So, migration and urban researchers must be very cautious in interpreting all such phenomena, and view them in correct perspectives, not in isolation. Only then, correct prescriptions will emerge for a sea of humankind in India!*

Table 12.11 *Relations between Marginal Workers in Districts and Volume of Male Out-migration, 2001 (N = 470, Beta = –.30, Sig. T = .01, Intercept = 102777.2)*

Dependent Variable	*Independent Variable*	*Mult R*	*R Sq.*	*Adj R Sq.*	*Expln.*	*Meaning of Relation*
Volume of male out-migration	Marginal workers	.36	.13	13	13%	Negative: the more marginal workers, the less male out- migration

Figure 12.9 *Relations between Marginal Workers and Volume of Male Out-migration, 2001*

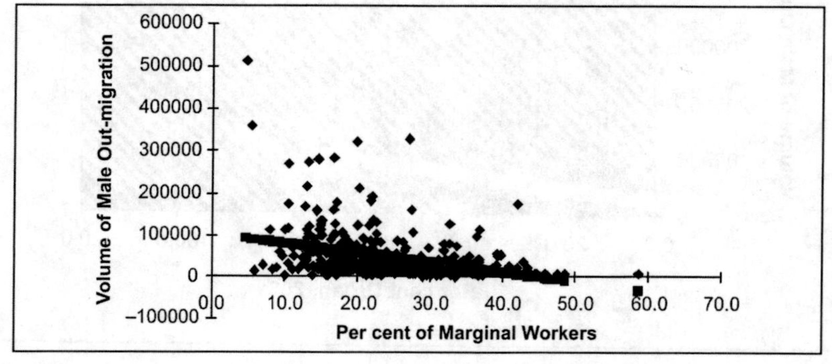

Relations between Urbanization of Districts and Net Migration of Districts, 2001

Figure 12.10 is very intriguing, as it depicts casual relation between urbanization and male net migration from districts. Relation is positive: as urbanization of the districts increases, net migration also linearly rises. The relation is *bi-polar: as net migration rises, so also urbanization, reinforcing each other.* In India, as elsewhere, in-migration into the cities contributes about 30–40 per cent of urbanization. Sometimes higher in case of large cities. These trends also have many ramifications. Such aspects are discussed in chapter 21, where future scenario of India's migration and urbanization are examined for 2001–51 period.

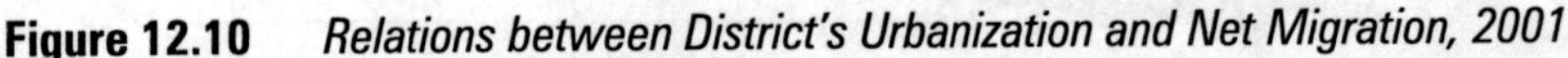

Figure 12.10 *Relations between District's Urbanization and Net Migration, 2001*

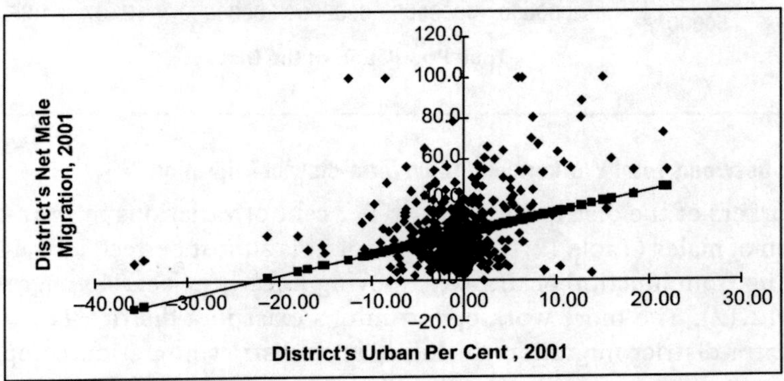

Table 12.12 *Links between Urbanization of the Districts and Male Net Migration, 2001 (N = 470 districts)*

Dependent Variable	*Indep. Variable*	*Adj R Sq.*	*Expln.*	*Meaning of Relation*
Male Net migration rates of district	Urban per cent of districts	.32	32%	Higher the urbanization of districts, the higher male net migration rates of districts

Causal Links between Total Population and Male Intra-district Migration, 2001

Larger the total population of the districts, the more volume of intra-district migration. That is, as population size of district increases, intra-district male migration also increases (Table 12.12, Figure 12.11). Adjusted R-square is 0.35, explaining 35 per cent (at 0.001 level). This relationship simply follows the Gravity model of migration, which spells that spatial interaction (migration) between two places is directly proportional to the product of size of population of two places and inversely proportional to distance between them. The finding has much utility in predicting volume of intra-district migration.

Table 12.13 *Links between Total Population and Male Intra-district Migration, 2001 (N = 470, Beta = .014, Sig. T = .001, Intercept = –989.4)*

Dependent Variable	*Indep. Variable*	*Adj R Sq.*	*Expln.*	*Meaning of Relation*
Male intra-district migration	Total population	.35	35%	More total population of districts, more male intra-district migration

Figure 12.11 *Causal Links between Total Population and Male Intra-district Migration, 2001*

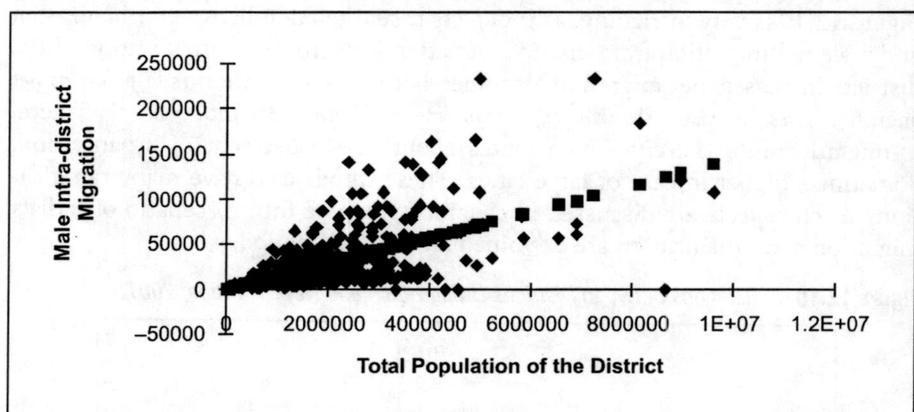

Relations between Total Workers and Male *Intra*-district Migration

Total workers of the districts explain 48 per cent of variations in intra-district migration of males (Table 12.13). The line of fit is almost perfect, a straight line originating from junction of the axes, moving linearly at near 45 degree angle (Figure 12.12). The more work opportunities exist in a district, larger is the size of intra-district migration. In India, intra-district migration comprises a very large segment of total migration of a district, and half of that is explained by this predictor alone. This finding is significant at 0.0001 level, i.e., error term is only 1 out of 10,000 observations that this findings could be wrong. Policy import is: we need real inclusive growth, instead of current jobless growth, which puts all benefits only to a handful of privileged business families. We urgently need real inclusive growth in favour of the poor and the under-privileged, both in deadly stagnant villages and slums, instead of government's only lip service to inclusive growth.

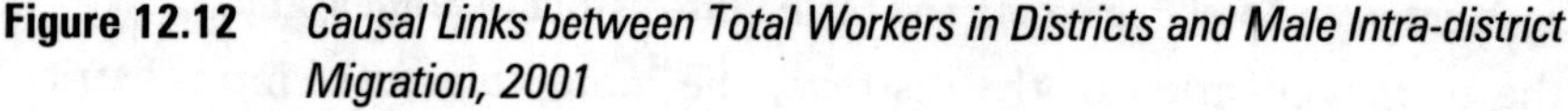

Figure 12.12 *Causal Links between Total Workers in Districts and Male Intra-district Migration, 2001*

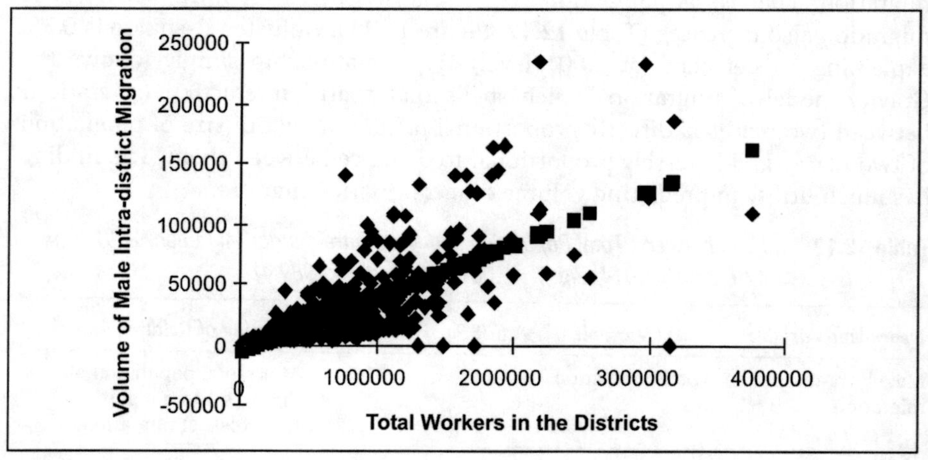

Table 12.14a *Links between Total Workers of the Districts and Male Intra-district Migration, 2001 (N = 470, Beta = .044, Sig. T = .0001, Intercept = –3.5)*

Dependent Variable	*Indep. Variable*	*Adj R Sq.*	*Expln.*	*Meaning of Relation*
Male intra-district migration	Total workers	.48	48%	More total workers in districts, more male intra-district migration

The More Marginal Workers, the More Intra-district Male Migration, 2001

More marginal workers in the districts, more intra-district male migration (explains 15%). More marginal workers in cultivation, agricultural labour, and plantations mean more temporary work for labourers, leading to rise in intra-district migration, mainly from rural to rural. This explains considerable male in-migration. Policy significance is that many labourers actually live on the fringe of livelihood, and need protection and more employment avenues in the countryside. The generation of more rural and agricultural work, both in primary and tertiary sectors, will fruitfully keep them well engaged in the villages themselves, instead of swelling in remote destinations, facing hostile environment (Figure 12.13). This can be a good migration strategy.

Table 12.14b *Links between Marginal Workers of the Districts and Male Intra-district Migration, 2001 (N = 470, Beta = .018, Sig. T = .001, Intercept = 803.0)*

Dependent Variable	*Independent Variable*	*Adj R Sq.*	*Expln.*	*Meaning of Relation*
Male intra-district migration	Marginal workers	.15	15%	More marginal workers in districts, more intra-district male migration

Figure 12.13 *More Volume of Marginal Workers, More Intra-district Male Migration, 2001*

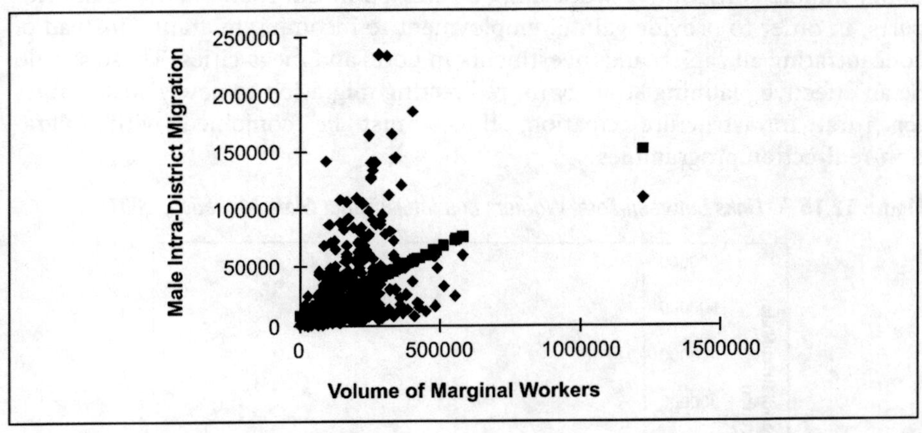

Causal Links between Total Population and Male Inter-district Migration, 2001

More total population, more inter-district male migration (explains 33%) (Figure 12.14, Table 12.15). This again follows "Gravity model" of migration, i.e., larger the population size of two districts, the more spatial interaction, or migration, between them.

Figure 12.14 *Causal Links between Total Population and Male Inter-district Migration, 2001*

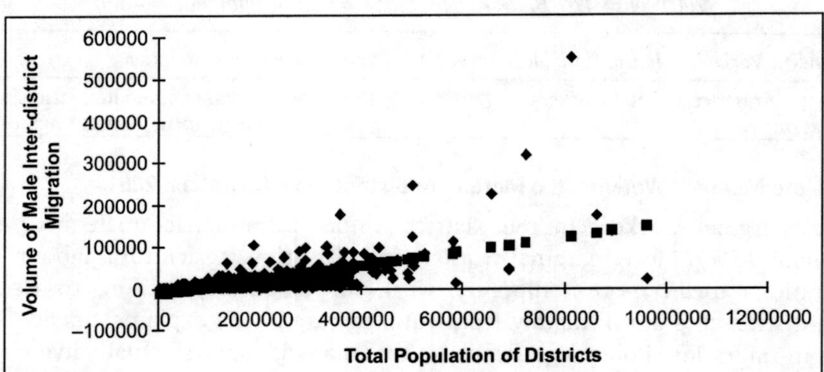

Table 12.15 *Links between Total Population of Districts and Male Inter-district Migration, 2001 (N = 470, Beta = .016, Sig. T = .0001, Intercept = –5.25)*

Dependent Variable	*Indep. Variable*	*Adj R Sq.*	*Expln.*	*Meaning of Relation*
Male inter-district migration	Total population	.33	33%	More total population, more inter-district male migration

Links between Total Workers and Inter-district Male Migration, 2001

More total workers, more inter-district male migration (explains 35%). Larger the scope of work opportunities, greater the volume of inter-district migration. Availability of work is the supreme determining factor of male migration in India. This is of paramount importance in movers' decision-making process. Policy import is that more work must be created in the countryside, in interior parts, in order to provide gainful employment to incoming migrants, instead of concentrating all capital and investments in ports and mega cities. These should be an effective planning strategy for redirecting migration to new vistas. Efforts for rural infrastructure creation, thus, must be conjoined with migration-redirection programmes.

Figure 12.15 *Links between Total Workers and Inter-district Male Migration, 2001*

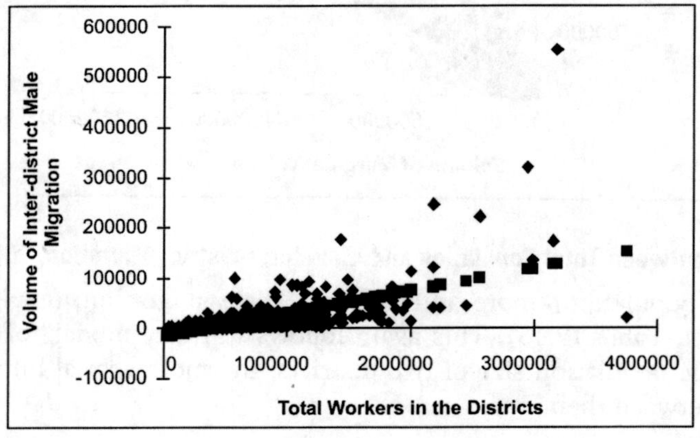

Table 12.16 *Links between Total Workers of Districts and Male Inter-district Migration, 2001 (N = 470, Beta = .045, Sig. T = .0001, Intercept = 15726.6)*

Dependent Variable	*Independent Variable*	*Adj RSq*	*Explanation*	*Meaning of Relation*
Volume of male inter-district migration	Total workers	.35	35%	More total workers, more volume of inter-district male migration

Causal Links between Tertiary Sectors and Volume of Male Inter-district Migration

More tertiary sectors, more inter-district male migration (explains 14%). Table 12.17 and Figure 12.16 present this interesting causal linkages between tertiary workers (trade-commerce, transport, and services) and volume of inter-district migration. Interpretation is almost the same as above (Table 12.16), and casual links are the same. Out of total workers, if there is a large part of tertiary workers (not manufacturing/secondary sectors, nor primary sectors), then, chances are high that it will attract more male inter-district migration. The only caveat, as noted before, that, unlike in the Western countries, where growth of tertiary sectors implies economic development, conversely in India, proliferation of low-grade tertiary sectors rather signify underdevelopment, or anti-development (as symptoms of mainly low-grade work). Of course, this is much better than unemployment or starvation in villages, and *hence much desirable.*

Table 12.17 *Links between Tertiary Sectors and Volume of Male Inter-district Migration, 2001*

Dependent Variable	*Indep.Variable*	*Adj R Sq.*	*Expln.*	*Meaning of Relation*
Male inter-district migration	Tertiary sectors	.14	14%	More tertiary sectors, more inter-district male migration

Figure 12.16 *Relations between Tertiary Sectors of Economy and Inter-district Migration of Males, 2001*

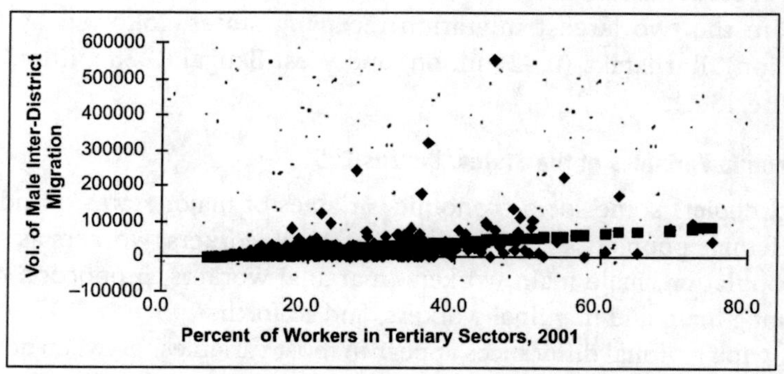

By creating backward and forward linkages between the organized and the unorganized sectors, we can easily transform this sea of semi-skilled and semi-educated migrants into highly trained and more productive workers. This is achieved in some Asian countries, e.g., China, South Korea and Indonesia. Definitely, India can also do that. Policy significance of this finding lies here.

13 Findings of State-level Analysis of Migration and Its Links with Regional Disparities, 2001

"Vow, then, to devote your whole lives to the cause of the redemption of these three hundred million, going down and down every day". (now 1.20 billion Indians on March 31, 2010)

Swami Vivekananda (1894)
(Complete Work, Centenary Volume V, 1963: 17)

State-level Analysis

In-migration into States, Males, 1991–2001

Inter-state migration matrix for the males and the females are presented in Tables 13.3 and 13.4 (see Appendix). These are also mapped in Figures 10.1 to 10.4. As regards the males, Maharashtra (1.76 million) and Delhi (1.06 million) are the two largest migration receiving states, followed by Gujarat (0.65 million), Karnataka (0.42 million) and West Bengal (0.28 million) (Table 13.1, Figure 13.1).

Socio-economic Variables of the States, Census 2001

Table 13.2 depicts some socio-economic variables of major states of India, viz., male and female populations, per cent urban, total workers, workers as per cent of total population, male main workers, marginal workers, proportion of cultivators among main and marginal workers, and so forth.

Very wide regional differences appear in most variables, between developed states like Punjab, Haryana, Maharashtra, Gujarat in the one hand, and comparatively less developed and neglected states like Uttar Pradesh, Bihar, Madhya Pradesh, Rajasthan, Orissa, West Bengal, Jharkhand, and Chhattisgarh. Evidently, massive migrants, of both the males and the females occur from less developed states to more favoured and developed states. These are also illustrated in four Maps (Figures 10.1 to 10.4).

Table 13.1 *Inter-state In-migration, Out-migration and Net Migration, All-India, Males, 1991–2001*

Major States	*In-migration*	*Out-migration*	*Net Migration*
Jammu Kashmir	34916	67408	–32492
Himachal Pradesh	88258	53077	35181
Punjab	384931	165487	219444
Delhi	1063812	176453	887359
Haryana	505702	179607	326095
Rajasthan	271231	438137	–166906
Uttar Pradesh	280225	1901431	–1621206
Bihar	54107	1156874	–1102767
Assam	47098	67670	–20572
West Bengal	283550	313053	–29503
Orissa	82718	217993	–135275
Madhya Pradesh	258191	292051	–33860
Maharashtra	1768112	182482	1585630
Gujarat	657621	343218	314403
Andhra Pradesh	175277	268829	–93552
Karnataka	418474	303505	114969
Kerala	117630	195671	–78041
Tamil Nadu	108707	287662	–178955
All-India In-migration and Out-migration (Males)	6, 600,560	6,600, 560	Nil

Source: Computed from Census of India, 2001, Migration Tables, D-Series, CDs, available only in 2006–7.

Figure 13.1 *In-migration to Indian States, 1991–2001, Males, Total In-migration 6.6 Million*

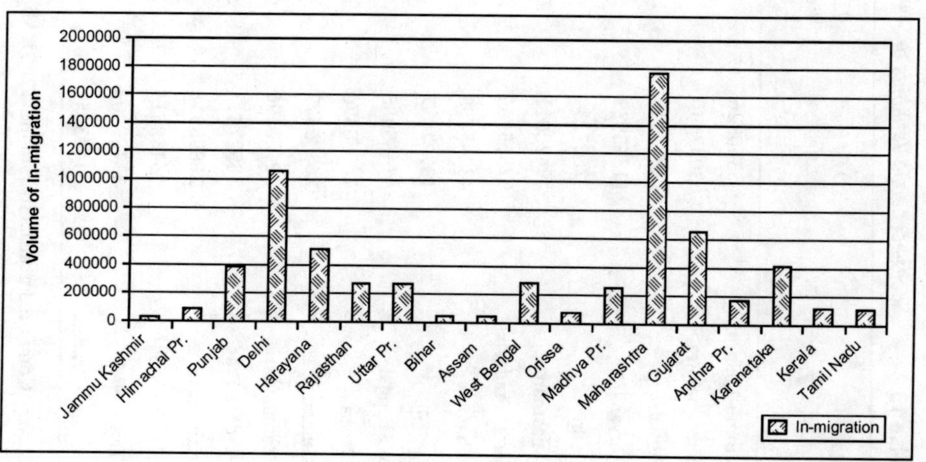

Table 13.2 *Socio-economic Variables of States, 2001*

States	*TOT-M Male*	*TOT-F Female*	*Urbanization(%)*	*General literacy (%)*	*Illiteracy (%)*	*TOT Workers Persons*	*Workers as % of Pop*	*Per cent Main Workers*	*Per cnet Marginal Workers*	*Main Cult %*
Jammu-Kashmir	5360926	4782774	25	47	53	3753815	37	70	30	42
Himachal Pradesh	3087940	2989960	10	67	34	2992461	49	66	34	65
Punjab	12985045	11373954	34	61	39	9127474	38	86	14	23
Haryana	11363953	9780611	29	57	43	8377466	40	75	26	36
Delhi	7607234	6243273	93	70	30	4545234	33	95	5	1
Rajasthan	29420011	27087177	23	49	51	23766655	42	73	27	55
Uttar Pradesh	87565369	78632552	21	46	54	53983824	33	73	27	41
Bihar	43243795	39754714	11	38	63	27974606	34	75	25	29
Assam	13777037	12878491	13	53	47	9538591	36	75	25	39
W. Bengal	41465985	38710212	28	59	41	29481690	37	78	22	19
Orissa	18660570	18144090	15	54	46	14276488	39	67	33	30
Gujarat	26385577	24285440	37	59	41	21255521	42	80	20	27
Maharashtra	50400596	46478031	42	66	34	41173351	43	84	16	29
Andhra Pradesh	38527413	37682594	27	52	48	34893859	46	83	17	23
Karnataka	26898918	25951644	34	58	42	23534791	45	82	18	29
Kerala	15468614	16372760	26	80	20	10283887	32	80	20	7
Tamil Nadu	31400909	31004770	44	65	35	27878282	45	85	15	18
Madhya Pradesh	31443652	28904371	27	52	48	25793519	43	74	26	43

Sources Computed from Census of India 2001. Migration Tables (D-series), and Economic Tables. Share of marginal cultivators and agricultural labourers not shown.

Typically, Uttar Pradesh (1.90 million) and Bihar (1.15 million) are the two largest migration-sending states, where from the movers crowd into Maharashtra, Delhi, and West Bengal. Thus, Utter Pradesh and Bihar are the net migration-loosing states, and Maharashtra and Delhi are the two net migration-gaining states. The same patterns can be seen, during 1981–91, or in all previous censuses. In fact, the patterns have not changed since last 130 years, since the first census taken in 1872 (Mukherji, 1981: 1–278). Everything changes in this world, but the typical inter-state migration patterns in India never change, simply because widespread spatial disorganization persisted in India, leading to a very marked regional disparities and social inequities. So, the poor migrants from the backward states of Uttar Pradesh and Bihar are virtually forced to move out and swell in the relatively forwarded states of Maharashtra and Delhi for survival since last 100 years. This migration pattern is also observed in a recent study (Dholakia, 2008: 15).

Inter-state Out-migration Matrix, All-India, Males, 1991–2001

Uttar Pradesh is the state of largest out-migration of males (1.9 million), followed by Bihar (1.1 million). From these two states, larger volumes of male out-migration occurs to Maharashtra and Delhi (Figure 13.2, Table 13.4, in the Appendix).

Figure 13. 2 *Total Out-migration from States, All-India, Males, 1991–2001, Total Out-migration 6.6 million*

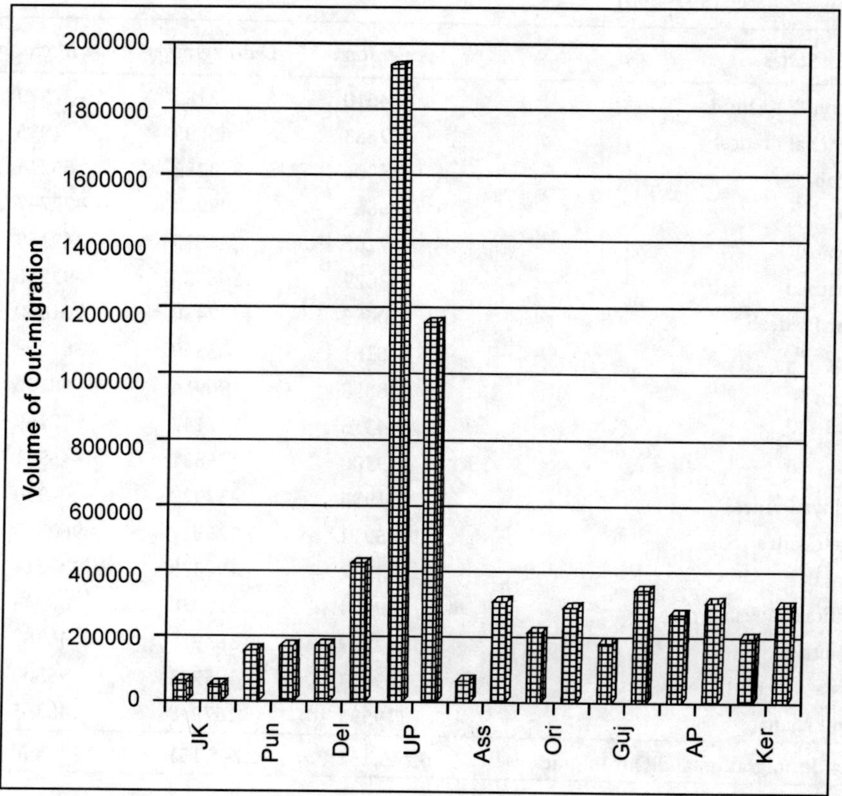

Reasons are elaborated above. Unless and until these two backward states are given all development inputs and infrastructure, and unless their governance are vastly improved, unfortunately, such typical migration due to poverty and under-development would continue for many more decades. *Migration policy-wise this is the greatest need of the hour. Specially when these migrants from Uttar Pradesh and Bihar are now facing considerable hostile oppositions from the local people at the destinations.* Unless these problems are urgently tackled, socio-economically and spatially, the path to the future is very tenuous and may lead to further inter-regional conflicts.

In the Appendix, two large Tables (Tables 13.3 and 13.4) are also presented, which show, respectively, inter-state migration matrix, to rural and to urban areas, for the males (during 1991–2001), and likewise, inter-state migration matrix for the females (during 1991–2001). They unravel important patterns which are also illustrated through maps and diagrams.

Inter-state In-migration Matrix, Females, 1991–2001

As usual with the males, for the female migration also, the largest receiving states are Maharashtra (1.2 million) and Delhi (0.8 million). The largest sending states are, again, Uttar Pradesh and Bihar. Inter-state migration patterns, thus, remain same for 1991–2001, as in earlier decades, and for both the sexes. These are age-old migration patterns of India, since last 130 years.

Table 13.5 *Inter-state in-migration, Out-migration and Net Migration, Females, 1991–2001*

Major States	*In-migration*	*Out-migration*	*Net Migration*
Jammu & Kashmir	34610	62189	–27579
Himachal Pradesh	67683	65698	1985
Punjab	318506	253282	65224
Delhi	826665	348918	477747
Haryana	587208	238039	349169
Rajasthan	413029	506585	–93556
Uttar Pradesh	520686	1422486	–901800
Bihar	216361	603369	–387008
Assam	38858	106964	–68106
West Bengal	244316	237147	7169
Orissa	79300	125881	–46581
Madhya Pradesh	431936	432922	–986
Maharashtra	1185912	225517	960395
Gujarat	412592	190378	222214
Andhra Pradesh	229104	318038	–88934
Karnataka	419339	383976	35363
Kerala	99453	195753	–96300
Tamil Nadu	119593	267948	–148355
Total In-migration and Out-migration	6,245,151	6,245,151	Nil

Figure 13.3 *In-migration to States, All-India, Females,1991–2001, Total In-migration 6.24 Million*

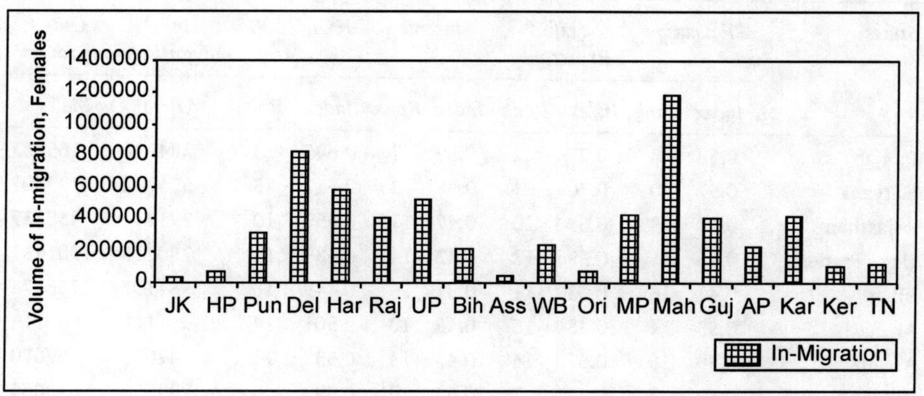

Inter-state Out-migration Matrix, Total, Females, 1991–2001

During 1991–2001, from Uttar Pradesh the largest volume of female out-migration occurs (1.4 million), followed by Bihar (0.6 million). They moved to Maharashtra and Delhi, as males also do. Patterns are almost same, as determining factors are alike.

Figure 13. 4 *Total Inter-state Out-migration, All-India, Females, 1991–2001*

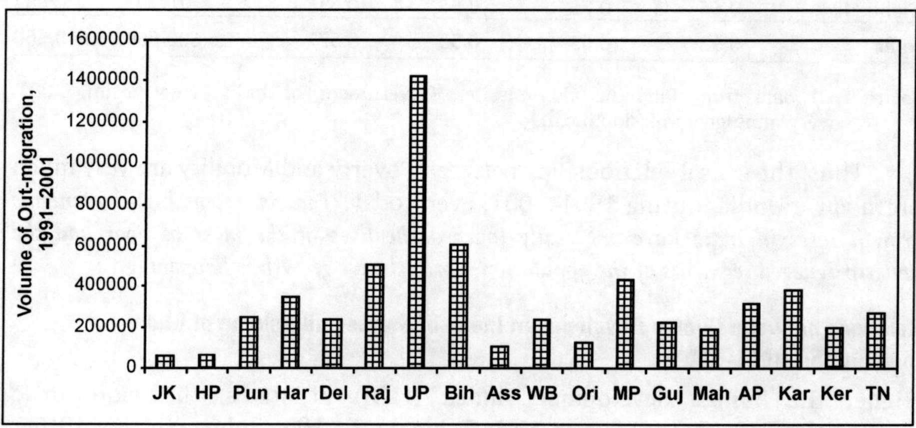

Human Development Index (HDI) and States of High Male In-migration and Out-igration

Table 13.6 indicates that Uttar Pradesh and Bihar with lowest HDI Index (in 2000) are perennially the regions of high male out-migration, and Maharashtra, Gujarat, Punjab and Haryana are perennially the regions of high male in-migration. West Bengal has moderate HDI index and also a moderate volume of male in-migration from Bihar. Such causal linkages become more evident when we notice Income Rank of these states, revealing wide regional disparities in income levels between forward states and back-ward states, consequently, causing almost an involuntary out-migration of male labourers from the lagging states to the prosperous and favoured states.

Table 13.6 *Human Development Index (HDI) 2000, and State's In-migration and Out-migration, 1991–2001*

States	*Education*		*Life Expectancy*		*Income*		*HDI, 2000*		*In-migration*	*Out-migration*
	Index	*Rank*	*Index*	*Rank*	*Index*	*Rank*	*Index*	*Rank*	*Males*	*Males*
Punjab	0.58	8	0.77	2	0.59	1	0.645	3	384931	165487
Haryana	0.57	10	0.70	4	0.58	3	0.617	5	505702	179607
Rajasthan	0.58	9	0.63	10	0.47	11	0.557	10	271231	438137
Uttar Pradesh	0.46	15	0.59	12	0.42	14	0.489	15	280225	1901431
Bihar	0.41	16	0.63	11	0.31	16	0.449	16	54107	1156874
Arunachal	0.53	14	0.48	16	0.49	10	0.501	14	NA	NA
Assam	0.59	6	0.57	14	0.43	13	0.53	11	47098	67670
W. Bengal	0.59	7	0.68	7	0.51	9	0.593	8	283550	313053
Orissa	0.56	12	0.58	13	0.40	15	0.515	13	82718	217993
Madhya Pradesh	0.57	11	0.55	15	0.45	12	0.523	12	258191	292051
Maharashtra	0.68	2	0.73	3	0.58	2	0.662	2	1768112	182482
Gujarat	0.61	4	0.66	9	0.54	5	0.606	7	657621	343218
Andhra Pradesh	0.54	13	0.67	8	0.51	8	0.575	9	175277	268829
Karnataka	0.61	5	0.69	6	0.53	7	0.608	6	418474	303505
Kerala	0.75	1	0.87	1	0.54	5	0.721	1	117630	195671
Tamil Nadu	0.66	3	0.70	5	0.55	4	0.638	4	108707	287662
India	0.57		0.63		0.53		0.577		6,600,560	6,600,560

Source: HDI data from Planning Commission, Government of India, New Delhi, 2001. www.planningcommission.nic.in

Thus, the causal relationships between Poverty and Mobility are very much prevalent in India, during 1991–2001, even today. *That is, recent higher economic growth rates in India have not really touched the lives of the most of poor and the under-privileged segments of the population, nor inclusive growth is happening.*

Relations between Human Development Index of States and Volume of Male In-migration, 1991–2001

Higher the human development index (HDI) of states, the more male in-migration into states (Figure 13.5, Table 13.7). HDI index explains 10 per cent of variations in volume of male in-migration into states (at 0.001).

Table 13.7 *Relations between HDI Index of States and Volume of Male In-migration into States, 1991–2001 (N = 17 Major States)*

Dependent Variable	*Indep. Variable*	*Adj R Sq.*	*Expln.*	*Beta*	*T.*	*Sig. T*	*Intercept*	*Meaning of Relation*
Vol. of male in-migration into states	Human development index of states	.10	10%	.65	1.5	.001	–1068611	Higher the human development index of states, the more male in-migration into them

Figure 13.5 *Relations between State's HDI and Volume of Male In-migration into States, 1991–2001*

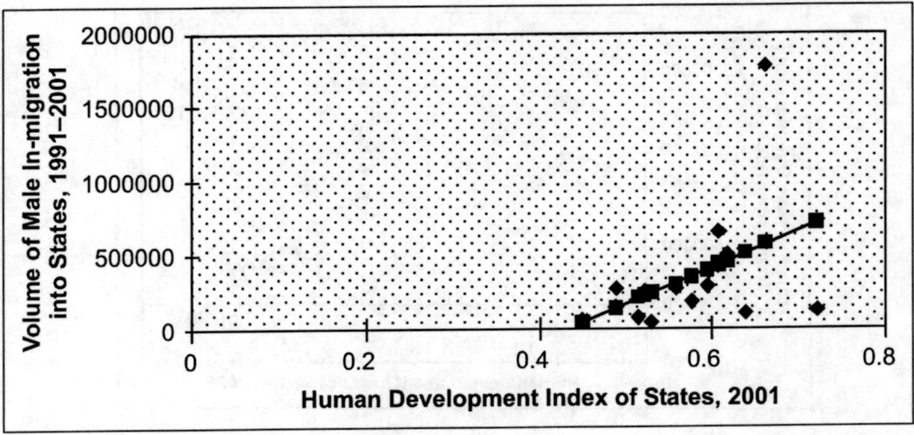

Relations between Human Development Index of States and Volume of Male Out-migration, 1991–2001

Lower the human development index of states, the more male out-migration from the states. Negative relationship emerges between the two, as expected (Table 13.8, Figure 13.6). It explains as high as 27 per cent of variations in the volume of male out-migration, almost three times higher than that of volume of male in-migration. This signifies that lack of socio-economic development in the states virtually impel the male labourers and workers to move out for somehow eking out their livelihood in the places of destinations, much more than the presence of development is effective in attracting male in-migration. The significance of this causal relationship is that it indicates the existence of a threshold value of tolerance of lack of development in a state, beyond which the people are virtually compelled to move out. *Policy import is that: migration in India is still very much poverty-induced, arises mostly due to lack of development, and not due to attraction of neon signs in the mega cities. Nor it is caused by aspirations or for better prospect in the places of destinations. No matter what other conventional migration or urban researchers may try to make us to believe, this is the hard reality. Planning-wise, thence, we must make every effort to provide at least minimum development and fulfillment of all basic human needs of the people in every village, every state, and every towns and cities of India. To ignore this hard reality, is at the cost of perils and catastrophe.*

Table 13.8 *Relations between HDI Index of States and Volume of Male Out-migration from States, 1991–2001 (N = 14 Major States)*

Dependent Variable	*Indep. Variable*	*Adj R Sq.*	*Expln.*	*Beta*	*T.*	*Sig.*	*T*	*Intercept Meaning of Relation*
Vol. of male out-migration	Human development index of states	.27	27%	–.65	2.9	.001	2674962	Lower the human development index of states, more male out-migration

Figure 13.6 *Relations between State's HDI and Volume of Male Out-migration from States, 1991–2001*

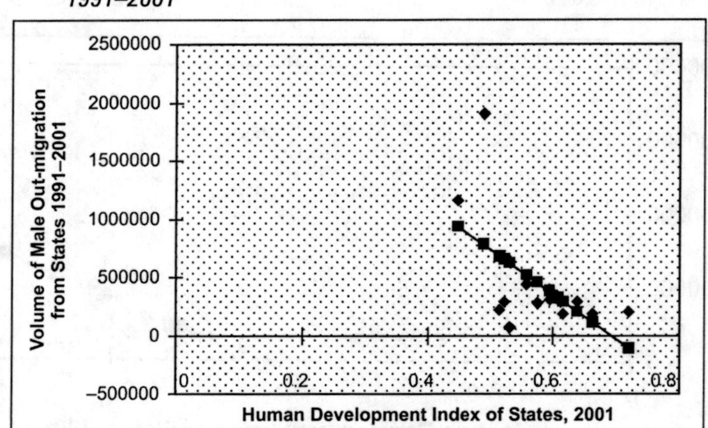

Male Inter-state In-migration, 1991–2001 and Economic Variables of States, 2001

Table 13.9 presents data of volume and rates of male in-migration and some socio-economic variables of the states, total population, male population, urbanization, and proportion of main workers to total workers. Urbanization is comparatively high in Gujarat, Maharashtra, Delhi Capital territory, Punjab, Haryana, and Tamil Nadu. These states also experience relatively higher male

Table 13.9 *Male Inter-state In-migration, 1991–2001 and Socio-economic Variables, 2001*

States	*Male In-migration*	*Total Population*	*Total Male Population*	*Urbanization*	*Percentage of Main Worker to Total Workers*	*Male In-mig. Rates*
Jammu-Kashmir	34916	10143700	5360926	24.8	69.3	0.65
Himachal Pradesh	88258	6077900	3087940	9.80	65.5	2.86
Punjab	384931	24358999	12985045	33.92	85.8	2.96
Haryana	505702	21144564	11363953	28.92	74.3	4.45
Delhi	1063812	13850507	7607234	93.18	95.0	13.98
Rajasthan	271231	56507188	29420011	23.39	73.3	0.92
Uttar Pradesh	280225	166197921	87565369	20.78	72.9	0.32
Bihar	54107	82998509	43243795	10.46	75.2	0.13
Assam	47098	26655528	13777037	12.90	74.7	0.34
West Bengal	283550	80176197	41465985	27.97	78.0	0.68
Orissa	82718	36804660	18660570	14.99	67.2	0.44
Madhya Pradesh	258191	60348023	31443652	26.46	74.1	0.82
Gujarat	657621	50671017	26385577	37.36	80.0	2.49
Maharashtra	1768112	96878627	50400596	42.43	84.3	3.51
Andhra Pradesh	175277	76210007	38527413	27.30	83.3	0.45
Karnataka	418474	52850562	26898918	33.99	82.2	1.56
Kerala	117630	31841374	15468614	25.96	80.0	0.76
Tamil Nadu	108707	62405679	31400909	44.04	85.2	0.35
Total In-migration	6,600,560					

in-migration rates. The causal relationship between the two is shown in Table 13.10, and illustrated in Figure 13.7. The more urbanization of the states, the higher male in-migration rates of states, both causally linked. Thus, both have a bi-polar relationship, each reinforces the other. This causal linkage explains as high as 71 per cent of variations in male in-migration rates (at 0.0001 level of significance). Such a very high statistical result is very rare in social sciences, which usually get between 10–15 per cent explanation. Policy significance is: in India, Migration and urbanization are progressing in tandem, in many progressive states (listed above), and may be further reinforced, if conjoined with higher level of industrialization, more job creation and inclusive growth that will take care of the poor and the downtrodden masses.

Figure 13.7 *Causal Links between Urbanization in States and Male In-migration Rates of States, 1991–2001*

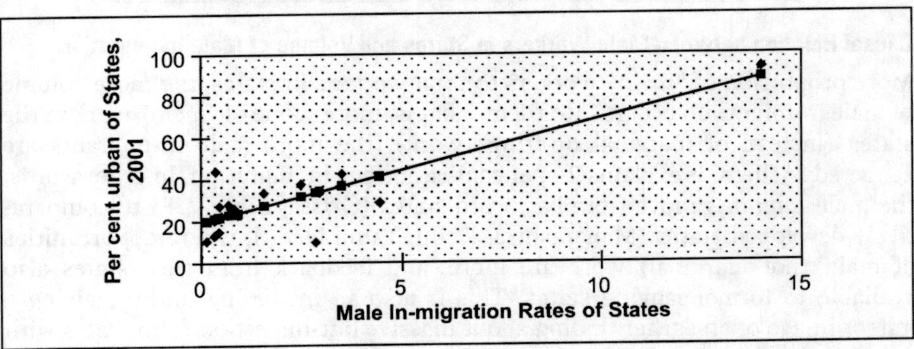

Table 13.10 *Relations between Urbanization in States and Male In-migration Rates, 1991–2001 (N = 17 States)*

Dependent Variable	*Indep. Variable*	*Adj R Sq.*	*Expln*	*Beta*	*T.*	*Sig. T*	*Intercept*	*Meaning of Relation*
Male In-migration rates	Urban per cent in states	.71	71%	.65	6.2	.0001	19.5	More urbanization in states, higher male in-migration rates of states (both causally linked)

Relations between Per cent Main Workers in States and Male In-migration Rates

More main workers in states, higher male in-migration rates in states; both causally linked, explaining 28 per cent (at 0.001 level of significance) (Figure 13.8, Table 13.11).

Table 13.11 *Relations between Main Workers in States and Male In-migration Rates, 1991–2001 (N = 17, Beta = .26, T = 2.7, Sig. T = .001, Intercept = –18.0)*

Dependent Variable	*Indep. Variable*	*Adj R Sq.*	*Expln.*	*Meaning of Relation*
Male In-migration rates	Per cent main workers	.28	28%	More main workers in states, higher male in-migration rates in states (both causally linked)

Figure 13.8 *Causal Links between percentage of Main Workers and Male In-migration Rates of States*

Causal Relation between Main Workers in States and Volume of Male In-migration

More proportion of "main" workers to total workers in states, the more volume of male in-migration occurs into them. That is, more scope of "main" work in the states (instead of marginal or fringe work), the more male in-migrants are attracted to them. It explains 24 per cent variations in migration. In other words, the male migrants move from backward states (Orissa, Bihar, UP) to comparatively developed states (Maharashtra, Delhi, Tamil Nadu), where opportunities of main (not marginal) work are more, and feedback from such states also available to former lagging states. This is also an intriguing finding, giving a mirror image of an earlier finding about massive out-migration from states with more workers that are marginal.

Figure 13.9 *Causal Links between percentage of Main Workers and Volume of Male In-migration, 1991–2001*

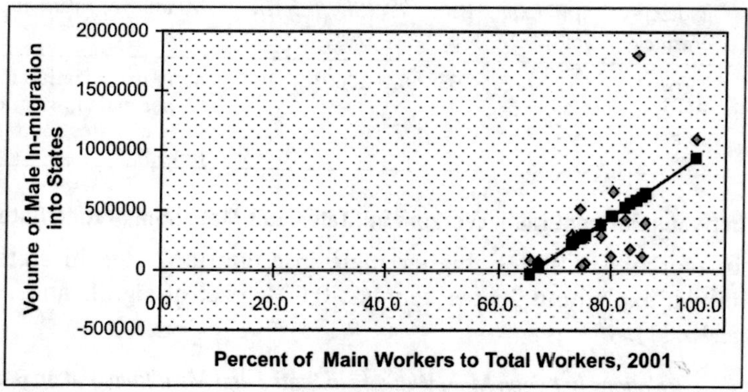

Table 13.12 *Relations between Percentage of Main Workers to Total Workers in States and Volume of Male In-migration, 2001 (N = 18 major states)*

Dependent Variable	*Indep. Variable*	*Adj R Sq.*	*Expln*	*Meaning of Relation*
Volume of male in-migration	Per cent of main workers to total workers	.24	24%	More percentage of main workers to total workers in states, more volume of male in-migration

Relations between Service Sectors and Volume of Male In-migration

More workers in service sectors in states, the more volume of male in-migration into them (explains 9%). This is very much akin to the next causal relations – where almost similar linkages emerge between tertiary sectors (which includes service sectors) and male in migration (Figure 13.10, Table 13.13). Also appears with the same significance of the result.

Figure 13.10 *Relations between Service Sectors of States' Economy and Volume of Male In-migration into States, 1991–2001*

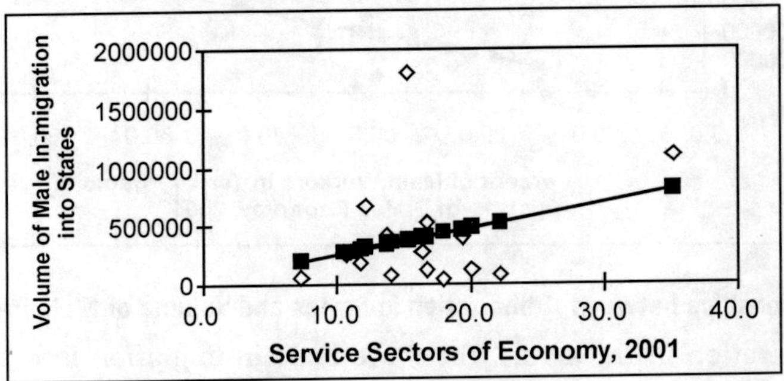

Table 13.13 *Relations between Service Sectors of States and Volume of Male In-migration, 2001 (N = 18, Beta = .32, T = 1.2, Sig. T = .01, Intercept = 507627)*

Dependent Variable	*Indep. Variable*	*Adj R Sq.*	*Expln.*	*Meaning of Relation*
Vol. of male in-migration into states	Per cent of workers in services	.09	9%	More workers in service sectors in states, the more volume of male in-migration into them

Relations between Tertiary Sectors and Volume of Male In-migration to State, 1991–2001

Figure 13.11 and Table 13.14 indicate that the more workers in tertiary sectors in states, the more volume of male in-migration into them. It explains 8 per cent of variations in male in-migration into the states. This proves that more migrants are moving where scope of only poor tertiary sectors exist, like trade-commerce, transport and low grade services, not so much manufacturing. Because, these are providers of more work opportunities to the incoming migrants, not capital-intensive manufacturing sectors, which generate very few jobs. This is clear evidence that many migrants find absorption only in lower-grade informal sectors, not in organized sectors. Policy-wise, this makes an urge for more forward linkages between informal and organized sectors of the economy, in order to generate more employment avenues for teeming millions of migrants.

Table 13.14 *Relations between Tertiary Sectors of States and Volume of Male In-migration, 2001 (N = 18 major states)*

Dependent Variable	*Indep. Variable*	*Adj R Sq.*	*Expln.*	*Meaning of Relation*
Volume of male in-migration into states	Per cent of workers in tertiary	.08	8%	More workers in tertiary sectors in states, more volume of male in-migration into them

Figure 13.11 *Causal Links between Tertiary Sectors of States' Economy and Volume of Male In-migration, 1991–2001*

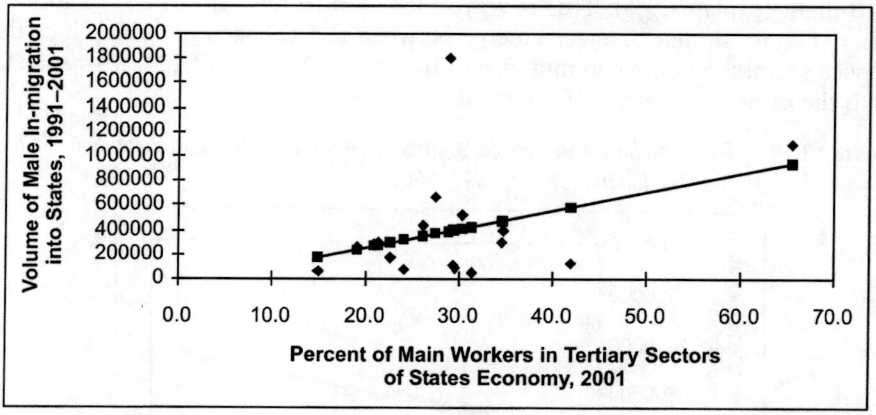

Volume of Male In-migration into States, 1991–2001
2000000
1800000
1600000
1400000
1200000
1000000
800000
600000
400000
200000
0
0.0 10.0 20.0 30.0 40.0 50.0 60.0 70.0
Percent of Main Workers in Tertiary Sectors of States Economy, 2001

Causal Relationships between Urbanization in States and Volume of Male In-migration

More urbanization in the states, the more male in-migration into them. Both increase linearly. Urbanization explains as high 36 per cent of variations in the volume of male migration into the states, with a very high level of significance (.0001). Error term is only one out of 10,000 observations or tests. This is simply remarkable. This points towards a synonymous or catalytic development relation between urbanization and in-migration in most states, each reinforcing the other (This result is different from Table 13.10). This also shows a healthy sign. But, there is a caveat, such rapid urbanization and spurt in male in-migration is not accompanied with industrialization, rather by mushrooming growth of low-grade tertiary sectors (see Figure 13.11, above). This demands more development of secondary sectors and the creation of jobs in these modern sectors in various states, instead of the poor tertiary sectors.

Table 13.15 *Relations between Urbanization in States and Volume of Male In-migration, 991–2001 (N = 17, Beta = .37, T = 3.1, Sig. T. = .0001, Intercept = –48810.3)*

Dependent Variable	*Indep. Variable*	*Adj R. Sq.*	*Expln.*	*Meaning of Relation*
Volume of male in-migration	Urban per cent in states	.39	36%	More urbanization in states, more male in-migration

Inter-State Male Out-migration, Population Pressure, and Primary Sectors of States

Table 13.16 presents data of volume and rates of male out-migration and related economic variables of states like proportion of main and marginal workers to total workers, per cent in primary work, and total male population. Uttar Pradesh and Rajasthan have both high per cent of marginal workers as well as large volume of male out-migration. Thus, these two variables are very highly causally linked. Similarly, male population pressure and volume of male out-migration are causally bound. These are further explained.

Figure 13.12 *Causal Relations between Urbanization in States and Volume of Male In-migration 1991–2001*

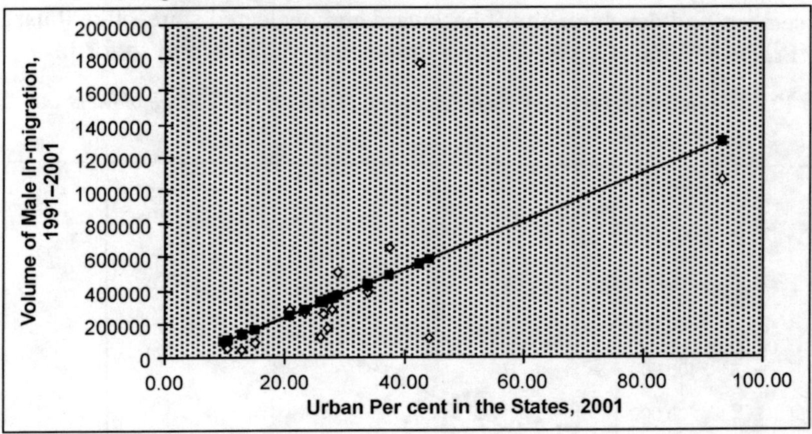

Table 13.16 *Inter-state Male Out-migration and Primary Sectors of Economy, 2001*

States	*Percentage of Main Workers to Total Workers*	*Percentage of Marginal Workers to Total Workers*	*Percentage of Primary Workers to Main Workers*	*Inter-state Male Out-migration, 0–9 Years*	*Total Male Population, 2001*	*Male Inter-state Out-mig. Rates*
J&K	69.3	30.7	44.2	40691	5360926	0.25
H. Pradesh	65.5	34.5	58.8	37826	3087940	0.30
Punjab	85.8	14.2	45.1	97623	12985045	0.22
Haryana	74.3	25.7	50.7	128141	11363953	0.22
Rajasthan	73.3	26.7	64.1	326214	29420011	1.01
Uttat Pradesh	72.9	27.1	63.8	1577893	87565369	1.09
Bihar	75.2	24.8	76.8	883896	43243795	0.77
Assam	74.7	25.3	58.1	44868	13777037	0.13
W. Bengal	78.0	22.0	42.8	245036	41465985	0.41
Orissa	67.2	32.8	61.1	159544	18660570	0.82
M. Pradesh	74.1	25.9	68.8	174740	31443652	0.59
Gujarat	80.0	20.0	50.5	133975	26385577	0.54
Maharashtra	84.3	15.7	53.5	221772	50400596	0.58
A. Pradesh	83.3	16.7	61.9	192110	38527413	0.66
Karnatka	82.2	17.8	56.4	191954	26898918	1.10
Kerala	80.0	20.0	32.4	159923	15468614	1.13
Tamil Nadu	85.2	14.8	48.3	195117	31400909	0.87
Total Male Out-migration				4948290		

Relations between Male Population of States and Volume of Male Out-migration

Male population pressure explains about 84 per cent of variations in the volume of male out migration (Table 13.17 and Figure 13.13). The causal relations is unbelievably high, 84 per cent, such high result is almost never found in social sciences, nor even in physical sciences. The level of significance is tremendously high, 0.00001. that's is, chances are that the result is true 99999 times out of 10,000 observations or tests. This indicates an *one-to-one relationship* between the two. The more population pressure in the states, higher is the volume of male out-migration from the states. Policy prescriptions are very evident: population control, fertility reduction, creation of more jobs in agricultural and nonagricultural sectors, and development of backward and neglected states, like Rajasthan, Uttar Pradesh, Bihar, Orissa, Madhya Pradesh, Karnataka, and so forth.

Figure 13.13 *Relations between Male Population of States, and Volume of Male Out-migration, 1991–2001*

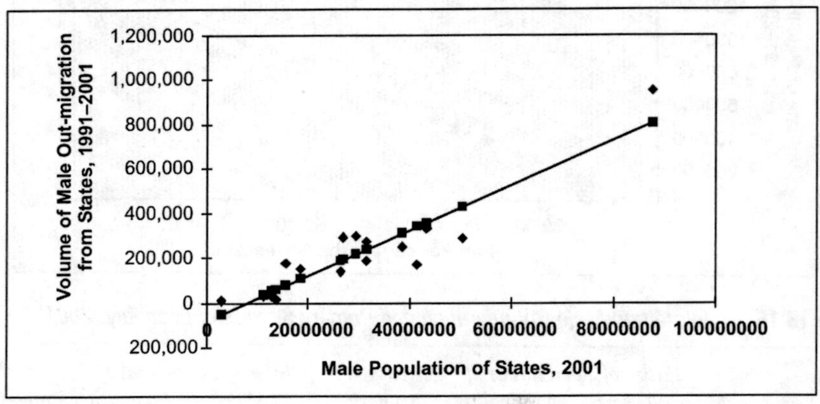

Table 13.17 *Relations between Male Population of States and Volume of Male Out-migration, 1991–2001 (N = 17)*

Dependent Variable	*Indep. Variable*	*Adj R Sq.*	*Expln.*	*Beta*	*T.*	*Sig. T*	*Intercept*	*Meaning of Relation*
Volume of male out-migration from states	Male population of states	.84	84%	.001	8.8	.0000 1	–81267.3	More male population pressure in states, higher volume of male out-migration

Relations between Male Population of States and Male Out-migration Rates

Male population pressure also explains about 15 per cent of variations in male out-migration rates (Figure 13.14, Table 13.18). This sounds almost axiomatic, but the statistical proof is here, with 0.001 level of significance. It is not a loose bunch of statements, rather a hard reality. Population control measures are not rigorously advocated in India by the state or central government, since declaration of emergency in 1975–77 and coercive excesses done during that period. The government fell in 1977. Since then, no government (state or central), nor any political party ever advocated strong implementation of population control measure, so now India is having 1.20 billion mouths to feed and provide jobs to a youthful population of about 500 million. No wonder, that male population pressures in various backward states impel them to move out elsewhere. Thus, policy-wise, family planning or population control measures are very much required to be rigorously implemented (as China did), and more jobs both in public sectors (i.e., government sectors) and private sectors are urgently need to be generated, both in agricultural sectors and urban-industrial sectors. Only then, an increasingly huge and youthful labour force can be provided with skill and gainful employment. Otherwise, the so-called "demographic dividends" of a youthful bulge in India (about which many population specialists delightedly write) may turn out to be its perils and catastrophe.

Figure 13.14 *Relations between Male Population and Male Out-migration Rates of States, 1991–2001*

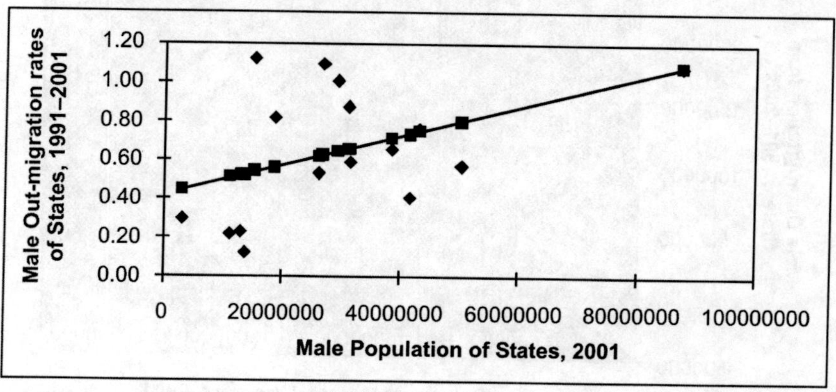

Table 13.18 *Relations between Male Population of States and Male Out-migration Rates, 1991–2001 (N = 17 States)*

Dependent Variable	*Indep. Variable*	*Mult. R.*	*Adj R Sq.*	*Expln.*	*Meaning of Relation*
Male out-migration rates	Male population in states	.45	.15	15%	More male population pressure in states, higher male out-migration rates

Strong Relations between Volume of Marginal Workers and Volume of Male Out-migration, 1991–2001

Figure 13.15 reveals that the more marginal workers persist in the states, the more male out-migration occur from it. This is a very intriguing finding, as regression line and statistics emphatically confirm that more male out-migration occur from those states, where the "main" workers are limited, rather more "marginal workers" predominate (like Bihar, UP, Rajasthan, Orissa, Jharkhand). This causal relation explains 72 per cent of variations in volume of out-migration. Such picture emerges in sharp contrast to tall claims of India's rapid economic development during the globalization decade (1991–2001). This must be a revelation to the conventional scholars, policy-makers, and the governments.

Table 13.19 *Relations between Volume of Marginal Workers in States and Volume of Male Out-migration, 2001 (N = 18 Major States)*

Dependent, Variable	*Indep., Variable*	*Adj R Sq.*	*Expln.*	*Beta*	*T.*	*Sig. T*	*Intercept*	*Meaning of Relation*
Volume of male out-migration	Volume of marginal workers	.72	72%	.18	12.5	.0001	−163111	More marginal workers in the states, the more male out-migration

Figure 13.15 *Relations between Marginal Workers and Male Out-migration (explains 72%)*

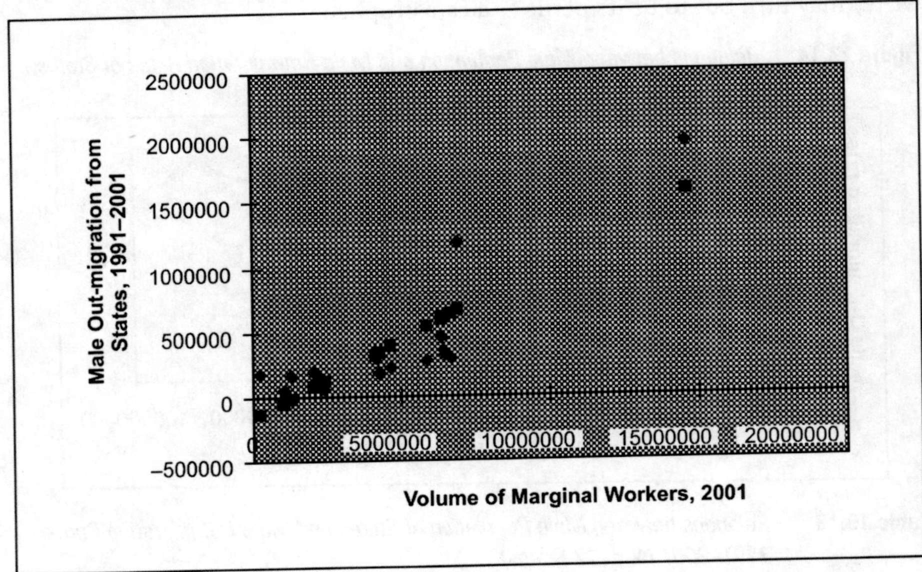

14 Findings of Class I City-level Analysis

Links between Migration and Urbanization, 2001

"Reason out what is true from what is untrue."

Swami Vivekananda (1896)
(Complete Work, Centenary Volume VIII, 1963: 228)

Occupational Absorption of Migrants in Selected 58 Class I Cities

Table 14.1 presents the volume of migration and percentage distribution of migrant workers by sex in seven occupational categories in 58 selected cities of India.

1. The percentage of migrant workers employed in the low grade production work category is significant as compared to other categories. As many as 17 (Ludhiana, Jamshedpur, Ahmedabad, Surat, Rajkot, Faridabad complex, Delhi, Durg-Bhilai Nagar, Dhanbad, Greater Mumbai, Pune, Nagpur, Nashik, Bhiwandi, Vijaywada, Coimbatore, Salem) out of the total 58 cities show more than 50 per cent male migrant workers employed in such low grade production-process work. These 17 cities also include metropolises like Greater Mumbai (57%) and Delhi (57%). Bhiwandi shows the highest proportion of male migrant workers employed in production work (86%), followed by Surat (77%), Ludhiana (67%), and Faridabad (61%). In 1991, their number was only 13; the situation appears to have further worsened.
2. Apart from these 17 cities another 26 cities show 40–50 per cent migrant workers joining in low-grade production-processing work. Notable among them also include Kolkata, Chennai, Bangalore, Vadodara, and Hyderabad. In other words, more than 40 per cent of the total migrant workers are engaged in low-grade production and related activities in 43 most important cities of India, out of 58 most relevant class I cities analysed. In 1991, their number was only 17. Hence, the situation of the migrant workers have not improved much, during 1991–2001
3. In case of female migrant workers, the scenario is different and interesting. It is true that a large chunk of female migration is employed in production work, but at the same time, a considerable chunk is absorbed in the administrative (5 to 20%) or clerical work (9 to 30%). In production-processing work, the proportion of females is low as compared to the proportion of males. However, in the administrative or clerical occupations in all cities

proportion of females is higher than that of the males, nevertheless, their volumes are very small. Another noteworthy aspect is that since their educational level is not very high (as revealed from other Tables), most such women as administrative or professional workers are actually primary school teachers or nurses, not technicians, doctors or engineers.

4. In 1991, whereas only five cities (Durg-Bhilai Nagar, Nagpur, Solapur, Aurangabad, Salem) showed more than 40 per cent females employed in low-grade production work, their number swelled to 35 cities in 2001. While 10 cities (Patna, Kozhikode, Ludhiana, Amritsar, Jalandhar, Jodhpur, Lucknow, Meerut, Allahabad, Bareilly) showed more than 40 per cent females employed in administrative-professional-clerical jobs, but in 2001, their number was reduced to 8 cities (Shimla, Chandigarh, Ghaziabad, Patna, Ranchi, Gwalior, Kozhikode, and Thirumallapuram). In most of 58 cities more than 20 per cent of female migrant workers are employed in administrative-professional jobs. *But, their absolute number is very small.*

Table 14.1 *Migrant Workers and Their Occupational Divisions, Selected 58 Class I Cities, 2001 (out of total 438 Class I cities analysed, data for only few shown here)*

Name of City	*Total Migrant Workers*		*Occupational Divisions of Migrants (%)*											
			Div 1 Prof. Workers		*Div 2: Admn. Workers*		*Div 3: Clerks*		*Div 4: Sales*		*Div 5: Services*		*Div 7–8–9: Production Process*	
	Males	*Females*	*M%*	*F%*	*M%*	*F %*	*M%*	*F%*	*M%*	*F%*	*M%*	*F%*	*M%*	*F%*
1	*2*	*3*	*4*	*5*	*6*	*7*	*8*	*9*	*10*	*11*	*12*	*13*	*14*	*15*
Shimla	35776	7192	7	3	11	18	14	29	11	14	21	13	34	20
Ludhiana	314570	35222	5	2	3	10	3	12	3	5	12	9	67	44
Chandigarh	201411	42821	7	4	8	19	9	20	6	11	20	9	47	33
Faridabad	215750	28118	6	3	7	14	5	16	6	7	11	7	61	41
Delhi	2294488	303132	6	4	7	14	5	14	5	7	17	11	57	42
Jaipur	211636	38138	7	3	10	12	7	18	7	4	19	9	46	43
Ghaziabad	145990	18476	6	4	10	20	6	17	13	11	16	9	43	23
Agra	56406	7620	3	1	4	8	4	9	7	4	24	12	42	27
Lucknow	208964	29946	7	4	11	16	8	15	13	9	20	11	35	34
Kanpur	196462	21472	3	2	6	11	5	9	9	5	20	14	48	36
Allahabad	55244	7450	6	2	12	18	5	10	14	7	23	11	26	25
Varanasi	67526	13472	4	1	8	9	5	9	7	3	23	10	38	33
Patna	134096	19398	8	3	14	20	10	21	12	6	25	13	24	23
Guwahati	184072	33690	6	3	8	14	8	16	9	10	28	11	33	26
Siliguri	53472	9006	4	2	5	11	4	9	10	6	38	18	35	38
Durgapur	83968	14000	5	1	6	11	7	10	12	5	20	13	44	47
Kolkata	1716178	303262	4	2	6	12	5	11	10	7	24	15	48	44
Jamshedpur	102200	12976	7	4	6	11	6	15	6	3	18	12	51	46
Dhanbad	131668	13024	5	3	7	8	6	11	5	3	14	13	54	46
Ranchi	77556	12080	9	3	11	16	7	23	9	6	25	14	31	26
Raurkela	86950	10982	8	3	6	10	8	15	4	3	20	12	47	48

Cont'd...

...Cont'd

Cuttack	76712	12922	7	2	9	12	7	15	7	5	22	7	42	47
Bhubaneswar	151632	24182	9	3	12	14	9	14	9	6	21	9	36	44
Durg-Bhilai	134084	28464	6	2	5	7	8	12	4	3	16	12	57	58
Gwalior	52570	12840	7	3	13	16	10	22	7	4	17	9	39	38
Ujjain	28990	10622	6	2	9	9	8	18	6	4	20	10	46	44
Indore	167148	36422	7	2	8	11	6	13	5	5	22	11	47	48
Bhopal	182780	40878	8	3	9	14	9	17	7	8	20	11	44	41
Ahmedabad	589286	78176	6	2	5	10	4	14	7	8	20	9	54	45
Rajkot	161636	20756	6	2	4	8	4	13	6	5	19	8	57	50
Vadodara	222408	39200	8	3	9	12	6	17	8	10	17	10	48	42
Surat	726696	45794	3	1	2	6	3	11	2	3	12	9	77	59
Amravati	57156	13222	4	1	7	9	9	17	9	6	21	12	46	51
Solapur	49230	19768	5	1	7	5	6	9	8	3	21	9	48	65
Gr. Mumbai	3296878	465058	5	3	5	10	5	13	6	11	20	11	57	45
Nagpur	217948	44402	6	2	6	8	8	16	7	7	20	13	52	49
Nashik	191268	39158	6	2	7	9	6	14	5	7	16	14	58	49
Bhiwandi	190628	9616	2	1	1	3	1	5	1	1	8	6	86	70
Pune	608896	141614	8	3	8	11	5	13	5	9	16	10	56	49
Kolhapur	44436	11252	9	2	10	12	7	15	9	8	20	14	42	42
Hyderabad	749398	151020	9	4	10	12	7	12	7	7	18	9	42	38
Vijayawada	111418	18126	8	2	6	9	5	11	8	5	19	14	50	45
Warangal	43908	12350	8	2	9	7	8	10	9	3	19	8	40	57
Nellore	38136	7462	6	2	7	8	5	10	8	4	20	14	48	49
Tirupati	44762	10204	7	2	9	10	7	14	7	5	23	18	43	44
Shimoga	31176	6566	10	2	8	8	7	19	7	9	26	15	39	38
Belgaum	50006	11082	10	3	8	9	6	18	7	8	22	13	43	38
Bangalore	871622	220716	10	4	10	10	6	12	5	7	18	8	47	50
Mysore	57826	12958	12	4	12	14	8	23	7	12	23	11	34	27
Kozhikode	42144	12814	6	3	8	18	7	26	4	10	22	7	47	31
Kochi	111826	49378	10	4	11	15	7	19	5	12	19	9	44	35
Thiru. puram	51058	20474	9	5	15	19	14	30	8	17	20	9	27	15
Chennai	709582	146180	8	5	8	14	7	13	6	8	20	11	43	34
Salem	67820	15504	5	2	6	10	5	11	5	4	20	14	52	44
Coimbatore	139030	32472	5	2	5	10	5	10	4	6	18	11	56	44
Tiru.palli	98248	23286	8	3	9	14	7	11	5	6	23	14	42	40
Madurai	91226	19688	4	2	5	9	5	10	5	4	26	16	49	46
Pondicherry	69519	19695	8	3	9	13	8	16	6	6	18	14	45	40

Source: Computed from Census of India, 2001(b), Migration Tables, D-Series, Census Commissioner and Registrar General's Office, New Delhi, CDs, data available only in 2008.

Note: To avoid wide table, some small percentages of Div 6 (farm workers), less than 1 per cent, Div 10 (unclassified) and Div 11 (unclassifiable) are not shown. For males, their total per cent vary between 2–6 per cent, rarely 10 per cent. For females, their per cent mostly vary between 2–10 per cent, sometimes over 20 per cent. These indicate more lower category workers, specially among the females. So, columns do not add upto 100%.

Occupational Divisions of Male Migrants, Class I Cities, India, 2001

Table 14.2 shows a picture of such occupational absorption of male migrants in main class I cities. Upper sectors includes professionals, administrative workers and clerks, and lower sectors involved illiterate and semi-educated (with less than secondary educated) low-grade production workers, services workers, farm workers and unclassified. The rest are in middle sectors, viz., sales or middle-grade production processing work (sales workers, and post-secondary educated workers in production work). This is not shown in table.

Table 14.2 *Occupational Divisions of Migrants (Males), 72 Class I Cities, India, 2001*

Name of Class I City	*Total Migrant Workers (Males)*	*Poor Sector (%)*	*Upper Sector (%)*	*Name of Class I City*	*Total Migrant Workers (Males)*	*Poor Sector (%)*	*Upper Sector (%)*
Srinagar	43040	66.2	10.8	Ranchi	77556	50.1	26.9
Jammu	72150	49.0	25.3	Raurkela	86950	52.5	22.0
Shimla	35776	42.0	31.4	Cuttack	76712	49.8	24.2
Ludhiana	314570	55.2	11.3	Bhubaneswar	151632	45.4	29.7
Amritsar	88172	57.4	12.6	Korba	55378	52.7	14.0
Jalandhar	89988	54.4	15.5	Durg-Bhilai	134084	51.5	19.1
Chandigarh	201411	48.6	23.9	Raipur	96108	52.8	18.4
Dehradun	65172	49.3	24.3	Gwalior	52570	46.0	29.8
Hardwar	28110	44.5	28.7	Ujjain	28990	49.7	23.4
Faridabad	215750	48.8	17.9	Indore	167148	53.0	20.8
Panipat	61778	56.1	9.6	Bhopal	182780	47.7	25.4
Delhi	2294488	63.2	17.2	Jabalpur	73416	49.7	24.7
Bikaner	25832	53.2	22.4	Ahmedabad	589286	53.5	15.5
Jaipur	211636	48.8	24.1	Rajkot	161636	53.8	14.3
Bhilwara	33940	51.2	18.0	Jamnagar	56966	58.1	12.9
Udaipur	27086	47.9	25.6	Bhavnagar	41938	50.8	18.1
Ganganagar	26054	62.8	12.4	Vadodara	222408	47.3	23.0
Jodhpur	35724	54.4	19.2	Surat	726696	55.9	7.9
Ajmer	18634	47.4	26.8	Amravati	57156	50.0	20.3
Kota	81832	51.6	18.8	Solapur	49230	52.7	18.1
Ghaziabad	145990	45.8	22.1	Gr. Mumbai	3296878	59.8	15.5
Noida	73670	52.0	23.1	Nagpur	217948	50.5	19.4
Muzaffarnagar	18800	56.7	18.4	Aurangabad	128858	47.9	22.0
Meerut	67838	52.2	16.3	Nashik	191268	50.0	18.4
Mathura	20674	56.4	16.2	Bhiwandi	190628	56.2	3.9
Agra	56406	63.2	10.7	Pune	608896	49.1	21.1
Bareilly	32584	48.0	24.9	Kolhapur	44436	47.0	25.5
Lucknow	208964	45.0	26.1	Hyderabad	749398	48.4	25.8
Kanpur	196462	56.4	13.7	Vijayawada	111418	50.5	19.0
Jhansi	28772	55.1	17.7	Warangal	43908	48.5	24.7
Allahabad	55244	52.0	22.6	Nellore	38136	52.6	18.0
Varanasi	67526	59.6	15.9	Tirupati	44762	50.3	23.7
Muzaffarpur	22010	46.6	32.4	H.Dharwad	63376	45.4	30.3
Patna	134096	44.7	31.9	Shimoga	31176	51.8	24.0
Gaya	14960	53.0	23.6	Belgaum	50006	50.3	23.6
Shillong	26820	58.7	19.5	Bangalore	871622	48.1	26.2
Guwahati	184072	54.2	21.5	Mangalore	55656	49.2	23.5
Siliguri (Part)	53472	61.5	13.1	Mysore	57826	45.9	31.9

Cont'd...

...Cont'd

Siliguri	34686	59.0	10.4	Kozhikode	42144	53.2	21.2
Durgapur	83968	50.7	17.8	Kochi	111826	47.8	27.0
Barddhaman	29768	53.4	16.8	T. Puram	51058	42.2	37.6
Kolkata	1716178	69.6	14.5	Chennai	709582	51.8	23.3
Asansol	93386	53.5	13.7	Erode	61128	59.6	12.7
Kharagpur	21280	49.4	24.1	Coimbatore	139030	55.7	15.6
Jamshedpur	102200	52.2	18.7	Tiruchirappalli	98248	52.3	23.2
Dhanbad	131668	53.0	17.8	Madurai	91226	58.8	14.7
Bokaro	74678	49.1	24.5	Pondicherry	69519	48.4	25.3

1. Out of selected 72 main class I cities, only 14 cities showed more than 25 per cent migrant male workers absorbed in upper class work (administrative, professional, and clerical). These are Jammu, Shimla, Muzzafarpur, Patna, Hardwar, Ajmer, Ranchi, Bhuvaneswar, Gwalior, Bhopal, Kolhapur, Hyderabad, Dharwar, and Bangalore. Most are second tier cities, except Bangalore and Hyderabad – which are metros.
2. Besides, there are 24 cities which have 20 to 25 per cent male migrant workers in upper sectors, and another 34 cities, mostly third-tier small cities, which have less than 20 per cent male migrant workers absorbed in upper class work. To some extent, these are positive signs that small cities are showing migrant workers being engaged in upper class work, instead of herding in shantytowns and urban slums in large metros. These tendencies must be encouraged.

Economic Structure of 438 Class I Cities, 2001

It is earlier surmised that there exist many causal relations between the economic structure of the cities and the kinds of migration to them. One of the objectives of this research is to untangle those hidden causal relationships. They cannot be achieved by simple discussions, rather can only be established through thread-bare statistical techniques, like regression or canonical analysis. Canonical analysis was very extensively employed in Part I, so here the emphasis is given mainly upon simpler regression technique (which most readers can easily understand). This has been done in following sections.

Table 14.3 presents a summary table of data of eight broad categories of workers in selected main 98 class I cities of India, along with the total workers. Here, both male and females workers are considered, as that truly depict the economic structure of cities, instead of only males taken. However, these are later correlated with male migrant workers. Obviously, there may arise some mismatch between the two; but the ensuing cause-and effect relations show that the extent of mismatch, if any, is insignificant (as we shall see).

As already pointed out, most of the class I cities, have a small manufacturing or secondary sectors (i.e., manufacturing, mining, household industry, and construction) that ranges between 15 to 25 per cent, and a large proportion under the poor tertiary sectors (i.e., trade and commerce, transport, and services) that comprises as large as 50–70 per cent. This becomes very evident from Table 14.3.

Table 14.3 *Economic Categories of 438 Class I Cities, 2001 (only selected 98 shown)*

Class I Cities	*Main Workers (Persons)*	*Economic Categories of Cities (Persons) (%)*							
		Primary Workers %	*Mining %*	*House-hold indus-tries %*	*Manu-factu-ring %*	*Constr-uction %*	*Trade-comm-erce %*	*Trans-port %*	*Servi-ces %*
Srinagar	237498	3.7	0.2	11.0	9.4	5.1	20.8	6.0	43.7
Jammu	113434	1.0	0.1	0.6	7.2	8.2	20.9	6.6	55.5
Shimla	52410	1.3	0.1	1.0	3.8	8.1	10.7	4.0	71.1
Amritsar	581122	3.5	0.1	4.1	21.9	6.8	25.6	8.0	29.9
Ludhiana	974380	2.5	0.4	6.1	40.0	5.4	17.6	6.1	21.9
Chandigarh	290821	0.9	0.1	0.9	12.9	8.8	17.0	6.3	53.1
Dehradun	110658	2.5	2.7	2.2	11.5	8.8	20.5	7.1	44.7
Hardwar	43722	2.2	0.4	2.4	14.9	8.1	24.5	9.1	38.6
Panipat	84338	1.9	0.3	6.9	39.2	4.6	21.4	4.8	21.0
Faridabad	300931	2.3	0.9	3.2	32.5	7.6	18.0	6.6	29.0
Delhi	3160618	0.7	0.3	3.1	21.9	6.2	23.4	8.6	35.8
Delhi (Part)	548806	0.8	0.2	1.9	19.7	7.4	18.2	7.5	44.2
Ganganagar	61466	3.0	0.0	4.3	11.7	6.0	27.5	8.7	38.7
Bikaner	139510	4.6	0.5	5.5	10.7	8.9	13.9	8.3	47.5
Jaipur	656888	4.3	0.3	5.3	23.1	8.4	18.4	7.4	32.8
Jodhpur	225869	2.0	2.3	4.6	16.0	9.8	19.1	9.9	36.4
Ajmer	124167	2.2	0.2	4.7	13.3	8.4	21.0	15.9	34.2
Bhilwara	84455	5.4	0.7	3.9	31.4	8.3	20.6	7.0	22.6
Udaipur	114078	1.8	2.0	5.1	14.1	6.2	23.5	9.6	37.8
Kota	174316	3.3	0.9	3.7	15.1	11.1	21.2	11.9	32.7
Muzaffarnagar	78263	2.9	0.1	3.9	15.4	6.7	31.0	10.2	29.7
Meerut	249271	4.2	0.1	4.9	22.4	9.2	23.5	7.9	27.8
Ghaziabad	247892	3.4	0.3	2.9	21.4	7.1	19.0	9.4	36.4
Noida	100153	4.0	0.4	3.0	15.3	7.4	13.6	5.4	50.9
Mathura	71186	2.8	0.3	7.0	19.7	4.9	23.3	9.2	32.9
Agra	285997	4.0	0.1	7.1	22.6	5.9	24.1	4.7	31.4
Bareilly	171994	4.9	0.1	6.4	22.2	5.5	21.8	9.9	29.2
Lucknow	536822	3.1	0.3	4.7	14.3	6.1	19.1	10.1	42.2
Kanpur	636525	2.4	0.2	3.5	22.7	5.2	24.6	7.9	33.5
Jhansi	86669	3.8	0.5	7.2	11.6	6.3	19.8	15.0	35.9
Allahabad	215952	2.8	0.4	5.9	9.8	3.8	23.0	7.4	46.9
Varanasi	274916	2.4	0.1	29.8	12.5	3.0	21.9	4.4	26.0
Muzaffarpur	144186	3.0	0.2	3.7	9.4	3.2	32.0	9.0	39.5
Patna	650388	7.7	0.2	4.1	9.2	4.9	22.8	8.5	42.7

Cont'd...

...Cont'd

Gaya	81822	9.7	0.4	7.5	11.8	3.9	27.0	8.0	31.6
Shillong	43250	1.6	0.4	1.5	5.7	7.1	20.2	4.5	59.0
Guwahati	269667	3.0	1.0	1.4	8.0	6.3	20.9	12.1	47.4
Siliguri	148313	1.8	0.5	1.7	10.4	7.1	30.4	14.5	33.7
Siliguri (Part)	90564	1.4	0.3	1.4	8.0	6.2	31.4	13.8	37.4
Asansol	114598	3.2	5.2	1.5	20.3	5.7	25.6	10.7	27.7
Durgapur	133536	4.1	2.1	1.2	25.2	6.9	19.2	7.4	34.0
Barddhaman	86790	3.0	0.6	2.2	12.2	7.5	24.3	13.5	36.7
Habra	40486	4.6	0.1	5.3	19.7	5.4	31.7	8.9	24.4
Kharagpur	47962	2.1	0.3	1.1	11.5	5.7	25.1	23.2	31.1
Kolkata	1624811	0.9	0.2	2.6	17.0	4.0	24.0	10.5	40.6
Dhanbad	50004	3.8	6.2	2.7	11.1	3.1	23.5	13.9	35.6
Bokaro	83074	6.2	2.5	2.7	47.4	4.5	10.4	6.4	19.9
Ranchi	200001	4.4	1.9	2.8	12.3	6.8	21.2	10.5	40.2
Jamshedpur	136735	1.6	1.2	2.4	36.3	7.9	15.3	9.1	26.3
Raurkela	59917	1.7	0.4	2.0	16.3	10.7	23.3	16.1	29.6
Cuttack	158219	3.3	0.2	3.0	13.0	7.9	23.7	11.0	38.0
Bhubaneswar	203792	3.5	0.3	2.0	8.1	14.7	16.3	8.5	46.5
Korba	78609	6.9	15.6	2.0	14.3	10.6	14.0	6.6	30.1
Bhilai Nagar	143812	3.3	1.9	2.0	37.1	11.4	16.0	8.4	19.9
Durg	67407	4.8	0.4	3.3	15.7	12.2	21.5	11.5	30.5
Raipur	181873	2.2	0.5	3.1	15.9	9.0	23.0	12.1	34.1
Gwalior	213957	3.2	0.6	3.9	15.9	9.5	20.3	9.5	37.0
Ujjain	117898	3.9	0.4	4.3	18.6	8.9	20.8	8.9	34.2
Indore	439494	1.4	0.2	4.8	21.3	9.0	24.1	8.7	30.5
Bhopal	385538	2.2	0.4	1.8	15.5	10.7	18.9	9.0	41.5
Jabalpur	258358	1.6	0.3	8.2	19.1	9.0	19.8	9.0	33.1
Ahmedabad	1070910	1.0	0.1	2.1	30.7	8.6	24.3	9.2	24.1
Rajkot	297289	1.5	0.2	2.2	31.9	9.0	22.9	9.4	23.0
Bhavnagar	148462	1.4	0.1	1.2	34.3	9.5	21.2	9.4	22.9
Vadodara	406877	1.4	0.7	1.1	23.5	8.8	20.8	10.1	33.6
Surat	908860	1.0	0.1	2.9	53.4	5.7	17.5	5.0	14.4
Gr. Mumbai	4087341	0.9	0.2	2.8	25.7	5.9	18.9	12.4	33.2
Amravati	148566	7.0	0.3	2.4	11.2	11.5	20.6	12.3	34.8
Nagpur	567541	1.8	0.7	2.7	15.2	11.5	21.1	12.5	34.6
Aurangabad	237087	3.7	0.2	1.3	19.1	16.1	17.4	10.0	32.3
Nashik	345757	7.9	0.2	1.5	24.1	12.4	15.1	9.0	29.9
Bhiwandi	242086	0.5	0.1	1.3	72.8	2.5	9.5	4.2	9.0
Gr. Mumbai (Part)	2836490	0.9	0.3	2.7	26.9	6.7	18.2	12.5	31.8

Cont'd...

...Cont'd

Pune	806320	2.0	0.1	3.2	18.8	12.4	15.8	9.8	37.8
Solapur	285310	3.8	0.2	17.3	26.7	6.7	16.1	7.0	22.3
Kolhapur	147885	4.4	0.2	3.8	17.5	9.2	20.2	10.2	34.5
Hyderabad	979238	1.9	0.4	2.6	12.4	8.8	23.5	11.1	39.3
Vijayawada	258242	2.8	0.3	2.8	13.5	10.6	25.5	16.9	27.7
Nellore	115333	6.3	0.4	3.6	15.8	12.6	22.0	10.2	29.2
Tirupati	68328	1.2	0.3	2.8	8.9	11.2	23.1	9.8	42.8
Belgaum	120945	3.8	0.2	5.5	22.0	6.4	21.7	9.1	31.3
Hubli-Dharwad	231638	7.3	0.2	3.5	14.2	9.4	21.3	12.5	31.5
Shimoga	87962	8.0	0.2	3.3	12.5	11.0	25.0	9.5	30.6
Bangalore	1536430	0.8	0.2	2.1	24.1	8.8	18.8	9.6	35.6
Mangalore	154934	3.8	0.6	14.3	14.1	11.0	16.1	10.2	30.0
Mysore	241893	1.9	0.2	3.6	17.7	8.7	21.4	11.5	35.2
Kozhikode	115849	7.6	0.2	1.7	13.6	11.5	23.0	11.7	30.6
Kochi	181024	4.1	0.2	2.4	14.6	11.7	18.7	13.6	34.7
Thiruvananthapuram	218876	9.4	0.4	1.7	9.1	10.0	15.3	11.3	42.7
Chennai	1382492	2.6	0.2	1.9	15.0	7.8	19.2	10.1	43.1
Salem	252955	3.2	0.5	13.1	24.8	7.2	18.0	5.9	27.3
Erode	59084	1.9	0.1	2.7	16.9	6.2	33.9	8.2	30.0
Coimbatore	340969	2.5	0.3	4.6	23.3	7.8	20.7	6.1	34.7
Tiruchirappalli	236732	3.9	0.8	4.2	16.1	6.9	22.4	10.6	35.2
Madurai	305541	2.0	0.2	3.1	21.5	7.4	25.1	8.4	32.3
Pondicherry	71108	5.0	0.2	1.6	18.1	8.2	17.3	8.4	41.2

Source: Computed from data of Census of India, 2001 (d), Economic Tables of Class I Cities, B-4 Series, Census Commissioner's and Registrar General's Office, New Delhi, CDs were available as late as in 2009. Data for smaller cities and towns are not even tabulated.

Note: Always analysis of all 438 selected class I cities are done. Due to shortage of space, detailed long tables of 438 cities (runs several pages) are not shown, only data of 98 short-listed major cities presented. The same procedure is also followed for other long tables.

Rural-Urban Migration and Economic Structure of Selected Class I Cities

Table 14.4, on the other hand, puts together the data of economic structure of class I cities, juxtaposed with the information on lifetime male migration and also their rural to urban, and urban to urban components, to those cities. The complex relationships hidden in these kinds of data matrix are gradually unfolded in subsequent analyses. Suffice may be here to point out that: (1) a causal relation emerges between tertiary sectors (trade-commerce, transport, services) of certain cities and large volume of migration to them, and (2) secondarily, a causal relationship also arises between secondary sectors (manufacturing or non-household industry, mining, and construction, etc.) of certain cities with a sizable segment of migration attracted to them. Both the relations are later testified by subsequent regression findings.

Table 14.4 *Rural-Urban Migration and Economic Structure of Selected Class I Cities, 2001 (out of total 338 cities analysed, few shown)*

City Nme	TotMig (LTMIGTOT)	LTMIGM	VOLTOURM	VRUTOTM	VUUTOTM	Industrial Categories of Main Workers (%) (Persons), 2001					
	Persons	Males	Males	Males	Males	HHI	Non-HHI	Cons	Trade/ Comm.	Trans	Serv
Srinagar	106935	62873	61725	56679	5046	11	9	5	21	6	44
Jammu	227056	114233	93121	63530	29591	1	7	8	21	7	56
Shimla	92548	53127	49028	37860	11168	1	4	8	11	4	71
Ludhiana	795972	459711	361223	223310	137913	6	40	5	18	6	22
Amritsar	232191	116996	63808	44043	19765	4	22	7	26	8	30
Jalandhar	245909	125792	73171	46054	27117	5	24	8	21	7	33
Chandigarh	517171	284281	266883	157245	109638	1	13	9	17	6	53
Dehradun	216823	109361	82594	45326	37268	2	12	9	21	7	45
Hardwar	83333	41154	35414	19629	15785	2	15	8	25	9	39
Faridabad	582861	314949	283836	175513	108323	3	33	8	18	7	29
Delhi	5550323	3111671	2766472	1918304	848168	3	22	6	23	9	36
Bikaner	88885	44777	34048	18682	15366	6	11	9	14	8	48
Jodhpur	122111	61677	48204	28963	19241	5	16	10	19	10	36
Ajmer	86909	34253	28810	12659	16151	5	13	8	21	16	34
Ghaziabad	472,126	238,305	205,319	96,291	109,028	3	21	7	19	9	36
Meerut	234,570	103,397	65,322	40,422	24,900	5	22	9	24	8	28
Agra	158,835	75,284	27,378	13,646	13,732	7	23	6	24	5	31
Bareilly	109,297	48,800	30,032	11,910	18,122	6	22	6	22	10	29
Lucknow	629,594	333,813	266,316	160,067	106,249	5	14	6	19	10	42
Kanpur	522,565	284,182	216,624	139,803	76,821	4	23	5	25	8	34
Jhansi	102,567	46,031	26,302	14,151	12,151	7	12	6	20	15	36

Cont'd...

...Cont'd

Allahabad	150,217	89,354	51,075	34,680	16,395	6	10	4	23	7	47
Varanasi	202,836	102,323	48,421	32,837	15,584	30	13	3	22	4	26
Patna	456526	231192	186895	132328	54567	4	9	5	23	9	43
Gaya	68212	25654	12749	9114	3635	8	12	4	27	8	32
Guwahati	378657	213669	169541	130483	39058	1	8	6	21	12	47
Siliguri	139418	73710	50036	27638	22398	2	10	7	30	15	34
Durgapur	258773	133894	106578	69140	37438	1	25	7	19	7	34
Kolkata	3735752	1994693	1297078	954276	342802	3	17	4	24	11	41
Asansol	306612	133149	96887	76617	20270	2	20	6	26	11	28
Jamshedpur	301475	151011	135853	96358	39495	2	36	8	15	9	26
Dhanbad	370327	183763	163725	138064	25661	3	11	3	24	14	36
Bokaro	219864	111791	102829	85661	17168	3	47	5	10	6	20
Ranchi	258859	133752	114618	73456	41162	3	12	7	21	11	40
Raurkela	228724	121339	112393	91299	21094	1	42	8	13	7	24
Cuttack	201361	104792	94601	76722	17879	3	13	8	24	11	38
Bhubaneswar	412829	231162	216650	166115	50535	2	8	15	16	9	47
Durg-Bhilai	399744	189482	179432	125562	53870	2	37	11	16	8	20
Gwalior	206117	90202	80381	43844	36537	4	16	10	20	10	37
Indore	474367	236415	185258	85913	99345	5	21	9	24	9	31
Bhopal	522735	269113	244116	121147	122969	2	16	11	19	9	42
Jabalpur	225782	105023	91172	44361	46811	8	19	9	20	9	33
Ahmedabad	1522148	793768	634641	440059	194582	2	31	9	24	9	24
Rajkot	415339	208541	166508	125264	41244	2	32	9	23	9	23
Bhavnagar	124578	60835	41731	30884	10847	1	34	10	21	9	23
Surat	1619967	963586	916421	756488	159933	3	53	6	18	5	14
Solapur	196600	87369	71863	42538	29325	17	27	7	16	7	22

Cont'd...

...Cont'd

Gr. Mumbai	7141583	4137467	3905038	2806380	1098658	3	26	6	19	12	33
Nagpur	647720	321902	299383	186847	112536	3	15	12	21	13	35
Aurangabad	396326	202883	191986	127964	64022	1	19	16	17	10	32
Nashik	577066	294021	284403	199431	84972	2	24	12	15	9	30
Pune	1673911	875694	791724	480928	310796	3	19	12	16	10	38
Hyderabad	1443983	776474	604551	367891	236660	3	12	9	24	11	39
Vijayawada	304565	154742	104768	79951	24817	3	14	11	26	17	28
Tirupati	127975	65076	56184	42061	14123	3	9	11	23	10	43
Belgaum	155810	71381	59864	35827	24037	6	22	6	22	9	31
Bangalore	2086719	1141021	914907	470988	443919	2	24	9	19	10	36
Kozhikode	160309	61671	42854	33299	9555	2	14	12	23	12	31
Kochi	408604	166016	130338	97613	32725	2	15	12	19	14	35
Thiru. Puram	171592	83750	53110	36782	16328	2	9	10	15	11	43
Chennai	1608299	855103	613692	332347	281345	2	15	8	19	10	43
Coimbatore	316020	168318	81021	55699	25322	5	23	8	21	6	35
Madurai	218272	113075	41946	29135	12811	3	22	7	25	8	32
Pondicherry	183384	84278	69753	36664	33089	2	18	8	17	8	41

Sources: Computed from Census of India, 2001 (b), Migration D-series and Economic series, New Delhi. Economic structure of cities are indicated by industrial categories of main workers, 2001 (d). Data CDs available only in 2005–6–7.

LTMIGTOT = Volume of lifetime migration (M+F)
VUUTOTM = Volume of urban to urban migration, males
LTMIGM = Lifetime migration, males.
VOLTOURM = Volume of total urban-ward migration, males
VRUTOTM = Volume of rural to urban migration, males

City-level Regression Analyses

Reasons for Migration (Males) and Economic Structure of Class I Cities, 2001

One of the purposes is to analyse causal relationships between the economic structure of the class I cities and the reason for migration to them. This is performed through a series of regression analyses, discussed below.

Table 14.5 *Reasons for Migration (Males) and Economic Structure of Class I Cities, 2001*

Name of Class I Cities	*Total Migrants*	*Reasons for Migration (Males) (%)*							*Industrial Categories of Main Workers (Persons) (%)*				
		Employment	*Business*	*Education*	*Marriage*	*Moved after birth*	*Moved with family*	*Other reasons*	*Manuf.*	*Constr.*	*Trade com.*	*Transport*	*Services*
Srinagar	62873	11	0	1	0	0	5	82	9	5	21	6	44
Jammu	114233	27	2	2	1	1	20	47	7	8	21	7	56
Shimla	53127	55	2	9	0	3	16	16	4	8	11	4	71
Amritsar	116996	29	1	1	1	2	13	54	22	7	26	8	30
Jalandhar	125792	33	1	1	0	2	17	46	24	8	21	7	33
Ludhiana	459711	45	1	1	0	3	16	34	40	5	18	6	22
Chandigarh	284281	55	3	4	0	5	21	12	13	9	17	6	53
Dehradun	109361	36	1	4	0	1	26	32	12	9	21	7	45
Hardwar	41154	46	1	4	0	2	20	27	15	8	25	9	39
Faridabad	314949	52	1	1	0	2	26	18	33	8	18	7	29
Delhi	3111671	57	1	2	0	2	22	15	22	6	23	9	36
Ganganagar	36955	44	1	2	0	4	23	25	12	6	28	9	39
Bikaner	44777	33	1	4	0	4	23	35	11	9	14	8	48
Jaipur	328403	46	2	4	0	3	25	20	23	8	18	7	33
Ajmer	34253	39	1	7	1	5	25	23	13	8	21	16	34
Jodhpur	61677	35	2	4	0	3	27	29	16	10	19	10	36
Bhilwara	49063	50	3	2	1	5	21	19	31	8	21	7	23
Meerut	103397	31	1	2	1	1	20	45	22	9	24	8	28
Ghaziabad	238305	41	1	1	1	1	29	26	21	7	19	9	36
Noida	116259	47	2	1	0	1	29	20	15	7	14	5	51
Mathura	32379	28	1	2	1	2	26	40	20	5	23	9	33
Agra	75284	13	1	1	1	1	13	72	23	6	24	5	31
Bareilly	48800	28	1	2	1	1	21	47	22	6	22	10	29
Lucknow	333813	40	1	5	0	2	21	30	14	6	19	10	42
Kanpur	284182	40	2	3	1	2	15	37	23	5	25	8	34
Jhansi	46031	25	1	1	1	1	16	54	12	6	20	15	36
Allahabad	89354	18	1	17	0	1	9	55	10	4	23	7	47
Varanasi	102323	20	1	8	1	1	11	60	13	3	22	4	26
Patna	231192	36	2	10	1	2	22	28	9	5	23	9	43
Gaya	25654	20	1	4	1	1	13	60	12	4	27	8	32
Imphal	17831	15	3	2	1	0	14	64	8	4	17	4	55
Shillong	37141	34	4	10	1	1	9	40	6	7	20	5	59
Guwahati	213669	33	17	4	0	1	12	32	8	6	21	12	47
Asansol	133149	38	5	1	1	4	17	35	20	6	26	11	28
Durgapur	133894	44	4	2	1	4	20	25	25	7	19	7	34
Kolkata	1994693	33	4	2	1	3	22	34	17	4	24	7	41

Cont'd...

...Cont'd

Dhanbad	183763	54	3	2	1	2	18	21	11	3	24	9	36
Bokaro	111791	55	3	1	0	2	23	17	47	5	10	14	20
Ranchi	133752	43	2	7	0	2	20	25	12	7	21	6	40
Jamshedpur	151011	54	2	2	1	4	18	19	36	8	15	13	26
Raurkela	121339	52	10	5	0	2	14	17	16	11	23	11	30
Cuttack	104792	47	10	6	1	1	17	19	13	8	24	9	38
Durg-Bhilai	189482	56	1	2	0	6	22	12	37	11	16	10	20
Raipur	133345	44	2	3	0	4	21	25	16	9	23	12	34
Gwalior	90202	41	1	6	1	2	30	19	16	10	20	7	37
Ujjain	47411	35	1	3	1	9	21	30	19	9	21	12	34
Indore	236415	40	2	5	0	5	18	30	21	9	24	7	31
Bhopal	269113	51	1	5	0	4	22	17	16	11	19	8	42
Jabalpur	105023	45	2	4	1	3	22	24	19	9	20	15	33
Korba	82685	56	2	1	0	6	25	10	14	11	14	14	30
Ahmedabad	793768	32	12	1	0	8	19	28	31	9	24	7	24
Rajkot	208541	18	23	2	0	9	23	25	32	9	23	9	23
Jamnagar	80471	14	15	4	0	6	17	43	31	8	20	6	28
Bhavnagar	60835	14	20	2	0	8	19	37	34	10	21	6	23
Surat	963586	48	15	1	0	8	19	11	53	6	18	12	14
Gr. Mumbai	4137467	60	2	2	0	9	13	15	26	6	19	6	33
Amravati	96058	41	1	7	1	12	21	17	11	12	21	9	35
Nagpur	321902	50	2	6	0	8	20	15	15	12	21	12	35
Aurangabad	202883	46	2	8	0	10	21	13	19	16	17	10	32
Pune	875694	48	1	5	0	12	18	16	19	12	16	11	38
Solapur	87369	32	2	4	1	16	16	30	27	7	16	9	22
Kolhapur	70937	39	2	5	1	19	17	17	18	9	20	4	35
Hyderabad	776474	41	4	4	1	4	15	33	12	9	24	9	39
Vijayawada	154742	33	4	3	1	5	15	39	14	11	26	9	28
Gudivada	19544	35	5	5	2	10	19	24	12	8	23	17	26
Nellore	48678	31	5	3	1	2	18	39	16	13	22	12	29
Belgaum	71381	35	2	5	1	13	18	25	22	6	22	13	31
Dharwad	112528	35	3	8	1	13	16	24	14	9	21	9	32
Shimoga	48744	38	5	4	1	8	19	26	13	11	25	10	31
Bangalore	1141021	46	4	4	1	5	13	28	24	9	19	10	36
Mangalore	78595	40	3	9	2	10	19	17	14	11	16	12	30
Mysore	93405	36	4	11	1	5	16	27	18	9	21	10	35
Kozhikode	61671	20	2	2	4	11	22	39	14	12	23	12	31
Kochi	166016	29	2	2	4	11	23	29	15	12	19	11	35
Thiruvanatha-puram	83750	29	2	3	6	3	15	42	9	10	15	11	43
Chennai	855103	35	2	2	1	5	17	37	15	8	19	8	43
Salem	84527	16	2	1	1	4	9	68	25	7	18	10	27
Erode	66447	33	2	1	1	5	18	40	17	6	34	6	30
Coimbatore	168318	24	1	1	1	3	10	59	23	8	21	3	35
Tiruchi	142329	30	2	4	1	7	16	39	16	7	22	8	35
Neyveli	26478	49	1	1	1	8	17	23	4	3	5	11	59
Madurai	113075	16	2	1	1	2	9	69	22	7	25	9	32
Thanjavur	23222	26	3	6	2	9	19	35	10	7	24	7	40
Pondicherry	84278	33	2	3	5	8	25	24	18	8	17	7	41

Note: Workers under mining and Household industries not shown, due to lack of space, though analysed in regression.

What cause-and-effect relationships the insightful regression technique can untangle, amidst masses of data and relations, that cannot be achieved by intuition or simple discussion. Canonical analysis is not performed in Part II, as requisite data not available, and the readers are also spared from that somewhat complex analysis!

Links between Manufacturing in Cities and Male Migration for Work, 1991–2001

Larger the manufacturing sectors in class I cities, the more male migration crowd there for work. This may seem an axiomatic or natural finding. A world-wide phenomenon. But it also have a caveat. In the Indian situation, this relation explains only 5 per cent of variation in male migration for work, implying that male employment migration occur more for other centres, where tertiary or service sectors, or construction work prevail. *Evidently, that is not a sign of development, rather anti-development!*

Table 14.6 *Statistics for Causal Links between Manufacturing Sectors of Economy of Class I Cities, and Male Migration for Work, 2001 (N = No. of class I cities studied 328, for which data available)*

Dependent Variable	*Indep. Variable*	*Adj R Sq.*	*Expln.*	*Beta*	*T.*	*Sig. T*	*Inter-cept*	*Meaning of Relation*
Male migration to class I cities for work	Manufacturing sectors in cities	.05	5%	.24	4.04	.0001	29.6	Larger manufacturing sectors in class I cities, the more male migration for work

Figure 14. 1 *Causal Links Between Manufacturing Sectors of Class I Cities and Male Migration for Work, 2001 Census*

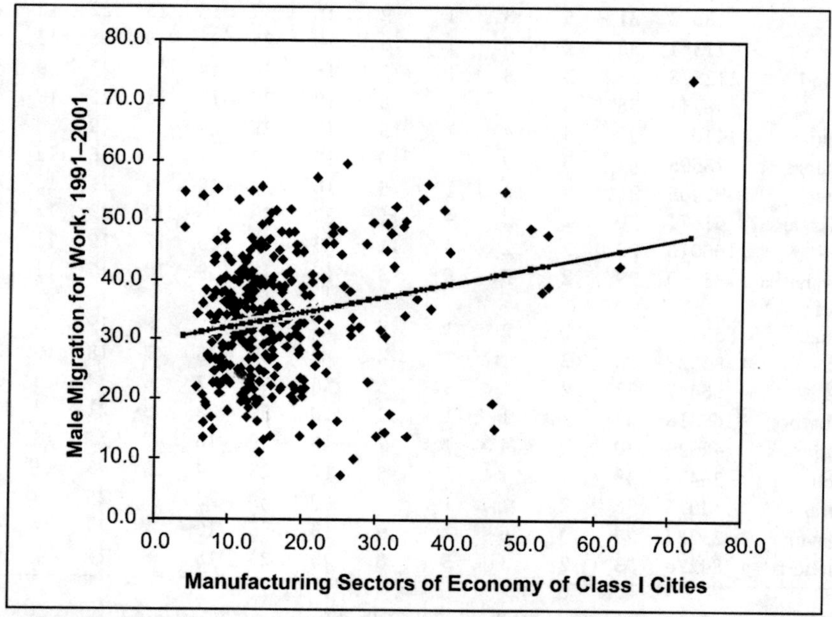

Source: Computed from Census of India, 2001

Links between Construction in Cities and Male Migration for Work, 1991–2001

The above observation is reinforced by this regression equation or regression line, which shows that more male migration for work occurs to those class I cities where construction sector is predominant. Migrant construction labourers in class I cities – quite a paradox! Rather, they are mostly expected in the villages. Thus, male migrants do not get absorption in administrative, professional, nor even in sales or services, rather get that mainly in labour construction work, in low-grade work characterized with low productivity and insecurity (explains 6%). Of course, it protects dispossessed people from poverty and immediate starvation, thus even such migration is very desirable.

Table 14. 7 *Links between Construction Sectors of Class I Cities and Male Migration for Work, 2001 (N = 328, Beta = .25, T = 4.5, Sig. T = .001, Intercept = 16.2)*

Dependent Variable	*Indep. Variable*	*Adj R Sq.*	*Expln.*	*Meaning of Relation*
Male migration for work	Construction sectors	.06	6%	Larger construction sectors of cities, the more male migration for work

Figure 14.2 *Causal Links between Construction Sectors in Class I Cities and Male Migration for Employment*

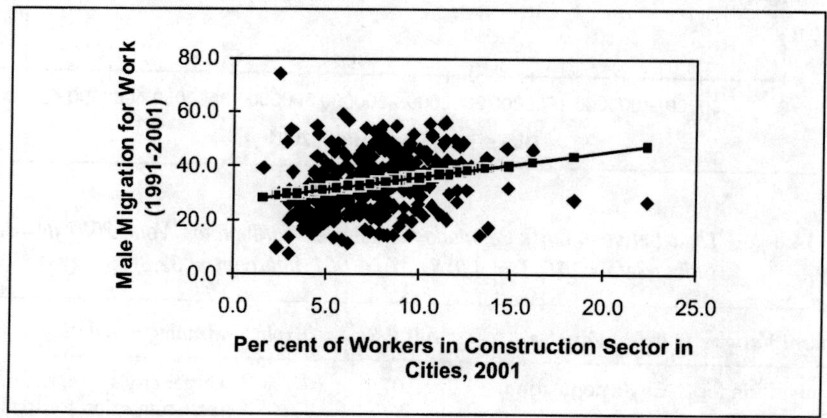

Source: Same as in Figure 14.1.

But to portray them as "migration leading to development", is untrue, wrong, misleading, and weakens the great need for economic reforms and planning for the poor migrants and common people. It is still wishful thinking! Truth must be told loud and clear, and the underlying unjust politico-economic processes be fully unfolded. Then only, correct planning prescriptions will emerge. Unfoldment of underlying processes is sadly and, most unfortunately, missing from migration-urbanization research. *This is my true perspective, all through life. I never wrote or prescribed "migration restriction" in my last 40 years of migration research (1969–2010), nor took a pessimistic view about migration in India. But the hiding the truth either, or misdirecting, does not uphold the great cause of helpless hundreds of millions of migrants in India, who urgently need our care, protection and pro-poor planning.*

Links between City's Total Population and Male Migration for Work, 1991–2001

Larger the size of class I city, the more male migrants are attracted to them for employment (explains 7%), because they have hunch that chances of getting any kind of subsistence work increases with the city size. Such kind of migration also reflects that most of them get absorption in urban informal sectors, whose size also increase with the city's population, where access to the low-grade sales or service or production work also becomes easy.

Figure 14.3 *Links between City's Total Population and Male Migration for Work, 2001*

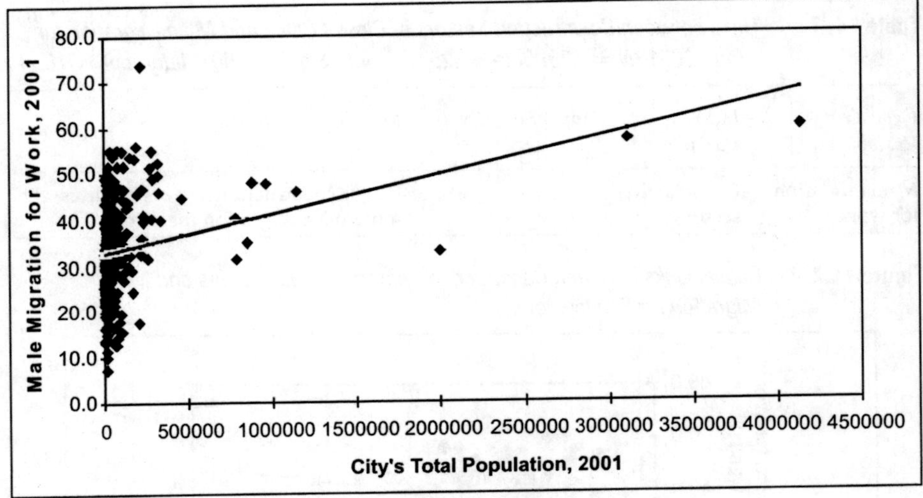

Table 14.8 *Links between City's Population and Male Migration for Work, 2001 (N = 328 Cities, Beta = .25, T = 4.0, Sig. T = .001, Intercept = 32.8)*

Dependent Variable	*Indep. Variable*	*Adj R Sq.*	*Expln*	*Meaning of Relation*
Male migration for work	City's population	.07	7%	Larger city's size, the more male migration for work

Links between Secondary Sectors of Cities and Male Migration for Work (1991–2001)

More secondary sectors in class I cities, the more male migration for work (explains 13%). This is quite a healthy sign, that more male migrants are moving into those class I cities, where secondary sectors of economy are predominating. This pattern emerges, irrespective of earlier equations and linkages that showed migrants are mostly absorbed in poor tertiary sectors, or construction work. In contrast, the secondary sectors comprise of manufacturing, as well as household industries, construction, and partly mining. So, construction work and poor household industries are also hidden here. So, out of total 13 per cent, pure manufacturing explains 5 per cent, construction (6%), and the rest 2 per cent by household industries and mining.

Table 14.9 *Links between Secondary Sectors of Cities and Male Migration for Work, 2001 (N = 388, Beta = .39, T = 6.9, Sig. T = .001, Intercept = 23.9)*

Dependent Variable	*Indep. Variable*	*Adj R Sq.*	*Expln.*	*Meaning of Relation*
Male migration for work	Secondary sectors of cities	.13	13%	More secondary sectors in class I cities, more male migration for work

Figure 14.4 *Causal Links between Secondary Sectors of Economy in Class I Cities and Migration for Employment Therein (1991–2001)*

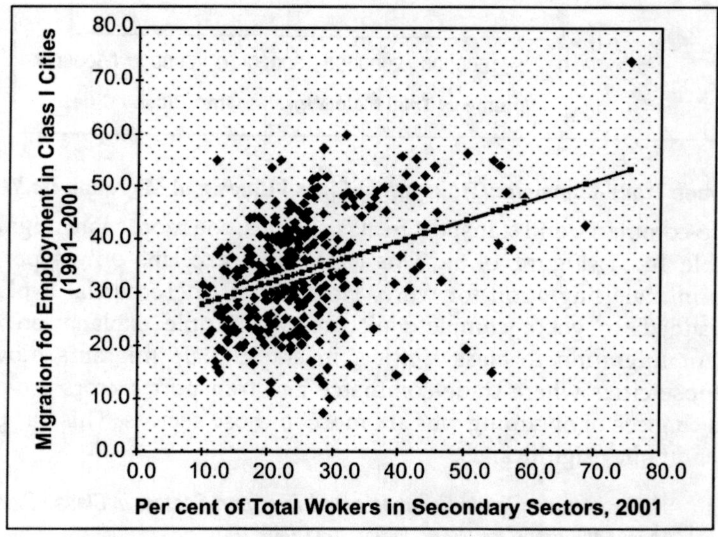

Volume of Total Male Migration into Class I Cities and Male Migration for Work

Larger the volume of male migration into class I cities, higher is the incidences of male migration for work (Figure 14.5, Table 14.10). This result explains 7 per cent of variations in male migration for employment to class I cities. In simple words, as the total male migration to class I cities increases, so volume of male employment migration to them also increases. This is quite reasonable and understandable, as people move mainly for work and survival strategy, and the chances of such subsistence increases with the city size, as providing various services to a large population itself generates some employment avenues, no matter how low is the pay, nor how informal work is (Mukherji, 1985b: 259–279).

Table 14.10 *Relations between Volume of Total Male Migration into Cities and Male Migration for Work, 2001 (N = 338, Beta = .009, T = 4.9, Sig. T = .001, Intercept = 32.8)*

Dependent Variable	*Indep. Variable*	*Adj R Sq.*	*Expln*	*Meaning of Relation*
Per cent of male migration for work	Volume of male migration to class I cities	.07	7%	Larger volume of male migration into class I cities, higher percentage of male migration for work

Figure 14.5 *Volume of Male In-migration into Class I Cities and Per cent of Male Migration for Work, 1991–2001*

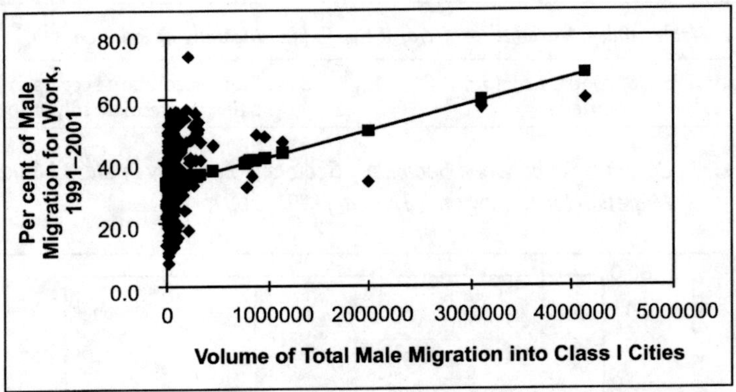

Links between Trade-Commerce/Transport in Class I Cities and Migration for Work

More trade-commerce and transport in class I cities, the more male migration for work (Table 14.11, Figure 14.6). This causal link explains only 4 per cent of variations in male migration for work. However all these partial explanations must be added, to get a complete picture of multiple explanation of male employment migration to class I cities. In short, male migrants move more towards those cities where trade-commerce and transport sectors are predominant, and chances of obtaining jobs are more in those sectors. This has practical meaning and policy significance.

Table 14.11 *Links between Trade-Commerce and Transport Sectors in Class I Cities and Male Migration for Work, India, 2001 (N=180)*

Dependent Variable	*Indep. Variable*	*Mult. R.*	*Adj R Sq.*	*Expln.*	*Meaning of Relation*
Male migration for work	Trade-commerce and transport in class I cities	.21	.05	4%	More trade-commerce and transport in class I cities, the more male migration for work

Figure 14.6 *Relations between Trade and Transport Sectors and Male Migration to Class I Cities for Work*

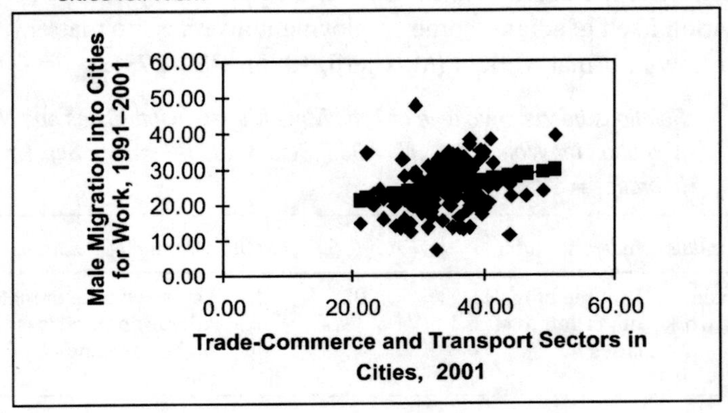

Links between Service Sectors in Class I Cities and Male Migration for Work

More service sectors in class I cities, the more male migration for work (Figure 14.7, Table 14.12). The linkage explains 9 per cent of variation in male migration for work. As expressed many time earlier, this result again reiterates that even in class I cities of India, most of the migration (both for males and females) occur, indeed, for absorption in the low grade urban informal sectors, specially in service sectors, not in manufacturing or secondary sectors. As I have indicated many times before in last 40 years migration research (1970–2010), of course, there is insecurity, low-grade work, low productivity, exploitation and cut-throat competition, but in spite of all these negative qualities, even these type of low-grade migration and low-grade absorption in urban informal sectors, have some positive benefits as well. That is, even these types of low-quality migration are much desirable as these help the poor rural people at least in the following *eight-fold* beneficial ways:

1. to escape poverty,
2. act as safety valve from suicide or further turmoil,.
3. to escape from the clutches of cruel village money lenders,
4. act as survival strategy,
5. to explore new work opportunities in new urban environment,
6. to struggle and fight out poverty, helplessness, and fatalism,
7. to escape from caste-ridden village society and its exploitation, humility and frustration,
8. expose them to urban ways of thinking and living.

Thus, even these kinds of low-quality migration in India are beneficial to the poor rural people or small town people, and hence much desirable. Thus, there should never be migration restriction. Rather, more encouragement.

Table 14.12 *Links between Service Sectors in Class I Cities and Male Migration for Work, 2001 (N = 328, Beta = .29, T = 4.1, Sig. T. = .001, Intercept = 17.1)*

Dependent Variable	*Indep. Variable*	*Mult. R.*	*Adj R Sq.*	*Expln.*	*Meaning of Relation*
Male migration for work	Service sectors of class I cities	.31	.09	9%	More service sectors in class I cities, the more male migration for work

Figure 14.7 *Links between Service Sector of Economy of Class I Cities and Male In-migration for Work, 1991–2001*

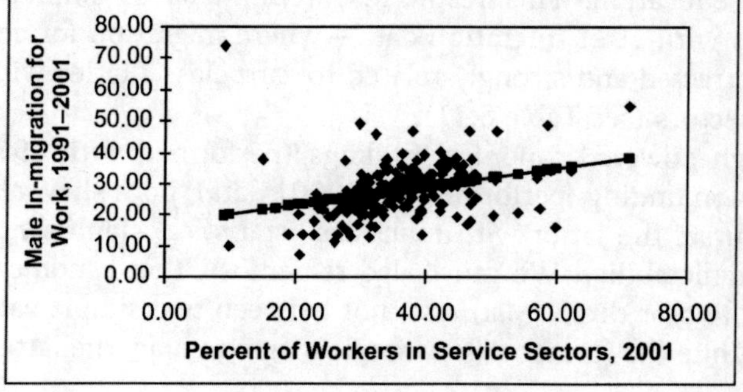

Relations between Male Migration for Business and Manufacturing Centres, 2001

Manufacturing sector in class I cities shows positive relation with the male migration for business. More manufacturing sectors in such cities, the more male migration for business purposes. It however explains only 3 per cent of variations. It also indicates that manufacturing and business are related in class I cities, and they together encourage such type of migration. The same result was also observed with 1991 data (Table 8.4). These are positive but yet feeble symptom of developmental migration. In future, such type of migration may show increasingly stronger signs.

Table 14.13 *Links between Manufacturing Sectors of Class I Cities and Male Migration for Business, 2001 (N = 328, Beta = .07, T = 3.0, Sig. T. = .01, Intercept = 2.12)*

Dependent Variable	*Indep. Variable*	*Mult. R.*	*Adj R Sq.*	*Expln.*	*Meaning of Relation*
Male migration for business	Manufacturing sector of cities	.17	.03	3%	Manufacturing in cities shows positive relations with male migration for business

Figure 14.8 *Links between Manufacturing Sectors and Migration for Business, 2001*

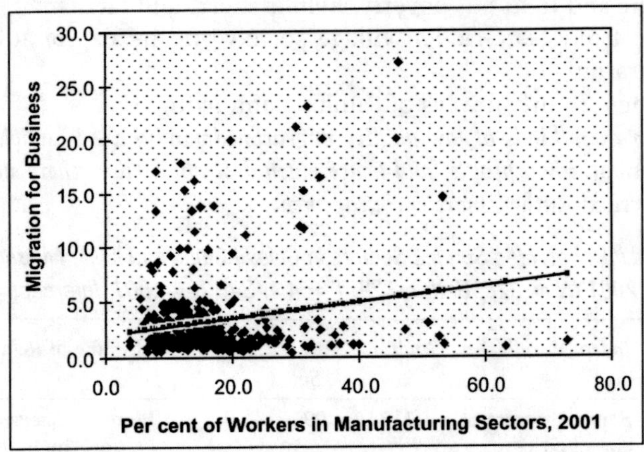

Links between Service Sectors in Cities and Male Migration for Education

Larger the service sectors in cities, the more male migration for education (Figure 14.9, Table 14.14). This explains 4 per cent of variations in male migration for education. This result may remind us of similar result from canonical tests with 1991 migration data – where migration for education was found to be attracted and strongly related toward class I cities with a predominant service sectors (see Table 8.11).

Thus, high powered canonical findings (performed with 1991 data) and simple regression finding (performed with 2001 data), both show almost similar results. Of course, the latter with much less statistical significance, statistical power, and predictability. We must also remember, that canonical analysis is done between two or three "*Matrices*", not between two simple variables (as in regression). While the former tells a classic magnum epic, the latter tells only a short story, without reference to vast sea of data, observations, and complex relationships (which canonical analysis does). I did not venture to do canonical analysis, again with 2001 migration data, because related data of bank investments, capital flows, and useful socio-economic variables were *not* available. This can be performed with 2011 census data.

Figure 14.9 *Causal Links between Service Sectors in Class I Cities, and Male Migration for Education*

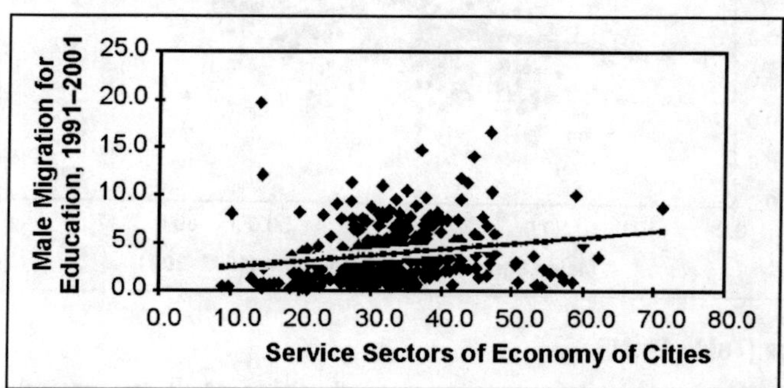

Table 14.14 *Links between Service Sectors of Class I Cities and Male Migration for Education, 2001 (N = Class I Cities Studied 328)*

Dependent Variable	*Indep. Variable*	*Mult. R.*	*Adj R Sq.*	*Expln.*	*Meaning of Relation*
Male migration for education	Service sectors	.19	.04	4%	Larger service sectors of cities, the more male migration for education

More male migration for familial reasons to cities, the more migration for work (bi-polar relations). Familial migration means that they moved with their families. This explains 4 per cent. This relation is also a bi-polar relationship, i.e., (a) the more migration for familial reasons promotes more migration for work, and also (b) the more male migration for work also promotes more moves with families (familial migration). Such picture also makes sense in India, because in census-taking, only main reason for migration is asked, so for many movers, who expressed that they had moved with their families, not for employment, take up employment later, but which is not revealed in census data. That information remains hidden. So, this hidden picture surfaces through such bi-polar relationship. Policy significance is that in future census-taking at least second reason for migration must also be asked. Then only, we can fathom magnitude of employment migration in India. I seriously believe this is much larger than census make us to believe. The same is very true for marriage migration among women.

Table 14.15 *Links between Male Migration with Family and Male Migration for Work*

Dependent Variable	*Indep. Variable*	*Mult. R.*	*Adj R Sq.*	*Expln.*	*Meaning of Relation*
Male migration for work	Migration for familial reasons	.20	.04	4%	More male migration for familial reasons to cities, the more migration for work (bi-polar)

Figure 14.10 *Relations between Male Migration with Family and Male Migration for Work (1991–2001)*

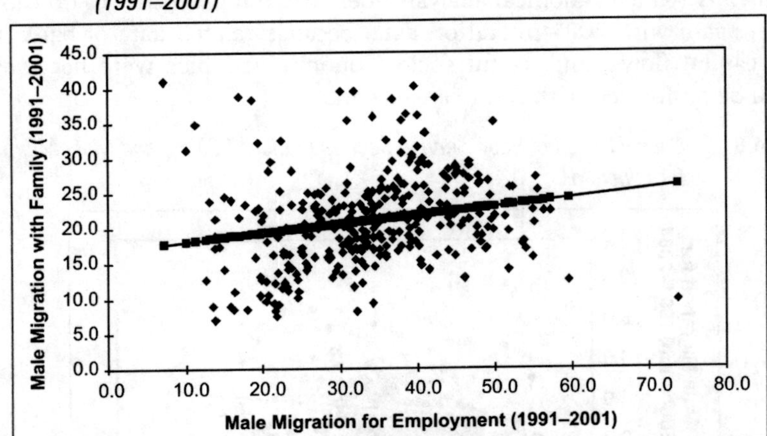

Other Findings (Table 14.16)

1. More manufacturing sector in class I cities, less migration for mixed reasons.
2. More household industries in class I cities, more male migration for other purposes.
3. More trade-commerce in class I cities, the more male migration for mixed purposes.

Table 14.16 *Other Regression Linkages*

Dependent Variable	*Indep. Variable*	*Mult. R.*	*Adj R Sq.*	*Expln.*	*Meaning of Relation*
Male migration for other reasons	Manufacturing sector	.19	.04	4%	More manufacturing in cities, the less male migration for mixed reasons
Male Migration for other purposes	Household industries of cities	.32	.10	10%	More household industries in class I cities, more male migration for other purposes
Male migration for other purposes	Trade-commerce sectors of class I cities	.21	.04	4%	More trade-commerce in class I cities, the more male migration for mixed purposes

Concluding Remarks

This chapter has revealed many interesting findings about manifold relationships between migration, urbanization, and various sectors of economy for Class I cities of India. Many findings were hitherto unknown, or some were only speculative in existing literature. But, here they were proved with concrete evidences and statistical analyses. Findings are not only statistically very powerful, but also have practical meaning and policy import. Their policy import are of immense value for further research and migration planning for the poor.

15 Findings of Million City-level Analysis

Links between Migration and Urbanization, 2001

"Serve as the worship of the Lord Himself in the poor, the miserable, and the weak."

Swami Vivekananda (1894)
(Complete Work, Centenary Volume IV, 1963: 246)

Million cities are of great importance in India, as they are regarded as generators of economic development and progress. Sometimes this is true, but not always. They have their share of positive and also negative aspects. Positively, they have the advantage of economies of scale, and more and more capital, finance, growth efforts, industries, and infrastructures are polarized there. Negatively, they have large, extensive and filthy slums, inhuman treatment meted out to the poor and destitute, and increasing social and economic inequities. Very frequent breakdown of essential urban services (like water, electricity, sanitation, transport) often plague such Million cities. Even then, we cannot do away with them, as these are generators of the National economy. We urgently need to sanitize them. Develop them. And, make them more livable. Some of these situations, specially in the context of masses of incoming migrants to million cities, are briefly discussed in this chapter.

Contribution of Migration to Urbanization in Million Cities, India, 1991–2001

Table 15.1 presents detailed calculation of contribution of migration (during 1991–2001) to decadal population increase in 35 million cities of India, during the same period. It is much interesting to estimate the contribution of migration to urbanization in India, which is roughly 30 per cent, on average. It ranges between as low as 9 per cent for Agra and as high as 75 per cent for Ludhiana, with many step like variations in between. For Mumbai, migration contributes 66 per cent of decadal urban growth, followed by Delhi (48%), and Kolkata (38%).

Besides, following two points are also noteworthy:

First, relationships between Total Population of Million Cities and Volume of Total In-migration (1991–2001): There emerges a very strong causal relationship between population size and total decadal migration to million cities, during the same period. This indicates a strong positive causal links between migration and urbanization in India, at least regarding million cities (Tables 15.3 and 4, Figure 15.1). This also implies that more migrants are drawn towards larger cities, as

Table 15.1 *Contribution of Migration to Urbanization in Million Cities, India, 1991–2001*

City	*Population in 2001*	*Decadal Population Increase*	*Migration to City 1991–2001*	*Contribution of Migration to decadal increase (%)*
Greater Mumbai	16368084	3771841	2489552	66
Kolkata	13216546	2194628	822389	38
Delhi	12791438	4372374	2112363	48
Chennai	6424624	1002639	435620	43
Bangalore	5686800	1556558	761485	49
Hyderabad	5533640	1189203	498483	42
Ahmedabad	4519278	1207062	328910	36
Pune	3755525	1261538	744194	59
Surat	2811466	1292516	869860	67
Kanpur	2690486	660597	138708	21
Jaipur	2324319	806084	250208	31
Lucknow	2266933	597729	208915	35
Nagpur	2122965	458959	241078	53
Madurai	1994665	108751	33540	31
Patna	1707429	607782	161372	27
Indore	1639044	529688	159191	30
Bhopal	1454830	392059	185597	47
Coimbatore	1446034	345288	68888	20
Ludhiana	1395053	352313	265003	75
Kochi	1355406	214801	166794	78
Visakhapatnam	1329472	272354	139003	51
Agra	1321410	373347	34227	9
Varanasi	1211749	180856	46989	26
Meerut	1167399	317600	71213	22
Nasik	1152048	426707	287017	67
Jabalpur	1117200	228284	68961	30
Jamshedpur	1101804	272633	80971	30
Asansol	1090171	326332	59501	18
Dhanbad	1064357	249362	86238	35
Faridabad	1054981	437264	237800	54
Allahabad	1049579	205033	41699	20
Amritsar	1011327	302492	56024	19
Vijaywada	1011152	165396	90894	55
Rajkot	1002160	347670	141177	41
Million Cities Total	106389439	27027698	12485364	46

Source: Computed from data of Census of India, 2001 (b), Migration Tables, D-Series, New Delhi.

they somehow know that the chances of eking out, even subsistence level of living, increases with the city size. *Thus, variations in population size explain as high as 67 per cent of variance in volume of migration to these cities (Table 15.2).*

Second, however, no such linear relationship emerges between the contribution of decadal migration to million cities and their decadal population increase. For instance, for Mumbai, a large mega city, migration contributes 66 per cent of decadal population increase of this city; which is also true for Surat (just 2.8 million population) and also Nasik (merely a small million city). Therefore, the relationship appears blurred. However, this could be due to faulty consideration of administrative boundaries of urban agglomerations for census purpose, even for Mumbai, Kolkata, Chennai, and Delhi, which are completely saturated in its main proper sites, but huge urban sprawls are still occurring at urban fringes of these mega cities, and where the new migrants are also drawn in. So, better Census data taking, or administrative consideration of boundaries, in future, may reflect this essential relationships, too. Further, due to such faulty consideration, often the conventional researchers wrongly conclude that rate of urbanization has decreased in India in recent decades, or migration to mega cities is also decreasing. While the truth is far from this faulty observation.

Figure 15.1 *Causal Links between Total Population of Million Cities and Total Migration to Them, 1991–2001*

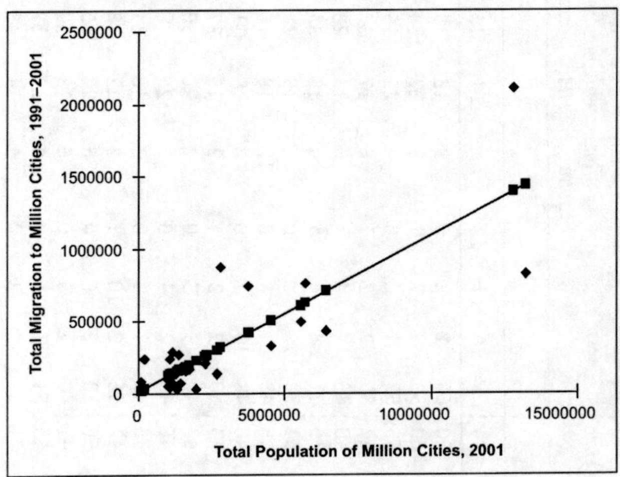

Table 15.2 *Regression Statistics of Relations between Total Population of Million Cities and Volume of Total In-migration, 1991–2001 (N = 35 Million Cities)*

Dependent Variable	*Indep. Variable*	*Mult. R.*	*Adj R Sq.*	*Expln.*	*Beta*	*T.*	*Sig. T*	*Intercept*	*Meaning of Relation*
Volume of total in-migration into million cities	Total population of million cities	.82	.67	67%	.11	8.1	.0001	11848.4	Larger the city size of million cities, larger the volume of total in-migration

Million City-level Analyses

Relations between Male Migration Variables and Economic Structure of Million Cities, and Reasons for Migration, 2001

Table 15.3 provides basic information about male migration variables and related socio-economic variables of the million cities. On the other hand, Table 15.4 presents the same for the female migrants. Tables are self explanatory. These are further analyzed through many bi-variate regression analyses.

Table 15.3 *Migration Variables (Males) and Economic Structure Variables, Million Cities, 2001 (selected cities)*

Million Cities	Total Population	Total Migrants (All durations)	Total Migrants	Duration of Migration (%)				Reasons for Migration (%)							Categories of Total Main Workers (Person) (%)						
				< 1 Yr	1–4 Yr	5–9 Yr	10 Yr +	Emp	Business.	Edu	Marriage	Moved after birth	Moved with HH	Other	Total Main Workers (Persons)	HHI	MNF	Cons	Tr-Cm	Tran	Serv
	Persons	Persons	Males												Persons						
1	2	3	4	5	6	7	8	9	10	11	12	13	14	15	16	17	18	19	20	21	22
Gr. Mumbai	16368084	7141583	4137467	3	17	16	60	60	2	2	0	9	13	15	4087341	3	23	4	21	12	36
Kolkata	13216546	3735752	1994693	2	10	9	60	33	4	2	1	3	22	34	2624811	3	17	4	24	11	41
Delhi	12791438	5550323	3111671	2	18	18	55	57	1	2	0	2	22	15	3160618	3	22	6	23	9	36
Chennai	6424624	1608299	855103	2	15	11	42	35	2	2	1	5	17	37	1382492	2	15	8	19	10	43
Bangalore	5686800	2086719	1141021	2	21	14	40	46	4	4	1	5	13	28	1536430	2	24	9	19	10	36
Hyderabad	5533640	1443983	776474	2	19	15	36	41	4	4	1	4	15	33	979238	3	12	9	24	11	39
Ahmadabad	4519278	1522148	793768	1	13	13	51	32	12	1	0	8	19	28	1070910	2	31	9	24	9	24
Pune	3755525	1673911	875694	5	24	17	46	48	1	5	0	12	18	16	806320	3	19	12	16	10	38
Surat	2811466	1619967	963586	3	27	25	40	48	15	1	0	8	19	11	908860	3	53	6	18	5	14
Kanpur	2690486	522565	284182	2	17	10	43	40	2	3	1	2	15	37	636525	4	23	5	25	8	34
Lucknow	2266933	629594	333813	2	18	14	42	40	1	5	0	2	21	30	536822	5	14	6	19	10	42
Jaipur	2324319	629012	328403	3	21	17	46	46	2	4	0	3	25	20	656888	5	23	8	18	7	33
Ludhiana	1395053	795972	459711	2	19	16	36	45	1	1	0	3	16	34	974380	6	40	5	18	6	22
Patna	1707429	456526	231192	2	20	16	42	36	2	10	1	2	22	28	650388	4	9	5	23	9	43
Nagpur	1657890	647720	321902	4	18	15	56	50	2	6	0	8	20	15	567541	3	15	12	21	13	22
Indore	1639044	474367	236415	2	19	14	41	40	2	5	0	5	18	30	439494	5	21	9	24	9	31
Bhopal	1454830	522735	269113	2	18	14	55	51	1	5	0	4	22	17	385538	2	16	11	19	9	42
Visakhapatnam	1329472	500246	265432	1	15	11	31	32	3	2	0	4	14	45	262897	4	12	15	15	14	37
Kochi	1355406	408604	166016	6	20	15	39	29	2	2	4	11	23	29	181024	2	15	12	19	14	35
Varanasi	1211749	202836	102323	3	15	8	22	20	1	8	1	1	11	60	274916	30	13	3	22	4	26

Source: Census of India, 2001, D-Series, Migration Tables, Registrar General's Office, New Delhi.

Note: Only main workers are considered, marginal workers are not included. Out of 35 million cities in 2001, data of only main 23 (and common with 1991) are shown here.

Table 15.4 *Migration Variables (Females) and Economic Structure Variables, Million Cities, 2001 (selected cities)*

Million Cities	Total Population 2001	Total Migrants (All durations)		Duration (%)				Reasons for Migration (%)							Total Main Workers (Persons)	Categories of Total Main Workers (Persons) (%)					
				< 1 Yr	1–4 Yrs	5–9 Yrs	10 Yrs +	Emp	Business	Edun	Marriage	Moved after birth	Moved with HH	Other		HHI	MNF	Cons	Tr-Cm	Trans	Serv
	Persons	Persons	Females																		
1	2	3	4	5	6	7	8	9	10	11	12	13	14	15	16	17	18	19	20	21	22
Gr. Mumbai	16368084	7141583	3004116	3	16	16	60	4	0	1	46	9	26	15	4087341	3	23	4	21	12	36
Kolkata	13216546	3735752	1741059	2	12	11	58	3	0	1	38	3	28	28	2624811	3	17	4	24	11	41
Delhi	12791438	5550323	2438652	3	18	18	55	4	0	1	33	2	48	12	3160618	3	22	6	23	9	36
Chennai	6424624	1608299	753196	2	15	11	38	6	1	1	25	4	23	40	1382492	2	15	8	19	10	43
Bangalore	5686800	2086719	945698	2	20	14	39	7	1	2	34	5	23	29	1536430	2	24	9	19	10	36
Hyderabad	5533640	1443983	667509	2	18	14	32	7	1	2	21	4	30	37	979238	3	12	9	24	11	39
Ahmadabad	4519278	1522148	728380	1	14	14	51	2	1	0	37	6	30	24	1070910	2	31	9	24	9	24
Pune	3755525	1673911	798217	4	23	17	46	4	0	2	39	10	31	15	806320	3	19	12	16	10	38
Surat	2811466	1619967	656381	3	26	23	41	2	1	0	31	9	46	11	908860	3	53	6	18	5	14
Kanpur	2690486	522565	238383	1	12	11	46	3	0	1	36	1	26	34	636525	4	23	5	25	8	34
Lucknow	2266933	629594	295781	2	16	14	42	4	0	1	28	2	38	28	536822	5	14	6	19	10	42
Jaipur	2324319	629012	300609	3	19	17	48	4	0	1	36	2	40	16	656888	5	23	8	18	7	33
Ludhiana	1395053	795972	336261	1	14	13	40	5	1	1	30	3	26	36	974380	6	40	5	18	6	22
Patna	1707429	456526	225334	2	16	16	49	3	0	2	42	1	31	21	650388	4	9	5	23	9	43
Nagpur	1657890	647720	325818	3	19	16	55	4	0	2	47	6	30	12	567541	3	15	12	21	13	35
Indore	1639044	474367	237952	2	17	14	45	4	0	1	41	4	25	26	439494	5	21	9	24	9	31
Bhopal	1454830	522735	253622	2	19	16	53	5	0	1	42	3	36	14	385538	2	16	11	19	9	42
Visakhapatnam	1329472	500246	234814	1	15	12	28	4	1	1	19	4	27	46	262897	4	12	15	15	14	37
Kochi	1355406	408604	242588	5	20	16	46	5	0	1	46	6	22	19	181024	2	15	12	19	14	35
Varanasi	1211749	202836	100513	2	11	9	34	2	0	2	31	1	15	49	274916	30	13	3	22	4	26

Source: Same as in Table 15.3.

Reasons for Migration to Million Cities by the Males, 2001

Employment is the main reason for male migration to million cities, it ranges between 30–60 per cent, viz., Mumbai (60%), Kolkata (33%), Delhi (57%). Chennai (35%), Bangalore (46%), and Hyderabad (36%) (Table 15.3). In rest of the cities, it varies between 40–50 per cent. Next important reason is miscellaneous reason, ranging between 15– 40 per cent, followed by 'moved with the family' (ranging between 15–25%). Migration for business and education are still very small, even for men, 2–4 per cent and 2–5 per cent, respectively.

Reasons for Migration to Million Cities by the Females, 2001

Conversely, for the females marriage migration comprises the most important reason for migration to million cities (ranging between 25–46%), viz., Mumbai (46%), Kolkata (38%), Delhi (33%), and Chennai (23%). This is followed by 'movement with the family', which ranges between 26 per cent and 48 per cent (e.g., Delhi, 48%, Mumbai, 26%). Other 'miscellaneous' reasons are quite important (ranges between 15% and 40%). For the females, moves for business (<1%) or education (1–2%) are still very negligible. So it is hard to explain migration of the females by economic factors.

Very strong Links between Population and Total Male Migration to Metros (All Durations), 2001

Larger the size of million cities, greater is the volume of male migration (all durations). It explains as high as 75 per cent of variations in male migration to million cities for all durations (Figure 15.2, Table 15. 5). Statistical significance is extremely high, (0.00001), i.e., error term is just 1 out of 100,000 tests, that this relationship could be wrong. Or the chances are 99,999 out of 100,000 tests that this is true. That is simply exceptional. Not only this is statistically very highly significant, but also practically very meaningful, proving that migration (all durations) makes great contribution to urbanization in India. They move together, in unison. In harmony! Only urbanization has outpaced industrialization, that lies at the root of all urban problems in India.

Figure 15.2 *Strong Causal Links between Total Population of Million Cities and Total Male Migration, 2001*

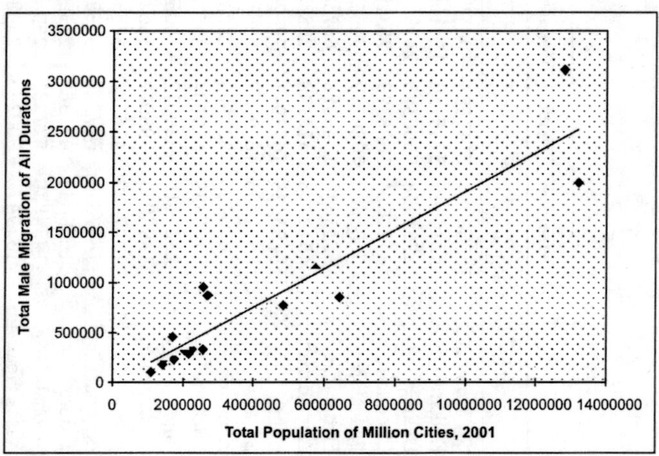

Table 15.5 *Links between Total Population in Million Cities and Total Male Migration to them (All Durations), 2001 (N=19)*

Dependent Variable	*Indep. Variable*	*Mult. R.*	*Adj R Sq.*	*Expln.*	*Beta*	*T*	*Sig. T*	*Intercept*	*Meaning of Relation*
Total male migration (all durations)	Total population	.88	.75	75%	.03	7.5	.00001	780430	Larger size of million cities, greater the volume of male migration (all durations)

Very Strong Links between Population of Million Cities and Volume of Male In-migration, 1991–2001

Larger the population size of metros and million cities, greater is the volume of male migration to them.(during 1991–2001). This reflects an exceptionally strong relation between the two. Population size of million cities explains as high as 85 per cent of variations in volume of male in-migration to them. As explained earlier in (chapter 3), in India, all the capital, investments, growth efforts and production units have markedly uneven concentration only at million cities and mega cities, and consequently, under centrifugal forces, labour are also forced to move towards these suctioning urban centres. These indicate spatial symptoms of migration under the nexus of poverty and underdevelopment in a developing economy. Such trends can also be seen in South East Asia, where most of the migrants are attracted to primate cities of respective countries (Bangkok, Jakarta, Manila) (Mukherji, 2006: 308–328). This also shows a *bipolar* relation.

Figure 15.3 *Causal Relations between Total Population of Million Cities and Male In-migration to Them, 1991–2001*

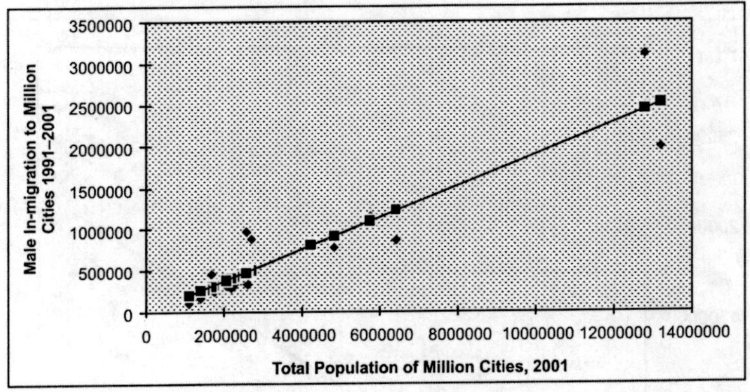

Table 15.6 *Links between Total Population of Million Cities and Male In-migration to Them, 1991–2001 (N = 19 selected million cities)*

Dependent Variable	*Indep. Variable*	*Adj R Sq.*	*Expln.*	*Beta*	*T*	*Sig. T*	*Intercept*	*Meaning of Relation*
Male in-migration to million cities	Total population of million cities	.86	85%	.92	10.4	.00001	–17291.6	Larger population size of million cities, greater volume of male migration to them

Links between Population in Million Cities and Total Volume of Female Migration to them, for All Durations

Larger the size of million cities, the more volume of female migration to them, for all durations (Table 15.7, Figure 15.4). It explains an unbelievably high, 90 per cent, of variations in volume of female migration for all durations to million cities. In India, the female migration invariably follows the patterns of male migration, because marriage migration constitutes 80 per cent all female migration. As per Indian traditions, after marriage, a wife invariably has to move to husband's home, or move with him. So when the husbands migrate to million cities, they also have to follow them. Thus, female migration shows the same causal relationship, as the males do. Female migration even represents a greater consonance with urbanization, more than even their counterparts, because while males migrate for economic purposes, but females migrate mostly for one single reason, "marriage". Even now, their moves for other purposes are not significant.

Table 15.7 *Links between Total Population in Million Cities, and Volume of Female Migration, All Durations, 2001 (N = No. of million cities 19)*

Dependent Variable	*Indep. Variable*	*Mult. R.*	*Adj R Sq.*	*Expln.*	*Meaning of Relation*
Volume of female migration to cities for all durations	Total population of million cities	.95	.91	90%	More size of million cities, more volume of female migration for all durations

Figure 15.4 *Causal Links between Total Population of Metros and Total Female Migration for All Durations*

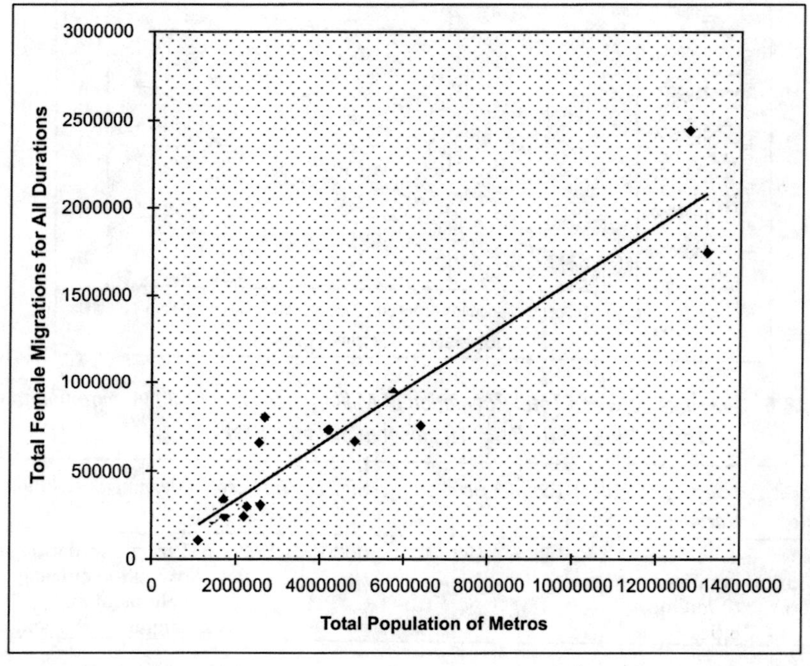

Strong Links between Service Sectors in Million cities and Female Migration for Work, 1991–2001

Strong positive causal relations emerge between service sectors of million cities and female migration to them for work (explains 18%). It implies that the females mostly migrate to those million cities where they get chances of absorption in poorly-paid 'services'. This confirms the phenomena of poverty-induced migration of the females and consequent proliferation of poor service sectors in large cities of India.

Table 15.8 *Links between Service Sectors in Million Cities and Female Migration for Work, 1991–2001 (N = 19, Beta = .44, Sig. T. = 2.2, Intercept = .911)*

Dependent Variable	*Indep. Variable*	*Adj R Sq.*	*Expln.*	*Meaning of Relation*
Recent female migration for work (1991–2000)	Service sectors	.18	18%	Strong positive relations emerge between service sectors and recent female migration for work

Figure 15.5 *Causal Links between Service Sectors and Female Migration for Work, 2001*

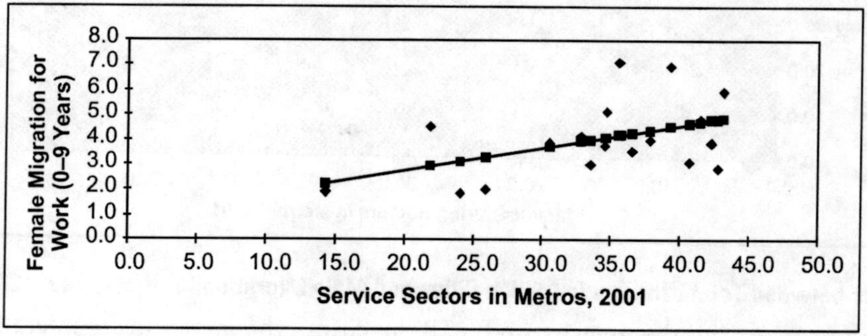

Links between Manufacturing in Million Cities and Male Migration for Work

More manufacturing industries in metros and million cities, the male migration to them for work. This relationship explains 11 per cent variations. This is a positive sign of development and needs to be further strengthened. In India, urbanization, migration and industrialization have querulous growth, i.e., migration and urbanization have outpaced industrialization. And, capital intensive industrialization has very limited employment generating capacity. These have created havoc in a very highly populous country, like India.

If it were planned effectively, then, this huge growing and youthful labour force could have been transformed into a vast army of skilled manpower. And, this country would have been one of the great economic super powers of world. But, there is no love for the poor, no empathy for them, no planning for the poor, no proper governance, and top of all, acute political corruption, and thus, this great Nation still remains a land of want, poverty, miseries and anarchy!.

Better governance, commitment to the Nation, and the planning for the poor are the real solutions for these great maladies. Bridging the development divide between the rich and the poor must be the mantra of Indian economy, not to be subservient to richie rich.

Table 15.9 *Links between Manufacturing Sectors in Million Cities, and Male Migration for Work, 1991–2001 (N = 19, Beta = .30, T = 1.44, Sig. T = .001, Intercept = 34.7)*

Dependent Variable	*Indep. Variable*	*Adj R Sq.*	*Expln.*	*Meaning of Relation*
Male migration to metros and million cities for work	Manufacturing	.11	11%	More manufacturing industries in million cities, more male migration for work

Figure 15.6 *Causal Links between Manufacturing Sectors in Metros and Male Migration for Work (1991–2001)*

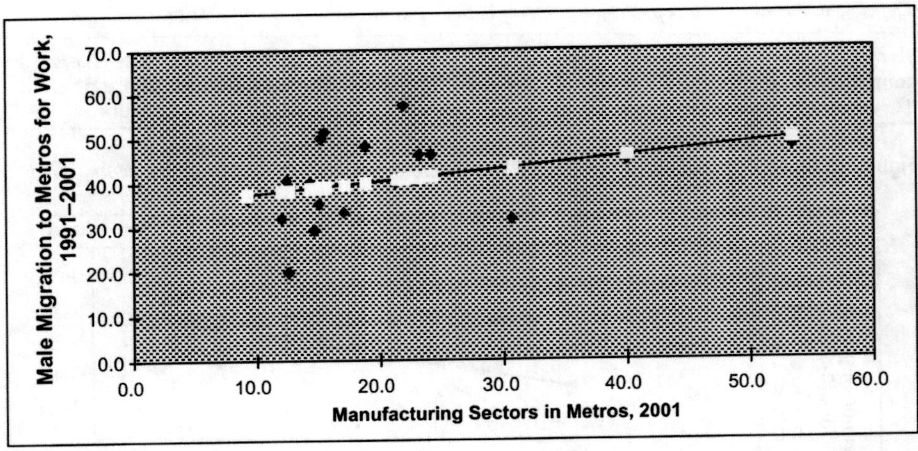

Links between Total Workers in Million Cities and Male Migration for Work, 1991–2001

More workers in the metros and million cities, the more male migration searching for work go there. It explains 6 per cent. That is knowledge network operates, attracting more workers into million cities where already huge number of workers have moved in. That is, the past migration flows determine current migration streams.

Figure 15.7 *Causal Links between Total Workers in Metros and Male Migration for Employment (0–9 Years)*

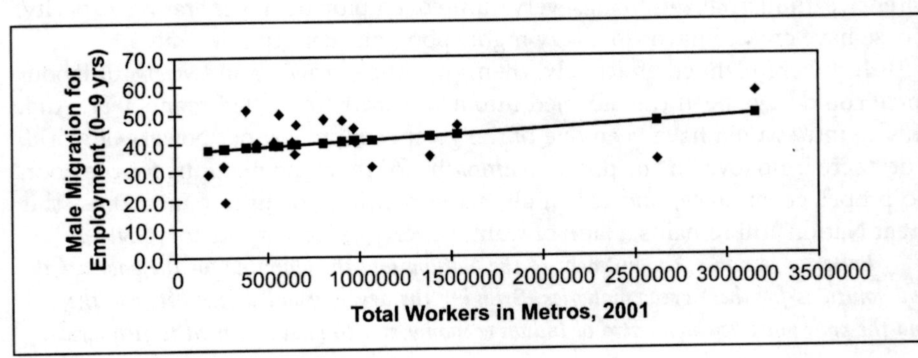

Table 15.10 *Links between Total Workers in Million Cities and Male Migration for Work, 2001 (N = No. of Cities 19, Beta = .039, Sig. T = .0001, Intercept = 36.8)*

Dependent Variable	*Indep. Variable*	*Adj R Sq.*	*Expln.*	*Meaning of Relation*
Male migration to metros for work (1991–2001)	Total Workers in metros	.06	6%	More workers in metros, the more male migration searching for work there

Relations between Secondary and Tertiary Sectors in Million Cities and Volume of Total Male Migration

More workers in secondary and tertiary sectors in million cities, the more volume of male migration into them, explaining about 11 per cent of variations in migration flows (Table 15.11, Figure 15.8). In the Indian situation, secondary sectors comprise of workers in mining, household industry, manufacturing and construction; and the tertiary sectors consist of workers in trade and commerce, transport and miscellaneous services. This finding indicates that in those million cities where these kinds of workers are predominant, they attract more male migrants for work. This is perfectly understandable and makes sense. Thence the corollary is also true: if we can generate more employment in these economic sectors in small towns and small cities, then they will succeed in redirecting the future migration flows into them. Besides, these will be more true for million cities, as well.

Table 15.11 *Relations between Secondary and Tertiary Sectors in Million Cities and Volume of Male Migration, 1991–2001 (N = 19, Beta = 0.27, Sig. T. = .001, Intercept = –33020096)*

Dependent Variable	*Indep. Variable*	*Adj R Sq.*	*Expln.*	*Meaning of Relation*
Volume of total male migration to million cities	Secondary and tertiary sectors	.11	11%	More workers in secondary and tertiary sectors in million cities, the more volume of male migration into them

Figure 15.8 *Causal Links between Main Sectors of Economy in Million Cities and Total Male Migration to Metros, 1991–2001*

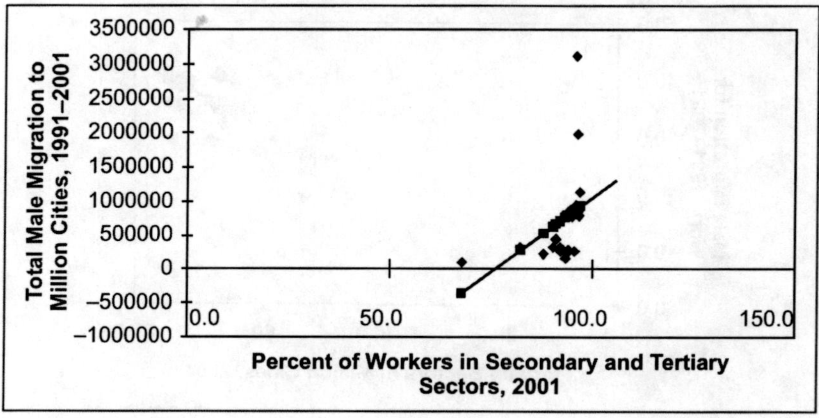

Links between Tertiary Sectors of Million Cities and Male In-migration for Work

Larger the tertiary sectors in the million cities, the more male migration to them for work (Table 15.12, Figure 15.9). This finding explains a very significant 26 per cent of variations in male migration for work. When seen, with the above regression equation (No 15.11), it points towards an intriguing finding: that is, tertiary sectors alone (services, transport and trade-commerce) explain as much as 26 per cent of variations in male migration for work, and its combination with secondary sectors explain only 11 per cent. That is, in fact it reduces its explanatory power, because of *variant* trend patterns of cities workers, which dance with cross purposes, canceling the cumulative benefits of workers in a million city. It also implies that, in reality, these tertiary sectors are the real harbingers of employment, even in such million cities. This re-confirms my age old thesis, that is, urbanization in India is propelled by proliferation of low-grade tertiary sectors, not strong manufacturing or secondary sectors (see Mukherji, 1975: 1–378; 1979, 1–89; 1981: 1–28). And, that migrants in India are absorbed in such poor and low productive tertiary sectors, where pay is low, cut-throat competition severe, and insecurity very high (Mukherji, 1985a:279–298; 1985b: 252–289; 2002: 525–562; 2006, 15–150). This re-confirmation rather makes me feel very sad, that even after 40 years, things have not improved in India a bit. Policy makers must take cognizance of such hard reality, and plan for the upliftment of the masses of the poor, both in the countryside and in the cities.

Table 15.12 *Links between Tertiary Sectors and Male In-migration for Work, 1991–2001 (N = 15. Beta = .61, T = 2.1, Sig. T = .0001, Intercept = –44.2)*

Dependent Variable	*Indep. Variable*	*Adj R Sq.*	*Expln.*	*Meaning of Relation*
Male in-migration for work	Tertiary sectors in million cities	.26	26%	Larger tertiary sectors of million cities, more male migration to work

Figure 15.9 *Causal Relations between Tertiary Sectors of Million Cities and Male Migration for Work, 1991–2001*

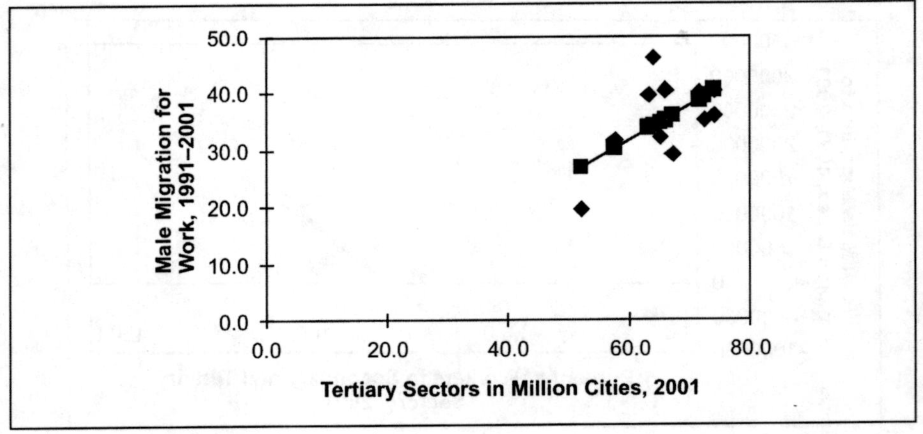

Links between Main Sectors of Economy in Million Cities and Total Male Migration to them, 1991–2001

More workers in million cities, the more male migration there searching work (Table 15.13, Figure 15.10). This explains 11 per cent. That is, higher the proportion of main workers (less marginal or temporary workers), the more male migrants are attracted to those million cities.

Table 15.13 *Links between Main Sectors in Million Cities and Total Volume of Male Migration, 1991–2001 (N = 19, Beta = 0.31, Sig. T = 1.8, Intercept = –3302096)*

Dependent Variable	*Indep. Variable*	*Adj R Sq.*	*Expln.*	*Meaning of Relation*
Vol of male migration to million cities	Main sectors of economy in million cities	.11	11%	More workers in million cities, the more male migration for work

Figure 15.10 *Causal Links between Main Sectors of Economy in Metros and Total Male Migration to Metros, 1991–2001*

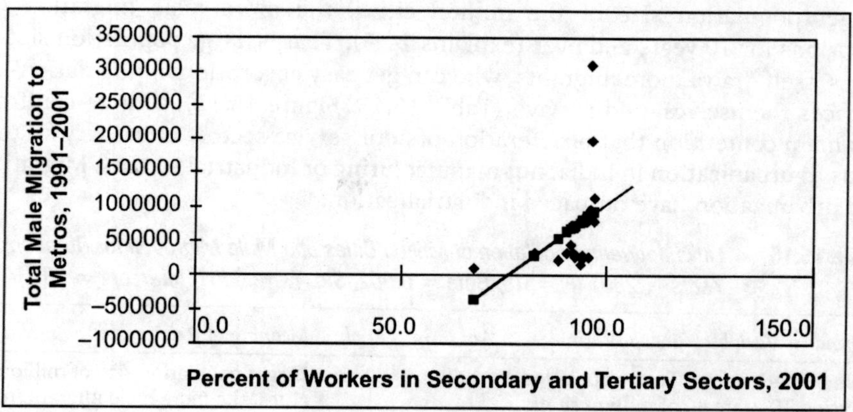

Links between Tertiary Sectors of Million Cities and Urbanization in India

More tertiary sectors in the million cities, the larger is the population size of them (explains 8%). Thus, one of the driving forces of rapid urbanization in India is the proliferation of the poor tertiary sectors, that is, growth of low-grade transport, trade and commerce and service sectors in the million cities. Therefore, unlike in the Western countries, in India, these low-grade tertiary sectors cater to the large population size of the million cities themselves, and they actually lie behind rapid urbanization in the country, not manufacturing or secondary sectors (Figure 15.11).

Table 15.14 *Links between Tertiary Sectors of Million Cities and Urbanization, 2001 (N =19, Beta = 0.32, Sig. T = 1.6, Intercept = –4278340)*

Dependent Variable	*Indep. Variable*	*Adj R Sq.*	*Expln.*	*Meaning of Relation*
Total population of million cities, 2001	Tertiary sectors of million cities	.08	8%	More tertiary sectors in million cities, the larger population size of them

Figure 15.11 *Causal Links between Tertiary Sectors and Urbanization in India, 2001*

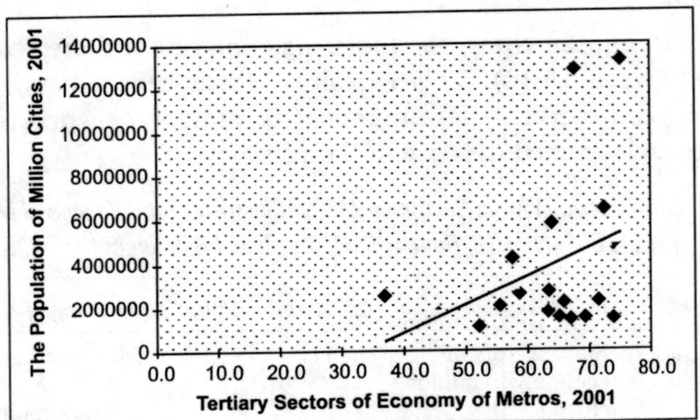

Relations between Population of Million Cities and Total Male Migration for Durations 10 Years+

Larger population size of the million cities, the more male migration for durations for 10 years and over (explains 24%). That is, large population size of cities itself draws more migrants, who can get easy absorption in population-led services themselves, and survive (Table 15.15, Figure 15.12). This re-confirms our main contention that proliferation of poor service sectors or tertiary sectors leads to urbanization in India, not manufacturing or industrial sectors. Migration and urbanization have outpaced industrialization.

Table 15.15 *Links between Population of Million Cities and Male Migration for Duration 10 Years+, 2001 (N = 19, Beta = 0.002, Sig. T. = .0001, Intercept = 38.1)*

Dependent Variable	*Indep. Variable*	*Adj R Sq.*	*Expln.*	*Meaning of Relationship*
Male migration for duration 10 years +	Total population of million cities	.24	24%	Larger population size of million cities, the more male migration for durations for 10 yrs +

Figure 15.12 *Causal Links between Total Population of Million Cities and Total Male Migration for Durations 10 Years+, 2001*

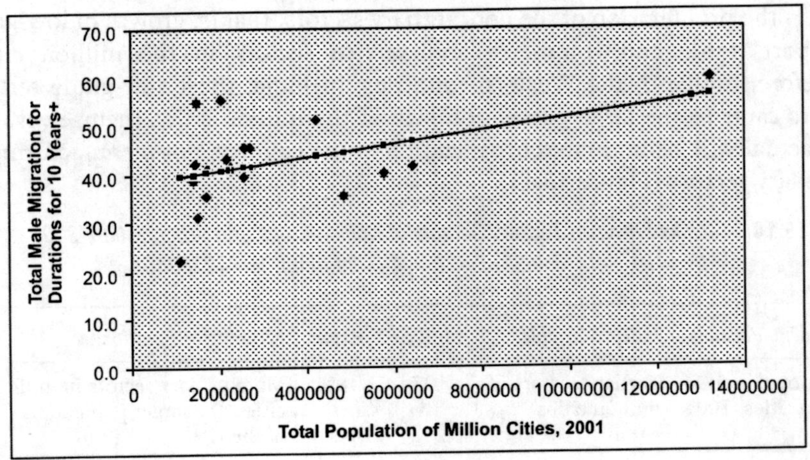

Estimated Population of Million Cities in 2011 and 2021 (If past trends continue)

If the present population growth trends continue, by 2021, Greater Bombay will reach 27.7 million, Delhi 29.5 million, Kolkata 19.0 million, and Chennai 9.0 million (Table 15.16, Figure 15.13 (a) and (b)). These assume that the current trends would continue in future, and as such, they slightly differ from UN estimates (2007), given in next chapter. Here, Delhi shows higher population, as it showed much recent growth.

Table 15.16 *Population in 1991 and 2001 of 20 Million Cities, and Their Estimated Population in 2021 (if past trends continue)*

	City	Tot. Pop. 1991	Tot. Pop. 2001	Difference	Decadal Growth Rate	Annual Growth Rate	Estimated Pop. 2011	Estimated Pop. 2021
1	Greater Mumbai	12596243	16372354	3776111	30.0	3.0	21280470	27659945
2	Kolkata	11021918	13208595	2186677	19.8	2.0	15829095	18969484
3	Delhi	8419084	12790376	4371292	51.9	5.2	19431297	29520265
4	Chennai	5421985	6422142	1000157	18.4	1.8	7606791	9009965
5	Hyderabad	4344437	4829753	485316	11.2	1.1	5369284	5969085
6	Bangalore	4130288	5759987	1629699	39.5	3.9	8032721	11202213
7	Ahmedabad	3312216	4215497	903281	27.3	2.7	5365114	6828244
8	Pune	2493987	2695911	201924	8.1	0.8	2914184	3150129
9	Kanpur	2029889	2185927	156038	7.7	0.8	2353960	2534909
10	Lucknow	1669204	2262369	593165	35.5	3.6	3066320	4155961
11	Nagpur	1664006	2052066	388060	23.3	2.3	2530625	3120788
12	Surat	1518950	2555811	1036861	68.3	6.8	4300451	7236012
13	Jaipur	1518235	2592067	1073832	70.7	7.1	4425409	7555456
14	Kochi	1140605	1410560	269955	23.7	2.4	1744407	2157268
15	Indore	1109056	1730363	621307	56.0	5.6	2699734	4212159
16	Patna	1099647	1432209	332562	30.2	3.0	1865346	2429476
17	Bhopal	1062771	1482718	419947	39.5	4.0	2068604	2886000
18	Vishakhapatnam	1057118	1507126	450008	42.6	4.3	2148699	3063386
19	Ludhiana	1042740	1693653	650913	62.4	6.2	2750888	4468083
20	Varanasi	1030863	1103952	73089	7.1	0.7	1182223	1266044

Even then, to provide basic essential urban facilities like water, electricity, housing, shelter, transport, employment, education and health to such burgeoning urban population will be really a Herculean task. But, the Indian government so far has no clearly envisioned urban policy, nor any migration policy, nor any kind of population control policy (due to narrow vote bank politics). Ad-hocism in planning, and a "total absence of planning for the poor" mark such slipshod efforts and their corrupt and unsuccessful implementation!

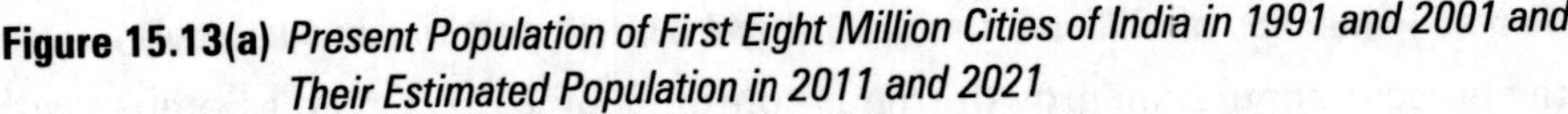

Figure 15.13(a) *Present Population of First Eight Million Cities of India in 1991 and 2001 and Their Estimated Population in 2011 and 2021*

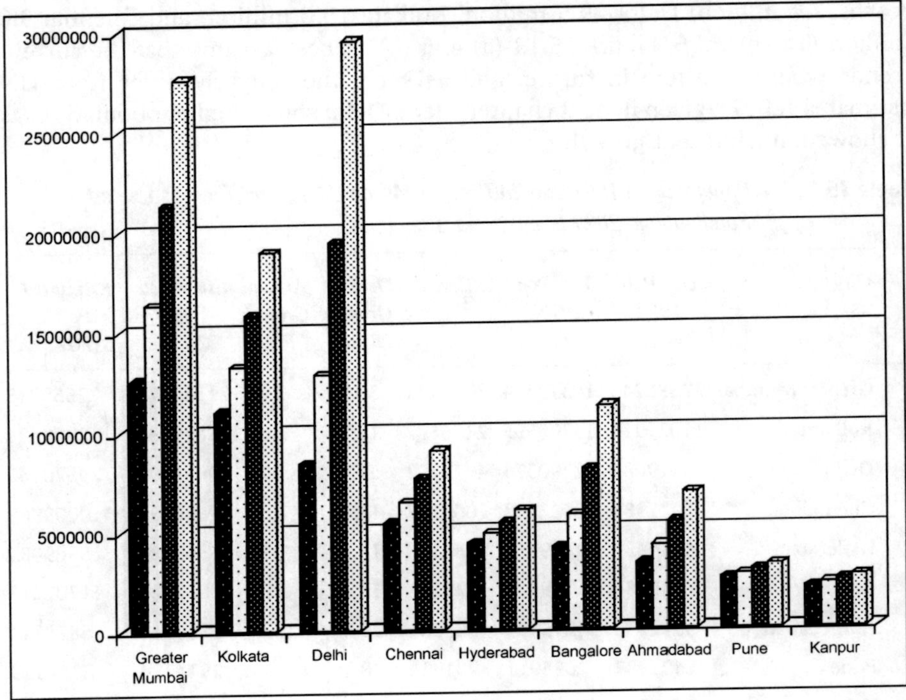

Figure 15.13(b) *Present Population of Next Eight Million Cities of India in 1991 and 2001 and Their Estimated Population in 2011 and 2021*

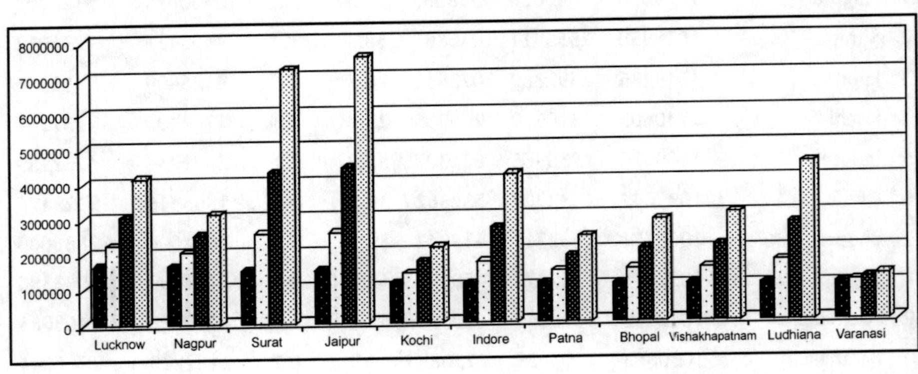

Poor and Upper Occupational Divisions of Migrants (Males), Million Cities, 2001

Even in the mega cities, majority of male migrants get absorption only in the poor services and low-grade production process sectors of the occupations: viz., Greater Mumbai (59.8%), Kolkata (69.6%), Delhi (63.2%), Chennai (51.8%), Hyderabad (48.4%), Bangalore (48.1%) and Ahmedabad (53.5%) (Table 15.17). Few are engaged in professional, administrative, or clerical jobs: Greater Mumbai (15.5%), Kolkata (14.5%), Delhi (17.2%), and Chennai (23.2%). Lower size million cities depict similar pictures.

Table 15.17 *Poor and Upper Occupational Divisions of Migrants (Males), Million Cities, India, 2001*

Name of the Million City	*Total Migrants Workers (Males), 1991–2001*	*Occupation Divisions of Male Migrants (%)*	
		Poor Sector (Illiterate and semi-educated workers in production, services, farms, unclassified)	*Upper Sector (Professionals, administrative and clerical services)*
Greater Mumbai	3296878	59.8	15.5
Kolkata	1716178	69.6	14.5
Delhi	2294488	63.2	17.2
Chennai	709582	51.8	23.3
Hyderabad	749398	48.4	25.8
Bangalore	871622	48.1	26.2
Ahmedabad	589286	53.5	15.5
Pune	608896	49.1	21.1
Kanpur	196462	56.4	13.7
Lucknow	208964	45.0	26.1
Nagpur	217948	50.5	19.4
Surat	726696	55.9	7.9
Jaipur	211636	48.8	24.1
Vadodara	222408	47.3	23.0
Patna	134096	44.7	31.9
Indore	167148	53.0	20.8
Bhopal	182780	47.7	25.4
Coimbatore	139030	55.7	15.6
Kochi	111826	47.8	27.0
Madurai	91226	58.8	14.7
Varanasi	67526	59.6	15.9

Note 1: Out of 35 Million cities in India in 2001, only selected 21 are discussed, for which migration data available.

Note 2: Proportion of production process workers who are illiterate or below high school are (semi-educated) estimated, based on similar data of 1991 (data for 2001 not available). Final poor sectors, thus comprised of such low grade production process workers, plus farm workers and service workers. Upper class workers comprised of professionals, administrative and clerks. Middle class composed of sales and rest of the middle-class production workers.

The reasons are: capital-intensive industrialization in such cities have failed to generate adequate employment in organized sectors, so illiterate and semi-literate migrants are absorbed only in low-grade informal sectors (Mukherji, 1995a: 1–45). *This is a grave symptom of poverty, underdevelopment and low quality migration and urban involution in India. Similar features can also be observed in South and Southeast Asia* (Mukherji, 1997b: 1–80; 2006: 45–330). Although, even these kinds of migration are desirable, as these help in reducing rural poverty and to escape from starvation, nevertheless, such low-quality migration and urban involution are not desirable in the long run, as they keep such developing countries under perpetual poverty, underdevelopment and serfdom! *Combating against such undesirable aspects must be given the top priority in the government's migration and urbanization policies (so far non-existing), and their right implementation.* These are subject matters of subsequent discussion (Chapters 21 and 22).

16 Findings of Metropolitan-level Analysis of Migration and Urbanization, 2001

> "Onward for ever! Sympathy for the poor, the downtrodden, even unto death – this is our motto. Onward, brave lads!
>
> **Swami Vivekananda** (1894),
> (Complete Work, Centenary Volume V, 1963: 30)

Future Population of Indian Mega Cities (UN Estimates, 2007)

United Nations report on World Urbanization Prospects (2007) presented a different projections of India's mega cities: Greater Mumbai will reach 26.4

Figure 16.1 *Present and Future Population of Mega Cities of South and South-East Asia, 1980–2025 (in millions)*

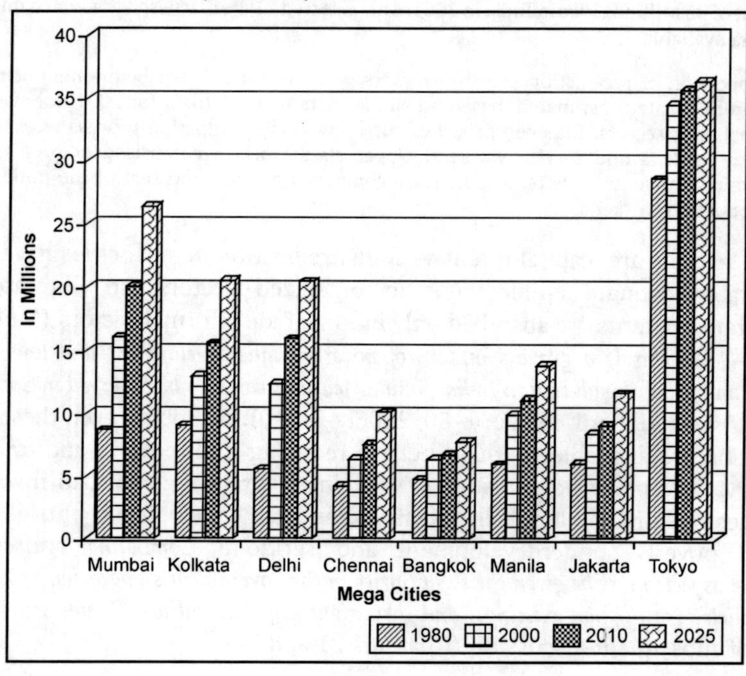

million, Kolkata 20.6 million, Delhi 20.5 million, and Chennai 10 1 million by 2025. (Table 16.1, Figure 16.1). Mumbai already has 56 per cent of its urban population under slums in 2001, followed by Kolkata (43%), Delhi (35% and Chennai (32%), and slums will proliferate in future also. Thus these mega cities would grow more as over-blown villages, not in prosperity! In comparison, by 2025, Tokyo, the world's largest city with 36 million population, will still remain a clean city, a green city, and a crime-free and slum-free city; but India's urban future does not seem to be that bright – it might have a more choking environment, more mushroom growth of slums, and a sea of people who would eke out their lives from hand to mouth.

Table 16.1 *Growth of Urban Population in Indian Mega Cities, 1980–2025 (millions)*

	1980	*2000*	*2010*	*2025*
Mumbai	8.66	16.09	20.07	26.39
Kolkata	9.03	13.06	15.58	20.56
Delhi	5.56	12.44	15.93	20.48
Chennai	4.20	6.35	7.56	10.13
Tokyo (for comparison)	28.55	34.45	35.68	36.40

Source: UN, 2007, World Urbanization Prospects, Various Tables.

Mega City-level Analysis

Components of Inter-state Migration to Mumbai, All durations, and 1991–2001

Mumbai is considered as the financial capital of India, while Kolkata as the cultural capital, Delhi the administrative capital, and Chennai, the commercial capital. Recently, Mumbai metropolis has metamorphosed into a megalopolis, like a *desi*-type of New York, with its glamorous sky-scrapers and psychedelic neon signs. But, behind Mumbai's opulence is hidden dark shadows of abject poverty, human miseries and severe exploitation. Mumbai attracts millions of migrants, both the males and the females, from all corners of the country, who have migrated into their *El-dorado*, or dream city, with great hopes and high aspirations. However, that frequently ends up with shattered dreams and battered lives!

In Mumbai, behind tall buildings and glitzy shopping malls, there exists a scary graveyard of dead aspirations and dying souls, surviving below the superficial glamour of India's commercial capital! Some writers have recently depicted life in Mumbai or in a Mega city in India as "a City within a City" and pointed out at the "City's Fault Lines" (Srivastava, 2010: 32). He evocatively narrated that: "It does take a high level of composure to walk from a street, crowded with makeshift homes and children in rags playing around dizzily speeding cars, and then walk into a mega mall lined with the latest branded items. It is still possible to see the shocked face of the girl behind the counter marveling at your ability to buy goods worth her entire year's salary." ... "For anyone in Mumbai with rolled up windows in an air-conditioned car in the face of a highly professionalized beggar economy, or has walked over a sleeping homeless body, ... it reminds you that there is world out there, which you see and need to respond to ..." (ibid.: 32). "It is about finding out where the fault lines actually are and preparing ourselves to see them and respond to them" (ibid.).

Table 16.2 *Migration to Mumbai, All Durations and During 1991–2001*

Last Residence	*All Durations (%)*	*Durations 0–9 Years (%)*
Total	100	100
Last residence elsewhere in India	98.5	99.0
Intra-District Migration (Within Maharashtra)	1.6	1.7
Inter-District Migration (Within Maharashtra)	39.4	34.2
Inter-State Migration (Outside Maharashtra)	57.4	63.1
Northern States	1.8	1.9
Rajasthan	3.8	4.2
Uttar Pradesh	21.8	25.7
Bihar	2.9	4.9
West Bengal	2.0	3.4
Central States	2.4	3.5
Gujarat	8.5	5.6
Andhra Pradesh	2.3	2.8
Karnataka	5.7	5.1
Goa	0.5	0.3
Kerala	2.5	2.5
Tamil Nadu	2.8	2.7
Last residence outside India	1.5	1.0

Source: Computed from Census of India, 2001(b), Migration Tables, D-Series.

Mumbai saw much ebbs and flows of the migrants during the last four decades. During 1961–71, Mumbai received a huge 3.4 million migrants, which decreased to 1.8 million during 1971–81, declining further to 1.6 million during 1981–91, but again rising to 2.5 million during 1991–2001 (Census of India, 2001b). As Mumbai gradually became the financial capital of India, its structure of migration also became increasingly inter-state. During 1981–91 while Mumbai received 43 per cent *intra*-state migrants, and 57 per cent inter-state migrants, but it further titled in favour of inter-state migrants recently (36% and 63%, respectively, during 1991–2001) (Table 16.2). But Mumbai's urban future does not seem to be bright – it might have a more choking city, more proliferation of slums, and a sea of sad faces!

Issue of the Outsiders and the Sons of the Soil

It is commonly believed that most of the migrants to Mumbai came from Bihar and Uttar Pradesh. The Census data of 2001 (b) reveal the true picture: during 1991–2001, 36 per cent of total migrants to Mumbai came from "within Maharashtra" and 63 per cent from outside Maharashtra; of which, about 4.9 per cent (0.22 million) came from Bihar, and 25.7 per cent (0.92 million) from Uttar Pradesh. Thus, *intra*-state migrants from within Maharashtra were still larger than (36%) migrants from Uttar Pradesh and Bihar combined (30.6%). However, recent agitation in Mumbai in favour of reserving jobs to the "sons of the soils" often turns violent, and are targeted towards the migrants from Bihar and Uttar Pradesh. Such political trends may have many ramifications in future. Migration streams from Bihar and Uttar Pradesh may considerably decline. When the benefits of development are small, and are regionally concentrated only to a few mega cities in India, then, such politically-motivated agitations are natural to arise. But they need not to be violent, nor should be inimical to unity of all Indians.

To understand the genesis of such critical problems, we need to have a correct and true historical and politico-economic perspectives. As described in Chapter 3, and elsewhere (Mukherji, 1981, 1982, 1997b, 2006) all such problems have roots in India's past colonial legacy and in induced spatial disorganization of the country, and also in Post-independent era of faulty economic policies. We must never forget that Mumbai, Kolkata and Chennai were totally absent 300 years ago, before the advent of British colonialism. These were artificially created as exporting centres – cum-ports-cum-military bases by colonial adversaries, for extracting raw materials, plantations, and minerals from all interior parts of India and to export to the master country at unfavourable terms of trade. New Delhi was also created for colonial administration and troop movements. Since capital, industries, and growth efforts were continuously pumped into these four growing villages, over time, they evolved into large towns. Under the *centrifugal forces,* when capital, investments, industries, and growth efforts moved therein, so also the labour also were also forced, under the *same centrifugal forces,* to migrate into these four evolving nodes. Labour had no choice, but to migrate to these port cities and the capital centre (New Delhi). So, everybody there were migrants and their progenies. Cheap labourers from Bihar and Uttar Pradesh were thus forced to migrate into these cancerous settlements, as the interior parts of the country were depleted from all resources, capital, finances, manufacturing, and production units, as these were mostly concentrated into those four evolving settlements-cum-exporting centres. No industries, nor any employment were created, nor available in Bihar and Uttar Pradesh. They were reeling under poverty and unemployment, because the finance were mopped out from all parts of the country and focused elsewhere, and industries were never located in those neglected states. Neither during colonial period, nor thereafter. So, hundreds of millions of migrants moved from Uttar Pradesh and Bihar, in the one hand, and four black-hole like large cities grew into cancerous mega cities, on the other. This is the true perspective of the genesis of the above crucial migration-urbanization problems in India. Unless corrected, such problems will soon grow into maximum entropy level and lead to a cataclysm, urban civil war, violence, crimes and greater turmoil will ensue!

The solution lies in developing hitherto-neglected Uttar Pradesh and Bihar, and to generate massive employment and development in the migrant-source regions. A battery of planning strategies are also recommended in last chapter for development of such hitherto-neglected and backward states. Only then, hapless migrants from these regions will not crowd into the filthy urban slums of Mumbai, Kolkata, Delhi and Chennai.

Figure 16.2(a) *Components of Migration to Mumbai, All Durations, 2001 (%)*

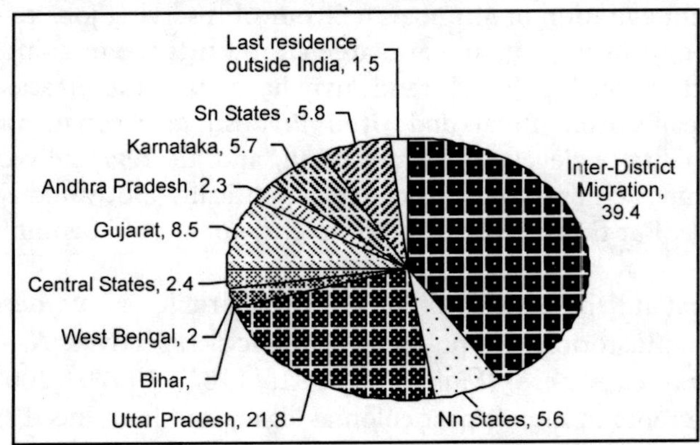

Figure 16.2(b) *Components of Migration to Mumbai, 1991–2001 (%)*

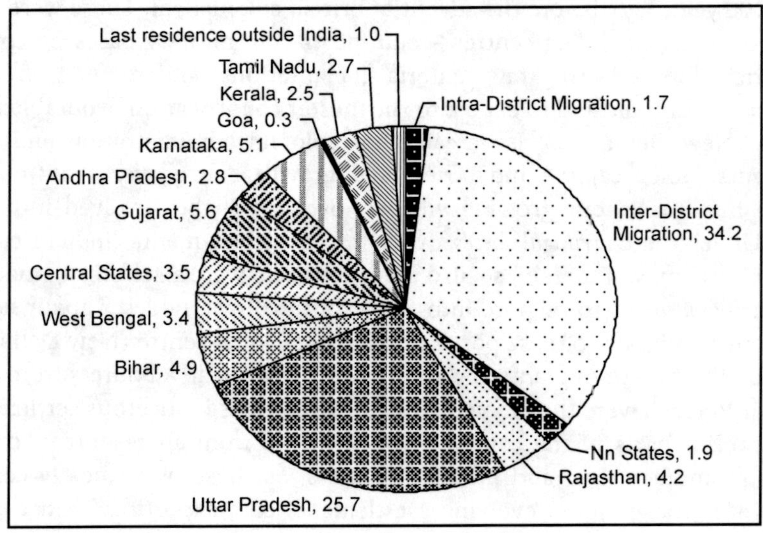

Figure 16.2(c) *Male Inter-state Migration to Mumbai, 1991–2001 (%)*

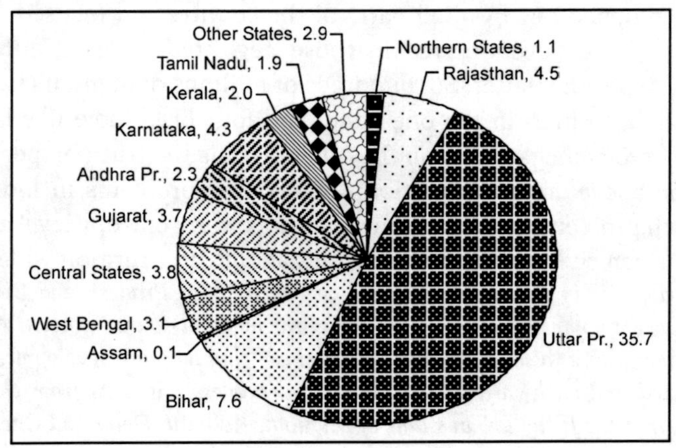

Figure 16.2(d) *Female Inter-state Migration to Mumbai, 1991–2001 (%)*

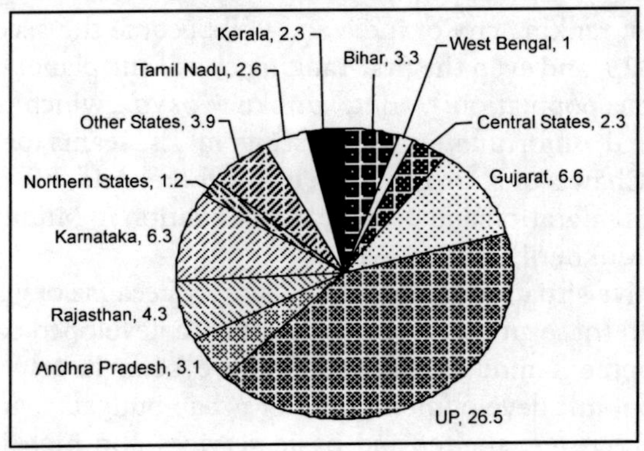

Rural-Urban Components of Migration to Mumbai

Table 16.3 depicts that during 1991–2001, majority of migrants, both males and females, came from far-flung rural areas, and both for inter-district and inter-state migration (Figure 16.3, two parts). Inter-state migration is male dominated, since finding shelter for the family is a big problem in Mumbai.

Table 16.3 *Rural-Urban and Male-Female Parts in Migration to Mumbai, 1991–2001*

	Last Residence	*Migration with Durations, 0–9 Years (1991–2001)*		
		Persons	*Males*	*Females*
Intra-district Migration	Rural	37765	19186	18579
Intra-district Migration	Urban	0	0	0
Inter-district Migration	Rural	592504	304911	287593
Inter-district Migration	Urban	237441	110962	126479
Total Intra-district and	Total	867710	435059	432651
Inter-district Migration	Rural	630269	324097	306172
Same as above	Urban	237441	110962	126479
Inter-state Migration	Total	1571181	992862	578319
Inter-state Migration	Rural	1047875	699341	348534
Inter-state Migration	Urban	488667	273254	215413

Figure 16.3(a) *Intra-state Migration to Mumbai, 1991–2001, Rural-Urban Parts and Male-Female Categories*

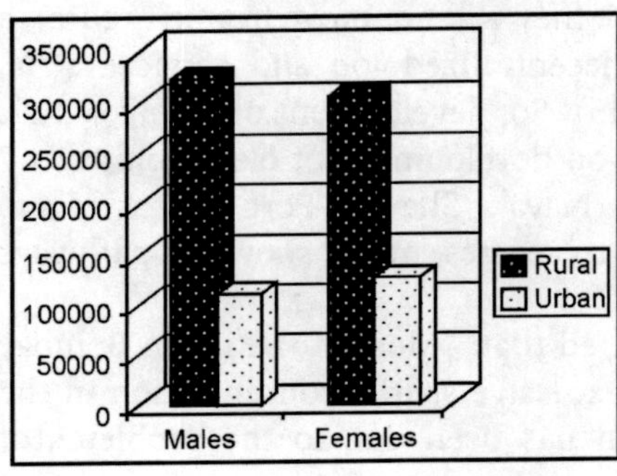

Figure 16.3(b) *Inter-state Migration to Mumbai, 1991–2001, Rural-Urban Parts and Male-Female Categories*

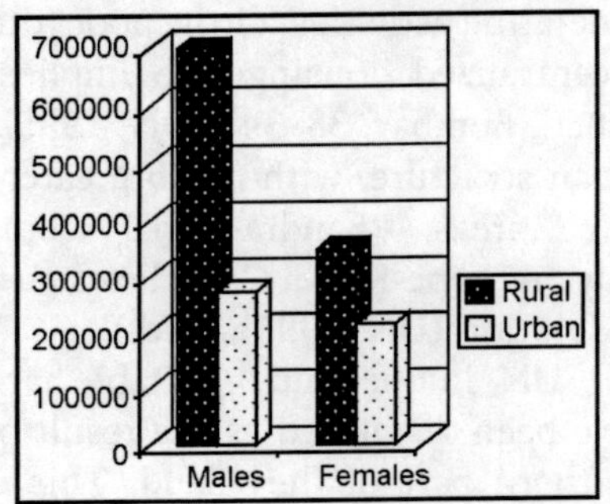

Concluding Remarks on Mumbai

Mumbai is the first ranking city of India and will become the second largest city of the world by 2025, and even the first-ranking city of the planet by 2050 (with a fearful 50 million population!). But, unlike Tokyo, which is growing in prosperity, Mumbai unfortunately is bursting in its seams only in size and growing poverty. Chawls or slums are seen everywhere. And, life flows miserably here. The details of migration and urbanization situation in Mumbai is presented in another book (Mukherji, 2006: 43–78).

Such oppressive situation has happened simply because of wrong policies of the city fathers. "In these cities, attempts to emulate developed countries' urban and social development models and trends have been largely unsustainable. Lower level of economic development, smaller urban budgets, shortage of entrepreneurial infrastructures, shelter and basic services and high levels of urban poverty have resulted in a different patterns of urban development and environmental degradation which look equally unsustainable" (Burgess, 2000: 12).

Moreover, when Tokyo, Hong Kong, or Singapore could grow in prosperity, Mumbai could also have grown equally well in happiness and well-being. City authorities should have taken a very firm policy of absolutely checking the exploitative activities of the land-speculators and housing-speculators who fleeced, and continue to fleece out, the skin of the common people. The estate developers have equally severely exploited the masses of urban residents and incoming migrants. The city fathers should have also developed all vacant land lying idle all around in Navi Mumbai and in between Mumbai and Navi Mumbai, and also in Thane districts. These areas can provide plenty of space for housing for urban poor and for the slum-dwellers. A more humane approach to the entire problem of sheltering urban poor should have been taken, instead of allowing a few privileged land-speculators, businessmen, and private estate-developers to fleece the common people by sky-rocketing the land and housing prices. The city cooperators and the state and the central government were mute spectators of such gross exploitation of the poor masses. The things have gone from bad to worst. But still it has not gone beyond the point of redemption. It needs iron will and crucial actions.

The concern for Mumbai's decentralization has to continue seriously in order to save the city from reaching crisis proportions. Development of a "poly-centric" spatial structure of Mumbai Metropolis has been feebly attempted so far; but it needs much sincere boosting. Since housing cannot be stimulated in outlying areas of Mumbai Metropolitan region, without providing employment generating activities for the poor (otherwise they will not move from city core), a decentralized housing also implies the decentralized job and services (UN, 1986d, Bombay, 33–34) (UN, 1995b, 41–45). So, development of a poly-centric urban structure, with much greater focus on development of New Bombay's 7 core areas, Bandra-Kurla complex, Nava Sheva Port areas, and Kalyan-Thane-Kalwa Complexes and Growth centres, might show the pathways to solution (UN, 1995b, ibid.).

UN, in one study (1995b), has indicated that: "Most of the ills in Bombay have been diagnosed as the result of the excessive spatial concentration in the southern part of the island. This concern has been due to the problems of increasing congestion, cost of building the infrastructure and the crisis of housing problem. A plan to build new housing in peripheral areas implies the decentralization of jobs and services as well, hence a polycentric metropolitan structure. However, this goal has remained elusive for many years" (UN, 1995b, ibid.).

"What we need now are fresh ideas, expert advice, social and political will and above all a determined government action" (David, 1996: 6). Besides, very efficient fiscal and administrative management of large cities like Mumbai (Delhi, Kolkata and Chennai, as well) are the most essential requirements of urban planning (Ghorpade, 1998: 361–380). Navi Mumbai, the planned twin city, has not taken on the scale earlier envisaged. Reasons behind the failure are the government's decision not to shift a large number of government jobs over there and the limited financial capacity of the CIDCO (City and Industrial Development Cooperation) authority. However, the plan of Nava Sheva port in the southern part of Navi Mumbai may well contribute in the development of the area (Mukherji, 2006: 75–78).

"Navi Mumbai is the result of following the Western pattern to provide healthier and greener towns to people. Planners wanted to make it a city in which common man would like to live. But the method of financing the new town has effectively skewed its class composition to middle and upper classes" (Jacquemin, 1999: 231–257). Navi Mumbai had to become a counter-magnet (Bhattacharya, 1995). But it failed to take population pressure off from Mumbai.

"Developments in the recent years have proved that not much remains of the original intentions of the entire New Bombay Project. The twin City has become no different from the numerous earlier experiences in urban planning and new town development, and has basically developed into a large real estate development project" (Jacquemin, 1999, ibid.). New Bombay Project which was to become "a city in which the common man would like to live". Yet, about 25 years later Navi Mumbai, indeed, has developed into a city in which the common man would like to live ... very much so. Unfortunately, for most families, it will never materialize" (UN, 1995b, ibid.). Indeed, Mumbai and Navi Mumbai both need much more effective decentralization and addressing acute housing and environmental problems. The issue of water and air pollution control must also be addressed with great urgency (Mukherji, 2006: 42–77).

Inter-state Migration to Kolkata, Males and Females, 1991–2001

Urban Situation in Kolkata

Kolkata was the largest city of India until 1990. It's population was 9.2 million and larger Kolkata Metropolitan District had 10.3 million population in 1981, which rose to 11.6 million in 1991. According to UN (UN, 1995a), Kolkata would have reached 15.6 million by 2001, and exceeded 24 million by 2010. But, compared to Mumbai, Kolkata considerably slowed down recently; specially its central city. Kolkata is often referred to as an example of urban pathology or a picture of urban future of most mega cities of developing countries – where scores of thousands are compelled to live on dirty pavements and where widespread unemployment and absolute poverty are visible everywhere (UN, Calcutta, 1986a: 1–2; UN, 1995d: 59–62).

Kolkata is not considered as world city, though big agglomeration, because not well connected to the world, and play a limited economic roles beyond the boundaries of its own state. Very severe congestion, extremely strained urban amenities, and acute shortage of basic infrastructure plague Kolkata. Kolkata Metropolitan area is a sheer example of very highly dense compact city, which caused extreme urban congestion, unruly traffic, and severe breakdown of basic civic amenities (Ghosh, 1998: 315–339). City's water supply system is most inadequate; the roads are extremely narrow, broken and over-burdened; sewerage system dates back to colonial period 250 years ago. Acute water logging and drainage problems mar daily lives of millions in rainy season every-year. Industrial stagnation continue since many decades. Kolkata is thus a city of nightmare to many outsiders. However, to the insiders, Kolkata is a great city of joy, India's great cultural centre, ideal intellectual paradise, a city of immense life, exuberance, intense creativities, matured political and social consciousness, and with total freedom of expression. So, there is a sharp contrast. An extreme contradiction.

Long ago, I had termed Kolkata as a "city of hallowed culture, but with a feet of clay"! (Mukherji, 1981b: 3–12). Besides, Kolkata is neither well connected with its hinterland, nor it allowed rise of second tier cities within its 500 miles radius, even after three centuries of domination (Mukherji, 2006: 78–110).

"Nevertheless, Kolkata is a unique city in the entire world, where one can immediately feel the pulse of people of the city, their intense struggle for life, non-stop creative activities, music, poetry (everybody were poets there sometime in their lives), frustration, hopefulness, sincere friendliness, and very warm hospitality. The city will immediately embrace you, even to strangers. It is a great friendly city – providing a feeling of great openness and warm heartedness – which one may not get in other great cities of the world, even after a long stay! Never in Delhi or Mumbai or Chennai. Nor in New York, Paris, London or Berlin. Nor in Bangkok, Hong Kong, Tokyo, or elsewhere. Kolkata is an unparalleled city in this sense" (Mukherji, 2006: 80–81).

Calcutta Metropolitan Development Authority (CMDA: 1995: 1–140) contributed a lot to upgrade lives in Kolkata, by slum uplifting, road construction, improving water supply, sewerage and drainage. Nevertheless, horrible traffic congestion, transportation bottlenecks, and very acute housing shortages continue; so also Calcutta's problems of very frequent labour strikes, lock-out, layoffs, and unemployment. Consequently, politico-economic atmosphere is so vitiated that no new industries have located itself to Kolkata since 1977.

Migration Situation in Kolkata

Kolkata has long been a paradise for the migrants. Details of urbanization and migration in Kolkata are discussed in another study (Mukherji, 2006: 78–110). Since 19th century, when Kolkata was the Capital of India, it was known to have drawn scores of thousands of migrants, both from adjoining districts of Bengal and from far-flung Bihar, Orissa, Assam and Uttar Pradesh. It was the main nerve centre of India during British rule till 1911, when capital shifted to New Delhi. Most of migrants were single males, who left their families behind in the villages. This happened due to extreme housing shortages. Most of the long distance migrants from northern India came to work in jute, textile, hosiery, iron and steel, paper, and other industries.

Most such migrants were huddled into slums or "bastees" which are like low grade shanty towns or squatter settlements. Recently, net migration to Kolkata has reduced. Planners are concerned with backlog of accumulated problems of migrants. Calcutta Metropolitan District (CMD) contains 82 per cent of West Bengal's total industrial units and generates about 88 per cent of total employment (UN, Calcutta, 1986a: 1–38). Calcutta with one-sixteenth of state's total population, generates about one-sixth of total income; and CMD having 20 per cent of state's total population, generates about 25 per cent of its total income (UN, ibid.: 15). So, Kolkata demonstrates considerable polarization of resources, population, income, industries, and factory employment. Kolkata is a typical example of poverty-induced migration and urban involution, and of polarization of investments and industries.

Industrial stagnation of Kolkata has been continuing since last two decades, and net migration to this city has been much less. Consequently, Kolkata is growing slowly, and West Bengal is also urbanizing slowly (UN, Calcutta, 1986a, 14–15). Situations of recent migrants are also not good, as revealed by annexed migration tables.

Table 16.4(a) *Kolkata: Intra-district, Inter-district and Inter-state Migration, 1991–2001*

Type of Migration	*Last residence*	*Duration of Residence 0–9 Years*			
	Rural/ Urban	*Males*	*M%*	*Females*	*F%*
1. Total Migration	Total	409231	100	413159	100
2. Total Internal Migration	Total	382980	93.6	384900	93.2
Total Internal Migration	Rural	281054	68.7	239995	58.1
Total Internal Migration	Urban	100960	24.7	144905	35.1
3. *Intra*-district and Inter-district Migration	Total	202882	49.6	267719	64.8
Intra-district and Inter-district Migration	Rural	137384	33.6	171973	41.6
Intra-district and Inter-district Migration	Urban	65499	16.0	95746	23.2
4. Inter-state Migration	Total	180098	44.0	117181	28.4
Inter-state Migration	Rural	123670	30.2	68022	16.5
Inter-state Migration	Urban	56428	13.8	49159	11.9
5. International Migration	Total	26251	6.4	28258	6.8

Table 16.4(a) indicates that during 1991–2001, about 822,390 persons migrated into Kolkata, of which 49.8 per cent were males and 50.2 per cent females. The majority of them came from rural areas: 69 per cent from rural and 25 per cent from urban areas among the male migrants; and 58 per cent from rural and 35 per cent from urban areas among the female migrants. Among the males, intra-district and inter-district short distance migration comprised 49.6 per cent and long distance inter-state migration, 44 per cent. Among the females, however, short distance intra-district and inter-district migration consists of as large as 65 per cent, while long distance inter-state migration, just 28.4 per cent. So, inter-state migration is male-dominated, because of acute housing shortages.

Inter-state migration from far flung rural areas is the major pattern for both the male and female migration to Kolkata.

Table 16.4(b) *Inter-state Migration to Kolkata, Males and Females, 1991–2001*

Major States	*Male (%)*	*Female (%)*
N-W States	2.7	2.7
Delhi	1.0	1.8
Rajasthan	2.2	3.3
Uttar Pradesh	12.1	13.8
Bihar	53.0	42.7
Assam	2.5	2.5
Jharkhand	7.4	5.1
Orissa	8.2	6.9
Madhya Pradesh	0.6	1.2
Gujarat	0.6	1.0
Maharashtra	1.1	1.9
Andhra Pradesh	1.0	1.7
Sn States	1.4	2.4
Other States	6.1	13.0
Total	100.0	100.0

Table 16.4(b) testifies that among inter-state migration to Kolkata, male migrants from Bihar consist 53 per cent, followed by Uttar Pradesh (12%), Orissa (8%), and Jharkhand (7%) (Figure 16.4(a) and (b)).

Figure 16.4 (a) *Inter-state Migration of Males to Kolkata, 1991–2001 (%)*

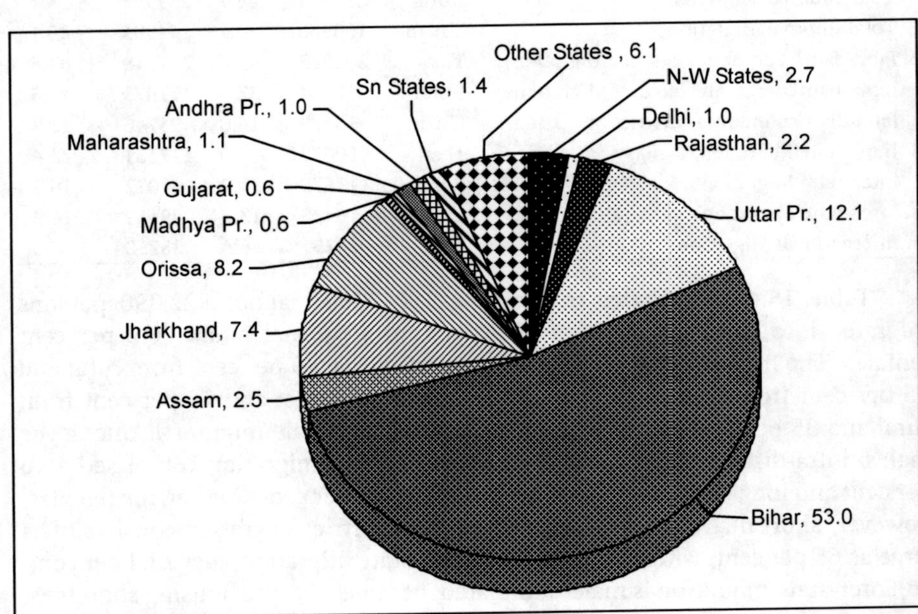

Figure 16.4 (b) *Female Inter-state Migration to Kolkata, 1991–2001 (%)*

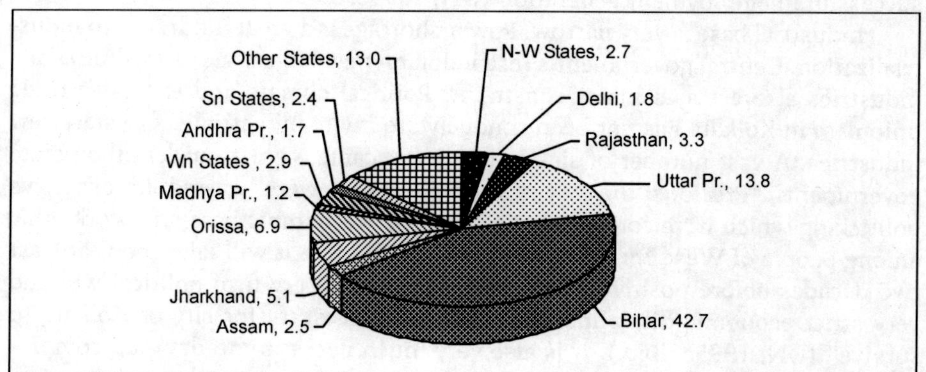

They mostly moved for eking out some subsistence in mega city by being absorbed into poor bazaar-type economy, as hawkers, vendors, transport workers, construction labourers, servants, watchmen, or sundry service workers. Almost similar patterns can also be seen among the female migrants: Bihari female migrants comprised as large as 43 per cent, followed by Uttar Pradesh (14%), Orissa (7%), and other states (13%). They form the counter parts of the male migrants, earning their livelihoods as hawkers, vendors, construction labourers, maid-servants, and so forth. These masses of illiterate and semi-educated migrants have no other choice left in a mega city, but to join in the lowest rungs of urban economy. But, they do serve city well, by providing many useful services, which the resident Bengali population shirks to do!

Concluding Remarks about Kolkata

Economically, Kolkata is now one of the poorest cities of the world (but it was not so during 1960's – my young days!). Slums constitute more than 43 per cent of its inhabitants. The condition of lower-middle class and middle class people is also no better either (Mukherji, 2006: 108–110). However, under the World Bank and IDA, CMD has upgraded considerably many civic facilities of the city (water, drainage, sewerage, electricity, sanitation). Kolkata also developed the first Metro railway system of India, which has been built after two decades of toiling. Kolkata is also a city where, for the first time, instead of slum eviction, tenure were officially granted to the millions of poor slum dwellers, squatter settlers and many colonies (refugees came after partition of India in 1947).

Slums are upgraded and developed: water provision, electrification, road construction, and sanitation are provided to many slums. In spite of these remarkable achievements, very acute urban crisis continues. Pavement dwellers are still scores of thousands. Water, electricity, and sanitation facilities are simply not available to one-third of city's population. Population grew very rapidly in suburbs, new towns, in Salt Lake city, Eastern Bypass zone, and elsewhere. People are swarming everywhere. The city is sprawling over miles and miles. Trains are over-jammed. The CMD is bursting at its seams. But the economic prosperity is not visible anywhere. It remains a distant dream. This is because the activities of CMDA remained as public work agency, not as the generators of industries, manufacturing, or income. Nor the government was successful in employment generation (UN, 1995c: 59–62).

Industrial base is very narrow. Power shortage is a great hindrance to industrialization. Central government's restriction on new large scale or medium scale industries also act as a major constraint. Political climate and excessive trade unionism in Kolkata has not been conducive to invite industrialists to start new industries. A vast number of sick industries became a great burden upon state government. "Precious thirty years (1977–2006) were wasted in excessive politicking which have completely destroyed the economic base and work ethic among people of West Bengal" (Mukherji, 2006: 110). It will take about at least two decades before positive results will show up. "Very firm political will and very strict economic discipline are very much necessary for city of Kolkata to survive" (UN, 1995c, ibid.). It is also very much necessary to draw up comprehensive urban development plan for Kolkata for its future growth and direction of development, which is lacking (UN, 1995c, 59–52). In 2009, the situation of Kolkata is no better either.

Male and Female Inter-State Migration to Delhi, 1991–2001

Table 16.5 provides details of interstate migration to India's national capital, Delhi. During 1991–2001, total 2,112,363 persons migrated to Delhi, of which 94 per cent were inter-state migration, and only 4 per cent intra-state migration, because Delhi is a small state also. Details of migration and urbanization situation in Delhi are provided in another volume (Mukherji, 2006: 111–140).

Table 16. 5 *Inter-state Migration to Delhi, 1991–2001*

Last residence	*Rural/Urban*	*Males*	*Females*	*Male (%)*	*Female (%)*
Total	Total	1191868	920495	—	—
Inter-state Migration	Total	1124569	863745	100	100
Inter-state Migration	Rural	795641	547322	70.8	63.4
Inter-state Migration	Urban	328928	288100	29.2	33.4
Jammu & Kashmir	R+U	8272	7718	0.7	0.9
Himachal Pradesh	R+U	11988	11033	1.1	1.3
Punjab	R+U	20434	26028	1.8	3.0
Uttaranchal	R+U	55693	46463	5.0	5.4
Haryana	R+U	63600	81046	5.7	9.4
Rajasthan	R+U	24938	39428	2.2	4.6
Uttar Pradesh	R+U	437784	350899	38.9	40.6
Bihar	R+U	257234	112054	22.9	13.0
West Bengal	R+U	46042	33432	4.1	3.9
Jharkhand	R+U	37334	20708	3.3	2.4
Orissa	R+U	13316	7834	3.0	0.9
Madhya Pradesh	R+U	20483	18763	1.8	2.2
Maharashtra	R+U	11645	13192	1.0	1.5
Kerala	R+U	15127	17478	1.3	2.0
Tamil Nadu	R+U	8806	9513	0.8	1.1
Other States	R+U	70848	68236	6.3	7.9

Figures 16.5(a) and (b) present the pictures of interstate migration of males and females to Delhi mega city. Among the males, 39 per cent come from adjoining Uttar Pradesh alone, followed by Bihar (23%), Haryana (5.7%), Uttaranchal (5%), West Bengal (4%), Rajasthan (3.7%) and northern states (3.6%). Among the females, again the majority come from nearby Uttar Pradesh (41%), followed by Bihar (13%), Haryana (9.4%), Uttaranchal (5.4%), Rajasthan (4.6%), West Bengal (4%), and Northern states (5.2%). After Mumbai, which acts as national destination of All-India migrants, Delhi also captures a similar position. As we will examine later, most of these migrants are illiterate and unskilled, and get absorbed mainly in low-grade urban informal sectors (see Table 16.8(b).

Figure 16.5(a) *Male Inter-state Migration to Delhi, 1991–2001 (%)*

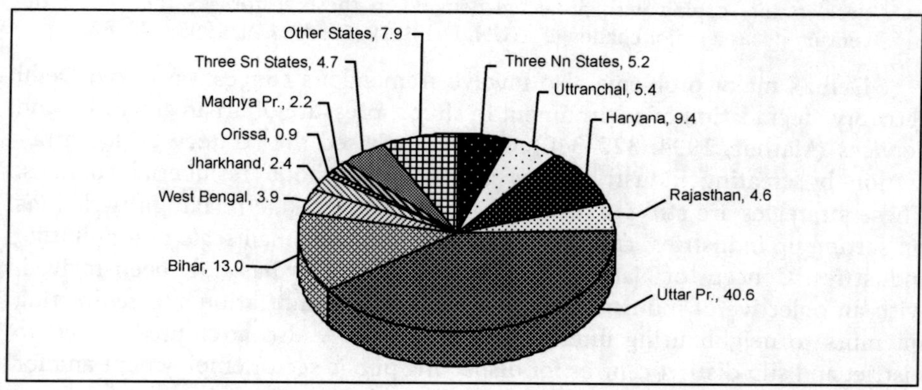

Figure 16.5(b) *Female Inter-state Migration to Delhi, 1991–2001 (%)*

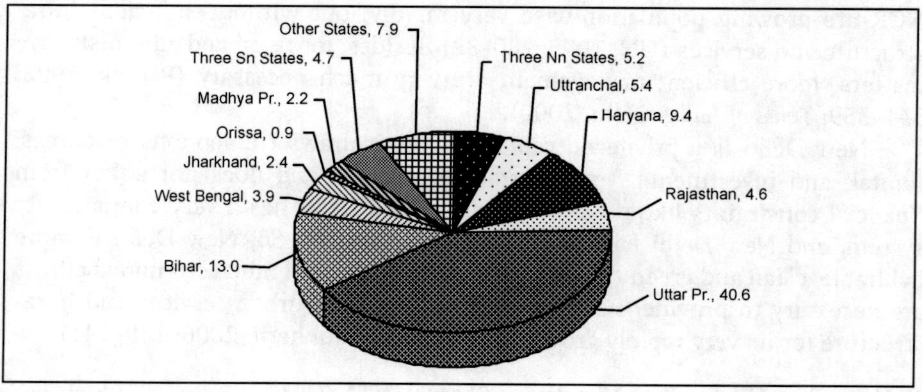

Concluding Comments on Delhi

Delhi can be considered as a model city by the standard of developing country. Because it has nicely preserved its old historical sites, relics, palaces and tombs, while maintaining features of a modern city of Delhi (Mukherji, 2006: 111–140). Road network and parks are well laid out in New Delhi. Moreover, Delhi Development Authority (DDA) constructs many housing complexes rapidly, with financial aids from the central government. Delhi is also a city of great contrast and contradictions – manifesting tremendous social, economic, income and political inequalities across various people, where high-density low-income houses exist side by side with affluent low density bungalow type houses, and filthy richness among a privileged few looks contemptuously over masses of the poor people down below. New Delhi is a city where some people have concentrated immense political and economic power, while the pangs of the hearts of the millions of the poor people living in Juggis and Jhopris are never atoned. Inadequacy of infrastructure, specially in old Delhi, is also troublesome. One UN report on Delhi has commented:

> "The city's power supply, water supply, sewerage network and solid waste treatment facilities are not capable of dealing even with current demand. Given the rapid growth of Delhi Metropolitan Area (DMA), which has yet to show signs of decelerating, coping with projected demand in these sectors by the end of the century poses a major challenge". (UN, Delhi, 1986b: 33; UN, 1995e: 78–82)

Delhi's major problems also involve tremendous congestion in old Delhi territory, degradation of environment in slums, pressure of urban amenities and services (Mathur, 1994: 320–340). Planners advised the strategy of decentralization by creating industrial sites and neighbourhood residential colonies. These strategies are still pursued with some changes, like relaxing restrictions on setting up industries, and promoting medium and small scale non-polluting industries. Concept of National Capital region (NCR) has now been revived, with an objective of industrial and residential decentralization and redirecting migrants to neighbouring intermediate cities. DDA also attempted to set up district and sub-district centres for dispersing public sector employment and for creating National Capital region. However, public sector jobs are rarely decentralized (UN, Delhi, 1986b, ibid.: 33–34). Instead, more offices are concentrated in city centre. Another hindrance is that many outlying urban centres within NCR are growing population-wise very rapidly, but without sufficient infrastructure and services (UN, 1995e, 80–82) Besides, for fiscal and administrative matters, more efficient management are very much necessary (Pathak, 1998: 341–359; *Times of India*, Delhi, 2000).

New Delhi is a privileged capital city as it draws tremendous resources, capital, and investments from central government and does not suffer from financial constraints like other mega cities. Old Delhi has a very compact city system, and New Delhi has less compact city system. So, New Delhi is more habitable, clean and green (Kumar, 2000: 301–310). Still much strenuous efforts are necessary to provide the basic needs of housing, urban services and infrastructure for its very rapidly growing population (Mukherji, 2006: 139–141).

Male and Female Inter-State Migration to Chennai, 1991–2001

Figures 16.6(a) and (b) respectively present pictures of interstate migration of males and females to Chennai. Details of migration and urbanization situation in Chennai is presented elsewhere (Mukherji, 2006: 141–170). Number of migrants to Chennai are small, only 435,620, of which within state migrants comprised 77 per cent and inter-state migrants, only 22 per cent. Among the males, the majority has moved from adjoining Andhra Pradesh (24%), followed by Kerala (22%), Karnataka (9%), Maharashtra (6.7%), and a mixture of

Northern states (15%). Among the females, likewise, the majority have come from neighbouring Andhra Pradesh (24%), followed by Kerala (23%), Karnataka (11%), Maharashtra (7%) and northern states (13%). Chennai, unlike Mumbai, caters as a regional centre, not as a National destination.

Figure 16.6(a) *Male Inter-state Migration to Chennai, 1991–2001 (%)*

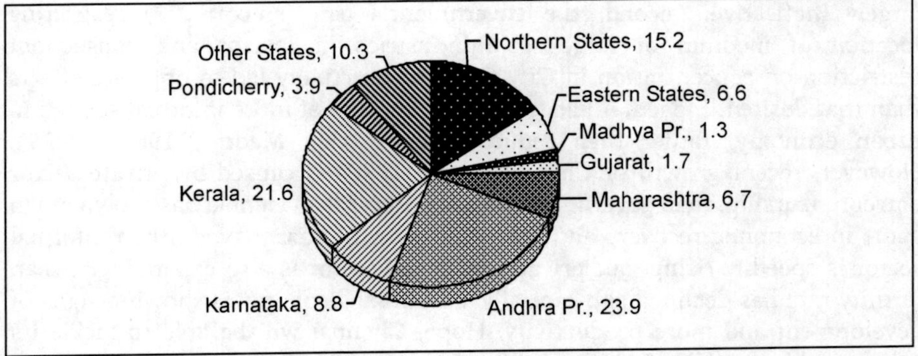

Figure 16.6(b) *Female Inter-state Migration to Chennai, 1991–2001 (%)*

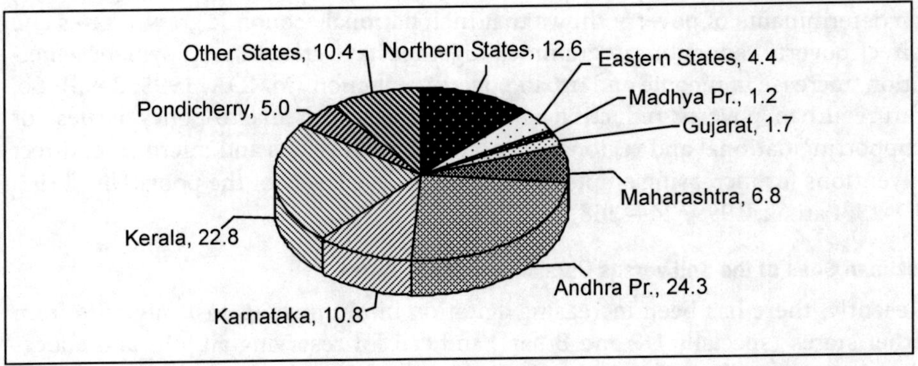

Concluding Remarks on Chennai

Although Madras Metropolitan Authority (MMA) had envisaged a spatial dispersal policy for Chennai, and thought to distract migration flows to the satellite towns and urban nodes in the periphery, but in reality, urban development of the city had progressed quite contrarily. Only a few of the proposed satellite towns (mainly Marai-Malai Nagar or MM-Nagar) and a few of the proposed urban nodes (mainly Manali) have been constructed and very few people have settled, when actually several hundred thousands were proposed to inhabit there. Of course, many constraints exist for achieving the envisioned goals; first, was slow pace of acquiring public land for satellite towns; second, providing housing in the satellite towns was not considered as the sufficient incentive for the middle income groups. Third, very inadequate provision was made for employment generation. Fourth, due to declining population growth rate of Chennai in later period, there was slackened pressure for sub-centre growth (UN, Madras, 1987a: 28–29). Indeed, urban growth has occurred, where it was actually prohibited. Central city became more densely settled, in spite of the government's declared policy on the contrary. Similarly, urbanized area has been expanding steadily outward, not only in linear corridors designated for development, but also in between them. Reasons for such haphazard urban development in Chennai are manifold: first, urban land-use controls have been largely ineffective. Second, the government's ban (since 1977) restricting location of medium or large scale industries in metros and consequent restriction on concentration in City Core, have actually led to opposite effects than that desired. Indeed, it has led to proliferation of more informal sectors in urban economy, rather than reducing them (UN, Madras, 1987a: 2–29). However, recent growth of Chennai in the 1990s is caused by private sector entrepreneurship, than government policies. Recently, Chennai has shown much spurt in economic recovery and economic growth. Bazaar type urban informal sector is speedily rising, but private organized sector is also expanding. Urban fertility rate has declined substantially, and urban economy is showing signs of development and more productivity. Hope, Chennai will be able to tackle its urban problems (UN, 1995b, 30–32; Mathur, 1994: 320–340). Like Kolkata, Chennai also has to solve crucial problems of urban poor. In spite of the declining trend in urban poverty, the number of urban poor is increasing. Studies on determinants of poverty shows that high national economic growth rates and direct poverty reduction programmes together have created employment generation, increase in income and urban poverty reduction (MMDA, 1995: 3–95). So, future urban poverty reduction should address both macro-policy issues for supporting national and regional economic growth issues and micro-level direct inventions for increasing employment and income levels of the poor (UN, 1992: 19–25; Pathak, 1999, 244–268).

Issue of Sons of the Soil versus Outsiders in Mega Cities

Recently, there has been increasing agitation in Mumbai against migrants from other states (specially UP and Bihar), and call for reserving all jobs and educational seats in colleges for the locals, the "sons of the soil" (*Marathi Manoos*). The annexed Table 16.6(a), however, shows that for Greater Mumbai, a large chunk of migrants comes from within the state of Maharashtra (43% during 1981–1991), and 57 per cent from the remaining 31 states of the country. During 1991–2001, their share changed into 36 per cent and 63 per cent, respectively; showing that segment of within state migration continuing to be large. Migration from UP and Bihar comprised only 26 per cent and 5 per cent during 1991–2001 (Table 16. 6(a), also Table 16.2). While there is genuine grievances of the local people for employment and education, the agitation for that must not be violent. Here, is also a strong plea for urgent development of hitherto neglected and undeveloped states of Uttar Pradesh and Bihar, so that they can be locally employed within their states, instead of crowding in stinking slums at Mumbai. As regards Delhi, majority comes from adjoining states, as Delhi Capital territory is a tiny state. In case of Kolkata, 57 per cent are from within state, and only 36 per cent from outside state. In Chennai, 77 per cent are from within state and 33 per cent from outside. However, even then the sheer volume of migrants from other states are considerable. Thus, almost similar story of unfriendly attitude to outsiders may begin to arise in Delhi, Kolkata, and Chennai and the same solution must be undertaken for such increasingly difficult problem of massive migration of the impoverished humanity to not-so-friendly destinations.

Table 16.6(a) *Intra-state and Inter-state Migration into Mega Cities, 1981–2001(%)*

Mega city	*Total Migrants*	*1981–1991*		*Total Migrants*	*1991–2001*	
		Intra-state Migration	*Inter-state Migration*		*Intra-state Migration*	*Inter-state Migration*
Greater Mumbai	1557040	43	57	2489553	36	63
Kolkata	692009	55	45	822389	57	36
Delhi	1160392	2	98	2112363	4	94
Chennai	677205	79	21	435621	77	22

Sources: Census of India, 1991(b) and 2001(b), Migration Tables, D-Series, CDs.

Contribution of Migration to Urban Growth of Mega Cities

One curious question is: to what extent migration contributes to urban growth of such mega cities? Table 16.6(b) provides answers to that. In 2001, Mumbai's population was 16.4 million, and lifetime migrants (for all durations) had contributed to 43.6 per cent of that. In Kolkata, migration had contributed to 28.3 per cent; as regards Delhi, 43.4 per cent and in Chennai, merely 25.1 per cent. In sum, Mumbai and Delhi perform as National centres attracting migrants from all parts of the country, whereas, Kolkata and Chennai cater as regional centres. *Certainly these testify more polarization of capital investments in these two megalopolises, neglecting others.*

Table 16.6(b) *Population and Migration Variables (Males), Four Mega Cities, 2001*

Mega Cities	*Total Population*	*Total Migrants (All Durations)*			*Migration as % of urban population*	*Duration of Migration (%)*			
		Persons	*Males*	*Females*		*< 1 Yr*	*1–4 Yr*	*5–9 Yr*	*10 Yr +*
Gr. Mumbai	16372354	7141583	4137467	3004116	43.6	2.5	16.8	15.9	59.6
Kolkata	13208595	3735752	1994693	1741059	28.3	1.5	9.7	9.3	59.6
Delhi	12790376	5550323	3111671	2438652	43.4	2.3	18.0	18.1	55.2
Chennai	6422142	1608299	855103	753196	25.1	1.5	14.6	10.8	41.7

Reasons for Migration to Four Mega cities

As regards male migration during 1991–2001, the purpose of move for "work employment" constituted as much as 59.6 per cent for Mumbai and 57 per cent for Delhi, but was considerably reduced to 33 per cent for Kolkata and 35 per cent for Chennai. Lack of new economic enterprises in Kolkata and Chennai are the underlying cause for such low state of economic affairs. Moves for education was only 2 per cent for all four mega cities, while migration for business comprised almost equally low proportion (1 to 4%). On the other hand, "other miscellaneous" purposes of moves were very large for Kolkata (34%) and Chennai (37%), compared to Mumbai (15%) and Delhi (15%). These facts reveal vibrant economic situation in Delhi and Mumbai, in the one hand, and relatively more familial or divergent reasons in case of Kolkata and Chennai, on the other.

Table 16.6(c) *Migration Variables (Males), Four Mega Cities, 1991–2001*

Mega Cities	*Reasons for Migration (%)*						
	Work	*Business*	*Education*	*Marriage*	*Moved after birth*	*Moved with family*	*Others*
Gr. Mumbai	59.6	1.5	2.1	0.4	9.2	12.6	14.7
Kolkata	33.3	4.3	2.2	0.6	3.3	22.4	34.0
Delhi	57.2	1.1	2.0	0.3	2.3	22.3	14.8
Chennai	35.2	2.4	2.4	1.3	4.5	16.9	37.4

Mushroom Growth of Poor Tertiary Sectors in Indian Metros, 1901–2001

Tables 16.7(a) and (b) present evidence of mushroom growth of poor tertiary sectors in Indian metros during 1901–2001. Most of illiterate and low-educated migrants find salvage in poor urban informal sectors, as domestic servants, maids, porters, road construction labourers, or hawkers. All are low-grade services with poor wages, cutthroat competition, and severe exploitation. Such distressed migration, thus, does not lead to development or high quality urbanization, neither in the past, nor now (Mukherji, 2005, 11–39).

Table 16.7(a) *Persistence of Poor Tertiary Sectors in Indian Metros, 1901–2001*

Metro City	*Econ. Sectors*	*1901*	*1951*	*2001*
Kolkata	Secondary	21.8	29.1	23.9
	Tertiary	75.8	70.3	75.2
Mumbai	Secondary	32.8	39.9	29.9
	Tertiary	64.5	58.8	69.4
Delhi	Secondary	41.0	29.4	31.5
	Tertiary	54.4	69.9	67.8
Chennai	Secondary	31.3	28.8	25.0
	Tertiary	62.5	68.5	72.4

Sources: Various Census Volumes of 1961–1991, and Census of India, 2001(c), All-India, and Various States-B Series, Economic Tables, Census Office, New Delhi, Various CDs, 2009.

Note: Tertiary sectors include: trade-commerce, transport, and services. In India, they comprise of low-grade services that population explosion itself creates (indigenous transport, hawkers/vendors, low services), not high level tertiary sectors as in the West. So, growth of low tertiary sectors is not sign of development!

Economic Structure in Four Mega Cities, 2001

Apropos to Table 16.7(a), further details abut the economic structure of these four mega cities reveal that manufacturing sector comprised of only 15 to 23 per cent of urban economy, while tertiary sectors, as large as 68 to 75 per cent (see Table 16.7(b)).Of these tertiary sectors, the poor service sectors constituted as high as 36 to 43 per cent of urban economy. Hence, Indian mega cities really have feet of clay, not strong manufacturing base, nor wide base of secondary sectors. No wonder that the incoming migrants can find salvage only in poor tertiary or service sectors, which mainly population explosion create, not vibrant urban economy.

Table 16.7(b) *Economic Structure Variables, Four Mega Cities, 2001*

Mega Cities	*Total Main Workers (Persons)*	*Categories of Total Main Workers (Persons) (%)*								
		Mining	*Household industries*	*Manufacturing*	*Construction*	*Trade-commerce*	*Transport*	*Services*	*Secondary sectors*	*Tertiary sectors*
Gr. Mumbai	4087341	0.1	2.8	23.1	3.9	20.7	12.4	36.3	29.9	69.4
Kolkata	2624811	0.2	2.6	17.0	4.0	24.0	10.5	40.6	23.9	75.2
Delhi	3160618	0.3	3.1	21.9	6.2	23.4	8.6	35.8	31.5	67.8
Chennai	1382492	0.2	1.9	15.0	7.8	19.2	10.1	43.1	25.0	72.4

Occupational Divisions of Male Migrants in Mega Cities, 2001

Now, the crucial question arises of providing for the evidence of absorption of incoming migrants to urban informal sectors of mega cities, which is testified in Tables 16.8(a) and (b).

Table 16.8(a) *Occupational Divisions of Migrants (Males), Mega Cities, India, 2001*

Name of Mega City	*Total Male Migrants Workers*	*Occupational Divisions of Migrants (%)*							
		Div 0–1	*Div 2*	*Div 3*	*Div 4*	*Div 5*	*Div 6*	*Div 7–8–9*	*Div 10–11*
	Males	*Prof*	*Admn.*	*Clerks*	*Sales*	*Services*	*Farm*	*Prod. process*	*Unclassified*
Gr. Mumbai	3296878	5.3	5.1	5.1	5.5	19.5	0.7	56.9	2.0
Kolkata	1716178	3.9	6.1	4.5	10.1	23.8	0.7	48.1	2.8
Delhi	2294488	5.6	6.6	5.0	4.9	16.9	0.9	56.8	3.3
Chennai	709582	8.0	8.3	7.0	6.0	20.4	0.8	42.9	6.6

Estimation of Different Sectoral absorption of Migrants, 1991–2001

First, proportion of production process workers among male migrants who are illiterate or below high school (or matric) are estimated for each mega city, based on similar data of 1991 (since similar data for 2001 not available). Finally, the poor sectors, thus, comprised of such low-grade production process workers, plus farm workers and service workers. Middle and higher sectors are estimated according to method provided below Table 16.8(b). Thence, poor sector comprised of half to two thirds of all migrants: namely, viz. Mumbai (60%), Kolkata (70%), Delhi (63%), and Chennai (52%). Upper class migrants constituted only 15 to 23 per cent, and middle class 15 to 25 per cent. The overall situation for migrants is relatively better in Mumbai and Chennai, while their work absorption is poor Delhi and Kolkata. The female migrants mostly move for marriage purposes, and partly for familial reasons, hence, not discussed.

Table 16.8(b) *Estimation of Three Sectors of Occupational Divisions of Migrants (Males), Mega Cities, 2001*

Mega City	*Occupational Divisions of Migrants (%)*										
	Poor prop. of produn. process workers	*Other Poor Sectors (farm, services, etc.)*	*Uncl-ssifieds*	***Poor Sectors***	*Div 0–1*	*Div 2*	*Div 3*	***Upper Sectors***	*Div 4*		***Middle Sectors***
					Prof.	*Admn*	*Clerks*		*Per cent of Middle class produn.*	*Sales*	
Gr. Mumbai	37.6	20.4	2.0	**59.8**	5.3	5.1	5.1	**15.5**	19.3	5.5	**24.7**
Kolkata	42.3	24.5	2.8	**69.6**	3.9	6.1	4.5	**14.5**	5.8	10.1	**15.9**
Delhi	42.0	17.8	3.3	**63.2**	5.6	6.6	5.0	**17.2**	14.8	4.9	**19.6**
Chennai	24.0	21.2	6.6	**51.8**	8.0	8.3	7.0	**23.3**	18.9	6.0	**24.9**

Notes: Proportion of production process workers who are illiterate or below matric (high school) are estimated for each mega city, based on similar data of 1991 (data for 2001 not available). Final poor sectors, thus comprised of such low grade production process workers, plus farm workers and service workers. Upper sector workers comprised of professionals, administrative and clerks. Middle sector workers composed of sales workers and rest of the middle-class production workers. Total is 100 per cent.

Absorption of Illiterate/Semi-educated Migrants in Informal Sectors in Mega Cities

Based on above Table 16.9 now testifies that most of illiterate and semi educated migrants find salvage in low-grade urban informal sectors. This holds true for both the sexes, during pre reform era and also during post-reform period

Table 16.9 *Absorption of Illiterate and Semi-Educated (below matric/secondary) Migrants in Low Grade Urban Informal Sectors in Mega Cities, 1981–2001 (migrants who moved for work)*

Metros	*Male Migrants (%)*					*Female Migrants (%)*				
	1981 (Life time migrants)		*1991 (0–9 years residence)*		*2001 (0–9 years residence)*	*1981 (Life time migrants)*		*1991 (0–9 years residence)*		*2001 (0–9 years residence)*
	Illite-rate and semi-educated (%)	*Absor-bed in low grade work*	*Illite-rate and semi-educated (%)*	*Absor-bed in low grade work*	*Absor-bed in low grade work*	*Illite-rate and semi-educated (%)*	*Absor-bed in low grade work*	*Illiter-ate and semi-educated (%)*	*Absor-bed in low grade work*	*Absor-bed in low grade work*
Kolkata	79.7	84.7	62.3	74.5	69.8	88.5	89.0	83.9	83.9	n.a.
Mumbai	68.6	79.6	57.0	58.8	59.6	64.0	66.5	54.5	57.6	n.a.
Delhi	63.4	72.3	58.7	57.5	63.2	65.3	65.8	49.5	49.5	n.a.
Chennai	48.9	62.6	41.3	39.4	51.8	43.7	48.2	41.5	41.0	n.a

Source: Computed from Census of India, 1981, All-India Migration Volumes, D Series,.Census of India, 1991, Migration Tables, and Census of India, 2001(b), Migration Tables, 2007–9, R. G. Office, New Delhi. Semi-educated means those below matric or secondary education, in fact, often below primary school education.

(1991–2001). During 1991–2001, 70 per cent of male migrants who moved for employment to Kolkata were absorbed in informal sectors, followed by Delhi (63%), Mumbai (60%), and Chennai (52%). Situation of female migrants are more precarious. Very little improvement occurred to their lives so far, in spite of 8–9 per cent economic growth rates in India. The picture of female migrants are not available for 2001, but it is not different from past situation.

Indian Mega Cities in the Global Context, 2000–2025

According to UN World Urbanization Prospects Report (2007), mega cities are urban agglomerations with at least 10 million inhabitants. In 2007, there were 19 mega cities in the world. By 2025 there should be 27. The share of people living in mega cities is still small. In 2007, only 9 per cent of the world's total

Table 16.10 *Mega Cities in the World and Asia, 1950–2025*

1950			*1975*			*2007*			*2025*		
Rank	*Agglomerations*	*Pop*	*Rank*	*Agglomerations*	*Pop*	*Rank*	*Agglomerations*	*Pop*	*Rank*	*Agglomerations*	*Pop*
1	New York	12.3	1	Tokyo	26.6	1	Tokyo	35.7	1	Tokyo	36.4
2	Tokyo	11.3	2	New York	15.9	2	New York	19.0	**2**	**Mumbai**	**26.4**
3	Mexico city	10.7	3	Mexico city	10.7	3	Mexico City	19.0	**3**	**Delhi**	**22.5**
						4	**Mumbai**	**19.0**	4	Dhaka	22.0
						5	Sao Paulo	18.8	5	Sao Paulo	21.4
						6	**Delhi**	**15.9**	6	Mexico City	21.0
						7	Shanghai	15.0	7	New York	20.6
						8	**Kolkata**	**14.8**	**8**	**Kolkata**	**20.6**
						9	Dhaka	13.5	9	Shanghai	19.4
						10	Buenos Aires	12.8	10	Karachi	19.1
						11	Los Angeles	12.5	11	Kinshasa	16.8
						12	Karachi	12.1	12	Lagos	15.8
						13	Al-Qahirah	11.9	13	Al-Qahirah	15.6
						14	Rio de Janeiro	11.7	14	Manila	14.8
						15	Osaka-Kobe	11.3	15	Beijing	14.5
						16	Beijing	11.1	16	Buenos Aires	13.8
						17	Manila	11.1	18	Los Angeles	13.7
.						18	Moskva	10.5	18	Rio de Janeiro	13.4
						19	Istanbul	110.	19	Jakarta	12.4
									20	Istanbul	12.1
									21	Guangzhou	11.8
									22	Osaka-Kobe	11.4
									23	Moskva	10.5
									24	Lahore	10.5
									25	Shenzhen	10.2
									26	**Chennai**	**10.1**
									27	Paris	10.0

Source: UN (2007), World Urbanization Prospects, 2006 Revision, UN, New York, Table 1.6.

urban population lived in mega cities. By 2025 the proportion would increase to 10 per cent. In relation to the world population, in 2007, mega cities accounted for 4 per cent of the Asian population. Asia has eleven mega cities; Latin America four; Northern America, two; and Africa and Europe have one each. Eleven of such mega cities are administrative capitals of their respective countries. By 2025, when the number of mega cities would rise to 27, Asia would have as many as 16 mega cities, Africa three, Europe only two, Latin America still four, and Northern America, still two.

By 2025, India will have four high ranking mega cities of the world (Table 16.10): Mumbai (26.4 million, ranking second), Delhi (22.5 million, ranking third), Kolkata (20.6 million, ranking eighth) and Chennai (10.2 million, ranking 26th). However, we wish that these burgeoning mega cities should grow, not only in population, but also in prosperity. They must grow as developmental nodes of India, sending development impulses to their hinterlands, and must not become cancerous and cruel metropolises!! For that, we need to have change-embracing urban policies in the country. More on these are discussed in chapter 22.

Brief Summary of This Chapter

The following points regarding migration-urbanization situation in Mega cities now can be highlighted:

- All four mega cities of India are having weak economic structure, with low manufacturing (15–23%) or secondary sectors base, and a very high poor tertiary sectors (comprising 68 to 75%).
- In 1901, they all had small secondary sectors (22 to 41%), and large poor tertiary sectors (54 to 78%). In 2001, secondary sectors further declined (24 to 32%), while poor tertiary sectors rose (67 to 75%).
- Unlike in the West, such mushroom growth of poor tertiary sectors do not reflect development, rather manifest anti-development, as they are created by population explosion, not by industrialization.
- Given these, the masses of incoming illiterate and unskilled migrants find salvage only in poor urban informal sectors, viz., domestic servants, road construction labourers, indigenous transport workers, watchmen, hawkers, vendors, in sundry services. Female migrants also reflect similar low-grade absorption as hawkers, vendors, road construction labourers, maid servants, ayahs, etc. Such informal sectors are characterized by cut-throat competition, low wages, hunger, insecurity, exploitation, and working and living under hazardous or unhealthy condition.
- *Although all such above conditions are negative, still such distressed migration of impoverished humanity is much more desirable, as these permit them to escape hunger and poverty in the origin villages, which are plagued by acute unemployment, recurrent underemployment, village stagnation, extreme poverty and lack of any work in deadly stagnant rural economy.*
- Population growth wise, all these mega cities will occupy distinguished ranks among the top twenty-five mega cities of the world by 2025. It is hoped that they will grow not only in population, but also in prosperity, both for local residents, and incoming migrants. They must serve as the

main nerve centres for the country, and will throw very strong development impulses to respective hinterlands, instead of growing as cancerous megalopolises.

- Such situation in Indian mega cities all the more urges for the need for vigorous development of small and intermediate towns and cities which are hitherto neglected, hence remained backward. This is, because the impending very huge population explosion in India in future will not be contained in villages, and vast streams of poor migrants would crowd into already overburdened mega cities in search for sustenance. Small and intermediate towns and cities must be developed, by channeling investments and creating infrastructures and industries, so that these become alternative centres for attraction for migrants.

17 Poverty and Mobility in India

Underlying Socio-economic, Spatial and Political Processes of Underdevelopment

"Awake, Awake, great one! The world is burning with misery. Can you sleep?"

Swami Vivekananda (1895)
(Complete Work, Centenary Volume VII, 1963: 501)

Six Basic Phenomena of Migration-Urbanization System of India

1. The Phenomenon of Induced Poverty and Underdevelopment in India

India was colonized by the British for 200 years (1757–1947), and some other parts by the French, the Dutch, and the Portuguese conquistadors during 1498–1962. Before that, India was colonized and severely exploited by the Pathans, the Turks, the Muslims and Mughal invaders and conquerors for 750 years (1020 AD till 1857). These were described in numerous books, especially in the famous book by Professor Basham (ANU, 1968): *The wonder that was India, till 1020 AD*. Also most notable study is *Advanced History of India* by R.C. Majumder, Kalikinkar Dutta, et al. (1950). No wonder, that India had undergone severe exploitation and tyrrany since last 1,000 years, manifested deep-seated and induced poverty and underdevelopment, and consequently, have experienced very low-quality migration and low-quality urbanization. Such induced poverty and underdevelopment persist even today (2001s). Indeed, current distressed migration and urban decay in India are just spatial symptoms of its deep-seated nexus of poverty and underdevelopment, which, in turn, were caused by the most cruel historic adversaries, and which had left their odd legacy on uneven spatial landscape, as socio-economic and regional disparities. In fact, distressed migration and urban decay are so insipid phrases for such an agonizing historic and politico-economic processes! (Mukherji, 1981: 1–190) No conventional theory can even barely touch the great truth of severe exploitation and induced poverty and underdevelopment that underlie the mechanisms of poverty-induced migration and urban involution in India. This also holds true for many colonized countries of Afro-Asia and the Pacific.

2. The Phenomenon of Spatial Disorganization

Spatial dimension of unequal socio-economic development, in the once-colonized country, has created disorganization and disintegration of the spatial structure of the economy. Spatial organization usually means the entire system of spatial arrangements of settlements (rural and urban) in a country, economic activities of peoples and places, trade linkages and transport network between them, land-use etc., the functional attributes of places and people and the complex inter-relationships between all those variegated elements. Spatial disorganization, on the other hand, implies distortions, disequilibrium, disharmony, hiatus in the spatial system, antagonism, decay, dependency and lack of internal cohesion and consolidation in that spatial organization of the country (Mukherji, 1981: 1–65). Such spatial disorganization lies at the roots of uneven spatial development, growing differences between favoured and neglected regions and the resultant distressed migration.

3. The Phenomenon of Regional Disparities

In such a former colonial country, as India, certain new ports and cities were set up, emerged and grew up at the expense of older towns and cities, and certain specific regions became favoured and prosperous (which helped in export), to the neglect of the interior regions of the country. Consequently, marked regional disparities and imbalances have sprung up and the gulf between the growing regions and the lagging regions were encouraged and widened. Under such a situation, evidently, labour migration of the males and the females occurred, and is still occurring, from neglected regions to relatively favoured regions. *These are the results of spatial disorganization* – created by the above unjust spatial processes. These are further accelerated by prolonged rural neglect and prolonged urban development bias and persistent regional disparities (Mukherji, 1985a: 252–279; 1991: 203–239).

4. The Phenomenon of Polarized Capital

To make the matter worse, there persisted a markedly uneven distribution of new production enterprises and excessive concentration of capital investments only to a few large metros, ports, and administrative centres (e.g., Kolkata, Mumbai, Delhi, Chennai), at the expense of vast majority of smaller cities, towns, and villages (Mukherji, 1985a, 250–79). But, this capital was not utilized to create more employment; not for incoming migrants. This aspect is called as the phenomenon of *"polarized capital"* in a few mega cities. Consequently, the majority of unskilled/semi-skilled and illiterate/semi-educated migrants, who moved from far-flung villages of surrounding hinterlands, are forced to take up whatever means of subsistence available to them in the overcrowded city slums. So, their distressed migration has ended up in low-grade urban tertiary activities. It is virtually a mobility from rural poverty to urban poverty.

5. The Phenomenon of Distressed Migration

With reference to rural-urban migration, a very complex scenario emerges. In such highly populous country, in the rural sector, such factors as demographic explosion, intense land inequality, continuous breaking of land holdings, disappearance and neglect of traditional village industries, and lack of rural industries or non-agricultural employment have compelled small farmers and landless agricultural labourers to leave poor villages and crowd in the cities (Mukherji, 1993: 1–56). They increasingly gravitate towards the metros, by-passing small towns and cities, as they somehow know that employment are more likely to be there, no matter how low is the pay, nor how low the productivity or job security (Mukherji, 1985a: 253–87). But, their dreams are often shattered, their lives end up in filthy urban slums. *Bastees*, shanty towns and pavement dwellers in many cities of India testify this. This is termed as phenomenon of *"distressed migration"* (Mukherji, 2001; 1–140; 2006, 20–150).

6. The Phenomenon of Urban Decay and Urban Involution

In urban sector, conversely, weak urban economic base, rapid urban population growth, heavy emphasis only upon export (mainly raw materials), neglect of development of domestic markets, growth of only light branches of industries, and very low technology, all have resulted in growth of parasitic urban centres, with a feet of clay !. In short, urban growth has occurred, but without development and socio-economic strength. Metros serve more as focal points of collection of raw materials for export, rather than as development poles to diffuse growth impulses to their respective hinterlands. Since these metros have very limited employment generating capacity, under capital-intensive industrialization and very limited absorptive capacity in the organized sector, the incoming illiterate and unskilled labour migrants, thus, find salvage only in bazaar-type or informal sector activities, such as, porters, domestic servants, hawkers, vendors, construction workers, etc. *So, urban involution, rather than evolution, is taking place.* That is, metropolises are now becoming merely overblown villages, without internal consolidation and prosperity. Quality of life is fast deteriorating, instead of evolving. This is termed as phenomenon of "*Urban Decay and Urban Involution*" (Mukherji, 1991: 203–49). Together, the entire aspect is called phenomena of "*Distressed Migration and Urban Decay*" (Mukherji, 1993: 1–86, 2005: 65–85). Hence, the *six* basic elements of the system are: (a) widespread poverty and underdevelopment, (b) spatial disorganization, (c) regional disparities (d) polarized capital mainly into primate cities, (e) distressed labour migration, and (f) urban involution, all are causally linked (Figure 17.1). These complex nexus are responsible for such low quality migration and low quality urbanization in India.

The Process: Broad Picture

As illustrated in schematic diagram (Figure 17.1), the causal widespread poverty and induced under-development led to spatial disorganization, which, in turn, led to regional disparities. Regional disparities are, in turn, accentuated due to further polarized capital around a few favoured ports and metropolises. This capital is not available for rural development. Consequently, the villages are reeling under abject poverty. Rural poverty and village stagnation have led to distressed migration of the rural poor and workers to escape from poverty. They have *a hunch that chances of getting some kinds of sustenance will increase with the city size. Finally, huge male migration of the millions occur to their urban El-Dorado's. This has led to acute urban decay, and swelling of urban poverty. Eventually, the result are urban involution and acute urban decay.* The annexed schematic diagram shows causal linkages in India. These are also valid for similarly placed developing countries.

Figure 17.1 *Schematic Diagram showing Processes of Poverty and Underdevelopment and Spatial Disorganization and Low Quality Migration and Urban Involution in India, and Similar Developing Countries*

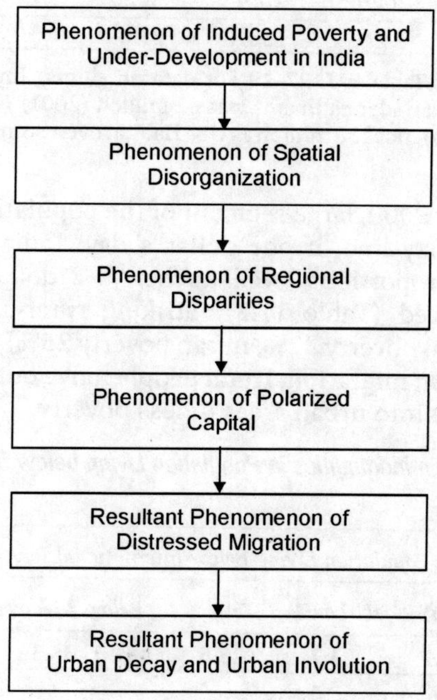

Source: Author (see Text)

In short, large cities and mega cities are growing everywhere in India, but slums also growing faster; and poverty, agony, exploitation; humiliation, inequalities, and unhappiness also multiply tremendously. These are indeed manifestations of iniquitous society and faulty planning. These are symptoms of under-development (or anti-development) and spatial disorganization, not development!

Some Evidences of the Process

Parasitic urban centres and proliferation of urban informal sectors: Rural migrants have to make quantum jumps to Mega cities or coastal metropolises, bypassing small local towns, because, like the flow of capital and commodities to such nodes, the human labour are also compelled to move under the pull of the same centrifugal forces. They somehow get absorbed in the urban informal sectors, because these are the only means available to the illiterate or semi-literate migrants for survival. *Some evidences of such situation of poverty and inequality in India are presented below* (see Mukherji, 2011, chapter 11).

1. *Urban Slums:* In 2001, India had 56 per cent of its urban population under slums (UN-Habitat, 2007: 27–29) (Table 17.1). Such huge proliferation of slums testifies massive migration of rural poor to large cities in a developing country, as well as incapability of cities to provide minimum shelter to such humongous ebbs of humanity!

Table 17.1 *Urban Slums in India, 2000–2020*

Country	Urbanization (%)		Slums (million)		Slums as (%) of Urban Pop.
	2000	2020	2001	2020	2001
India	27.7	34.4	158.4	219.8	55.5

Source: UN-Habitat (2007), Table B-3: 27–29 For data on slums, Town and Country Planning Organization of India under-estimates it as 62 million (2001) (vide UNDP, Urban Poverty Report of India, 2009), not 158 million as UN-Habitat overestimates. True figure seems lies in between.

2. *Poverty:* Even in 2000, large segment of the population in India live below the international poverty line of one dollar a day: India (35%) (UN-Habitat, 2007: 48–50). Their proportions swell further, if 2 dollars a day poverty line estimates are considered (Table 17.2). Striking rural-urban differences also emerge, viz. India (rural poverty 32%, urban poverty 25%) – which lie at the root of massive rural to urban migration. Rural people move out to escape widespread rural poverty and move into urban areas of less poverty.

Table 17.2 *Rural-Urban Inequalities in Population Living below International Poverty Line, 2000*

Country	Year	Population Living Below International Poverty Line (%) (2000)				
		Rural%	Urban%	Total%	Below $1/day (%)	Below $2/day (%)
India	2000	30.2	24.7	28.6	35.3	80.6

Source: UN – Habitat (2007), Table B-10: 48–50.

Migration only as survival strategy: Although they somehow survive in the Mega city at the most minimum level of living, there is very little scope for upward social mobility. They continue to live at the same low level of existence in the cruel city, even after 30 or 40 years. This results in massive waste of human resources and national potential. Briefly this is the central idea of underlying processes. Planning strategies are discussed in the last section.

3. *Income Inequality and Land Inequality:* Wide socio-economic inequalities are prevalent in India, which cause people to migrate (UN, 2007: 48–50). Income inequality is considerably high in India (0.33) (Table 17.3). Land inequality is also very much prevalent, i.e., large land holdings are owned by a few privileged people, while the masses of petty farmers own very small parcels of land. Their hand-to-mouth existence triggers their out-migration from tottering villages!

Table 17.3 *Income Inequality and Land Inequality, India, 2000*

Countries	Income/Consumption Inequalities: Gini Coefficients (2000)	Year	Land Inequalities: Gini Coefficients
India	0.33	1980	0.55

Source: UN-Habitat (2007), Table B-10: 48–50.

Note: Land Inequality data for recent year is not available in UNDP. Agricultural census of 1980 provided data, based on which Gini coefficient for land inequality computed, which comes about 0.55 in 1980. Recent data must be showing much higher land inequality (also see Mukherji and et al. (1980), *Population, Land Inequality and Insecurity: A Geography of Hunger in India,* for details of land inequality in India.

4. *Income Level and Income Inequalities between the Rich and the Poor:* UN (2009: 52–54) provides very useful data regarding per capita GDP and degree of income inequality (Table 17.4). In 2007, India had US (PPP) $2753. Noteworthy features are: (a) one third (31%) of income are shared by the richest 10 per cent, (b) only less than 4 per cent of income are shared by the poorest 10 per cent, (c) thus, it has deep-set income inequality, apart from poverty. Such complex web of factors like widespread poverty and intense income inequality act as drivers for human mobility in such formerly colonized developing nations. So, poverty is the socio-economic context or "social field" from which migration arises in developing countries and the poor try to escape to survive elsewhere.

Table 17.4 *GDP and Measures of Inequality in India, 2007*

HDI Rank	*Country*	*Per Capita GDP (PPP, US$)*	*Per Capita GDP annual growth rate (%)*	*Share of (%) income*		*Inequality Measure*	
				by Poorest 10%	*by Richest 10%*	*Richest 10% to Poorest 10%*	*Gini index (out of 100)*
2007		*2007*	*1990–2007*	*2007*	*2007*	*2007*	*2007*
134	India	2753	4.5	3.6	31.1	8.6	36.8

Source: UNDP, 2009, Table M.For per capita GDP growth rate, average of period taken. PPP means purchasing power parity in income (in a local currency (Rs) converted into US dollar equivalent, in terms of purchasing power parity).

5. *Comparative Human Development Index (HDI) of India:* UN (2009: 62–66) used three indicators for determining HDI: per capita GDP, life expectancy at birth, and adult literacy rate (above 15 years). Table 17.5 presents UN Human Development Index for India as 134, out of total 195 countries. Thailand has 87 rank, followed by the Philippines' 105, and Indonesia's 111 rank. Their lower HDI ranks testify that they belongs to lower middle income level and also lower HDI level. Besides, in last column another measure is given: per capita GDP rank minus HDI rank. Here, positive sign in per capita GDP rank minus HDI rank means that the country has performed better in HDI index than in GDP index. Negative sign means just the opposite. Here, India has performed better in GDP index than in HDI index. That is, social inequalities are much more in India, compared to other countries. For example, in India, in spite of 8–9 per cent annual growth of economy during last decade (1991 onwards), poverty, inequality, and backwardness are still very rampant; consequently, massive migration of 96 million occurred during 1991–2001. Combined with income inequality and poverty, such manifold indices testify the presence of many socio-economic maladies in India, even today. These are also persistent reflection of their past historical colonial (or neo-colonial) legacy. Migration of rural agricultural labourers arose in the past, and arises even now, from such iniquitous socio-economic-spatial context in which they are imbedded. Policy wise, we must provide remedies to such maladies.

Table 17.5 *HDI Index, GDP Index, and Difference between Them in South and South-East Asia, 2007*

HDI Rank	*Countries*	*HDI Index*		*Life expectancy at birth (in years) @*	*Adult literacy rate (15 yrs+) @*	*GDP index @*	*Per capita GDP rank minus HDI rank*
2007		*2000*	*2007*	*2007*	*1999–07*	*2007*	*2007*
134	India	0.55	0.61	63.4	66.0	0.55	–6
111	Indonesia	0.67	0.73	70.5	92.0	0.60	10
105	Philippines	0.72	0.75	71.5	93.4	0.59	19
87	Thailand	0.75	0.78	68.7	94.1	0.73	–5

Source: UNDP (2009), Tables M, G, H. @ show indicators used for calculating HDI index. For Adult literacy rates average of period taken. Positive sign in per capita GDP rank minus HDI rank means country performed better in HDI index than in GDP index. Negative sign means just the opposite.

6. *International and Internal Migration in Four Asian Countries:* In the context of afore-mentioned socio-economic situations, we need to view their impacts on internal migration (also international migration). But, lack of detailed migration data is a great hindrance to such an attempt. Whatever rudimentary data are available (UN, 2009: 100–126), show massive internal migration in India (42 millions during 1990–2005) (Table 17.6). However, here data for lifetime internal migration in India is shown wrong, which should be 314 millions in 2001 (not mere 42 millions) and 96 millions during 1991–2001 alone (Census of India, 2001(b). *Such massive flows of humanity (continuously 10 million per year in India) definitely arise, not out of simple rural push and urban pull mechanism, rather arise out of a complex syndrome of poverty-underdevelopment-spatial disparities-socio-economic inequalities (discussed above), and it demands Himalayan task of socio-economic reconstruction*! Also noteworthy aspects (Table 17.6) are: high emigration rates of the Philippines (4%) and Thailand (1.3%), and high internal migration rates of the Philippines (12%) and Indonesia (4%). Internally displaced people are also considerable.

7. In sum, such migrations are spatial symptoms of induced spatial disparities, poverty and social inequalities. The complex nexus of rampant poverty, intense income inequality and land inequality, low levels of human development, lopsided urbanization, high urban primacy, neglect of other urban nodes, huge urban slums, very wide regional disparities, so forth – the conditions which arose during past historical adversaries, and continued during Post Independent and planning era, are still operating even today. And, these are determining massive human mobility in such countries, both in the past and the present, as well. Such situations and their spatial symptoms – migration and urbanization – will aggravate in future, especially when accelerated by globalization processes! (Mukherji, 2011, chapter 11).

Table 17.6 *International and Internal Migration in South and South-East Asia, 2007*

HDI Rank	*Country*	*Immigration Share of Pop (%)*		*Emigration Rate (%)*	*Lifetime Internal Migration*		*Total internally displaced people (000)*
					Total migration (000)	*Migration rate (%)*	
2007		*1960*	*2005*	*2000–2*	*1990–2005*	*1990–2005*	*2008*
134	India	2.1	0.5	0.8	42,000	4.1	500
111	Indonesia	2.0	0.1	0.9	8,100	4.1	150–250
105	Philippines	0.8	0.4	4.0	6,900	11.7	314
87	Thailand	1.8	1.5	1.3	n.a.	n.a.	n.a.

Source: UNDP (2009), Tables A and L. For internal migration rate, average of period taken. For total migration, most recent data for country taken. For India, data here for lifetime internal migration is wrong, which should be 314 million in 2001, and for 1991–2001, 96 million.

Problems of Migration in India and Required Planning Perspectives

The crucial problems of migration and economic underdevelopment in India and similar developing countries are fully discussed in another detailed study (Mukherji, 1981: 1–189). And, some strategies are also highlighted there for relieving human problems associated with migration and economic underdevelopment. Over time, as I have made many migration and urbanization studies, these were updated, but mostly remained the same (over last 30 years 1981–2010). In India changes do not occur over night, and modernization of economy of villages are almost rare and the towns remain same parasitic. Top of all, there is an utter lack of "Planning for the Poor", all through these 63 years (since Independence in 1947). All planning and development are made for the handful of rich, the privileged and the educated few, at the expense of over 500 million poor in India.

Some such discussions were also detailed in chapter 3 of this book. Presently, in chapter 17, a summary and an overall insight into the underlying processes that are still continuing during last 63 years are highlighted.

These problems and underlying causes and processes are very briefly highlighted in the following (Figure 17.1)

Problems of Low Quality Migration and Urbanization in India

1. Peasants, labourers and other workers are not gainfully employed in rural areas.
2. Acute village stagnation, and poor level of living.
3. Underdeveloped areas and regions within the country.
4. Migrants are uprooted and forced to move to urban centres and other regions.
5. Migrants not gainfully employed in the destinations.
6. Migration moves do not improve their economic condition much.
7. Waste of human resources and human potentials.
8. Urban decay, congestion, and urban involution.
9. Draining out of rural human potentials.
10. Backward migrant-source regions remain backward.

11. National growth and development process remain slow.
12. National reconstruction efforts not integrated.
13. The problem perpetuates and continually aggravates over time.
14. No migration planning, nor awareness of these problems among scholars, planners and administrators.

Causal Reasons and Underlying Processes

15. Overall poverty in India induced due to 1,000 years of foreign rules, repeated invasions, tyranny and colonization (since 1020 AD).
16. Colonial adversaries.
17. Induced poverty in India and its persistence even now.
18. Induced underdevelopment in India which was once a wonder and a very rich country with great resources and people (that's why invaders came to loot since one millennium). Since then, plundering and induced poverty continued unabated.
19. People were enslaved the during past 1,000 years (since 1020 AD).
20. Thus, utter slave mentality became imbedded and continued even today (2000s).
21. Unfavourable terms of colonial trade, and unfavourable balance of payments.
22. Distorted spatial economy of the country and various regions.
23. Regional economic imbalances, and disparities.
24. Certain regions and foreign enclaves grew more rapidly than others (due to export, cash cropping, plantations, favoured trade linkages, favoured ports, and capital investment therein).
25. Neglect and disappearance of all village crafts and rural industries.
26. Disarticulations between rural and urban areas.
27. Disarticulations between agriculture and industry.
28. Spatial inequalities and social inequities.
29. Agricultural underdevelopment.
30. In Post-independent period, neo-colonialism pervaded in all sections of government and its policies.
31. Population pressure on meagre amount of land and population explosion continued unabated.
32. No effective fertility control measures were ever advocated, nor practiced due to evil some minority vote bank politics. So, India now has 1.25 billion population in 2010, and soon going to be the largest populous country in the world, without jobs for hundreds of millions of unemployed youths.
33. It will aggravate problems of crime, violence, violent Naxal (Maoist) movements, more corrupt governments and bureaucrats, grabbing limited power and limited money, and all attendant population problems of high infant mortality, high fertility, acute child malnutrition, and widespread social, economic and political inequities.
34. Mal-distribution of income between different social classes, and different regions.
35. Consequent persistent regional disparities and social inequities, triggering massive migration of poor peasants, landless labourers and artisans. to relatively prosperous rural regions, cities and mega cities.

36. Planning never took account of migration problems, never in the past, nor even now in 1990s and 2000s.
37. Planning not oriented to use local manpower supply and human or economic resources in rural regions.
38. Planning never meant for the poor.
39. Planning never made to benefit 500 million poor in India, living in stagnant villages and dirty urban slums (in 2005, World Bank Report, 2008).
40. Planning not geared to provide labour-intensive industries, neither in villages, nor in towns. Where will labourers go? Such questions never given due focus in studies, in planning, or in government's policies.
41. Planning overburdened with the Western models and sectoral development. Ad-hocism in planning persisted, not total planning for solution of the problems, nor for the future.
42. Neo-colonialism pervades through the minds of the planners and administrators, and lack of commitment to development of the Nation,
43. Increasing socio-economic-spatial inequalities, and thus movement of people from rural to urban poverty.
44. During the last 63 years (1947–2010) very acute and very widespread poverty deepened in villages, in interior parts of country, and in backward and neglected regions.
45. Backward and neglected states always remained backward and neglected (viz., Uttar Pradesh, Bihar, Madhya Pradesh, Rajasthan, Orissa, West Bengal, and North-Eastern Indian states) – from where the poor migrants continued to move to favoured and more developed states, as they did since last 100 years.
46. Rampant and most evil politics has pervaded and ruled India since Independence and increasingly more evil politics became ingrained in all political parties of the country. Consequently, the common people suffered and still suffering greatly. Evidence: about 100,000 poor farmers have committed suicide in Maharashtra and Andhra Pradesh alone in last 5 years (2004–9), but not a ripple came in the news-media or electronic media, nor government's policies or actions. Same way in all other fields.
47. Another very crucial evidence: over 50 millions illegal Bangladeshi in-migrants have invaded India and illegally settled all over India, but neither common people raised this as most important issue, nor any political parties did anything to urge this as the most dangerous issue, which challenge the very core of India's demography, politics, economy and society, and eventually will usurp India's very existence! This problem is more dangerous than nuclear bombs from Pakistan.
48. In this respect, the states' and central Governments are not only mute spectators, rather great facilitators of such evil practices (by providing them with ration cards and voters identity cards), simply for narrow minority vote bank politics. Eventually, this terrible problem will cause India's great disaster and ultimate dissolution! But everybody is mute spectator, rather many are providers of this illegal and anti-national activities (for few bucks).
49. Very rampant and acute corruption have spread in all spheres of lives and all activities in India, specially in politics, judiciary, police, *babu-dom* (administration and public offices), executives, administrations, all

government bodies and functions, machineries and policies and their implementation. No wonder that the poor masses suffer silently, without any solutions in sight. They migrate to their dream cities, but with no permanent redress to their poverty situation. Immobile majority are mute sufferers.

50. *Thus, the same poignantly sad story of migrants and common people continues, as expressed in the beginning of chapter 11.*
51. Thus, no change came in "Spatial Structure of economy" of India, consequently, nor in migration patterns.
52. Globalization, privatization and liberalization are indeed cruel forces and unjust processes, which are really meant to immensely benefit a handful of excessively privileged and exploitative groups, at the cost of the poor masses who are now pushed to the wall, and they are increasingly compelled to out-migrate from acutely poverty-stricken villages for survival, elsewhere. Violent Naxal or Maoist movements, spreading over 200 disrticts of India, are also rooted therein.
53. Unless these evil forces and processes are changed, the same uneven spatial structure of India will remain, the same unjust socio-economic and regional inequities will continue, and as results, the same distressed migration and urban decay will continue for many decades, even many centuries!! More than that, it is feared that, violent Naxalite movements may soon spread to all 605 districts of India!!!

Required Changed Planning Perspectives

54. Need land reforms to benefit the rural poor.
55. Need "Planning for the Poor".
56. Need restructuring the space economy.
57. Rural regeneration and irrigation facilities.
58. Area development and regional development.
59. Rural industrialization.
60. Reduce regional economic imbalances.
61. New orientation in community development programmes: participatory, administrative, institutional.
62. More equitable distribution of income, wealth, consumption and investment among classes.
63. More equitable distribution of means of production, and consumption, and productive units among regions.
64. Fertility control and more comprehensive population policies for all communities.
65. Raising the status of women and women empowerment, and consequent dampening of fertility levels.
66. Maximum efforts of providing mass employment.
67. Identification of backward regions and their development.
68. Optimum rural-urban balance policy for their respective growth and development.
69. Identify and eliminate barriers from the migration fields of people, castes and communities for their free field adjustments according to their basic needs, resources and field forces. In short, make their migration and adjustment to new destinations easy and comfortable. These ideas were

suggested 35 years ago by the present author (Mukherji, 1975: 1–378; 1981, 2006). Very recently UNDP (New York, Jakarta and Bangkok, 2009) have borrowed these ideas of present author (published many times four decades ago), without acknowledging it, and have advised to free all barriers from the migrant's work and all activities in the destinations.

70. Reorient spatial linkages from external dependency to internal domestic markets within the country.
71. Relieving the country and regions from poverty and underdevelopment.
72. Migration planning for the poor labourers/workers so that they are gainfully employed, contributing to National development.
73. Need deep-seated love for the Motherland, India, at all levels, in child rearing, education, work, everyday living, politics, planning, administration, government's activities and all programmes.

Required Paradigm Shift for Migration Planning

74. Integrate people's migration-mobility with programmes for agricultural development in rural India.
75. Integrate migration planning with economic planning of the country.
76. More allocation of growth efforts and investments to migrant-source regions, for their development.
77. No migration-restriction from rural areas should be advocated. Rather need more constructive efforts for self-sustained growth and development of villages.
78. Provide short and effective training to migrants to cities, transforming them into skilled operatives.
79. Rural plans and programmes so that villagers derive more benefits from their labour and produce, and required to pay less to urbanites for goods and services of daily needs.
80. Reorient exports, such that, instead of raw materials, processed goods and commodities are exported from villages and local people draw their due share of benefits, and raise levels of consumptions, income and productivity.
81. Urban renewal programmes for urban evolution, instead of the present-day trends of urban involution.
82. Mass employment generation in rural and urban areas, by maximum utilization of local human and physical resources.
83. Transfer of surplus army of unemployed from agriculture to cottage and agro-industries, dairying and livestock rearing, consumer goods and capital goods industries.
84. Reorient credits, institutional agencies, trade and transport linkages, resources use, investment and growth efforts, away from excessive exportation and external dependency relations, rather towards development of poorer people in hitherto-neglected regions within India.
85. Development of small towns, by setting up more productive units and making institutional changes.
86. Transform the roles of present-day parasitic cities, making them centres of development that will diffuse development impulses to surrounding regions.
87. Integrated area development programmes to be thoroughly envisaged and rigorously implemented.

88. Need very strong political will, stringent economic discipline, and sense of commitment to the Nation, India, without which none of above objectives can be actualized (evidence of last 63 years prove that).
89. Needs real character-building, high moral living, Patriotism and Love for the Motherland, India. Without these, present-day mad race among the youth and everyone, just living only for self-aggrandizement, result in no concern for the nation, and fast leading this noble country, to further turmoil.
90. Repeated violent terrorist attacks are hell bent on fragmenting and bleeding this country, India. But, alas, no body cares. The police, military, intelligent services, and big government – no body really cares. Rampant corruption at every level, dirty politics only for grabbing power and money for selfish motives, total lack of concern for the poor masses, and utter absence of concern for the Nation – all these are, unfortunately, leading to ultimate calamity and devolution of this former great Nation.

In India, now no body even talks about such turmoil and no body even ready to listen. It appears that scholars and planners are not ready to even discuss such crucial processes and evil forces that are leading to India's destruction. Most of one billion plus population of this former great Nation now prefer to remain mute spectators, as ever ...

The same Poverty-Induced Migration and Urban Decay May Continue for Decades

If these evil and unjust socio-economic and political processes are not completely wiped out, I am very much afraid, that the same kinds of poverty-induced migration and acute urban decay will continue for many decades, until the entire migration-urbanization system will break open, leading to utter catastrophe. Recent violent agitation and protests by some political parties in Mumbai and Maharashtra – "against the outsiders" (i.e., migrants from Uttar Pradesh and Bihar) have created a most volatile situation. Additionally, recent violent protests from the (un)civil urban societies against the hapless peasant migrants to the city of Mumbai and New Delhi are unholy symptoms of persistent problems (Raju, 2009: 1–45). Dangers are lurking at large: soon Kolkata, Chennai, Hyderabad, Ahmedabad or Bangaluru or other million cities may catch up such undesirable violence against the migrants. In turn, the migrants may also be tempted to take up to violence, and India will be shattered into pieces. That will be very hefty price to be paid, for our centuries-old neglect of this crucial syndrome of poverty-underdevelopment- low-quality- migration-urbanization!

Top of all, there are other dangerous signals of ultimate dissolution of this great nation, briefly discussed above. Without character-building and Nation-building education of all its citizens, as propounded by Swami Vivekananda long ago (1896), it seems that very little prospects lie for India in future.

18 Summary of Findings

2001 Census Situations

"Be fearless, the Lord is with you, and He will yet raise the starving and ignorant millions of India"

Swami Vivekananda (1894)
(Complete Work, Centenary Volume V, 1963: 23–24)

Summary of Findings of Part II

First, the volume and patterns of migration of 2001 census are meticulously analysed at *six* different scales of investigation: (1) All-India, (2) district, (3) state, (4) class I city, (5) million city, and (6) mega city levels. A series of simple bi-variate regression analyses were performed between: (a) volume and rates of migration in the geographical units (districts, states, class I cities, or million cities) (as dependent variable), and (b) socio-economic variables of those units (independent variables). This is performed at each level of investigations. A series of regression equations were generated, linking each time, a specific migration variable with a specific socio-economic variable. *Such regression linkages have yielded, as we shall summarize later, many useful and meaningful results.* These comprised the subject matter of Chapters 10 to 16. Chpter 17 presents spatial and socio-economic-political processes underlying poverty-induced migration and urban decay in India, and similar countries, and now summarized here. Chapter 18 briefly summarizes all major findings of data analysis of 2001 census (chapters 10 to 17).

I. All-India Findings

According to 2001 Census, a total 314.6 million people were recorded as migrants for all durations. In a country of 1.016 billion population (in 2001), this implies almost every third Indian is a migrant (31%). Of them, 93.4 million were males and 221.2 million were females; indicating the predominance of female mobility. This is because of massive marriage migration among the females, due to prevalent social custom of migration of the wives to the husband's village/towns after marriage.

1. Broad Migration Patterns

During 1991–2001, however, 98.3 million were migrants: 32.9 million males and 65.4 million females. Considerable variations between male and female migration patterns are also notable:

- As regards internal migration, the females move from rural to rural (64%); for males this share is much less (36%).
- Rural-urban migration is predominated by the males (31%); the female's share is only 16%.
- Females primarily move short distances, within the district (61%), between rural areas (47%). About 26 per cent are inter-district migrants and only 13 per cent are inter-state migrants. Corresponding proportion for the males are 43, 22, 30 and 26 per cent, respectively. So, inter-state migration is more male dominated.
- With respect to rural-urban migration, volume-wise male and female migrants are not much different at intra-district, inter-district and inter-state levels. But, proportion-wise the females depict decreasingly a smaller share of the total female migration. Therefore, rural-urban migration is also relatively male selective.
- Similar patterns are seen for urban-urban migration.
- In general, the females are in majority in urban-urban migration, while males predominate in rural-urban migration, especially at longer distances.

2. Four Components of Migration, 1991–2001

- Out of total 98.3 million during 1991–2001, 61.8 million (63%) moved to rural areas and 36.5 million (37%) moved to urban areas. During 1991–2001, rural to rural migration was 53.4 million (56.8%), rural to urban 20.6 million (22%), urban to rural only 6.3 million (6.6%) and urban to urban, 14.4 million (15%). Majority was rural-ward migration (63%) and urban-ward migration, only 37 per cent.
- Rural-urban migration was still mere 22 per cent of total decadal migration. However, it increased substantially from 16.8 million (21%) during 1981–1991 to 20.6 million in 1991–2001, an increase of 23 per cent. Even such increase in rural-urban migration may cause great urban problems in future.

3. Variations in State-level Migration Patterns

Specific concern here is migration of men and women for employment, about which notable features are:

- Compared to the males, the females make much less moves for employment in all the states.
- Males report 30–60 per cent rates for employment migration (higher than 1981–1991); rates for females vary between 4 and 8 per cent in most states.
- For most of the states, migration rates for both males and females are comparatively higher for rural-urban and urban-urban patterns than for rural-rural and urban-rural components; because the chances of obtaining work are higher in urban nodes; except in a few exceptions, where rural development have progressed to some extent (Kerala, Tamil Nadu, Andhra and Karnataka).

4. Inter-state Migration Flows, 1991–2001

Noteworthy features are:

- Uttar Pradesh, Bihar, Tamil Nadu, Kerala, Madhya Pradesh and Rajasthan are main migration-source regions both for males and females. Karnataka and Andhra Pradesh are secondary sending regions. These are all less economically developed states from which they move out.
- Maharashtra, Delhi, Gujarat, Karnataka, Madhya Pradesh, Punjab, Haryana, and West Bengal are main migration-destination states for both males and females. They are economically developed states towards which workers move for employment. Kerala, Tamil Nadu, and Andhra also get some migrants from neighbouring states.
- In most states, both the males and the females are drawn towards urban nodes, to the centres of production and trade-commerce; with exceptions in rural parts of Haryana, Kerala, Karnataka and Gujarat – where agricultural development has recently occurred.
- Notable point is that migration occur as spatial responses to regional disparities in the levels of economic development in India: moves arise from less economically developed states (Uttar Pradesh, Bihar, etc.) to comparatively more developed states (Maharashtra, Delhi, Punjab, Haryana and partly West Bengal).
- Maps of inter-state migration of males and the females are almost identical; only difference is that volumes are much higher for the males. Migration-source states and migration-receiving states are the same; so also underlying macro socio-economic-political-spatial forces that cause regional disparities in economic development, inducing migration over space.
- Likewise, migrations patterns towards main mega cities (Mumbai, Kolkata, Delhi, Chennai), by both the sexes, are strikingly very similar to that of inter-state patterns. The difference is only in volumes. These patterns remarkably indicate spatial responses to distinct regional disparities.
- The same patterns can also be seen, if compared with that of prior five decades (since 1951–61). In fact, the same patterns were prevailing since the first Indian census, from 1872 onwards. The migration patterns did not change since last 130 years, because the spatial disorganization persisted all these years in the country. Unfortunately, it might also continue another many decades, unless and until we make very strong efforts to develop small towns and small cities and re-configure India's spatial organization in favour of development of internal domestic markets.
- In India, both the males and the females, are under the influence of the same nexus of macro historic-economic-political forces and spatial processes that generated and still maintain poverty, regional imbalances and under-development over the national space and induce migration to arise and proliferate. These are still in force. And will continue in future.

5. Various Aspects of Migration According to 2001 Census

(a) *Migration according to Place of Birth statistics:* About 181.8 million people were enumerated in other places but within the district of enumeration. Additionally, 76.8 millions were enumerated in other districts within the same state. Thus, *intra*-state migration is very large, 258 millions.

(b) *Inter-state Migration (according to Birth-Place statistics):* Besides, 42 millions migrated from other states (47% males, 53% females, males' share slightly increased from last census). Of them, the largest number of migrants moved from Uttar Pradesh, followed by Bihar, and some from Madhya Pradesh, Karnataka and Andhra Pradesh. Moreover, substantial volume of migrants was also displaced from Kerala, Rajasthan and Orissa. These ebbs and flows are shown in the four migration maps (Chapter 10). Such massive migration streams prove that the migrants move towards all parts of India and very unique in the world.

(c) *Migration according to Place of Last Residence, 2001:* Total migrants, according to place of last residence, were 314.5 millions; of which majority are females (232 millions). Compared to 1981–91 period, volume of migration has considerably increased during 1991–2001. During earlier decade, total migrants were 227 millions, it rose to 314.5 millions by 2001. In a country of 1.016 billion population, this emerges as 31 per cent (27.3% in 1991), or *almost every third person in India is a migrant.*

(d) *Rural-Urban Components and Short-distance vis-à-vis Long-distance Migration:* Within short distance (*intra*-state) migration, majority of the male migrants moved from rural areas (54%), 46 per cent moved from urban places (changed much from 1991). Corresponding share of female migrants were 80 per cent and 20 per cent (same as before). However, their proportions changed much in regard to long-distance (inter-state) migration: viz., rural male migrants share 63 per cent (59% in 1991) and urban male migrants comprised only 37 per cent (31% in 1991); whereas corresponding share of the rural female migrants were 65 per cent (66% in 1991) and urban female migrants, 35 per cent (34% earlier). Thus, for longer distances both the sexes appear equally mobile. So, *intra*-district migration is 61.5 per cent, inter-district migration 23.7 per cent, inter-state migration merely 13 per cent and international migration, just barely 1.6 per cent. Other features are as follows:

- *Total Population Migration, Persons, All-India, 1991–2001 and Its parts:* During 1991–2001, 98.3 million migrated, of which majority were *intra*-district migrants (51%), followed by inter-district migration (26%), inter-state migration (20%) and international migration (3%).
- *Total Male Migration, All-India, 1991–2001 and Its parts:* However, for the males, those migration components changed considerably: out of total 32.9 million male migrants, only 43 per cent performed *intra*-district, 29 per cent moved for inter-district, and another 26 per cent moved for inter-state migration. These emerge in much contrast to the picture of total migration (for all persons).
- *Total Female Migration, All-India, 1991–2001 and Its parts:* In comparison, for the females, those components changed substantially: out of a total 65.4 million female migrants, a huge 60 per cent moved for short distance *intra*-district migration, whereas 26 per cent did for inter-district, and only 13 per cent performed inter-state migration. Thus, majority of the females moved short distances (*a la* marriage migration).

6. Reasons for Migration

According to 2001 Census, 315 million migrants moved in between different parts of India. Of which, 30 per cent were males, and 70 per cent were females. Of these migrants, the majority came from within the state (268 million, 85%) and 41.2 million (13%) came from other states. For the males, the most important reason was employment (28%), followed by other miscellaneous (34%), family moved (19%), business (3%), and education (3%). For the females, marriage (70%) was the most important reason, followed by family moved (11%) and miscellaneous (14%). Among the females, education, or business was still not so prominent reason, less than 1 per cent. Thus, for the males the economic motives are the most supreme reasons for migration; whereas for the females, marriage or familial migration is still very important. Indeed, patterns have not changed, in spite of the so-called recent economic development in India.

However, migration for employment is a very important reason for males in states like Uttar Pradesh (64%), Bihar (66%), West Bengal (65%), Orissa (72%), Madhya Pradesh (52%), and also in Tamil Nadu (56%), Kerala (57%), Karnataka (52%) and Andhra Pradesh (52%) – because these states have less economic development. Female employment migration is also significant in Tamil Nadu and Kerala, because of high female literacy.

Reasons for Migration, All-India, All Durations, Males, 2001: Table 10.9 and Figure 10.8 indicate the male migration for all durations: employment migration becomes increasingly important, as we move from *intra*-district migration (15%) to inter-state migration (52%). To a lesser extent, similar trend is also noticeable in migration for business (*intra*-district 1.8%; inter-state 3.9%). The importance for miscellaneous purpose linearly decreases, as migration distance increases (48% for *intra*-district, and 16% for inter-state migration), as cost for moves increases with the distance. So, a distance-decay function operate here.

Reasons for Migration, All-India, all Durations, Females, 2001: Even in 2001, the females moved much less for employment (only 1.7%), and marriage migration consists a huge proportion (70%). Familial reason was also significant (11%), and other purposes (14%). However, as mentioned earlier, a large chunk of those females who moved for familial reason also take up work later in the destinations. Only minute field based investigation of their migration-mobility may reveal such truth. Here, lies the tremendous importance of field-based migration studies and detailed circulation research (*a la* Professor Chapman).

Reasons for Migration, All-India, 1991–2001, Males: During 1991–2001, male migration for employment shoots up noticeably from 25 per cent for *intra*-district moves to as high as 57 per cent for inter-state moves, viz., long-distance migration were undertaken only with a major trigger effect of the dire need for work.

Reasons for Migration, All-India, 1991–2001, Females: Similarly, one notable aspect regarding employment migration among the females is that they are more visible with respect to long distance inter-state migration, rather than short distance *intra*-state migration. Likewise, the same holds true for familial moves (moved with the family). Conversely, female marriage migration represents a distinct distance-decay function (decreasing from *intra*-district to inter-state migration). That is, the females take up long-distance inter-state migration mainly for work, or for familial purposes.

Reasons for Intra-district Migration, Males, 1991–2001: In *intra*-district migration, male employment movements were only 25 per cent, while movements after birth 16 per cent, movements with family 25 per cent, and for other purposes, 21 per cent. Migration for education (7%) or business (3%) was still small.

Components of Inter-district Migration, All-India, 1991–2001, Males: During 1991–2001, notice that employment migration among the males suddenly increases to 39 per cent with respect to inter-district moves, while all other types remain more or less same as in *intra*-district moves.

Components of Inter-district Migration, All-India, 1991–2001, Females: Female inter-district migration is still dominated by marriage migration (58%), followed by familial moves (22%), and other purposes (7%). Migration for education among women is still very tiny (1.7%) and for business almost insignificant (0.3%).

Reasons for Inter-state Migration, All-India, 1991–2001, Males: Most important reason is moves for work (57%), followed by familial moves (22%), and other purposes (10%). Migration for education (3.8%) and for business (3%) are still very minor.

7. Literacy and Illiteracy among Migrants for Employment, 1991–2001

Information about illiteracy and illiteracy of the migrants is a revelation. It shows educational status of two main categories of migrants, who migrated for employment:

(a) the migrants from rural and urban areas within the state, and
(b) the migrants from rural and urban areas, outside the state.

In India, total migration for "employment" for 1991–2001 was mere 14 millions. Of this, 12.0 million (86%) were performed by males, and only 2 million (14%) by females. Majority (74%) moved from rural areas; the rest from urban centres (26%). Strangely, one fifth of all rural male migrants were illiterate; and their share rose even to two-thirds among rural female, who moved for employment. The proportion among urban males and urban females were 9 and 22 per cent, respectively. In sum, considerable proportion of male migrants (60% from rural and 33% from urban areas), who moved for employment, were actually illiterate or semi-educated (below secondary school). Plus, more than 80 per cent of rural female employment migrants were either illiterate or with less than secondary education (40% among urban female migrants). These characteristics reflect a very dismal situation!

However, during 1981–91, only 9.9 million were employment migrants, it rose to 14 millions during 1991–2001, and as such, there were about 41 per cent increase. This is remarkable.

Out of a total 14 million migrants who moved for employment (1991–2001), 8.7 million or 62 per cent came from within state (74% from rural, and 26% from urban). Another 5.3 million (38%) came from outside the state (73% from rural, 27% from urban). Migration from rural still comprised 74 per cent; while from urban areas only 26 per cent. The following additional features may appear:

(a) Among rural "*Intra*-state" migrants, the proportion of illiterate plus semi-educated migrants comprised 53 per cent among males, rising to 75 per cent among females. Corresponding picture of urban illiterate and semi-educated migrants with all durations are slightly better: 29 per cent among males and 41 per cent among females (little improved from past).

(b) Among rural "Inter-state" migrants, the share of illiterate and semi-educated migrants are 66 per cent among males, and 86 per cent among females. Corresponding share of urban illiterate and semi-educated among Inter-state migrants are 37 per cent among males, and 40 per cent among females (improved from the past).

(c) In sum, over half of male migrants from rural areas (53–66%), both from *intra*-state and inter-state migration, comprised of illiterate and semi-educated migrants (with < secondary education). Their share improves to 30–37 per cent among urban male migrants. Corresponding picture is further frustrating among females (75–86% among rural female; and 40% among urban females). Compared to earlier decade, situation further deteriorated among rural female migrants, though some improvements are seen among urban female migrants. More precarious situation also arise among all kinds of migrants, who moved for various reasons, but also seeking employment.

(d) Such low quality migration of poor and distressed people only confirm one of the basic findings of this volume: i.e., poverty-induced migration and urban involution are occurring in India, not yet migration for prospect or high quality urbanization. Indeed, these are signs of anti-development!

(e) Crucial question is: what could be expected from masses of such illiterate/semi-educated migrants? Indeed, it is human mobility from rural to urban poverty. Involves much waste of human potentials and national productivity!

(f) *However, it is never implied that "migration restriction" could be any solution. Contrarily, it is always advised in this volume – that such masses of deprived people would die in the villages, if their only escape route – "migration" is restricted. Thence, even such a low-quality migration is far more desirable than starvation or slow death in stagnated villages. Even such distressed migration is much more beneficial. It is only meant here, that in India, the migrants are not receiving adequate scope for vertical social mobility in urban or rural destinations, and, as such, their lives and rights must be protected. For that, relevant and humane policies should be urgently envisaged and properly implemented.*

8. Illiterates and Semi-educated are Majority among Migrants, 1991–2001

- Total male migration for all durations were 94 millions, and total female migration for all durations 222 millions. Of them, the share of illiterate among male migrants was 28 per cent and among females, 58 per cent.
- Situation worsens among recent migrants with duration less than one year (2000–01): 50 per cent of male migrants were illiterate, rising to 59 per cent among females.

- When semi-educated migrants (less than secondary education, in fact, less than primary), are also considered, their share rise to 65 per cent among males, and 86 per cent among females (for all durations). For migrants with less than 1 year duration, these rise to 79 per cent and 83 per cent, respectively. Similar picture also arises when migrants with duration of residence for 1 to 4 years or 5 years+ seen. The condition of recent migrants (less than 1 year duration) has further deteriorated.
- When semi-educated (less than secondary education) are also included, their proportion shoots up to 66 per cent and 77 per cent (among 1–4 years duration). This is very saddening, given India's recent high economic growth (above 8%), which have failed to give "inclusive growth" to the poor masses!

9. Occupational Categories of the Migrants (All Durations and Rural-Urban), 2001

- With respect to total male migrants, with all durations of residence, 50 per cent are engaged in low-grade production – processing work (Div. 7–8–9). They comprise a large bulk of total male migrant workers, not engaged in sales, services, and not in professional or administrative work. Similar features are also seen among the females migrants (44%).
- Some male workers are also engaged in sales (5% in rural, 8% in urban) and services (18% in rural, 21% in urban). Situation for females follows the suit. Females are comparatively more engaged in services (9% in rural, and 11% in urban), and few in sales (1% in rural, 7% in urban); but these are in fact very low-grade services in informal economy (servants, domestic help, hawkers, vendors).
- With respect to *intra*-district migration, most of the males are engaged in low-grade production process work (49% in rural, 43% in urban), only few in administration (6% in rural, 8% in urban), or clerical work (8% in rural, 7% in urban). Substantial segment are also engaged in services (19% in rural, 22% in urban). Among females, similar features are seen; however, more are engaged in clerical work (5% in rural, 15% in urban), or in services (8% in rural, 11% in urban).
- Among "inter-district" migrants, most males are engaged low-grade production process work (53% in rural, 36% in urban), but a small percentage of males got absorption in professional (9% in rural areas, 9% in urban areas), or administrative (7% in rural, 12% in urban), or clerical work (7% in rural, 9% in urban). Likewise, among the females, a large chunk mainly work in low-grade production-processes (44% in rural, 32% in urban). But, some also work in administrative (4% in rural, 15% in urban), or clerical work (8% in rural, 19% in urban), or sales or services (9% in rural, 11% in urban). However, their number are still very few.
- The position of the males is very precarious. And, the condition of the female migrants are further dismal!
- If all low-grade occupational groups of migrants are added up, it comprises as high as 60 per cent low grade workers among the males, and 65 per cent among the females (for all durations). The majority of them were absorbed only in a *bazaar* type or low-grade urban informal sectors, which are characterized by cutthroat competition, low wages, low productivity, insecurity,

exploitation, and humiliation. These are indeed symptoms of underdevelopment, or anti-development, not development! In fact, *these are symptoms of syndrome of poverty and mobility!!*

- Almost similar features also emerge among the "inter-state" migrant workers, separately for males and females. As high as 66 per cent of rural male workers got absorbed only in low-grade production-process work. Likewise, 57 per cent of the rural females also absorbed. Their urban proportions are 41 per cent and 30 per cent, respectively. Proportions of clerks or service workers, however, increased among both the sexes, in urban nodes.
- In sum, the situation has not improved much in recent years, in spite of tall claims of fast economic spurts during the development decade (8–9% growth, 1991–2001). The poor remained in the same darkness as before. Development has not touched their lives. *Happiness has not visited their homes!* This is the most pitiable condition of the migrants. Indeed, it is a continuing trends of movement of distressed people from one region of poverty to another. From rural unemployment to urban under-employment. From one region of stress to another. Whatever dismal situations were found during 1981–91, have not changed much even during 1991–2001 inspite of globalization! And, whatever rudimentary news are available in 2008–2009, the things appeared to have rather worsened recently.
- Indeed, these are symptoms of persistent poverty and anti-development. In India, recent economic growth and corrupt governance actually help a handful of corporate houses to amass immense super profits, hurting 600 million poor population of India. These findings about migration in India must act as revelations to the students, scholars, social scientists, planners, administrators, and the government.
- *We really need to act urgently for the upliftment of these millions of poor migrants in India, before these lead to a great calamity and a point of no return!*

10. Characteristics of Migrants, Main/Marginal Workers, and Non-workers, All Durations, 2001

- Out of total 93 million male migrants (for all durations), 26 per cent were illiterates, 74 per cent literates (by definition, they can only sign), only 57 per cent were main workers (work more than 6 months/year) and another 6 per cent marginal workers (work less than 6 months/year). Proportionally, male non-workers are quite large (38%). Corresponding pictures of 221 million female migrants for all durations are far more worse: 58 per cent illiterates, only 42 per cent literates, merely 22 per cent main workers, additionally 17 per cent marginal workers, and large chunk (62%) non-workers! Such facts unravel a very pathetic condition of movers. Rural situations are more negative than this overall scene, while urban picture is slightly better.
- Among recent migrants, with duration less than one year, the share of male illiterates increased to 50 per cent, whereas of female illiterates remained 58 per cent, as before. Share of male "main" workers worsens to 45 per cent, while female "main" workers to 19 per cent. Male non-workers swelled to 46 per cent and that of female to 69 per cent!. Compared with

older migrants (with 5–9 years duration), the condition among recent migrants (less than 1 year duration) has further degraded. The lives of helpless hundreds of millions of movers remained untouched, in spite 8–9 per cent economic growth in the development decade. Inclusive development is a myth!

- *Indeed, the government has institutionalized a globalized, liberalized and privatized economy in India, sub-servient to a handful of privileged business families, permitting an increasing number of dollar billionaires among them, in the one hand, and allowing them to enslave over five hundred millions of impoverished humanity of the country, on the other! A great paradox that both exist side by side in India.*
- *Nowadays, the number of (US dollar) billionaires are swelling everyday in India, while at the same time the number of extremely poor people have already crossed 500 million in 2005 (who survive less than Rs 24 per day per capita, i.e., less than US$ 1.25 PPP, at purchasing power parity)(World Bank, 2008).Other estimate puts their number as 77 per cent of total population or over 924 million (chapter 21).*

11. Characteristics of Recent Migrants by Literacy, Main Workers, Marginal Workers, 1998–2001

- Compared to Migration with all durations, situations have not improved, rather deteriorated among the recent migrants, with less than 1 year or 1 to 4 years duration. For instance, share of male illiterates have risen from 21 per cent among older movers (with 5–9 year duration) to 31 per cent among recent movers (1–4 years duration); so also the share of "main" workers among them (declined from 54 to 49%). Similar trends are also noticeable among the females.
- Regarding Circular Migration: statistics from 55th Round of National Sample Survey (1999–2000) put the number of short term circular migrants at 12.6 million. Recent micro-studies documenting large and increasing numbers of internal migrants (often hundreds of thousands) suggest this is an underestimate, could be 30 million, or more.

II. District-level Findings

1. High In-migration Districts and their Socio-Economic Correlates

47 high in-migration districts are identified, out of total 470 districts studied. This set indicates comparatively high in-migration rates (above 4%). Corresponding socio-economic variables of those 470 districts are also analysed, as the correlates. Results are also statistically significant and practically very meaningful.

2. High Out-migration Districts and Their Socio-Economic Correlates

Likewise, 67 high out-migration districts are identified (rates above 4%), out of 470 districts studied. Socio-economic variables of all 470 districts are also analysed.

3. District-level 15 Regression Analyses

Many analyses are performed and briefly discussed in chapter 12. Here, only brief summary is highlighted. Analysis of *intra*-district and inter-district migration (males) and socio-economic variables are performed (2001). Most tables are self-explanatory, and major causal relations are elaborated in the last column, titled "meaning of relationship" in each table.

4. Positive Links between Total Workers of Districts and Male In-migration Rates, 2001

The more volume of total workers of the districts, higher is the male in-migration rates of the districts. Adjusted R-square is 0.25, showing that 25 per cent of variation in male in-migration rates is explained by variations in total workers. Statistical significance is 0.001, i.e., error term is only 1 out of 1,000 observations. Not only this is practically very meaningful, but also statistically very significant. Policy implication: more male in-migration will occur into those districts where more jobs will be generated.

5. Links between Urbanization and Male In-migration Rates of Districts

The more urbanization of the districts, the more male in-migration occurs into them. Relationship is bi-polar, i.e., acts in both directions: more male in-migration also leads to more urbanization. Adjusted R-square is 0.31, explaining 31 per cent of variations (highly significant at 0.001 level). Finding has great policy import. More urbanization and more male in-migration are working in unison, reinforcing each other. This will have attendant plus and minus points also, i.e., swelling of urban poverty, urban slums, urban congestion and shortages of urban services. But, migration *per se* is not at fault, rather lack of government's clear urban and migration policies are.

6. Relation between Male In-migration Rates and Service Sectors of Districts

The more workers in service sectors in districts, higher is the male in-migration rates. Adjusted R-square is 0.16, explaining 16 per cent (at significance 0.001). Policy import: more services will attract more in-migration into districts themselves, instead of their out-migration. So, generating local self-employment in services within the villages will pay great dividends.

7. Links between Tertiary Sectors and Male In-migration Rates of Districts

The more tertiary sectors in economy of the districts, higher is the rates of male in-migration into them. (explains 21% at 0.001 level). In India, tertiary sectors comprise of trade-commerce, transport and services. *This testifies one of the main tenets of this volume that, in India, most of the migrants find salvage mainly in poor tertiary sectors, not in manufacturing/secondary sectors.* So, swelling of tertiary sectors does not signify development. Still, it acts as a safety valve to incoming migrants, who eke out livings in low-grade unorganized work. *Hence, even this is highly desirable to the migrants. Simultaneously, such dismal findings only urge us to seriously "Plan for the Poor" and provide more protection to hundreds of millions of poor migrants in India. Dodging the truth will not help. It will only strengthen the hands of the exploiters and the pseudo-scientists!!*

8. Relation between Secondary Sectors of Districts and Male In-migration Rates

Regression fit is almost perfect, showing that, as secondary sectors increases, the male in-migration also rises linearly (explains 19%). It has great policy import for migration planning: development of manufacturing and construction sectors will re-direct new migrants to such districts.

9. Relation between Total Population of Districts and Volume of Male Out-migration

More population pressure in districts, the more male out-migration from them (explains 18%). This is again a classic example of population dynamics: as population pressure increases, out-migration also linearly increases. Policy implications are: urgent need for fertility control, generation of rural employment, diversification of agriculture and creation of more employment.

10. Less Primary Sectors and Larger Volume of Male Out-migration from Districts

Male out-migration from districts increases as primary sector (cultivation, agricultural labour etc.) decreases, indicating uprooting and out-migration from villages, confirming the same sad story of exploitation and humiliation (explains 7%).

11. More Urbanization, More Out-migration from Districts, 2001

More urbanization, larger is the volume of male out-migration from districts. This reflects the aspiration of some of the youth, explaining 14 per cent (at 0.001). Moves may be education-related or for better prospects. Policy-wise, this finding has much significance, i.e., recent increased urbanization (1991–2001) in some districts is found to be in tandem with both in-migration and out-migration in those districts. Higher quality migration and urbanization are perhaps initiated in India. However, it has a caveat: only small privileged segment of village society usurps such benefits. In general, in India more urbanization has its benefits, as it breaks shackles of barriers of migrants, in which he/she is previously bound in caste-ridden village society, and prompts him/her to search for better luck in free urban settings. So, urbanization and migration are not evil *per se*. Policy-wise, better urban governance and gainful migration must be encouraged. Urban slums are creation of evil builders and slum-lords, who keep artificially sky-rocketing urban land and housing prices, aided with city authorities. Such corruption must be stopped, rather than migration-restriction!.

12. Links between Marginal Workers in Districts and Volume of Male Out-migration

Relation is negative – the more marginal workers, the less male out-migration from districts. But, the meaning is rather positive: less male out-migration occurs where more scope of marginal work is available within the district, no matter how small is the pay, nor how short is working period. This acts as *a safety valve* for the migrants (explains 13%). Conversely, as shown above, a privileged section of community (14%), also move out from more urbanized districts for better prospects, education or business. Both exist side by side in India. Since globalization (1991), now many billionaires live side by side with 500 millions of very poor. Indeed, India has now become a land of unspeakable social and economic inequities! Unjust policies of the government complicated adversities.

13. Relation between Urbanization of Districts and Net Migration of Districts

It is very intriguing, as depicting casual relation between urbanization and male net migration from districts. The relation is positive and *bi-polar: as net migration rises, so also urbanization, reinforcing each other*. In India, in-migration contributes 30 to 40 per cent of urbanization: sometimes, more in case of large cities. They also have concomitant ramifications, discussed in chapter 21.

14. Links between Total Population and Male Inter-district Migration

Larger the total population size, the more inter-district male migration (explains 33%). This follows Gravity model of migration: i.e., the larger the population size of two districts, the more spatial interactions between them!

15. Relation between Total Workers and Male Intra-district Migration

Amazingly high, 48 per cent of variations in the *intra*-district migration are explained by total workers. Regression line makes an almost perfect fit. Finding is significant at 0.0001 level (i.e., the error term is *only* 1 out of 10,000 observations or tests!). Unbelievable Policy import is: we need more inclusive growth, instead of the present-day jobless growth, which puts all benefits only to a handful of privileged families. We urgently need real inclusive growth in favour of the masses of the poor and the under-privileged, both in deadly stagnant villages and urban slums.

16. More Marginal Workers, More Intra-district Male Migration, 2001

More marginal workers in cultivation, agricultural labour and plantation mean more temporary work for them, thus increasing *intra*-district migration, between rural areas (explains 15%). Policy significance is that many labourers actually live on the fringe of the lives, and need protection and more work avenues in countryside. Generation of more rural and agricultural work, both in primary and tertiary sectors, will fruitfully keep them engaged in villages themselves, instead of swelling in remote and hostile places. This will be a good migration strategy.

17. Links between Total Population and Male Intra-district Migration, 2001

Larger the total population of districts, the more volume of intra-district migration (explains 35 per cent, significant at 0.001). This relation simply follows the Gravity model: which spells that spatial interaction (migration) between two places is directly proportional to the product of population of those two places (origins/destinations), and inversely proportional to intervening distances. It has utility in predicting future *intra*-district migration.

18. Links between Total Workers and Inter-district Male Migration, 2001

More total workers, more inter-district male migration (explains 35%). Economic considerations are paramount in movers' decision-making process. Policy import is: more job opportunities must be created in the countryside, in all interior parts of India, to provide gainful employment to incoming migrants, instead of concentrating all capital nodes investments in few ports, and mega cities. There should be an effective planning strategy for redirecting migration to new vistas. Rural infrastructure creation must be coupled with migration-redirection programmes.

19. Links between Tertiary Sectors and Volume of Male Inter-district Migration

More tertiary sectors, more inter-district male migration (explains 14%). Interpretation is same as item above, and casual links are also same. Only caveat is, as noted before, that unlike in the West, in India the proliferation of low tertiary sectors signifies underdevelopment. Still, this is much better than unemployment or starvation in villages, and hence much more desirable! By creating backward and forward linkages between organized and unorganized sectors, we can also easily transform this sea of semi-skilled and semi-educated migrants into an army of highly trained and more productive workers. This is achieved in China, Korea, Malaysia, Taiwan, and Indonesia. Surely, India can also achieve that. Policy significance of this finding is rooted there.

III. State-level Findings

1. Inter-state In-migration Matrix, Males, 1991–2001

As regards males, Maharashtra (1.76 million) and Delhi (1.06 million) are two largest migration receiving states, followed by Gujarat (0.65 million), Karnataka (0.42 million) and West Bengal (0.28 million). Uttar Pradesh (1.9 million) and Bihar (1.15 million) are two largest migration-sending states, where from the movers crowd into Maharashtra, Delhi, and West Bengal. The same patterns can also be seen, during 1981–91, and in all previous censuses. The patterns have not changed since last 100 years, since first census done in 1872 (Mukherji, 1981: 1–278). Everything changes in this planet, but the typical inter-state migration patterns in India never change, simply because wide-spread spatial disorganization persist in India, leading to a very marked regional disparities and social inequities. So, the poor migrants from backward Uttar Pradesh and Bihar are forced to move out and swell in relatively forwarded Maharashtra and Delhi for survival.

2. Inter-state Out-migration Matrix, All-India, Males, 1991–2001

Uttar Pradesh is the state of largest out-migration of males (1.9 million), followed by Bihar (1.1 million). From them, large volume of male out-migration occurs to Maharashtra and Delhi. Reasons are elaborated before. Unless and until these two backward states are given development inputs and infrastructure, and unless their governance is vastly improved, such typical migration due to poverty and underdevelopment would continue for many more decades. *Policy-wise this is the greatest need of the hour. Specially when these migrants from Uttar Pradesh and Bihar now face considerable hostility from local residents at the destinations. Unless these problems are urgently tackled, these dangerous trends may lead to further strife, inter-regional conflicts and extreme violence in the near future.* Indeed, we are making picnics, sitting over eruptive volcanoes.

3. Inter-state In-migration Matrix, Females, 1991–2001

As with the males, so also for the female migrants, the largest receiving states are Maharashtra (1.2 million) and Delhi (0.8 million). Largest sending states are, again, Uttar Pradesh and Bihar. Inter-state migration patterns remain same for 1991–2001, as in earlier decades, and for both the sex. These are age-old migration patterns, since last 100 years!

4. Inter-state Out-migration Matrix, Total, Females, 1991–2001

During 1991–2001, from Uttar Pradesh largest volume of female out-migration occurs (1.4 million), followed by Bihar (0.6 million). They moved to Maharashtra and Delhi, as males also do. Patterns are almost same, as determining factors are also alike.

5. Human Development Index (HDI) and States of High Male In- and Out-migration

Uttar Pradesh and Bihar with lowest HDI Index (in 2000) are the regions of high male out-migration, and Maharashtra, Gujarat, Punjab and Haryana are the regions of high male in-migration. West Bengal has moderate HDI index and also attracts a moderate volume of male in-migration from Bihar. Such causal linkages become more evident when we notice Income Rank of these states, revealing a clear picture of wide regional disparities in income levels between the forward states and the backward states, consequently, causing almost an involutionary out-migration of male labourers from the lagging states to relatively prosperous states. Thus, the causal relationships between "Poverty and Mobility" is very much prevalent in India, during 1991–2001, even today (Mukherji, 2006). *That is, recent higher economic growth in India has not really touched the lives of the poor and the under-privileged, nor is inclusive growth really happening!!*

6. Relations between Human Development Index of States and Volume of Male In-migration, 1991–2001

Higher the human development index (HDI) of states, the more male in-migration into them. HDI index explains 10 per cent of variations in volume of male in-migration into the states (at 0.001 significance).

7. Relations between HDI of States and Volume of Male Out-migration, 1991–2001

Lower the human development index of states, the more male out-migration from them. Negative relationship emerges between the two (explains 27%), almost three times higher than that of male in-migration. This signifies that lack of socio-economic development in the states virtually impel the male labourers to move out for livelihood in the destinations, much more than development is effective in attracting in-migration. Policy import is that, migration in India is still very much poverty-induced, arises mostly due to lack of development, and not due to attraction of neon signs in the mega cities. Nor caused by better prospect. No matter what conventional migration or urban researchers make us to believe, this is the hard reality. *Planning-wise, thence, we must provide minimum development and fulfill their all basic human needs in each village, in each state, and every towns and cities of India. To ignore this reality, is at the cost of our own perils.*

8. Male Inter-state In-migration Rates, 1991–2001 and Urbanization of States, 2001

Urbanization is comparatively high in Gujarat, Maharashtra, Delhi, Punjab, Haryana, and Tamil Nadu. The more urbanization of the states, the higher male in-migration "*rates*" of them, both causally linked. Thus, they have a bi-polar relation, each reinforcing the other. This explains 71 per cent (at 0.0001 level). Such very high statistical result is very rare in social sciences, which usually get 10 to 15 per cent explanation. Policy significance is: in India, migration and urbanization are progressing in tandem, in many progressive states, and may be further reinforced, if conjoined with more industrialization, more employment and inclusive growth that will take care of the poor and the downtrodden.

9. Relation between Main Workers in States and Volume of Male In-migration

More proportion of "main" workers to total workers in states, the more volume of male in-migration into them.(explains 24%). In short, the male migrants move from backward states (Orissa, Bihar, UP) to comparatively developed states (Maharashtra, Delhi, Tamil Nadu), where opportunities of main (not marginal) work are more. This is a mirror image of another finding about massive out-migration from states with more marginal workers.

10. Relation between Service Sectors and Volume of Male In-migration

More workers in service sectors in states, the more volume of male in-migration into them (explains 9%).This is very much akin to the next causal relations – where almost similar linkages emerge between tertiary sectors (which includes services) and male in migration. Significance of the result is also same.

11. Relation between Tertiary Sectors and Volume of Male In-migration into States

The more workers in tertiary sectors in states, the more volume of male in-migration into them (explains 8%). This proves that more migrants are moving where only poor tertiary sectors exist, like trade-commerce, transport and low services, not manufacturing. Because, these provide more work avenues to migrants, not capital-intensive manufacturing, which generates few jobs. Policy-wise, this urges for more forward and backward linkages between informal and organized sectors, to generate more employment for teeming millions of migrants.

12. Relation between Urbanization in States and Vol. of Male In-migration

The more urbanization in the states, the more "*volume*" of male in-migration into them Both increase linearly. Urbanization explains as high 36 per cent of variations in *volume* of male migration (0.0001 level) (*wow*!). Error term is only one out of 10,000 observations, simply remarkable! This shows a catalytic development relation between urbanization and in-migration in developed states, each reinforcing other. But, there is a caveat, such rapid urbanization and male in-migration is not accompanied by industrialization, rather by mushroom growth of low-grade tertiary sectors. Policy-wise, this calls for more development of secondary and modern sectors!

13. Relation between Male Population Pressure of States and Volume of Male Out-migration from them

Male population pressure explains 84 per cent of variations in volume of male out migration. Causal relation is unbelievably high, 84 per cent; such high result is almost never found in social sciences, nor even in physical sciences. Level of significance is tremendously high, 0.00001(error term is only 1 out of 100,000 tests, Unbeatable!!). This indicates an *one-to-one relationship* between the two. The more population pressure in the states, higher is the volume of male out-migration from them. Policy prescriptions are evident: population control, fertility reduction, more job-creation in agricultural and non-agricultural sectors, and development of backward/neglected states, viz., Rajasthan, UP, Bihar, Orissa, MP, West Bengal, and Karnataka.

14. Relation between Male Population of States and Male Out-migration Rates

Male population pressure also explains 15 per cent of male *out-migration rates*. Population control are not rigorously advocated in India by state or central governments (due to narrow minority vote bank politics). So India now has 1.20 billion mouths to feed. Has 500 millions of youthful population to provide jobs. No wonder, that male population pressures in backward states impel them to move out. Thus, policy-wise, family planning and population control measures must be rigorously implemented. More jobs both in public sectors (government sectors) and private sectors are urgently needed, both in agricultural and modern-urban sectors. Only then, an increasingly huge and youthful labour force can get necessary skill and gainful employment. Otherwise, the so-called "demographic dividends" of a youthful population in India may turn out to be a great curse.

15. Very Strong Relations between Volume of Marginal Workers in States and Volume of Male Out-migration

Finding reveals that the more marginal workers persist in the states, the more male out-migration from them. This is a very intriguing finding which very emphatically confirm that more male out-migration prevail from those states, where the scope of "main" workers are limited, rather more "marginal work" predominate (Bihar, UP, Rajasthan, Orissa, Jharkhand, explains as high as 72%. Such picture emerges in sharp contrast to tall claims of India's rapid economic development during the globalization decade. This must be an eye-opener to the scholars, planners, policy-makers, administrators and the governments!

IV. Class I City-level Findings

1. Links between Manufacturing of Class I Cities and Male Migration for Work

Larger the manufacturing sectors in class I cities, the more male migration crowd there for work. This may seem an axiomatic finding. But, this explains only 5 per cent of variation, implying that male employment migration occur more for other centres, where tertiary, services or construction work prevail. *Evidently, that is not a sign of development!*

2. Links between Construction Sectors in Class I Cities and Male Employment Migration, 1991–2001

Male migrants are not absorbed in administrative, professional, nor even in sales or services, rather mainly in construction labour work, in low-grade jobs, that are characterized with low productivity and insecurity (explains 6%). Of course, it protects *dispossessed people from poverty and immediate starvation*, thus even *such migration is desirable*. But, to portray migration in general occurring in India – as "migration leading to development", is untrue, wrong, misleading and weakens the great need for economic reforms and planning for the poor migrants and the common people! Some conventional studies have mis-understood my emphasizing upon the hard reality that migration in India is still "poverty-induced" ("arising out of rural poverty, not due to glitzy pull factors of mega cities"; "migration is still distressed, not leading to much upward social mobility in destinations", or "most migrants absorbed in low-grade sectors"). But the hard reality are just these, as innumerable evidences, even in this volume, testify! Truth must be told bravely, and the underlying unjust processes be unfolded. Then only, correct planning prescriptions will emerge. *This is my true perspective, all through life. But, I never prescribed "migration restriction" in my last 40 years of migration research (1969–2010), nor took a pessimistic view about migration in India. But the hiding the truth either, or misdirecting, does not uphold the great cause of uplifting the lots of hundreds of millions of poor migrants in India, who urgently need our care, protection and pro-poor planning!*. Poverty in India must be liquidated, very soon. Totally! There must not be a conspiracy of silence. Nor misdirecting truth. Let such stereotyped studies, first, explain, why over 500 millions poor exist in India, even in 2005 (World Bank, 2008)? Why are their numbers daily swelling, even in 2010 (perhaps exceeded over 600 millions)? Why urban slum population have risen to 95 million in 2009 (UNDP, Delhi 2009)? Why do mental bankruptcy and paralysis exist among academia and governments regarding great need for planning for the poor? Conventional migration-urbanization research remains mute, blind and without social commitments!

3. Links between City's Total Population and Male Migration for Work, 1991–2001

Larger the size of class I city, the more male migrants attracted to them for employment (explains 7%), because they have the hunch that chances of getting any kind of manual work increases with the city size, where access to low-grade sales, service, or production work also becomes easy.

4. Links between Secondary Sectors of Class I Cities and Male Migration for Work

More secondary sectors in class I cities, the more male migration for work (explains 13%). This is quite a healthy sign. However, the secondary sectors comprise of manufacturing, as well as household industries, construction, and mining. So, the point to be emphasised is that construction and poor household industries are also hidden here. So, out of total 13 per cent, pure manufacturing explains only 5 per cent (item 1 above), construction (6%), and the rest 2 per cent, by household industries and mining!

5. Volume of Total Male Migration into Class I Cities and Male Migration for Work

Larger the volume of male migration into class I cities, higher is the incidences of male migration for work (explains 7%). This is understandable, as people move mainly for work, and the chances of such subsistence increases with the city size, as large city size itself generates many work avenues (Mukherji, 1985b: 259–279).

6. Links between Trade-commerce and Transport in Class I Cities and Migration for Work

More trade-commerce and transport in class I cities, the more male migration for work (explains 4%). However, all these partial explanations must be added, to get a complete picture of multiple explanations of male employment migration to class I cities.

7. Links between Service Sectors in Class I Cities and Male Migration for Work

More service sectors in class I cities, the more male migration for work (explains 9%). As expressed earlier, this result reiterates that even in class I cities, most of migration occur for absorption in the low-grade informal sectors, specially in services, not in manufacturing or secondary sectors. As I indicated before in many years of migration research that there are, of course, insecurity, low-grade work, low productivity, exploitation and cut-throat competition, but in spite of all such negative qualities, even these kinds of low-quality migration and low-grade absorption, have positive benefits. Even these types of migration are very much desirable, as they benefit the poor rural people at least in *eight-fold* ways:

(a) to escape poverty,
(b) to act as safety valve from suicide and further turmoil,

(c) to acts as survival strategy,
(d) to fight out poverty, helplessness, and fatalism,
(e) to escape from the clutches of cruel village money lenders,
(f) to escape from caste-ridden village society and exploitation, humility and frustration,
(g) to explore more new work opportunities in new urban environment,
(h) to expose them to urban ways of thinking, living and aspiring!

Thus, even these kinds of low-quality migration in India are beneficial to the poor rural people or small town residents, and hence much more desirable. So, there should never be migration control or restriction, rather more encouragement and fredom (see Mukherji, 2001, chap. 11).

8. Relations between Male Migration for Business and Manufacturing Centres, 2001

More manufacturing sectors in such cities, the more male migration for business (explains only 3%). The same result was also observed with 1991 data. These are positive but yet feeble symptom of developmental migration.

9. Links between Service Sectors in Cities and Male Migration for Education

Larger the service sectors in cities, the more male migration for education (explains 4%). This result reminds us of similar result from canonical tests with 1991 data – where migration for education was found to be strongly related to class I cities with strong service sectors (Table 8.11). Thus, high-powered canonical findings (performed with 1991 data) and simple regression finding (performed with 2001 data), both show almost similar results, of course, the latter with much less statistical significance, power and predictability. Canonical analysis was done between three "*matrices*" of data, not between two simple variables (as in regression). While the former tells a classic magnum epic, the latter tells only a short story, without reference to vast sea of data and complex relations (which canonical model did). I did not venture to do canonical analysis with 2001 migration data, because related data on investments, capital and socio-economic indices were simply *not* available. This may be taken up with 2011 data.

10. Relation between Male Familial Migration and Male Employment Migration

More male migration for familial reasons to cities, the more migration for work (explains 4%). This has a bi-polar relationship, i.e., it works in both directions: (a) the more migration for familial reasons promotes more migration for work, and also (b) the more male migration for work also promotes more familial migration. This also makes sense in India, because in census-taking, only the 'main' reason for migration is asked, so for many movers, who expressed that they had moved with their families, not for employment, later also take up employment, but which is not revealed in census data. That information remains hidden. Policy significance is that in future census data collection, at least the 'second' reason must also be asked. Only then, we can really fathom the real magnitude of employment migration in India, which I seriously believe, is much more in magnitude. The same is also true for female marriage migration.

Concluding Remarks

Findings of immense value for further research and migration planning for the poor: This section has revealed many useful findings about manifold relationships between migration, urbanization, economy and various aspects of class I cities of India. Many findings were hitherto unknown, or a few were only speculative in literature, but here they were proved with concrete statistical analyses and tests of significance. The findings are not only statistically very powerful, but also have practical meaning and policy importance. They are very useful for migration planning.

V. Million City-level Findings

1. Contribution of Migration to Urbanization in Million Cities, India, 1991–2001

Overall contribution of migration to urbanization in India is roughly 30 per cent. It ranges between 9 per cent for Agra and 75 per cent for Ludhiana, with many step-like variations in between. For Mumbai, migration contributes 66 per cent of decadal urban growth, followed by Delhi (48%), and Kolkata (38%). Besides, following two points are also noteworthy:

First, relation between Total Population of Million Cities and Volume of Total In-migration (1991–2001): A very strong causal relationship emerges between population size and total decadal migration to million cities. *Variations in population size explain as high as 67 per cent of variations in volume of migration to these cities.* This implies that more migrants are drawn towards larger cities, as they know that the chances of eking out a living increases with the city size.

Second, however, no such linear relationship emerges between the contribution of 'decadal' migration to million cities and their decadal population increase. For instance, for Mumbai, a large mega city, migration contributes 66 per cent of decadal population increase; which is also true for Surat (just 2.8 million population) and also Nasik (merely a small million city). Thus, the relationship appears blurred. However, this could be due to faulty or very restrictive consideration of administrative boundaries of urban agglomerations for Mumbai, Kolkata, Chennai and Delhi, which are completely saturated in main proper sites, but huge urban sprawls are still occurring at their urban fringes, where new migrants are also drawn in (Jones, 2004). Due to such faulty considerations, conventional researchers often wrongly conclude that rate of urbanization has recently decreased in India, or migration to mega cities also decreasing. While the truth is just the opposite!

2. Very strong Links between Total Population and Total Male Migration to Metros (All Durations)

Larger the size of million cities, greater is the volume of male migration (all durations) (explains 75% of variations!). Statistical significance is extremely high, 0.00001, i.e., error term is just 1 out of 100,000 observations (or the chances of this finding could be true are 99,999 out of 100,000 tests!). It is also practically very meaningful, proving that migration (all durations) makes great contribution to urbanization in India. They move together in unison. Only urbanization has outpaced industrialization, that lies at the root of all urban are problems in India.

3. Exceptionally Strong Links between Total Population of Million Cities and Volume of Male In-migration

Larger the population size of metros and million cities, greater is the volume of male migration to them (1991–2001) (explains 85%). As explained in Chapter 3, in India, all capital, investments, growth efforts, and production units have markedly uneven concentration only at million cities/mega cities, consequently, under centrifugal forces, labour is also forced to move towards those suctioning urban centres. These indicate spatial symptoms of migration under the nexus of poverty and underdevelopment. Such trends are also visualised in South-east Asia, where most migrants are attracted to primate cities (Bangkok, Jakarta and Manila) (Mukherji, 2006: 308–328; 2011: 246–271). This also shows *bipolar* relations.

4. Links between Population in Million Cities and Total Volume of Female Migration, for All Durations

Larger the size of million cities, the more volume of female migration to them, for all durations (explains an incredible 90%). In India, the female migration invariably follows the patterns of male migration, because marriage migration constitutes 80 per cent all female migration. As per Indian traditions, after marriage a wife invariably has to move to husband's place, or move with him. When the husbands migrate to million cities, they also follow them. Consequently, female migration shows the same causal relationship, as the males do. The female migration even represents a greater consonance with the urbanization, more than their male counterparts, because while the males migrate for economic purposes, but the females migrate mostly for one single reason, "marriage". Even now, their moves for other purposes are not significant.

5. Strong Links between Services in Million Cities and Recent Female Migration for Work, 1991–2001

Strong positive causal relations emerge between service sectors of million cities and recent female migration for work (explains 18%). It implies that the females mostly migrate to those million cities where they get chances of absorption in poor service sectors. This confirms the phenomena of poverty-induced migration of the females and consequent proliferation of poor service sectors in large cities.

6. Links between Manufacturing in Million Cities and Male Migration for Work

More manufacturing industries in million cities, the more male migration to them for work (explains 11%). This is a positive sign of development and needs further strengthening. In India, urbanization, migration and industrialization have querulous growth: migration and urbanization have outpaced industrialization. And, capital intensive industrialization has very limited employment-generating capacity. These have created havoc in a very highly populous country, like India. Were it planned effectively, this huge growing and youthful labour force could have been transformed into a vast army of skilled manpower. And, the country would have evolved as one of the great economic super powers. But, there is no love for the poor, no planning for the poor, no proper governance, and top of all, acute and all pervading political corruption, and thus, this great Nation now remains a land of poverty, miseries, and anarchy! *Better governance, commitment to the Nation, and the planning for the poor are the real solutions for such great maladies.*

7. Links between Total Workers in Million Cities and Male Migration for Work, 1991–2001

More workers in million cities, the more male migration searching for work there (explains 6%). So, past migration flows determine current migration streams.

8. Relation between Secondary/Tertiary Sectors in Million Cities and Volume of Total Male Migration

More workers in secondary and tertiary sectors in million cities, the more volume of male migration into them, explaining 11 per cent. This makes sense. The corollary is also true: if we can generate more employment in these economic sectors in small towns/cities, then they will succeed in redirecting the future migration flows into them. These will be true for million cities, as well.

9. Links between Tertiary Sectors of Million Cities and Male In-migration for Work

The larger tertiary sectors in the million cities, the more male migration to them for work (explains 26%). When seen, with the above regression equation, it points towards an intriguing finding: i.e., tertiary sectors alone (services, transport and trade-commerce) explain as much as 26 per cent of variations, and its combination with secondary sectors explain but only 11 per cent. That is, it reduces its explanatory power, because of *varian*t patterns of city's workers, which move with cross purposes, canceling cumulative benefits of workers in a million city. In reality, tertiary sectors are the real harbingers of employment, even in million cities. This re-confirms my age-old thesis, i.e., urbanization in India is propelled by proliferation of low-grade tertiary sectors, not manufacturing/secondary sectors (Mukherji, 1975: 1–378; 1979b, 1–80; 1981: 1–28). And, that migrants are absorbed in low productive tertiary sectors, where pay is low, competition severe, and insecurity high (Mukherji, 1985b: 252–289; 2002: 525–562; 2006, 15–150). Such re-confirmation rather make me sad, that even after 40 years, things have not improved in India. Policy makers must take cognizance of such reality, and plan for the upliftment of the poor masses, both in villages and cities.

10. Links between Main Sectors of Economy in Million Cities and Male Migration, 1991–2001

More workers in million cities, the more male migration for work (explains 11%), i.e., higher the proportion of "main" workers (less marginal workers), the more male migrants are attracted to those million cities.

11. Links between Tertiary Sectors of Million Cities and Urbanization in India

More tertiary sectors in million cities, the larger is the population size of them (explains 8%). Thus, one of the driving forces of rapid urbanization in India is the proliferation of the poor tertiary sectors, i.e., growth of low-grade transport, trade-commerce and service sectors in million cities. Unlike in the West, in India, such low-grade tertiary sectors conversely cater to the large population of cities themselves, and they actually lie as causal reasons for rapid urbanization in the country, not manufacturing/secondary sectors.

12. Relation between Total Population of Million Cities and Total Male Migration for Durations 10 Years +

Larger population size of the million cities, the more male migration for durations for 10 years and over (explains 24%).

13. Estimated Population of Million Cities in 2021 (If Past Trends Continue)

If the present population growth trends continue, by the year 2021, Greater Mumbai will reach 27.7 million, Delhi 29.5 million, Kolkata 19.0 million, and

Chennai 9.0 million. Thence, to provide essential urban facilities like water, electricity, housing, shelter, transport, employment, education and health services to such burgeoning urban population will be really a Himalayan task. But, the Indian government so far has no clear urban policy, nor any migration policy, nor any population control policy (due to minority vote bank politics). A total absence of "planning for the poor" mark such slipshod planning, and most unsuccessful implementation!

14. Poor and Upper Occupational Divisions of Migrants (Males), Million Cities, 2001

Even in the mega cities, the majority of male migrants get absorption only in the poor services and low-grade production-process sectors of occupations: Greater Mumbai (59.8%), Kolkata (69.6%), Delhi (63%), Chennai (52%), Hyderabad (48%), Bangalore (48%) and Ahmedabad (54%). Very few of them are engaged in professional, administrative, or clerical jobs: viz., Greater Mumbai (15.5%), Kolkata (14.5%), Delhi (17%), and Chennai (23%). Lower size million cities also depict the similar pictures.

The reasons are: capital-intensive industrialization in such cities have failed to generate adequate employment in organized sectors, so illiterate and semi-educated migrants are absorbed only in low-grade informal sectors (Mukherji, 1995a: 1–45). *This is a grave symptom of poverty, underdevelopment and low quality migration and urban involution in India. Similar features can also be observed in South and South-east Asia* (Mukherji, 1997b: 1–80; 2006: 45–330). Although, even these kinds of migration are desirable, as they help in reducing rural poverty and opening avenues to escape from rampant poverty; nevertheless, such low-quality migration and urban involution are not at all desirable in the long run, as they keep them under perpetual poverty, underdevelopment and serfdom! *Combating against such undesirable aspects must be given the top priority in the government's migration and urbanization policies (so far non-existing), and their right kind of implementation.* These are subject matters of subsequent chapters (21 and 22).

VI. Mega City-level Findings

1. Future Population of Indian Mega Cities (UN Estimates, 2007)

United Nations report on World Urbanization Prospects (2007) presented a different projections of India's mega cities: Greater Mumbai will reach 26.4 million, Kolkata 20.6 million, Delhi 20.5 million, and Chennai 10.1 million by 2025. Mumbai already has 56 per cent of its urban population under slums in 2001, followed by Kolkata (43%), Delhi (35% and Chennai (32%), and slums will also proliferate in future. Thus, these mega cities would grow more as over-blown villages, not in prosperity!

2. India's Urban Future

In comparison, by 2025, Tokyo, the world's largest city with a stable population of 36 millions, will still remain a clean and a green city, and a crime-free and slum-free city. But, India's urban future does not seem to be that bright – it might have a more filthy environment, more proliferation of slums and a vast ocean of faceless people who would live from hand to mouth.

3. Mumbai

By 2025, Greater Mumbai will reach 26.4 million, Kolkata 20.6 million and so forth, but India's urban future does not appear to be glitzy – it might have more urban congestion, bursting slums, and more strife-ridden and iniquitous urban society! The more and more people would be compelled to live below-the-human-dignity-level of existence in stinking slums in future!

4. Migration to Mumbai

Mumbai saw much ebbs and flows of migrants during last four decades. As Mumbai gradually rose as financial hub of India, its pattern of migration also became more inter-state.

5. Sons of The Soils in Mumbai

During 1991–2001, *intra*-state migrants from within Maharashtra (36%) were still larger than migrants from Uttar Pradesh and Bihar combined (30.6%). However, recent agitation in Mumbai of reserving jobs and education in favour of the "sons of the soils" often turns violent. Such trends may have many ramifications in future. When the benefits of development are small, and are concentrated only to a few mega cities, then, such politically-motivated agitations tend to arise. But they must not be violent, nor be inimical to the unity of all Indians. This rather urges for development of UP and Bihar, migrant source regions – which remained neglected since many decades! Historically, coal and mining resources from Bihar and very cheep labour from UP were forced to move to Bombay for its enrichment. Consequently the migrant-scarce regions remained backward. Now, these states must be given much more development impetus. Then, migrants will be absorbed locally, , instead of toiling in the filthy urban slums in Mumbai!

6. Planning for Mumbai

Mumbai and Navi Mumbai both need much more effective decentralization and addressing acute housing, traffic, and environmental problems. The issue of water and air pollution must also be tackled with great urgency.

7. Migration to Kolkata

Among inter-state migration to Kolkata, male migrants from Bihar consist of 53 per cent, followed by Uttar Pradesh (12%), Orissa (8%), Jharkhand (7%), and other states (6%). They move for eking out subsistence in the mega city, and are absorbed into the poor bazaar-type economy.

8. Development of Kolkata

Very firm political will and very strict economic discipline are very much necessary for Kolkata to survive. It is also very much necessary to draw up comprehensive urban development plan for Kolkata for its future development, which are terribly lacking. Industrialization of Kolkata and its hinterlands are of supreme requirement. Political instability and Maoist violence in West Bengal are sapping out its all growth prospects! The city of joy is fast becoming a city of despair! (Recent political rout of the Marxist government may usher in new hopes!)

9. Migration to Delhi

In Delhi, among males, 39 per cent comes from adjoining Uttar Pradesh, followed by Bihar (23%), Haryana (6%), Uttaranchal (5%), West Bengal (4%),

Rajasthan (4%) and northern states (4%). Among female migrants, again, majority comes from nearby Uttar Pradesh (41%), followed by Bihar (13%), Haryana (9%), Uttaranchal (5%), Rajasthan (5%), West Bengal (4%), and Northern states (5%). After Mumbai, which acts as national destination of All-India migrants, Delhi also acts likewise.

10. Inequality in Delhi

Delhi is a city of great contrast – manifesting tremendous social, economic and political inequalities, where filthy affluence among a privileged few looks contemptuously over masses of the poor down below. These need urgent corrective measures. Otherwise, the urban systems may soon burst open, leading to a catastrophe. However, this might happen sooner in Mumbai (greater affluence and extreme inequities), than in Delhi (where ugly political sycophaney might avert volatile eruption!).

11. Migration to Chennai

Number of migrants to Chennai are small, only 435,620, of which within state migrants comprised 77 per cent and inter-state, only 22 per cent. Among the males, the majority has moved from adjoining Andhra Pradesh (24%), followed by Kerala (22%), Karnataka (9%), Maharashtra (7%), and Northern states (15%). Among females, likewise, maximum have come from neighbouring Andhra Pradesh (24%), followed by Kerala (23%), Karnataka (11%), Maharashtra (7%) and northern states (13%). Chennai acts as a regional migration centre. And, this helps to maintain its relative sensibility!

12. Development of Chennai

Studies on determinants of poverty show that high national economic growth rates and direct poverty reduction programmes together have created employment, increase in income and urban poverty reduction. Still, Chennai has to address the problems of urban poor. In spite of declining trend in urban poverty, their number is increasing.

13. Economic Structure

Further, the following points regarding migration-urbanization situation in Mega cities also can be highlighted: all four mega cities of India are having weak economic structure, with low manufacturing or secondary sector base (15 to 30%), and a very high poor tertiary sectors (65–74%).

14. Proliferation of Tertiary Sectors

In 1901, these cities all had inadequate secondary sectors (22 to 41%), and a very large poor tertiary sectors (54 to 78%). By 2001, secondary sectors further declined (24 to 32%), while poor tertiary sectors further rose (67 to 75%).

15. Signs of Anti-Development

Unlike in the West, such rapid growth of poor tertiary sectors of urban economy do not reflect development, rather anti-development, as these poor sectors are created mainly by population explosion, not by industrialization.

16. Low Grade Absorption of Migrants

Given these context, the masses of incoming illiterate and unskilled migrants find salvage only in poor urban unorganized sectors, viz., as domestic servants, road construction labourers, indigenous transport workers, hawkers, vendors, and sundry services. The female migrants also reflect similar low-grade absorption as hawkers, vendors, road construction labourers, maid-servants, etc. Such informal sectors are characterized by cut-throat competition, low-grade wages, hunger, insecurity, exploitation, and working and living under hazardous condition.

17. Still Such Migration Desirable

Although all such above conditions are negative, still such distressed migration of impoverished humanity is much more desirable, as these permit them to escape prolonged hunger and poverty in deadly stagnant origin villages, which are plagued by acute unemployment, recurrent underemployment, village stagnation, exploitation, humiliation, extreme and lack of any kinds of work in tottering rural economy.

18. Mega Cities Must Grow in Prosperity, not in Population

Population wise, all these mega cities will occupy distinguished ranks among the top twenty-five mega cities of the world by 2025. Hoped that they will grow not only in population, but also in prosperity! For both residents and migrants. These must serve as main nerve centres for the country, throwing very strong development impulses to respective hinterlands, instead of growing as cancerous nodes!

19. Need Urgent Development of Small Towns and Small and Medium Class Cities

Such adverse situation in Indian mega cities all the more urges for development of the small and intermediate towns and small and medium cities which are hitherto neglected, and hence remained backward (Mukherji, 1993b: 1–196). This is very urgently required because the impending very huge population explosion in India will not be contained in the villages, and vast streams of poor migrants would be forced to crowd into already overcrowded mega cities in search for survival. So, small and intermediate level towns and class I cities must be developed soon, by channeling investments and necessary infrastructures and industries, so that these become alternate attractive centres for the migrants (Mukherji, 1997c; 2006). One, of the strategies would be the issuance of governments bonds for development of small towns and small cities (just like existing rural infrastructure bonds, or *Kisan Vikas Patras* (farmers development savings schemes). Another impetus would be ten-year tax-free investment and industrialization schemes for the private sectors, encouraging them for locating enterprises in the villages, small towns, and small/medium level cities. Such strategies may boost the development of smaller urban nodes, and gainful employment for the incoming migrants.

Part III

Issues, Challenges and Development Policies

19 Massive Illegal Immigration from Bangladesh and Its Adverse Consequences upon India

"Do not be afraid. Tell the truth boldly."

Swami Vivekananda (1893)
(Complete Work, Centenary Volume II, 1963: 55)

Massive Illegal Immigration of Muslims from Bangladesh

Recently, one very important study about India's changing religious demographic structure was made in a book titled *"Religious Demographic Changes in India" by Joshi, Srinivas, and Bajaj, and published by Centre for Policy Studies, Chennai* (2003: 87–110). They examined census-based religious population data of all districts of India, over the period 1901–1991, specially over 1951–91, and found that religious demographic structure of many bordering districts of India have drastically changed, specially due to massive illegal migration of Muslims from Bangladesh.

> "The Muslim population is present in large segments and are very much growing in recent decades over a vast continuous stretch of border districts, from Assam, West Bengal, Bihar and Uttar Pradesh. It is a huge belt that starts from Goalpara, Kamrup, Darrang, Nagaon, Dhubri, Barapeta, and Marigaon districts in Assam, continuing on to West Dinajpur, Maldah, Murshidabad, Birbhum, Hooghly, Nadia, and Twenty-Four Paraganas districts in West Bengal. It stretches further to Purnia, Champaran, Muzaffarpur, Darbhanga, Saharsa, and Santhal Parganas districts in Bihar, and spreading over to Deoria, Gorakhpur, Basti, Bahraich, Bareilly, Rampur, Moradabad, Bijnor, Meerut, Muzzaffarnagar, Haridwar, and as far as Saharanpur districts of Western Uttar Pradesh (ibid. 2003: 100–109). This belt of illegal Muslim migration stretches over 1500 miles, from Assam to Western Uttar Pradesh, and widens as far as 300–400 miles, from North to South West Bengal" (Joshi, Srinivas, and Bajaj, 2003: 85–87).

The authors have also noted that in Assam, the proportion of Muslims in total population was 32.42 per cent in 1951, which rapidly increased to 37.15 per cent in 1991. In West Bengal, their comparative proportion rose from 39.9 per cent in 1951 to 47.1 per cent in 1991. Most illegal infiltration of Muslims was in West Bengal, because of active political support from Marxist governments in the State. In Bihar, comparative figures are 14.56 per cent (1951) and 21.00

per cent (1991). In Eastern Uttar Pradesh, it rose from 15.40 per cent in 1951 to 20.47 per cent in 1991. Comparative figures in Western Uttar Pradesh were much higher, 29.93 and 36.33, respectively (ibid.: 2003: 107–108).

Authors have thus noted that, "Proportion of Muslims in this belt as a whole is 27.67 per cent: their share has grown by more than 7 percentage points since 1951, when they formed 20.49 per cent of the population of this belt. If we add only the relevant component districts rather than the composite districts, then the proportion of Muslims in this belt turns to be higher at 32.77 per cent in 1991" (ibid., 2003: 107–108).

The obvious conclusion is that, the share of Muslim population has grown from one-fifth in 1951 to one-third of the total population, within a very short span of 40 years (1951–91). The situation have further worsened in 2001 census, and thereafter. These pose the greatest dangers to India, its demography, economy, politics, culture and its very existence in near future.

That is the most frightful change and it have already transformed the demographic character of population of these states. If these trends continue unabated, then, very soon, the Muslims will constitute the majority of the population of these states, and of entire India (over 50%). This is the result of their comparatively higher fertility levels, but *much more compounded by very massive illegal immigration of Muslims from Bangladesh over last 63–64 years, and higher fertility trends of their progenies, over successive generations.*

Evidences and Ongoing Processes

1. These ominous signs are revealed in the above-mentioned study (Joshi, Srinivas, and Bajaj, 2003: 87–110). They found that a vast stretch of border districts from Bahraich, Gonda, Basti, Gorakhpur, Deoria, (in UP), Champaran, Muzaffarpur, Darbhanga, Saharsa, Purnia, Santhal Paragnas (in Bihar), and West Dinajpur, Malda, Birbhum, Murshidabad, (in West Bengal) and Goalpara, Kamrup, Darrang, Nagaon, etc. (in Assam) have very rapid rise of Muslim population during last 6 decades. Obviously, they have spread out to the interiors of India, crossing from Bangladesh border, and spread all over India. The book did not deal specifically with Maharashtra, but from other reports and daily newspapers it is very evident that many hundreds of thousands of illegal Bangladeshi Muslims are found working in Mumbai, more than 2000 miles from the *International border*! The same way in other remote places, like Delhi, Hyderabad, Kerala, Karnataka, and so forth.
2. But that study, *although a very good and a pioneering attempt,* only analysed past census records, and did not study differential fertility patterns among the two communities, nor the extent of "illegal immigration" patterns. Nor did it pinpoint ramifications and consequences. Nor it studied phenomena by two major communities of India, rather focused on Hindu and co-religionists (combining also Jains, Sikhs, Buddhists, etc.), and thus blurred the pictures. It has a great limitation of not exploring future demographic trends and patterns for India, nor was based on formal rigorous demographic study of fertility, mortality and migration trends. So a very rigorous and very systematic investigation must be taken up urgently.

3. Since Independence (in 1947), over last 63 years, successive governments at the Centre, and in Assam, West Bengal and Tripura (specially Marxist governments in last two states since 1977) always encouraged such massive illegal immigration from Bangladesh for their very evil some minority vote-bank politics, very frequently providing them with ration cards, identity cards, and voter identity cards. Most political parties of India also preferred to look to other ways for the same reasons and stakes. Most Indian demographers, population specialists and the social scientists preferred to remain, not only mute, but also deaf, to the entire issues (*see Economic and Political Weekly, Special volume, Sept 2004*). Administrators and policy makers remain gutless and totally paralysed. And, the common people of India remain absolutely mute spectators, unconcerned, defense-less and totally fatalistic – as they always remained throughout the Indian history, specially since last two Millenniums!
4. In spite of comparatively high Muslim fertility in India (evidenced by NFHS – I (1992–93), NFHS-II, (1998–99) surveys, Census 2001, and other studies (Moulasha and Rama Rao, 1999), and in spite of clear evidence of very massive infiltration of Bangladeshi Muslims into India – both the print media and electronic media – totally dismiss these crucial issues. They label these as myths of "Saffron Demography of Hindu Communalists" (Rao, *Times of India*, 2006: 30). During 1991–2001 census period, the Hindu population grew by 19.9 per cent, while the Muslim population by 29.9 per cent! (Census of India, 2001), but that was also severely brushed aside and ignored by the vested interests. Such spurt in population rose massively due to great illegal invasions from Bangladesh and Pakistan. But the governments never took seriously this most crucial issue, nor investigated such ominous signs.
5. The greatest crime in India is being born into the Hindu community! If you ever raise the crucial issue of self survival, you are sure to be branded as the "communalist", by pseudo-intellectuals, the leftists, Marxists, Hindu-baiters, and by so-called pseudo-secular Hindus themselves. A paradox! a paradox!! A great paradox!!!
6. Swami Vivekananda thus thundered over a century ago: "Do not ever make the mistake of considering your laziness, ignorance and weakness as pious divine traits; these are sheer lower Tamasic (cowardice) traits" ... "*Strength, O man, strength, says the Upanishads, stand up and be strong*" (Vivekananda, 1893: 237).
7. According to NFHS-1 report (National Family and Health Survey, Ministry of Health and Family Welfare, New Delhi, and done by International Institute for Population Sciences, Mumbai, 1992–93 round), the Total Fertility Rate (TFR) among the Muslims was 4.2 (children per mother), compared to 2.7 (children per mother) among the Hindus, about 40 per cent higher. But, NFHS-I report *did not write* more than 2–3 lines on this grave issue, nor drew National attention to this very serious issue. The situation did not improve much by 1998–99 round of NFHS – II survey, and currently in 2005–2006. These are further greatly compounded by very massive illegal immigration of Bangladeshi Muslims. Sadly, conventional

demographic, or fertility or migration studies in India *do not even consider such massive illegal immigration in their population projections, observations and conclusions (as evidence, see Economic and Political weekly, Sept 2004 special issue), which did not even discuss massive illegal immigration from Bangladesh in their calculations and conclusions!*

8. Unfortunately, there is a complete lack of knowledge and utter lack of any concern about such imminent dangers, among the population specialists, demographers, social scientists, so-called intellectuals, among the pseudo-secularists, the political parties and leaders, and in the society at large. Such very grave National issues must be debated, investigated and prevented soon, before the onset of the great calamity, arising out of such massive illegal immigration from Bangladesh, and their high fertility.
9. There is a very planned and systematic illegal immigration of Bangladeshi Muslims across the borders. During last 63 years, specially during last 33 years (1977–2010) of Marxist rule in West Bengal and Tripura, about 30–40 millions or more illegal Bangladeshi Muslims have illegally migrated into West Bengal *alone*, due to minority vote bank policy and encouragement from the Congress Government (1947–1977) and later Marxist government of West Bengal (1977–2010). After entering, soon those illegal Bangladeshi migrants spread out to all other parts of India, as far as Bihar, UP, Delhi, Mumbai, Gujarat, Jammu-Kashmir and everywhere, as workers and often as terrorists!
10. Likewise, millions of illegal Bangladeshi Muslim migrants have entered into *all over Assam and North Eastern Indian states, since the Independence*. Prolonged Congress rules (both in the Centre and in the States) and their allies in Assam always kept a blind eye to such perennial infiltration problems, rather always encouraged this for the minority vote bank policies. Recent killing of Bihari labourers in Assam (2007–9), it is alleged, is prompted by ULFA terrorists, in order to settle further illegal Bangladeshi migrants into Assam and to reciprocate the shelter facility given to ULFA terrorists in Bangladesh.
11. Neither rigorous prevention are ever made, not Central and State Governments ever took effective policies and stringent actions to perennially stop such massive illegal immigration. Total illegal Bangladeshi immigration is estimated to be over 60 millions, as in 2008, and their numbers are swelling daily, through daily infiltrations, and their high fertility and progenies. *Recent 2010 report* (*Times of India*, October 8, 2010) *estimates about 2 million illegal Bangladeshi migrants in Mumbai city alone! Their magnitude all over India will be many times more, and daily rising*. But, India sleeps on ... as it did since last two millenniums. Besides, Pakistan is hell bent on cutting India into thousand pieces! It had sent just 10 terrorists to Mumbai in terror attacks on November 26, 2008, who killed 300 innocent people and inflicted devastating wounds. Nothing has been done to avert recurrence of such dangers. India sleeps on ....
12. According to one 2010 news, already 90 districts, out of total 605 districts of India, have more than 25 per cent Muslim majority. Another 45–50 districts have more than 15 per cent Muslim majority (more than National average), and they demand more Muslim quota in government and private jobs, school and college admissions, and in all other facilities (*Times of India,*

April 8, 2010). It is seriously suspected that, if fertility differentials between the two communities are not much (as *conventional population scientists make us to believe,* vide *Economic and Political Weekly,* Sept, 2004), then, a great majority of such sudden spurts in minority population surely arises out of *very massive illegal Bangladeshi Muslim immigration or invasions.* Those demographers very conveniently ignored this factor of massive illegal migration of Bangladeshi Muslims in their population projections, predictions, and conclusions, and their likely share in future populations of India. There must be a *conspiracy* of silence and omission, misdirecting the Nation. Serous investigation must be made on all such crucial issues.

13. Unfortunately, India follows the blind strategy of proverbial ostrich (putting its head into the sand) and is totally immune to the ominous dangers lying ahead. Such blind behaviour on the part of Indian government and the population and the society, the population-specialists and so-called intellectuals will not save India from its ultimate dissolution. India cannot escape from such ultimate calamity, due to ongoing processes of systematic attempts of disintegration of India, if the evil processes go unchecked.
14. And, top of all, if India continues neglecting such critical issues, then all those features which epitomise "Indian Civilization and Characteristics" will soon be wiped out. India, then, will be completely dissolved into thin air! And, the next progeny would struggle very hard to find even the name, India, in the Internet!

Need Very Urgent Actions

1. First, all illegal immigration from Bangladesh must be stopped immediately and permanently.
2. Second, the entire length of India-Bangladesh borders must be immediately sealed, for all times.
3. All illegal immigration from Pakistan, and of Pakistanis through open Nepal border, must be stopped immediately and permanently.
4. All illegal Bangladeshi immigrants must be expatriated back to Bangladesh.
5. All *terrorist infiltrations* through Bangladesh borders must be stopped permanently.
6. Promotion of literacy, education and employment must be made among the Muslim population. When widespread illiteracy and poverty among them will be reduced, their fertility level will also decline. This is also necessary for their own benefits: to escape from poverty, illiteracy and unemployment.
7. Sadly, India is the only country in the *entire world,* which keeps its border *open to all invaders and illegal migrants from across borders.* These are *unthinkable* that countries, like USA, Canada or Israel, even Pakistan or Bangladesh will never tolerate such massive illegal immigration from their international borders!! But, unfortunately, in India, various political parties and the governments (central and states), not only tolerating, rather very much *encouraging* such mischievous and nefarious activities, by providing the voter's identity cards, rations cards, passports, and all facilities and services to the illegal migrants. And, 1.20 billion voiceless people remain mute spectators of such evil-some activities, since last six decades! The entire population is entirely mute, entirely silent on such most crucial issues.

8. *Moreover, now, Unique National Identity Cards (UIDs) are very soon going to be issued to all people present (along with benefits to holders of the cards), without ever "checking" who are* illegal trespassers, *and who are the* real citizen of this country!! *Consequently, those 60 millions Bangladeshi Muslim tresspassers (and their progenies) would become legal citizens of India!! This is sheer act of stupidity (rather great crime) and inviting great disasters for the Nation for all time to come!!*
9. There are masses of Hindu-baiters, pseudo-secularists, marxists, leftists, so-called intellectuals, and even Hindu *netas* and political leaders, who love to see India fully disintegrated and vanish into thin air! Print and electronic media are persistently anti-Hindu! Such nefarious activities must stop for all time. All are hell-bent on in the devilish competition for bashing out the majority citizens of this country!
10. *There are about two hundred nations in this planet Earth, but you will not find a single nation, like India, who most unfortunately encourages such suicidal activities for its own destruction!*
11. There should be all-pronged sincere efforts to ensure complete solidarity among the Hindus, encompassing the Dalits, scheduled castes, scheduled tribes, hill tribes, and tribal populations. There should not be any trace of caste-based politics, any infightings, and enmity among all such diverse groups. Historically, India was internally so divided and weakened, thus repeatedly devastated by the invaders and plunderers. This happened mainly because of such infightings and lack of internal solidarity among them. This is now the fundamental requirement for continuation of India's very existence. Otherwise, in the near future, the name India will be found *only* in the Internet! This may happen even within this century!
12. *Top of all, in this context we should rather remember and abide by what the greatest Soul of this country, nay of this Universe, Swami Vivekananda thundered in 1894, 116 years ago, that: "Each country has a specific inner spirit which it upholds, and through which it expresses its specific role in the world. India is the only country in this entire World which has "spirituality" as its inner spirit for its very existence! India has this specific role to play in this world, as the Spiritual Teacher of all other countries. Bereft of its deep-set Indian spiritualism, India will cease to remain India."*
13. To this I must add, if India is dissolved then the *traits of spirituality itself* will be wiped out from this Planet. Swamiji also cautioned in the same way 116 years ago. Because Indian spirituality was the mother of all other spiritual systems of this Earth, since many millenniums. It had never gone out of its borders to colonize earth and impose Hinduism over other countries during its 10,000 years of existence (which cannot be said about other religions).
14. *We must always strive to reach above Divine goal, and try to keep India as True India.*

20 India's Growing Population and Growing Economy

Crucial Challenges and Required Perspectives

"Continue to exercise your will and it will take you higher still".

Swami Vivekananda (1893)
(Complete Work, Centenary Volume II, 1963: 356)

This chapter very briefly discuses India's two burgeoning issues: population explosion and recent rapid economic growth. There are various ramifications of India's population explosion that demand urgent relief of high infant mortality rates, high fertility rates and rapid poverty reduction. Conversely, India's so-called rapid economic growth, without inclusive growth and without benefits to half a billion poor Indians, urgently demands sincere paradigm shift in favour of the poor masses of the country (Mukherji, 2009: 7–12). Such crucial challenges and required planning perspectives in favour of the Poor are very briefly highlighted here.

Part I
Growing Population of India and Its Various Aspects

India's Future Population, 2001–2101

Population Foundation of India, New Delhi, and Population Reference Bureau, Washington, have made population projections of India for 2001–2101 (2007: 1–15). They presented two scenarios, A and B, with slightly different fertility assumptions. These differ only in one aspect. The 'target' TFR (total fertility rates), used as a final value. Scenario A, the higher projection case, assumes that 2.1– replacement level fertility – will be the final value for highly populous and high fertility states – where it is currently much above 2.1 (3.5 to 4.5 children per mother). In Scenario B, the target is 1.85 (children per mother) for those states above that value. For low TFR states, like Kerala and Tamil Nadu, the TFR are assumed to remain constant throughout projection period.

For projections, simple assumptions were also used regarding other factors, like mortality, life expectancy, migration, and sex ratio at birth. Life expectancy widely differs in India: from 57 years in Madhya Pradesh to 74 years in Kerala.

Similarly, infant mortality rates (IMR) differ from 14 in Kerala to 76 in Madhya Pradesh in 2005. For projections, it is assumed, like fertility assumptions, that gradually declining level of mortality will operate, based on ongoing trends. For these, standard model life tables were used for varying levels of IMR, but for the same level of life expectancy. Sex ratio at birth are very skewed in India, only 927 female births per 1,000 male births, often vastly declining in many northern states (Punjab, Haryana, Himachal Pradesh). This is caused by pre-birth sex selection, abortion of female fetuses, and utter neglect and discrimination against female infants and children, regarding nutrition, health care and treatment. All these evils are primarily caused due to cruel age-old dowry system at the time of daughter's marriage. Government's half-hearted measures have not yet made any dent upon these problems. For projection purpose, however it is assumed that sex ratio at birth will return to global normal value of 95 female births per 100 male births during the first 35 years of the projection.

Net migration figures for states were used for projections, but assuming very little international migration for projection purpose. However, this is a very grave mistake, made in all projections by all agencies, because, increasingly scores of millions of illegal Bangladeshi infiltrators are invading India, annually, and very rapidly changing India's demographic, religious, economic, cultural and political scenarios. However, for the present purpose, international migration is assumed negligible, as projection experts have made us to believe. Summary details are given in Table 20.1 and illustrated in Figure 20.1.

Table 20.1 *India's Future Population, 2001–2101 (in billions)*

Population of India	*2001*	*2011*	*2021*	*2031*	*2041*	*2051*	*2061*	*2071*	*2081*	*2091*	*2101*
Scenario A	1.03	1.20	1.38	1.55	1.69	1.82	1.93	2.02	2.09	2.14	2.18
Scenario B	1.03	1.20	1.37	1.52	1.65	1.75	1.82	1.86	1.88	1.87	1.85

Source: Population Foundation of India and Population Reference Bureau (2007), "The Future Population of India," New Delhi and Washington: 6–15.

Figure 20.1 *India's Future Population (billions), 2001–2101*

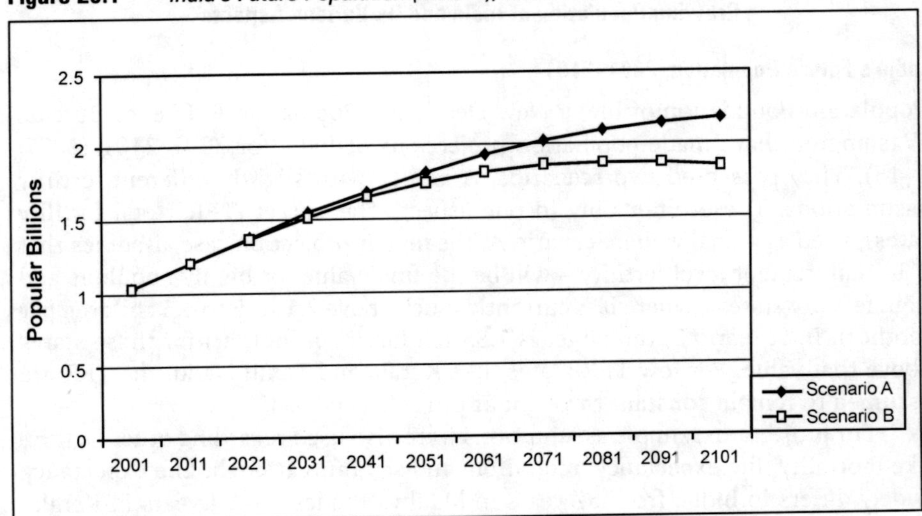

Scenario A with a final total fertility rate (TFR) of 2.1 for high fertility states (like Bihar, Uttar Pradesh, Madhya Pradesh, and Rajasthan), India's population would reach about 2 billion by 2066–2071,.and it will rise to 2.18 billion by 2101 (Table 20.1). Above four currently high fertility states would contribute half of the total population of the country. In *Scenario B,* conversely, with a final TFR of 1.85, population of India would not reach 2 billion, rather would peak at 1.88 billion by 2081–2086; after which population would start declining (Tables 20.1 and 20.2).

What scenario is more likely? Most probably, the future population may follow a path in between the two scenarios, or even show higher population by 2101. Low fertility states, like Kerala, Tamil Nadu and Goa, may achieve faster population decline, than assumed. Conversely, currently high fertility states, like Bihar and Uttar Pradesh may not achieve replacement level of fertility of 2.1 by stipulated time, resulting in greater population explosion. Besides, lack of agricultural land may induce larger magnitude of rural to urban migration and greater urbanization, but faster fertility decline. All such complexities may offer variant pictures, but all said and done, the overall future population of India may appear as in Scenario A.

India's Demographic Transition

While China achieved much rapid fertility transition, during the 1980–90s, facilitated by its strict and totalitarian regime and one child policy, India has faltered, due to lack of 'political will' for executing demographic decline over different religious groups, being set in the context of the world's largest democracy and its attached strings. Although, democracy is a greatly desirable aspect of life and existence (as in Japan and USA), but it has myriad limitations for ensuring rapid population control (so also achieving rapid economic growth and development). India is only now experiencing somewhat rapid fertility decline, during 1990s and 2000–08s, first in south India, and later in western and northern India (NFHS-III, 2007: 1–18). Its proportion of working ages will steadily increase, overtaking an aging Japan in 2010, and will finally reach its peak in the mid-2030s (Population Foundation of India and Population Reference Bureau, 2007: 1–20), Thus, India will be experiencing a demographic transition which Japan has undergone in the 1970–1980s, and China, 1990–2005.

India's Demographic Dividends and Need for Massive Employment Generation

This demographic dividend, thus, becomes a very important strength in India's favour. As the developed economies ages, India will flourish with her most youthful, energetic and productive population. Even when China begins to age rapidly, during 2005–2020, India will enjoy and blossom with her most prosperous dividends of having the world's largest labour force, from 2020–2031 onwards (Table 20.2) (Population Foundation of India and Population Reference Bureau, 2007: 1–15).

Greatest challenge for India will be to provide full and gainful employment to this huge labour force. India will need to create additional 200 million jobs by 2030, apart from 34 million of currently unemployed backlogs (Gupta, 2002: 29–45; Planning Commission, 2002b). Without providing necessary skills, education and proper employment, the benefits of demographic dividends, unfortunately, might turn sour. Evidently, neither can agriculture provide that magnitude of massive employment; nor can IT, IT-based jobs, or private organized sectors, as these sectors offer only 2.5 per cent of all jobs, now. Largest number of new jobs will need to be generated by *small and medium enterprises* (SMEs) in the private sectors, which contribute massive employment in USA, Japan and Germany. Besides, in India, forging backward and forward linkages between organized and unorganized sectors, coupled with transformation of technology, will also be required for generating massive employment in these SMEs. Moreover, high employment-generating sectors will need to be greatly expanded, like, commercial agriculture, agro-industry, agri-business, forestry and horticulture, retail and wholesale trade, commerce, tourism, housing and construction, IT and IT-based services, manufacturing, cottage and household industries, transport and communications, health and financial services, and myriad of modern and technology-enabled services. Mining and industries ought to be energized for generating greater number of jobs. Topmost, industrialization of agriculture and intensive integration between industry and agriculture also require to be tremendously activated – which may create massive number of jobs.

Table 20.2 *India's Demographic Dividends: Very Large Labour Force, 2001–2101 (%)*

Year	*2001*		*2011*		*2021*		*2031*		*2041*		*2061*		*2101*	
Age groups	*15–65*	*65+*	*15–65*	*65+*	*15–65*	*65+*	*15–65*	*65+*	*15–65*	*65+*	*15–65*	*65+*	*15–65*	*65+*
Scene A	60.9	4.8	64.1	5.2	65.7	6.2	**66.4**	7.9	66.2	10.1	64.1	15.1	59.7	**22.0**
Scene B	60.9	4.8	64.2	5.2	66.2	6.2	**66.7**	8.0	**67.1**	10.3	64.7	16.1	59.2	**24.7**

Source: Same as in Table 20.1. Bold figures for 2031 and 2101 show peak in demographic dividends and aging population, respectively.

Future Burden of Huge Aging Population

Table 20.2 shows that India had only 4.8 per cent in old ages (65+) in 2001, which (scenario B) will grow first slowly to 8.0 per cent by 2031, thereafter progressively to 16 per cent by 2061, and to a fearful 24 per cent by 2101. This implies an unbelievable burden of providing food, shelter and health care to 470 millions aged and dependent population. Scenario A will be more critical, 484 millions. Unthinkable! But, Indian government, policy makers or demographers have not yet even thought about such burgeoning problems. Evidently, India will face much greater crisis than Japan or China. Unfortunately, then, India's great population *dividends* will fail to mitigate crisis.

Gender Imbalance

India experience declining sex ratios during 1981–2001 and acute problems of gender imbalance in India (Census of India, 2001a). These problems are most acute in northern states of Delhi (only 821 females per 1,000 males), Haryana (861 females), Uttar Pradesh (898), Jammu and Kashmir (900), Bihar (921), Rajasthan (922), even in Maharashtra (922). Reasons are: female infanticide, killing of female fetuses, and utter neglect of nutrition and health-care, and discrimination against female infants/children done by parents themselves – due to cruel age-old practice of giving away heavy dowry during daughter's marriage.

These result in to declining sex ratios and gender imbalance. Southern states show more balanced situation ... where sex selective female infanticide is less. Gender imbalance is already creating great havoc in northern states of Haryana, Jammu-Kashmir, Rajasthan, Uttar Pradesh and Bihar – leading into purchase of brides, or women trafficking from West Bengal, Tripura, Orissa, Assam, and even Bangladesh and Nepal. Such problems will greatly magnify in near future.

Poverty and Female Illiteracy in India

India's greatest challenge is to combat widespread poverty, prevailing even now. According to National Sample Surveys (NSSO), poverty in India has considerably declined, from 36.6 per cent in 1992–93 to 26.6 per cent in 1990–2000. But, considerable doubts also arise; and recently NSSO estimated it at 28.3 per cent for 2004–5 (rural 28.7%, and 25.9% urban). However, in the absence of poverty data in all National Family Health Surveys (NFHS), and lack of continuous and recent NSSO estimates, I consider, proportion of adult female illiteracy (age 15–49) as better indirect index of poverty (Mukherji, 2007: 69–93): which puts it at 44.2 per cent, as per census 2001. This is very close to another indirect poverty measure considered here: per cent of non-bricked houses (39% in 2001). These two indirect indices are indeed very close to World Bank's recent estimate of poverty in India, 42 per cent in 2005 (World Bank, 2008), which portrays true reality.

Unfortunately, as per this estimate, about 450 million people live below the poverty line in India and go to bed hungry every night. Thus, although poverty is being reduced in India, but their absolute number and proportion virtually remained almost same over time; due to high population explosion and government's half-hearted measures to combat this greatest menace. Deep-seated multi-level corruption prevents benefits to reach the poor, as middlemen usurp all! *Thus, in my opinion, to realize India's dream of becoming a vibrant and a great Nation, again, as in ancient times, will supremely depend upon success in this realm!*

Table 20.3 *Poverty and Female Illiteracy in India, 1992–2005*

Characteristics	*1992–3 (NFHS-1)*	*1998–9 (NFHS-2)*	*2001 (Census)*	*2004–5 (NSSO)*	*2005 (World Bank)*
Population Below Poverty Level (NSS) (%)	36.6*	26.9**	***26.6	28.3	42.0.
Per Cent Adult Female Illiteracy (15–49 (%)	62.0	56.0	44.2	NA	NA
Per cent of Kutcha (non-bricked) houses (Indirect Poverty Index) (Census 2001)	NA	NA	39.0	NA	NA

Sources: (1)* National Sample Survey (NSSO, 1996), 50th Round (1992–3); (2)** NSSO (2002), 55th Round (1998–9); (3)*** NSSO (2001), 1999–2000 survey, (4) National Sample survey, 2006 (61st Round) for poverty data, 2004–5, (5) Census of India 2001 (a) for data for illiteracy and (*Kutch*a) or non-bricked houses in 2001, (6) World Bank 2008 Report for 2005 new estimates of poverty.

India's Recent Fertility and Mortality Levels

Fertility Levels

According to National Family Health Survey-III of 2005–6 (NFHS-III, 2007: 4–5), total fertility rate in India (TFR) was 2.7 children, i.e., a woman would have on average 2.7 children in her entire reproductive period. As per NFHS-I survey, done during 1992–3 (NFHS-1, 1995: 1–10), TFR was 3.4, which decreased to 2.9, as per NFHS-II survey (done during 1998–9) (NFHS-II, 2000: 1–20) (Table 20.4). But TFR declined to 2.7 children in 2005–6 (NFHS-III, 2007), thus fertility reduction has been quite slow in India, compared to Japan and China. However, it is quite a good achievement, compared to South Asia, considering India's huge population, incredible demographic diversity having multi-ethnic, multi-religious population, with huge minority population that oppose fertility reduction – due to evil vote bank politics. Thus, unlike China, which is under totalitarian rule and enforced one child policy, conversely in India, democratic polity greatly hinders fertility control (also rapid development), because here each person has a vote, also *veto*! Hence, like a huge elephant, under democracy, India moves very slowly, both demographically and economically. It must also be clearly borne in mind that syndrome of poverty and high fertility in India must be de-linked very soon, before onset of real fertility decline can be ensured permanently (Mukherji, 1995c: 1–36).

Table 20.4 *India's Level of Fertility, Infant Mortality and Family Planning, 1992–2006*

India	*1992–3 NFHS-I*	*1998–9 NFHS-II*	*2005–6 NFHS-III*
Total Fertility Rate (TFR) (children/mother)	3.4	2.9	2.7
Infant Mortality Rate (IMR)	77	72	57
Child Mortality Rates (CMR) (under-5 child deaths)	107	95	74
Contraceptive Use: % of currently married women, 15–49	41	48	56
Female Sterilization (% of total contraceptive use)	76	71	66
Child Vaccinations Got: % of children 12–23 months age	35	42	44
Child Malnutrition (low weight for age)	50	43	40
Maternal Care (3+ visits for ante-natal care, % of mothers)	44	44	51
Safe deliveries in hospitals (% of all deliveries)	26	34	41

Sources: NFHS-I (1995), NFHS-II (2000), NFHS – III (2007), IIPS, Mumbai.

Figure 20.2 *Total Fertility Rate*

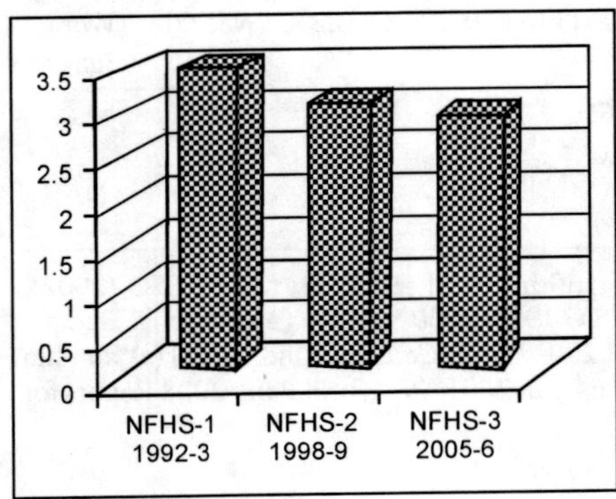

Figure 20.3 *Infant Mortality Rate*

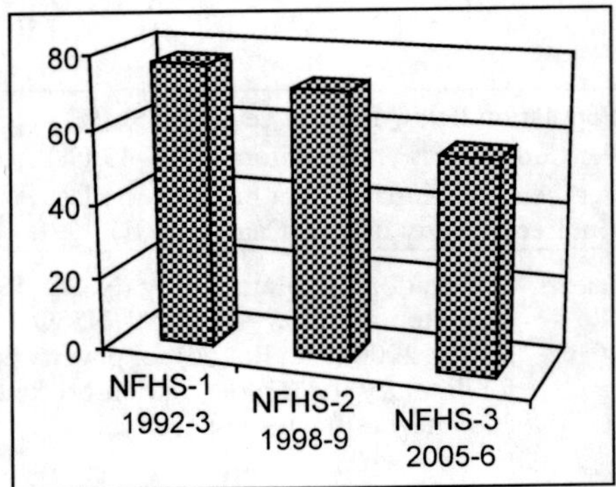

Infant Mortality Rates (IMR)

IMR is considerably decreasing from 77 infant deaths before attaining age 1, per 1,000 live births (in a year) in 1992–93 (NFHS-I), to 72 deaths in 1998–9

(NFHS-II), and 57 deaths in 2005–6 (NFHS-III). Such decline is not spectacular, compared to Sri Lanka (10 in 2001). Rural IMR (62.2) is 50 per cent higher than urban IMR (41.5). High IMR is caused due to widespread female illiteracy among mothers(70), sharply declining as the education of mothers improves to 10 years schooling (26) (NFHS-III: 183). Widespread regional disparities also prevail, Uttar Pradesh in the north has IMR of 70, while Kerala in the south, about 15 (NFHS-III: 8–10). "Combating widespread female illiteracy and providing essential child health care to rural areas and all backward and neglected states are urgently needed for IMR reduction. Without IMR decline, fertility transition will not occur in India" (Mukherji, 2007: 173–180). One important field-based -investigation showed that efficient management of rural Primary Heath Centres (PHCs) are very much required in order to enhance their delivery services to the poor rural people (Mukherji, 1989b: 1–125).

Family Planning

Contraceptive prevalence rate among currently married women is 56 per cent in 2005–6 (NFHS-III), considerably improved from 41 per cent in 1992–3 (NFHS-I) and 48 per cent in 1998–9 (NFHS-II). Muslim women use much less contraceptives (46%) than Hindu women (58%) (NFHS-III: 6–7). Contraceptive use is still responsibility of women, men still do not share, by using condoms. Female sterilization is the primary method used, 66 per cent. This is highly practiced mainly in southern states: Andhra Pradesh (63%), Karnataka (57) and Tamil Nadu (55). Median age of female sterilization in Andhra Pradesh is 23 years, which led to its recent fertility decline. Four northern states, Uttar Pradesh (17%), Bihar (24), Rajasthan (34) and Madhya Pradesh (43) are still lagging. Drastic poverty reduction and rigorous family planning in such highly populous and highly fertile states are most urgently required, because they will contribute to half of the future demographic explosion!

Child Health Care and Child Malnutrition

Sadly, even in 2005–6, only less than half (44%) of Indian children of 12–23 months got fully vaccinated against 6 major childhood illnesses (BCG, Polio-3, DPT-3, Measles, TB, Tetanus), and over half are not protected fully. Vast rural-urban differences also stare at our face (rural only 38.6% and urban 57.6%) (NFHS-III: volume 1: 231–2). Wide regional disparities also prevail: northern states of Uttar Pradesh (only 23%), Rajasthan (26.5), Bihar (33), and Madhya Pradesh (40) stand in sharp contrast against southern states like Kerala (75%) and Tamil Nadu (81) (ibid.: 231). Children of educated mothers and less deprived families are better vaccinated, so also children of developed states, as compared to neglected and backward northern states. Besides, it is a great pity that *providing child nutrition remains still an unfulfilled goal, even in 2005–6: over 40 per cent of children age 12–23 months remain under weight* (NFHS-III: Volume 1: 274). Tremendous efforts are thus necessary to achieve UN's Millennium Development Goals (MDG) for child health care and nutrition by 2015.

Maternal Health Care: Ante-natal Care and Safe Child Delivery

Even in 2005–6, only half of mothers, who gave births in preceding 5 years, were given adequate ante-natal care of three visits or more, and about half of Indian mothers remain only partially attended, or unattended. Safe deliveries occurred only to 41 per cent cases; however, another 49 per cent were assisted by a health professional (NFHS-III: 11–12). No wonder that maternal mortality is still very high in India. Again, educated mothers, non-poor mothers and mothers in relatively developed states get more ANC, Tetanus injections, folic acid tablets, and safe child delivery services than the illiterate mothers, poor mothers and mothers in backward states. These leave much to be desired for maternal health care in India. Indeed, better MCH care will greatly help in achieving faster and stable fertility transition (Mukherji, 2007: 205–258).

Trends of Urbanization in India, 1951–2021

As per Census 2001, though only 28 per cent of India's population was urban; but its total urban population was massive 285 million. Indian cities and metropolises are already bursting in their seams, manifesting very acute problems of housing, slums, traffic, steep land and housing prices, over-congestion, failing urban services and pollution (Figure 20.4). They are growing mainly in size, not in prosperity (Mukherji, 2006: 21–43). If present trends continue, then, by 2021, India will be 43.5 per cent urban, with 578 millions urban population (Figure 20.4 and Table 20.5) (Census 2001a), tremendously over-straining urban infrastructure, urban services and employment situation (Dholakia, 2008b: 163–175). *Hope, India's 9 per cent growing economy, rapid industrialization and globalization may turn numerous metros and large cities as vibrant new centres of buoyancy and engines of development, instead of faltering urban nodes!*

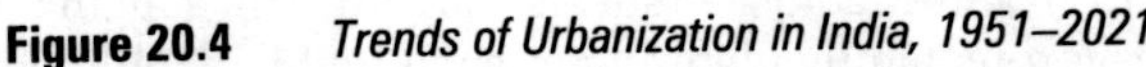

Figure 20.4 *Trends of Urbanization in India, 1951–2021*

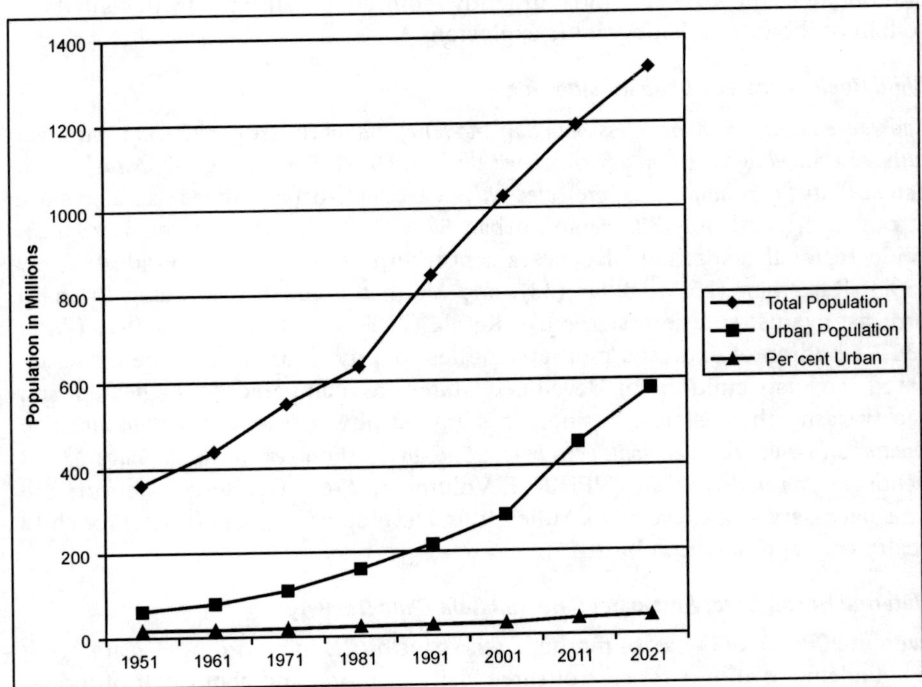

Table 20.5 *Trends of Urbanization in India, 1991–2021 (millions)*

Year	*Total Population*	*Urban Population*	*Per cent Urban*
1991	844.32	217.17	25.72
2001	1027.00	285.35	27.78
2011	1194.40	453.85	38.00
2021	1328.33	577.83	43.50

Sources: Censuses of India, 1991 (a) to 2001 (a).

Internal Migration

Natural increase in population in towns and cities is the major contributing factor in India's urbanization, and will remain so in future. Besides, contribution of rural to urban, and urban to urban migration to urban population has been about 27.3 per cent, which has increased to 34 per cent by 2001 (Table 20.6). In future, huge population pressure on limited agricultural land will lead to tremendous surge in rural to urban migration, thus, further accentuating the crucial problems of migration-urbanization in India (Mukherji, 2006: 17–170). The present patterns of massive labour migration from backward northern states of Bihar, Uttar Pradesh, and Madhya Pradesh to burgeoning metropolises of Mumbai, Kolkata, New Delhi and Chennai will multiply manifold, with future streams directed towards emerging new mega cities of Hyderabad, Bangalore, Ahmedabad, Gurgaon, Surat, Pune and others. Future urbanization and massive urban-ward migration will require challenging efforts for evening out economic and social disparities over India's national space, very efficient urban management, rural regeneration, rural industrialization, development of small and medium towns and cities, spatial restructuring of economic space and massive generation of jobs for incoming migrants to their urban El–Dorado's (Mukherji, 2006: 315–339).

Figure 20.5 *India: Per cent Urban*

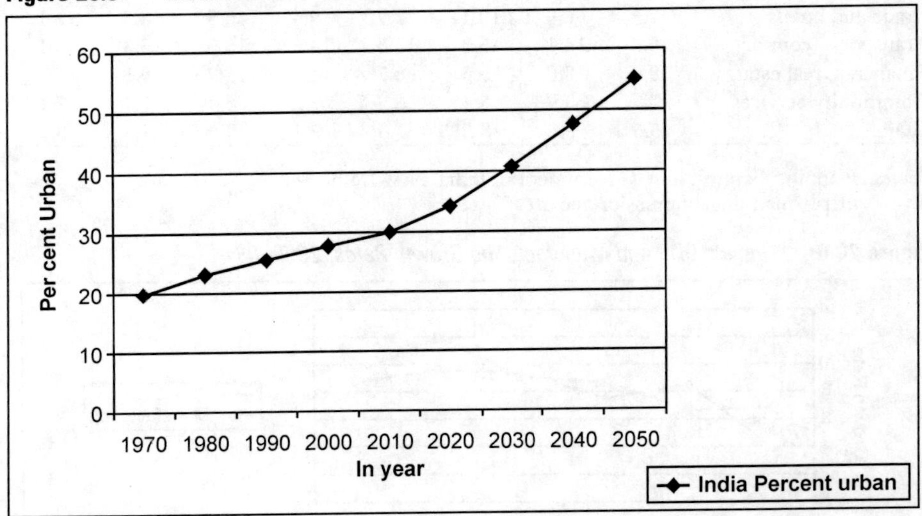

Source: UN: (2007)

Table 20.6 *Contribution of Migration to Urbanization (millions)*

Year	Total Population	Urban Population	No. of Migrants (all durations)	Migrants as % to Total Population	Components of Decadal Migration (millions)				Vol. of Decadal Urban-ward Migration (millions)
					Rural-Rural	Rural-Urban	Urban-Rural	Urban-Urban	
1981	659.3	159.6	206.5	31.32	46.26	15.33	6.45	12.39	27.72
1991	816.2	217.3	226.7	27.77	46.25	16.76	6.08	11.58	28.34
2001	1027.0	285.4	307.0	30.00	53.35	20.59	6.27	14.39	34.78

Source: Computed from Census 2001(a) and (b) Data.

Part II
Growing Economy of India

Since April 1991, the government of India's new open economic policies have unfolded new vistas and led to unprecedented economic growth and development, Thus, previous 44 years of very stifling license and permit Raj (administration) have ended, encouraging greater integration with International markets, and have led to very fast and incredible economic growth. Indian economy continued to grow very fast, averaging above 8 per cent during last 17 years, 1991–2007. Often, annual growth reached 10 per cent plus (Planning Commission, 2002a).

Table 20.7 *Some Indicators of India's Growing Economy, 2002–08*

Items	IX Plan	2002–3	2003–4	2004–5	2005–6	2006–7	X Plan	2007–8
Agriculture-Allied	2.5	–7.2	10.0	0.0	5.9	3.8	2.5	2.6
Mining	4.0	8.8	3.1	8.2	4.9	5.7	6.1	3.4
Manufacturing	3.3	6.8	6.6	8.7	9.0	12.0	8.6	9.4
Electricity	4.8	4.7	4.8	7.9	4.7	6.0	5.6	7.8
Construction	7.1	7.9	12.0	16.1	16.5	12.0	12.9	9.6
Trade and hotels	7.5	6.9	10.1	7.7	9.4	8.5	8.5	12.1
Transport – comm.	8.9	14.1	15.3	15.6	14.6	16.6	15.3	15.1
Financing, real estate	8.0	8.0	5.6	8.7	11.4	13.9	9.5	11.7
Community Services	7.7	3.9	5.4	6.9	7.2	6.9	6.1	7.1
GDP	5.5	3.8	8.5	7.5	9.4	9.6	7.5	8.7

Source: Planning Commission, Government of India, New Delhi. See http://planningcommission.nic.in/

Figure 20.6 *India's GDP and Manufacturing Growth Rates, 2000–08*

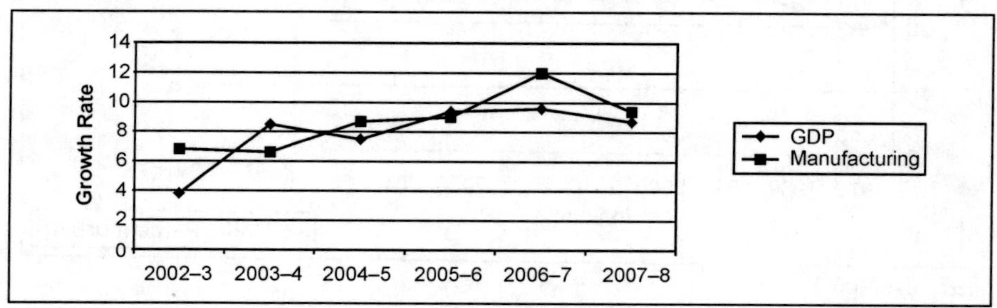

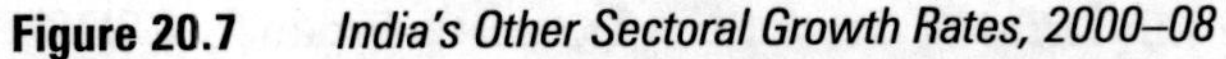

Figure 20.7 *India's Other Sectoral Growth Rates, 2000–08*

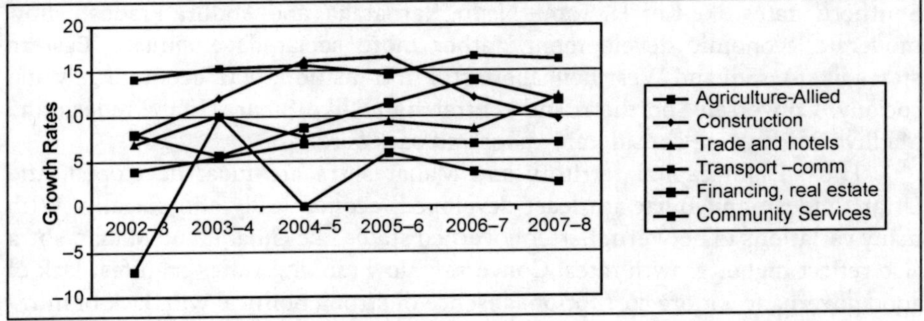

Spatial Differences in the Levels of Development

Tremendous spatial variations prevail over India in the levels of economic development-Table 20.8 presents some economic and social indicators showing these regional differences. States like Delhi capital territory, Maharashtra, Gujarat and Haryana are economically more developed, showing higher Per Capita Income

Table 20. 8 *Regional Differences in Levels of Economic Development, India, 2007*

Rank	*States Ranked According to More to Less Developed status, considering these 6 criteria.*	*Per Capita Income, 2003–4 at 1993–4 prices (Rs) (Planning Commission)*	*State Gross Domestic Product (GSDP) Growth Rate, 2002–7*	*Literacy (Census 2001)*	*Population below Poverty level, 2004–5 (Head count Ratio), (NSSO)*	*Per cent Urban, Census 2001*	*Electricity Available 2006–7 (000 GWh)*
1	Delhi (Union Territory)	29231	8.0	81.6	10.5	93	21.9
2	Maharashtra	16479	7.9	76.9	29.95	42	91.1
3	Gujarat	16779	10.6	61.1	16.75	37	54.3
4	Haryana	15721	8.7	67.9	13.92	29	24.9
5	Tamil Nadu	12976.	6.8	73.5	28.31	44	62.4
6	Punjab	15800	5.7	69.7	8.12	34	35.9
7	Karnataka	13141	6.6	66.6	27.15	34	41.4
8	Kerala	12101	7.4	90.9	14.48	26	13.9
9	Andhra Pradesh	11333	7.4	60.5	14.8	27	56.4
10	Himachal Pradesh	12302	7.6	76.5	11.61	10	5.3
11	West Bengal	11612	6.0	68.6	25.67	28	29.6
12	Jammu-Kashmir	7591	5.2	55.5	4.81	25	8.4
13	Rajasthan	8571	5.0	60.4	21.48.	23	31.1
14	Madhya Pradesh	8284	3.9	63.7	37.21	27	33.1
15	Orissa	6487	8.6	63	47.07	15	16.1
16	Assam	6520	6.4	63.3	20.46	13	3.9
17	Uttar Pradesh	5702	5.1	56.3	33.25	21	51.1
18	Bihar	3557	6.4	47	41.53	10	7.8

Sources: (1) For State Domestic Product (SDP) data and electricity data, Planning Commission (2009), Various reports and data, 2007, (2) NSSO (2006) reports for poverty estimates of 2004–5, (3) Census 2001(a) for literacy and per cent urban data. Due to space shortage, only major 17 states and Delhi Union Territory are shown, out of total 28 states and 7 Union Territories.

and also higher growth rates in terms of Gross State Domestic Product (GSDP). Southern states like Kerala, Tamil Nadu, Karnataka, and Andhra Pradesh show moderate economic development, rather more social development. Eastern states like Assam and West Bengal are still in transition, both economically and socially. Conversely, northern and central states like Bihar, Uttar Pradesh and Madhya Pradesh are considerably poor and backward.

Thus, Delhi capital territory and Maharashtra are most developed, and Uttar Pradesh and Bihar are least developed, economically and socially. With many variations in between. Better governed states like Gujarat and Maharashtra also reflect higher growth rates. Conversely, low ranking states manifest lack of good governance, more corruption, absence of strong political will, lack of infrastructure, and of strong motivation and skills for growth and development. Comparatively developed states also fail in terms of poverty alleviation and literacy, and will need better education, health and more social justice. On the other hand, the lagging states will need much better governance, stronger infrastructure, and proper implementation of Five Year Plans so as to reach the Target Poor and Rural population. Top of all, the greatest need is to wiping out corruption from the surface of India. Entirely and urgently. Recently, Gujarat and Bihar are showing better economic performances (2010).

Poverty in India

Various reports of the National Sample Survey Organization (NSSO) indicate that poverty at All-India level was reduced, relatively faster, from 45 per cent to 39 per cent, during 1983–88 period (6 percentage points during 5 years), than the next 6 years (1988–94) which recorded only 3 percentage point decline (39% to 36%) (see Table 20.9). But, some studies (Himanshu, 2007: 497–508; Dev, 2007: 509–521) unravel that poverty levels remained virtually untouched during India's so-called fast economic growth period, 1995–2000. Although India's economy was liberated since 1991 and increasingly integrated with global economy, but it led to *jobless growth*, without touching the lives of the dispossessed millions. Whatever poverty declined, it actually happened during 2000–2005 (reduced from 36% in 1993–04 to 28.3% in 2004–05).

Table 20.9 *Estimated Level of Poverty Head-count Ratio (%)*

	Estimated Level of Poverty Head-count Ratio (%)			
	1983	*1987–88*	*1993–94*	*2004–05*
Rural India	46.5	39.0	37.2	28.7
Urban India	43.6	38.7	32.6	25.9
All-India	44.9	38.9	36.0	28.3

Sources: Himanshu (2007: 497– 508) and Dev and Ravi (2007; 509– 521); their estimates are based on data of National Sample Survey Organization (NSSO, 2006) Report 508 (61st round for 2004–5); and earlier rounds of consumer expenditure surveys or indirect poverty surveys (1996), 50th round (1993–4), 43rd round (1987–8), and for 1983 estimates, Sarvekshana, vol. 13, 1989.

Due to jobless growth during 1991–2005 (even in 2008–09) and lack of strong political will and economic discipline, the absolute number of poor in India virtually remains same: 503 millions in 1983, and 430 millions in 2004–05 (Tables 20.9 and

20.10). *Economic growth must occur with social justice, otherwise it is no development, rather may lead to dangerous exploitation and endless miseries of the Poor.* "Sustained growth remains a high priority. But it is not just how fast a country grows; crucially, it is also *how* it grows. Widening gaps between rich and poor dampen the impact of growth on poverty" (Thomas, 2008: 20).

Table 20.10 *Number of Very Poor and Poor Remained Constant in India, 1983 and 2004–05 (millions)*

		1983	*1983 Total*	*2004–05*	*2004–05 Total*
Rural	Very Poor	140.6		76.7	
	Poor	252		232.2	
	Sub-Total		**392.6**		**308.9**
Urban	Very Poor	38.4		38.4	
	Poor	72.3		83.3	
	Sub-Total		**110.7**		**121.7**
All-India	Very Poor	178.9		115.1	
	Poor	324,3		315.5	
	Sub-Total		**503.2**		**430.6**

Source: Same as in Table 20.9, and as estimated by Dev and Ravi (2007: 510–511).

Figure 20.8 *Poverty Decline in India, 1983–2005*

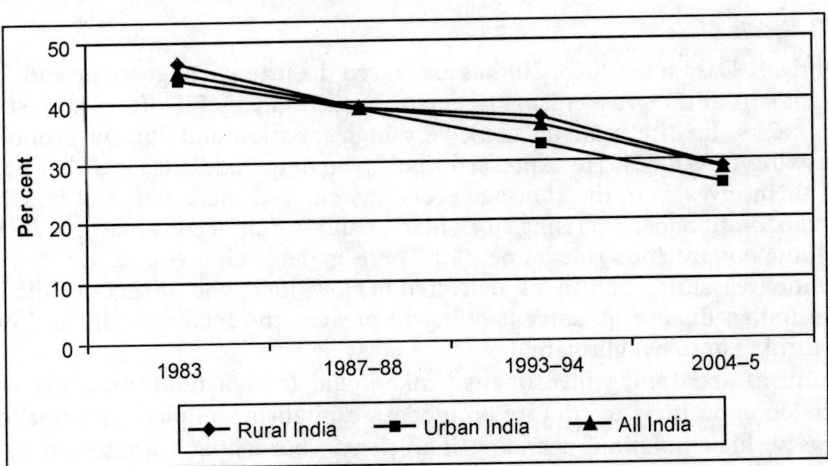

"The new poverty estimates from the World Bank incorporates the findings that living costs are actually higher than estimated before, reflected in a global poverty line of $1.25 a day (roughly Rs 24 per day). These calculations suggest that as of 2005 there were 1.4 billion people world wide living in extreme poverty. One third of them would be in India, signifying the largest number of the poor compared to other countries ..." (ibid.)

"Regardless of precise numbers, the urgency is clearing India for achieving more inclusive growth. It is important to get at the inequalities, but in ways that do not derail growth .... Generating opportunities and jobs for the poorer segments of the population would seem to be the best way forward. India needs to spur more actions and achieve results in these respects"(ibid.). "Poverty data reminds us that it is not enough to grow, it is also vital that increasing numbers of people benefit from the growth. India can generate high growth with a far greater impact on poverty through policy actions. As it turns out, inclusive growth is not only key to social progress, it is indispensable to sustain growth itself" (ibid.).

Need Inclusive Growth and Rapid Poverty Alleviation Measures

More inclusive growth will require actions to address disparities in education that contribute to large earning differentials, specially, the relevance and quality of education and learning outcomes that determine its usefulness in workplace and its contribution to growth (Thomas, 2008). Also need to solve problems of growing skill differentials, mobility and functioning of labour markets. Urgently required is to reduce rural-urban and regional income disparities. Raising agricultural productivity, all-weather rural roads and rural electrification are very essential for rural poverty reduction (Mukherji, 2006: 314–330).

Another urgent measure will be to provide income support *directly to the poor,* totally dispensing with illusory idea of trickle-down effect from top-down. Because, in India, the subsidized programmes very seldom reach to the poor, due to rampant corruption at all levels, specially at village execution levels. So, these are rarely effective. Cash support to the poor must be provided, coupled with subsidized education and health services; thence these may really help in poverty reduction (Mukherji, 2007: 266–305).

India's Middle Class

Recently, S. Dasgupta (2008: 20) has expressed the fear and anger of new middle class Indians at the gross mismanagement of economy by FII (financial institutions, banks, finance ministry etc.), very high inflation and current economic downswing (2007–09). He expressed that, "The new middle classes that extricated themselves from the shortage economy, enjoyed the benefits of housing, car and education loans, a rising stock market and surfeit of consumer goods, the party-poopers are (now) at home. "... There is deepening realization that no amount of reassuring platitudes, delivered in slow, loud, and impeccable diction by the Indian finance minister is going to prevent the Incredible India dream from turning in to a nightmare"

Causes are: "smug investment bankers and foreign fund managers who descended upon India to educate on modern capitalism; coupled with financial profligacy, high inflation, spending inefficiency, burdening with severe fiscal deficit, touching 10 per cent of GDP; further aggravated with rampant consumerism and reckless speculation" (ibid.). Even a neighbourhood shopkeeper is more cautious not to lend credit, beyond one's repayment capacity.

But, further mis-management of economy continues, like many developed countries, the Indian government and the Reserve Bank of India (RBI) are also pouring in huge amount of public money to such inefficient banks and FIIs – which, in reality, resulting in *privatizing personal greed and socializing debts*. Such mismanagement are hurting the poor most and mars the lives of common people of India. "Middle India is thus both fearful and angry. It knows what it doesn't want: terrorist attacks, job insecurity, dwindling purchasing power and political chaos. It is less sure how such goals can be achieved" (ibid.).

Sensex Declines: Worldwide Meltdown also Affects Indian Economy

During March 2007–Sept 2008, Indian share market index, sensex, grew very fast from 8,000 to 22,000 points, mainly due to recently-introduced convertibility of Indian rupees to world's major foreign currencies, and concurrent stable financial returns made available to foreign financial investors and institutions. These returns became very attractive and stable, compared to major international markets. Thus, during that period, increasingly more and more foreign investments kept pouring into Indian share markets, boosting huge spurts in Indian sensex and Indian economy. All major foreign players found it more lucrative to invest in India's growing economy and in the world's largest market of middle class consumers (250–300 million), who were bent on buying any consumer goods (car, freeze, mobile, computer, house).

Then, suddenly, from mid-September, 2008, devastating economic downslide, havoc and very acute credit crunch started in the USA, followed by all major World economies –worldwide meltdown, caused mainly by sub-prime investments to unscrupulous creditors by international financial institutions and banks, gross financial inefficiency, and rampant speculations. Governments of the developed countries are now desperately trying to bail out such agents of private greed, sadly, by socializing the debts. Ripple effects of such international economic downswing are also felt in Indian economy and sensex, that rapidly slid to below 8,000 points by end-October 2008. This downslide occurred because of very rapid withdrawal of dollars by major foreign financial investors, who have to repay their creditors back home. Consequently, dollar reserve of India has dwindled from 310 billion to 292 billion, during March to October 2008, and Indian rupee is sharply devalued, at Rs 50 to one US dollar (in Nov 2008).

Although the sensex has declined (restricting unscrupulous share speculations), and may remain low for next 6–12 months; however, credit crunch may not adversely affect the Indian manufacturing, industries and overall Indian economy. Because, it has strong economic fundamentals (sufficient foreign exchange (forex), good balance of payments, very high individual savings rate (over 34%), good tax outcomes, low fiscal deficit (3% of GDP), high rate of car and other export, etc.).

Such factors make Indian economy capable of withstanding dollar withdrawal shocks, coupled with Reserve Bank of India's (RBI) efforts – constantly monitoring and providing credits to banks and industries – such that Indian economy remains 7.5–8.0 per cent growth, and money flows are constantly available. Many Indian economic experts recently have expressed hopes for economic revival and return to high growth trajectory in near future (Dasgupta, 2008: 12–14).

Present Global Crisis Needs Extraordinary Regulations

Current global meltdown is akin to classic crisis in a joint family, where pampered eldest son squanders away all money in racing, alcoholism and greedy market speculations (as in developed economy), thus, adversely affecting all in the joint family (worldwide). And, eventually, the poor junior-most son suddenly face loss of job and savings, and forced to commit suicide (poor worker in a remote Third World country)! Sadly, the parents in the joint family further pampers the eldest son (financial speculator) by bailing him out, scattering away leftover crumbs. Entire joint family is enslaved (entire world)! *Privatizing personal greed and socializing debts* cannot go on. Global turmoil very urgently requires very extraordinary regulations. International body polity needs drastic actions.

My Vision of Future India

Indeed, India is a rich country in resources, but is still inhabited by the poor people. On the one hand, there is one small tiny *India Shining*, on the other hand, there is a vast *Deprived India*, still in darkness, poverty, misery and exploitation. India cannot become a super-power, until her massive poverty is completely wiped out. And, the Rich India must stop trampling the Poor India. Rampant and very widespread corruption, existing at all levels, political, bureaucratic, administrative, corporate, business and academic systems, must soon be uprooted entirely. Only then, India will be unchained and emerge again as a great Nation and the World's wonder, as before (Mukherji, 2009: 7–12).

Let me conclude this chapter by recalling the divine message of the greatest monk of the World, Swami Vivekananda (1863–1902) – indeed a reincarnation of God Buddha himself. He promised 112 years ago, that: "*Until even a stray dog remains hungry and unfed in India, I cannot take rest and feel complacent, and I will take many re-births and continue to do my work of serving the poor in India*" (Vivekananda, 1896: 150).

Current one and a quarter billion Indians must aspire to live for that supreme goal and touch the divinity!

21 Major Issues in Migration, Urbanization and Regional Disparities in India

Implications and Challenges for the Future

"Do not say we are weak; we can do anything and everything. What can we not do? Everything can be done by us; we all have the same glorious soul, let us believe in it."

Swami Vivekananda (1894)
(Complete Work, Centenary Volume III, 1963: 244)

"This is a lesson for all life. Face the terrible, face it boldly. Like the monkeys, the hardships of life fall back when we cease to flee before them. If we are ever to gain freedom, it must be by conquering nature, never by running away. Cowards never win victories, we have to fight fear and troubles and ignorance if we expect them to flee before us."

Swami Vivekananda (1893)
(Complete Work, Centenary Volume II, 1963, Various pages)

Growing Poverty in India and Utter Neglect of the Poor by the Governments

India's greatest challenge is to combat abject poverty, spread over all corners of the country. Planning commission (2009) estimates that 37.2 per cent of India's population live below the poverty level (in 2005), that is, they cannot get even one square meal a day, required for survival with minimum nutrition. That amounts to 409 million in 2005, and 446 million in 2010 (Table 21.1). However, this is a very conservative estimate. There is an alternative method of measuring poverty, not based on calorie intake, but in terms of consumption expenditures. If poverty is defined as the ability to make minimum consumption expenditure of Rs 20 per capita per day, then people living poverty line implies those unable to spend even Rs 20 per person per day (in 2005). According to this definition, as per Arjun Sengupta Committee, a humungous 77 per cent of India's population lives below poverty level. This amounts to 847 million poor in 2005, or a whooping 924 million in 2010. Thirdly, as recent World Bank report (2008) defined, people living below poverty level are those who cannot afford to spend even $1.25 a day (or Rs 24 per day at PPP, Purchasing Power Parity), and according to this norm, India's poor amounts to 500 million in the year 2005, or 545 million in 2010. So, whichever norm we may take, a big substantial segment of Indians are poor, and another large chunk live on the border fringe of poverty lines. According to these definitions, by 2020, minimum 521 million would be poor according to Planning commission's index, or 636 million by the World Bank norm, or an unbelievable 1078 million, as per Sengupta Committee's yardsticks. These are all very frightening numbers.

Table 21.1 *Estimates of Population below Poverty Line, India, 2001–2010 (millions)*

Year	*2001*	*2005*	*2010*	*2020*
Population (millions)	1016	1100	1200	1400
Poverty Estimates				
(1) Planning Commission (based on minimum food intake needed) **(37.2% poor)**	378	409	446	521
(2) Arjun Sengupta Committee (based on minimum Rs 20 expenditure per capita per day) **(77% poor)**	782	847	924	1078
(3) World Bank estimates (based on $1.25 per day or roughly Rs 24 expenditure per day) **(45. 4% poor)**	461	500	545	636

Sources: Planning Commission (2009) (*www.planningcommission.nic.in*), *Arjun Sengupta Committee Report (2006)*, *and World Bank (2008).*

A recent study (Gupta, 2010: 22) also observed that "Low poverty rates appear good only if the cut-off point is set off at Rs 11.8 consumption expenditure per capita per day in the rural areas and Rs 17.9 in urban areas. Are these yardsticks at all rational in today's prices?" Can really anyone survive with such a meagre amount of subsistence? "If these cut-off points are raised even slightly, by Rs 3.0 for rural areas and Rs 2.0 for urban areas, the proportion of the poor goes up to 38 per cent. Slowly raise the bar by another tiny fraction, say, to Rs 22, and this figure swells to amazing 70 per cent" (ibid.) *Thus, poverty in India is still very rampant, and cannot be just wished away.*

Thus, even after 63 years of India's Independence, and even after 20 years of economic reforms (started in 1991), poverty remains stubbornly high in the country. And, their numbers are swelling very rapidly. Still many academicians, especially the demographers, population specialists, geographers, economists and other social scientists keep denying India's acute poverty problems, and a vast majority of them appear not at all concerned with India's most burning issues of extreme poverty and social injustice! This is most unfortunate. During last 50 years (1959–2010), whenever I tried to talk about poverty in India, and the great need for planning for the Poor, I was very badly humiliated and insulted many times. Saddest thing is that it happened repetitively not by the illiterate people, rather by the fellow academicians, by the university professors themselves and by the elite society! *That is, there is an increasingly hostile attitude of the Indian academicians towards the poor people, arising out of a guilt feeling* (as if feelings still left there!). If the so-called civil society were really civil, then, India would have returned to her timeless wonder, long ago!.

"There is no point denying the vast extent of poverty. There are other evidences and various symptoms of poverty coming from different sources"(Ranade, 2010: 30). For example, very widespread Naxalite (as it started in 1968 in Naxalbari village in Darjeeling district) or Maoist movements and violence occur in 200 districts of India (out of total 605 districts). Such symptoms are: rapidly increasing in stinking urban slums; such as, high incidences of infant mortality rates (above 75 infant deaths per 1,000 live born infants per year); such as, very widespread adult female illiteracy rates in most states (above 40–60%, even 60–80%, or over, in 2004–05) (Mukherji, 2007: 100–280). It comes from such evidences as more than 100,000 farmers' suicides in Maharashtra and Andhra states alone, or incidences of very high child malnutrition among 1–4 years age (about 50%). Lack of empathy from the scholars, planners and policy makers, and utter neglect by the politicians and the governments to the challenging issues of poverty eradication lie at the root of such a great malady in India. Ranade (ibid.) has rightly, opined, "Our rich politicians' neglect of poverty and governance can be considered a much bigger scandal than their involvement in ongoing IPL (Indian Premier League) drama."

In 2006, the Government of India launched *National Rural Employment Guarantee Act* (NREGA) programmes, under which one individual of the BPL (below poverty level) families will get 100 days of guaranteed work each year, with around Rs 100 as daily wages. So far, only 160 districts, out of total 605 districts of the country, were brought under this NREGA programme. On paper, this looks good, and this is just an old wine in a new bottle, because Food for Work (FFW) Programme were very much prevalent in India in the 1960s and 1970s. This is just a revival of that old scheme. But now supposed to be spread all over India. But, there are many caveats, and many failures in its implementation. First, identification of BPL families are not properly done, and actual poor families are often left out, due to political mischief, political parties' arm-twisting, sectarian conflicts between the higher castes denying basic rights to the lower castes, and so forth. Second, the entire implementation is heavily bureaucratized and tainted with widespread corruption, at all levels.

Third, its ground level implementation is entrusted with the Panchayati Raj organizations (local village self-governments), and their vested interest groups commit many corrupt practices, such that the entire purpose is defeated. The government has no mechanisms to supervise proper implementation of NREGA programmes. Thus, most frequently it is the rich middlemen who are benefited, rather than the actual poor. Huge money is wasted and goes down the drains. And, the vast sea of the poor humanity remains in the same darkness, as before. So, NREGA is a great failure. Although the central government and the congress party keep trumpeting its so-called grand success. It really needs tremendous overhauling and freedom from all pervading corruption, and uplift of the mind sets of all involved. Similar programme for Public Distribution Systems (PDS) of Food to the poor at the subsidized prices are also very seriously infected with deep-seated corruption and non-implementation, due to the same ineffective delivery systems and very corrupt governance.

Recently, Mundle (2010: 20) has also observed that "Delivery is the Key" in channeling food and other BPL entitlements to the poor, and recommended that: "if self-help groups are used to distribute PDS grain, BPL cards or NREGA job cards, we would see a sharp improvements in the effectiveness of anti-poverty programmes" (ibid.) In fact, these need vast systems transformations and committed officers and institutions.

Another very recently initiated programme is *Jawaharlal Nehru National Urban Renewal Mission (JNNURM)* for affordable housing for the urban poor and the slum dwellers. The purpose is commendable. On paper the scheme is excellent. Nevertheless, its implementation is plagued by many serious lapses. Namely, inadequate financial provision in the budget, or continued eviction of the slum dwellers in the mega cities. The onus of developing the slums of cheap housing given to the same groups of developers, who are primarily responsible of artificially sky-rocketing the urban land prices and urban housing beyond the reach of the poor masses and the migrants (UNDP, India, 2009; Raju, 2009). These processes thus create stinking slums, and play dirty politics in the entire slum redevelopment programmes.

The greatest paradox is that now India is having very fast growing economy (above 7.5% growth annually). But this growth is usurped by a handful of business families or corporate houses, at the cost of an ocean of dispossessed and exploited humanity! It appears that India's Planning commission, the government's top economists, and the business houses do understand well *only* the economic growth rates, but they do not understand that more than 500 million Indian poor cannot *eat* growth rates, they need rice and flour to eat and to survive!

These trends soon might lead to most calamitous civil war and most dangerous catastrophe, beyond a point of no return! Already, excessively violent Naxal or Maoist movements have created very serious law and order problems in 200 districts of the country and the great danger of ultimate dissolution of India! Such violent movements get easy fodder from the local tribal and the poor people who have been denied the fruits of development, since many centuries. Very recently (*Times of India*, April 4, 2010), about 75 para-military forces were ambushed and mercilessly killed by the Maoist insurgents at Dantewada village in Chhattisgarh. And, the government was just a mute spectator of such a great killing by the Naxals or the Maoist insurgents. Lack of development is one of the reasons for such violent agitation, but the real goal of such Maoist insurgents is to capture political power of the entire nation. However, if the benefits of development reach to such poor and dispossessed people, surely it will make an effective dent upon their such violent movements. But, the Naxals want all round destruction of the entire country and capture of absolute power, not development of poor people or the tribal, because otherwise, they would not have bombarded schools, railways, roads, dams, power stations and all signs of development, in less developed tribal zones!

A very recent study (Ganguly, 2010: 14) also opined in the same vein: "There are reasons to worry about the quality of this growth, which doesn't seem inclusive enough" ... "The benefits of India's growth, by contrast, haven't percolated significantly beyond the middle class. This means India hasn't made a serious enough dent upon poverty – it ranked 65 out of 84 countries in the Global Hunger Index of 2009, below North Korea, Sudan and Zimbabwe."

The government, the official economists, and planning machinery trumpet only about 8 or 9 per cent growth rates, but India's 500 million poor can not chew growth rates, they utterly need rice and food for survival, which the governments neither understand, nor provide. All high-flying talks about so-called " inclusive growth" are mere lip service to social justice and eye wash, while even mid-day meals to primary school children are frequently stopped due to abysmal poverty and frequent political bungling (Mukherji, 1997f: 1–12). *"India is a strange country where the so-called demographers and population specialists make study of population and undertake National Population Surveys, without ever touching and investigating the basic premise, "poverty", in which hundreds of millions of people are deeply imbedded" (Mukherji, 1997h: 1–6; 1997g: 1–21; 2007).* Recently one journalist have also lamented: "Millions go to bed in the night hungry, while millions of tons of food-grains are rotting in the open" (Nandy, 2010: 3).

Thus, in short, very poor governance at every level of the governments, panchayats, local, district, state and the Central, lie at the roots of such dismal situation, and the continuation of abysmal poverty and inequities in India (Mukherji, 1998a: 250–270). Even after 63 years of independence from the colonial rules! Even after 63 years of continued Planning Era!! Required planning strategies are discussed in last chapter (22).

Table 21.2 *Estimates of Poverty in India, 2001–2051 (if per cent under poverty level remain unchanged, and decline in poverty trends continue) (millions)*

	2001	*2004–5*	*2011*	*2021*	*2031*	*2041*	*2051*
Total Population (millions)	**1027**	**1104.2**	**1220**	**1379**	**1525**	**1656**	**1758**
Total Poverty – Estimate I (*) (millions)	380	409	452	511	565	613	651
Total Poverty – Estimate II ($) (millions)	407	438	484	547	605	657	697
Total Poverty (NSSO) (millions)	339	312	285	258	231	204	177

(*) Following Tendulkar Committee estimate of 2005 as base and if same per cent of poverty continues unchanged. ($) Following World Bank 2008 estimates of 2005 as base and if same per cent of poverty continues unchanged.

Sources: World Bank Report, NSSO Reports, and Tendulkar Committee Report. Only baselines of these estimates for 2005 are taken, then future extrapolations are made independently, by the author, assuming proportion under poverty remain unchanged. For NSSO estimates, however, 1993–4 and 2004–5 estimates and their expected changes are taken into consideration for future extrapolations, but with much reservation (see notes below).

Figure 21.1 *Estimates of India's Future Poverty, 2001–2051 (if current per cent below poverty remain unchanged, and if decline in poverty continues)*

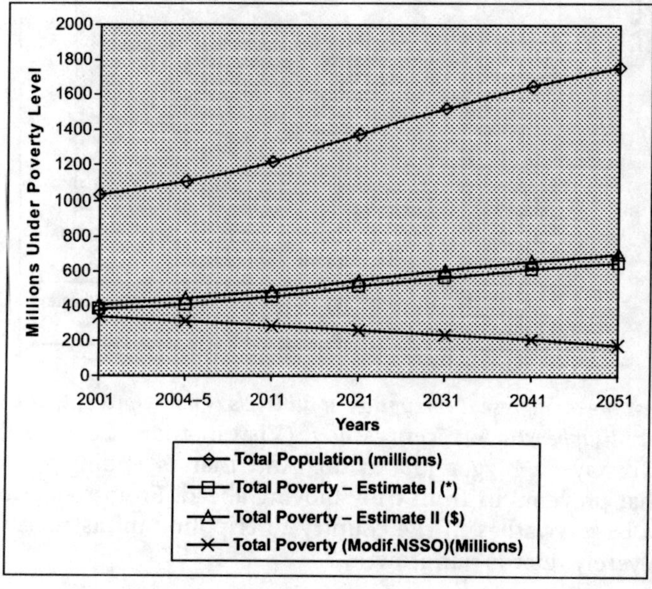

Estimates of Rural and Urban Poverty, India, 2001–2051

Here one important point must be stated right at the outset. Although NSSO Reports on Consumption Expenditures, 61st Round (2004–5) and 50th Round (1993–4) and per cent under poverty are considered as starting points, but, future estimates of poverty reduction *are independently* extrapolated by me here, *not* based on NSSO's probable future trend lines. This is because as Dev and Ravi (2007), Himangshu (2007) and others have doubted, NSSO estimates are much biased, protecting the government's image in poverty reduction. As Dipankar Gupta (2010: 22) also revealed "according to one tally, just about 28 per cent of India's population lives below the poverty line. This is clearly India shining. But, then our nose tells us something different. Tendulkar committee and World Bank estimates themselves have also doubted their reliability. So, my estimates of India's future success in poverty reduction, thus, takes NSSO future estimates with much pinch of salt, and makes a more realistic estimates (considering the "art of the possible" and government's "utter lack of political will and determination" to combat hunger and poverty in India (Mukherji et al., (1980), *Population, Food and Land Inequality: Geography of Hunger in India*). It will be a great achievement, if India's number of the poor comes down to less than 200 million, even by the year 2051!

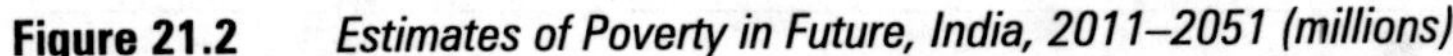

Figure 21.2 *Estimates of Poverty in Future, India, 2011–2051 (millions)*

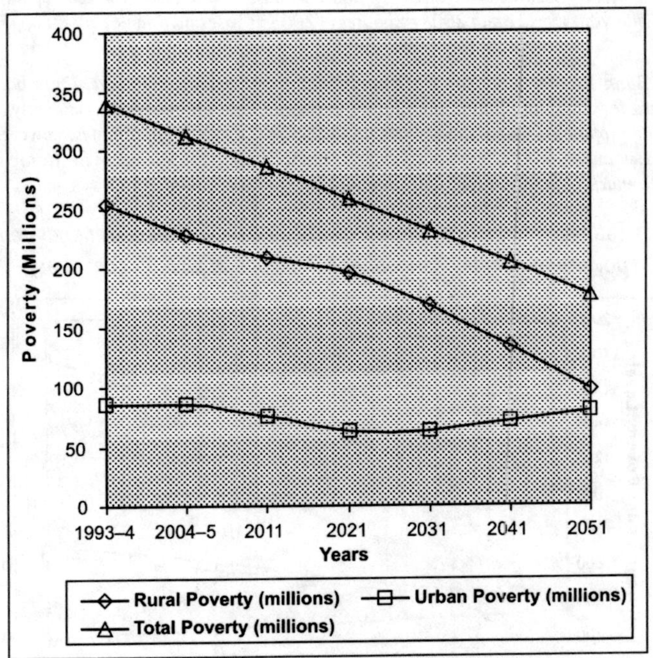

But, unless the omnipresent corruption at all levels is not wiped out, abject poverty in India will not disappear!! A recent study (Viswanathan, 2010: 16) similarly observed, "we have a bigger job to do. And that is ending the systematic corruption that prevents us from truly moving ahead. From rendering the PDS ineffective in large swathes of the country to crippling infrastructure projects, corruption severely retards our growth."

Table 21.3 *India: Estimates of Rural and Urban Poverty, 2011–2051*

	1993–4	*2004–5*	*2011*	*2021*	*2031*	*2041*	*2051*
Rural Poverty (%) (see text)	37.2	28.7	24.5	21.5	18.5	15.4	12.4
Urban Poverty (%) (see text)	32.6	25.6	20.7	13.3	10.2	8.9	8.2
Total Poverty (%) (see text)	36.0	28.3	23.4	21.1	15.2	12.3	10.1
Rural Poverty (millions)	254	227	209	195	168	133	97
Urban Poverty (millions)	85	85	76	63	63	71	80
Total Poverty (millions)	339	312	285	258	231	204	177

Note: NSSO Reports on Consumption Expenditures, 61st Round (2004–5) and 50th Round (1993–4) and per cent under poverty are independently extrapolated based on computations of their 2004–5 estimates See explanations given below.

End of corruption demands character building of all citizens of India, and sincere feelings of patriotism for the Motherland, India. Alas! All those good qualities have completely disappeared since 1947, since India won freedom after great sacrifice of millions of citizens. It appears that the nation's all energy was spent in just achieving Independence from foreign rules that enslaved India for 1,000 years, and nothing was left for nation-building and character-building!! This is the greatest requirement now.

Estimates of Future Urban Slum Population, India, 2001–2051

Town and Country Planning Organization of India (TCPO) estimated that India's total slum population was only 45.7 million in 1991, which increased to about 61 million by 2001. They also observed that slums are more in million cities (41.3% in 1991 and estimated to be 35.45% in 2001), and less slums are

Figure 21.3 *Estimates of Total Urban Slum Population, India, 2001–2051*

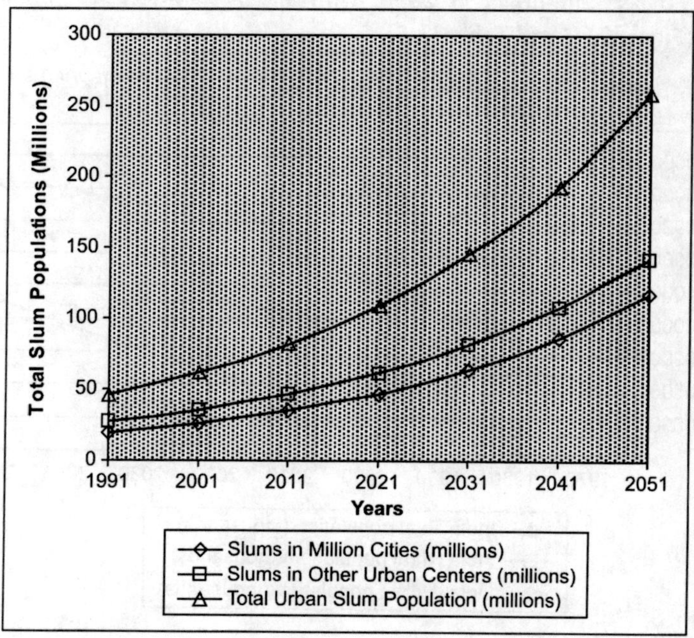

found in other urban centres. Over all slums constitutes 21.06 per cent of total urban population of India in 1991, which would rise to about 26.5. per cent in 2051. More or less, TCPO's trend lines are considered in extrapolating urban slum population in future, from 2001–2051. By 2051, India would have 259 million of slum population, which would comprise about 26.5 per cent of total urban population of the country. To provide clean and potable drinking water, sanitation, electricity, drainage, affordable housing and adequate shelter to this humongous population will need Himalayan tasks!

Table 21.4 *Estimates of Future Urban Slum Population, India, 2001–2051*

	1991	*2001*	*2011*	*2021*	*2031*	*2041*	*2051*
Slums in Million Cities (millions)	18.9	25.6	34.7	47	63.7	86.3	116.9
Slums in Other Urban Centres (millions)	26.8	35.4	46.7	61.7	81.4	107.4	141.7
Total Urban Slum Population (millions)	45.7	61	81.4	108.7	145.1	193.7	258.6

Sources: Town and Country Planning Organization (TCPO), 1996 and 2005.

India's Urban Future: Migration and Urbanization Situation, 1970–2050

Urbanization in India has been quite rapid, with slums growing very faster. In 1951, India's total urban population was just 62.4 millions (17.2%), which rose to a staggering 285.4 millions in 2001 (27.8%), showing a great spurt in urban population, an increase of 223 millions in mere 50 years! Table 21.5 provides UNDP's (2007) estimates of India's urban future: *it will increase from 289 millions in 2000 to a burgeoning dimension of 473 millions by 2020, and a fearful 915 millions by the year 2050! Urban percentages will rise from 28 per cent in 2000 to 34 per cent by the next 20 years, to 55 per cent by the year 2050! That means India will be more than 50 per cent urban in 2050, with an unbelievable 915 millions urban population (Figure 21.4 and Table 21.5).*

Figure 21.4 *India: Total Population, Rural and Urban Population, 1970–2050*

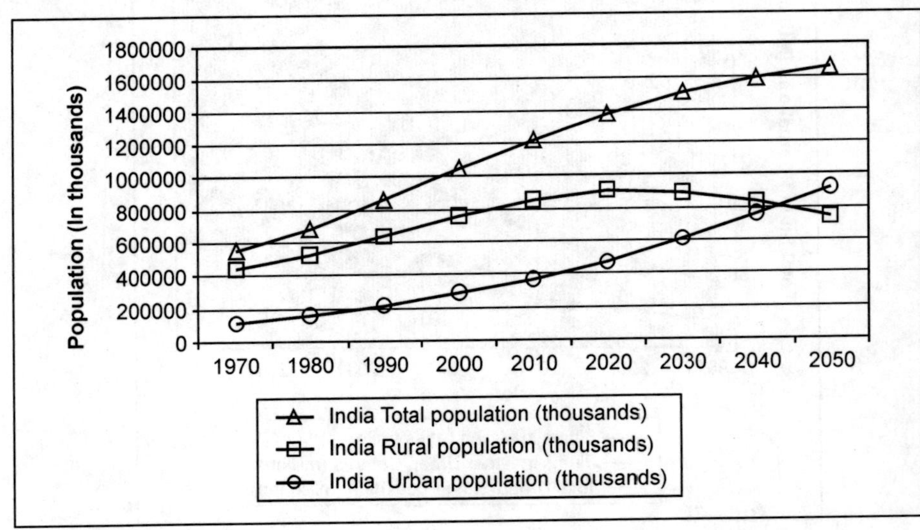

Table 21.5 *India: Total Population, Urban and Rural Population and Per cent Urban, 1980–2050 (thousands)*

	1980	*1990*	*2000*	*2010*	*2020*	*2030*	*2040*	*2050*
Total population	688575	860195	1046235	1220182	1379198	1505748	1596719	1658270
Rural	529529	640437	756797	853324	906638	894341	832814	743382
Urban	159046	219758	289438	366858	472561	611407	763905	914888
Urban (%)	23.1	25.5	27.7	30.1	34.3	40.6	47.8	55.2

Sources: *UNDP, World Urbanization Prospects (2007) (2006 Revision). (According to UNDP, 2007)*

Figure 21.5 *India: Per cent Urban*

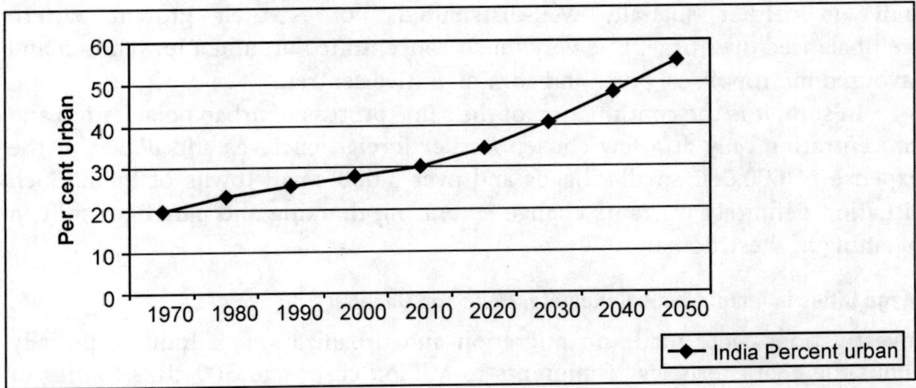

It was feared that the total urban slum population would double from its 80 millions in 1988 to 160 millions within the short span of just 15 years (NIUA, 1988; Ministry of Urban Development, Urban Commission, 1988).

Indian Mega Cities Show the Following Characteristics

Fuchs. et al. (1994: 1–2) noted: "Mankind's future will unfold largely in urban settings ... a major challenge for mankind is, therefore, an informed response to such unprecedented urban growth and intelligent management of urban settlements, which in future, will serve as abiding place of majority of mankind". Given this context, it is notable to examine the following characteristics of India's large urban centres Census of India 2001 (a and b) (2005: various tables):

(a) These metropolises are still growing at much alarming rate,

(b) They remain main centres of survival for large masses of migrants from distant rural areas,

(c) They remain the main source of employment for the distressed rural migrants,

(d) Satellite towns/new towns/suburbs are growing very fast mainly because these are primarily dormitory towns.

Mega cities like Mumbai, Kolkata, Delhi (and others) show the following characteristics mainly used as night-time dormitory places for the million of daily commuters and new migrants, who are compelled to move to the cruel metropolis, as tiny cogs in a giant wheel.

Most of these daily commuters are compelled to travel as much as 100 miles daily, wasting several hours of their precious lives everyday. Lives of these millions of daily commuters are routine, robot-like, completely mechanistic, deadly stable, totally involuted, and perennially joyless. Such lifeless lives are signs of human underdevelopment! This is the process of anti-development, not development. Such is the tremendous social-psychological-economic- spiritual prices that people are forced to pay for lopsided, unplanned, iniquitous, and socially and spatially unjust urbanization.

Polarization of urbanization emerges during last 6 decades (1950–2010), in spite of some attempts at decentralization. Contrary to what National Commission on Urbanization (1988, ibid.) believed, level of urbanization in India is neither spatially well-distributed, nor is their growth pattern well-balanced over time. It is very much concentrated around a few chosen and favoured metropolises, ports and administrative centres.

In sum, it is the continuation of the same process of urban polarization and concentration only at a few chosen former foreign enclaves and nodes, at the expense of 600,000 small villages and over 5,000 small towns of India. Such situation definitely warrants change-embracing thinking and paradigm shift in planning in these domains.

Mega Cities in India: Mumbai, Kolkata, Delhi and Chennai

Investigations were made on migration and urbanization in India, especially about the characteristics of migrants to Million cities and 300 class I cities in 1991 (with more than 100,000 populations), have revealed the following basic trends (Mukherji, 2001b: 79–121; 2001c: 1–26):

- Most such cities indicate that migrants largely come from far flung rural areas;
- Most of these migrants are either illiterate, or having less than primary education;
- Most of these migrants are absorbed in low-grade production process work, or low grade sales and services – where wages are low, competition severe, and insecurity predominate. So it is very low quality migration of poor and illiterate people; who are compelled to crowd in city slums as low grade workers. It leads to tremendous waste of human and national potentials.
- Most such cities are also having poor tertiary sectors as the main component of their economic structure, not manufacturing sectors or strong secondary sectors.
- In sum, the patterns of poverty-induced migration of masses of illiterate and unskilled migration occurs to Indian metropolises and class I cities, even in 1981–91 and 1991–2001 decades, and these lead to acute urban involution and acute urban decay.

Further on Economy of Mega Cities

- Indian mega cities' urban economy reflect growth of only poor tertiary sectors: Mumbai (54% in 1991, rose to 69% in 2001), Kolkata (57% in 1991, 75% in 2001), New Delhi (64% in 1991, 68% in 2001) and Chennai

(62% in 1991, 72% in 2001) (Census of India, 1991(d) and 2001(d): Workers Tables).

- Among migrants who moved for employment, Census 1991 revealed that majority are either illiterate or semi-literate (less than high school, indeed primary): Mumbai (62%), Kolkata (66%), New Delhi (58%) and Chennai (50%).
- Majority of all employment migrants absorbed only in low-grade work viz., production-processing, petty sales/services, low-grade transport: Mumbai (61%), Kolkata (69%), New Delhi (63) and Chennai (51%) (Census of India, 2001(b), Migration Tables). What could be expected from such a sea of illiterate/semi-literate migrants, somehow eking out their miserable life in their urban El-Dorado?
- Filthy slums are visible everywhere (Table 21.2(a) and Table 21.2(b)): Mumbai (56%), Kolkata (43%), New Delhi (35%), and Chennai (33%) (Ministry of Urban Development, 1988: 1–32; Mukherji, 1996a: 26–54; 1996b: 41–91).
- Many recent studies have also revealed manifold urban problems of Indian mega cities (Chapman, Dutt, and Bradnock, 1999: 1–15; Dutt and Parai, 1999: 93–107; Census of India, 2001(a to d), various volumes). Such sordid facts amply testify main tenet of this study, and warrant our urgent actions (see Table 21.6 in two parts).

Table 21.6(a) *Recent Characteristics of Migration and Urbanization in Mega Cities, 2001 (continued)*

Metros	*Estimated Population (millions)*		*Migration Characteristics*			
	2010	*2025*	*Main reasons for migration*	*Main purpose of move*	*Educational level (%) (1991)*	*Absorption of migration in urban informal sectors*
Mumbai	20.1	26.4	Unemployment, poverty	Search unskilled jobs	38% male illiterates	Above 60% in construction, poor production process work
Kolkata	15.6	20.6	Poverty, unemployment	Unskilled jobs	32% male illiterates	Above 69% in informal sectors
Delhi	15.9	20.5	Unemployment	Search jobs	26% male illiterates	63% in informal sectors
Chennai	7.6	10.1	Unemployment	Search jobs	14% male illiterates	51% in informal sectors

Sources: *(1) UN, World Urbanization Prospects, 2006 Revision (2007), Various tables; (2) UN-Habitat Report (2007), Various Tables; (3) UNDP Report on World Population (2007), (4) Kothari (2002); (5) Census of India, 1991 (a to c) and 2001 (a to d), Population, Urbanization, Migration and Economic Data Series, Various Data CDs (2005–8); (6) Raju, S.(2009); (7) Bery, S (2008), Delhi; (8) Srivastava, R. (2010): Mumbai: 32; (9) Kurosaki. T., et al. (2007), on Delhi. Note: Differences exist between urbanization estimates in UN 1993 Report (Ch. 2) and that of UN 2007. This arises due to referring (in 2007) only to proper administrative limits, not to Greater Metropolitan Areas of respective metropolises.*

Table 21.6(b) *Recent Characteristics of Migration and Urbanization in Mega Cities, 2001 (concluded)*

Metros	*Characteristics of Urban Decay*						*Urban Polarization*	
	Urban congestion and decay	*Urban slum (% of urban pop.)*	*Large slums and squatters*	*Housing problems*	*Traffic congestion*	*Environmental problems (air, water pollution)*	*Industries, banks, political power*	*Concentration of country's total urban pop.*
Mumbai	Extreme congestion and decay	56.5	Chawls, Jhoparhpattis	Tremendously extreme	Extreme	Dangerous	40% of country's all banks	5.4%
Kolkata	Extreme decay	43.0	Bastees	Extreme	Extreme	Dangerous	State's industries, finance	4.6%
Delhi	Acute decay	35.0	Juggis	Extreme	Extreme	Acute	Extreme admin. Concentration	4.5%
Chennai	Considerable	33.0	Chawls, slums	Very acute	Extreme	Considerable	State's industries	2.2%

Sources: Same as in Table 21.6(a).

Urban Concentration in Mega Cities and Neglect of Small Towns/Cities, 1951–2001

Total Urban population of these 4 mega cities comes to 49 millions which accounts for 16.7 per cent of total urban population of India, or about 29 per cent of total population of all Class I cities. These indicate tremendous lop-sided urbanization in the country. Further, if two new mega cities of 2001, namely Bangalore (5.68 millions) and Hyderabad (5.53 millions) are also added, then these six mega cities will have a total population of 60 millions, and that would make 21 per cent of total urban population of India (285.35 millions in 2001). Table 21.7 presents distribution of India's urban population according to six size class of towns (I to VI).

Table 21.7 *Percentage of Urban Population by Size-Class of Towns, 1951–2001*

Size Class of Towns	*I (over 100,000)*	*II (50,000–100,000)*	*III (20,000–49,999)*	*IV (10,000–19,999)*	*V (5,000–9,999)*	*VI (below 5,000 population)*	*Urban Inequality* (Gini coefficient)*
1951	44.6	9.9	15.7	13.6	12.9	3.1	0.658
1961	51.4	11.2	16.9	12.7	6.8	0.7	0.673
1971	57.2	10.9	16	10.9	4.4	0.4	0.689
1981	60.3	11.6	14.3	9.1	3.5	0.5	0.711
1991	65.2	10.9	13.1	7.7	2.6	0.3	0.720
2001	68.6	9.7	12.2	6.8	2.3	0.2	0.741

* Urban Inequality is computed (Mukherji, 1991: 203–49).

Source: Census of India, 1961(1967a) to 2001(a).

Most noteworthy features are that:

(a) Most of the urban population are unevenly concentrated in class I cities (over 100,000 population), constituting 69 per cent of the country's total urban population,

(b) Only 2.5 per cent are found to be in small towns, with less than 10,000 population, and

(c) Small or medium towns (between 10,000 and 100,000) account for the rest 28.7 per cent, These show haphazard or completely unplanned urbanization in India. One recent study also observes that, "It would be wrong and dangerous to let the process of urbanization and migration be planned around a few mega cities despite their lower levels of poverty, better resource mobilization. ... Smaller towns lack these and yet they need attention if poverty issues are to be addressed effectively" (Raju, 2009).

(d) In two separate studies (Mukherji, 1993b: 1–149; 1997c: 69–113), a multitude of effective steps is elaborated for the regeneration of small and intermediate towns and cities of India (also see chapter 22).

(e) *Index of Urban inequality (Gini urban concentration ratio)* has rapidly increased from 0.658 in 1951 to 0.721 in 1991 and to 0.741 in 2001, indicating very pronounced and prolonged urban inequalities. In simple words, more and more uneven distribution of urban population is occurring in India, with tremendous pro-metropolitan development bias, resulting in utter neglect of small and medium towns and small cities.

(f) Mega cities are bursting at their seams. Social, psychological and spiritual costs of wasting lives of the millions in such cruel megalopolises are huge and inestimable. Urban economists who advocate economies of scale in living and locating industries and infrastructures in such mega cities have never estimated such huge and inestimable socio-psychological and spiritual costs. Once we start doing that, we would begin developing our stunted small cities and towns, which are very much neglected since many centuries.

Figure 21.6 *Change in Per cent Urban Population by Size-Class of Towns, 1951–2001*

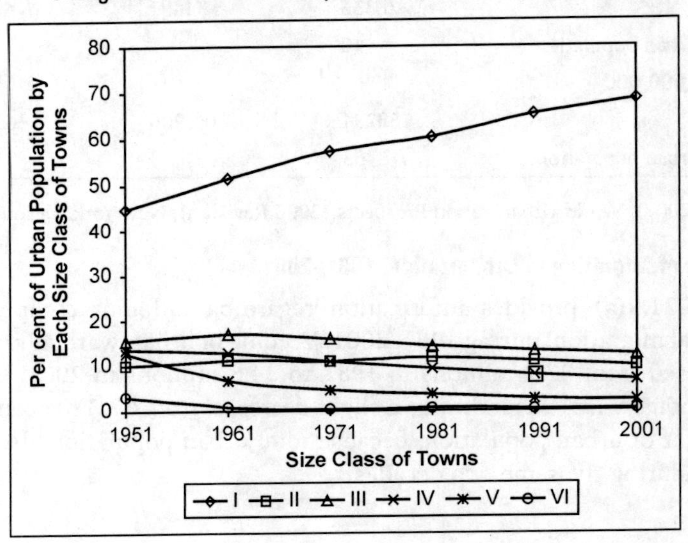

(g) According to UN projections, by 2025, the number of 1 to 5 million cities in India will increase from 26 to 56, that of 5 to 10 million cities will rise from 3 to 5, and number of mega cities of above 10 million population will increase from 3 to 4. Correspondingly, urban inequality will also accentuate greatly, with attendant ramifications (Table 21.8).

(h) India's urban future, thus, seems quite bleak, unless we drastically modify the current unequal and lopsided urbanization processes (having pro-metropolitan development bias), and instead focus on developing the small towns and small cities (numbering around 5,000).

Table 21.8 *Size-Class Distribution of Large Urban Centres in India, 2000–2025 (population in thousands)*

Size Class	*2000*	*2010*	*2025*
10 million or more			
No. of agglomerations	3	3	4
Population	41585	52664	79572
Per cent of urban population	14	14	15
5 to 10 million			
No. of agglomerations	3	5	5
Population	17365	32285	39047
Per cent of urban population	6	9	7
1 to 5 million			
No. of agglomerations	26	40	56
Population	43858	65513	105587
Per cent of urban population	15	18	20
500,000 to 1 million			
No. of agglomerations	39	51	70
Population	28336	34491	49858
Per cent of urban population	10	9	9
Fewer than 500,000			
Population	158294	181906	263991
Per cent of urban population	55	50	49

Source: UN (2007), World Urbanization Prospects (2006 Revision), New York: various pages

Contribution of Migration to Urbanization, 1981–2001

1. Table 21.9(a) provides information regarding different components of decadal migration, during 1981–2001. Volume of urban-ward migration has increased from 27.7 millions in 1981 to 34.8 millions in 2001. However, percentage-wise, this indicates a slight decrease, from 17.3 per cent to 12.2 per cent of urban population, because total urban population also swelled much during the same two decades.

Table 21.9(a) *Contribution of Migration to Urbanization (millions)*

Year	Total Population	Urban Population	No. of Migrants	Per cent Migrants to Total Population	Components of Decadal Migration (millions)				Volume of Decadal Urban-ward Migration (millions)	Urban-ward Migrants as % of Urban Pop
					Rural-Rural	Rural-Urban	Urban-Rural	Urban-Urban		
1981	659.3	159.6	206.5	31.3	46.26	15.33	6.45	12.39	27.72	17.36
1991	816.2	217.3	226.7	27.8	46.25	16.76	6.08	11.58	28.34	13.04
2001	1027.0	285.4	307.0	30.0	53.35	20.59	6.27	14.39	34.78	12.19

Source: Computed from Data of Census of India, 2001 (b), Migration Tables.

2. However, closer examination of data reveal more intriguing things (Table 21.9 (b)): contribution of urban-ward migration to decadal urban increase was 55 per cent during 1971–81, which decreased to 49 per cent during 1981–91, and again rose to 51 per cent during 1991–2001. That is, contrary to common believe (of contributing just 40%), actual contribution of urban-ward migration to urban increase move round 50 per cent during respective decades. This trend is used in estimating future urban – ward migration (Table 21.9 (a) and (b)).
3. *Notable thing is that during 1971–2001, a total of 91 million urban-ward migration occurred in India, which is almost unparalleled in human history.* In China, a recent study (Meng et al., 2010) shows that about 135 million rural to urban migration were recorded, but that have occurred during a much longer period of many decades. And in China, a settlement of only 2,000 people is termed as urban, while in India the population yardstick is 5,000. So both are not actually comparable.

Table 21.9(b) *Migration and Urbanization in India, 1981–2001 (population in millions)*

Year	Urban Pop (millions)	Decadal Urban Increase (millions)	Decadal Total Migration (millions)	Decadal Total Ruralward Migration (millions)	Vol. of Decadal Urbanward Migration (millions)	Contribution of Urbanward migration to Total urban increase (%)
1981	159.6	50.4	80.4	52.7	27.72	55.0
1991	217.3	57.7	82.1	53.8	28.34	49.1
2001	285.4	68.0	98.3	63.5	34.78	51.1

Source: Computed from Census Data, Census 1981 (1988–89), 1991 (a to d) and 2001 (a to b).

Note: During 1971–2001, a total of 91 millions urbanward migration occurred in India, which is almost unparalleled in human history.

Distribution of Different Parts of Migration and Future Trends, 2001–2051

Table 21.9 (c) presents the past trends of four components of migration, rural to rural, urban to rural, rural to urban and urban to urban, at All-India level. Based on these past trends (1971–2001), the future trends in each of this components of migration are estimated, for the period 2001-2051. Care has been taken for making separate estimates of trends for the "decadal" migration and migration for "all durations". Their future percentage distribution are also shown in Table 21.9 (c). In short, decadal rural-rural migration would decrease from 56.8 per cent in 2001 to 43.8 per cent in 2051, while decadal rural-urban migration would increase from 21.8 per cent in 2001 to 30.6 per cent in 2051. Urban to urban migration would also increase from 15 per cent to 19 per cent during the same period, while urban-rural migration will decline. Almost similar trends can be noticed for migration for all durations. These trends are applied in estimating future migration patterns, shown in Table 21.10, and illustrated in Figures 21.4 to 21.7.

Table 21.9(c) *Percentage Distribution of Different Components of Migration and Their Future Estimates, 2001–2051*

	1971	*1981*	*1991*	*2001*	*2011*	*2021*	*2031*	*2041*	*2051*
Decadal Urban-Ward Migration and Parts									
Decadal R-U Migration (%)	18.0	19.1	20.8	21.8	23.3	24.9	26.7	28.6	30.6
Decadal U-U Migration (%)	15.0	15.4	14.4	15.2	15.0	16.0	17.0	18.0	19.0
Decadal Urban-ward Migration (%)	33.0	34.5	35.2	37.0	38.3	40.9	43.7	46.6	49.6
Decadal Rural-Ward Migration and Parts									
Decadal R-R Migration (%)	58.0	57.5	57.3	56.8	56.4	52.9	49.7	46.7	43.8
Decadal U-R Migration (%)	8.0	8.0	7.5	6.6	5.3	6.2	6.6	6.7	6.6
Decadal Rural-Ward Migration (%)	67.0	65.5	64.8	63.4	61.7	59.1	56.3	53.4	50.4
All Duration Migration and Its Parts									
All Duration R-R Migration (%)	n.a	n.a	63.8	63.0	62.2	61.4	60.6	59.8	59.0
All Duration U-R Migration (%)	n.a	n.a	6.2	5.2	4.2	3.2	3.2	3.0	3.0
All Duration R-U Migration (%)	n.a	n.a	18.0	19.1	20.3	21.5	22.8	23.2	24.7
All Duration U-U Migration (%)	n.a	n.a	11.9	13.5	13.3	13.9	13.4	14.0	13.3

Sources: Computed from Data of Census of India, 1971–2001, Migration Tables. n. a. means data not available.

Procedures for Estimating Future Migration, India, 2001–2051

The procedure is simple but tedious. This involves many complicated steps in estimating all related demographic elements of population, urbanization, decadal urban increase, migration and its various components, separately for each decadal period, as well as for migration for all durations. The procedure follows the component projection methods. First step is to adopt the population projection (scenario B) of Population Foundation of India's projections, 1991–2051, as given in chapter 20. Second, is to adopt UN (2007) estimates of India's urban population projection, for the period 2000–2050 (ignoring just one year time lag) (as in chapter 20). Third, rural population is estimated accordingly. Fourth, is to compute decadal future urban population increase. Fifth, is to estimate "decadal" urbanward migration, as per urban population increase, and as per the future trends of rural to urban, and urban to urban, migration, both as percentages, as well as in volumes (in millions). These steps follows the trend patterns given in Tables 21.9(b) and 21.9(c). That is, it follows the future trend lines of per cent contribution of urbanward migration to urban population increase, estimated *a priori*, as given in above two tables. Likewise, based on past decadal patterns of rural to rural migration and urban to rural migration, their future trends are estimated (as in Table 21.9(c)), and corresponding volume of migration are estimated. Similarly, the migration for all durations and their four parts are also estimated.

Estimates of Future Migration and Their Components, India, 2001–2051

Table 21.5 presents all the details of future size of India's urbanization, and future migration and their all four components (rural-rural, urban-rural, rural-urban and urban-urban), both for decadal periods, and for all durations. These future trend lines are also illustrated in figures 21.7 to 21.10.

Table 21.10 *Estimates of Future Migration and Its Parts, 1971–2051 (estimates of future trends based on past trends) (millions)*

	1971	*1981*	*1991*	*2001*	*2011*	*2021*	*2031*	*2041*	*2051*
Total Population (millions)	**548**	**633**	**844**	**1027**	**1220**	**1379**	**1525**	**1656**	**1758**
Rural (millions)	439	474	627	742	853	906	907	864	782
Urban (millions)	**109**	**159**	**217**	**285**	**368**	**473**	**621**	**793**	**976**
Urban per cent	19.8	23.3	25.7	27.8	30.1	34.3	40.6	47.9	55.5
Urban Population Increase (millions)	41.2	.50.4	57.7	68	83	105	148	172	183
Total Migrants (% of Population)	**30.6**	**31.3**	**27.8**	**32.6**	**34.7**	**36.9**	**39.4**	**41.9**	**44.7**
Total No. of Migrants (millions)	**162**	**207**	**227**	**315**	**424**	**509**	**601**	**694**	**785**
Decadal Migration as % of Total Migration	38.7	38.8	36.2	31.2	36.2	38	39.9	41.9	44
Decadal Migration in millions as per cent of Total Migration	62.7	80.3	82.2	98.3	153.5	193	239	290	345
Decadal Urbanward Migration as per cent to Urban Increase	45.0	55.0	49.1	51.1	53.2	55.3	57.6	60	62.5
Decadal Urbanward Migration in millions as per cent to urban increase	18.5	27.7	29.5	34.7	44	58	85	103	114
Decadal Ruralward Migration (millions)	44.2	52.6	52.7	63.6	109.5	135	154	187	231
Total Migration over 10 years durations (millions)	99.3	127	145	217	270.5	316	362	404	440
Decadal R-U Migration (millions)	10.1	15.3	17.4	20.5	26.8	35.3	51.9	63,2	70.3
Decadal U-U Migration (millions)	8.4	12.4	12.1	14.3	17.2	22.7	33.1	39.8	43.7
Decadal Total Urbanward Migration (millions)	**18.5**	**27.7**	**29.5**	**34.8**	**44**	**58**	**85**	**103**	**114**
Decadal R-R Migration (millions)	38.3	46.1	46.6	56.9	100.1	120.8	135.9	163.5	200.8
Decadal U-R Migration (millions)	5.9	6.4	6.1	6.6	9.4	14.2	18.1	23.5	30.3
Decadal Total Rural-Ward Migration (millions)	**44.2**	**52.6**	**52.7**	**63.6**	**110**	**135**	**154**	**187**	**231**
All Duration Migration and Its Parts (millions)									
All Duration Migration, R-R (millions)	n.a	n.a	145	198	263	312	364	415	463
All Duration Migration, U-R (millions)	n.a	n.a	.14	16	18	16	19	21	24
All Duration Migration, R-U (millions)	n.a	n.a	41	60	86	110	137	161	194
All Duration Migration, U-U (millions)	n.a	n.a	27	42	56	71	81	97	104

Sources: *Computed from Census, 1971–2001. Future estimates of urban population, volume of future migration, and their components are computed, based on past trends of respective demographic elements, viz., urbanization, migration rates, contribution of urbanward migration to urbanization, volume of ruralward and urbanward migration, volume of total migration, and rural-rural, urban-rural, rural-urban and urban-urban components, for both decadal migration and migration for all durations.*

Figure 21.7 *Estimates of Future Population, Urbanization and Migration, India, 2011–2051*

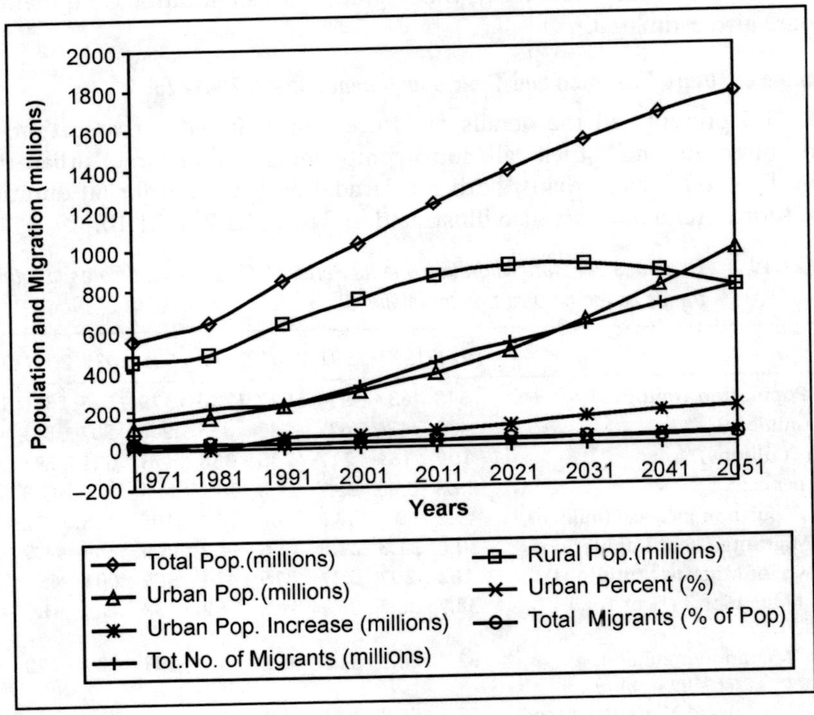

Figure 21.8 *Estimates of Future Decadal Migration, India, 2011–2051*

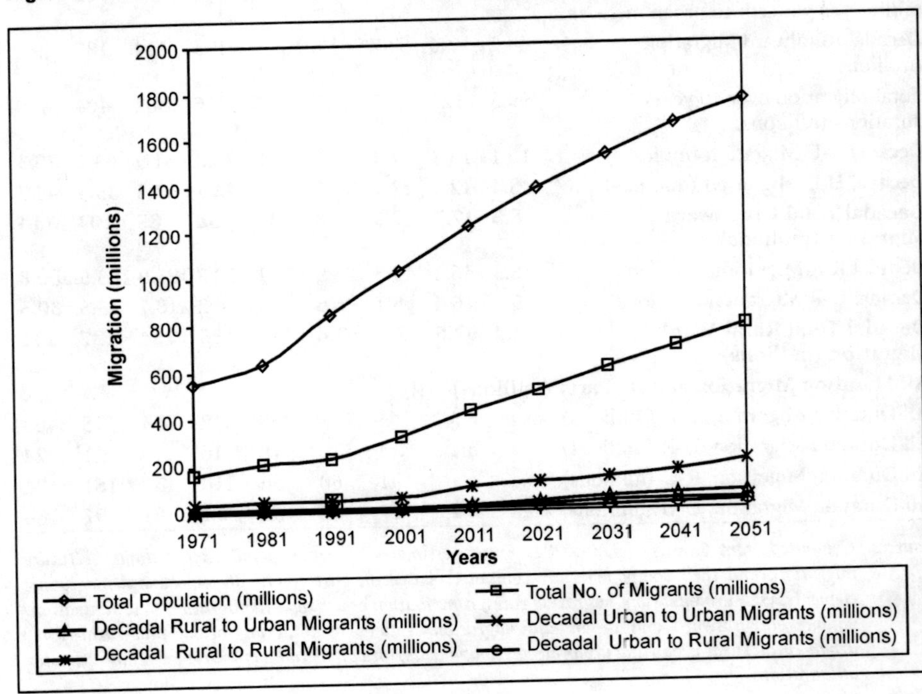

Figure 21.9 *Estimates of Future Migration, Urban Increase and Urbanward Migration, 2001–2051*

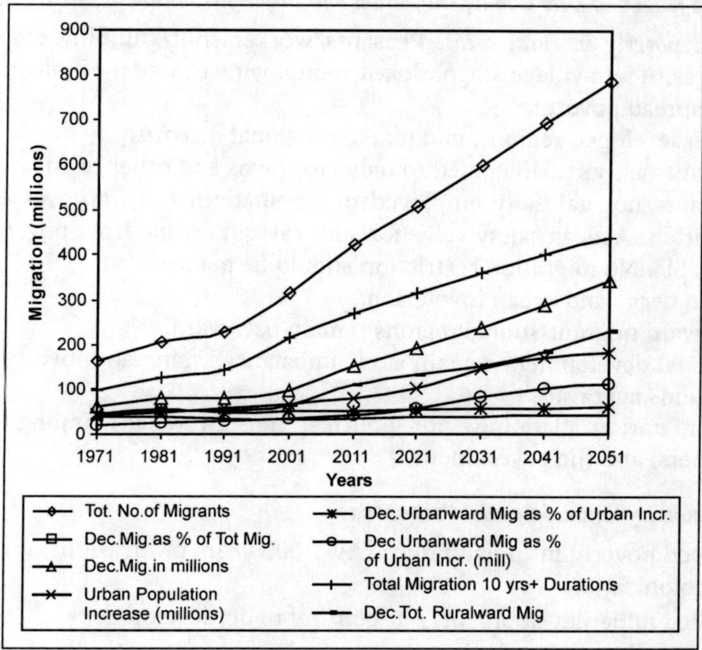

Figure 21.10 *Estimates of Future Migration for All Durations, India, 2011–2051*

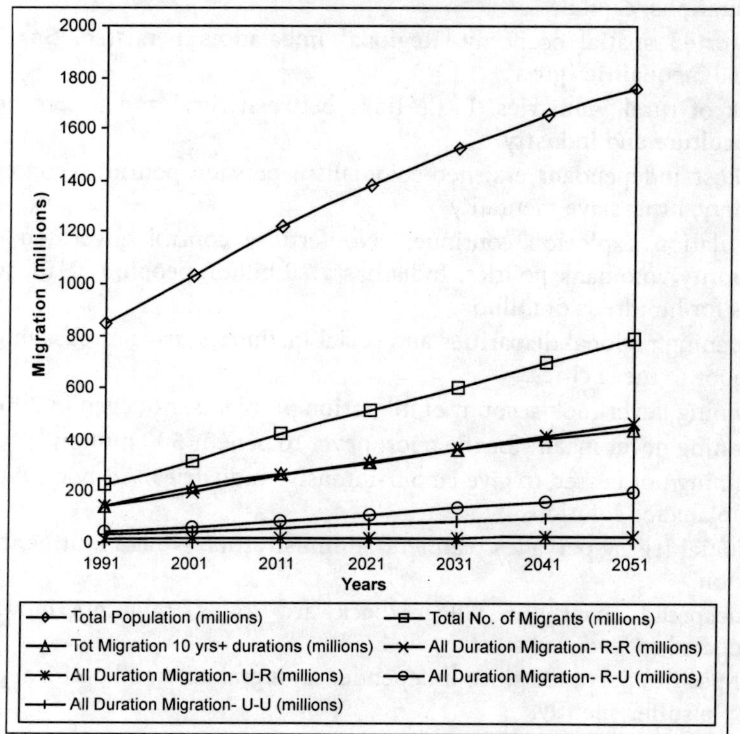

Determinants and Consequence of Migration in India

Challenging Issues of Low Quality Migration and Urban Involution in India

1. *Abject poverty in rural areas.* Peasants/workers not gainfully employed in villages. Acute village stagnation. Unemployment, under-employment, and widespread poverty.
2. Underdeveloped regions, and marked regional disparities.
3. Migrants are virtually forced to move to towns and other regions.
4. Migrants not gainfully employed in destination: not improves economic condition. Acts as safety valve for survival and escape from poverty; hence desirable. No migration restriction should be made.
5. Urban decay and urban involution.
6. Backward migrant-source regions remain backward.
7. National development remain slow, imbalanced, rampant poverty persists. Problems aggravate.
8. No migration planning, nor policies, nor awareness among scholars, planners, and the government.

Causal Economic-Political-Spatial Processes

9. Induced poverty in India, induced by 1,000 years of invasions, foreign rule and colonization.
10. Induced underdevelopment. Agricultural underdevelopment
11. Unfavourable terms of colonial trade, and problems of balance of payments.
12. Foreign enclaves/ports grew rapidly than others, due to export, cash crops, plantations, capital.
13. Distorted spatial economy. Regional imbalances persisted. Spatial and social inequalities grew.
14. Lack of rural industries. Little links between rural and urban, between agriculture and industry.
15. In Post Independent era, neo-colonialism pervade politics, economy and society, utter slave mentality.
16. Population explosion continues. No fertility control advocated due to minority vote bank politics. India has 1.20 billion people (2010), without jobs for hundreds of millions.
17. Widening regional disparities and social inequities: trigger mass migration of poor to mega cities.
18. Planning never took account of migration problems, not even in 2000s.
19. Planning never meant for the poor: never to benefit 500 millions poor.
20. Planning not geared to give labour-intensive industries. Ad-hocism persist, not plans for solution.
21. Colonial legacy pervades planners/administrators. No commitment to the Nation.
22. Widespread poverty in villages/backward states. Migrants move from neglected to favoured states.
23. Evil politics pervaded since Independence; ingrained in all political parties. People suffer silently.

24. Evidence: over 60 millions illegal Bangladeshi immigrants invaded India, everyday increasing, but none raised this crucial issue as most dangerous problem – which is challenging India's very existence!
25. Evidence: widespread corruption spread in all spheres: masses suffer; and forced to migrate to cities.
26. The same sad story of migrants continues, as given in the beginning of chapter 11.

Required Improved Development Policies and Implementation

27. Need land reforms to benefit the rural poor, in yet unfinished (land reforms) states.
28. Need Planning for the Poor.
29. Need restructuring of space economy, and reduce regional economic imbalances.
30. Rural regeneration, irrigation development, raising agricultural productivity.
31. Regional development and rural industrialization. Development of backward and neglected areas.
32. Encourage more people-participation in community development programmes.
33. Need more equitable distribution of income, investment and means of production among classes.
34. Fertility control for all communities. Raise status of women and empowerment: dampen fertility.
35. Need greatest efforts for massive employment generation.
36. Eliminate barriers from migration field for free field adjustment according to the needs, and field forces.
37. Reorient spatial linkages from external dependency to internal domestic markets, instead of excessive export of raw materials.
38. Relieve country from poverty and underdevelopment by creating massive labour intensive jobs.
39. Need full commitment to Nation: at all levels, education, work, politics, planning and governance.

Need for Migration Planning

40. Migration planning for poor workers for gainful employment, so that they contribute to national development. Integrate migration planning with economic planning.
41. Integrate people's migration-mobility with agricultural development programmes.
42. Allocate more growth efforts to migrant-source regions.
43. No migration-restriction from villages to cities be made, more efforts need for development.
44. Provide short effective training to migrants: transforming them into army of skilled workers.
45. Industrialize villages so they derive benefits from labour/products, and pay less to city for services.
46. Reorient export: instead of raw materials, processed goods be exported and people may draw benefits.

47. Urban renewal programmes for urban evolution and affordable shelter, instead of urban involution. Rampant corruption be wiped out.
48. Mass employment generation in villages/towns: by maximum use of local human/natural resources.
49. Transfer of surplus unemployed to cottage/agro-industries, consumer/capital goods industries.
50. Reorient credits, trade-transport, resources, investment/growth efforts, away from export and external dependency, rather towards development of internal domestic markets.
51. Develop small towns/cities by setting up industries, infrastructure, institutions, and tax incentives.
52. Transform parasitic cities, making them centres of development – diffusing growth impulses to surroundings.
53. Integrated area development programmes must be fully implemented, making them corruption free.
54. Need strong political will, economic discipline, freedom from corruption, without which none can be realized.
55. Needs character-building and Patriotism for the Motherland, India – utter lack of which very fast leading this noble country to turmoil!

Same Poverty-induced Migration and Urban Decay May Continue for Many Decades

If these evil and unjust socio-economic and political processes are not completely wiped out, I am very afraid, then, the same kinds of poverty-induced migration and acute urban decay and urban involution may continue for many decades, until the entire migration-urbanization system will reach the maximum entropy level and break open, leading to utter catastrophe.

Recent violent attacks from the (un) civil societies against the hapless peasant migrants to the city of Mumbai and New Delhi are unholy symptoms of accentuating the problems. Dangers are lurking large elsewhere also: soon Kolkata, Chennai, Hyderabad, Ahmedabad or Bangaluru or other million cities may catch up this undesirable tendencies of violence against the migrants. In turn, the migrants may also be compelled to take up violence, and India will be shattered into pieces. That will be very hefty prices to be paid, for our centuries-old neglect of this crucial problem of the nexus between poverty-underdevelopment and distressed migration and low quality urbanization in India.

Problems of Acute Urban Poverty in India and Their Alleviation

In a recent article title "Our Choking City", Bery (2009: 1–3), expressed the similar views. "Our policies need to be driven by three broad concerns – improve linkages between the city and its hinterland; make our towns a productive setting for growth, entrepreneurship and innovation; and develop a distinctive approach to addressing issues of urban poverty with the same energy we have traditionally devoted to rural poverty". "It is imperative to introduce urban reforms now, so that infrastructure that is laid down reflects a competitive, sustainable spatial pattern rather than the ugly sprawl that is so often seen today" (ibid. 3).

Another paper noticed, that: "We tend to overlook this (recent slower urbanization rates) as our towns are crowded and filthy. But they are not filthy because they are crowded; they look crowded because they are filthy. Had they been better planned, they would smell differently" (Gupta, 2010: 22) .... "The Indian route to urbanization is like the flyovers in our metros. Traffic jams are now at an elevation and pedestrians don't know which way to go" (ibid.).

In a recent study on *Urban Poverty in India* (Raju, 2009, UNDP, India, 2009) have also observed that: "Despite being projected as engines of growth, towns and cities in India have a high incidence of poverty. However, the poverty rates vary significantly across states as also across urban centres". Some of the important points the report made are as follows:

1. One of the most interesting findings is that, "Poverty levels in small size towns are high, in the middle size towns poverty levels are lower and is the lowest for large towns, thereby lending credence to theories that the metros and mega towns have been the engines of growth in recent years. It finds that the infrastructure facilities, quality of employment, productivity and returns to education are likely to be better in large cities than in small towns" *(summary,* ibid.) (see Table 21.11).

Table 21.11 *Per cent of Poor in Different Size-Class of Urban Centres, India, 1993–94 and 1999–2000*

City/Town Size	*1993–94*	*1999–2000*
Large towns/Cities	18.4	14.2
Medium Towns/cities	27.6	20.4
Small Towns	33.2	24.2
All Urban Areas	27.4	19.9
Rural Areas	35.7	23.9

Source: UNDP (2009): India: Urban Poverty Report 2009; Raju (2009). These data are based on NSSO Consumer Expenditure Survey Reports. Thus, these poverty estimates have the same limitations as discussed below.

2. "Migrants in cities are economically better off and are placed at higher economic stratum than the natives of cities on poverty indices. Rural migrants into urban areas have been found to have a lower probability of being poor than the local population, therefore making urbanization an important prong in the poverty reduction strategy".
   However, this finding is rather debatable, because their study mostly relies on NSSO sample survey data on migration (1999–2000), which is rather heavily biased against the poor and illiterate migrants and gives highly skewed results in favour of the literate and better off sections of the respondents or migrants. Thus, it fails to catch the weaker sections of the migrants and distorts the findings. Because, then the question arises: how come over 500 millions poor people exist in India in 2005 (World Bank, 2008)? And still growing?
   Further, another serious question arises: how come urban slums are growing very fast in all large cities and mega cities? These hard truth rather stare at our faces, and prevent us from reaching that kind of conclusion. Of course, the migrants have to be more struggling and more hard working in a cruel metropolis, in order just to survive, as new entrants in an unknown city environment, and they have only their own hands of labour to rely upon. Consequently, they might be earning little more than the local "poor"

urban residents. But, that might not mean they are much better off than the local urban residents (who usually have shelters, no matter how small, nor how dilapidated).

3. "The failure of the small and medium towns to attract migrants, despite policy statements and programmatic interventions by the government ... has been identified as a major problem intercepting the process of balanced urbanization" (Raju, 2009, ibid.).
4. "Urban poverty has to be seen in the context of the growing importance of the unorganized workforce .... This has led to out migration of the poor from backward rural areas and their absorption within the urban informal economy .... The importance of education and skill in poverty reduction has to be adequately understood" (ibid.). *This in reality just echoes the findings of this book and my life-long migration-urbanization research result!*
5. "It would be appropriate to design micro-finance systems around multiple objectives and integrate them with the existing service delivery structure in the public sector" (ibid.).
6. "The incidence of poverty is observed to be high in case of female-headed households. ... need modifications in future poverty alleviation programmes that are gender sensitive and pro-gender" (ibid.).
7. "The issue of denial of housing and basic amenities to the urban poor within the larger framework of social security needs attention. Increased privatization of housing and basic services will reduce their availability to the poor." (ibid.).
8. "Cities are increasingly becoming hostile to poor migrant as informal as well as formal institutional structure makes urban spaces scarce, manifested through an ongoing trend towards slum evictions ... (needs) tenure regularization, backed by the strengthening of infrastructure .... Large cities have the problem of elite capture and marginalization of the poor" (ibid.). (This echoes my findings, described under "sons of the soil"!).
9. "Two landmark urban initiatives, the 74th Constitutional Amendment Act and the Jawaharlal Nehru National Urban Renewal Mission (JNNURM) ... designed to empower local governments (and) helps inclusive growth and can serve the interests of the poor. But, there is skepticism regarding their success in bringing in the functional and financial reforms at the grassroots level" (ibid.). (I doubt, often JNNURM projects just help plunder of the funds by the political leaders and bureaucrats).

So, much of the above findings also emphasize upon the great need to combat war on poverty.

Migration, Poverty Reduction and Economic Development

Recently, there has been increased interests, both in developing and developed countries, in visualizing migration as a means of poverty reduction. See for instance, a study by Skeldon, titled "Migration and Poverty" (2003) in which he opined:

1. "The weight of the evidence provides support for a very different conclusion: that the movement of population can be a significant factor for the alleviation of poverty. The principal reason lies in the nature of the migration process itself. Their movement is a complex system of circulation

between two, or among several, destinations. Migrants, rather than individual income maximizes, can be conceptualized as existing within a communal risk-minimizing strategy" (p. 10).

2. "Migration, both internal and international, is thus an integral part of the whole process of economic development which must underlie any attempt to alleviate poverty"(p. 12).
3. "The weight of the evidence is that mobility enhances economic growth and improves the lot of most, but not all, of the population" (p. 14).
4. "Attempting to limit or restrict migration is likely to be much less productive. The words of John Kenneth Galbraith capture the essence of the whole relationship: "migration is the oldest action against poverty. It selects those who most want help. It is good for the country to which they go; it helps to break the equilibrium of poverty in the country from which they come" (cited in Harris, 2002: 119).
5. "However, it is important to recognize that migration can involve costs, economic and social, as well as benefits. The challenge to policy makers is to facilitate the types of movement that are most likely to lead to an alleviation of poverty while protecting migrants from abuse and exploitation" (p. 15).
6. "The immediate challenge remains the need to incorporate an appreciation of the potentially positive role of migration in poverty reduction programmes" (p. 15).

However, there are also some current studies which emphasize that 'migration for development' are recently occurring in large scale in India, and/or 'migration is actually much successful in poverty reduction', etc. and so forth, and rather questioned and termed my discussion on "poverty-induced migration" is a misnomer or misleading (vide Deshingkar, 2005; Kundu et al., 2007).

But, at the same time, it is much wise to remember that migration is primarily the individuals or family's "personal" efforts to combat poverty. By labeling and linking such personal efforts as "migration occurring for development", or "migration acting as poverty reduction strategy" etc., cannot shirk the responsibility of the scholars, the society, the planners, and the government from the sacred duty to alleviate rampant poverty among the Indian masses! By wrongly depicting an undue "rosy" picture of the hundreds of millions of poor and helpless migrants may tempt the scholars, planners, the society, and the government to shirk from their most essential duty of providing helping hands to an ocean of over 600 millions of utterly poor people in India! Some such studies often are tempted to make those kind of mistakes and thereby strengthen the hands of the exploiters! Such studies should first ask the basic question: "why do 600 millions poor people still exist in India even today?" Why 150 millions slum dwellers struggle to survive in most filthy Slums? They have no answers!

Need Overcoming Barriers of Migrants and Protection and the Rights

In this context, one point must be stated very clearly right at the outset. This concept of *"eliminating barriers from the individual's mobility"* was first developed by the present author in his second PhD thesis on "Mobility Field Theory" (Mukherji, 1975: 1–378) in University of Hawaii (published as Microfilm version, University of Michigan, Ann Arbor, 1976). These ideas were further elaborated in various papers and books (Mukherji, 1979a, 45–61; 1979b, 1–81;. 1981: 150–173; 1982a: 1–280). It was clearly enunciated 35 years ago in 1975, and in three other books (Mukherji, ibid.) that:

"There are different kinds of socio-economic-cultural-political – linguistic barriers in the individual's mobility fields (or life space of the individual(s) in which he/she can move for basic need fulfillment), which block need gratification and restrain free field adjustments within the life space of the individuals, and the urgent need is eliminating barriers from the individual's mobility fields and permit them to adjust their own lives" (Mukherji, 1975: 316–318).

But recently, UNDP's "Human Development Report 2009: Overcoming Barriers: Human Mobility and Development" (UN, 2009) seems to have borrowed above ideas of the present author, and emphasized that main migration-related problems in many developing countries arise due to inappropriate policies and regulations. Report urges for better policies to protect migrants as large gains to human development may be achieved by *lowering barriers to movement* and improving treatment of movers. In fact, these echo the above ideas of the present author, repeatedly preached 35 years ago!!!

Again, in a recent UNDP sponsored study on "Urban Poverty in India" (Raju, ed. 2009; UNDP India, 2009) have also recommended for protection of migrants in mega cities from the aggression from urban elites and the middle class, who become increasingly hostile to them (see Ranade, 2010).

Another, recent study on 'Migration and Development in Asia' has also observed that: "Migrant workers are discriminated against and paid less than non-migrant workers. Poor workers are unlikely to be able to educate their children properly and are therefore unlikely to break the inter-generational transmission of poverty. Unless migrant workers are supported by policy through better services, social protection and remunerative wages, migrant are less likely to reach MDG" (Deshingkar, 2006: 1–6). It also suggested: "Circular labour migration can yield strong win-win outcomes for most concerned. For sending households, migration is a source of additional income and for receiving areas and employers, migrants are a source of cheap labour" (ibid.).

Another study on India observed that: "Studies show that migrant labourers live and work in extremely difficult and dangerous conditions" (Deshingkar and Akter, 2009: 1–90). "They are on the margins of society both economically and socially and face unnecessary high costs and risks because of non-recognition at the policy level and faulty implementation of labour laws". "India needs to take a stronger position on protecting migrant workers" (ibid.).

Wang (2008) also observed that the government of China recently understood the need for protection of internal migrants. It felt that more protection of migrants leads to more development and policy needed to provide public services and protect rights of rural migrants, and started extending training, services and social security to them.

Natali (2009) has also observed that, like international migration, internal migration can potentially be a good development and livelihood improvement strategy, difference being that development opportunities from internal migration are more likely to reach a significantly higher number of people.

Well, a good beginning! Four decades ago(in 1970s), I was the lone ranger in the forest of despair! Now at least some migration-urbanization researchers have joined me (without acknowledging the pioneer), in advocating the great need for "protecting the migrants" and "eliminating barriers from their mobility fields", and their lives!! More will be discussed on these at the end of chapter 22.

Concluding Remarks

This chapter has highlighted many burgeoning and challenging issues:. abject poverty, distress migration, low quality urbanization and widening socio-economic and regional disparities. It has also recommended some pathways for planning for the poor, and to address those challenges. Without such planning for the poor and proper implementation of pro-poor policies and strategies, a very large segment of India's population will continue to suffer in poverty, despair and human miseries. Absolute elimination of poverty from the surface of India should be given the top priority in all actions and programmes. Without these policies of inclusive development, India will remain a poor nation, in spite of the so-called software superpower and high growth economy!

Although this chapter often makes dismal reading, but it ends with optimistic notes. It was absolutely necessary that all such problems should have been vividly narrated and their underlying causes unraveled, because only then with scientific mind and brave courage to face the fear and troubles, can we muster steely nerves and Himalayan strength to wipe out poverty and hunger from the surface of India. And, redress inequities and all such problems. All these problems are not insurmountable. If many nations of the world have succeeded in solving them, then India can also achieve so. India can also win, with her great functioning democracy, growing economy, vast youthful population, knowledge society, software superpower, expanding middle-class markets and her eternal values and ideals!

Only things necessary are: good governance, corruption-free society, and eradication of poverty. In one word, Indians only need a soulful commitment to this Great Nation!!

22 Future Development Policies and Strategies for Migration Planning, and Urban and Regional Development

"Fill the brain, therefore with high thoughts, highest ideals, place them day and night before you and out of them will come great work".

Swami Vivekananda (1893)
(Complete Work, Centenary Volume II, 1963: 86)

Encourage Migration, Not Migration-restriction

It must be very clearly stated at the outset, that migration-restriction never can be a desirable option or strategy. Control of migration is never meant, nor advocated anywhere in this book, nor in any of my previous writings, because that will be the most undesirable and most undemocratic action. Although for most of the migrants, the choice is limited between quick death in the villages, or slow starvation in the stinking urban slums, still migration is their only escape route from rural poverty, hence, very much desirable, no matter how small is the pay, nor how unbearable is the stay in the urban slums. If migration is not allowed, then most would probably die in the stagnant and tottering villages. Hence, migration is most desirable for these poor masses as a survival strategy, and as an escape route from poverty. Often, it also enhances their incomes and skills, no matter how small is the betterment, nor how long is the waiting time to get opportunities in the new destinations. Furthermore, in the Indian situation, rural-to-urban migration unshackles the movers from the tyranny of caste-ridden village society and consequent oppression by the upper castes and the rich on the poor and the downtrodden. In the new urban setting, no body enquires about his or her caste or community, and he or she is free to move around and feel free to take up any work. So, migration must be more encouraged and migrants must be protected from exploitations and hardship.

Migration Planning

The reversal of migration streams away from metro cities to local or district headquarters and small towns and small cities require tremendous structural transformations in the urban economy of both small towns/intermediate cities, as well as of the metropolises. Neither were such measures thought about in the existing studies or planning designs, nor are such transformations easy to take place. For such changes call forth vast transformations in the existing polarized investment patterns, in concentrated industrial licensing policies, in employment-generating capacities of towns. It lies in promoting pro-rural against pro-urban development policies, restructuring of spatial structure of economic activities of the entire national space, changes in rural and regional development policies, and so forth.

This total package is termed as essential steps for *Migration planning* – that is, planning strategies for more beneficial migration for the Nation and for the migrants themselves (for details, see Mukherji, 1981, 1–278; 2000e: 45–178; 2001(b): 1–225; 2001(c): 1–26; 2001(d):1–20)).

Set within these contexts, briefly, the following policies and strategies may be envisaged and implemented (Mukherji, 1983c: 1–32; 2004: 151–163). These are merely suggestive, not an exhaustive list of measures. Some focus upon rural development, some focus on urban development, and still some other upon regional development. All these are very intimately connected and need our serious attention (Figure 22.1). The discussion is deliberately brief and to the point.

Rural Development Strategies

Need More Effective Rural and Regional Development

To save such metropolises, it is very necessary that all-round socio-economic development of all rural and interior parts of India be urgently made, which are hitherto neglected, and from which massive migration of poor people occur to metros. Unless these are done, the problems of distress migration, over-congestion, and urban involution of metros and larger cities, will continue unabated. Thus, problems must be attacked and solved at its roots, where it arises, that is, in the rural areas (Mukherji, 2000a: 15–27; 2000d: 171–182).

Eliminate Rural Poverty

- Eliminating rural poverty must be given maximum focus in "Planning for Poor", without which, low quality migration will remain in India, for many decades! (Mukherji, 2005d: 38–75).
- A major study by ESCAP (1993: 92–98) on poverty-population linkages and poverty alleviation strategies, has recommended a number of policies and strategies aimed at limiting population growth and alleviating poverty, namely (a) those which rely on increasing economic growth strategies (growth-mediated strategies), and (b) those which provide immediate public action for the poor (public-support mediated or basic-need fulfilling strategies). It is also opined that both growth and basic needs satisfaction strategies are to be considered as mutually reinforcing each other.
- In a recent book on "Poverty and Fertility in India", Mukherji (2007: 259–305) has very much emphasized on strategies for reduction of rural poverty for fertility decline and for uplifting low quality migration in India (also see Mukherji, 1988: 1–68; 1997e: 1–40; 2001a: 1–150; 2000g: 1–25;

Udupa and Mukherji, 1988: 1–175). More serious efforts must also be made to achieve UN *Millennium Development Goals* (MDGs) of reducing infant mortality, achieving safe motherhood and child survival, and promote literacy and gender equality within 2015 (UN Millennium Project, 2005).

- Generate more non-agricultural employment in rural and neglected areas, which will reduce poverty-induced migration, and high fertility (Mukherji, 1997h: 1–6; 1998a: 250–270).
- Also, ensure that benefits of economic development are not eaten up through income inequality and unjust social development, without which it is difficult to break vicious cycle of poverty and fertility, and poverty and migration (UN, 1997: 90–115; UN, 1998: 87–88; Mukherji, 2000f: 1–6).

Figure 22.1 *Migration of Workers and Labourers and Required Planning Strategies*

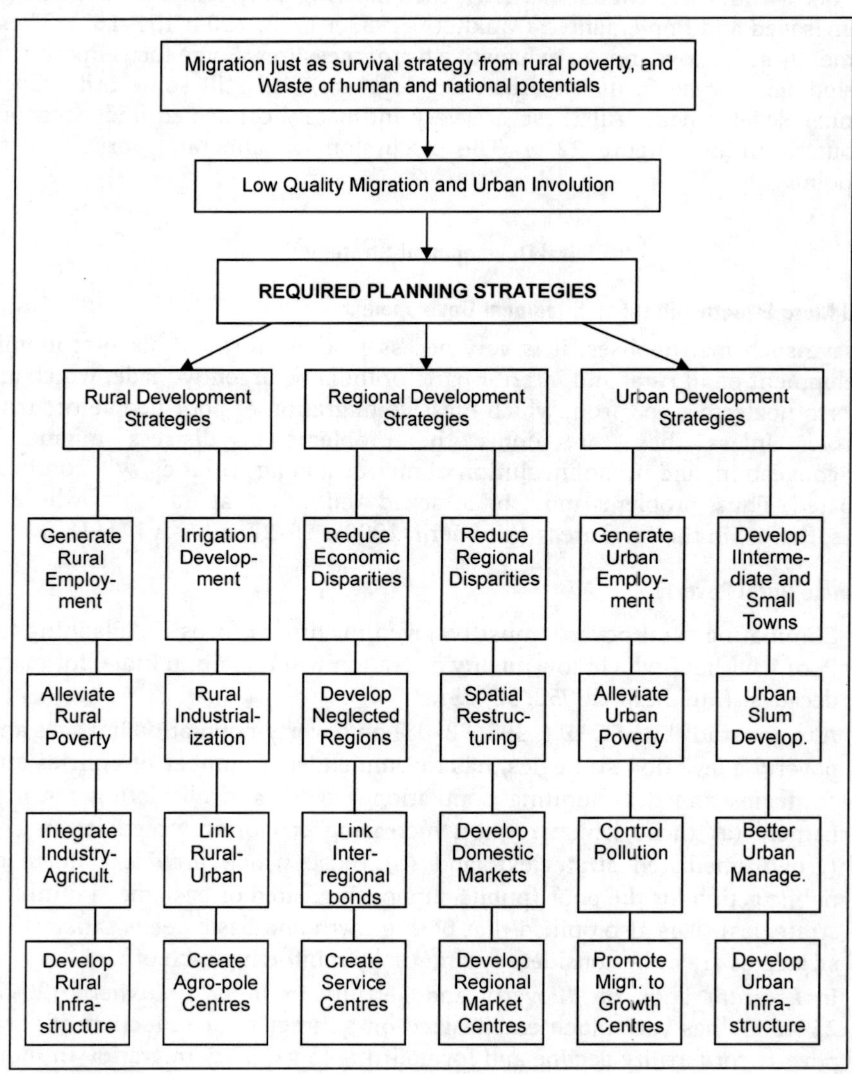

Source: Author

Generate Massive Rural Employment for Eliminating Rural Poverty

(a) Tremendous efforts are needed for massive generation of employment in villages, through

- rural industrialization,
- irrigation development,
- land conservation,
- land redistribution,
- multiple cropping, and
- development of village crafts and cottage industries (Mukherji, 2001b: 1–11).

(b) Rural poverty can only be reduced:

- If purchasing power of rural people are sufficiently enhanced by generating massive rural employment (Bihari, 1990: 101–102; Dev, 2000: 823–836).
- By proper distribution of benefits to total village society, specially for weak and under-privileged (Sinha and Singh, 1999: 143–151; Basu, 2000: 161–166).
- Unless such attempts made for uplifting the pauperized rural people, nothing really can be done for controlling current migration flows from rural poverty to urban poverty (Mukherji, 1996b: 41–91).
- These steps will require very strong political will and determined economic discipline at all levels of the government: local, district, state and All-India (UN-ESCAP, 1992: 3–4; UN-ESCAP, 1995: 7).
- Elimination of rural poverty must be taken up on a war footing (Mukherji, 1992b: 1–92; 2006: 304–330).

Irrigation Development

- Thus, needs massive irrigation development programmes in villages for:
    - Canal irrigation,
    - River irrigation,
    - Well irrigation,
    - Reconstructing field drains
    - Other irrigation channels (ponds), etc.
- These steps will considerably add to the total land capable of cultivation and to the agricultural productivity.
- These will create jobs for the landless labourers and the seasonally unemployed (Mukherji, 2000a: 15–27).
- Irrigation is the main panacea for rural development and agricultural development in India. Two-third variations in agricultural productivity in India depends solely upon this, not upon High Yielding Variety (HYV) seeds, fertilizers, or other inputs or subsidies (Mukherji, 1981: 150–190; 1983b, 121–140).
- Therefore, we must create irrigation channels, deep tube-wells, pond irrigation, and do water harvesting (Mukherji, et al., Geography of Hunger and Insecurity in India, 1980).

- These steps will greatly raise the agricultural productivity, create massive rural employment, raise their levels of living and purchasing power, and rejuvenate the entire village systems (Mukherji, 1992b: 54–91; 2000a: 15–27).

Top Priority Must be Given to Eliminate Rural Poverty

- Tremendous efforts must be made for massive generation of employment in the villages, through rural industrialization, irrigation development, land conservation, land redistribution, multiple cropping, and development of village crafts and cottage industries (Mukherji, 1999b).
- Rural poverty can only be liquidated, if the purchasing power of rural people is sufficiently enhanced by generating massive rural employment, both for males and females, and by proper distribution of benefits to all sections of village society, specially for the weak and the under-privileged.
- Unless such vigorous attempts are made for the up-liftment of the lot of pauperized rural people, nothing really can be done for the controlling of their present-day migration in India from rural poverty to urban poverty,

Rural Industrialization and Economic Value-Enhancing Process

- Great efforts are required to ensure that raw materials are processed within villages, in finished/semi-finished form, before sent to towns.
- So, that economic values are enhanced to the products locally, before they are transferred to the cities for consumption.
- Need to set up many rural industries and cottage industries, like rice-milling, indigenous sugar-making, oil-pressing, weaving, garment-making, handicrafts, etc. (with subsidies from the government and under co-operative management). These must be set up at properly chosen, centrally located villages, each serving about 10 or 20 surrounding villages (Mukherji, 1991: 203–249) (Figure 22.1).
- Such value-enhancing process will raise rural productivity, improve levels of living and motivate them to work more productively, as they will derive benefits of their work themselves (Mukherji, 2006: 315–330).
- When more rural work will be created, then, it will reduce current mass migration from rural poverty to urban poverty. This must be considered as one of the top migration-influencing strategies for India.

Integration of Industry and Agriculture

- We must dispense with two great disarticulations between towns and villages, and between industry and agriculture: based upon which many contradictions between growing and lagging regions are founded. Resolution of these problems can be achieved through following steps:
    - Creation of new division of agricultural labour: by transferring part of food-producing labour to industrial crop-growing, livestock-breeding, fishing, forestry, horticulture; and another part to agro-industries, small-scale industries, transport and communications.

- Thus, needs conversion of huge masses of unskilled labour to semi-skilled and skilled labour through short but effective training, and raising the per capita labour productivity to higher levels (NIRD, 1999, 120–121).
- Also very much required are: industrialization of agriculture, implementation of industry into rural areas, and for general integration of industry and agriculture.

To Change Unequal Rural-Urban Linkages and Relations

- The thrust of rural transformation programme must be to accelerate rapid development of villages and to reduce rural-urban disparities in wages, amenities, income, growth efforts, investment, education, nutrition, and overall well-being (Mukherji, 1981: 150–190).
- Thus, needs definite pro-rural development policy and all-pronged attack at the roots of rural poverty and rural underdevelopment. So, many essential corrective steps are needed for changing existing unjust rural-urban relations and linkages (Mukherji, 1987: ch. 15).
- For that, we must dispense with the false notion of downward-filtration of development from the towns to the villages, rather adopt direct programmes which will benefit the rural poor directly.
- We must act to free villages from excessive dependence upon cities, and from expropriation of rural agricultural surpluses for the benefits of urbanites.
- The governments should fix proper pricing policy in favour of the peasants, so that they derive due share of their hard labour.
- Strengthen rural-urban relations and linkages in favour of the villages, through marketing of agricultural goods, road development, electrification, tele-communications, and so forth.
- To enable rural economic surplus for reinvestment in rural development
- To focus both subsidy-oriented "Food for Work" or "Relief Programmes" and on self-generating and capital-producing productive and construction work. Current simple *NREGA* (National Rural Employment Guarantee Act) type of providing only village relief work will not really help the farmers to escape from rampant rural poverty. It really needs entirely corruption-free and most effective rural poverty-eradication programmes, totally free from political bungling and widespread corruption among rural bureaucrats in the delivery system (which saps out all good efforts).
- To provide basic amenities of life to villages like school, dispensary, rural health centres, drinking water, roads and village cooperatives.
- To adopt full-fledged programmes to create economically viable villages by generating employment to seasonally unemployed and totally unemployed, and thereby arresting the current trends of massive rural-urban migration of marginalized labourers or idle workers.
- Extension of cheap and affordable credit services and other monetary facilities to the rural poor and rural artisans at minimum rate of interests.

- To impart short but useful training, vocational and non-formal education for skill development and creation of village leadership and entrepreneurship within villages themselves. The governments (local, district, state, and Central) should not treat these as doles to the villagers, rather consider as the most essential National duty for total rural poverty eradication.
- To encourage decentralization of economic and political power in favour of rural folks. This really needs total overhauling of current most corrupt Panchayati Raj systems (local self-governments) in villages, where actually local criminals loot the poor villagers (Mukherji, 2005a: 11–36).
- To encourage better and more active participation of rural communities in plan formulation and implementation for rural transformation programmes.

Create More Rural Banks for Rural Industrialization

- The crucial problems of arresting out-ward flows of rural agricultural surpluses, capitals, and savings to the urban centres, and re-orienting their use for rural development locally, also have to be resolved with firm decision and control. This is a difficult task, evidently. *NABARD* (National Agricultural Banking for Rural Development) and other rural banks in India have started some initial endeavours, but much more strenuous efforts towards this goal will be greatly needed.
- To provide higher incentives and higher interest rates to the investments made for rural reconstruction programmes may have to be worked out at central and state levels in order to attract surpluses of rural novo-rich and urban elites. Novel and innovative approaches are urgently necessary.
- Rural farmers and rural people must be given easy and most affordable finance and credits at a very low interest of (say, 3% annually), in the rural banks located in the villages themselves. and made free from conmen and middlemen who usurp the hapless illiterate rural people. So far very little is done in this respect (Mukherji, 2011 chap. 11).
- When easily finance will be available for rural people, they may be encouraged to industrialize their agricultural products and make more agro-industries. These will pay dividends in the form of more rural employment, and consequent reduction of poverty-induced urban ward migration (Mukherji, 2006; and 2007).

Develop Agro-pole Centres

One of the crucial steps for rural reconstruction should be to create and develop "*Agricultural Growth Pole Centres*" in central locations in the rural setting itself, where agricultural goods and commodities from surrounding villages may be marketed, and the farmers may derive their own benefits, without being looted or plundered by the middlemen, rural Panchayati-Raj officers, and village money lenders. Existing agricultural collecting centres may also be promoted to perform these roles. Further details are given elsewhere (Mukherji, 1983b: 1–192; 1983d: 171–192).

Urban Development Strategies

Development of Small Towns and Intermediate Cities

- Restructuring of the space economy of the hinterland of large cities is thus urgently necessary. That is, the need for providing much greater capital investment, growth efforts, industrial licenses in the rural areas, smaller towns, and intermediate cities, as well as making them as poles of development that will diffuse growth waves to the surrounding villages, instead of the present day excessive reliance only upon a few primate cities and larger cities (Mukherji et al., 1982; Mukherji, 2006: 305–330; also see Chapman, Dutt and Broadknock, 1999: 5–11; Chapman and Pathak, 1999: 135–153).
- Such spatial restructuring also implies development of and use of vast unutilized internal domestic markets within the country and internal orientation, rather than excessive dependence upon export activities. *For, development means internal development, not external dependency* (Mukherji, 2000 (a): 15–27; 2006: 285–330; 2008a: 308–328).

Massive Employment Generation in Cities

- Objective should be to generate massive employment, productive self-employment, and gainful employment, both for migrants and urban residents, by strengthening and expanding better and productive linkages between urban formal and informal sectors, and by increasing their productive efficiency and transfer of technology (Mukherji et al. 1981: 32–121).
- We must make all-pronged efforts for the creation of employment for rural masses in the villages themselves. Irrigation development, transfer of technology to villages, and rural industrialization of villages will be means, which are greatest generators of employment in countryside. No doubt, these are difficult tasks. But many developing Asian nations (China, Indonesia, Thailand) (Passy, 1990: 69–79; UN, 1991a: 1–25; UN, 1992: 19–115) are succeeding in such efforts, and there could be no reason why India cannot achieve equal or better success.

Eliminate Urban Poverty

- Urban poor are very rapidly swelling everywhere. To eliminate poverty among urban poor, ensure that value received by them must enhance. They must derive benefits of their only capital – labour – and they should be asked to pay less for goods and urban services that they receive from cities.
- One World Bank policy study (1975) suggested two interventions: one, we should increase the value of labour by increasing the demand for their labour and by upgrading the quality of labour; and other, improve quality and quantity of public services available to the urban poor. Providing quick but useful training for their skill development and providing cheap and subsidized school and health services to urban poor, especially slum dwellers, will reduce urban poverty and human resource development.

- Standing (1985: 1–55) had emphasized on the relations between increased migration to metropolises, proliferation of urban informal sectors and consequent severe exploitation of labour. Rodgers (1989: 1–17) unfolded relationships between growing urban poverty and distortions in labour market in the Third World cities. Many UN and World Bank studies, and other studies also have indicated the great problems of growing poverty and unemployment in metropolises of the developing countries (Singh and De Souza, 1980: 3–56; Todaro and Stillkind, 1981: 11–77; Singh, 1989: 1–38; UN, 1991b: 85–95; UN, 1992: 19–115; UN, 1993a: 1–11; UN, 1993b: 126–127; 1993c: 92–104).
- Oberai (1987, 1993) noted "coping with employment and poverty problems in large cities is thus the major challenge facing developing countries. There is urgent need to examine current policies related to employment promotion, particularly in informal sectors, promotion of small scale industry, and employment generation through investment in housing and community infrastructure for poor".
- Skill development will provide more self-employment or upgraded employment, both in formal and informal sectors (Rodgers, 1989; Ruiter, 1999: 205–221). Skill development will provide more self-employment or upgraded employment both in formal and informal sectors and will reduce poverty among them through income generation (Rodgers, 1989: 1–17; Pathak, 1999: 244–268; Mukherji, 2004: 156–165).
- Many recent UN and World Bank studies have also emphasized upon the great need for generation of employment and reduction of urban poverty and for slum redevelopment in the metropolises of the developing countries (UN, 1995b: 25–166). And, by providing security for the urban poor, and by giving them the basic amenities and essential services (like schools, health services) (UN, 1995a: 10–150; UN, 1995 (b) to (e): 25–166; UN, 1997: 90–115; World Bank, 1995: 165–228; 1996: 79–98; and W.B., 2003b: 86–106).

More Humanistic Urban Planning and Housing for Slum People

- The objective should be to give a better deal to the slum-dwellers and ensure a more humanistic approach to urban planning for their welfare. Specifically, concrete programmes must be made for construction of inexpensive, heavily-subsidized, low-rise apartments for slum dwellers within the slum areas, each apartment with 150–200 sq. ft and designed to accommodate a 6–7 person family (Mukherji, 2005e: 11–36).
- Toilets and bathroom facilities can be centrally located and commonly operated. Free labour of slum-dwellers for construction of own houses at present sites can be ensured. Expenses can be met by subsidies from city corporations, state government, voluntary organizations, and some monthly levy from not-poor segments of metro residents (as slum development tax).
- Goal will be to provide cheap housing and sanitary facilities to slum people within slums; instead of perpetuation of such problems. So, cities and

metropolises hopefully will become self-sustained, more habitable and more egalitarian. A more humanistic approach to these entire problems of slum development and shelter of urban poor is very urgently needed.

Need Efficient Metropolitan Management

- Regarding this, all mega cities of developing countries must learn a few lessons from very efficient Tokyo Metropolitan Government and Japanese Urban management experiences. In extremely competitive and strenuous world, efficiency has no alternative (Tokyo Metropolitan Government, TMG, 1994, 1996, 1998; Mukherji, 2000c: 1–10).
- TMG has a very large, very organized, and very efficient work-force. It takes care of efficient management of Tokyo Metropolitan region's all aspects of development, people's problems, care: right from urban traffic, transport, communications, statistics, administration, resources, planning, implementation, housing, health care, social welfare (TMG, 1994, 1996, 1998).
- Their efficiency is manifest in concrete plans, updated every 2 years, and their implementation in right earnest as well as in city life which flows smoothly in Tokyo, in spite of very big population (32 million). Efficient management of TMG should be replicated in metropolitan management of Indian mega cities, Kolkata, Mumbai, Delhi, Chennai. Better management skills of Japanese people, discipline, orderliness, work ethic, even innovativeness to elicit financial resources from urban residents can be applied to other cities (TMG, 1998: 1–5; Shimodaira, 1997; Mukherji, 1997b: 61–81).
- These are the one of most important lessons that all the mega cities of India and the Asia Pacific must learn from very efficient Tokyo Metropolitan Government and Japanese urban management experiences (Mukherji, 1997b: 61–81; 2000b, 1–12; 2000c: 1–10; Mukherji and Otomo, 2000: 19–35; World Bank and ARMEC, 1998: 1–120).

Develop Urban Infrastructure

- Many cities have inadequate essential urban infrastructure like surfaced roads, electricity, water, parks, utilities and means of transport-communications. Frequent breakdown of essential urban services very acutely hamper urban lives and productivity. Developing such most essential urban infrastructure must be a top priority (WB, 2003a: 31–125; Mukherji, 2000b: 1–12).

Redirect Migration to Growth Centres

- This avowed goal may not be possible, unless and until we make a paradigm shift towards development of small cities and small towns and re-orient our present iniquitous planning bias towards only metropolitan and mega city development. Promoting new growth centres and redirecting migration flows to district headquarters and small cities must be encouraged.
- The next six steps *broadly* elaborate various aspects of such programmes for restructuring of the spatial organization of the country.

Regional Development Strategies

Spatial Restructuring

- In order to relieve acute problems associated with such migration-urbanization and for achieving economic development, a major requirement is to re-orient the country's spatial-economic structure and spatial linkages to internal domestic markets.
- Reorient credit services, institutional agencies, trade and transport linkages, resources use, investment and growth efforts, away from export activities and external dependency relations, but rather towards development of poor people in hitherto neglected regions. And, in the interior parts of the country.
- Spatial restructuring implies development of and use of vast unutilized internal domestic markets within country and internal orientation, rather than excessive dependence upon exporting. *Because, development means internal development, not external dependency* (Mukherji, 2006: 260–330).

Evening Out Spatial and Socio-economic Disparities

- Strenuous attempts ought to be made for achieving a more equitable distribution, over whole national space, of productive forces and units, and of means of production, employment, consumption, and investments, as well as of services, e.g., schools, hospitals, vocational training, and all basic amenities of life. That is, an even distribution for all the people over the nation of what I would like to call *"per capita civilization"*.
- It requires an evening-out of social and economic disparities among social classes and among regions throughout India.

Focus Upon Neglected Regions and Enhance Their Potentials

- Problem of balance between production and consumption must be worked out at all levels. For that, we need to develop latent possibilities and expand each small region's productive base in accordance with its potentialities and basic human needs.
- The present-day much accentuated concentration of per-capita consumption only among the privileged few and widening gap between the growing and the lagging regions must be given a final burial.

Reduce Regional Disparities

- Tremendous attention should be given to reduce all kinds of regional disparities, specially that arise due to faulty planning, excessive pro-urban development bias, political bungling, excessive corruption at all levels, lack of regional development planning prescriptions (instead of all time ad-hoc planning) and basic lack of 'planning for the poor'.
- Traditionally Uttar Pradesh, Bihar, Orissa and interior parts of India always remain neglected, backward, and tottering under widespread poverty, because no industry were created in these regions since last 300 years, not even during last 63 years (since Independence). Consequently, hundreds of

millions of poor migrants are forced to move to favoured and comparatively developed states of Maharashtra, Delhi, Punjab and Haryana (where they are increasingly treated as unwelcome movers).

- Thus, planning for the poor is a must. So also, to achieve a balanced regional growth and development over entire national space must get top priority. Then only, any fruitful *"Migration Planning"* can occur in India (Mukherji, 1981: 1–300; 2006: 250–330; 2007: 265–280).

Fostering Inter-regional Developmental Bonds

- Adequate attention should be given to the development of inter-regional economic bonds through proper extension and re-orientation of transport and communication links and forging mutually beneficial inter-local and inter-regional trade links.
- This re-orientation should be away from current excessive focusing of rails and roads and trade links towards exporting ports and large metros, and must be towards small, local headquarters, and micro-regional and meso-regional centres, so that future migration streams can be attracted to them.

Create Agricultural Market Centres at Central Locations

- This step will be similar to creation of agri-pole centres, but may have more spatial field or wider "sphere of influence" than the former. These may be set up at district level or wider regional level, at central locations in order to serve a broader rural community.
- Thus, generating *"Agricultural Market Centres"* in central locations in rural and regional setting itself, where agricultural commodities from surrounding areas may be brought, marketed and linked with agro-industries.

Create Service Centres at Central Locations

- Likewise, setting up *new* "service centres" and growth of existing "service centres" must be encouraged at regional level, to be located at central position, where rural community may get urban services, agricultural repair services, rural bank services, micro finance services, communications and marketing information.
- These will make farmers to derive their own benefits, without being deceived by conmen, unscrupulous rural bureaucrats and village money lenders. Existing service centres may also be promoted to achieve such goals.

Needs Rapid Business Innovations for Massive Job Creation

- Recently, some business experts advocate rapid and innovative business expansion in India, at multi-tier market levels: (a) global, (b) glocal, (c) local, and (d) BoP or Bottom of the the Pyramid level (Chakravarthy, January 2010: 18; *Times of India*, March 2010: 24). Indian business circles can produce goods and services at each tier of these markets, and consequently, generate massive job opportunities.

- "*Global* product market tier represents customers that are multinational companies as well as select Indian customers who are willing to pay for products and services which have been created primarily to serve customers in developed markets". "The *glocal* tier consists of customers who are unwilling to pay global prices, but seek products and services that are close to global standards" ... "The *local* tire represents customers who are happy with less sophisticated and often lower quality products and services, but offered at local prices that are considerably cheaper than global prices. The country's middle class belongs mostly in the local tier ...." (Chakravarthy, ibid.: 18).
- "The final tier is the so-called *Bottom of the Pyramid (BOP)*. This tier represents customers who have been traditionally excluded from the market' .... It is possible to identify similar tiers in the case of talent market .... If business stays only with these tiers, India will not alleviate its poverty. What is needed is business innovation that finds creative ways of serving customers at the bottom of the pyramid using an unskilled and semi-skilled workforce from lower tiers of the talent market" (ibid.).
- "Indian companies have started offering products and services that appeal to the local and BOP tiers. The innovative Indian company Bharti offers the world's cheapest telecommunications service at just one cent per minute. This service is offered through retailers and micro-entrepreneurs who sell prepaid telephone cards in every nook and corners of India. It is service for the poor by the poor ... India needs more innovations of this kind ..." (ibid.).
- Although these business ideas *smack* of promoting a class-ridden fractured society, nevertheless, I feel that still it is worthwhile to give a try, as it might generate enough jobs for the poor masses. Hunger is the greatest evil! And, that must be fought out on the top priority!

Policies for Poverty Alleviation and Fertility Decline

1. One UN study (UNDP, 1997: 41–120) recommended the following steps for poverty reduction: *To empower the individuals, households and communities to gain greater control over their life and resources by:*

- Ensuring their access to assets as a protection against vulnerability: access to credit and other financial services are vital, especially security of tenure, housing, and land.
- Ensuring food security for households and families.
- Ensuring education and health for all, along with access to reproductive health care, family planning and safe water and sanitation.
- Building social safety nets to prevent people from falling into destitution and disaster (UNDP, 1997: 90–115).

2. *Strengthen gender equality in order to empower women and to release their vast underused energy and creativity. Poverty eradication without gender equality is impossible.*
3. Accelerate pro-poor growth., which will:

- Restore full employment and opportunity expansion as a high priority.
- Create an enabling environment for small-scale agriculture and the informal sector.

- Restructure public expenditure and taxation to support poverty reduction.
- Reverse environmental degradation.
- Create more employment.

4. *To ensure an active state, committed to eradicating poverty and providing an enabling environment for political participation and partnership for pro-poor growth (UNDP, 1997: 105–110, Also see Mukherji, 2000h: 1–35).*

Strategies for Poverty Eradication and Fertility Control

- Widespread illiteracy and pathetic poverty are two great curses in India. The great majority of people, specially in villages, are reeling under extreme poverty. According to Swami Vivekananda (1894): "This poverty is man-made, not God-made. It is the educated and privileged elites who deliberately maintain poverty among the poor and the downtrodden, and do nothing to alleviate it." He further thundered: "I hold all such educated people as traitors, who being educated at the expense of the illiterate masses, do nothing for them" (ibid.: 1894, Volume III: 105).
- *The rural people, denied of education, denied of employment, denied of any scope for upliftment, are bound to remain in the shackles of poverty, fatalism, and utter despair* (Mukherji, 1975: 260–325; 1979b: 1–80). *We need real planning for the poor and their true implementation* – which will benefit directly the poor; not be usurped by middlemen; nor disappear in political bungling, nor camouflaged under illusory theory of downward-filtration from rich to the poor!
- So, our most sacred duty is to uplift the poor masses from poverty, in the same way as handful of educated classes got affluence. Fertility level of the poor will automatically decline, as has already declined among advantageous groups, because scientific rule states that, under a given condition (i.e., *no poverty*), if an event has occurred once (i.e., fertility declined), then, it will definitely recur again, if the same conditions are brought forth again (Mukherji, 2005c: 1–38; 2007: 265–285).
- Only pseudo-scientists are unable to face this truth; and ritualistically preach about on-setting fertility decline, without ever changing abject poverty. You cannot force contraceptive down the throats of hungry women and men, and expect fertility decline! (Mukherji, 2007: 270–305).

Reduction of Rural Poverty through Economic Growth and Development

- "Major poverty alleviation programmes include self-employment programmes, wage employment programmes, PDS (public distribution system of food), nutrition, and social security programmes. Employment creation through infrastructure development,. and pension schemes for the elderly are recent initiatives" (Radhakrishna and Ray, 2005: 40).
- "For reducing rural poverty, agricultural growth is important. Low relative food prices are needed for reduction in both rural and urban poverty. Any strategy for reducing poverty has to concentrate both on employment intensity as well as labour productivity" (Dev, 2000: 823–836).
- "Direct poverty alleviation programmes are also needed to raise the incomes and purchasing power of the poor ... Investments in rural roads and

agricultural research and development have the greatest impact ... Rapid economic growth remains the best bet for reducing India's immense problems of inequality and poverty. ... Efforts must (also) be made to see that that the distribution of consumption does not get skewed further" (ibid.).

- "Need to promote agricultural intensification for both higher and low potential regions. Striking the right investment balance between irrigated and rain fed regions, and between high and low potential rain fed areas will be particularly important" (ibid.).

Poverty Alleviation through Agricultural Growth

- "Data on regional variation of poverty reduction through income growth shows that it has a strong agricultural link (Radhakrishna and Ray, 2005: 57–58). Green revolution mainly occurred in "irrigated" regions of Punjab, Haryana and Western Uttar Pradesh, and in delta areas of Andhra Pradesh, Tamil Nadu and Karnataka. Here even small farmers were benefited, and poverty was least. In contrast, green revolution bypassed "rain-fed" (and non-irrigated) regions of Andhra Pradesh, Maharashtra, Madhya Pradesh, West Bengal, and arid regions of Gujarat and Rajasthan. In such areas, depths of poverty were in abundance" (ibid.: 56–57).
- The authors further argued that, "If it were possible to refocus agricultural growth to extend to the vast geographical areas under the 'rain fed' agro-ecological system areas (AES), considerable progress could be made in poverty reduction" ... "These are the major pockets of poverty. It is the map of agricultural growth that could be modified with considerable mileage for poverty reduction" (ibid.: 57).
- "It is imperative, therefore, agricultural growth be stepped up and its thrust should be on the hitherto bypassed regions of central and eastern India .... So emphasis on irrigation development – which is in some sense difficult but crucial in parts of these regions – agricultural technology – to sustain growth in them – and requisite policy support – to spur growth – would be critical in this quest" (ibid.: 58).
- As noted elsewhere (Mukherji, 1981: 24–140; 2006: 65–121), the majority of urbanward migrants come from the same rural backward regions of Bihar, Uttar Pradesh, Madhya Pradesh, Orissa, Andhra Pradesh, etc., to metropolitan cities of Kolkata, Mumbai, New Delhi, Chennai, Bangalore, Ahmedabad or Hyderabad, and million cities like Kanpur, Lucknow, Jaipur, Patna and Pune. They are poor illiterate and unskilled migrants from the villages, who move out and somehow eke out their living in their urban El Dorado.
- Besides, massive migration of unskilled and illiterate labourers also occur from "agriculturally backward and hitherto neglected states" of Bihar, Orissa, Eastern Uttar Pradesh, and Madhya Pradesh to "agriculturally prosperous states" of Punjab, Haryana, Western Uttar Pradesh, and also to Karnataka and Maharashtra (Mukherji, 2002: 525–559; 2006: 21–170). To this vast hinterland of poverty where the programmes for poverty alleviation must be mainly focused.

Rural Development and Agricultural Development Strategies

- There are innumerable ways for poverty alleviation, if we are soulfully sincere to find ways and implement them. Rural industrialization, the creation of widespread network of surface and underground irrigation, multiple cropping, rural construction, integrating industries and agricultural products, value-adding process of agricultural goods, etc., will be the greatest generators of rural employment. Such steps will raise the levels of agricultural productivity, household income, and consumption. Massive generation of rural employment for women and men is a great necessity, which can be actualized by the creation of household industries, village industries, agro-industries, horticulture, food processing, handicrafts, weaving, oil pressing, sugar making, and other cottage industries (Mukherji, 1977a: 1–56; 2005b: 75–95). Some UN (UN-ESCAP, 1977, 17–18, and 21–27; UN, 1997) and World Bank reports have also emphasized upon similar steps for rural employment generation (World Bank, 1993; and 2003a: 31–125).
- Besides, changes in iniquitous patterns of land ownership and adequate safeguards against drought, floods, and seasonal unemployment are very essential to alleviate poverty. Rural cooperative societies for credits, *grameen* (rural) banks, and marketing cooperatives for village products will be extremely necessary. Many farmers and workers are forced to commit suicide, because of very high interest rates of village money-lenders, and due to lack of credit facilities at reasonable rates. These must stop immediately. Rural micro-finance organizations, rural credit societies and marketing cooperatives must emerge and operate in every village.
- "Land reform is not just distribution of land. Its aims are to break the land-and-caste based political controls, loosen the interlocking behaviour of factor markets, guarantee access to technology and credit, and create conditions for maximum production and marketable surplus, all so necessary for rural transformation. All its elements need to be addressed in a holistic, rather a piecemeal, fashion" (NIRD, 1999: 121).
- Land reforms, co-operative farming, irrigation, innovative measures for agricultural development, rural banks, adequate marketing facilities, multiple cropping, agro-industries, etc., are the only answers to such rural maladies. Decentralization of economic power, more even distribution of development facilities and credits, and lessening of socio-economic inequities between the owning and non-owning classes, should also get priority to ameliorate the miserable condition of the poor rural masses, and for both men and women. Too much politicking in village societies, political bungling in all political parties, and a very deep-seated corruption among village panchayats, power-hungry village elites, novo-rich, and village development agencies have usurped all the forces and capabilities of village regeneration in India. All such evil practices soon must be completely liquidated.

Rural Development through Decentralization and Panchayati Raj

- There is a great need for people's participation in rural development programmes. One important study notes: "Central to the overall failure are excessive reliance on top-down centralized bureaucracy and scarcity of funds" ... "An elaborate system of patronage, thriving on disempowerment of the poor and hapless, distributes largesse to a chosen few at the cost of multitudes. As for the funds, rural development, meaning about half the country's development, has attracted less than a tenth of the expendable funds at any time. An acute urban bias is all pervasive" (National Institute of Rural Development in India, (NIRD, 1999: 119).

- "Without a positive trust towards the socio-economic transformation of the marginalized groups, growth may bypass the poor and safety net schemes may only remain short-term palliatives. Thus, economic growth *per se* is not the solution" (NIRD, 1999: 120). It further emphasized upon the great need to decentralize and to develop the Panchayati Raj Institutions (PRI) (rural self-government organizations), and opined that: "The need of the hour is to strengthen the localized elected base in contrast to the appointed authorities" (ibid.: 120).
- "Government interventions should not only improve the incomes of the poor but their bargaining power *vis-à-vis* the moneylenders, landlords, and bureaucracy. Such empowering measures need to be distinguished from the popular measures, which merely act as doles and do not enable the poor to stand on their own legs or fight for their rights. Empowerment is good in itself, leads to higher incomes, checks corruption, and arbitrary use of power" (ibid.:120)
- NIRD emphasizes upon the *two* basic requirements for effective rural development in India: *First,* "The ultimate goals should be to achieve rural prosperity through participatory development process .... No such development is possible without bestowing the real decision making power on the community" (ibid.: 121–122). Regarding scarcity of resources, it suggests that: "What can still be expected is reduction of excessive expenditures on the bureaucracy, both administrative and political, non-productive budget expenditures, and concealed subsidies, particularly to the non-poor segments of the population. This would release a significant amount of resources for deployment in social sectors" (NIRD: 122).
- *Second,* people's active participation in designing, implementing and controlling the entire budget and all the processes of rural development work, without the intervention of the bureaucrats and, even powerful elite of the Panchayati Raj, should be activated (ibid.).
- *Otherwise, I strongly believe that the happiness will be an unfortunate lady, who will miss seeing the faces of an ocean of the rural poor in India!*

Generate Massive Rural Employment through Rural Industrialization

- "To generate growth the main policy components are ensuring sound macro-economic management and macro-economic stability, boosting domestic demand, adopting fiscal discipline, accelerating industrial production, reforming financial sector institutions and promoting good governance" (ICSI Herald, 2000: 13–18). The study further observed that, "Pro-poor growth is needed both for reducing poverty and for making growth a stronger and a more indigenous process ... Maximization of employment and through this maximization of welfare of individuals shall have to be defined as the goal of economic programme" (ibid.).

- "Speedy expansion of small business seems to be a viable alternative for India" ... We need to encourage small scale industries and enterprises because "this sector can promote large scale employment with relatively much less capital requirement, a more equitable distribution of income, effective mobilization of resources and promotion of dispersed growth" (ibid.: 13–14).

Special Rural Development Programmes and Employment Generation

- Recently Bhaduri (2005: 1–90)) opined that market economy is not at all capable of poverty reduction and mass employment generation in India. For these objectives, we need to devise *special rural development programmes* for generating mass employment among the poor unemployed rural workers, and to create national assets. It needs programmes that will benefit the poor directly. According to him, there are roughly 35 million unemployed rural people (but too low estimate?). If employment is to be provided to these people for 300 days per year, at the rate of Rs 60 per day, that would cost Rs 630,000 million (Rs 63,000 crores (billions). Plus, if cost of essential materials are also added, then, the total cost would be only 4 per cent of the Gross National Product – two and half per cent of GNP for wages, and only one and half per cent for required materials (Bhaduri, 2005, ibid.).
- According to Bhaduri (2005: 10–90), the entire work will be executed through Panchayati Raj systems, through government's recent Information Right Act (in order to curtail corruption and misappropriation of funds). His argument is that the benefits will work in two ways: (1) first, it will provide money in the hands of the workers, which, in turn, will create demands for consumer goods, which in turn will generate additional mass employment. every where; thereby starting a wheel of economic prosperity; and (2) second, the project will also create permanent national assets and by raising national productivity, eventually, it will generate National wealth. Additionally, the greatest benefits will be encouraging people's massive and active participation in the National Re-construction.
- Although the above ideas are profound, however, some questions also arose (Sarkar, 2006: 95–96); first, the estimate of only 35 million rural unemployed is untenable, it must be three times more; second, thus, the cost of wages will be also three times more Rs 1,900,000 million (Rs 190,000 crores). Plus, the cost of materials will also be three times more to make it meaningful, and permanent assets. Thus, total cost of the project will be 12 per cent of GNP, not just 4 per cent, as the author dreamt.
- In spite of these limitations, I strongly think that such Rural Massive Employment Generation Programme (RMEGP) is much more commendable, and it should be seriously attempted, rather than government's presently envisaged National Rural Employment Generation Act (NREGA) which has very much limited scope and coverage. NREGA is a half-hearted programme, taken mainly for vote-bank politics, not really to ameliorate widespread poverty and hunger in India. Otherwise, much greater fund would have been allocated and countrywide coverage would have been made.

- Besides, it must also be reiterated that the current on-going NREGA programme (started from 2006) is just a variation of the former "Food for Work" Programme of 1960–70's, and that also will not make much dent upon rampant poverty in India. Reports of rampant corruption in NREGA programme implementation have already vitiated its success.

Need Rural Infrastructure Improvement and Rural Employment

- "The poor need a ladder to climb out of poverty, not palliatives that keep them dependent on government handouts. Subsidies for rural power, canal water and fertilizers benefit mainly large farmers. Subsidies for food, education, and health overwhelmingly benefit urban folk and richer rural areas. Rural employment schemes are a palliative that help greatly in droughts when agricultural jobs plummet, but they are plagued by corruption and waste. They have failed to create durable assets" (Aiyar, 2005: 18).
- "Many studies have shown that all – weather roads (need capital-intensive construction) are the best way to reduce rural poverty, while temporary roads built by labour-intensive employment schemes achieve little. Even illiterate Bihari villagers will tell you that if every village has a paved road plus electricity plus telecom, businesses will spring up all over place and provide millions of new jobs. Talent is in place, even the finance is in place, only the infrastructure is missing. Provide that and rural India will take off" (Aiyar, 2005: 18, also see Mundle, 2010: 20).
- *Thence, massive investments for infrastructure development (roads, electricity, water, school, post offices, mobile towers, means of transport and communications, and so forth) must be given the top priority for rural reconstruction. And, dividends will be the generation of massive rural employment.*

Policies for Agricultural Development and Security of the Poor

- We need to strengthen agricultural research and extension systems. Need is also to establish clear, long term property rights over land, and access to credit.
- We need to promote sustainable intensification of agriculture and sound management of natural resources, especially in areas with fragile soils, limited rainfall and widespread poverty.
- We need to develop low cost markets and transport networks for inputs and outputs.
- We need to expand and improve assistance in food and agricultural development (UNDP, 1998: 87).

Promotion of Agri-Business and Rural Employment

- Recently, some experts suggest the benefits of agribusiness and bio-energy for creating massive rural employment in each village by "focusing on export of a variety of processed food, seafood, herbal products and flowers, with the help of friendly bank loans, and insurance companies for necessary cover" (Firodiya, 2006: 30). It is opined that, it will create mass of rural employment. Textile export will provide another opportunity. Agribusiness and textiles will generate crores (tens of millions) of new well-paid jobs. It is also suggested that, "oil companies should create a bio-energy cluster in each village, which will use local feedstock to produce biogas, bio-diesel, and ethanol. Biogas may be used for electricity, bio-fertilizers, and bio-pesticides; while bio-diesel and ethanol may be further processed and blended with diesel and petrol for energy. It will generate further crores of rural employment (ibid.).

- For promotion for agri-business management, we also need to enhance value addition. and marketing. Singh and Sharma suggest (2006: 456– 458) such steps as:
  (1) Post-harvest management of agro-products, e.g., pre-processing facilities, washing and packaging.
  (2) Agro-processing facilities like cold chain, pre-cooling facilities close to production areas to avoid wastage and reduce transportation costs.
  (3) Technology for agro-industrial processing.
  (4) Warehouses and infrastructures for storage and transportation of unprocessed goods.
  (5) Integration of small and unorganized processing units and transforming them into national and global players, with incentives for optimum marketing (ibid.).
- But, Ghosh (2006: 4) pinpointed various dangers of further penetration of capitalism, both Indian and international, into agri-business and commercialization in Indian agriculture. "The dangers lie in the fact that: all risks of agricultural failure or marketing uncertainties will have to be borne by petty farmers, not by MNCs." They thus would have no responsibilities. They will harvest only the heaps of benefits at the cost of the poor peasants, and the petty farmers will be bound by endless bondages!
- However, we also need to explore innovative options for rural employment, albeit with much cautions. Thus, many-pronged efforts for poverty alleviation are required now.

Education and Development

- Radhakrishna and Ray (2005: 59–60) rightly indicated that among the tribal North Eastern states of India, incidence of "very poor" is absent and the people enjoy inalienable rights on land and assets. They also show better indicators of human development. So, education has contributed a lot for their development. Thus, education is an important component of health, nutrition, and material well being of this people and this has reduced poverty in the region." So, as lessons for poverty reduction, human development components, like education, health, and nutrition, must be given due priorities.

Need Tremendous Efforts for Development of Small and Medium Towns/Cities

- In another major study the present author made very detailed investigations of the problems of small and medium towns of India (Mukherji, 1993b: 1–146; 1997c: 68–113). The main recommendations are very briefly highlighted. The same findings are valid even today, in 2009, as in India change occurs at snails pace (also see Mukherji, 1993d: 75–94).

- "In 1991, there were about total 3609 towns in India. Of which, there were about 1466 non-agricultural towns and about 1700 small agricultural towns. Of total non-agricultural towns, there was persistent proliferation of 665 underdeveloped small non-agricultural towns, which remain virtually stagnant during 1971–1991" (Mukherji, 1993b: 21–146). "These small underdeveloped and neglected towns actually require and should get much more development efforts than the so-called large cities and metropolises whose present day very high maintenance costs far exceed their so-called advantage of economies of scale and which are generating very degraded urban environment, stinking filth and squalor, and extreme social inequities (Mukherji, 1997c: 68–113).
- "The crucial point requiring our serious attention is that such small towns and agricultural towns urgently need economic regeneration, growth inputs, capital investments, infrastructure development, and all pronged efforts for industrialization (agro-industries, small scale industries, cottage and household industries, and handicrafts)." (ibid.: 110) .... "If these essential growth inputs are provided, soon they will turn out to be the agents of change for the vast surrounding countryside which for too long a period, has been reeling under extreme poverty, lack of any basic amenities of life and civilization, prolonged neglect and utter stagnation" (Mukherji, 1997c: 110).
- "The findings of cluster analysis of towns (Mukherji, 1993b: 105–106) show that the majority of non-agricultural towns of India have very low value on most urban functions, or have low manufacturing-cum-service-cum-trade/commerce functions. They invariably show a low mixture of manufacturing-service trade type, or slight variations of these with some low proportions of household industries, or mining, or construction or transport activities. The basic patterns remains more or less unchanged" (Mukherji, 1997c: 111).
- "As regards agricultural towns, the majority of cluster types are found to be finally clubbed into a single large cluster, represented by mixed cultivation and agricultural labourer-cum-low proportion of manufacturing/service/trade functions, with slight variations here and there with construction, livestock or household industry. Basic patterns of cluster types remain unaltered over time. Pattern can be termed as deadly stable, without much structural or functional transformations, in spite of planning era" (ibid., 1997c: 111).
- "These findings show that the entire urban situation of India calls for the vast systems transformations – the changes which ought to place more capital, investments, and growth efforts in favour of the hitherto neglected towns and small towns/cities, instead of catering and feeding only the metropolitan cities.
- In the context of very rapid population explosion in the country, a huge population bomb will explode in the rural area, who cannot get even minimal subsistence in the agricultural sectors. This sea of humanity will

be forced to migrate to towns and cities which are already over crowded and cannot provide employment, shelter and even the basic urban amenities of water, sanitation and electricity. Set against these setting, it is all them ore very imperative, that the innumerable small towns and intermediate towns and cities must get our utmost attentions and growth efforts. Only then, they will be able to attract future streams of migrants, and provide employment, education, health and shelter. Urban policy makers and the governments must pay immediate attention to such problems of catastrophic magnitude (Mukherji, 2006: 305–330).

- "In sum, a total awakening and a total change in our conventional perspectives of urban development, urban policies and urban planning is thus urgently needed" (Mukherji, 1997c: 110–111).

Generate More Urban Employment

- "Jobs should be indeed India's new *mantra.* In a fast growing and domestic-driven country, urban and rural consumers are on an aspirational spiral", one recent article has opined (Editorial, *Times of India,* March 24, 2010: 24). "The youth bulge is growing, and with it the productive potential of our human resources. Farming barely sustains the majority of Indians. We need greater agriculture-industry interface, such as agro-processing. NREGA cannot substitute for mass labour absorption into manufacturing. Such shifts will need private capital and reformed labour laws and new land requisition laws. To ease out the setting up of factories. Investment friendly policymaking for key labour intensive sectors, including real estate and tourism, can have multiplier effects in terms of empowering people, creating skills, and generating jobs" (ibid.: 24).
- "With demands for services in short supply, education is emerging as a labour magnet. Creaking government infrastructure barely satisfies India's mammoth student population, so more private players need to take up a supporting role. On health, let us think both ends of the social spectrum by building and running rural assets as well as promoting top medical tourism. Boosted construction, a key growth driver, can serve social goals by creating affordable housing and spur infrastructure building ... providing jobs on a vast scale" (ibid.: 24).
- "India's employment trends are, however, marked by a increasing unorganized labour that translates into large-scale labour insecurity. The reason is that employers are forced to tap informal hiring systems since labour laws do not permit flexibility. The gainers are labour contractors and the losers are workers, who remain underpaid and do not get on-the-job training. Labour reform has long been sidelined in the name of workers interests. All this does is cosset a labour aristocracy while denying millions of labour market entrants a better chance to participate in India's economic transformation. If inclusive growth is the goal, this situation needs to change, and fast" (ibid.: 24). However, I think that this issue of labour reform is also a double-edged and ticklish issue, because under the garb of generating more employment, often organized formal sectors and corporate houses also take advantage of quick hiring and firing of employees, nor provide them adequate protection or job security.

- Another study suggests: "To alleviate poverty and distress, let's think of beyond food subsidy and loan waivers. Let's create manufacturing jobs on a mass scale to stem casualisation of work and absorb rural labour. 21st century India can no longer delay labour reform, modernization of agriculture or the trimming of wasteful subsidies (*Times of India*, January 26, 2010: 18).
- Develop small towns, by setting up more productive units, infrastructure and making institutional changes. Generate more urban employment in such towns and cities in real estate, tourism, local handicrafts and local industries (Mukherji, 2005a: 20–40; 2006: 274–325).
- Transform present-day parasitic cities, making them centres of development, diffusing development impulses to surrounding regions and towns and villages (Mukherji, 2005b: 75–95). Utilize the present-day huge growth of telecommunications in India (growing by 19 million cell-users per month, in 2010) for more urban employment in formal and informal sectors.

Other Important Strategies

Overall General Strategy: Eliminate Barriers for the Migrants and Protect their Rights

As briefly explained at the end of chapter 11, there are many different kinds of socio-economic-cultural-political barriers in the individual mover's mobility fields, which block need gratification and restrain free field adjustments within the individual's life space (Mukherji, 1975: 316–18; 1979b: 75–77, 1982: 265–278).

In this context, one point must be emphasized very clearly here. The concept of *"Eliminating Barriers from the Individual's Mobility Fields"* was first developed by the present author in his second PhD thesis on "Mobility Field Theory" (Mukherji, 1975: 1–378) in the University of Hawaii and East West Center (published as Microfiche version, University of Michigan, Ann Arbor, 1976). These innovative ideas were further elaborated in various papers and books (Mukherji, 1979a: 45–61; 1979b:1–81, 1976a: 1–25; 1976b: 12–20). It was clearly enunciated 35–36 years ago in all four books (Mukherji, 1975, 316–18; 1979a, 1–81; 1981: 150–173; and 1982a: 250–280) that

> "There are different kinds of socio-economic-cultural-political-linguistic barriers in the individual's mobility field (life space of the individual(s) – in which he/she can move for basic need fulfillment), which block need gratification and restrain free field adjustments, within the life space of the individuals. Caste system is one such barrier. Deprivation is another. Bonded land tenancy, land mortgage and debt are some other kinds of barriers which bind the rural folks to perpetual serfdom. Sometimes, the government's coercive actions against the hawkers, vendors or squatters in the urban areas, and lack of encouragement or subsidy to small-scale entrepreneurs act as barriers in their mobility fields, hampering free field adjustments" (Mukherji, 1975: 316–318).

> "Such barriers could be innumerable in number, diverse in character and variant in degree. The field solution, then, involves identifying these different kinds of barriers in the individual's mobility fields and findings ways and means of eliminating them from the social mix of the population. The purpose would be to eliminate them so that individuals and people are enabled to forge out their best abilities and right to decide their own lives" (Mukherji, 1975: 316–318; 1981: 172–73; 1982a: 250–280).

The above ideas were first developed and written extensively by the present author in 1975, and subsequently and repeatedly published also in 1983, 1985a, 1985b, and later. Strangely enough, very recently, UNDP (Human Development Report 2009, titled as "Overcoming Barriers: Human Mobility and Development", New York, 1–250) is recommending almost the same things, that is, "overcoming barriers in human mobility and development". Besides, UNDP, Jakarta (2009: 1–45) and UNDP, Bangkok (2009: 1–30) are also recommending the same ideas. They are emphasizing, 35 years after, what I had first evolved and propagated those ideas. It seems that these ideas are borrowed, without acknowledging or referring to the original thinker!

The UNDP's "Human Development Report 2009: Overcoming Barriers: Human Mobility and Development" (UN, 2009) emphasizes that the main migration-related problems in many developing countries, including South Asia, arise due to inappropriate policies and regulations. The report urges for better policies to protect migrants as large gains to human development may be achieved by *"lowering barriers to movement and improving the treatment of movers."*

Set within these context, notice almost similar ideas, similar phrases and similar recommendations of UNDP *(Overcoming Barriers: Human Mobility and Development*, New York, 2009; and UNDP, Jakarta, 2009) (given below and italicized) which borrowed the same concepts and policies written 35 years ago by the present author.

Human Development Report (Overcoming Barriers: Human Mobility and Development, 2009, summary, 1–6) opines: "Migration, both within and beyond borders, has become an increasingly prominent theme in domestic and international debates, and is the topic of the of this Report. *The starting point is that the global distribution of capabilities is extraordinarily unequal, and that this is a major driver for movement of people*. Migration can expand their choices – in terms of incomes, accessing services and participation, for example – *but the opportunities open to people vary from those who are best endowed to those with limited skills and assets. These underlying inequalities, which can be compounded by policy distortions, is a theme of the report"* (UNDP, Human Development Report, 2009, Summary: 1–2).

"There is a range of evidence about the positive impacts of migration on human development, through such avenues as increased household incomes and improved access to education and health services. *There is further evidence that migration can empower traditionally disadvantaged groups, in particular women. At the same time, risks to human development are also present where migration is a reaction to threats and denial of choice, and where regular opportunities for movement are constrained"* (ibid.: 2).

"National and local policies play a critical role in enabling better human development outcomes for both those who choose to move in order to improve their circumstances, *and those forced to relocate due to conflict, environmental degradation, or other reasons*. Host country restrictions can raise both the costs and the risks of migration. Similarly, *negative outcomes can arise at the country levels where basic civic rights, like voting, schooling and health care are denied to those who have moved across provincial lines to work and live. HDR09 shows how a human development approach can be a means to redress some of the underlying issues that erode the potential benefits of mobility and/or force migration"* (ibid.: 3).

Thence, UNDP report offers some recommendations to be taken into account by governments as guidelines to seek solutions: "The six 'pillars' as key policy reforms are: (a) Opening existing entry channels for more workers, especially those with low skills; (b) Ensuring basic human rights for migrants, from basic services, like education and health care, to the right to vote; (c) Lowering the transaction costs of migration; (d) Finding collaborative solutions that benefit both destination communities and migrants; (e) Easing internal migration; and (f) Adding migration as a component for origin countries' development strategies" (UNDP, 2009: 4–5).

Such research findings are indeed emphasizing the main point of "*eliminating barriers from the migrant's mobility fields and lives*" – the original ideas of the present author (Mukherji, 1975: 1–378). *Then, it is greatly amusing: whom shall I quote and refer? To my own original ideas of 1975? Or UNDP (2009)? These are examples of sheer plagiarism!*

However, the crucial issue here is to help the poor masses of illiterate/semi-literate and unskilled/semi-skilled migrants, the world over. If UNDP researchers at New York (2009), Jakarta (2009) and Bangkok (2009) and elsewhere, have found their ways and propagates these useful ideas and programmes, even after 35 years of its origin and evolution, then, very good for the humanity!

A Spatial Paradigm of Village Clusters and Central Villages for Rural Development

The spatial paradigm of clustering of villages and developing central villages, within each sub-block or Panchayat level, involves the following principles All the details are given in another study (Mukherji, 1983: 179–192):

(a) Central villages, within a cluster of contiguous villages (and within sub-block territory), may provide the basis for better rural interaction, spatial transformations and implementation of rural regeneration programmes.

(b) In India, there are over 600,000 villages, of which 50 per cent have less than 500 persons, and most of them are without any basic amenities like school, post-office, rural health centre, agricultural depot, all-weather roads, or even potable drinking water. Providing all such amenities to all these numerous villages will not be possible even in near future, nor would they be economically viable. Therefore, in order to optimize the best use of scarce capital, it would be economically practicable to provide most such centralized goods and services to the cluster of the villages as a whole by locating them in the *central village*, within the *village cluster*. Such a central village must be at easy transportation distance of surrounding 5 or 10 villages, and should cater for the needs of the total rural community of that *village cluster*. Within each sub-block, there may be a hierarchy of such central villages, surrounded by respective clusters.

(c) Central village-cum-village cluster will forma viable community, the *lowest-tier spatial unit* of rural development plans.

(d) There must be a well-planned and well-organized attempt to identify and develop these lowest level central villages (and village clusters), by channeling to them most of afore-mentioned goods and services that are required for an integrated rural development in India.

(e) A great care should be taken that these central villages do really diffuse development impulses to the surrounding village cluster for an *integrated area development* – they should not usurp the growth efforts and benefits only for their own cancerous growth, as conventional strategy of growth centre, or service centre, or central place development did.

(f) Therefore, plan for development of *central village-cum-village cluster* should be so envisaged as to develop infrastructure facilities for *agricultural development-cum-rural industrialization,* for the fullest utilization of human and natural resources, and for more even distribution of essential goods and service over sub-block or panchayat territory.

(g) Certain agro-processing industries, specially those offering centralized services, may be located at the central village; but other cottage and village industries may well required to be located at numerous surrounding villages within the cluster, specially those which can use local skill and resources. Thus *a policy of decentralization* must be given due prominence, without which integrated rural development might remain a difficult task.

(h) *For identification of central villages,* either of the following three methods or their combination may be adopted:
  (1) *Weighted Composite Ranking Method:* based on number and kinds of central functions offered by the villages.
  (2) *Ray-diagram Method:* based on travel patterns of villagers for different goods and services.
  (3) *Bi-Section Method*: delineating respective service areas of the central villages, by delimiting the sub-block territory on the maps.

(i) Further details about such methods, principles and the implementation of the entire idea are greatly elaborated in another volume (Mukherji, 1983b: 1–192), and hence not repeated here.

Need to Totally Stop Illegal Migration from Bangladesh

One of the greatest needs of India, now, is to prevent all illegal immigration of Muslims from Bangladesh. Indeed, grave dangers from India's eastern borders are thousand times greater than that from Pakistan borders. Massive and invisible daily illegal infiltrations from Bangladesh are changing the demography, politics, economy, culture, elections and the governments, and saps out the very existence of Indian Nation.

Evidences are plenty. Result of recent Assam state elections (May 2006), where massive illegal Muslim migration from Bangladesh continued since last 63 years, show that they became majority in many border districts, have determined not only winners through consolidated vote banks, but also controlled entire formation of Assam government (*Times of India,* May 23, 2006). Now, political parties in Kerala in the extreme south are also planning to follow this path (*Times of India,* May 25, 2006). Also see *Times of India* (October 2010, p. 4), for evidences of 2 million illegal Bangladeshi migrants in Mumbai. Ominous signs are everywhere for all to visualize!

Not only illegal migrants, but terrorists, ammunitions, explosives, disintegrating forces and militants are also exported from Bangladesh to India, through those routes: West Bengal, Assam, Tripura, even through Nepal. But, these state governments, and the Central government, are not only mute spectators, rather give the infiltrators all support and welcome reception for evil-some minority vote bank politics, without ever realizing that such anti-India activities are destroying the very existence of these states, and India, as a nation, in entirety! India is known as a very tolerant and soft nation. But, this is not a sign of proverbial Indian tolerance, rather cowardice. No other country in the World will ever tolerate such evil designs! Thus, the following stringent actions are very necessary:

1. Entire Nation must be made very urgently aware of these issues that threaten India's very existence. No political parties should play selfish political games on these issues of supreme National importance!
2. Very strict military solution of sealing of Bangladesh border permanently is very urgently required.
3. Solution lies in providing very urgent and complete sealing of entire borders with Bangladesh, heavily fencing with barbed wires and military installations, and constant army vigilance.
4. Benefit of this step alone will exceed that of endless Five Years Plans, over many millenniums!
5. In this regard, the most stern border policy of USA must be strictly followed.

The Problems of Financial Scarcity and Resources

Question of financing all above strategies and resources is not really a big problem. The government has been envisaging most of these programmes through successive Five Year Plans. Now the country is amidst the 11th Five Year Plans (2007–2012). What is really missing is a lack of proper co-ordination and proper implementation of various programmes (Mukherji, 2006: 310–330). The issue of restructuring iniquitous village society is also an untouched phenomenon that hinders progress (Mukherji, 1983c: 30–31). So also the crucial issue of spatial restructuring of the space economy of the country and development of interior markets. When most of the programmes will be geared towards that goal, and domestic markets given growth impetus, consequently the space economy will also be restructured (Mukherji, 1981: 124–190; 2006: 276–330).

Often arguments are made that the above-mentioned policies and strategies are utopian, and they can not be implemented due to shortage of funds. In reality, these arguments are mischievous designs by vested interest. Well, where money for the government's extravaganza come from? For every expensive perks and wasteful expenditures of all political representatives (Mukherji, 2007: 301–303)? Why is hundreds of billions of rupees always available for the rich 350 universities, but not even a *Naya Paisa* for village primary schools? Why are subsidies, meant for the poor, always usurped by middle class and the rich? Why are funds always available for very expensive fly-overs in the mega cities for the motorists, but not for the basic roads in the villages?

Why does Reserve Bank of India always protect interests of super-rich, corporate houses and business sectors, draining out scarce money from common people? Why is burden of indirect taxes so heavy upon common people, and why are direct taxes on business houses so disproportionately low? Why are trillions of trillions of dollars of Black money secretly stashed in private accounts in Swiss Banks, while the basic minimum programmes of rural development in the country suffer tremendously? Why are trillions of bank loans, scattered to defaulting business families and corporate houses never recovered, while over

100,000 poor farmers (in Maharashtra and Andhra Pradesh) are made to commit suicides annually for their outstanding bank loans? Why are vast black money, manifold larger than the government's entire exchequers, never confiscated? The funds and resources for the above-mentioned development strategies for the poor should come from the same sources! Planning thus must be made for the poor, and the poor only! (Mukherji, 2007: 301–305).

John Kampfner (2010: 22) thus succinctly observed: "The problem in India, particularly, since economic liberalization in 1991, is not wealth creation. Nor is it democratic institutions. It is governance, the inability to deliver freedoms for the vast majority of its people. Politics and business have worked together to use power as means of enrichment ... *India's selfish elite holds the Republic back*" (italics mine).

Top of all, currently, in Delhi preparations are going on for impending Commonwealth Games, 2010. Billions and billions of scarce public money are wasted in financial bungling and corruption in a country, India, where – as recent World Bank Report (2010) showed that eight Indian states (UP, Bihar, Orissa, West Bengal, Chhattisgarh, Rajasthan and Madhya Pradesh) have very deeply-incised poverty, much worse than even world's poorest African countries, like Ethiopia or Tanzania (World Bank, 2010; Dwivedi, 2010).

A recent *Times of India* report (*TOI*, August 25, 2010) showed a more than Rs 80,000 crores (1 crore = 10 million) is so far spent in preparing for Commonwealth Games in Delhi for October 2010. Wasted in political bungling and rampant corruption, in a country, where half of total 1.20 billion population live less than Rs 24 per capita per day! With that kind of huge money (Rs 800,000,000,000), all the 580,000 tottering villages of India could have benefited. Each village could have roughly Rs 1,380,000 – that would have been enough to provide drinking water facilities, a primary school, minimum rural electrification and a health dispensary in each village. Benefits could have reached to an ocean of impoverished humanity! Such a callous government – for whom "inclusive growth" is mere an election slogan! And, what limitless insensitiveness of a billion plus mute spectators!! Strange. All these can happen only in India!!

Most crucial questions are: where such money come from? Why are the top priorities (combating rampant poverty) thrown into dustbins? Why are bridges not built over development divide between the rich and the poor? Why is the government hell bent upon developing a high growth, but most unjust economy, which is merely enslaving itself to a handful of private business houses and dollar billionaires, while cruelly trampling over 600 millions very poor Indians? The masses of the poor – who are forced to live at less than Rs 24 per day per head ($1.25 per person per day)? What kind of cosmetic democracy is this?

Such gross social and economic inequities very soon will create a very dangerous volcanic eruption in India. Evidences provided in this book unfortunately herald the onset of such a catastrophe. Our future, and the future of our progenies, lies in our real awakening and consciousness for the Nation and soulful efforts to overcome such a calamity, before it is too late!

Need Education for Character Building and Nation Building

Swami Vivekananda thundered more than 117 years ago (1893): "A nation-wide real educational effort for character-building of all men and women and children of India, and their transformation for Nation building seem to be the only panacea." ... "You should go to the sinking millions of India, and take them by the hand" (*Swami Vivekananda, 1893,* Complete Work, Centenary Vol. III, 1963: 433).

Most unfortunately, since Independence, this greatest requirement of human-building is entirely missing from India's educational and developmental efforts, due to utter pseudo-secularism. India was a land of supreme spiritualism. Two hundreds years of Macaulay's (1835) evil design of imparting *colonial education* to generate a country of slaves and clerks for dominating Indian Nation were complete in its goals. It continued even after Independence, as the colonial legacy. After Freedom, secularism and secular education were imposed by children of Macaulay, agnostics, pseudo-secularists, and pseudo intellectuals. They threw away the baby with the bath water. By imposing secular education in a land of supreme spiritualism, India, the moral and ethical teachings were also thrown away through the windows! Now, bereft of its inner core, *spiritualism*, India has degenerated into a weak and a miserably failed state. Presently, we have scores of expert engineers, doctors, management specialists and computer experts from IITs and IIMs, but seldom real human beings, who would have sincere feelings for the masses of the poor, or true sense of duty to the Motherland! In India, all education must be woven round the deep-seated teachings and revelations of spiritualism – which is the core inner spirit of India and Indians. Bereft of that education, we in fact only generate millions of expert robots, not real human beings, who will have deep-set patriotism, spiritualism, and ethical values. Only this can fight out rampant and omnipresent corruption. Only this will raise India again as a great Nation! Sooner the leaders and common people of India will understand this greatest requirement (character building and Nation-building education), and will ceaselessly strive for achieving this, the better for India's survival and real inner development!

Conclusion

This book has discussed the acute problems of distressed migration and urban involution in India. It has also discussed essential *five Ps*: *(a) widespread and rampant poverty in India, (b) patterns of migration in India, (c) phenomena of migration-urbanization system, (d) socio-economic and political processes underlying the nexus of poverty-underdevelopment and migration-urbanization, and (e) the policies and strategies required. All these five P's are very much inter-related. Each of them are vividly highlighted and discussed.*

An entire set of economic development policies and strategies are also recommended which include: steps for poverty eradication, reduction of rural poverty and economic development, poverty alleviation programmes through agricultural growth and rural development through agricultural development. Besides, the book also recommended rural industrialization through decentralization and Panchayati Raj, rural industrialization for massive employment generation, special rural development programmes for employment creation, rural infrastructure improvement, policies for security of the poor, promotion of agri-business for rural employment and social development through education Further details for rural development and poverty reduction are presented elsewhere (Mukherji, 2007: 270–305). And, it also suggested effective steps for reduction of urban poverty and better urban and metropolitan management. And, top of all, it very strongly urged for the greatest need for education for character building and nation building.

In conclusion, I must state that such problems cannot be fully redressed unless we realize that these are consequences of spatial imbalances in economy, which, in turn, is consequence of excessively polarized economic activities and resources at a few centres and improper policies.

So, indeed great efforts are required to restructure the spatial organization of economy over national space of India. These means more emphasis on development of internal markets, rather than only upon external markets and export activities. These will require tremendous reorientation of trade-transport links, resource-use, growth and investment, capital, credits and subsidies, and functions of urban centres, all away from the currently excessive concentration only at the larger metropolises and mega cities, rather towards the development of hitherto neglected villages and small urban centres and small cities. These will also require greater welfare for the poor and to raise their purchasing power. In sum, these efforts must aim at more equitable distribution of income, wealth, and means of production and consumption. This implies the total elimination of poverty from the surface of India and making all people, specially the poor, the humiliated and the downtrodden, free from all human bondages and fully liberate them for their sojourn towards higher human and spiritual fulfillment!

What is very essential is *not* a super-fined and supra-organized formulation of a plan or a strategy, rather rigorous implementation of whatever programmes and strategies we may have. Corrective measures to arrest bungling, misappropriation, and inefficiency are very much the need of the day. It is also very much necessary to instill a sense of commitment to National reconstruction and development among the minds of all people, students, scholars, technicians, administrators, policy makers, politicians, bureaucrats down to village level workers. As a short-term strategy, *this commitment can be inculcated through proper kind of education, an educational system which will make people to be honest, just, egalitarian, rational, humanist, and profoundly compassionate and committed to the cause of upliftment of the poor people and complete eradication of poverty from India. No nation can prosper without a high standard of character and morality of its people. Thence, our long term need is to create proper human beings, a billion strong army of people having character and morality, possessing steel nerves, compassionate heart and sincere dedication to the Nation, India!!*

This book sometimes presented a dismal picture, but it ends with a clear note of optimism about a bright future for India. There is a clear road ahead. Let me conclude this book with the Divine messages of the greatest savior, Swami Vivekananda (1863–1902): "*Arise, awake, for your country needs this tremendous sacrifice*" (Swami Vivekananda, 1893) (Centenary Volume III, 1963: 318). He also urged all of us to arouse inherent Divinity in ourselves, to arouse in all others, and work for the country and the entire humanity.

His inspiring message brings great hopes for the future: "*We are responsible for what we are, and whatever we wish ourselves to be. We have the power to make ourselves. You cannot believe in God until you believe in yourself. Never loose faith in yourself. You can do anything in the Universe*" (Swami Vivekananda, 1896, Centenary Vol. VII, 1963: 331).

Message of Swami Vivekananda to the Nation

"India, which was once the wonder of the world, the mother of all the civilizations of this planet, had gone to a millennium of humiliations due to endless tyranny and foreign dominations. But, India will rise again, like a giant leviathan, to such an unimaginable heights, far surpassing her all past glories, that the entire world will be surprised with great amazement."

Swami Vivekananda (1896)

Appendix

Tables of Chapter 1

Table 1.5(a) *State-level Variations in Migrants Classified by Place of Last Residence and Duration, India, 1991 (only major states shown)*

Place of last residence	*Total/ Rural/ Urban*	*Total migrants*			*Duration of Residence in Place of Enumeration (%)*									
					Less than 1 year		*1–4 years*		*5–9 years*		*10–19 years*		*20+ years*	
		P	*M*	*F*	*M %*	*F %*	*M %*	*F %*	*M %*	*F %*	*M %*	*F %*	*M %*	*F %*
	1	*2*	*3*	*4*	*5*	*6*	*7*	*8*	*9*	*10*	*11*	*12*	*13*	*14*
Total Migrants		**232112973**	**64308038**	**167804935**	**5**	**2**	**22**	**15**	**16**	**15**	**20**	**25**	**23**	**36**
States in India beyond the state of enumeration														
	Total	26689595	11883886	14805709	6	4	22	19	17	17	23	25	25	29
	Rural	16216380	7001731	9214649	6	4	21	17	17	16	24	26	25	32
	Urban	10268141	4778773	5489368	5	4	24	22	16	18	22	25	25	25
Andhra Pr.	Rural	720899	285490	435409	6	4	19	17	15	16	23	25	28	32
	Urban	493685	225222	268463	5	4	26	22	15	17	20	24	24	25
Bihar	Rural	2297573	1197675	1099898	6	3	21	16	17	16	25	27	26	32
	Urban	687249	375999	311250	5	3	24	20	18	18	24	27	22	25
Gujarat	Rural	514642	225415	289227	4	2	14	15	12	14	22	25	41	37
	Urban	415511	191682	223829	6	3	17	19	12	15	19	23	36	31
Haryana	Rural	954154	267329	686825	6	4	21	16	18	16	25	27	25	35
	Urban	464604	182576	282028	4	3	21	20	16	18	24	28	30	28
Karnataka	Rural	854096	320637	533459	7	4	20	18	15	16	21	23	23	30
	Urban	568375	248063	320312	5	4	22	21	15	17	21	23	26	26

Cont'd...

...Cont'd

Kerala	Rural	457636	238837	218799	5	4	25	24	16	17	22	23	26	24
	Urban	497355	262797	234558	4	4	26	25	16	17	22	23	25	23
Madhya Pr.	Rural	1000042	272826	727216	12	4	22	16	15	15	21	25	20	34
	Urban	477489	171270	306219	5	3	24	21	16	18	23	26	22	26
Maharashtra	Rural	876681	319667	557014	10	6	20	18	15	16	21	23	22	30
	Urban	888495	384588	503907	8	4	24	23	16	18	20	24	21	22
Orissa	Rural	472815	207509	265306	8	4	23	17	16	16	22	25	24	32
	Urban	143493	72945	70548	5	4	29	25	18	18	21	24	19	22
Punjab	Rural	714503	297418	417085	4	3	17	16	12	15	21	24	39	38
	Urban	651613	300736	350877	5	4	22	22	14	17	19	24	34	31
Rajasthan	Rural	1332206	491896	840310	8	4	21	16	16	16	22	25	24	35
	Urban	608884	273307	335577	4	3	21	19	15	17	22	25	27	29
Tamil Nadu	Rural	645649	307831	337818	6	4	25	21	17	17	23	24	24	28
	Urban	808407	402564	405843	6	4	26	24	17	18	22	24	22	23
Uttar Pr.	Rural	3893910	2028402	1865508	5	4	21	19	20	18	28	27	23	29
	Urban	1834731	930361	904370	4	3	22	21	18	19	26	27	25	25
W. Bengal	Rural	560313	177571	382742	5	2	21	15	15	16	22	29	31	36
	Urban	572278	254162	318116	6	3	24	21	17	18	22	27	23	26
B. Last Residence outside India														
		5927882	3068146	2859736	3	2	8	9	7	8	15	17	59	57

Table 1.6(a) *Migration with 0–9 Years Durations, 1981–91, and State-level Variations*

Last residence	*Total Migrants*			*Reasons for Migration (%)*											
				Emp-loyment		*Busi-ness*		*Educa-tion*		*Moved with family*		*Marri-age*		*Others*	
	P	M	F	M %	F %	M %	F %	M %	F %	M %	F %	M %	F %	M %	F %
Total	Duration of residence 0–9 Years														
Migrants	82107175	27255302	54851873	30	3	7	1	9	2	30	19	3	66	20	10
A. Last residence in India															
	80948404	26681723	54266681	31	3	7	1	9	2	30	18	3	66	20	9
I. Within the state of enumeration															
	69859268	21442906	48416362	27	3	6	1	10	2	31	17	3	68	21	9
(a) Elsewhere in the district of enumeration															
	46952579	12974057	33978522	22	2	5	1	11	2	32	14	4	72	25	10
(b) In other districts of the state															
	22906689	8468849	14437840	35	4	7	1	9	2	30	23	2	60	16	9
II. States in India beyond the state of enumeration															
	11089136	5238817	5850319	44	5	10	1	5	2	27	34	1	49	12	9
Andhra Pr.	492030	217828	274202	36	5	8	1	9	2	29	34	1	46	15	10
Bihar	1226839	700317	526522	53	6	9	1	6	2	20	33	1	50	10	8
Gujarat	305738	131623	174115	28	3	15	2	7	2	30	32	1	48	19	13
Haryana	561504	196323	365181	37	2	8	1	5	1	36	26	1	62	13	8
Karnataka	582750	241915	340835	34	5	14	3	4	2	27	28	1	48	19	13
Kerala	439285	228684	210601	54	14	8	1	7	6	20	33	1	34	11	12
Madhya Pr.	597184	209693	387491	33	4	10	2	5	1	31	24	2	60	18	9
Maharashtra	770030	324888	445142	35	6	9	2	4	1	32	34	1	45	19	12
Orissa	267594	135333	132261	57	7	6	1	6	1	20	30	1	53	10	8
Punjab	513763	222972	290791	30	3	11	1	4	2	39	39	1	46	15	8
Rajasthan	769967	335695	434272	40	4	18	2	4	1	26	28	1	56	11	9
Tamil Nadu	679280	344542	334738	49	10	7	1	4	2	25	38	2	38	12	10
Uttar Pr.	2457996	1317662	1140334	51	4	11	1	5	2	25	42	1	44	8	7
West Bengal	454862	193802	261060	44	4	10	1	6	2	26	27	1	60	13	6
Delhi	281946	109318	172628	29	3	6	1	7	2	40	36	1	51	16	7
B. Last residence outside India															
	1079945	546649	533296	20	4	4	1	3	1	27	33	1	27	46	34

Only major states and Delhi Union territory are shown.

Tables of Chapter 4

Table 4.1(c) *Socio-economic and Migration Variables, Selected 56 Districts (showing high out-migration rates), India, 1991*

S. No.	DISTRICT	CULT	AGL	LIVES	MINS	HH	MNF	CONS	TC	TRA NS	SERV	PCBD EP	PCBC RED	PCBC AGI	PCBC SSI	PCBC IND	PER WOR	PERF AREA	PER NSA
1	Srikakulam	32.69	41.45	4.02	0.23	3.78	2.32	0.58	5.81	1.54	7.58	867	483	154	43	104	48.6	12.0	54.3
2	Vizianagaram	38.37	34.19	2.16	0.30	3.35	3.79	0.75	6.55	2.30	8.22	791	525	168	96	213	50.3	17.7	49.4
3	West Godavari	15.06	55.19	1.74	0.20	2.21	5.10	1.01	7.33	2.66	9.51	1767	1333	505	108	340	43.3	10.4	53.3
4	Krishna	15.73	48.60	1.95	0.45	2.39	6.18	1.61	8.60	5.30	9.19	2348	1598	446	125	361	43.2	7.5	56.1
5	Guntur	20.46	51.48	1.35	0.54	1.21	5.35	1.34	7.18	3.03	8.06	2094	1577	390	176	426	47.8	13.7	52.9
6	Prakasam	26.47	50.86	2.11	0.32	2.50	3.37	1.22	4.85	1.70	6.60	1547	1234	493	51	128	48.6	12.3	33.6
7	Warangal	32.42	42.08	1.05	0.48	3.54	5.05	1.58	4.59	2.25	6.96	1295	846	344	70	181	47.7	28.8	31.8
8	Goalpara	54.89	18.82	1.44	0.04	1.49	1.76	1.63	6.72	1.74	11.46	511	263	112	122	314	33.6	14.0	42.6
9	Barpeta	58.38	16.62	1.31	0.02	1.21	2.43	1.64	6.92	2.16	9.30	426	246	62	15	37	30.0	17.2	53.4
10	Nalbari	49.77	18.40	3.46	0.03	1.94	2.65	1.85	6.56	2.35	13.00	414	321	69	25	89	33.1	4.9	72.7
11	Jorhat	44.23	5.33	19.38	0.55	1.06	3.31	1.90	7.52	2.65	14.08	1844	736	135	144	366	38.3	12.5	43.3
12	Sibsagar	44.58	6.24	24.57	3.39	0.45	2.09	1.00	5.43	1.65	10.59	1340	508	135	109	336	41.9	12.6	53.4
13	Jamnagar	39.72	14.43	3.43	0.57	2.07	11.60	2.03	9.77	4.74	11.65	3594	1239	200	202	849	36.6	3.4	58.6
14	Bhavnagar	29.38	24.32	2.27	0.14	2.18	21.66	1.54	7.78	3.60	7.12	2275	1461	135	169	573	38.3	3.1	63.2
15	Amreli	39.88	24.02	3.30	0.27	1.16	15.63	1.12	6.20	2.07	6.35	1173	534	218	14	203	39.8	1.3	69.1
16	Gandhinagar	18.11	21.38	3.05	1.76	0.91	12.36	4.16	7.77	4.75	25.74	6388	5614	1224	221	1671	32.9	0.0	73.5
17	Bharuch	26.70	40.17	1.86	1.14	1.14	9.36	2.52	5.93	3.34	7.83	2277	1615	205	303	1333	43.2	18.6	54.0
18	The Dangs	70.52	16.14	1.28	0.03	1.38	1.12	1.28	1.76	0.53	5.98	840	308	86	3	5	50.5	98.4	0.0
19	Hamirpur	61.48	1.85	1.04	0.07	1.83	2.92	4.49	5.34	2.44	18.55	4479	734	150	35	199	41.8	18.2	35.3
20	Lahul and Spiti	51.69	5.15	3.86	0.01	0.77	0.64	12.29	2.03	1.17	22.39	3346	646	102	14	35	64.9	6.1	1.5

Cont'd...

...Cont'd

21	Bangalore Rural	49.65	21.31	3.09	0.63	2.88	8.04	1.20	5.48	1.51	6.22	915	751	420	50	194	43.0	10.5	47.1
22	Chikmagalur	35.93	24.72	17.46	0.83	1.04	2.91	1.67	5.97	1.47	8.00	2252	1867	965	55	180	44.9	24.7	38.3
23	Dakshin Kannad	19.72	16.08	6.73	0.42	1.09	28.13	3.15	10.44	3.89	10.36	6021	2826	416	389	771	43.1	27.0	26.0
24	Hassan	57.04	14.44	7.42	0.49	0.91	2.96	1.58	5.75	2.07	7.33	1601	1159	520	43	92	44.2	8.1	51.2
25	Mandya	53.22	24.96	2.65	0.54	1.12	3.36	1.58	5.25	1.18	6.12	1053	738	338	36	79	44.5	4.7	50.6
26	Shimoga	37.50	35.26	1.94	0.37	1.58	5.24	1.82	7.11	1.89	7.28	1720	1596	468	113	473	40.8	31.0	29.8
27	Tumkar	54.62	21.16	2.21	0.41	2.60	4.24	1.43	5.34	1.51	6.48	1223	757	248	50	122	47.6	4.2	47.3
28	Ernakulam	9.30	15.79	7.12	0.95	1.57	16.16	7.16	15.27	9.29	17.39	7136	5880	330	472	2223	33.4	3.4	75.8
29	Idukki	19.43	22.16	35.24	0.25	0.64	3.20	1.62	6.33	2.39	8.74	1176	1016	398	49	115	39.7	50.6	32.2
30	Kottayam	15.70	23.35	10.59	0.55	2.25	8.24	3.52	13.25	5.51	17.03	4789	2066	304	238	489	31.2	3.7	83.1
31	Alappuzha	7.97	24.17	7.99	0.46	9.72	12.94	3.31	12.25	5.19	16.01	4342	1645	241	195	622	34.0	0.0	75.7
32	Pathanamthitta	25.82	27.11	6.37	0.55	1.18	5.83	3.15	9.59	4.53	15.87	10227	1479	183	73	121	29.7	57.7	37.6
33	Ujjain	40.77	23.83	1.18	0.14	1.78	9.34	2.48	7.22	2.50	10.76	2239	1722	283	156	777	39.8	1.2	75.2
34	Hosangabad	36.38	32.66	2.26	0.14	2.28	4.35	2.59	6.11	3.01	10.22	1374	956	349	50	241	37.4	36.0	45.5
35	Raigarh	44.81	17.65	2.95	0.37	1.52	11.39	2.77	6.33	3.36	8.84	2189	808	131	183	1036	43.8	23.4	26.7
36	Ratnagiri	63.48	9.63	3.04	0.61	1.38	4.03	2.61	5.04	2.28	7.91	1940	507	92	106	198	45.0	1.1	28.8
37	Sindhudurg	60.49	12.19	3.09	1.45	1.10	3.88	2.32	5.23	2.16	8.10	1998	544	125	75	130	47.4	6.7	21.0
38	Jalgaon	30.02	44.32	1.42	0.06	1.28	5.03	1.37	6.01	2.83	7.65	1122	784	163	58	124	42.8	14.8	69.9
39	Ahmadnagar	47.35	26.59	1.48	0.14	1.38	7.56	1.57	5.05	1.81	7.07	11330	879	325	70	250	45.9	10.8	68.1
40	Pune	31.38	14.01	1.60	0.16	1.50	16.32	5.47	9.81	4.79	14.96	5386	3416	300	437	2106	40.3	11.8	63.6
41	Sangli	43.44	24.19	2.04	0.13	1.29	7.76	1.99	6.94	2.78	9.42	1722	1124	331	135	377	44.1	5.4	69.5
42	Solapur	33.73	31.56	2.07	0.16	2.36	10.35	1.95	6.76	2.72	8.34	1256	890	333	84	239	43.0	2.3	75.6
43	Satara	49.28	21.58	1.80	0.21	2.22	6.18	1.78	5.46	2.72	8.76	1497	877	293	96	234	44.5	13.7	53.7
44	Bid	49.13	30.51	1.69	0.11	1.18	3.04	1.54	4.31	1.54	6.96	655	426	158	14	46	47.0	1.8	72.6

Cont'd...

...Cont'd

45	Osmanabad	40.51	41.09	1.15	0.19	1.42	2.65	1.45	3.41	1.33	6.80	615	435	185	11	31	45.3	0.5	76.1
46	Akola	26.13	50.83	0.86	0.10	1.00	3.66	1.57	5.92	2.44	7.49	847	674	154	48	79	43.7	6.7	75.7
47	Amravathi	21.53	52.42	1.47	0.04	1.31	3.42	2.00	6.02	2.52	9.25	1278	634	285	51	85	44.3	27.2	59.1
48	Wardha	27.79	46.15	1.60	0.20	0.73	5.41	1.89	4.91	2.11	9.21	1378	846	315	204	709	44.5	10.6	70.0
49	Madurai	17.17	43.74	0.91	0.27	1.35	9.47	1.98	11.27	3.39	10.45	2116	1844	415	194	576	43.9	20.0	21.3
50	Kamarajar	19.35	32.69	0.68	0.15	3.75	23.41	1.82	8.44	2.00	7.70	1732	1793	195	341	608	50.0	6.1	44.0
51	Chidambaranar	18.86	33.43	3.01	0.23	3.70	13.87	2.24	10.44	3.83	10.40	2118	1399	272	119	311	41.5	—	—
52	Tirunelveli Kat	22.72	31.56	1.56	0.22	5.17	8.38	1.29	8.15	1.98	8.97	1894	907	272	107	318	47.1	12.0	35.5
53	Tehri Garhwal	77.93	1.01	1.27	0.05	0.30	1.20	4.20	2.82	1.15	10.07	1869	295	91	5	18	45.3	68.9	12.7
54	Garhwal	62.40	1.80	2.45	0.03	0.50	2.08	2.61	4.31	1.90	21.91	2938	431	52	26	55	39.4	61.3	13.3
55	Pithoragarh	73.46	0.77	1.13	0.21	1.62	0.82	1.74	3.51	0.99	15.74	1663	438	38	13	154	48.5	50.3	13.5
56	Almora	76.49	0.93	1.39	0.28	0.71	0.89	1.74	3.27	1.04	13.25	1858	392	65	34	88	47.0	54.5	14.8

CULT – Per cent cultivators, total workers
AGL – Per cent agricultural labourers, total
LIVES – Per cent livestock workers, total
MINS – Per cent mining workers, total
HH – Per cent workers in household industry, total
MNF – Per cent workers in manufacturing, total
CONS – Per cent workers in construction, total
TC – Per cent workers in trade/commerce, total
TRANS – Per cent workers in transport, total

PCBDEP – Per capita bank deposit
PCBCRED – Per capita bank credit
PCBCAGI – Per capita bank credit to agriculture
PCBCSSI – Per capita bank credit to SSI industries
PCBCIND – Per capita bank credit to industry
PERWOR – Percentage of workers to total population
PERFAREA – per cent forest area
PERNSA – Per cent net sown area
SERV – Per cent workers in services, total

Table 4.1(d) *Economic and Migration Variables (Males) of Selected 56 Districts (showing high out-migration rates), India, 1991*

S. No.	*DISTRICT*	*POP GRO*	*POPD ENS*	*URBA NISA*	*GLIT ERA*	*VINM IGM*	*VOM IGM*	*INMI GRTM*	*OMIG RTM*	*INTRA DMA*	*INTE RDM*	*TOT MIGM*	*INTR ADMR*
1	Srikakulam	1.7	398	12.5	36.2	17950	84415	1.6	7.3	136983	18090	166221	82.4
2	Vizianagaram	1.6	323	17.2	34.2	36760	74076	3.5	7.0	125051	36880	169263	73.9
3	West Godavari	2.1	454	20.7	53.4	89563	169211	5.1	9.6	304862	119213	430185	70.9
4	Krishna	1.9	424	35.8	53.2	151581	140887	8.1	7.5	316367	152711	482338	65.6
5	Guntur	1.8	361	28.9	46.4	103152	149663	5.0	7.2	300734	103662	412536	72.9
6	Prakasam	1.7	157	16.5	40.3	41998	125252	3.0	8.9	144431	41998	189639	76.2
7	Warangal	2.0	219	19.4	39.3	50712	91492	4.5	8.1	152418	95122	254175	60.0
8	Goalpara	2.1	0	7.8	46.8	17666	41297	5.2	12.0	38561	17746	61157	63.1
9	Barpeta	1.8	427	7.0	43.2	11360	63619	1.6	8.9	70097	11560	86477	81.1
10	Nalbari	2.0	450	2.3	56.0	26473	41950	5.0	8.0	37890	26693	70620	53.7
11	Jorhat	1.4	305	15.3	65.5	16044	38585	3.5	8.5	25083	16254	53593	46.8
12	Sibsagar	1.6	340	7.2	64.5	13800	38354	2.9	8.1	27070	13900	52400	51.7
13	Jamnagar	1.0	110	40.4	59.0	36642	66223	4.6	8.3	73778	36712	120780	61.1
14	Bhavnagar	2.0	205	35.1	57.9	50695	124372	4.3	10.6	112898	50805	175713	64.3
15	Amreli	1.5	185	21.5	60.1	35568	98441	5.6	15.6	53575	35618	93096	57.6
16	Gandhinagar	3.4	630	40.9	87.1	64259	16246	30.1	7.6	8680	64459	86059	10.1
17	Bharuch	1.8	171	21.3	61.9	55340	76112	6.9	9.5	103850	55450	189012	54.9
18	The Dangs	2.4	81	11.0	47.6	4041	8050	5.6	11.1	7560	4071	13541	55.8
19	Hamirpur	1.2	330	6.2	74.9	5430	15468	3.1	8.8	16314	5453	25541	63.9
20	Lahul and Spiti	0.4	2	0.0	56.8	1673	2762	9.7	16.0	1740	1677	3756	46.3
21	Bangalore Rural	1.4	288	18.1	50.2	31270	76779	3.6	8.9	34071	32100	73941	46.1

Cont'd...

...Cont'd

22	Chikmagalur	1.1	141	16.9	61.1	56136	42619	10.9	8.3	61950	56746	130576	47.4
23	Dakshin Kannad	1.3	319	28.3	75.9	34072	99565	2.6	7.6	228621	34782	309940	73.8
24	Hassan	1.5	230	17.4	56.9	45370	68394	5.8	8.7	91822	45560	145220	63.2
25	Mandya	1.5	331	16.2	48.2	47899	62617	5.7	7.5	67970	48639	126889	53.6
26	Shimoga	1.4	181	26.5	61.5	92961	73710	9.5	7.6	124143	93391	238074	52.1
27	Tumkar	1.5	218	16.6	54.5	48100	94390	4.1	8.0	121911	48780	185087	65.9
28	Ernakulam	1.0	1170	48.7	92.4	96500	113728	6.9	8.1	144713	96790	261783	55.3
29	Idukki	1.1	214	4.7	86.9	123475	44693	22.6	8.2	61427	124435	216672	28.4
30	Kottayam	0.7	829	17.6	95.7	53560	233948	5.9	25.6	122782	53760	186152	66.0
31	Alappuzha	0.7	1415	30.5	93.9	47970	89100	4.9	9.1	90600	48150	144570	62.7
32	Pathanamthitta	0.5	449	13.1	94.4	45450	70865	7.9	12.3	59464	45590	113664	52.3
33	Ujjain	2.2	227	39.5	49.1	59464	52958	8.3	7.4	54448	60714	137502	39.6
34	Hosangabad	2.4	126	27.3	52.5	44567	50415	6.7	7.6	77499	44837	135246	57.3
35	Raigarh	2.0	255	18.0	64.0	73388	104760	8.1	11.5	104905	73828	221701	47.3
36	Ratnagiri	1.1	188	8.9	62.7	44444	233319	6.4	33.3	93273	44514	154159	60.5
37	Sindhudurg	0.6	160	7.6	75.8	25820	134014	6.6	34.4	48807	26040	87327	55.9
38	Jalgaon	2.0	270	27.4	64.3	98173	149953	6.0	9.1	329501	98403	462242	71.3
39	Ahmadnagar	2.2	197	15.8	61.0	112898	149540	6.5	8.6	257385	121388	388903	66.2
40	Pune	2.8	353	50.7	71.1	236192	202260	8.3	7.1	226085	238632	573927	39.4
41	Satara	1.8	233	12.9	66.7	118423	201010	9.8	16.6	255998	118793	396281	64.6
42	Sangli	1.8	257	22.7	62.6	79904	150724	7.1	13.4	141175	80114	257628	54.8
43	Solapur	2.2	216	28.8	56.4	97635	174035	5.8	10.4	240557	97935	380030	63.3
44	Bid	2.6	170	17.9	49.8	40073	127135	4.3	13.6	79697	40153	122410	65.1
45	Osmanabad	2.1	168	15.2	54.3	38392	89351	5.8	13.6	57625	38392	100727	57.2

Cont'd...

...*Cont'd*

46	Akola	1.9	209	28.7	65.8	86410	93280	7.6	8.2	162888	86560	260558	62.5
47	Amravathi	1.7	180	32.6	70.1	53517	87602	4.7	7.7	127798	54067	201315	63.5
48	Wardha	1.4	169	26.6	70.0	55636	48560	10.1	8.8	84401	56026	150337	56.1
49	Madurai	1.5	525	44.7	66.4	95800	154374	5.5	8.8	147521	100630	254664	57.9
50	Kamarajar	1.5	365	37.4	62.9	36956	57454	4.7	7.3	61575	38976	102231	60.2
51	Chidambaranar	0.8	315	41.2	73.0	38054	70590	5.4	10.0	73417	43771	119441	61.5
52	Tirunelveli Kat	1.2	367	31.7	65.6	26380	143976	2.1	11.7	95883	37520	137583	69.7
53	Tehri Garhwal	1.5	131	5.7	48.4	12870	31865	4.6	11.3	20900	12920	38490	54.3
54	Garhwal	0.6	126	11.9	65.4	17702	40468	5.3	12.2	24017	18362	46705	51.4
55	Pithoragarh	1.4	63	7.4	59.0	8809	34388	3.1	12.1	22283	8949	32862	67.8
56	Almora	0.8	155	6.4	58.7	10511	57506	2.6	14.3	26267	10671	39378	66.7

POPGRO – Population growth rate
POPDENS – Population density
URBANISA – Urbanisation
GLITERA – General literacy
VINMIGM – Volume of in-migration, males
VOMIGM – Volume of out-migration, males

INMIGRTM – In-migration rate, males
OMIGRTM – Out-migration rate, males
INTRADMA – *Intra*-district migration, males
INTERDM – Inter-district migration, males
TOTMIGM – Total migration, males
INTRADMR – *Intra*-district migration rate, males

Tables of Chapter 5

Table 5.9(b) *Findings of Step-wise Regression Analysis between District-level Migration Variables and Socio-economic Variables, Various States of India, 1991 Census (Males)*
Equation 1: VINMIGM (Volume of In-migration, males)

Eq. No.	Dependent Variable (y)	State	Step No.	Independent Variable (x)	Adj. R-sq.	Ind. Expl. (%)	Cum. Expl. (%)	Beta	T	Sig. T	Constant (a)	Explanation
1	*2*	*3*		*4*	*5*	*6*	*7*	*8*	*9*	*10*	*11*	*12*
1	Volume of In-migration, Males (VINMIGM)	Andhra P.	1	Population Growth (POPGRO)	.60	60	60	.8	5.8	.000	–75063.8	High rate of population growth, more in-migration
			2	Per cent General literacy (GLITERA)	.76	16.	76	.4	4.0	.001	–166992.2	More general literacy, more in-migration
		Assam	1	Per Capita Bank Credit (PCBCRED)	.68	68	68	.8	6.7	.000	8457.0	More bank credit, more in-migration
			2	Per cent General literacy (GLITERA)	.74	6	74	-.3	-2.5	.021	49103.4	Less general literacy, more in-migration
		Bihar	1	Per cent Workers in Mining (MINS)	.78	78	78	.9	12.1	.000	138.9	More workers in mining, more in-migration
			2	Per cent Workers in Service (SERV)	.94	15	94	.4	9.7	.000	–21406.7	More workers in service, more in-migration
		Gujarat	1	Per cent Workers in Trade/Commerce (TC)	.64	64	64	.8	5.7	.000	–80028.5	More workers in trade/comm., more in-migration
			2	Population Growth (POPGRO)	.76	12	76	.4	3.1	.007	–186671.8	High rate of population growth, more in-migration
			3	Per cent Transport Workers (TRANS)	.85	9	85	–.5	–3.2	.006	–162833.3	Less workers in transport, more in-migration

Cont'd...

...Cont'd

Haryana	1	Urbanization (URBANIZA)	.21	21	21	.5	2.2	.042	7175.1	More urbanization, more in-migration
	2	Per cent Livestock Workers (LIVES)	.41	20	41	.5	2.4	.032	–4029.5	More livestock workers, more in-migration
Himachal P.	1	Per Capita Bank Credit to Agriculture (PCBCAGI)	.71	71	71	.9	5.3	.000	–110.6	More bank credit to agriculture, more in-migration
	2	Per cent Forest Area (PERFAREA)	.87	16	87	.4	3.7	.005	–6223.7	More forest area, more in-migration
Karnataka	1	Urbanization (URBANIZA)	.89	89	89	.9	12.4	.000	–43670.2	More urbanization, more in-migration
	2	Per cent Workers in Mining (MINS)	.93	.93	93	–.2	–3.3	.004	–25972.2	Less workers in mining, more in-migration
Kerala	1	Per cent Livestock Workers (LIVES)	.39	39	39	.7	3.0	.011	48831.2	More livestock workers, more in-migration
	2	Per cent Transport Workers (TRANS)	.57	18	57	.5	2.5	.031	8636.1	More transport workers, more in-migration
Madhya P.	1	Per cent Workers in Manufacturing (MNF)	.56	56	56	.8	7.4	.000	10951.9	More manufacturing workers, more in-migration
	2	Per cent Workers in Mining (MINS)	.61	5	61	.2	2.4	021	6176.3	More manufacturing workers, more in-migration
Maharashtra	1	Per Capita Bank Credit (PCBCRED)	.62	62	62	.8	6.6	.000	24358.2	More bank credit, more in-migration
	2	Per cent Workers in Construction (CONS)	.69	7	69	–.6	–2.6	.017	43251.8	Less construction workers, more in-migration
Orissa	1	Per Capita Bank Credit to Industry (PCBCIND)	.64	64	64	.8	4.7	.001	15750.3	More bank credit for industry, more in-migration

Cont'd...

...Cont'd

Punjab	1	Per Capita Bank Credit (PCBCRED)	.84	84	84	.9	7.4	.000	9386.9 More bank credit, more in-migration
	2	Per cent Workers in Household Industry (HH)	.93	9	93	.3	3.7	.006	–4290.0 More workers in household industry, more in-migration
Rajasthan	1	Per Capita Bank Deposit (PCBDEP)	.71	71	71	.8	8.0	.000	–13135.7 More bank deposit, more in-migration
	2	Per Capita Bank Credit to Agriculture (PCBCAGI)	.75	4	75	.2	2.2	.038	–19782.8 More credit for agriculture, more in-migration
Tamil Nadu	1	Per cent Transport Workers (TRANS)	.68	68	68	8	6.2	.000	–19595.0 More transport workers, more in-migration
	2	Population Growth (POPGRO)	.84	16	84	.4	4.2	.001	–142959.0 High rate of Population Growth, more in-migration
Uttar P.	1	Per Capita Bank Deposit (PCBDEP)	.57	57	57	.8	8.2	.000	–1303.0 More bank deposit, more in-migration
	2	Per Capita Bank Credit to Agriculture (PCBCAGI)	.63	6	63	.3	3.2	.002	–19881.0 More credit for agriculture, more in-migration
W. Bengal	1	Per cent Workers in Mining (MINS)	.59	59	59	.8	4.4	.001	33003.3 More workers in mining, more in-migration
	2	Per Capita Bank Credit to Industry (PCBCIND)	.82	23	82	.5	4.0	002	15399.7 More bank Credit to industry, more in-migration

Table 5.10 *Findings of Step-wise Regression Analysis between District-level Migration Variables and Socio-economic Variables, Various States of India, 1991 Census (Male), Equation 2: VOMIGM (Volume of Out-migration, males)*

Eq. No.	Dependent Variable (y)	State	Step No.	Independent Variable (x)	Adj. R-sq.	Ind. Exp. (%)	Cum. expl. (%)	Beta	T	Sig. T	Constant (a)	Explanation
1	2	3		4	5	6	7	8	9	10	11	12
2	Volume of Out-migration, Males (VOMIGM)	Andhra P.	1	Cultivators (CULT)	.20	20	20	–.5	–2.5	.0200	132998.5	Less cultivators, more volume of out-migration
			2	Per cent workers in Construction (CONS)	.46	26	46	–.7	–3.4	.0030	209073.7	Less construction workers, more volume of out-migration
		Assam	1	Per cent Net Sown Area (PERNSA)	.59	59	59	0.8	5.6	.0000	8014.5	More net sown area, more volume of out-migration
			2	Per cent Workers in Trade/Commerce (TC)	.68	9	68	.3	2.6	.018	–9179.9	More workers in trade/commerce, more volume of out-migration
		Bihar	1	General Literacy (GLITERA)	.24	24	24	0.5	3.7	.0010	–17937.5	More general literacy, more volume of out-migration
			2	Per cent of Manufacturing Workers (MNF)	.43	19	43	–.5	–3.7	.001	–35014.9	Less manufacturing workers, more volume of out-migration
		Gujarat	1	Per cent Net Sown Area (PERNSA)	.25	25	25	.5	2.7	.016	18708.4	More net sown area, more volume of out-migration
			2	Per Capita Bank Credit to Agriculture (PCBCAGI)	.45	20	45	–.5	–2.7	.017	25984.5	Less bank credit, more volume of out-migration
		Haryana	1	Population Growth (POPGRO)	.37	37	37	–.6	–3.2	.007	36766.9	Low rate of population growth, more volume of out-migration
			2	Per Capita Bank Credit to Industry (PCBCIND)	.52	15	52	.6	2.3	.041	47573.6	Less bank credit to industry, more volume of out-migration

Cont'd…

...*Cont'd*

Himachal P.	1	Population Density (POPDENS)	.43	43	43	.7	3.0	.0130	3121.8	More population density, more volume of out-migration
	2	Per cent Forest Area (PERFAREA)	.68	25	68	.5	3.0	.0160	–319.6	More forest area, more volume of out-migration
	3	Per cent of Manufacturing Workers (MNF)	.80	12	80	–.4	–2.6	.0340	1441.6	Less manufacturing workers, more volume of out-migration
Karnataka	1	Per cent workers in Mining (MINS)	.23	23	23	–.5	–2.5	.023	87548.1	Less mining workers, more volume of out-migration
	2	Per cent Livestock Workers (LIVES)	52	29	52.	–.5	–3.3	.004	98418.5	Less livestock workers, more volume of out-migration
Kerala	1	General Literacy (GLITERA)	.42	42	42	.7	3.2	.007	–666275.9	More general literacy, more volume of out-migration
Madhya P.	1	Transport Workers (TRANS)	.18	18	18	0.4	3.2	.003	22725.6	More transport workers, more volume of out-migration
	2	Per cent Workers in Trade/Commerce (TC)	.27	9	27	–.2	-2.5	018	32621.8	Less workers in trade/commerce, more volume of out-migration
Maharashtra	1	Agricultural Labourers (AGL)	.32	32	32	–.6	–3.7	.0010	186719.2	More agricultural labourers, less volume of out-migration
	2	Per cent workers in Mining (MINS)	.41	9	41	–.3	–2.1	.042	203320.0	More mining workers, less volume of out-migration

Cont'd...

...*Cont'd*

Orissa	1	Population Density (POPDENS)	.57	57	57	.8	4.1	.0020	–1184.6	More population density, more volume of out-migration
	2	Population Growth (POPGRO)	.79	12	79	–.5	–3.5	.005	145826.6	Low rate of population growth, more volume of out-migration
	3	Per Capita Bank Credit to Industry (PCBCIND)	.98	19	98	–.4	–2.5	.049	93261.4	Less bank credit to Industry, more volume of out-migration
Punjab	1	Per cent Workers in Trade/Commerce (TC)	.30	30	30	.6	2.3	.049	–5732.4	More workers in trade/commerce, more volume of out-migration
Rajasthan	1	Transport Workers (TRANS)	.37	37	37	.6	4.0	.001	4157.4	More transport workers, more volume of out-migration
	2	Per cent Livestock Workers (LIVES)	.51	14	51	–.4	–2.9	.007	8217.3	Less livestock workers, more volume of out-migration
Uttar P.	1	Population Density (POPDENS)	.20	20	20	.5	3.7	.000	16985.0	More population density, more volume of out-migration
	2	Population Growth (POPGRO)	.50	30	50	–.6	–5.5	.0000	41715.1	Low rate of population growth, more volume of out-migration
W. Bengal	1	General Literacy (GLITERA)	.27	27	27	.6	2.4	.034	–23921.3	More general literacy, more volume of out-migration
	2	Per cent Workers in Household Industry (TC)	.73	46	73	.7	4.7	.0010	–62311.8	More workers in HH industry, more volume of out-migration

Table 5.11 *Findings of Step-wise Regression Analysis between District-level Migration Variables and Socio-economic Variables, Various States of India, 1991 Census (Male),*
Equation 3: INMIGRTM (In-migration rate, males)

Eq. No.	*Dependent Variable (y)*	*State*	*Step No.*	*Independent Variable (x)*	*Adj R-sq.*	*Ind. Expl. (%)*	*Cum. Expl. (%)*	*Beta*	*T*	*Sig. T*	*Constant (a)*	*Explanation*
1	*2*	*3*		*4*	*5*	*6*	*7*	*8*	*9*	*10*	*11*	*12*
3	Rate of In-migration, males (INMIGRTM)	Andhra P.	1	Population Growth Rate (POPGRO)	.74	74	74	.9	7.9	.000	–6.0	Higher population growth rate, higher in-migration rate
			2	Per cent General literacy (GLITERA)	.78	4	78	.2	2.3	032	-9.4	More general literacy, more in-migration
		Assam	1	Population Growth (POPGRO)	.56	56	56	.8	5.2	.000	–6.8	Higher population growth rate, higher in-migration rate
			2	Agricultural labour (AGL)	.79	23	79	-.5	-4.9	.000	–2.4	Less agricultural labourers, more in-migration
		Bihar	1	Per cent of mining workers (MINS)	.76	76	76	.9	11.1	.000	1.4	More mining workers, higher in-migration rate.
			2	Per Capita Bank Credit (PCBCRED)	.93	17	93	.4	10.2	.000	–0.2	More bank credit, higher in-migration rate.
		Gujarat	1	Per cent Service Workers (SERV)	.76	76	76	.9	7.5	.000	–5.0	More service workers, more in-migration rate
			2	Population Growth (POPGRO)	.86	10	86	.4	3.7	.002	–10.5	Higher rate of population growth, higher in-migration rate
		Haryana	1	Agricultural labour (AGL)	.35	35	35	.6	3.0	.009	1.1	More agricultural labourers, higher rate of in-migration
			2	Population Density (POPDENS)	.57	22	57	.5	2.8	.014	–0.7	More population density, higher in-migration rate

Cont'd...

...*Cont'd*

Himachal P.	1	Per cent Livestock Workers (LIVES)	.40	40	40	.7	2.9	.017	0.1	More livestock workers, higher in-migration rate
	2	Per cent Forest Area (PERFAREA)	.67	27	67	–.5	–3.1	.014	3.2	Less forest area, higher in-migration rate
Karnataka	1	Per cent Service Workers (SERV)	.37	37	37	.6	3.4	.003	0.9	More service workers, higher in-migration rate
	2	Per Capita Bank Credit to Agriculture (PCBAGI)	.56	19	56	.5	2.9	.010	–0.9	More bank credit, higher in-migration rate.
Kerala	1	Per cent Livestock Workers (LIVES)	.83	83	83	.9	8.2	.000	0.9	More livestock workers, higher in-migration rate
	2	Per Capita Bank Credit to Agriculture (PCBAGI)	.91	8	91	.4	3.3	.007	–1.1	More bank credit to agriculture, higher in-migration rate
Madhya P.	1	Per cent of Manufacturing Workers (MNF)	.57	57	57	.8	7.5	.000	2.1	More manufacturing workers, higher in-migration rate.
	2	Agricultural labour (AGL)	.62	5	62	.3	2.7	.011	0.4	More agricultural labourers, higher rate of in-migration
Maharashtra	1	Per cent General literacy (GLITERA)	.17	17	17	.4	2.5	.019	–0.2	More livestock workers, higher in-migration rate
	2	Per cent Workers in Household Industry (HH)	.41	24	41	–.5	–3.4	.002	–0.2	Less workers in household industry, higher in-migration rate
Orissa	1	Urbanization (URBANIZA)	.42	42	42	.7	3.1	.010	1.3	More urbanization, higher in-migration rate
Punjab	1	Agricultural labour (AGL)	.56	56	56	–.8	–3.7	.005	14.9	Less agricultural labourers, higher in-migration rate

Cont'd...

...Cont'd

Rajasthan	1	Cultivators (CULT)	.40	40	40	–.6	–4.3	.000	9.2	Less cultivators, higher in-migration rate
	2	Per Capita Bank Credit (PCBCRED)	.47	7	47	.4	2.1	.042	6.2	More bank credit, higher in-migration rate.
Tamil Nadu	1	Per cent Transport Workers (TRANS)	.61	61	61	.8	5.4	.000	1.0	More transport workers, higher in-migration rate
Uttar P.	1	Per cent Livestock Workers (LIVES)	.67	67	67	.8	10.1	.000	–1.5	More livestock workers, higher in-migration rate
	2	Per Capita Bank Deposit (PCBDEP)	.77	10	77	.4	4.9	.000	–1.9	More bank credit, higher in-migration rate
W. Bengal	1	Urbanization (URBANIZA)	.85	85	85	.9	8.7	.000	0.5	More urbanisation, higher in-migration rate
	2	Population Density (POPDENS)	.90	5	90	–.3	2.7	.020	1.0	Less population density, higher in-migration rate

Table 5.12 *Findings of Step-wise Regression Analysis between District-level Migration Variables and Socio-economic Variables, Various States of India, 1991 Census (Male), Equation 4: OMIGRTM (Out-migration rate, males)*

Eq. No.	*Dependent Variable (y)*	*State*	*Step No.*	*Independent Variable (x)*	*Adj. R-sq*	*Ind. Expl. (%)*	*Cum. Expl. (%)*	*Beta*	*T*	*Sig. T*	*Constant (a)*	*Explanation*
1	2	3		4	5	6	7	8	9	10	11	12
4	Out-migration rate, males. (OMIGRTM)	Andhra P.	1	Population Growth Rate (POPGRO)	.13	13	13	–.4	–2.1	.0490	8.3	Low rate of population growth, higher out-migration rate
			2	Per cent Forest Area (PERFAREA)	.28	15	28	–.4	–2.3	.0310	10.2	Less forest area, higher out-migration rate
		Assam	1	Per cent Net Sown Area (PERNSA)	.48	48	48	.7	4.5	.0000	2.6	More net sown area, higher out-migration rate
		Bihar	1	General Literacy (GLITERA)	.28	28	28	.5	4.0	.0000	–0.9	More literacy, higher out-migration rate
			2	Urbanization (URBANIZA)	.63	35	63	–.9	–6.0	.0000	–3.4	Less urbanization, higher out-migration rate
		Gujarat	1	Per Capita Bank Deposit (PCBDEP)	.21	21	21	–.5	–2.4	.0280	10.1	Less bank deposit, higher out-migration
		Haryana	1	Population Growth (POPGRO)	.43	43	43	–.7	–3.5	.0040	6.2	Low rate of population growth, higher out-migration rate
			2	Population Density (POPDENS)	.63	20	63	.6	2.9	.0120	5.8	More population density, higher out-migration rate
		Kerala	1	Per cent General literacy (GLITERA)	.35	35	35	.6	2.8	.0150	–68.3	High literacy, higher out-migration rate

Cont'd…

...*Cont'd*

	Madhya P.	1	Per cent of mining workers (MINS)	23	23	23	–.5	–3.7	.0010	5.2	Less mining workers, higher out-migration rate
		2	Agricultural labour (AGL)	.46	23	46	.5	4.3	.0000	2.7	More agricultural labourers, higher out-migration rate
	Maharashtra	1	Cultivators (CULT)	.48	48	48	.7	5.0	.0000	–9.7	More cultivators, higher out-migration rate
		2	Population Growth (POPGRO)	.70	22	70	–.5	–4.4	.0000	6.9	Low rate of population growth, higher out-migration rate
	Rajasthan	1	Urbanization (URBANIZA)	.24	24	24	.5	3.0	.0060	1.6	More urbanization, higher out-migration rate
	Tamil Nadu	1	Population Growth (POPGRO)	.26	26	26	–.5	–2.7	.0150	12.3	Low rate of population growth, higher out-migration rate
	Uttar P.	1	Per cent Net Sown Area (PERNSA)	.49	49	49	–.7	–7.1	.0000	8.7	Less net sown area, higher out-migration rate

Tables of Chapter 7

Table 7.11 *Factor Results of Migration Variables of Indian States, 1991*

Migration Variables	*Factors*			
	1	*2*	*3*	*4*
Proportion of Migration	*Migration from UP to Maharashtra/ Madhya Pradesh*	*Migration from Bihar to West Bengal and UP*	*Migration from Tamil Nadu to Kerala, Karnataka and Andhra Pradesh*	*Migration from Kerala and Karnataka to Tamil Nadu*
Haryana as destination (HRD)	**0.94**	0.18	–0.05	–0.11
Madhya Pradesh as destination (MPD)	**0.92**	0.22	0.07	0.06
Maharashtra as destination (MAHD)	**0.91**	0.01	0.15	0.12
Punjab as destination (PUND)	**0.86**	0.38	–0.05	–0.13
Rajasthan as destination (RAJD)	0.85	0.24	–0.07	–0.10
Himachal Pradesh as destination (HPD)	0.78	0.32	–0.11	–0.21
Gujarat as destination (GJDES)	0.73	–0.01	0.14	0.10
Bihar as destination (BIDES)	0.54	0.05	–0.05	0.15
Uttar Pradesh as destination (UPD)	0.06	**0.96**	–0.02	–0.08
Assam as destination (ASSDES)	0.27	**0.94**	–0.02	–0.02
West Bengal as destination (WBD)	0.23	**0.93**	0.01	–0.10
Orissa as destination (ORRD)	0.19	**0.88**	0.02	0.19
Kerala as destination (KERD)	–0.07	–0.04	**0.96**	–0.20
Andhra Pradesh as destination (APDES)	0.12	0.03	**0.90**	0.11
Karnataka as destination (KARD)	–0.02	–0.01	**0.89**	0.30
Tamil Nadu as destination (TAMD)	0.03	–0.01	0.13	**0.94**
Eigen values	5.67	3.83	2.61	1.22
Per cent of Variance explained	35.44	23.93	16.33	7.60
Cumulative per cent of variance	35.44	59.37	75.70	83.31

Table 7.12 *Factor Score of Migration Variables, States, 1991*

S. No.	*State*	*Migration from UP to Maharashtra/ Madhya Pradesh*	*Migration from Bihar to West Bengal and UP*	*Migration from Tamil Nadu to Kerala, Karnataka and Andhra Pradesh*	*Migration from Kerala and Karnataka to Tamil Nadu*
		Fs1	*Fs2*	*Fs3*	*Fs4*
1	Andhra Pr.	–0.29	0.22	0.22	1.71
2	Assam	–0.47	–0.24	–0.38	–0.30
3	Bihar	0.26	4.75	0.00	–0.41
4	Gujarat	–0.20	–0.32	–0.31	–0.21

Cont'd...

...Cont'd

5	Haryana	–0.02	–0.17	–0.44	–0.56
6	Himachal Pr.	–0.32	–0.24	–0.42	–0.41
7	Karnataka	–0.13	–0.38	0.60	0.49
8	Kerala	–0.02	–0.11	0.46	4.10
9	Madhya Pr.	0.00	0.24	–0.28	–0.20
10	Maharashtra	0.48	–0.41	0.77	0.44
11	Orissa	0.13	–0.13	0.17	–0.09
12	Punjab	0.31	–0.11	–0.44	–0.80
13	Rajasthan	0.54	–0.23	0.01	0.11
14	Tamil Nadu	–0.36	–0.17	4.59	–1.09
15	Uttar Pr.	4.63	–0.56	–0.15	–0.34
16	West Bengal	0.09	0.71	–0.35	0.93

Tables of Chapter 8

Table 8.2 *Result of Factor Analysis of Socio-economic Variables of Indian States, 1991*

Variables	*Factors*			
	1	*2*	*3*	*4*
	Service as an important section of the economic structure	*Manufacturing as the important aspect of the economic structure*	*Trade/ commerce an important aspect of the economic structure*	*Construction as important aspect of economic structure*
Percentage of workers in service (SERV)	**0.94**	0.24	0.18	0.02
Percentage of workers in manufacturing (MNF)	–0.85	**0.43**	0.14	0.06
Percentage of workers in transport (TRANS)	0.01	–0.83	–0.03	0.13
Percentage of workers in trade/commerce (TC)	0.04	–0.61	**0.54**	–0.11
Percentage of workers in mining (MINS)	–0.04	–0.01	–0.95	0.05
Percentage of workers in household industry (HHIND)	–0.10	–0.05	0.17	–0.82
Percentage of workers in construction (CONS)	–0.14	–0.15	0.21	**0.71**
Eigen values	1.64	1.33	1.32	1.22
Percentage of variance explained	23.46	19.00	18.80	17.43
Cumulative per cent of variance	23.46	42.46	61.26	78.69

Note: The data for input of factor analysis are taken from the Table 8.1

Table 8.13 *Migration Variables (Females) and Economic Variables of 22 Million Cities and Investment, India 1991 (cities whose data available shown)*

S. No.	CITY	MIG (< 1 YR)	MIG (1–9 YR)	MIG (10+ YR)	RMEMPF	RMBUSIF	RMEDUF	RMFMOV	RMOTHER	TOTPOP
1	Greater Mumbai	3.0	37.4	59.6	4.2	1.1	2.7	36.0	16.7	12,596,243
2	Kolkata	2.7	27.0	70.3	5.7	0.5	1.7	32.4	15.0	11,021,918
3	Delhi	2.9	40.4	56.7	3.5	0.6	1.4	55.4	4.9	8,419,084
4	Chennai	1.5	42.0	56.5	8.2	1.0	2.7	40.2	10.7	5,421,985
5	Hyderabad	3.3	52.6	44.1	9.7	0.8	2.8	46.8	9.9	4,344,437
6	Bangalore	4.1	45.6	50.3	7.7	0.6	3.2	40.4	9.6	4,130,288
7	Ahmedabad	2.1	38.8	59.1	5.3	3.8	2.3	31.2	11.7	3,312,216
8	Pune	4.8	47.4	47.8	3.7	2.1	2.4	40.5	16.1	2,493,987
9	Kanpur	2.1	37.3	60.7	3.7	1.6	2.8	28.5	9.2	2,029,889
10	Lucknow	2.9	43.0	54.1	3.2	1.1	4.0	41.3	8.0	1,669,204
11	Nagpur	2.5	40.0	57.4	3.5	2.2	4.5	36.6	10.5	1,664,006
12	Surat	3.6	55.2	41.1	5.3	2.8	1.5	47.5	9.9	1,518,950
13	Jaipur	2.8	42.9	54.3	4.5	1.2	2.7	39.7	6.8	1,518,235
14	Kochi	5.7	44.0	50.3	8.3	0.4	4.0	37.7	11.2	1,140,605
15	Vadodara	3.2	41.6	55.1	4.6	2.5	2.4	37.8	13.6	1,126,824
16	Indore	2.8	40.1	57.1	4.6	0.9	2.3	29.6	8.7	1,109,056
17	Coimbatore	3.5	44.7	51.8	10.3	1.2	2.2	35.3	11.8	1,100,746
18	Patna	3.1	34.2	62.8	2.8	0.8	6.0	25.0	6.1	1,085,914
19	Madurai	2.2	41.0	56.8	7.5	1.8	4.1	30.9	16.7	1,062,771
20	Vishakhapatnam	3.3	52.4	44.4	9.4	1.0	2.4	41.8	12.8	1,057,118
21	Ludhiana	3.0	39.1	57.9	6.8	0.6	1.6	28.0	7.6	1,042,740
22	Varanasi	2.7	35.6	61.7	3.5	1.2	7.2	23.8	4.1	1,030,863

(contd.)

S. No.	CITY	MINS	HH	MNF	CONS	TC	TRANS	SERV	PCBDEP	PCBCSSI	PCBCIND
1	Greater Mumbai	0.2	1.4	35.7	4.7	24.1	11.2	21.6	52985	1515	10578
2	Kolkata	0.2	1.4	34.5	3.5	24.9	10.1	23.3	34856	1621	9117
3	Delhi	0.1	1.4	23.5	7.6	25.1	8.2	33.1	25009	1194	4948
4	Chennai	0.1	1.1	25.9	6.6	23.0	10.2	30.2	22630	1714	9417
5	Hyderabad	0.4	0.5	23.1	8.4	24.3	11.3	28.6	12826	831	4934
6	Bangalore	0.2	1.4	31.1	8.4	24.3	8.8	24.2	12402	1165	4435
7	Ahmedabad	0.4	0.8	35.7	4.7	25.1	9.2	22.4	8478	700	3113
8	Pune	0.2	1.7	30.7	11.1	18.3	7.9	27.4	5386	437	2106
9	Kanpur	0.0	0.7	27.9	2.0	27.4	7.6	30.6	7974	695	1991
10	Lucknow	0.1	2.8	13.4	5.0	23.1	7.9	40.6	8345	267	1159
11	Nagpur	0.8	3.0	20.8	9.6	23.0	12.5	27.3	4082	259	643
12	Surat	0.2	2.2	55.7	3.4	18.7	4.5	13.3	4958	522	1254
13	Jaipur	0.6	3.9	22.2	6.4	24.0	8.1	31.8	3934	234	655
14	Kochi	0.5	1.1	20.4	9.6	21.4	13.9	23.4	7136	472	2223
15	Vadodara	1.1	0.6	31.9	5.7	20.1	9.0	27.7	6758	567	3061

Cont'd...

...Cont'd

16	Indore	0.1	1.3	26.5	5.6	26.2	9.3	27.9	6442	732	2886
17	Coimbatore	0.1	2.5	36.9	6.1	20.0	7.4	20.1	5294	1005	2630
18	Patna	0.1	2.6	27.0	5.5	29.3	9.3	20.5	2116	194	576
19	Madurai	0.4	1.1	18.4	11.0	20.3	8.9	35.3	8740	NA	NA
20	Vishakhapatnam	0.6	0.8	19.3	7.9	15.0	15.2	34.6	3147	107	906
21	Ludhiana	0.0	0.2	44.5	6.3	20.5	6.2	14.1	8726	1504	2705
22	Varanasi	0.0	23.4	16.3	2.4	27.1	6.1	20.8	2968	282	386

MIG (<1 YR) – Migration for < 1 year, females
MIG (1–9 YR) – Migration for 1–9 years, females
MIG (10 + YR) – Migration for 10 years + females
RMEPF, RMBUSIF, RMEDUF, RMFMOV – Reasons for moves are employment, business, education, family move, others (females)
PCBDEP – per capita bank deposit
PCBCSSI – Per capita bank credit to SSI
MINS – Per cent total workers in mining
PCBCIND – Per capita bank credit to ind.
MNF – Per cent total workers in manuf.
HH – Per cent total workers in household ind.
TRANS – per cent total workers in transport
CONS – Per cent total workers in const.
TC – Per cent total workers in trade/commerce
SERV – Per cent total workers in services

Table 8.14 *Canonical Structure Matrix: Linkages between Migration Variables and Economic Structure of Million Cities and Investment, 1991, Females*

Variables	*Canonical Variate Pairs*			
	1	2	3	4
A. Dependent Matrix (Migration Variables)	*Canonical Loadings*			
1. Vol. of Lifetime Migration (females)	**0.73**	–0.03	–0.02	–0.01
2. Per cent Migrants (< 1 yr.)	0.10	0.05	0.17	0.10
3. Per cent Migrants (1 to 9 yrs.)	0.40	**0.65**	**0.64**	0.68
4. Per cent Migrants (10 yrs.+)	**0.55**	**0.76**	**0.75**	0.73
B. Independent Matrix (Socio-economic Variables)				
1. Total population	0.70	0.04	0.19	–0.25
2. Mining workers	0.05	0.19	0.04	–0.17
3. Household industry	–0.02	0.05	–0.25	–0.08
4. Manufacturing workers	0.01	–0.12	**–0.69**	0.07
5. Construction	0.05	**–0.47**	–0.08	0.22
6. Trade/Commerce	0.03	0.29	–0.16	0.28
7. Transport	–0.07	0.13	–0.23	–0.11
8. Services	0.06	0.15	**–0.58**	0.01
9. Bank Deposit	**0.55**	–0.25	–0.03	0.37
10. Credit to SSI	0.16	**0.64**	0.01	–0.71
11. Investment in Industry	**–0.41**	–0.36	–0.06	0.35
C. Canonical Correlations	**0.99**	**0.83**	**0.66**	0.02

Cont'd...

...Cont'd

D. Meaning of Canonical Linkages	Female lifetime and 10 yrs+ migration linked to total population and deposit, not to investment	Female 1–9 yrs and 10 yrs+ migration linked to SSI and industrial investment	Some 1–9 yrs mig and 10 yrs+ migration not linked to MNF and service centres	Not Significant
E. Trace Correlation	= **0.72**			
Chi Square	= 75.9			
Significance	= 0.0001			

Table 8.15 *Canonical Structure Matrix: Links between Reasons for Migration of Females, and Economic Structure of Million Cities and Investment, 1991*

	Canonical Variate Pairs				
	1	*2*	*3*	*4*	*5*
		Canonical Loadings			
A. Dependent Matrix (Reasons for Migration)					
1. Employment	–0.11	–0.63	–0.32	0.22	**0.50**
2. Business	0.30	–0.15	0.14	**0.89**	0.16
3. Education	–0.75	0.40	–0.62	0.35	0.27
4. Family Moved	0.38	**0.58**	–0.25	–0.01	0.64
5. Others	**0.43**	0.30	–0.66	–0.17	–0.50
B. Independent Matrix (Economic Structure of Cities)					
6. Total population	0.14	–0.05	–0.11	0.02	0.33
7. Mining workers	0.01	0.06	0.05	0.14	–0.01
8. Household	0.04	0.20	0.21	0.12	0.30
9. Manufacturing	**0.79**	0.30	**0.51**	0.29	0.33
10. Construction	0.17	0.33	0.04	–0.07	0.24
11. Trade/Commerce	0.10	0.12	0.15	0.10	–0.02
12. Transport	0.13	–0.21	0.09	–0.09	0.15
13. Service	**0.46**	**0.39**	**0.52**	0.02	**0.42**
14. Bank Deposit	–0.12	**0.61**	0.20	–0.44	–0.57
15. Credit to SSI	–0.23	–0.41	0.36	–0.57	0.31
16. Credit to Industry	0.15	–0.09	–0.47	**0.59**	–0.11
C. Canonical Correlations	**0.96**	**0.91**	**0.87**	**0.79**	**0.54**
D. Meaning of Links	Females move for other purposes to manufacturing and service centre metros	Family moves to service centres, and where bank deposit high	Migration to service-MNF centres, but for no clear purpose	Business mig. where investment to industries	Employ-mig. to service centres
E. Trace Correlation	= **0.83**				
Chi Square	= 95.3				
Significance	= 0.0001				

Tables of Chapter 13

Table 13.3 *Inter-state Migration Matrix, to Rural and to Urban, Males, 1991–2001 (only selected major states shown)*

States	*Direction*	*Pun*	*Har*	*Del*	*Raj*	*UP*	*Bih*	*Ass*	*WB*	*MP*	*Guj*	*Mah*	*AP*	*Kar*	*Ker*	*TN*	*T. Out-M*	*Tot. Out-mig*
Pun	To Rural	0	20239	1243	13193	6645	3120	322	1414	1302	1122	2224	325	429	251	128	67864	165487
	To Urban	0	26072	20453	7330	6402	727	660	1768	3599	2897	11031	1115	2228	293	518	97623	
Har	To Rural	11256	0	6732	15837	4082	1103	205	827	915	1180	1387	259	521	188	63	48312	176453
	To Urban	19533	0	63762	10924	8071	693	444	1367	3437	3525	8272	973	2381	302	397	128141	
Del	To Rural	1418	11659	0	3227	10921	3712	285	2111	743	563	1471	464	470	1124	446	42640	179607
	To Urban	6037	31201	0	6214	49570	872	398	2464	4007	3231	17142	2883	5562	1087	2703	136967	
Raj	To Rural	9642	33091	3358	0	3694	603	815	1473	17154	19652	13048	2938	2243	678	410	111923	438137
	To Urban	8979	21602	41467	0	9257	848	2234	4999	21202	79788	101400	6804	18444	939	4741	326214	
UP	To Rural	42547	81156	38760	21736	0	6750	1769	6976	23929	31193	46523	2160	2822	945	538	323538	1901431
	To Urban	109015	114616	438586	40078	0	8514	2724	28836	75136	139589	580077	6166	13674	1310	2594	1577893	
Bih	To Rural	35225	45766	26410	12076	35555	0	6931	37324	5587	20476	24839	2985	3496	777	1337	272978	1156874
	To Urban	77494	57510	257890	22292	56554	0	15304	126751	19871	58113	149644	6089	11745	646	2475	883896	
Ass	To Rural	1053	1220	488	1040	1985	2003	0	10844	278	731	1020	488	363	395	191	22802	67670
	To Urban	1542	1194	8070	1742	7642	1472	0	9242	1143	2185	5865	761	2130	256	542	44868	
WB	To Rural	4878	9953	2357	3751	6057	6617	3866	0	2561	3099	9166	1944	2277	962	594	68017	313053
	To Urban	10605	11908	46114	13251	12896	4721	5924	0	6999	12485	80690	6200	12068	1198	2887	245036	
MP	To Rural	2046	3076	1886	20148	9376	323	205	903	0	15157	58839	1321	647	718	301	117311	292051
	To Urban	3094	5319	20550	20228	15557	434	222	1723	0	24249	71296	2513	3134	560	1402	174740	

Cont'd...

...Cont'd

Guj	To Rural	589	806	299	14427	1584	1752	108	1312	2730	0	17260	1219	1073	1244	356	48507	182482
	To Urban	1211	1340	5342	8562	2739	831	249	1723	5312	0	94183	2703	6026	817	1472	133975	
Mah	To Rural	1523	1451	609	7885	3877	1663	220	2272	12464	39239	0	10525	30677	4609	2012	121446	343218
	To Urban	3634	3562	11647	7498	5484	1332	343	3008	26425	100302	0	16038	27672	4781	7423	221772	
AP	To Rural	570	762	210	1683	491	314	285	720	2347	1783	23382	0	31320	1886	5293	76719	268829
	To Urban	1013	1172	5188	2193	1956	469	522	2929	3914	7672	70170	0	65953	2345	17330	192110	
Kar	To Rural	915	326	181	1299	508	258	140	514	448	847	77757	12315	0	9129	6284	111551	303505
	To Urban	871	810	4188	1191	1728	171	138	832	1714	3774	143163	16201	0	5547	10762	191954	
Ker	To Rural	393	475	429	848	506	92	224	467	755	1591	6125	2293	14188	0	6498	35748	195671
	To Urban	912	1444	12655	2213	2878	268	351	1278	3644	8269	50490	5869	42736	0	25551	159923	
TN	To Rural	479	583	282	1196	310	165	212	501	324	1112	3424	14084	24039	45010	0	92545	287662
	To Urban	1021	1141	8806	1715	1879	247	247	1517	2435	5283	48109	17999	76198	27064	0	195117	
Tot In-mig		384931	505702	1063812	271231	280225	54107	47098	283550	258191	657621	1768112	175277	418474	117630	108707	6600560	6600560

Source: Same as in Table 13.4.

Note: Some discrepancies in total figures may be noticeable between Table 13.3 and 13.4, specially in the last columns, and last rows, because in Table 13.3 unclassifiable are excluded. Data of Jammu-Kashmir, Himachal Pradesh and Orissa are also not shown, though included in all analyses.

Table 13.4 *Inter-state Migration Matrix, to Rural and to Urban, Females, 1991–2001 (only major states shown)*

States	Direction	Pun	Har	Del	Raj	UP	Bih	WB	MP	Guj	Mah	AP	Kar	Ker	TN	Tot. Out-mig	Tot. Out-mig
Pun	To Rural	0	55677	1254	22778	7452	1981	1444	967	626	821	274	218	213	78	124171	253282
	To Urban	0	44087	26054	11621	8540	812	1862	4397	2724	10453	998	1688	317	478	129111	
Har	To Rural	47681	0	16886	74478	23165	4091	963	797	867	652	236	676	180	30	176129	348918
	To Urban	33178	0	81538	17588	14716	830	1229	4283	3154	7708	757	1960	311	370	172789	
Del	To Rural	2367	28987	0	3251	21117	922	1473	753	440	885	438	269	1120	404	65031	238039
	To Urban	9930	48154	0	9181	63843	760	2667	4990	3105	15933	2408	4703	1233	2520	173008	
Raj	To Rural	19568	96449	3055	0	28545	2836	1601	45825	18412	4971	1589	1244	490	291	227869	506585
	To Urban	12391	28420	39550	0	14251	1011	5041	33267	56050	63104	4740	11425	591	3498	278716	
UP	To Rural	28521	86446	31765	39885	0	78648	5930	84774	11974	16318	1224	1105	647	316	397098	1422486
	To Urban	56235	95955	351554	43829	0	12199	23392	94801	61537	258883	3939	6764	937	1838	1025388	
Bih	To Rural	10042	20631	13716	4266	84466	0	43891	3245	5771	5797	1840	757	344	373	203883	603369
	To Urban	23370	25794	112259	11627	40581	0	81628	14820	17194	43472	3400	3611	427	1281	399486	
WB	To Rural	3490	6029	1803	2417	19754	20804	0	1868	1266	2521	1404	554	411	190	82018	237147
	To Urban	5887	7487	33455	8516	13246	8319	0	6139	6769	33798	4461	5378	751	1749	155129	
MP	To Rural	1990	2938	1481	59944	82245	804	928	0	14260	70289	1246	360	737	271	239634	432922
	To Urban	3147	4935	18812	34468	30883	684	2087	0	17864	70476	2245	2013	524	1069	193288	
Guj	To Rural	699	857	302	22882	2375	13069	943	4112	0	22279	907	796	983	311	71404	225517
	To Urban	1496	1516	5783	13178	3146	1159	1887	8368	0	106547	2326	4722	841	1383	154113	

Cont'd…

...Cont'd

Mah	To Rural	2264	1753	661	3345	4518	6871	2083	39251	41531	0	21811	58884	3578	2231	190378	190378
	To Urban	3511	3463	13195	7202	7154	1968	2964	48230	104936	0	15994	35980	5141	7112	260061	
AP	To Rural	827	1027	222	2119	788	3798	838	5481	1167	27187	0	59681	1565	9645	125461	318038
	To Urban	1257	1297	5716	2414	2034	581	3232	5801	7305	69140	0	61932	2370	17665	192577	
Kar	To Rural	564	489	198	1435	1679	1777	622	817	637	97649	51178	0	11115	12589	181372	383976
	To Urban	881	755	4364	1409	1944	256	837	1988	3506	146015	19797	0	5213	14524	202604	
Ker	To Rural	680	612	526	945	932	152	655	782	1127	2697	2851	15717	0	8078	36702	195753
	To Urban	1313	1583	17480	3038	3769	688	1333	5166	7370	40608	6960	38378	0	29352	159051	
TN	To Rural	561	683	314	856	485	407	564	190	688	1824	24477	24428	36212	0	92396	267948
	To Urban	1150	1055	9514	1916	1971	261	1492	2398	4091	39325	19021	70133	21532	0	175552	
Tot In-mig		318506	587208	826665	413029	520686	216361	244316	431936	412592	1185912	229104	419339	99453	119593	6245151	6245151

Source: Computed from Census of India, 2001, Migration Tables, Census Commissioner and Registrar General's office New Delhi, CDs, available in 2005–6. Data of Jammu-Kashmir, Himachal Pradesh, Assam and Orissa not shown in Tables, though included in all analyses. So, Grand row total and Grand column total may show some discrepancies.

References

Abler, A.B., Adams, J. and Gould, Peter (1971), *Spatial Organization,* Wiley, New York.

Aiyar, Swaminathan S.A., (2005), "Globalising Rural India", *Times of India,* Dec 18: 18.

Anderson, T.W. (1958), *An Introduction in Multi-variate Statistical Analysis.* Wiley, New York.

Armstrong, Warwick and T.G. McGee (1985), *Theatres of Accumulation: Studies in Asian and Latin American Urbanization,* London: Methuen, 88–110.

Basham, A.L. (1968), *The Wonder that was India, Till 1020 AD.* Picador, London.

Basham, A.L. (1970), *The Wonder that was India: A Survey of the Culture of the Indian Sub-continent before the Coming of the Muslims,* Picador, London.

Basu, Rumki (2000), *Economic Liberalization and Poverty Alleviation,* Deep and Deep Publications, New Delhi: 161–166.

Bedford, R. (1999), "Mobility in Melanesia: bigman bilong circulation." *Asia Pacific Viewpoint,* Vol. 40 (1): 3–17.

Behari, Bipin (1990), *Rural Poverty and Unemployment,* Vikas Publishing House, New Delhi: 101.

Bery, Suman (2009), "Our Choking City", *Outlook,* Sept: 2–4.

Berry, B.J.L. (1966), *Essays on Commodity Flows and the Spatial Structure of the Indian Economy.* University of Chicago Research Paper No 111, Chicago: University of Chicago.

Berry, B.J.L. (1969), "Interdependency of Spatial Structure and Spatial Behaviour: A General Field Theory Formulation", *Papers, Regional Science Association,* Vol. 19.

Bhaduri, Amit (2005), *Development with Dignity: A Cass for Full Employment,* National Book Trust, New Delhi: 1–90.

Bhattacharya, A. (1995), "An integrated approach to urban Development." *A CIDCO Paper for All-India Housing Board Association,* Mumbai.

Bose, A. (1978), *India's Urbanization, 1901–2001,* Tata McGraw Hill Publishing Co. Ltd. New Delhi.

Breman, Jan (2000), "Even dogs are better off': The ongoing battle between capital and labour in the cane-fields of Gujarat", *Journal of Peasant Studies,* Vol. 17, Issue 4, July: 546–608.

Breman, Jan and Das, Arvind (2000), *Down and Out: Labouring under Global Capitalism,* Delhi, Oxford University Press: 12–48.

Burgess, Rod (2000), "Introduction" in *Compact Cities: Sustainable Urban Forms for Developing Countries*, by Jenks, Mike and Burgess, Rod (eds) Spon Press, New York: 10–12.

Census of India (1961(a)/1967), *Census of India, 1961, India, Paper 1 of 1967*, Tables B Series, Registrar General Office, New Delhi.

Census of India (1961(b)/1967), *Census of India, (1961), India, Series I, General Economic Tables, B Series*, Census Commissioner and Registrar General's Office, New Delhi, various volumes.

Census of India (1971), *Census of India, 1971, India, Population Totals*, Registrar General Office, New Delhi.

Census of India (1981(a)/1982), *Census of India, (1981), India, Series I, General Economic Tables, B series*, Census Commissioner and Registrar General's Office, New Delhi.

Census of India (1981(b)/1988), *Census of India, (1981), India, Series I, Part V (A and B) (i) to (viii), Migration Tables, D-I and D-III Series*, Census Commissioner and Registrar General's Office, New Delhi, various volumes.

Census of India (1981(c)/1989), *Census of India, (1981), India, Series I, Part V (A and B) (vi) to (viii), Migration Tables, D Series*, Registrar General's Office, New Delhi, various volumes.

Census of India (1991(a)/1992), *Census of India, (1991), India, Series I, Provisional Population Totals: Rural and Urban Distribution*, Paper 2 of 1991, Registrar General and Census Commissioner's Office, New Delhi: 1–94. Also see Census of India (1991), *Census of India, (1991), India, Series I, Population Total Tables*, Registrar General's Office, New Delhi.

Census of India (1991(b)/1999), *Census of India, 1991(b), India, Series I, Part V (A and B) (i) to (viii), Migration Tables, D-I Series, and D-III Series*, Registrar General and Census Commissioner's Office, New Delhi, Various CDs for Migration data (1999). Also Census of India, 1991, Series B, Economic Tables.

Census of India (1991(c)/1998), *Census of India, (1991)(c) India, D-Series, Migration Tables*, Registrar General's Office, New Delhi (Unpublished data), (Floppy Disks). Also see some published volumes on Migration Tables (1998/2000).

Census of India (1991(d)/1994), *Census of India, (1991)(d), India, Series I, Workers Data in Urban Areas*, Registrar General's Office, New Delhi (Unpublished data), (Floppy Disks), 1994.

Census of India (2001)(a), *Census of India, 2001, India, A-Series, Population Tables*, Registrar General and Census Commissioner's Office, New Delhi, 2002–3.

Census of India (2001)(b), *Census of India, 2001, India, D-Series, Migration Tables*, Registrar General and Census Commissioner's Office, New Delhi (CDs available only in 2005–6, some not even in 2008).

Census of India (2001)(c), *Census of India, 2001, India, B-Series, Economic Tables*, Registrar General and Census Commissioner's Office, New Delhi (Data CDs available in 2005–6).

Census of India (2001)(d), *Census of India, (2001), India and States, Series B, Economic Series, Workers* Data *in Million Cities and Class I Cities*, Registrar General's Office, New Delhi (Unpubl/CDs in 2009).

Centre for Monitoring Indian Economy (1990–3), *Indian Economy*, CMIE, Various Reports (1991, 1992, 1993) Mumbai.

Calcutta Metropolitan Development Authority (CMDA) (1995), *Master Plan for Calcutta Metropolitan Area,* CMDA, Calcutta: 1–140.

Chakravarthy, S. (2010), "Rapid and Innovative business expansion in India," *Times of India,* Jan 10: 18.

Chapman, Graham P. and Dutt, Ashok K. and Bradknock, Robert W. (1999), *Urban Growth and Development in Asia, Vol. I and II,* Ashgate: Brookfield, USA.

Chapman, Graham and Pathak, Pushpa (1999), "Indian Urbanization and the Characteristics of Large Indian Cities Revealed in the 1991 Census", in *Urban Growth and Development in Asia,* by Graham Chapman, A.K. Dutt, and R.W. Bradknock (eds), Vol. I and II, Ashgate: Brookfield, USA: 135–153.

Chapman, Murray (1970), *Population Movements in Tribal Society: The Case of Duidui and Pichahila, British Solomon Islands,* PhD Dissertation, Department of Geography, University of Washington, Seattle.

Chapman, Murray (1975), "Mobility in a non-literate Society: Method and Analysis for two Guadalcanal communities", in *People on the Move: Studies on Internal Migration* by L.A. Kosinski and R.M. Prothero (eds), Methuen, London: 129–145.

Chapman, Murray (1976), "Tribal mobility as circulation: a Solomon Islands example of micro/macro linkages", in L.A. Kosinski and J.W. Webb (eds): *Population at Micro scale,* Conference Series 8A, Christchurch: New Zealand Geographical Society and International Geographical Union, Commission on Population Geography: 127–142

Chapman, Murray (1978), "On the cross-cultural study of circulation", *International Migration Review,* 12: 558–69.

Chapman, Murray (1979), "The cross-cultural study of circulation", *Current Anthropology* 20:111–114.

Chapman, Murray (1981), "Policy Implications of Circulation: Some Answers from the Grassroots" in *Population Mobility and Development: Southeast Asia and the Pacific,* by G.W. Jones and H.V. Richter (eds), Development Studies Center Monograph No. 27, Australian National University, Canberra: 71–87.

Chapman, Murray (1985a), "Introduction", *Pacific Viewpoint (now Asia Pacific Viewpoint),* Vol. 26 (1): 1–6.

Chapman, Murray (1985b), "Policy-makers and Circulation at the Grass Roots: South Pacific and South-east Examples", in *Labour Circulation and Labour Policies* by Guy Standing (ed.), An ILO-WEP Study, Croom Helm, London: 382–407.

Chapman, Murray (1985c), (ed.): *Mobility and Identity in the Island Pacific,* special issue of *Pacific Viewpoint,* 26(1): 1–371.

Chapman, Murray (1991a), "Population Movement: Free or Constrained?" in *Independence, Dependence and Interdependence: A Review of the First Ten Years of Solomon Islands Independence,* by R. Crocombe and E. Tuza (eds) Honiara; Solomon Islands College of Higher Education, Institute of Pacific Studies, and Solomon Islands Centre, University of South Pacific: 75–98.

Chapman, Murray (1991b), "Pacific Island Movement and Socio economic Change: Metaphors of Misunderstanding", *Population and Development Review,* Vol. 17, No. 2, June 1991: 263–292.

Chapman, Murray (1992), "Pacific Island Movement and Socio economic Change: Metaphors of Misunderstanding", *East West Population Institute, Reprint Series, East West Center,* Honolulu: 262–293.

Chapman, Murray (1995), 'Island autobiographies of movement: alternative ways of knowing?' in P. Claval and Singaravelou (eds) *Ethno geographies*, Paris, L'Harmattan: 247–259.

Chapman, Murray and Prothero, R. Mansell (1977), "Circulation between Home places and Towns: A Village Approach to Urbanization", Paper for the *Working Session on Urbanization, Pacific Association for Social Anthropology in Oceania*, Monterrey, California.

Chapman, Murray and R. Mansell Prothero (1983), "Themes on circulation in the Third world", *International Migration Review*, 17: 597–632.

Chapman, Murray and R. Mansell Prothero (1985a), "Themes on Circulation in the Third World", in *Circulation in Third World Countries* by Prothero, R. Mansell and Murray Chapman (eds), London: Routledge and Kegan Paul: 1–26 and Conclusion Part: 436–440. Routledge Library Edition (2011), London and New York.

Chapman, Murray and Prothero, R. Mansell (eds) (1985b), *Circulation in Population Movement: Substance and Concepts from the Melanesian case*, Routledge and Kegan Paul, London.

Chapman, Murray and R.M. Prothero (1985c), "Circulation between "home" and other places: some propositions", in M Chapman and R M Prothero (eds), *Circulation in Population Movement: Substance and Concepts from the Melanesian Case*, London: Routledge and Kegan Paul, 1–12.

Cooley, W.W. and P.R. Lohnes (1962), *Multivariate Procedures in the Behavioural Sciences*, New York: 35–45.

Dasgupta, Swapan (2008), "Beware of Middle India," *Times of India*, Oct. 19, Mumbai: 20.

Dasgupta, Dipankar (2008), "Fall of Sensex: Waves of world market downswing have also reached India," *Desh: A Bengali Fortnightly*, October 17, Kolkata: 12–14.

David, M.D. (1996) (ed.), *Urban Explosion of Mumbai*, Himalaya Publishing House, Mumbai.

Desai, A.R. (1974), "An alternative approach to development", in *Population in India's Development, 1947–2000*, by A. Bose et al. (eds), New Delhi, Vikas Pub. Co.

Deshingkar, Priya (2005), "Improved Livelihoods In Improved Watersheds: Can Migration Be Mitigated?", Paper, *International Workshop on Watershed Management Challenges*, Indian Council of Agricultural Research-International Water Management Institute-International Crops Research Institute for the Semi-arid Tropics, 2004, New Delhi.

Deshingkar, Priya (2006), "Internal migration, poverty and development in Asia", Overseas Development Institute, Brief Paper 11, London: 1–6.

Deshingkar, Priya and Saheen Akter (2009), "Migration and Development in India", *UNDP Human Development Report*, London: 1–90.

Dev, S. Mahendra (2000), "Economic Reforms, poverty, Income Distribution and Employment", *Economic and Political Weekly*, Vol. 35, No. 10: 823–836.

Dev S. Mahendra and Ravi, C. (2007), "Poverty and Inequality: All-India and States, 1983–2005," *Economic and Political Weekly*, February 10: 509–521.

Dholakia, J.R. (2008a), "Basic Concepts of Migration and Urbanisation", in *Urbanisation: Issues and Perspectives* by J.R. Dholakia (ed.), The ICFAI University Press, Hyderabad: 1–15.

Dholakia, J.R. (2008b), "India's Future Urbanisation", in *Urbanisation: Issues and Perspectives* by J.R. Dholakia (ed.), the Icfai University Press, Hyderabad: 163–175.

Dixon. M and Massy, W. (1970), *Introduction to Statistics.* Wiley, New York.

Dos Santos, T. (1973): "The Crisis of development theory and the problem of dependence in Latin America", in *Underdevelopment and Development in Third World,* by Henry Bernstein (ed.): 76–77.

Dubey, et al. (2006), "Surplus Labour, Social Structure and Rural to Urban Migration: Evidence from Indian Data", *The European Journal of Development Research,* Vol. 18 (1): 86 – 104.

Dutt, Ashok K. and Parai, Anindita (1999), "Defining Urban Corridors: Case Studies of Four Mega Cities of India", in *Urban Growth and Development in Asia, Vol. I and II,* Ashgate: Brookfield, USA:93–107.

Dutt, R.C. (1892), *The Economic History of India under Early British Rule,* McMillan, London.

Dwivedi, S. (2010), "Political mess in India", *Nabha Bharat Times,* July 10, Mumbai.

Economic and Political Weekly (2004), "Differential Fertility among the Hindus and the Muslims", *Economic and Political Weekly, Special Issue,* September, Mumbai.

ESCAP (1993), "Population-Poverty Inter-linkages and Poverty Alleviation Strategies", ESCAP Secretariat, Development Planning Division, *The Fourth Asian and Pacific Population Conference, Bali Conference,* Aug, 1992, Selected papers, Asian Population Studies Series No 124, New York: 92–98.

Firodiya, Arun (2006),"Back to Roots: Agribusiness and Bio-energy can create 27 Crore Jobs", *Times of India,* January 4, Edit Page Article: 30.

Fuchs, Roland, J. Ellen Brennan, Joseph Chamie, Fu-Chen Lo, and Juha I. Uitto (eds) (1994), *Mega City Growth and the Future.* United Nations University Press, Tokyo: 1–420.

Ganguly, Saugoto (2010), "New Labour Dies, Long Live New Labour," *Times of India,* May 11: 14.

George, Abraham (2004), *India Untouched: The Forgotten Face of Rural Poverty,* George Foundation, Bangalore.

Ghorpade, K.R. (1998), "Mumbai Metropolitan Region, India." in *Metropolitan Governance and Planning in Transition: Asia-Pacific Cases,* by Josefa S. Edralin, (ed.), UNCRD Research Report Series, no. 31. Nagoya, Japan: United Nations Centre for Regional Development: 361–380.

Ghosh, Santosh. (1998), "Calcutta Metropolitan Area, India." in Josefa S. Edralin, (ed.), *Metropolitan Governance and Planning in Transition: Asia-Pacific Cases,* UNCRD Research Report Series, no. 31. Nagoya, Japan: United Nations Centre for Regional Development: 315–339.

Ghosh, Shankar (2006), "Dangers of Contract Farming in West Bengal ", *Ananda Bazaar Patrika,* May 21, 2006: 4.

Gupta, Dipankar (2010), "Busting Urban Legends," *Times of India,* March 10: 20.

Gupta, Dipankar (2010), "Smell check your numbers: Sniff out what statistics about socio-economic progress conspire to conceal," *Times of India,* May 7: 22.

Gupta, S.C. (1969), *Statistics,* Vikas Publishing Co., New Delhi.

Gupta, S.P. (ed.) (2002), "Summary and Overview: India, Vision: 2020", in *Report of the Committee on India: Vision 2020,* Planning commission, New Delhi: Government of India: 29–45.

Harris, N. (2002), *Thinking the Unthinkable: the Immigration Myth Exposed*, London.

Himanshu T. (2007), "Recent Trends in Poverty and Inequality: Some Preliminary Results," *Economic and Political Weekly*, February 10: 497– 508.

Hotelling, H. (1936), "Relation Between Two Sets of Variates", *Biometrika*: 321–377.

Indian Council of Small Scale Industries (2000), "The Situation of Small-Scale Industries in India", *ICSI Herald*, August 2000, New Delhi: 11–14.

Jacquemin, Alain (1999), "The Politics of Urban Development in New Bombay", in *Urban Growth and Development in Asia, Vol. I and II*, Ashgate: Brookfield, USA: 231–257.

Joshi, A.P., Srinivas, M.D. and Bajaj, J.K. (2003) *Religious Demography of India*, Centre for Policy Studies, Chennai: 40–133.

Kampfner, John (2010), "India's Selfish Elites holds the Republic Back," *Times of India*, January 24: 22.

Kothari, Uma (2002), "Migration and Chronic Poverty", *Institute for Development, Policy and Management, University of Manchester*, Working Paper No 16: 1–32.

Kumar, Ashok (2000), "New Delhi: Inverted Compact Systems", in *Compact Cities: Sustainable urban Forms for Developing Countries*, by Jenks and Burgess, Spon Press, New York: 301–310.

Kundu, A. and N. Sarangi (2007), "Migration, Employment Status and Poverty: An Analysis across Urban Centres," *Economic and Political Weekly*, January 27: 299–306.

Kurosaki, T., Y. Sawada, A. Banerji and S.N. Mishra (2007), "Rural-Urban Migration and Urban Poverty: Socio-Economic Profiles of Rickshaw Pullers and Owner-Contractors in North-East Delhi", CIRJE Discussion Paper CIRJE., University of Tokyo, Tokyo.

Lewin, Kurt (1951), *Field Theory in Social Sciences*. New York.

Lokeshwarananda, Swami (1988), "Introduction" to the Book *Divine Messages of Swami Vivekananda*, Sri Ramakrishna Institute of Culture, Kolkata: 3–5.

Macaulay. Thomas B. (1835), "Lecture to the British Parliament, February 2, 1835", Modern History Feedback.: Thomas Babington Macaulay (1800–1859). www.fordhams.edu/halsell/mod/1833macaulay.

Majumder, R.C., Roychoudhuri, H.C. and Dutta, Kalikinkar (1953) *The Advanced History of India*, Macmillan, London.

Mathur, O.P. (1994), "Indian Mega cities", in *Mega City Growth and the Future* by Fuchs, Roland, Brennan, Chamie, Fu-Chen Lo, and J. Uitto (eds) (1994), United Nations University Press, Tokyo: 320–330.

McGee T.G. (1973), "Peasants in the cities: A paradox, a paradox, a most ingenious paradox", *Human Organization*, Vol. 32, No. 2: 135–42.

McNeil, Mary (1995), "Bombay: One City – Two Worlds", *The Urban Age: The Human Environment of Cities*, 3(2) June: 1–4.

Meng, Xin and Manning, Chris (eds) (2010), *The Great Migration: Rural-Urban Migration in China and Indonesia*, Edward Elger Publishing, London and Cheltenham (UK).

Ministry of Health and Family Welfare (MOHFW), Government of India (1994) *National Population Policy, 1994* (NPP, 1994), Government of India (GoI), New Delhi.

Ministry of Health and Family Welfare (MOHFW), Government of India (2000) *National Population Policy, 2000* (NPP, 2000), Government of India (GoI), New Delhi.

Ministry of Health and Family Welfare (MOHFW), Government of India (2004) *National Rural Health Mission (NRHM)*, Government of India (GoI), New Delhi

Ministry of Urban Development, India (1988), *Report of National Commission on Urbanization, Vol. I–II and Interim Report*, New Delhi.

Madras Metropolitan Development Authority (MMDA) (1995), Master Plan of Madras Metropolitan Area-2011, Madras: 3–70.

Moulasha, K. and Rama Rao, G. (1999), "Religion Specific Differences in Fertility and Family Planning", *Economic and Political Weekly*, October 16–23: 3047–3051.

Mukherji, Shekhar (1971a), "A Field Theory Approach to the Study of Migration Flows through the Settlement Hierarchy in India", *Department of Geography, University of Hawaii*, Honolulu (mimeo): 1–45.

Mukherji, Shekhar (1971b), "Inter-State Migration and Economic Distances between States, India: A Field Theory Perspective, *East West Population Institute, East West Center, and Department of Geography, University of Hawaii*, Honolulu (mimeo): 1–35.

Mukherji, Shekhar (1973), "Migration Field Notes from Varanasi to East West Population Institute, East West Center", Hawaii.

Mukherji, Shekhar (1974), "A Spatio-Temporal Model of the Mobility Patterns in a Multi-ethnic Population, Hawaii", in *People on the Move: Studies in Internal Migration*, by L.A. Kosinski and R.M. Prothero (eds), *Proceedings of 22nd International Geographical Congress Symposium on Population Geography* at Edmonton, Canada, Methuen, London: 245–261.

Mukherji, Shekhar (1975), *The Mobility Field Theory of Human Spatial Behaviour: A Spatial Behavioural Approach to the Study of Migration and Circulation in the Indian Situation, PhD dissertation*, Department of Geography, University of Hawaii (Xeroxed University Microfilms, Ann Arbor, Michigan, 1976): 10–378.

Mukherji, Shekhar (1976a), "A General Field Theory of Movement Dynamics", *Paper presented to 47th Conference of Australian and New Zealand Association of Applied Scientists (ANZAAS)*, Seminar on Population Geography and Geographical Methodology, Hobart, Tasmania, May 10–14: 1–25.

Mukherji, Shekhar (1976b), "A General Field Theory of Movement Behaviour: A Pathway to Micro-Macro Generalization for Migration Planning in Underdeveloped Countries", *Paper, XXIII International Geographical Congress, Symposium on Population at Micro Scale, Minsk*, Kiev, USSR, July (Published in Proceedings, *Geography of Population*, Minsk, USSR, in *Russian*).

Mukherji, Shekhar (1977a), "Spatial Disorganization and Internal Migration in India: Alternative Strategies for Restructuring the Space Economy and Development", *Paper presented at ESCAP Expert Group Meeting on Population and Economic Development in Sub-National Areas, UN-ESCAP*, Bangkok: 1–56. Also see *summary of paper in Report of Expert Group Meeting, Asian Population Study Series No 40*, Bangkok, 1977: 17–18.

Mukherji, Shekhar (1977b), "Assessing Inter-relationships between Population Policies, Socio-Economic Systems, and Demographic Behaviour in India: An Analytical Framework," *Demography India*, 6, Nos. 1–2: 250–266.

Mukherji, Shekhar (1977c), "Circular Mobility, Wage Labor Displacement and Policy: A cross-cultural comparison in Hawaii and India", Paper, 8th Summer Seminar on Population, East-West Population Institute (EWPI), East West Center, Honolulu Hawaii: 1–12 (mimeo).

Mukherji, Shekhar (1979a), "Spatial Disorganization and Internal Migration in India: Probable Strategies for Restructuring of the Space Economy and Development", *Canadian Studies in Population,* Vol. 6: 45–61.

Mukherji, Shekhar (1979b), *The Mobility Field Theory: A Spatial-Behavioural Foundation to the Movement Dynamics, With Application to Indian Situation.* International Geographical Union's and National Geographical Society of India's Research Monograph No. 25, Department of Geography, Banaras Hindu University, Varanasi: 1–80.

Mukherji, Shekhar (1979c), "A General Field Theory", *Indian Journal of Regional Sc.,* Vol. 11 (2): 40–51.

Mukherji, Shekhar (1979d), "Understanding Canonical Analysis through Human Mobility Research", *Geographical Review of India,* Sept: 234– 249.

Mukherji, Shekhar (1980a), "A General Field Theory of Movement Behaviour: A Pathway to Micro-Macro Generalization for Migration Planning in Underdeveloped Countries", *Geografiska Annaler, Series B, Human Geography,* Vol. 62: 46–60

Mukherji, Shekhar (1980b), "Understanding Mobility Field Theory," *Demography India,* 8(4–6): 254–284.

Mukherji, Shekhar (1980c), "A General Field Theory of Movement Dynamics", *Indian Journal of Regional Science,* IIT, Kharagpur: 39–66.

Mukherji, Shekhar (1981), *Mechanisms of Underdevelopment, Labour Migration and Planning Strategies in India,* Prajna, Calcutta: 1–190.

Mukherji, Shekhar (1982a), *Poverty and Mobility in India: The Mobility Field Theory Perspective,* Prajna, Calcutta, 1–280.

Mukherji, Shekhar (1981b), "Kolkata: Sonar Mukut, Maatir Paa" (Kolkata: City of Hallowed Culture, but with a Feet of Clay), *Desh: Weekly Bengali Journal,* May 21, 1981: 3–12.

Mukherji, Shekhar (1982b),"Mobility Field Theory of Migration Behavior", *Journal of Manpower Research,* Delhi, Ch. 3.

Mukherji, Shekhar (1982c), "Demographic Field Theory: Theoretical and Empirical Example of Geo-Demography", *International Geographical Union (IGU)* Congress, Sao Paulo: 1–30 (mimeo).

Mukherji, Shekhar (1983a), *The Demographic Field Theory: Population Policies and Demographic Behaviour in India.* Thinkers Library, Allahabad: 1–145.

Mukherji, Shekhar (1983b), *Essays on Rural Development.* Utsargo Publications, Varanasi: 1–192.

Mukherji, Shekhar (1983c), "Integrated Rural Transformation Programme: An Alternative Strategy of Rural Development in India," in *Essays on Rural Development* by Shekhar Mukherji, Utsargo Publications, Varanasi: 1–32.

Mukherji, Shekhar (1983d), "Further Thoughts on Rural Development," in *Essays on Rural Development* by Shekhar Mukherji, Utsargo Publications, Varanasi: 179–192.

Mukherji, Shekhar (1985a), "The Process of Wage Labour Circulation in Northern India", in *Labour Circulation and Labour Process* by Guy Standing (ed.), *International Labour Office,* Croom Helm, London: 252–289.

Mukherji, Shekhar (1985b), "The Syndrome of Poverty and Wage Labour Circulation: The Indian Scene", in *Circulation in Third World Countries by* R. Mansell Prothero and Murray Chapman, (eds), London: Routledge and Kegan Paul: 279–299 (Library Edition, 2011) .

Mukherji, Shekhar (1985c), "A Canonical Model of Migration to Cities", *Espace, Population, Societies, Migrations and Cities, International Geographical Union's Symposium*, Rouen, France, August, Vol. I: 54–61.

Mukherji, Shekhar (1987), "Alternative Strategy of Integrated Rural Transformation Programme", in *Regional Planning and Rural Development*, by L.R. Singh (ed.), Thinkers Library, Allahabad, Ch. 15.

Mukherji, Shekhar (1988), *Operation Research on Delivery of Rural Health Services in Varanasi District.* Indian Council of Medical Research Project, Institute of Medical Sciences, Banaras Hindu University, Varanasi: 1–68.

Mukherji, Shekhar (1989a), "Application of the Demographic Field Theory to Study Linkages between Demographic Behaviour, Geo-Socio-Economic Systems, and Population Policies in India", in *Dynamics of Population and Family Welfare* by K. Srinivasan and K.B. Pathak (eds), Bombay: Himalaya Publishing House: 342–373.

Mukherji, Shekhar (1989b), *Systems Analysis of PHCs of Varanasi District.* ICMR Health Project, Institute of Medical Sciences, Banaras Hindu University, Varanasi: 1–126.

Mukherji, Shekhar (1990), "Underdevelopment and Migration of Women for Employment in India: Patterns, Processes, and Policies", *Paper presented in All-India Seminar on the Status of Women and Demographic Change in India,* Oct 1990, IIPS, Bombay; 1–38.

Mukherji, Shekhar (1991), "The Nature of Migration and Urbanization in India: The Search for Alternative Planning Strategies", in *Dynamics of Population and Family Welfare* by Srinivasan and Pathak (eds), Himalaya Publishing Co., Bombay: 203–249.

Mukherji, Shekhar (1992a), *The Application of Demographic Field Theory to Developed and Developing Countries,* Research Monograph, International Institute for Population Sc. (IIPS), Bombay: 1–96.

Mukherji, Shekhar (1992b), *Migration, Regional Disparities and Urbanization in India,* Research Monograph, International Institute for Population Sciences (IIPS), Bombay: 1–121.

Mukherji, Shekhar (1993a), *Poverty-Induced Migration and Urban Involution in India: Causes and Consequences.* I.I.P.S. Research Monograph: 1–135.

Mukherji, Shekhar (1993b), *Functional Classification of Indian Towns by Factor Cluster Method, 1981 and 1991*, IIPS Research Monograph, Mumbai, 1–196.

Mukherji, Shekhar (1993c), "A Canonical Model of Migration and Regional Disparities in India: Linking Spatial Structure to Spatial flows", in *Dynamics of Population and Family Welfare, 1993,* by K B. Pathak et al. (eds), Himalayan Publishing House, Bombay, 250–280.

Mukherji, Shekhar (1993d), "A Critique of Spatial Strategy of National Commission on Urbanization in India", in *Urbanization: Trends, Perspectives, and Challenges* by Jaymala Diddee and Vimla Rangaswamy (eds), Jaipur and New Delhi, Rawat Publications, 75–94.

Mukherji, Shekhar (1993e), *Nature and Characteristics of Migrants to Greater Bombay,* IIPS, Research Monograph, Mumbai, 1–32.

Mukherji, Shekhar (1994a) "Rapid Metropolitan Growth and Alternative Perspectives of Urban and Regional Development in India", *Tech Workshop on Environment, Management and Urban-Regional Development, Delhi, 1993. Published in Indian Journal of Social Sciences (ISSA),* New Delhi: 9–21.

Mukherji, Shekhar (1994b) "Urban Atrophy: Bombay will cross 24 Million by 2010", *Independent*, Mumbai: 1.

Mukherji, Shekhar (1995a) "Poverty-Induced Migration and Urban Involution in ESCAP Region," *Background Paper for UN-ESCAP Expert Meeting on Population and Poverty, Bangkok, Sept 1995*: 1–65. Summary and Recommendations published in *UN-ESCAP Expert Group Meeting's Proceedings Volume*, June 1996.

Mukherji, Shekhar (1995b), "Distressed Migration and Urban Involution in ESCAP Region: Needed Planning Strategies", *News Letter, International Institute for Population Sciences*, Mumbai: 1–8

Mukherji, Shekhar (1995c), "The Syndrome of Poverty and High Fertility in India and The Third World: Strategies Required for Fertility Decline and Better Health Deliveries", *Paper presented to International Seminar on Population, Development and Health in Developing Countries*, Dept of Geography, Banaras Hindu University: 1–36.

Mukherji, Shekhar (1996a), "The Nature of Migration to Greater Bombay: The Need for Alternative Development Perspective", in *Urban Explosion of Mumbai* by M.D. David (ed.) Himalaya Publishing House, Mumbai: 26–54.

Mukherji, Shekhar (1996b), "Poverty-Induced Migration and Urban Involution in India: Alternative Planning Strategies", in *Census as Social Document* by S.P. Mohanty and A.R. Momin (eds), Jaipur and New Delhi, Rawat Publications: 41–91.

Mukherji, Shekhar (1997a), "Underdevelopment and Migration of Women for Employment in India ", Published in *Proceed. International Geographical Congress, Migration and Gender*, Dept of Geography, University of Pretoria, South Africa: 283–304.

Mukherji, Shekhar (1997b), *Poverty-Induced Migration and Urban Involution in ESCAP Region: And Urban and Regional Planning Lessons from Japan*. Research Monograph No 300, Institute of Developing Economies, Tokyo: 1–81.

Mukherji, Shekhar (1997c), "Problems of Small and Medium Towns of India: Their Inadequate Economic Characteristics," in *Indian Medium Towns: An Appraisal of Their Role as Growth Centres* by Jaymala Diddee (ed.), Rawat Publications, Jaipur and New Delhi: 68–113.

Mukherji, Shekhar (1997d), "Poverty and Fertility and other Demographic Elements in India", *Presidential Address, Population Science Section, 21st Indian Social Science Congress, Tamil University, Thanjavur*, Tamil Nadu, Dec: 1–65.

Mukherji, Shekhar (1997e), "Causal Linkages between Syndrome of Poverty and High Fertility in India: A Very Neglected Aspects of Population Studies in India", *Presented in International Seminar on Environment, Energy and Technology: Regional and Global Perspectives*, Banaras Hindu University, Dept of Geography, Dec.: 1–40.

Mukherji, Shekhar (1997f), "Syndrome of Poverty and Fertility in India", Paper, *International Geographical Union (IGU) Seminar on Gender, Environment, and Health*, Dept of Geography, Chiang Mai University, Thailand, 1–12.

Mukherji, Shekhar (1997g), "Poverty Index and High Fertility and Mortality in India: Required Strategies", *Paper, Population Science Section, 21st Indian Social Science Congress, Tamil University, Thanjavur*, Tamil Nadu, Dec. 1997: 1–21.

Mukherji, Shekhar (1997h), "Poverty and Fertility in India: Findings of the Demographic Field Theory – Linking Demographic Behaviour, Socio-economic System, and Population Policies in India", *International Institute for Population Sciences (IIPS) News Letter*, Mumbai, Jan, Nos. 4–6: 1–6.

Mukherji, Shekhar (1998a), "Poverty and Fertility in India: Required Policy Changes", *IGU Symposium on Changing Health Problems in Developing Countries*, MS University of Baroda, Proceedings Volume, March 1998: 250–270.

Mukherji, Shekhar (1998b), "Poverty-induced Migration and Urban Involution in ESCAP Region," *IIPS News Letter*, Jan–Feb: 10–20.

Mukherji, Shekhar (1999a), "Poverty and Fertility in India." Paper, *Nihon University Seminar in Population and Socio-economic Transformations. in Asia, UN Population Project, Nihon University*, Tokyo, March 3: 1–25.

Mukherji, Shekhar (1999b), "Demographic and Socio-economic Conditions in India", *Paper presented, Seminar in Japan Women's University, Kawasaki, Japan. July 1999.*

Mukherji, Shekhar (2000a), "Stressful Migration and Urban Involution in Mega Cities of India: Required Planning Strategies," *Geographical Review of India*, Kolkata: 15–27

Mukherji, Shekhar (2000b), "Urban Planning of Tokyo: Metropolitan Management Lessons for Asian Mega Cities", *Nagarlok: Journal of Urban Studies*, Indian Institute of Public Administration, New Delhi: 1–12.

Mukherji, Shekhar (2000c), "Tale of Tokyo: Metropolitan Planning Lessons for Asian Mega Cities", *IIPS News Letter*, June 2000: 1–10.

Mukherji, Shekhar (2000d), "Urban Decay in India: A Plea for Sustainable Planning", *International Sem. on Land-use and technology in Developing Countries*, Dept of Geography, Banaras Hindu University, Pub in *Changing Land and Environment Systems: Scenario to Sustainability* by S.B. Singh, R.P.B. Singh and V.K. Kumra (eds), Nat. Geog. Soc. of India (NGSI), Varanasi: 171–82.

Mukherji, Shekhar (2000e), *Poverty-Induced Migration and Urban Involution in ESCAP Region: Needed Planning Strategies*, International Instt. for Population Sciences (IIPS) Research Monograph 25, Mumbai: 1–178.

Mukherji, Shekhar (2000f), "The Syndrome of Poverty and Fertility in India", *Yojana, Ministry of Information and Broadcasting*, New Delhi, May 2000: 1–5.

Mukherji, Shekhar (2000g), "Poverty Index and Its Linkages to Demographic Behaviour in India", presented to *National Seminar on Land-use, Rural Development and Transfer of Technology*, Dept of Geography, Banaras Hindu University, Feb: 1–25.

Mukherji, Shekhar (2000h), "Poverty and Fertility in India and Andhra Pradesh: A Demographic Field Theoretic Perspective", *Seminar on Rapid Fertility Decline in Andhra Pradesh*, Hyderabad, Mar. 2000: 1–35.

Mukherji, Shekhar (2001a), *Application of The Demographic Field Theory to India: Linkages between Demographic behaviour, Socio-Economic Systems and Population Policies.* IIPS Research Monograph, 27, Mumbai: 1–150.

Mukherji, Shekhar (2001b), *Causal Linkages between Migration, Urbanization, and Regional Disparities in India: Required Planning Strategies*, IIPS Research Monograph, 29, Mumbai: 1–226.

Mukherji, Shekhar (2001c), "Low Quality Migration and Urban Decay in India: Processes and Planning Strategies", *Paper, International Union for the Scientific Study of Population (IUSSP), Salvadore, Bahia, Brazil*, Aug: 1–26.

Mukherji, Shekhar (2001d), "International Mobility Field Theory: Linking Internal and International Migration," *Paper, 24th IUSSP Conference, Spatial Mobility*, Salvatore, Brazil, Aug 2001: 1–20.

Mukherji, Shekhar (2002), "Urbanization and migration in India: a different scene", in H.S. Geyer (ed.), *International Handbook of Urban Systems: Studies of Urbanization and Migration in Advanced and Developing Countries*. London and Cheltenham, UK and Massachusetts, USA: Edward Elgar, 525–559.

Mukherji, Shekhar (2004), "Poverty-Induced Migration and Urban Decay in India", in *Space, Society, and Geography* by Banerjee-Guha, S. (ed.), Jaipur and New Delhi, Rawat Publications: 156–165.

Mukherji, Shekhar (2005a), *Poverty and Population in India: Three Essays*, R.N. Dubey Foundation, Allahabad: 1–95.

Mukherji, Shekhar (2005b), "Distressed Migration and Urban Decay in India: Required Planning Strategies", in *Poverty and Population in India*. by Shekhar Mukherji, Professor R.N. Dubey Memorial Lectures, 2004, Prof. R.N. Dubey Foundation, Allahabad: 75–95.

Mukherji, Shekhar (2005c), "The Syndrome of Poverty and High Fertility in India: Programmes for Poverty Eradication and Health Services", in *Poverty and Population in India* by Shekhar Mukherji, Professor R.N. Dubey Memorial Lectures, 2004, R.N. Dubey Foundation, Allahabad: 1–38.

Mukherji, Shekhar (2005d), "Syndrome of Poverty and High Fertility in India', in *Poverty and Population in India*, by Shekhar Mukherji, Professor R.N. Dubey Memorial Lectures, 2004, Prof. R.N. Dubey Foundation, Allahabad: 38–75.

Mukherji, Shekhar (2005e), "Migration and Urban Decay in India", in *Oriental Geography, Golden Jubilee Volume* by Rosie Majid Ahsan (ed.), Dept of Geography, Dhaka University, Dhaka: 11–36.

Mukherji, Shekhar (2005f), "Migration Field Notes", Mumbai.

Mukherji, Shekhar (2006), *Migration and Urban Decay: Asian Experiences*. Rawat Publications: Jaipur and New Delhi: 1–330. Also see, www.shekharmukherji.com/site.

Mukherji, Shekhar (2007), *Poverty and Fertility in India: The Demographic Field Theory Perspectives*. Rawat Publications: Jaipur and New Delhi: 1–278.

Mukherji, Shekhar (2008a), "Distressed Migration and Urban Decay in Some Asian Metropolises: Phenomena, Processes, and Planning", in *Explorations in Applied Geography* by Ashok K. Dutt, H.N. Misra and Meera Chatterjee (eds), Prentice-Hall of India: New Delhi: 308–328.

Mukherji, Shekhar (2008b), "Migration Field Notes," Mumbai.

Mukherji, Shekhar (2009), "India's Growing Population and Growing Economy: Issues and Perspectives", *Tokei: Japan's Statistical Journal*, 2009, January *(in Japanese, with English Abstract)*: 7–12.

Mukherji, Shekhar (2011), "Urban-Rural Inequalities in South and South East Asia: Colonial Policy Impacts and Current Spatial and Economic Disparities", in *International Handbook of Urban Policy, Volume III*, by H.S. Geyer (ed.), London and Cheltenham, UK and Massachusetts, USA: Edward Elgar Publishing Inc, Chapter: 246–271.

Mukherji, Shekhar *et al.* (1980), *Population, Food, and Land Inequality: The Geography of Hunger and Insecurity in India*, Indian Council of Social Science Research (ICSSR), and Allied Publishers, New Delhi: 32–121 *(Shekhar Mukherji is the Principal Author of this Seminal Book)*.

Mukherji, Shekhar *et al.* (1981), *Indian Cities: Their Economic Structure, In-migration and Capital Investments*, Indian council of Social Science Research (ICSSR), New Delhi *(Shekhar Mukherji is the Principal Author of this Seminal Book)*.

Mukherji, Shekhar *et al.* (1982), *Functional Classifications of Indian Towns (1961 and 1971) by Factor-Cluster Method*, Indian council of Social Science Research (ICSSR), New Delhi *(Shekhar Mukherji is the Principal Author of this Seminal Book)*.

Mukherji, Shekhar and Otomo, Atsushi (2000), "Metropolitan Planning of Tokyo: Urban Planning Experiences of Japan," *Journal of Graduate School of Integrated Arts and Sciences, Japan Women's University*, Kawasaki, Japan: 19–35.

Mundle, Sudipto (2010), "Delivery the Key: We need parallel Institutions of the poor to channel food and other BPL Entitlements," *Times of India*, April 29: 20.

Naoroji, Dadabhai (1889), *Poverty and Un-British Rule in India*, Ranima Union Press, Bombay,

Natali, Claudia (2009), "Linkages between Internal and International Migrations: Policy Implications for Development", *Conference* on Urban-Rural Linkages and Migration, Sept. 16th, 2009, Plenary Session 1, *Urban-Rural Linkages and Migration: A Potential for Poverty Alleviation in Developing Countries*, Dortmund, Germany.

National Family and Health Survey (NFHS-I) (1995), *India: National Family and Health Survey–I Report (1992–1993), (NFHS-I)*, International Institute for Population Sciences, (IIPS), Mumbai, and Ministry of Health and Family Welfare (MOHFW), New Delhi.

National Family and Health Survey (NFHS-II) (2000), *India: National Family and Health Survey–II Report (1998–1999) (NFHS-II)*, International Institute for Population Sciences, (IIPS), Mumbai, and Ministry of Health and Family Welfare (MOHFW), New Delhi.

National Family and Health Survey (NFHS-III) (2007), *India: National Family and Health Survey–III Report (NFHS-III, 2005–06)*, Volume I, International Institute for Population Sciences, (IIPS), Mumbai, and Ministry of Health and Family Welfare (MOHFW) New Delhi.

National Institute of Rural Development. (NIRD) (1999), "Rural Development Programmes", in *India: Rural Development Report, 1999, Regional Disparities in Development and Poverty*, NIRD, Hyderabad: 99–122.

National Institute of Urban Affairs (NIUA) (1988), *State of India's Urbanization*, New Delhi: 66–70.

National Sample Survey Organization (NSSO) (1989), *Sarvekshana*, Vol.13 (1983 estimates) various pages.

National Sample Survey Organisation (NSSO) (1993), *Consumer Expenditure Surveys, 1987–88 (43rd round)*, NSSO, New Delhi.

National Sample Survey Organization (NSSO) (1996), *Consumer Expenditure Surveys, 1993–94 (50th round)*, NSSO, New Delhi.

National Sample Survey Organisation (NSSO) (2001), *Migration in India 1999–2000, NSS (55th round)*, Report No. 470, National Sample Survey Organisation, Ministry of Statistics and Programme Implementation, Government of India., New Delhi.

National Sample Survey Organization (NSSO) (2002), *Consumer Expenditure Surveys, 1999–2000 (55th round)*, NSSO, New Delhi.

National Sample Survey Organization (NSSO) (2006), *Consumer Expenditure Surveys, 2004–5 (61st round)*, NSSO, New Delhi.

Nivedita, Sister (Margaret Noble) (1903), *The Master as I Saw Him*, Calcutta.

Oberai, A.S. (1987), *Migration, Urbanization and Development*. ILO, Geneva.

Oberai, A.S. (1993), *Population Growth, Employment, and Poverty in Third World Mega Cities*, New York, St Martin's Press: 1–180.

Onyeiwu, Steve et al. (2007), "Distributional Impact of Globalization Induced Migration: Evidence from a Nigerian Village", UNU-WIDER Research Paper, Vol. 66. Wider, Stockholm.

Pasay N. Haidy, et al. (1991)," Indonesia" in *Small Town and Rural Human Resources Development to Reduce Migration to Large Cities: China, India, Indonesia, Nepal, and Papua New Guinea.* Asian Population Studies Series No. 110, United Nations, New York, 1–232.

Pathak, Pushpa (1998), "Delhi, India" in *Metropolitan Governance and Planning in Transition: Asia-Pacific Cases,* by Josefa S. Edralin, (ed.), UNCRD Research Report Series, no. 31. Nagoya, Japan: United Nations Centre for Regional Development: 341–359.

Pathak, Pushpa (1999), "Two Decades of Urban Poverty reduction through Income Generation", in *Urban Growth and Development in Asia, Vol. I and II* by Graham Chapman, A.K. Dutt, and R.W. Bradknock (eds), Ashgate: Brookfield, USA: 244–268.

Phillip, Warren (1973), "Understanding Canonical Analysis", Department of Political Science, The Ohio State University, Columbus, Ohio (mimeo).

Planning Commission (2001), *Human Development Index of States (HDI data)*, Government of India, New Delhi, 2001. *www.planningcommission.nic.in*, Planning Commission (2001).

Planning Commission of India (2002a), *Indian Planning experience – Indian Agenda for 21st Century,* New Delhi: Government of India.

Planning Commission of India (2002b), *India Vision: 2020 Report of the Committee on India: Vision 2020,* New Delhi: Government of India: 29–45 and 139–143.

Planning Commission of India (2009), "Indicators of India's Economy", Government of India, New Delhi. www.planningcommission.nic.in, Planning Commission.

Population Foundation of India and Population Reference Bureau (2007), "The Future Population of India: A Long-range Demographic View," *Population Foundation of India,* New Delhi, and *Population Reference Bureau,* Washington: 1–20.

Prothero, R. Mansell and Murray Chapman (eds) (1985a), *Circulation in Third World Countries,* London: Routledge and Kegan Paul, Introduction and Last Chapter: 1–26 and 436–440. Routledge Library Edition (2011), London/New York.

Radhakrishna, R. and Ray, Shovan (2005), "Poverty in India: Dimensions and Character", in *India Development Report, 2004–05,* by Parikh, Kirit and Radhakrishnan R. (eds): 40–61.

Raju, Saraswati (2009), *Urban Poverty in India, 2009, UNDP Sponsored Report,* Centre for Regional Development, Jawaharlal Nehru University, New Delhi.

Ranade, Ajit (2010), "Poor People's Rich Representatives", *Mumbai Mirror,* April 24: 30.

Rao, Mohan (2006), "Saffron Demography: Hindu Communalists Spread Population Myths", *Times of India,* Edit Page article, April 20, 2006, p. 30.

Rao, V.L.S Prakasa, Mishra, R.P. and Sundram, K.V. (1974), *Regional Developmental Planning in India: A New Strategy,* Vikas, New Delhi.

Rodgers, Gerry (ed.) (1989), *Urban Poverty and Labour Market*. ILO, Geneva: 1–256.

Ruiter, Wilke (1999), "Equity and Slum Redevelopment in Mumbai", in *Urban Growth and Development in Asia, Vol. I and II*. Ashgate: Brookfield, USA: 205– 221.

Rummel, Rudolf J. (1965), "A Field Theory of Social Action with Application to Conflict within Nations", *General Systems*, 10: 183–197.

Rummel, R.J. (1970), *Factor Analysis*, Sage Publishers, Los Angeles.

Rummel, R.J. (1975a), *Dynamic Psychological Field: A Psycho-Philosophical Prolegomenon to the Dynamics of Conflict and War*. Sage Publication, Beverly Hills, Los Angeles.

Rummel, R.J. (1975b), "Analyzing Population Policy and Demographic Change", A Research Proposal for National Science Foundation (USA), *Dimensionality of Nation's Project, Department of Political Science, University of Hawaii, Hawaii*: 1–46 (mimeo).

Rummel, R.J. (1980), *Field Theory Evolving*, Sage Publication, Beverly Hills, Los Angeles.

Rummel, R.J. and Mukherji, Shekhar (1981), *Analyzing Population Policies and Demographic Behaviour*, Prajna, Calcutta: 1–90.

Sarkar, Avirup (2006), "Exceptional and Straightforward: A Critique of the Book on Development with Dignity" by Amit Bhaduri (in Bengali), *Desh: A Bengali Fortnightly*, April 12: 95–96.

Sengupta, Arjun (2006), *Sengupta Committee Report on Unorganized Economic Sector*, Government of India, New Delhi. www. democraticunderground.com.

Sharma, R.N. and Narender, A. (1996), "Policies and Strategies for Slum Improvement and Renewal – The Bombay experience", in David, M.D. (ed.) *Urban Explosion in Mumbai*, op cit.: 199–223.

Shimodaira, Hiromi (1998), "Slums of Tokyo: Their Changing Phases with Economic Development", in *Shrinkage of Urban Slums in Asia and their Employment Aspects* by Tatsuru Akimoto (ed.), ILO Regional Office for Asia and the Pacific, Bangkok: 65–169

Shreshta, N. (1989), *Underdevelopment and Migration in Nepal*, Boulder, Colorado: West View Press: 1–11.

Singh, Ajit (1989), *Urbanization, Poverty and Employment: The Large Metropolis in the Third World*. ILO working Paper, Geneva: 1–38.

Singh, Amarendra P. and Sharma, J.K. (2006), "Management Strategies for Promotion of Agriculture", *Journal of Rural Development*, Vol. 24 (4): 445–458.

Singh, Andrea M. and A. de Souza (1980), *The Urban Poor, Slum and Pavement Dwellers in Major Cities* of *India*, Manohar, New Delhi: 3–56.

Singh, L.R. (ed.), (1987), *Regional Planning and Rural Development*, Thinkers Library, Allahabad.

Sinha, R.K. and Singh, B.D. (1999), "Rural Development through Poverty Alleviation", in Singh, J.L. and Gaur, K.D. (eds), *Need for New Strategies to Eradicate Poverty*, Manak Publications, New Delhi: 143 – 151.

Skeldon, Ronald (2003), "Migration and Poverty," Paper presented at *Conference on "African Migration and Urbanization in Comparative Perspective"*, Johannesburg, South Africa, June, 2003.

Srivastava, Rahul (2010), "Finding the City's Fault Lines," *Mumbai Mirror*, February 3, Mumbai: 32.

Standing, Guy (ed.) (1985), *Labour Circulation and Labour Policies. ILO-WEP Study*, Croom Helm, London, Introduction and first chapter: 1–55.

Tendulkar, Suresh (2008), *Tendulkar Commission Report on Poverty*, Government of India, New Delhi. www.indianexpress.com.

Thomas, Vinod (2008), "Don't Ignore Poverty Data: Latest figures show an urgent need for inclusive growth," *Times of India*, Oct. 17, Mumbai: 16

Times of India, (2000), "Jobless in Bhiwandi, Maharashtra", *Times of India*, May 16, 2000, Mumbai.

Times of India (2000), "Delhi," *Times of India*, Mumbai, Dec 1, 2000

Times of India (2006), "Bangladeshi Migrants form Ministry in Assam," *Times of India*, May 23, 2006: 8.

Times of India (2006), "Kerala follows Assam Patterns," *Times of India*, May 25, 2006: 10.

Times of India (2010), "Republic of Hope: Let's transform the Country in the next 20 years," Editorial, *Times of India*, January 26, Mumbai: 18.

Times of India (2010), "It's Jobs, Stupid: Fast growing India must generate employment on a vast scale," Editorial, *Times of India*, March 24, Mumbai: 24.

Times of India (2010), "Dantewada Killings of CRPF by the Naxalites and Maoists", *Times of India*, April 4, Mumbai: 1.

Times of India (2010), "Government Committed to Muslim Quota: Khurshid wants more minority districts", *Times of India*, April 8, Mumbai: 10.

Times of India (2010), "India's richie rich: Millionaire count climbs to 126,700", *Mumbai Mirror*, June 24, Mumbai:14.

Times of India (2010), "Huge Waste in the Commonwealth Games, Delhi, 2010", *Times of India*, August 25, 2010:16.

Times of India (2010), "Police gear up to flush out Illegal Bangladeshi", *Times of India – Times of Navi Mumbai*, October 8, 2010: IV.

Todaro, Michael P. and Jerry Stillkind (1981), "City Bias and Rural Neglect: The Dilemma of Urban Development", New York, The Population Council: 11–77.

Tokyo Metropolitan Government (1994), *Planning of Tokyo, 1994*. Bureau of City Planning, Tokyo: 1–25.

Tokyo Metropolitan Government (1996), *Planning of Tokyo, 1996*. Bureau of City Planning, Tokyo: 1–35.

Tokyo Metropolitan Government (1998), *Planning of Tokyo, 1998*. Bureau of City Planning, Tokyo: 1–5.

Town and Country Planning Organization (TCPO) (1996), *A Compendium of Urban Slums in India*, TCPO, New Delhi.

Town and Country Planning Organization (TCPO) (2005), *A Compendium of Urban Slums in India*, TCPO, New Delhi.

Udupa, K.N. and Mukherji, Shekhar (1988), *Knowledge and Utilization of Primary Health Services by Rural Women of Varanasi District*. ICMR Health Project, Institute of Medical Sciences, Banaras Hindu University, Varanasi: 1–175.

Underhill-Sem, Yvonne (2004), "Fertility of the Mobility: Impulses from Hawaii", *Geo-journal*, Vol. 59: 55–58.

UN-ESCAP (1977), *Summary of Expert Group Meeting on Population and Economic Development in Sub-National Areas of Asia-Pacific Region, Asian Study Series No. 40*, UN-ESCAP, Bangkok, 1977: 14–17 and 21–27 *(also see summary of paper by Shekhar Mukherji: 17–18)*.

UN-ESCAP (1992), *Migration and Urbanization in Asia and the Pacific: Interrelationship with Socio-Economic Development and Evolving Policy Issues*, Asian Population Studies No. 111: 3–4.

UN-ESCAP (1995), *Trends, Patterns and Implications of Rural-urban Migration in India, Nepal and Thailand*: United Nations, New York: 7.

United Nations (1986a), *Population Growth and Policies in Mega Cities, Calcutta*, New York, UN: 1–38.

United Nations (1986b), *Population Growth and Policies in Mega Cities, Delhi*, New York, UN: 1–34.

United Nations (1986c), *Population Growth and Policies in Mega Cities, Bombay*, New York, UN: 1–34.

United Nations (1987a), *Population Growth and Policies in Mega Cities, Madras*, New York, UN: 1–29.

United Nations (1991a), *Small Town and Rural Human Resources Development to Reduce Migration to Large Cities: China, India, Indonesia, Nepal, and Papua New Guinea*. Asian Population Studies Series No. 110, UN, New York: 1–232.

United Nations (1991b), "Urbanization and Human Development", Chapter 5 of *Human Development Report 1990*. New York: 85–95.

United Nations (1992), *Migration and Urbanization in Asia and the Pacific: Interrelationships with Socio-economic Development and Evolving Policy Issues*. Selected papers of Pre-Conference Seminar, Fourth Asian and Pacific Population Conference, Seoul, 21–25 Jan, 1992, New York: 19–115.

United Nations (1993a), *Urbanization and Socio-economic Development in Asia and the Pacific: The Philippines, Sri Lanka, Thailand, and Viet Nam*, Population Studies Series No 122, New York: UN.

United Nations (1993b), *World Urbanization Prospects: the 1992 Revision*, United Nations, New York 36, 126–127.

United Nations (1993c), *The Fourth Asian and Pacific Population Conference, Bali Conference*, August, 1992, Selected papers, Asian Population Studies No 124, New York: 92–104.

United Nations (1995a), *World Urbanization Prospects: the 1994 Revision*, United Nations, New York: 30–32, 120–150.

United Nations (1995b), *The Challenge of Urbanization: The World's Largest Cities*, New York: UN: 10–166.

United Nations (1995c), "Bombay", in *The Challenge of Urbanization: World's Largest Cities*. ibid.: 41–44.

United Nations (1995d), "Calcutta", in *The Challenge of Urbanization: World's Largest Cities*. ibid.: 59–62.

United Nations (1995e), "Delhi", in *The Challenge of Urbanization: World's Largest Cities*. ibid.: 78–82.

United Nations (1997), Human *Development Report, 1997: Poverty*, UN, New York

United Nations (1998), *Human Development Report, 1998*, UN, New York.

United Nations (2005), *Summary: Human Development Report 2005: International Cooperation at a Crossroads – Aid, Trade, and Security in an Unequal World*, UNDP, 2005: 19–26.

United Nations (2007), *World Urbanization Prospects, 2006 Revision*, United Nations, New York.

United Nations, Habitat, (2007), *Report on Urban Safety and Security, 2007*, New York: Various Tables.

United Nations Millennium Project (2005), *Investing in Development: A Practical Plan to Achieve the Millennium Development Goals*, UNDP, New York.

UNDP (2003), *Human Development Report 2003*, UNDP, Oxford University Press, New Delhi.

UNDP (2007), *The State of World Population 2007: Unleashing the Potential of Urban Growth*, United Nations, New York: Various Tables.

UNDP (2009), *Human Development Report 2009, Overcoming Barriers: Human Mobility and Development*, UNDP, New York: 1–250, Summary and Various Tables.

UNDP (2009), *Human Development Report: Overcoming Barriers: Human Mobility and Development*, Bangkok: 1–50.

UNDP (2009), *Human Development Report 2009: Overcoming Barriers: Human Mobility and Development*, Jakarta: 1–45.

UNDP (2009), *Urban Poverty Report of India, 2009*, UNDP, Oxford University Press, New Delhi.

Viswanathan, Vishal C. (2010), "Ending Corruption,". *Times of India*, May 18, Mumbai: 16.

Vivekananda, Swami (1893), *The Complete Works of Swami Vivekananda, Centenary Edition*, 1963, Vol. 1–8, Advaita Ashram, Mayavati, Uttranchal, India.

Vivekananda, Swami (1893), *Complete Work of Swami Vivekananda, Centenary Volume I*, Advaita Ashram, Mayavati, Uttaranchal, 1963: 5, 108, and various pages.

Vivekananda, Swami (1893), *Complete Work of Swami Vivekananda, Centenary Volume II*, Advaita Ashram, Mayavati, Uttaranchal, 1963: 55, 86, 237, 304, 356, 410, and various pages and letters.

Vivekananda, Swami (1894), *Complete Work of Swami Vivekananda, Centenary Volume III*, Advaita Ashram, Mayavati, Uttaranchal, 1963: 105, 193, 244, 318, 368, 433, 461, and various pages.

Vivekananda, Swami (1894), *Complete Work of Swami Vivekananda, Centenary Volume IV*, Advaita Ashram, Mayavati, Uttaranchal, 1963: 1246, 352, 480, various pages.

Vivekananda, Swami (1894), *Complete Work of Swami Vivekananda, Centenary Volume V*, Advaita Ashram, Mayavati, Uttaranchal, 1963: 17, 23–24, 29, 30, 38, 57–58, 61, 227, various pages.

Vivekananda, Swami (1895), *Complete Work of Swami Vivekananda, Centenary Volume VI*, Advaita Ashram, Mayavati, Uttaranchal 1963: 264, 295, various pages.

Vivekananda, Swami (1895), *Complete Work of Swami Vivekananda, Centenary Volume VII*, Advaita Ashram, Mayavati, Uttaranchal, 1963: 331, 501, 504, and various pages.

Vivekananda, Swami (1896), *Complete Work of Swami Vivekananda, Centenary Volume VIII*, Advaita Ashram, Mayavati, Uttaranchal, 1963: 150, 228, 353, various pages.

Wang, Dewan (2008), "Rural-Urban Migration and Policy Responses in China: Challenges and Options", *Working Paper No.15, ILO Asian Regional Programme on Governance and Labour Migration*. ILO Regional Office for Asia and the Pacific, Bangkok.

Wolpert, Julian (1965), "Behavioural Aspects of the Decision to Migrate", *Papers, Regional Science Association*, 15: 152–180.

Wood, Donald A. (1973), "Toward the Interpretation of Canonical Dimensions", *Multivariate Behavioural Research*, October: 477–482.

World Bank (1975), *The Task Ahead for the Cities of the Developing Countries*. Bank Staff Working Paper No 209, Washington, D.C.: 47–56 (as in Todaro et al.)

World Bank (1990), *World Development Report 1990: Poverty, World Development Indicators*, The World Bank, Washington D.C.: 56–89.

World Bank (1993), *World Development Report, 1993*. New York.

World Bank (1995), *World Development Report, 1995*. Delhi: Oxford University Press: 165–228.

World Bank (1996), *India: Five Years of Stabilization and Reforms and the Challenges Ahead*, A World Bank Country Study, World Bank, Washington, D.C.: 77–98.

World Bank (1997), *World Development Report 1997: The State in a Changing World*, The World Bank, Washington, D.C: 111–130.

World Bank (1998), "Study on Japanese and Asian Experiences in Urban Development: Final Report", June 1998, *World Bank Report*, Washington D.C. and ARMEC Corporation, Tokyo.

World Bank (2003a), "India's Sustaining Reforms, Reducing Poverty," *Development Policy Review*, July, World Bank: 1–125.

World Bank (2003b), *World Development Report 2003, Sustainable Development in a Dynamic World: Transforming Institutions, Growth and Quality of Life*, The World Bank, Washington D.C.: 83–106.

World Bank (2008), *New Estimates of Poverty in the World*, Washington, D.C: World Bank.

World Bank (2010), *Current Estimates of Poverty in the World*, Washington, D.C.: World Bank.

Index